"Karen Jobes' survey is clearly written, critically informed, beautifully illustrated, background-enlightening, and theologically rich. As a bonus, Jobes regularly links the biblical text to current issues of Christian belief and behavior. This volume is an ideal textbook for the study of the letters that it covers."

—Robert H. Gundry, Westmont College

"Professor Jobes combines lively prose and scholarly depth to make the most neglected books in the New Testament come alive for students. Her textbook is not only academically challenging, but filled with interesting, illuminating illustrations, insightful applications, and wise theological counsel. This is, without rival, the most engaging introduction available to these important but difficult biblical books."

—Frank Thielman, Beeson Divinity School of Samford University

"*Letters to the Church* is a highly accessible guide to the General Epistles. Jobes insightfully addresses the historical, literary, and theological features of these letters and does so with a conversational and engaging demeanor. The text itself is visually appealing, with photographs, maps, illustrations, and panels that include chapter goals and review questions for the reader. *Letters to the Church* is a comprehensive introduction to these letters and a great textbook choice for college and seminary classrooms.

—Jeannine Brown, Bethel Seminary

"This clear, accessible, thorough, and well-organized study of Hebrews and the General Epistles is an ideal text for survey courses. Jobes utilizes the best of biblical scholarship but presents it in a manner that beginning students will understand."

—Mark L. Strauss, Bethel Seminary San Diego

"This is the textbook on the General Epistles I have been waiting for. It is thorough and accessible, even for students with little biblical background knowledge. Dr. Jobes provides an informed and judicious overview of the normal introductory questions (author, date, audience, genre, social setting, etc.) for each of the General Epistles (including Hebrews), along with astute and penetrating summaries of the contents and theological concerns of each."

—Dan McCartney, Redeemer Theological Seminary, Dallas, Texas

FREE Resources!

textbook*plus*+

Equipping Instructors and Students with *FREE RESOURCES for Core Zondervan Textbooks*

Available Resources for Letters to the Church

Teaching Resources

- Instructor's manual
- Presentation slides
- Chapter quizzes
- Image/map library
- Midterm & final exam
- Sample syllabus

Study Resources

- Quizzes
- Flashcards

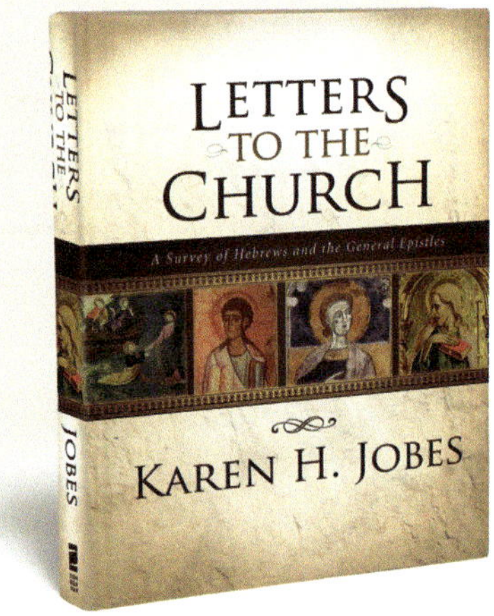

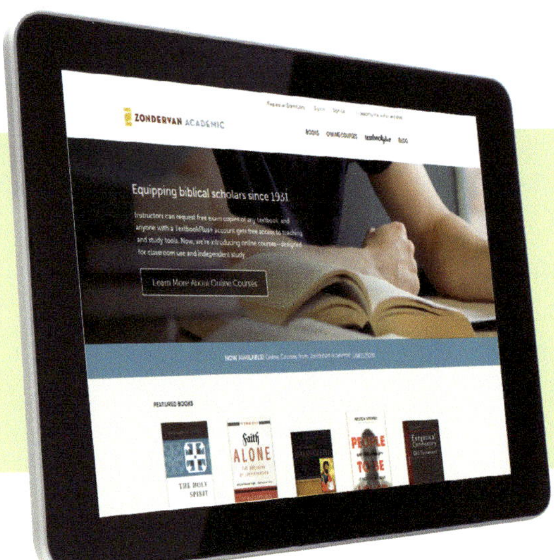

**How To Access Resources*

- Go to www.ZondervanAcademic.com
- Click "Sign Up" button and complete registration process
- Find books using search field or "Browse Our Products" feature
- Click "Teaching Resources" or "Study Resources" tab once you get to book page to access resources

www.ZondervanAcademic.com

LETTERS TO THE CHURCH

LETTERS TO THE CHURCH

A Survey of Hebrews and the General Epistles

KAREN H. JOBES

ZONDERVAN ACADEMIC

ZONDERVAN ACADEMIC

Letters to the Church

Published in Grand Rapids, Michigan, by Zondervan. Zondervan is a registered trademark of The Zondervan Corporation, L.L.C., a wholly owned subsidiary of HarperCollins Christian Publishing, Inc.

Requests for information should be addressed to customercare@harpercollins.com.

Zondervan titles may be purchased in bulk for education, business, fundraising, or sales promotional use. For information, please email SpecialMarkets@Zondervan.com.

ISBN 978-0-310-49479-9 (ebook)

Library of Congress Cataloging-in-Publication Data

Jobes, Karen H.
Letters to the church : a survey of Hebrews and the General Epistles / Karen H. Jobes.
p. cm.
Includes bibliographical references and index.
ISBN 978-0-310-26738-6 (hardcover)
1. Bible. N.T. Hebrews—Textbooks. 2. Bible. N.T. Catholic Epistles—Textbooks. I. Title.
BS2775.55.J63 2011
227'.061—dc22 2010051062

Cover design: www.wdesigncompany.com
Cover photography: Bridgeman Art Library
Interior illustration: Brett M. Hoffman
Interior design: Ben Fetterley

Printed in the United States of America

---

26 27 28 29 30 31 32 33 34 35 36 /TRM/ 22 21 20 19 18 17 16 15 14 13 12 11

Lovingly dedicated to my mother, Dorothy E. Hill
1928–2009

Contents

List of Abbreviations

AB	Anchor Bible
ABD	*Anchor Bible Dictionary*
ACCS	Ancient Christian Commentary on Scripture
ACNT	Augsburg Commentaries on the New Testament
ANF	*Ante-Nicene Fathers*
Ant.	*Jewish Antiquities*, Josephus
Ara.	Aramaic
BAR	*Biblical Archaeology Review*
BBR	*Bulletin for Biblical Research*
BECNT	Baker Exegetical Commentary of the New Testament
BETL	Bibliotheca ephemeridum theologicarum lovaniensium
Bib	*Biblica*
BJRL	*Bulletin of the John Rylands Library*
BV	*Biblical Viewpoint*
CAH	Cambridge Ancient History
CBC	Cornerstone Biblical Commentary
CBQ	*Catholic Biblical Quarterly*
CTJ	*Calvin Theological Journal*
EBS	*Encountering Biblical Studies*
EQ	*Evangelical Quarterly*
ESV	English Standard Version
ExAud	*Ex auditu*
FC	Fathers of the Church
FRLANT	Forschungen zur Religion und Literatur des Alten und Neuen Testaments
Ger.	German
Gk.	Greek
Heb.	Hebrew
HTKNT	Herders theologischer Kommentar zum Neuen Testament
IBT	*Interpreting Biblical Texts*
ICC	International Critical Commentary
IDBSupp	*Interpreter's Dictionary of the Bible: Supplementary Volume*
IVPNTC	InterVarsity Press New Testament Commentary
JBC	*Jerome Biblical Commentary*
JBL	*Journal of Biblical Literature*
JETS	*Journal of the Evangelical Theological Society*
JSNTSup	Journal for the Study of the New Testament: Supplement Series
JTS	*Journal of Theological Studies*

J.W.	*Jewish War*, Josephus
KJV	King James Version of the Holy Bible
Lat.	Latin
LCL	Loeb Classical Library
LW	Luther's Works
NASB	New American Standard Bible
NICNT	New International Commentary on the New Testament
NIGTC	New International Greek Testament Commentary
NIV	New International Version
NIVAC	New International Version Application Commentary
NKJV	New King James Version
NovT	*Novum Testamentum*
NovTSup	Novum Testamentum Supplements
NRSV	New Revised Standard Version
NTL	New Testament Library
NTS	*New Testament Studies*
OG	Old Greek
PNTC	Pillar New Testament Commentary
RevQ	*Revue de Qumran*
SBLDS	Society of Biblical Literature Dissertation Series
SBLMS	Society of Biblical Literature Monograph Series
SBLSymS	Society of Biblical Literature Symposium Series
SCJ	*Stone Campbell Journal*
ScrHier	Scripta hierosolymitana
SJT	*Scottish Journal of Theology*
SNTSMS	Society for New Testament Studies Monograph Series
STDJ	Studies on the Texts of the Desert of Judah
StPB	Studia post-biblica
TJ	*Trinity Journal*
TNIV	Today's New International Version
TNTC	Tyndale New Testament Commentaries
TynBul	*The Tyndale Bulletin*
WBC	Word Bible Commentary
WTJ	*Westminster Theological Journal*
WUNT	Wissenschaftlichte Untersuchungen zum Neuen Testament
WW	*Word and World*
ZECNT	Zondervan Exegetical Commentary on the New Testament
ZIBBC	*Zondervan Illustrated Bible Backgrounds Commentary*
ZNW	Zeitschrift für die neutestamentliche Wissenschaft und die Kunde der älteren Kirche

Acknowledgments

The writing of a book spans several years and involves many people other than the author. Special thanks must go to the several research assistants who helped me in one way or another by gathering information for the bibliography, fetching materials, proofreading chapters, and thinking up visuals: Dr. Chee-Chiew Lee (2006–7), Andrew Carr (2006–8), Laurie Norris (2005–6; 2007–8), Matt Newkirk (2008–9), Cassandra Blackford (2008–9), Ben Ribbens (2009–10), Daniel Crickmore (2010–11), and especially Charlie Trimm (2010–11), who prepared the indices. I have appreciated the fellowship of working with each of you more than I can say.

I am grateful for the opportunity to write this book and must thank Jack Kuhatschek (then at Zondervan) and Katya Covrett for initiating it and especially to Katya for her oversight and encouragement along the way. Kim Tanner has brought her expertise to bear in preparing the visual content. I thank editors Laura Weller and Jim Ruark, whose fine work has made me sound like a better writer than I am.

Much appreciation goes to Wheaton College and Graduate School for the sabbatical leave needed to bring this work to its completion. The Gerald F. Hawthorne Chair of New Testament Greek and Exegesis that I hold has provided resources necessary to support this work; I gratefully acknowledge the donor and pray that this volume might be a fitting tribute to the chair's namesake.

I remember with gratitude the many friends and colleagues who supported me through prayer during the difficult time of my mother's long illness and passing while writing this book. To my late mother, Dorothy E. Hill, I dedicate this work with deep appreciation for her example of unwavering Christian faith through the darkest valleys of life. I thank my husband, Forrest, for his patience and his continued support of my writing, especially when it has consumed so many hours of our life together.

Finally and supremely, my heart is filled with gratitude to the Lord, who called me to this task and has given me strength for each new day to bring it to completion.

How to Use This Book

When an author writes a textbook, he or she always has in mind a type of student audience and envisions how the book will be used. Here are a few assumptions I have made and suggestions that will hopefully enhance the benefit this book might bring to your studies.

TO THE STUDENT

You are embarking on the study of a sequence of books in the New Testament that are often grouped together in academic courses as "Hebrews and the General/**Catholic** Epistles." This sequence of books usually includes the relatively lengthy book of Hebrews and the much shorter James, 1 and 2 Peter, and Jude. Sometimes the three **epistles** of John are also included, as they are in this volume.

There is no substitute for reading the biblical text itself, and I assume that you will do that for each book before reading the corresponding chapters in this book. Hopefully you will read the biblical book in its entirety in just one or maybe two sittings.

A glossary is provided, and for greatest comprehension, you should look up each word introduced in boldface type.

The Questions for Review or Discussion at the end of each chapter are intended to draw your attention to the key points of the chapter, giving you an opportunity to reflect on or to review points more deeply. If you are using this book for an academic course, I encourage you to form a study group and talk through the questions.

To keep the size of this book practical and affordable, many topics are introduced that could not be discussed at greater length. Please note that a Going Further bibliography is provided at the end of each chapter for those who wish to pursue further study of a topic or who need to find additional resources for a term paper. When I was a student, I tended to skip over bibliographies, but reading through them as a part of your study time will acquaint you with resources to further your study efficiently.

I realize that not everyone who reads this book will be a believing Christian, though I suspect that many, if not most, will be. For those who come to this as agnostic or skeptical, remember that "to learn a belief without belief is to sing a song without the tune."[1] In any case, I pray that your study of the New Testament through using this book will further God's purposes in your life.

1. Ursula K. LeGuin, *The Telling* (New York: Harcourt, 2000), 97–98, quoted by Joel B. Green, "Living as Exiles," in *Holiness and Ecclesiology in the New Testament*, ed. Kent E. Brower and Andy Johnson (Grand Rapids: Eerdmans, 2007), 312.

TO THE INSTRUCTOR

An author is always grateful when someone actually reads his or her book, so I thank you for choosing this book for your course. Please assign the biblical text to be read in one, or at most two, sittings as homework along with the corresponding chapters of the book.

You will notice that not every topic relevant to these New Testament books is pursued in depth, giving you as the instructor opportunity to supplement those you deem worthy of more time in the classroom. Although I hold conclusions resulting from my years of study and teaching Hebrews and the General Epistles, I have intended to present them in such a way that leaves adequate room for other viewpoints to be engaged in the classroom.

Please use the Questions for Review or Discussion at the end of each chapter as assigned written homework or as classroom discussion as you see fit. They are designed to reinforce the major points of the chapter and provide a starting point for lengthier or more complex discussions.

The bibliographical information provided at the end of each chapter and in the footnotes will provide you with additional resources, should you need them, and will help your students get started on further research for term papers.

May the Lord bless your teaching of these fascinating New Testament books that are too often overlooked in the academic curriculum.

Karen H. Jobes
Gerald F. Hawthorne Professor of New Testament Greek and Exegesis
Wheaton College and Graduate School

Introducing Hebrews and the General Epistles

WHAT ARE THE "GENERAL EPISTLES"?

Many of the books of the New Testament that originated as letters from an apostle were addressed to a specific congregation, such as Paul's letters to the Corinthian church, the Roman church, and others. The books of Hebrews, James, and 1 and 2 Peter, John's letters, and Jude are not explicitly addressed to a specific location, although they were no doubt written with a particular audience in mind. Therefore, they are books that have the appearance of being originally written for a broader audience and more generally for the whole church.

The designation of these books as "general" **epistles** is rather recent. Previously for many centuries, these books were referred to as the "**catholic**" epistles. The terms "catholic" and "epistle" come from the period of time when the Christian church spoke ***koine* Greek**, the language in which the New Testament was originally written. The term *epistle* comes into English from the Greek noun *epistolē*, which refers to written correspondence. This book uses the words *epistle* and *letter* as virtually synonymous, while recognizing that *epistle* is a word that is becoming archaic.

The term *catholic* epistles derives from the Greek phrase *kath holou*, "referring to the whole," which came into English through its Latin translation *catholicus* ("universal"). It is this use of the term *catholic* that is to be understood in the phrase "catholic epistles" as well as in the statement in the Apostles' Creed that is sometimes expressed as "I believe in the holy catholic church." This section of the New Testament canon is designated as letters for the entire church (not that Paul's letters are any less universally applicable). But later in history, after the Reformation, and particularly in the English language, the term *catholic* came to refer more specifically to the Roman Catholic Church. Many Protestants might be confused about why they confess belief in the "catholic" church when reciting the Apostles' Creed, and that phrase is now the "universal church" in some versions of the creed. The term *General Epistles* has been adopted to avoid the mistaken idea that these books of the New Testament have something to do distinctively with Roman Catholicism or hold a special place in Roman Catholic tradition.

Although Hebrews and 1 John are considered to be "epistles," they don't use the standard letter opening at all, suggesting that perhaps they began as an essay or sermon for a congregation in one location and subsequently were copied and circulated as a letter would have been. Moreover, Hebrews and, to a lesser extent, 1 John, include many rhetorical qualities that are not found in common correspondence of that time. The author of Hebrews seems to have thought of it as a work for a much broader audience that may not have been personally known to him. And while James, 1 and 2 Peter, and Jude do have opening statements that conform at least in part to the standard Hellenistic letter opening, their recipients are referred to in such a general way as to suggest that the letter opening is a literary device to clue the original readers on how to read the contents. For instance, when 1 Peter addresses chosen exiles of the **Diaspora** in 1:1 and mentions that he is writing from "Babylon" in 5:13, he is framing his thoughts as a Diaspora letter rather than specifying the location of the original readers. Although each of the General Epistles was sent to an intended audience originally, the authors of these books were not writing personal correspondence (with the exception of 3 John), but intended their writings for a more general audience.

WHAT WAS HAPPENING WHEN THESE BOOKS WERE WRITTEN?

The attempts to date each of the specific books will be discussed in the appropriate corresponding chapter. However, it should be helpful to locate these books broadly by considering what the church was facing in the period of New Testament history in which these books originated. All books of the New Testament refer to events that happened in the first century of this era (i.e., **AD** 1 – 100 as the modern calendar numbers years), and the New Testament books were themselves written in the second half of that century. The focus of the New Testament is on one person who lived in the early third of the first century, Jesus Christ, and the significance of his life, death, and resurrection. As almost everyone knows from Christmas carols and TV programs, if not from the Bible itself, Jesus was born in Bethlehem near Jerusalem, which was at that time in the Roman province of Judea. But even the Gospels written to tell about the life, death, and resurrection of Jesus were written a few decades afterward and within particular circumstances that motivated their authors to write as each did. And so when we study the Gospels, we are concerned with two distinct time periods and their events: first, the recorded events of Jesus' lifetime and, second, the events taking place in the churches to which each of the Gospels was addressed. When we get to the book of Acts, Luke tells about events that happened generally in the third through sixth decades of the first century, but he wrote after those events had occurred and with a particular purpose in mind that motivated him to select certain material and present it in a certain way.

The New Testament epistles are different from these narrative accounts, because the authors of the letters address real questions, issues, and circumstances that were of concern at the time rather than recounting events from a previous time period. Consequently, the New Testament writings allow us to distinguish three periods of the first century and place the events and the origin of the books within each period.

1. The Period of Gospel Origins

No New Testament books were written during the lifetime of Jesus (c. 6 **BC** – c. AD 33).

2. The Period of Church Expansion (AD 33 – 60)

This was a time of great missionary activity both within Palestine and throughout the Roman world. The New Testament writings focus especially on the apostle Paul's trav-

Much of the New Testament was written during the time of the initial expansion of the church, and addresses issues and problems which arose as the gospel crossed cultural boundaries.

els, but Peter and other of Jesus' disciples were also actively preaching and teaching. This period was characterized by questions and issues that arose as the gospel crossed beyond the borders of Palestine to other nations and peoples, issues such as whether **Gentile** believers needed to be **circumcised** and whether Christians had to keep the food laws of Judaism.

3. The Period of Doctrinal and Ecclesial Unification (AD 60 – 100)

This period was a time when individual, far-flung congregations began to see themselves as part of one larger body, the body of Christ in this world, and embrace the apostolic teaching as applicable to believers everywhere. But it was also within this period that the church faced huge obstacles, namely, organized persecution of Christians by the Roman government; heresy infiltrating the church, especially from the various Greek philosophies; and a crisis of church leadership, especially as the apostles died and the Lord had not returned.

At that very time when Caesar Augustus was being hailed as son of God and savior, Jesus of Nazareth came as the long-promised Messiah of the Jews. Judaism, the religion of Jesus and most of the writers of the New Testament, had been shaped for the previous four centuries by its interaction with foreign religions and philosophies, resulting in much turmoil and conflict in the land into which Jesus was born. However, Jesus brought a kingdom of God that was not to be contained within geopolitical, ethnic, or national

Mount Sinai.

boundaries. And so the story of Jesus' life, death, and resurrection had to be told to audiences that included Jews, with their knowledge of God's ancient work in the world, as well as to Gentiles who came from backgrounds of other religions and pagan worldviews.

Immediately after the death and resurrection of Jesus, there was a period of about three decades that the New Testament writings (especially the Acts of the Apostles) describe as a time of explosive growth in the numbers of people who were putting their faith in the resurrected Jesus Christ, and as a time when the Christian church expanded outside of the Judaism of Palestine and throughout the Gentile Roman Empire. This expansion of the Christian faith to peoples coming from many diverse ethnic groups, pagan religions, and schools of Greek philosophy raised many important issues for the apostles to resolve. Throughout many previous centuries, God's redemptive work in the world, as far as Scripture reveals, was achieved through the nation with which he had a covenant—ancient Israel. That covenant defined ancient Israel, and anyone wanting to worship the one, true, creator God was expected to enter the covenant and live as an Israelite (for instance, as Ruth, a Moabite, did). God established the covenant relationship with his people on Mount Sinai when he gave the Law to Moses and prescribed **circumcision** as the sign of that covenant relationship. Women were included in the covenant by being the daughter or wife of a circumcised man. The new covenant described in the New Testament had been established by the death and resurrection of Jesus Christ. When Gentiles began to put their faith in Christ, the first issue the apostles had to hammer out, of course, was whether Gentile believers in the Jewish Messiah needed to be circumcised and obey the law of Moses (Acts 15:1). When Peter, Paul, and James decided at the Council of Jerusalem in AD 49 that, no, Gentiles did not need to become Jews in order to be Christians, the whole issue of the role and purpose of the Law and the basis of Christian morality and ethics was brought into play. From these issues come Paul's instructions in Galatians and possibly the book of

James, with its famous statement that "faith without works is dead" (James 2:20 KJV), to clarify the role of good works in Christian living.

The relationship between the old and new covenants, with animal sacrifices made by the **Aaronic priesthood** as the basis of the former and the death of Jesus establishing the latter, needed to be thought through and articulated. Where were the continuities and discontinuities between the old covenant and the new, given the death and resurrection of Jesus Christ? The writer of Hebrews took up this challenge and produced a profound exposition of this topic.

Although the Gospels are first in the sequence of books we call the New Testament, they were almost certainly not the first of the New Testament books to have been written. That distinction probably goes to the letters of the apostle Paul to the Thessalonians or to the Galatians that date from about AD 49 or 50. Some would date James and possibly 1 Peter and Jude as among the earlier books of the New Testament as well. Other books, like Hebrews, were most likely written decades later. The three letters of John were probably among the last books of the New Testament to have been written near the end of the first century. It is helpful when studying each of these books to have in mind the types of issues that would have characterized the time when they were written. And so James, if written during the period of expansion, could be seen as balancing Paul's proclamation of righteousness by faith in Christ alone and answering the question of where good works fit into Christian life. John's letters, written during the period of unification when heresy was a major problem, open a window to the way **Christology** was being distorted by Christians who had an improper understanding of the nature of Jesus Christ.

Baker Photo Archive

The Mamertine Prison, where it is believed both Peter and Paul were imprisoned.

For various reasons, persecution of Christians increased as the decades of the first century advanced. Even before the Roman government began to imprison and sometimes execute Christians in the second half of the century, Christians faced social ostracism and hostility from local rulers. These forms of persecution took place from the very beginning, starting with Jesus and then experienced by his apostles as well. The newly formed church needed instruction on how to live in such a climate so that they would neither assimilate to the expectations of a pagan society nor become so separatist that they would fail in their mission of evangelization. The book of 1 Peter provides an insightful analysis of this situation as it was unfolding in Asia Minor (the modern country of Turkey), with challenging advice about the Christian's engagement with society viewed as the sojourn of an alien residing in a foreign land.

Once Gentiles began to come to faith in Christ in great numbers, it did not take long for heresy to become a problem for the apostles. Tendencies in Greco-Roman philosophy, such as **Neoplatonism** and incipient **Gnosticism**, were influential in first-century thinking and caused distortions of the perception of who Jesus was, of the goal of salvation, and consequently, of moral issues concerning how Christians were to live. The books of 2 Peter and Jude and the **Johannine** epistles take on the important task of correcting various types of heresy that caused wrong beliefs and behavior in the church.

Because these books are in the New Testament, Hebrews and the General Epistles are theological writings. They are about God, Jesus Christ, the Holy Spirit, and the necessary implications that follow for Christian faith, life, and morality. Millions of Christians rightly read the words of these books in worship and devotions. But these writings didn't drop out of heaven into our laps yesterday. These are ancient books that were written in a time and place quite unlike the modern setting in which we read them today. To understand the books of the Bible as theological writings, we must understand the authors' ideas within each book's original historical setting. To appreciate the original historical setting, we must have knowledge of the who, what, when, and why. The biblical authors assumed that their original readers shared a vast amount of knowledge about the people, places, customs, religions, society, politics, and philosophies of that moment simply because both author and reader were alive at the same time and shared many common experiences. For modern readers today, that needed knowledge can come only by study, which is why I have written this book. Without such knowledge, the risk of misunderstanding the biblical books is great.

Furthermore, the books of the New Testament not only have historical settings and references that must be correctly understood; they are themselves literary texts produced in a culture that is not our own. This means that each book was written in a particular genre, has a structure to its discourse, involves the use of ancient images and rhetorical features, and alludes to other ancient writings. All of these things were no doubt commonly understood by the original readers in the first century; however, because we have not grown up in that culture, reading texts in koine Greek or biblical Hebrew and Aramaic, our work is to study to learn as best we can about those things that will inform our reading of the New Testament books. This book should help inform its readers of such issues in general terms and prepare them for further reading in the commentaries and monographs pertaining to each of the General Epistles.

WHO WROTE THE GENERAL EPISTLES? THE ISSUE OF PSEUDEPIGRAPHAL AUTHORS

The great consensus of modern New Testament scholarship is that few of the New Testament books were actually written by the authors traditionally assumed or explicitly stated within the texts. A text is said to be **pseudonymous** "when the author is deliberately identified by a name other than his own."[1] The term derives from the Greek words *pseude* ("false") *onoma* ("name"). In our day, authors have sometimes adopted a pen name for various reasons, such as Samuel Clemens adopting the pen name Mark Twain. The difference is that a modern writer generally makes up a new name for himself or herself and does not try to impersonate a well-known writer. The practice of ancient **pseudonymity** as it relates to the Scripture is a very different thing, because the actual author is not the same person as

1. K. Koch, "Pseudonymous Writing," *IDBSupp*, 712, quoted in David G. Meade, *Pseudonymity and Canon: An Investigation into the Relationship of Authorship and Authority in Jewish and Earliest Christian Tradition* (Grand Rapids: Eerdmans, 1986), 2.

the named author, and the named author is generally someone of renown whose authority and reputation would be assumed for the text.

The term *pseudonymity* focuses on the identity of the author; the related term ***pseudepigrapha***, from the Greek *pseude* ("false") *grapha* ("writings"), identifies a type of writing that is known or believed to be pseudonymous. Serapion, the second-century bishop of the church at Antioch, used the word to refer to texts that were falsely attributed to a New Testament writer, for instance, the *Gospel of Peter* and the *Acts of Paul* (Eusebius, *Hist. eccl.* 6.12). The *Testament of Adam* is a text that likely dates to the Christian era in which the actual author adopted the name of an Old Testament personality and wrote as if he were Adam. There are many such ancient texts that are obviously pseudonymous. Collectively, ancient texts that are believed to be pseudonymous and not part of the biblical canon are referred to as the Pseudepigrapha. They can be read in English translation in Charlesworth's edition.[2]

An author dictates to a scribe.

The common practice of using an **amanuensis** in the ancient world needs to be distinguished from pseudonymous authorship. An amanuensis was a scribe who put pen to **papyrus** on behalf of an author, who for various reasons (e.g., disability, old age, imprisonment, other pressing tasks), was not in a position to take up the pen himself. Without doubt, some of the New Testament epistles were penned by an amanuensis, and some have attributed the quality of the Greek to him when it seems beyond the ability of the stated author (e.g., Peter's first letter). But at what point does an amanuensis shade into a pseudepigrapher? The common assumption is that an amanuensis worked during the lifetime of the person who commissioned him. But what if an amanuensis wrote after the death of the author? Within what time period after the death would an amanuensis have become in fact a pseudepigrapher? I. Howard Marshall's definition of pseudonymity is helpful: "A text is pseudonymous when it is not by the person whose name it bears in the sense that it was written after his death by another person or during his life by another person *who was not in some way commissioned to do so*" (italics added).[3]

And so New Testament books written by an amanuensis should be considered an authentic work of the person who commissioned it. The key is whether the person who put pen to papyrus and wrote in the name of another was granted that task by the person whose name appears in the text. So if the apostle Peter used an amanuensis to write 1 Peter

2. James Charlesworth, ed., *Old Testament Pseudepigrapha*, 2 vols. (New York: Doubleday, 1983).

3. I. H. Marshall, "The Problem of Non-Apostolic Authorship of the Pastoral Epistles" (paper presented at the annual meeting of the Tyndale Fellowship New Testament Study Groups, Cambridge, England, 1985), 1 (italics added), quoted in Terry L. Wilder, *Pseudonymity, the New Testament, and Deception: An Inquiry into Intention and Reception* (Lanham, Md.: University Press of America, 2004), 2.

on his behalf, it is authentic; if not, it is pseudonymous. The trickier hypothetical situation is if a disciple of an apostle decided to write in the name of the apostle after his death without express permission but with an assumed permission based on the closeness of the relationship. This is the primary option argued by those who wish to retain the apostolic authority of the text while granting its pseudonymity (such as is often argued in the case of Paul's pastoral letters).

The topic of pseudonymity in the ancient world is taken up in a vast corpus of literature; this discussion will be limited to the idea so prevalent in New Testament studies today, that some, perhaps most, of the New Testament epistles were not actually written by their stated author. The idea of pseudonymous epistles should be distinguished from anonymous New Testament books, such as the Gospels and the epistle to the Hebrews. Even though virtually all New Testament scholars reject Paul's authorship of Hebrews and many argue that none of the Gospels was actually written by the apostle named in their titles—which were later added by the church—the claim that New Testament texts were not written by the authors stated in the texts themselves presents a challenge to the doctrine of inerrancy as it has traditionally been understood, as well as to two thousand years of Christian tradition. Inerrancy claims that what the Scripture says is true when read as the inspired author intended it to be read. A Hellenistic letter opening, which is where the name of the alleged author is found, could be read in no other way except to take the letter as having come from the stated person.

> "We may lay down as a general principle that, when biblical books specify their own authorship, the affirmation of their canonicity involves a denial of their pseudonymity. Pseudonymity and canonicity are mutually exclusive."
>
> J. I. Packer

But, some ask, could there not be a legitimate pseudonymity that wouldn't incur the ethical violation of forgery? Needless to say, those scholars who come to the topic of pseudonymity with no belief in, or concern with, the inerrancy or infallibility of the Bible bring a different bias than those who affirm that doctrine.

The idea that the New Testament epistles are probably pseudonymous has become so commonplace, even among many evangelical scholars, that it may seem futile to argue that those whose names are stated in the letter openings actually did write the letters. Some have described such attempts as desperate, as if no historical argument can plausibly be made. There is even disagreement about whether it matters who wrote the New Testament books. People who are otherwise on opposite ends of the theological spectrum sometimes argue that this topic is irrelevant. On one end of the spectrum are those who have no belief in a unified canon of the New Testament and who do not see these ancient texts as normative for life today. Their study of the New Testament is purely a historical inquiry into an artifact from the ancient world. Therefore, it matters little to them who actually wrote the letters that came to comprise so much of the New Testament, except perhaps as a point of historical information. At the other end of the spectrum are those Christians who regard the New Testament as inspired by the Holy Spirit and infer from that belief that even if a letter wasn't written by the specified author, it is nonetheless a canonical text inspired by the Spirit, and so again, the issue of human authorship may be judged moot. Clearly, by my devoting space in this book to the topic, I judge the topic of pseudonymity to be both relevant and significant to the well-informed and thinking Christian.

The concept of a pseudonymous New Testament text arose in the mid-nineteenth century when the German scholar F. C. Baur proposed that the Pastoral Epistles had not been written by the apostle Paul.[4] Nineteenth-century German biblical scholarship was largely based on antisupernatural presuppositions that flowed from the Enlightenment. If supernatural miracles did not happen, how can their presence in the Gospels be explained? It must be because the Gospels are not eyewitness accounts but are the much later ruminations about Jesus by otherwise unknown Christian communities that included miracle stories for a variety of reasons. That general antisupernatural approach to Scripture, coupled with the influence of **dialectical Hegelian philosophy** on historical reconstructions of those communities, led to dating most of the New Testament books into the second century, well past the lifetimes of any of Jesus' contemporaries and therefore necessarily making them pseudonymous. While Baur's legacy and that of those who followed in his footsteps has been challenged and weakened on many fronts (e.g., the discovery of the **Rylands fragment**), the idea of the pseudonymous authorship of most New Testament books has persisted as an assumption by many New Testament scholars. Although internal evidence based on the texts themselves has been argued to support pseudonymity—such as the quality of the Greek of 1 Peter and the testament genre of 2 Peter—the weight of such evidence strikes some as compelling and others as not.

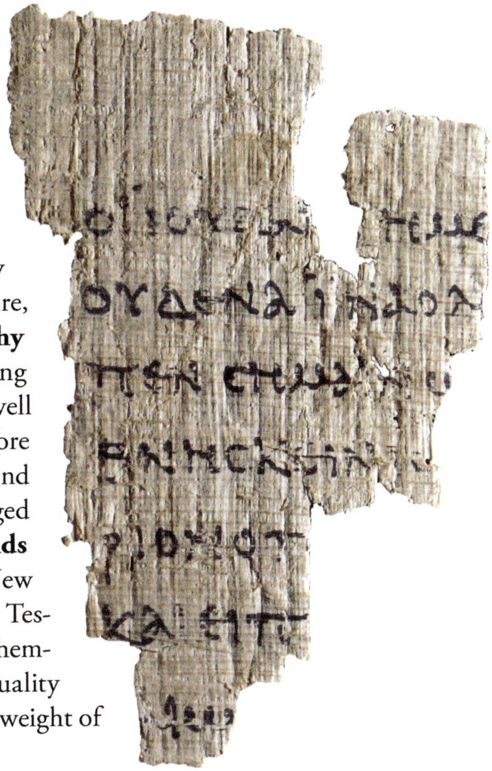
Mal Hamilton

$\mathfrak{P}^{52}$, the Rylands fragment

Those scholars who argue for pseudonymous New Testament epistles but nevertheless value the theological concept of the authority of the canon reach for ways to understand pseudonymity as a legitimate and acceptable practice in the ancient world. Such arguments include the following:[5]

1. The claim that a pejorative evaluation of pseudonymity is anachronistic because the correct attribution of authorship was of little concern in an age prior to copyright laws.
2. The claim that pseudonymity was an acceptable literary device conventionally employed in ancient genres such as wisdom literature, **apocalyptic**, and even epistles.
3. A view of divine inspiration that involves an author essentially channeling an apostolic personality.

---

4. F. C. Baur, *Die sogenannten Pastoralbriefe des Apostels Paulus aufs neue kritisch untersucht* (Stuttgart: Cotta, 1835).

5. For a list of several types of pseudonymous texts, see James H. Charlesworth, "Pseudonymity and Pseudepigraphy," *ABD*, vol. 5 (New York: Doubleday, 1992), 540–41. For a fuller discussion of legitimate ancient pseudonymity, see Meade, *Pseudonymity and Canon*, 4–23.

4. The idea that a disciple could legitimately write something in his master's name. If everything he knew was from the master, the master should get the credit. This thought developed into the idea of "schools" of disciples — for example, the Johannine school, the Pauline school, and others — that is so widely accepted in New Testament studies today.

There is much debate about whether pseudonymity was acceptable in the ancient world and, if so, in what circumstances, and whether the intent to deceive was or was not involved. But it is clear that the forgery of texts with the intent to deceive was not acceptable in the ancient world. The great Hellenistic libraries, such as those at Ephesus and Alexandria, purchased rare copies of books by well-known writers, and that provided financial incentive for newly created texts to appear that had allegedly been written by famous Greek authors. Consequently, well before the Christian era, in Alexandria, Egypt, techniques were employed to detect and reject literary forgeries. In some cases, pseudonymity was interpreted by the law as criminal forgery. Seutonius reports that the Emperor Claudius had a man's hands cut off because he had forged a document (Seutonius, *Claud.* 5.15.2). Clearly, not every use of someone else's name was acceptable practice.

What remains of the library at Ephesus.

Within early Christian circles, orthodoxy and orthopraxy motivated well-meaning but deceptive people to write in the name of the apostles, resulting in many New Testament pseudepigraphical books, such as the apocryphal *Gospel of Peter* and the *Acts of Paul.* Even letters appeared, allegedly written by an apostle, such as 3 Corinthians, written in Paul's name in the second century. When it was discovered that the letter was pseudonymous, and had actually been written by an elder of a church in Asia Minor, Tertullian reports that the elder was removed from office in shame, even though he confessed to being motivated only by love for Paul (*Bapt.* 17).[6] Two other letters attributed to Paul circulated in the second century, a letter to the Laodiceans and a letter to the Alexandrians. Both were condemned and rejected as forgeries by the **Muratorian Canon.**[7] Bishop Serapion of Antioch in the late second century rejected the *Gospel of Peter*, knowing that it had "not been handed down to us" (Eusebius, *Hist. eccl.* 6.12.2–4).

Such historical evidence does not explain how pseudonymous works were detected, but it does clearly show that when it came to letters allegedly written by apostles, pseudonymity was not an acceptable practice. Furthermore, Serapion's comment that such books had not "been handed down" suggests that it would have been difficult in the second century

6. For other examples and the responses of early Christian leaders, see Wilder, *Pseudonymity.*
7. Wilder, *Pseudonymity*, 132.

New Testament Writers Warned against Pseudonymous Use of Their Names

"We ask you, brothers and sisters, not to become easily unsettled or alarmed by the teaching allegedly from us — whether by a prophecy or by word of mouth or by letter."

The apostle Paul,
2 Thessalonians 2:1 – 2

for a pseudepigrapher to present his newly written text as authentic, for it lacked the sustained recognition within the church that the genuine apostolic books apparently enjoyed. Serapion's statement has important implications for how the canon was formed — not by a politically motivated selection process employed by the councils, but by a lineage of recognition from one generation to the next that went back to the apostles themselves.

The issue of pseudonymous texts also has significant exegetical implications. Only if the letters attributed to an apostle actually originated with him do we have enough **extant** historical context to make sense of the New Testament. Although we may wish we knew more about Peter, Paul, John, and the other apostles, there is much more known about these men that informs exegesis than if the actual author was an unknown believer in an unknown place who wrote for unknown reasons. To embrace such a scenario is like deliberately locking your car keys in the trunk and then expecting to drive the car. Furthermore, the embrace of pseudonymous New Testament writings insidiously turns the study of the New Testament into a study, not of what Jesus and his chosen eyewitnesses said and did, but merely of the religious ruminations of some anonymous people in the Roman period, and it effectively cuts off any genuine knowledge of Jesus and his first followers.

"We receive both Peter and the other apostles as Christ, but the writings which falsely bear their names we reject ... knowing that such were not handed down to us."

Bishop Serapion of Antioch,
second century

Against all arguments for pseudonymous New Testament books is the further question of whether it is psychologically conceivable that the men Jesus chose to be his witnesses, who saw him die and then be resurrected from the grave, could have passed from this life without writing anything down about the most awesome and magnificent event of human history, but that much later anonymous believers would have been both motivated and able to create the texts that came to be the New Testament. It seems to me that the idea that the New Testament books are largely a created fiction of the later church apart from the apostolic witness, as many critical scholars would argue, calls into question the resurrection of Jesus as a historical event by rejecting it as sufficient motivation for those alive at the time to have written about it. And if the story of Jesus ended in the grave, that raises the question of how the later church came to be the church without any other historically identifiable event to give energy and momentum to a movement that swept the Roman world.

There is "very little space for the common modern assertion that pseudonymity was a widely acceptable practice in the ancient world. That pseudonymous apocalypses were widespread is demonstrable; that pseudonymous letters were widespread is entirely unsupported by evidence; that any pseudonymity was knowingly accepted into the New Testament canon is denied by the evidence."*

*D. A. Carson, Douglas J. Moo, and Leon Morris, *An Introduction to the New Testament* (Grand Rapids: Zondervan, 1992), 495.

There is much debate over how to interpret the historical evidence available to us and how it answers the questions raised by the theory of pseudonymous authorship. How one evaluates the evidence depends on what assumptions, theological and otherwise, one brings to the task. But to me, the historical evidence suggests that if there are letters in the New Testament that were not written by the apostle named, they were written by a close personal associate of the apostle and enjoyed a lineage of recognition in the churches going back to their apostolic origin, and that corroborated their authenticity.

READING OTHER PEOPLE'S MAIL

All of the New Testament letters, including Hebrews and the General Epistles, are what are called "**occasional writings**." Each letter is a discourse written by an individual author who wrote for a purpose that arose from a specific occasion or situation that has been largely lost to us. Therefore, we must infer from the contents of the epistle what might have prompted the author to write as he did. It's like eavesdropping on only one-half of a phone conversation and trying to figure out from what you hear what the person on the other end is saying. Or it's like finding a bundle of old letters in your grandmother's attic and trying to imagine what the other half of the correspondence that she had written must have said.

If you have come to read the Bible through the church and for devotional purposes, you might not appreciate that these texts that seem so familiar—the Psalms, Gospels, and Epistles—are actually quite foreign to us. They were not only written thousands of years ago, but they were written in and for an ancient culture vastly different from our own. So, for instance, a modern, scientifically minded reader might be amazed to read that Jesus changed water into wine because of the complex molecular transformation that such a feat would require. That same reader might completely miss the point that the original Greco-Roman reader would have seen a power at work in Jesus that rivaled the Greek wine god Bacchus. And so when we read the New Testament epistles, we are actually reading letters originally sent to other people who were in a much bet-

The Drinking Contest of Dionysus and Heracles, found at Antioch, Roman, (2nd century AD)/Worcester Art Museum, Massachusetts, USA/The Bridgeman Art Library

Bacchus, the Greek god of wine.

ter position to understand them, because they knew very well what their situation was and how the letter they had received from an apostle addressed it.

The question of pseudonymity is important for the exegetical task as well. It is one thing to read a letter from James, the brother of Jesus; it is quite another to read a letter from someone trying to "channel" James and write what he thought James would have said. In the first case, the goal of studying the letter of James is to better understand what a firsthand witness of Jesus can tell us about Christian faith. But if it is a pseudonymous writing, then James himself implicitly becomes the object of study through a letter that only tells us what somebody later thought James might have written.

And so none of the historical information we have about James as leader of the Jerusalem church who was stoned to death by the Sanhedrin before AD 62 (Josephus, *Ant.* 10.9.200) can be brought to bear with confidence in understanding this letter. The historical framework defined by the name of the author better serves the exegetical task, which would indeed be how a pseudepigrapher would have intended it to be read.

Scala/Art Resource, NY

James stoned to death by the Sanhedrin sometime before AD 62.

Reading other people's mail might seem like an odd way for God to have given us his Word. We might wish that Jesus himself had written a systematic theology book that summed up all the things we need to know and believe about him. But in his wisdom, God instead gave us, among the inspired writings, the letters of the apostles to specific Christians living in very concrete situations during times that were very trying to the Christian faith. Because of that, we get to see how the Christian life was to be lived out in the context of first-century culture, and we can identify the same or similar issues today that challenge us. Rather than giving us a book of abstract philosophy or theology, God's Word has come in the form of very practical and specific situations. It is another instance of God's incarnational intent, to be Immanuel, God with us.

When we pick up the Bible in an academic program, we are about the work of *biblical studies*, which is a task involving a wide range of disciplines, such as ancient languages, historical method, ancient philosophy, sociology, classical rhetoric, and literary analysis. Many of the foundational principles of these disciplines are learned in other academic courses commonly found in a college liberal arts curriculum. It is no longer sufficient to simply read the Bible and reflect on what it means "to me," although the importance of personal spiritual formation should never be abandoned. But full academic rigor is needed for understanding the Bible as the original authors intended, which is implicitly how God intended it.

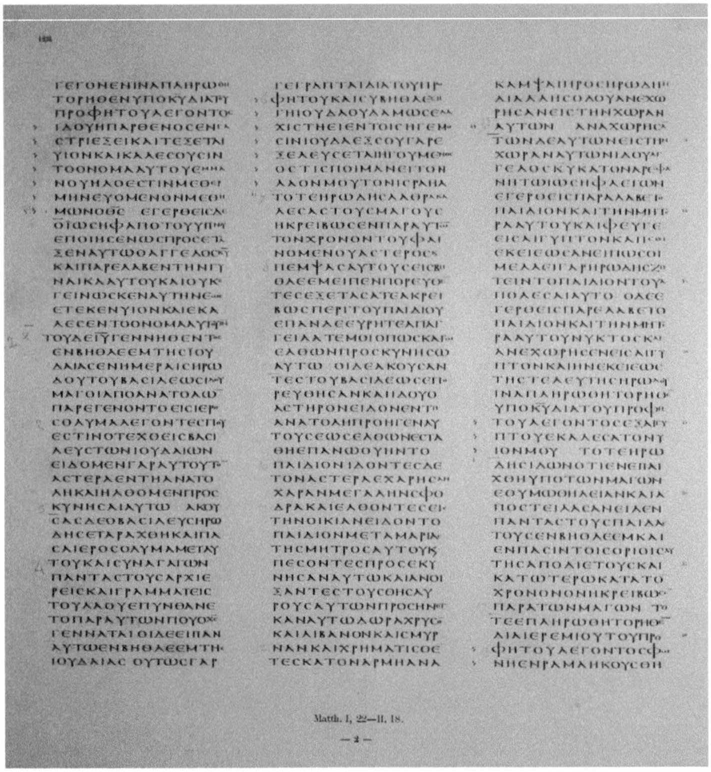

Wikimedia Commons

Codex Vaticanus, an almost complete 4th-century Bible lacking Gen. 1:1 – 46:28 and the New Testament from Heb. 9:14 on.

Often the academic pursuit of biblical studies brings new knowledge that challenges or threatens what one thought he or she believed about the Bible; that is a very common occurrence. It is helpful to realize that God has given us his Word, even if he didn't do it quite the way we naively supposed he did. Even after decades of Christian life and academic biblical studies, I am still surprised by God's mysterious workings through human beings the Holy Spirit chose to inspire.

Or perhaps the academic study of the New Testament seems too dry and disconnected from Christian life. It doesn't seem as exciting as the spiritual experiences we have previously had that drew us to study the New Testament in the first place. It takes time and effort to more deeply comprehend God's Word by understanding it in its original historical context. Old ideas may need to be left behind; new languages, methodologies, and approaches may need to be adopted. But the fruit of that labor is sweet as we grow in our knowledge and understanding of the Lord's marvelous work in human history. It is to that purpose of biblical studies in service to a deeper understanding of God's Word that this book introducing Hebrews and the General Epistles is dedicated.

THE GENERAL EPISTLES IN THE DEVELOPMENT OF THE NEW TESTAMENT CANONICAL PROCESS

Another issue that arises if the Bible has been read only devotionally is the issue of how the canon developed. If pressed to think about it, most people would realize that the Bible did not drop from heaven with sixty-six books neatly bound in black leather (or pink suede), but most would be at a loss to say how it came to be in the form we have it today. There was a time when the New Testament did not exist. Four centuries after Jesus, the full canon of the twenty-seven New Testament books we know today did exist. How did that happen, especially when several different human authors were involved in the production of the individual books and they were composed before the time of printing presses and corporate publishers? Clearly, at some point the books of the New Testament came together into a corpus, but that process did not bring all the books together all at one time and available for the church everywhere. Without the mass production and widespread distribution used by publishers today, it could take many years for a work to be copied, circulated, and eventually gathered as part of the New Testament corpus. We have evidence that the Gospels may have been gathered and circulated as a collection, and that Paul's letters may have been gathered at a different time and place. The canon of the New Testament developed gradually, and each section of books took its place during that long development. One topic of study involving Hebrews and the General Epistles is why they were put in the position they occupy — after the Pauline corpus and before Revelation — and why within that section of canon the books are ordered as we have them.

Any discussion of canon needs to distinguish between two usages of the Greek word *kanōn*, from which the English word derives. In the period in which the New Testament developed, the word *canon* was used to refer to a standard or text that was authoritative and normative. It also was used to refer to the list of such texts. These two concepts must be kept clearly distinguished, for while it is true that *canon* in the second sense, as a list of texts authoritative for the universal church, did not come to its completion until the fourth century, the individual books of the New Testament were canonical in the first sense of the word, as authoritative and normative, from the time of their origin. Certainly apostolic authority was being asserted when James or Peter or John wrote to an audience and expected to be heard and obeyed. The writings of the New Testament find their origin in the apostolic authority of the men chosen by Jesus to be his witnesses, including the apostle Paul, and their writings to and for the church carried normative authority for their audiences as soon as they came into existence. The historical process of forming a list of canonical texts, the second sense of *canon*, involved the apostolic texts written to one geographical area becoming available to and accepted by more far-flung congregations of Christians. Necessarily, not every apostolic writing was known everywhere at once or even quickly; it took time, and for some books quite a long time, before all of the apostolic writings were known and accepted by all churches and the list of canonical books we know today could be finalized in the fourth century.

Because the story of Jesus' life, death, and resurrection is foundational for the Christian faith, the four gospels came together at some point as the first section of the New Testament canon. This is first evidenced by **Tatian's Diatesseron**,[8] a second-century text that interweaves the four gospels as we know them into one continuous narrative. The Diatesseron suggests that the four gospels we know from the New Testament were the same four authoritative gospels known to Tatian. In the New Testament canon, Matthew's gospel was placed first perhaps because it is the most Jewish of the four, contains an account of Jesus' birth, and therefore is an apt introduction to the New Testament era following the Old Testament.

The book of Acts provided the story of the apostles Peter, James, Paul, and to a lesser degree, John. These are the men who rose to prominence in the earliest stage of the church and who contributed to its expansion through their individual missions in various geographical areas. It is certainly no accident that the epistles written by these men were regarded as authoritative and subsequently were gathered into the New Testament collection. Their

8. See William L. Petersen, *Tatian's Diatessaron: Its Creation, Dissemination, Significance, and History in Scholarship* (Leiden: Brill, 1994).

travels and work recorded in the book of Acts provides the narrative introduction to the entire corpus of New Testament epistles.

𝔓46 dates from about A.D. 200 and contains both Paul's epistles and the book of Hebrews.

Evidence exists that Paul's letters were first collected, copied, and circulated as a corpus.[9] Perhaps from the initial collection, but certainly at some later time, the book of Hebrews was considered part of his writings. In some manuscripts, it follows directly after Romans. The position it occupies today, following the Pauline corpus, may reflect the understanding that its author was closely associated with Paul, even if not with Paul himself.

The General, or Catholic, Epistles were apparently also gathered, and it appears that the letter of James, leader of the Jerusalem church and half brother of Jesus, was positioned after Paul's epistles possibly as a counterbalance to his message of justification by faith alone. Regardless of whether James was aware of Paul's writings, the epistle he left defines the nature of saving faith to deter misuse or distortion of the Pauline doctrine. Then follow the writings of Peter, whose role in the early church dominates the first twelve chapters of the book of Acts but who is not mentioned after chapter 15. It was by Peter's authority that faith in Christ was first opened to the Gentiles living within Palestine (Acts 10), paving the way for Paul's mission to the Gentiles throughout the empire. Next in the sequence of the General Epistles comes the letters of John, who partnered with Peter in the earliest days of the Jerusalem church as told in the first twelve chapters of Acts. And finally, comes the letter of Jude, brother of James (and therefore half brother of Jesus), whose magnificent doxology is a fitting ending to the collection of the General Epistles. The collection opens with the writing of one of Jesus' half brothers, James, and closes with the letter of a second half brother, Jude. This sequence draws together the apostolic authority of two of Jesus' twelve disciples, Peter and John, with two from Jesus' earthly family, James and Jude.[10] Because Jude is not mentioned in the book of Acts and his leadership enjoyed only a relatively small and local area of influence, it is not surprising that this epistle may have been slow to be universally recognized as canonical.

It is not necessary to speculate that James was written pseudonymously at a very late date when the collection was forming to appreciate how it aptly provides a bridge between Paul and the General Epistles.[11] In fact, the unifying coherence between all the New Testament epistles in their themes and concerns suggests an underlying historical reality that they would

9. D. Trobisch, *The First Edition of the New Testament* (Oxford: Oxford University Press, 2000).

10. See Richard Bauckham, *Jude and the Relatives of Jesus in the Early Church* (Edinburgh: T&T Clark, 1990).

11. As does David R. Nienhuis, *Not by Paul Alone: The Formation of the Catholic Epistle Collection and the Christian Canon* (Waco, Tex.: Baylor University Press, 2007), esp. pp. 163–231.

not display if written in far-flung reaches of the empire by anonymous individuals at random times long after the lives of the men in whose names they wrote. As Robert Wall observes:

> The working relations between Peter and Paul, or Paul and James, or James and Peter, or even Peter and John as depicted within Acts are generally collaborative rather than adversarial, and should frame the interpreter's approach to "their" biblical writings as essentially complementary in meaning and purpose even though certainly not uniform and sometimes even in conflict. For example, if Peter and John or James and Paul are enjoined as partners in this narrative world, then we should expect to work with their written traditions in a partnered way that assumes their theological distinctiveness and interdependence.[12]

The study of a unifying theology of the General Epistles, or of the entire New Testament, both assumes and demonstrates an underlying historical reality that connects the authors of these books in some substantial way. Wall has presented a summary of the themes the General Epistles share, presented here with some modifications:

1. Human suffering tests the faith community's love for God.
2. In response to suffering, God has disclosed the way of truth that leads to salvation.
3. In obedience to this way of truth, Christian believers must live in a way that publicly declares them to be followers of Christ.
4. Theological orthodoxy by itself is inconclusive to declare a profession of faith in Christ when it is not embodied in loving works.
5. The reward of steadfast obedience to God's Word even in the face of suffering is eternal life with God.[13]

Wall's study of the unifying theology of the General Epistles did not include the book of Hebrews. But the placement of Hebrews—with its major theme of the high priesthood of Jesus Christ who is himself the final **atoning** sacrifice—is appropriate and effective when the General Epistles are joined to Paul's writings. Reading Hebrews before James picks up the gospel story again, to remind the reader of the narrative of the cross before he or she launches into James and the letters that follow.

The underlying historical reality that allows the books of the New Testament canon to be read as substantially connected works is undercut by the assumption that many, if not most, of the books are pseudonymous. That underlying historical reality would be tenuous, resting upon what unknown individuals happened to believe about the beliefs of the apostles in whose name they wrote, perhaps separated by many years and many miles from where the apostles lived. The source and reliability of the pseudepigrapher's beliefs cannot be anchored in anything but the scholarly imagination of reconstructed "schools" or "communities" that are believed (by faith) to represent the apostolic tradition. A radical skepticism about the historical reliability of the New Testament books is not only unwarranted, but it undercuts the very aim of New Testament studies by distancing the origin of the primary texts from the historical reality in which they are moored and which provides the context in which they can be best understood.

---

12. Robert W. Wall, "A Unifying Theology of the Catholic Epistles: A Canonical Approach," in *The Catholic Epistles and the Tradition*, ed. J. Schlosser (Leuven: Leuven University Press, 2004), 56.
13. Ibid., 61.

The resurrection of Jesus Christ is the center and underlying unity of New Testament theology.

The unity of the messages of the General Epistles originates in the common experience of the men who wrote them—James, Peter, John, Jude, and their close associates—who knew each other personally, preached, evangelized, and supervised the churches during the same decades, and who had all experienced firsthand or by one degree of separation the resurrection of Jesus Christ, the incarnate Son of God. That historical reality provides the soundest foundation for seeking a unified New Testament theology and the most reasonable context in which to read and understand these books.

THE TEXT OF THE GENERAL EPISTLES

The Institute for New Testament Textual Research at the University of Münster in Germany publishes the standard Greek New Testament text used by scholars, the Nestle-Aland 27th ed. (NA27). The institute is currently producing a new critical edition of the New Testament, *Editio Critica Maior*. Their printed Greek text of the Catholic Epistles is available from Deutsche Bibelgesellschaft. Those readings in *Editio Critica Maior* that vary from NA27 can be found in Peter M. Head, 'Editio Critica Maior: An Introduction and Assessment', *Tyndale Bulletin* 61.1 (2010), 149–152, available online at https://www.academia.edu/3633883/_Editio_Critica_Maior_An_Introduction_and_Assessment_Tyndale_Bulletin_61.1_2010_131-152 (accessed May 2, 2016).

The Earliest Surviving Manuscripts of Hebrews and the General Epistles

Book	Siglum	MS name	Date	Contents
Hebrews	$\mathfrak{P}^{46}$	P. Chester Beatty II	c. AD 200	1:1–9:16; 9:18–10:20, 22–30; 10:32–13:25
James	$\mathfrak{P}^{20}$	Am 4117 P.Oxy. 1171	3rd century	2:19–3:9
	$\mathfrak{P}^{23}$	P.Oxy 1229	3rd century	1:10–12, 15–18
1 Peter	$\mathfrak{P}^{72}$	Bodmer VII–IX	3rd/4th century	complete text
2 Peter	$\mathfrak{P}^{72}$	Bodmer VII–IX	3rd/4th century	1:1–3, 18
1 John	$\mathfrak{P}^{9}$	P.Oxy 402	3rd century	4:11–12, 14–17
2 John	$\mathfrak{P}^{74}$	Bodmer XVII	7th century	1, 6–7, 12–13
3 John	$\mathfrak{P}^{74}$	Bodmer XVII	7th century	6, 12
Jude	$\mathfrak{P}^{72}$	Bodmer VII–IX	3rd/4th century	1–25

Courtesy of The Spurlock Museum, University of Illinois at Urbana-Champaign

Papyrus P.Oxy 1229 ($\mathfrak{P}^{23}$) from the 3rd century is one of the earliest extant manuscripts containing portions of the General Epistles.

PART 1

Hebrews: The Book of Better Things

CHAPTER 1

Introducing Hebrews

THE BOOK OF BETTER THINGS

Your Goals for This Chapter

- To know the range of dates scholars give for the writing of Hebrews and the reasons why.
- To be able to list the evidence for identifying the various possible authors of Hebrews and why most today do not believe it is the work of the apostle Paul.
- To better understand the situation of the original readers of Hebrews and why this **epistle** was written to them.
- To be able to list literary characteristics of the book of Hebrews.
- To be able to discuss how the original situation addressed by Hebrews compares to contemporary situations.

WHY THE BOOK OF HEBREWS IS IMPORTANT TO YOU

The book of Hebrews is important to you for three primary reasons. First, it has been compared to Romans for the magnitude of its theological significance. It is the book of the New Testament that is most devoted to explaining the relationship between the old covenant God made with ancient Israel and the new covenant established by the death of Jesus Christ. And so it presents profound insight into how Jesus Christ, particularly in his death, relates to the important elements of the Old Testament priesthood and sacrificial system. If you wish to better understand the Old Testament and why Christians no longer live under the old covenant, you need to understand what the author of Hebrews says about the new covenant's relationship to the old. And the better your knowledge of the theology and practices of ancient Israel, the better you will understand Hebrews.

Second, there is probably no other book of the New Testament that so clearly explains why the Christ had to be fully human in order to bring God's redemptive plan to its culmination. The glory of Christ's divinity sometimes obscures in Christian thought the necessity of his humanity. Christians often fail to appreciate how Jesus Christ lived with the same human frailities, fears, and temptations that each one of us faces. Jesus Christ's full participation in all that it means to be human was a qualification for his redemptive work on the cross, a work that Hebrews describes in terms of him being both priest and sacrifice.

Key Verses

2:3b:	This salvation, which was first announced by the Lord, was confirmed to us by those who heard him.
5:12:	In fact, though by this time you ought to be teachers, you need someone to teach you the elementary truths of God's word all over again....
10:32–35:	Remember those earlier days after you had received the light, when you endured in a great conflict full of suffering. Sometimes you were publicly exposed to insult and persecution; at other times you stood side by side with those who were so treated. You suffered along with those in prison and joyfully accepted the confiscation of your property, because you knew that you yourselves had better and lasting possessions. So do not throw away your confidence; it will be richly rewarded.
12:4:	In your struggle against sin, you have not yet resisted to the point of shedding your blood.
13:22:	Brothers and sisters, I urge you to bear with my word of exhortation, for in fact I have written to you quite briefly.
13:23:	I want you to know that our brother Timothy has been released. If he arrives soon, I will come with him to see you.
13:24b:	Those from Italy send you their greetings.

Challenges Presented by the Book of Hebrews

- Identifying its author.
- Appreciating its use of the Old Testament.
- Understanding its relationship to Philo and **Neoplatonic philosophy**.
- Comprehending its teaching on the possibility of **apostasy**.
- Rising to its challenge of pressing on to spiritual maturity.

It also allowed God to share in the experience of all that it means to be human—the temptations and fears as well as the sweetness of life and love and beauty.

Third, the book of Hebrews explains the incentive for faithful living. In a Christian culture that so puts the emphasis on "being saved," Hebrews issues the most disturbing warnings found in the New Testament. Its teaching on apostasy must be understood in the original historical context of the book and taken to heart by anyone who wishes to press on to Christian maturity. For these and other reasons, no Christian should pass over the book of Hebrews lightly.

CHAPTER OUTLINE

I. Who Were the People Originally Addressed?
II. Where Were the Original Readers Living?
III. When Was the Book of Hebrews Written?
IV. Who Wrote the Book of Hebrews?
V. Is Hebrews Really a Letter?
VI. An Overview of the Theology of the Book of Hebrews
  A. **Christology** in Hebrews
  B. God the Father
  C. The Holy Spirit
  D. The New Covenant
  E. The Reality of Heaven
  F. The Dualism of Hebrews
  G. The Definition and Practice of Faith
  H. Angelology
VII. The Text and Canonicity of Hebrews
  A. The Greek Text of Hebrews
  B. Canonicity
VIII. Outline of the Book of Hebrews

Please read the book of Hebrews in one or two sittings before reading this chapter.

WHO WERE THE PEOPLE ORIGINALLY ADDRESSED?

Have you ever grown bored with Christianity and been tempted to experiment with a new, more glamorous religion? Would you go to church this Sunday if you knew there was a high risk you would be arrested by hostile authorities on your way? Have you ever been mocked for your Christian faith and tempted to quietly distance yourself from Jesus Christ? Has the thought ever gone through your mind that, because you once said the "sinner's prayer" and meant it, that it now matters little how you live for Christ, since you have your ticket to heaven? Judging from the exhortations in the book of Hebrews, the Christians to whom it was originally addressed may have faced issues like these.

Considering the pervasive references throughout the book to Israel's history and practices, the epistle of Hebrews apparently was written by an author who was thoroughly steeped in the theology of Judaism and wrote to Christians who also presumably would understand his references and arguments, at least to a great extent. The Jewish nature of the book conclusively says something about its author, but it is a little less certain what we can infer from this about the original audience. It would have been especially important for Christian converts from Judaism to understand the relationship of Christ to the religion of Israel. But even **Gentile** converts would have had the Scriptures of Israel available to them in its Greek translation (the **Septuagint**). So it is less certain whether the audience was Jewish Christian, Gentile Christian, or mixed. It can be inferred with more confidence that regardless of their ethnic origin, the people to whom Hebrews was originally written were beginning to waver in their faith because of some kind of persecution, whether it was a form of social ostracism or more menacing acts by government officials (e.g., Heb. 12:4). And if the Christians to whom Hebrews was originally sent were, in fact, converts from Judaism, it is easy to imagine how they would be tempted to slip quietly back into the synagogue to worship God and to forget all about this man Jesus. Maybe they had been mistaken that he was Israel's long-awaited Messiah after all.

As Christians reading the Bible today, we think of it as God's Word speaking directly to us. This is a true and right way to read the Bible, but we must not lose sight of the fact that the books of the New Testament were originally written to Christians who lived more than two thousand years ago, who read the New Testament in its original language (***koine* Greek**), and who were living in times when society, politics, religions, and philosophies were vastly different from our own. And so to better understand what God *is* saying to us today through the book of Hebrews, we need to consider those circumstances originally addressed when the book was first written.

We can infer from the content of the book of Hebrews that its author was intensely interested in teaching the original audience about the relationship of Jesus Christ to the old covenant between God and ancient Israel as revealed in the Hebrew Scriptures. The book of Hebrews is filled with references to the sacrificial system and priesthood of ancient Israel and explains how the new covenant established by Christ's death has replaced the old covenant in God's redemptive dealings with humanity. Such matters would have been vitally important to converts from Judaism, whose families had for generations practiced the religion of Israel. Gentile Christians may have found the supersession of the old covenant by the new of interest, but not with the same existential zeal (or perhaps angst).

All New Testament books originally were written in Greek, but the authors did not assign the titles that have come down to us. This suggests that the circumstances in which the books were produced were specific and personal, such that a writing, whether gospel or epistle, passed between author and original readers with no need for a title. Titles certainly had to be added when the individual books of the New Testament began to be collected and bound together.

Although the titles of the New Testament books were not assigned by their authors, they are nevertheless quite ancient. The title of Hebrews, "To the Hebrews" (Gk. *pros hebraious*; Lat. *ad Hebraeos*), apparently was assigned before the end of the second century, as attested by Tertullian, who provides the earliest **extant** reference to the book by name (*Pud.* 20). Perhaps the title reflects a reliable memory of the book's original audience even though, unlike Paul's letters, the book doesn't specify it was written "to the Hebrews." Neither the word *Hebrew* (Gk. *hebraios*) or *Jew* (Gk. *ioudaios*) appears in the book, making one wonder what motivated the ascription "To the Hebrews." The title "To the Hebrews" may indicate that when it was assigned, the book was thought to be addressed to Jewish Christians, for ancient evidence shows the term *Hebrews* (Gk. *hebraioi*) was generally used to refer to Jews in distinction from Gentiles. However, a synagogue in first-century Rome was known as the "synagogue of the Hebrews," and an inscription in Corinth bears the same phrase.[1] Since all synagogues were presumably attended by Jewish people, these inscriptions may indicate a sect of Judaism that, though located geographically in the **Diaspora**, maintained the language and customs of Jerusalem. Even in Jerusalem itself there were both Hellenistic Jews—those more amenable to the influence of Greek culture—and Hebraic Jews (Acts 6:1). Perhaps Hebrews was written to an audience of Jewish Christians who had not yet fully understood that Christ's death replaced the ancient sacrificial system.

In fact, some scholars have attempted to identify Hebrews as a sermon preached in a synagogue of Jewish converts, since early Christian worship was patterned on the synagogue liturgy. Some argue Hebrews originated as a **midrash** preached on Psalm 110.[2] Another sees it as a sermon preached on Tisha Be-Av, a day of fasting and mourning that was a solemn day in the Jewish liturgical year commemorating the broken covenant. The Palestinian Triennial Cycle (PTC) of lectionary readings observed this day by pairing Exodus 31:18–32:35 with Jeremiah 31:31–34, a reminder of both the breaking of the covenant and the promise of a new covenant written on hearts. The PTC took a congregation through the Torah in three years and was used in ancient Palestine and Palestinian Diaspora communities, perhaps such as the "synagogue of the Hebrews" in Rome.[3] While the message of Hebrews would be very apt on such an occasion, it is probably not possible to tie it to so specific a setting with current evidence.

---

1. Ben Witherington III, *Letters and Homilies for Jewish Christians* (Downers Grove, Ill.: IVP Academic, 2007), 24–25.

2. George W. Buchanan, *The Book of Hebrews: Its Challenge from Zion* (Eugene, Ore.: Wipf & Stock, 2006); D. R. Anderson, *The King-Priest of Psalm 110 in Hebrews*, Studies in Biblical Literature 21 (New York, Bern: Lang, 2001).

3. Gabriella Gelardini, "Hebrews, an Ancient Synagogue Homily for Tisha Be-Av," in *Hebrews: Contemporary Methods—New Insights*, ed. G. Gelardini, Biblical Interpretation Series 75 (Leiden: Brill, 2005), 107–27, esp. 110, 122.

Other scholars argue that the title of the book does not compel the conclusion that the original readers were necessarily converts from Judaism or that they spoke the Hebrew language. You will note that Abraham's relationship to Melchizedek is of great importance in the argument that the author of Hebrews makes for the priesthood of Jesus (7:1–10). At the time Abraham lived (about two thousand years before Christ), God had not yet established his chosen nation, ancient Israel, so there were no people called "Hebrews." Abraham, a pagan man, is the first person in the Bible to be called a "Hebrew" (Gen. 14:13) because he was chosen by God to be the ancestral father of the nation of ancient Israel. Therefore, the ascription "To the Hebrews" may not so much reflect the ethnic identity of the original readers, but their embrace of the religion established by God and foreshadowed by Abraham, the first Hebrew, and as culminating in the new covenant based on Jesus Christ. Paul similarly describes all who believe in Christ as the children of Abraham, regardless of their ethnic identity (Gal. 3:7).

> "Abraham is father of Hebrews and gentiles alike."
>
> Clement of Alexandria, *Stromateis* 3.8.6

Nevertheless, the content of the book is so steeped in the practices of ancient Israel—practices that centered on the **tabernacle**, priesthood, and sacrificial system—that many interpreters argue it is very likely that the author is addressing Christian converts from Judaism who would most appreciate the substantial exposition of the Old Testament. This inference assumes that Gentile converts to Christ would not have been sufficiently familiar with the Scriptures and practices of Judaism to make good sense of the extensive discussions of Jesus as High Priest and ultimate sacrifice. But because the Hebrew Scriptures had existed in Greek translation (the Septuagint and others) long before Jesus was born, there would have been no reason why Gentile Christians could not have read and studied the Old Testament, especially since that was the Bible of the church before the New Testament books were brought together. Access to the Septuagint and knowledge of the Old Testament would have been available especially in areas with a substantial Jewish population. Just as Gentile Christians today gain a great deal of insight into the Old Testament through their reading of Hebrews, one cannot infer with certainty from the content of the book that it was composed exclusively for a Jewish Christian audience.

Regardless of the ethnic background of those originally addressed, the author of Hebrews passionately used ancient Greek rhetoric to persuade his readers to persevere and to continue in their Christian faith. The people he addressed had experienced difficult times:

> Remember those earlier days after you had received the light, when you endured in a great conflict full of suffering. Sometimes you were publicly exposed to insult and persecution; at other times you stood side by side with those who were so treated. You suffered along with those in prison and joyfully accepted the confiscation of your property, because you knew that you yourselves had better and lasting possessions. So do not throw away your confidence; it will be richly rewarded. (10:32–35)

We do not know the specific circumstances that were apparently tempting these believers to turn from faith in Christ. There was likely more than one. Perhaps it was harsh persecution, either actually occurring or only a distant threat (Heb. 10:32–35; 13:3). Perhaps a more general spiritual malaise had set in as these Christians aged in years but not in maturity (Heb. 5:11–14). Regardless of the motivation of their temptation, he warns them that if they do turn away from Christ for any reason, there is nowhere to go but toward apostasy, which would be a spiritually fatal mistake (Heb. 6:4–12; 10:26–31).

Putting these observations and inferences together, the author of Hebrews wants to explain to the readers how there is no turning back to the familiar ways of the old covenant God made with ancient Israel now that Jesus Christ has come. That was then; this is now. The incarnation of Jesus Christ has begun nothing less than a new epoch of God's dealings with the inhabitants of planet Earth. The message from God that Jesus Christ is the full and final revelation of his relationship with humanity is relevant as much today as it was when originally written, regardless of who is reading it.

WHERE WERE THE ORIGINAL READERS LIVING?

If the original audience was at least predominantly Jewish, they could have been from one of the three major cities in the Roman world of New Testament times that had a large Jewish presence: Jerusalem, Alexandria, or Rome.

Furthermore, while not centered in any one city, a large Jewish population had lived in Asia Minor since the time of the Hellenistic kings. A small number of scholars in past generations have supported Jerusalem as the original destination of the letter.[4] But the persecution of Christians there that resulted in the deaths of Stephen and the apostle James was very early, even before the apostle Paul's conversion (Acts 7:58–8:3; 12:1–2; 1 Thess.

4. George W. Buchanan, *To the Hebrews*, AB 36 (Garden City, N.Y.: Doubleday, 1972); Philip E. Hughes, *A Commentary on the Epistle to the Hebrews* (Grand Rapids: Eerdmans, 1977); Marie E. Isaacs, *Sacred Space*, JSNTSup 73 (Sheffield: JSOT, 1992); William M. Ramsay, *Luke the Physician* (New York: Hodder and Stoughton, 1903); Ceslas Spicq, *L'Epître aux Hebreux*, 2 vols., Études bibliques (Paris: Gabalda, 1952–53).

Alexandria, Jerusalem, and Rome are commonly considered probable destinations for the letter to the Hebrews, but there was also a sizable Jewish population in western Asia Minor as well.

2:14–16). Hebrews 2:3 implies that the original readers did not personally hear the Lord Jesus teach, or even his twelve apostles, which makes an early Jerusalem destination more unlikely, depending on when the epistle was written. Moreover, the exclusive use of the Septuagint and the high literary style of the Greek may also weigh against Jerusalem as the original destination, though there is increasing evidence that Greek was in common use even in first-century Jerusalem.

The mid-twentieth century saw some views arise that have not been widely accepted. One minority view is that Apollos wrote Hebrews in the early 50s while at Ephesus and sent it to the church in Corinth (cf. 1 Cor. 3:4–6, 22; 16:12).[5] The ruins of a large synagogue at Sardis, and other similar ruins in that general vicinity, attest to the presence of a sizeable Jewish population from which early Christians may have come. Another theory not widely accepted is that Hebrews was originally written to the churches of the Lycus Valley in Asia Minor, possibly written by Apollos or Epaphras, to combat the "Colossian heresy" that diminished Christ to the status of an angel and tried to observe Jewish rituals (Col. 2:16, 18).[6] Whether or not it was written to combat the "Colossian heresy," Jewish Christians in any location would have unlikely found the message of Hebrews of pressing interest.

Alexandria, Egypt, was for centuries another Eastern center of both a large Jewish population and Greek culture. Both the content of Hebrews and the style of rhetoric presented in the epistle would have been at home in Alexandria. Furthermore, the Greek version of the Old Testament had its origin in Alexandria and was the Jewish Scripture for that city, accounting for the form of the Old Testament quotations as found in Hebrews. Moreover, there was persecution of the Jewish population in Alexandria during the reign of Caligula (**AD** 37–41), which, while earlier than most scholars would date Hebrews, may account for the reference of past persecution in Hebrews 10:32–34. Although the persecution was of the Jewish population in the earliest days of the church, the Roman officials often con-

5. E.g., Hugh Montefiore, *A Commentary on the Epistle to the Hebrews* (London: Black, 1964).

6. T. W. Manson, "The Problem of the Epistle to the Hebrews," *BJRL* 32 (1949): 1–17. Also Robert Jewett, *Letter to Pilgrims: A Commentary on the Epistle to the Hebrews* (New York: Pilgrim, 1981), 5–10.

Clement Knew Hebrews

By the end of the first century, Clement of Rome clearly knew the text of Hebrews as reflected in his letter to the Corinthian church:

> This is the way, dear friends, in which we found our salvation, namely *Jesus Christ, the High Priest* of our offerings, the Guardian and Helper of our weakness. Through him let us look steadily into the heights of heaven.... Through him the Master has willed that we should taste immortal knowledge, for *"he being the radiance of his majesty, is as much superior to angels as the name he has inherited is more excellent."* For so it is written: "He makes his angels winds and his ministers flames of fire." But of his Son the Master spoke thus: "You are my Son; today I have begotten you.... Sit at my right hand, until I make your enemies a footstool for your feet."
>
> Clement of Rome
>
> *1 Clement* 36.1–6 (emphasis added)

sidered Christians to be Jews and didn't spare Jewish Christians from persecution as Jews. On the other hand, one argument against Alexandria as the original destination is that if the Timothy mentioned in Hebrews 13:23 is the apostle Paul's associate, how likely would it be that he would have been known in Alexandria? But with the relative ease of travel by sea, it is plausible that Timothy and others associated with the Christian mission in the northern Mediterranean area could have visited Alexandria. But had Hebrews been originally sent to the church in Alexandria, it seems odd that the Alexandrian fathers, Clement and Origen, would not have known this. Instead, they seemed to think it was originally addressed to Christians of Palestine.[7]

The character of any given writing more certainly reflects its author, and only to a lesser degree its audience. And so even if Hebrews reflects the character of the Christian message in Alexandria, that doesn't determine the destination of the letter, for an Alexandrian author could have been writing to readers in Alexandria, Jerusalem, Rome, or elsewhere. More on this below in the discussion of who wrote Hebrews. And so all considered, there is not a sufficient basis on which to claim Alexandria as the original destination, especially when there is stronger evidence to identify Rome as the original destination.

Because of strong connections with Rome, most scholars today support the imperial city as the original destination of Hebrews, though this theory is also not without its problems. The book seems to have been known first, or at least very early, in the city of Rome, as is evident in Clement of Rome's letter to the Corinthian church that dates from before AD 100 (*1 Clement* 36.1–6). Although Clement does not refer to the book of Hebrews by name, he clearly quotes material from its opening chapter in the same sequence in which it appears in Hebrews 1. While this hardly proves the theory, it is certainly consistent with Rome as the original destination.

The oldest manuscript containing the book of Hebrews places it following Romans.

In spite of apparently having known of the book from its early days, for centuries the Roman Church was very reluctant to accept the canonicity of Hebrews. In contrast, the Eastern churches argued for its canonicity from at least the second century onward on the basis of Pauline authorship. (See discussion of canonicity below.) This could be construed as evidence for Alexandria being the original destination (or possible origin) of the letter, though the early Alexandrian fathers apparently believed it had been originally sent to another Eastern city, Jerusalem. The Roman reluctance to accept it as canonical possibly may have been because of a latent memory of having received the letter now known as Hebrews, but from an author other than the apostle Paul (Eusebius, *Hist. eccl.* 3.3.5; 6.20.3). But the authority on which the original readers accepted the epistle might be expected to carry its canonicity in that geographical area—an argument against a Roman destination. The earliest extant manuscript of Hebrews is $\mathfrak{P}^{46}$, in which Hebrews is located in the middle of Paul's letters, right after Romans. While this is usually construed as suggesting

7. Eusebius, *Hist. eccl.* 6.14.2, 6.25.12, respectively.

those who so ordered the books believed the apostle Paul wrote Hebrews, it may instead reflect a Roman destination for both letters.

An explicit association with Rome might be inferred from Hebrews 13:24, where the author sends greetings from "those from Italy." This could be construed as greetings from Italy to another location if the author was writing from Rome; or if he was writing from another place outside Italy, as greetings from some Italians who happened also to be at that location. But in either case the reference to Italy strengthens the association of Hebrews with Rome. For these reasons, and because there is no comparable evidence to tilt the conclusion toward Alexandria or Jerusalem, Rome is most often inferred today to have been the original destination of Hebrews. However, the inference that Rome was the original destination of the book doesn't necessarily mean that the author was also in Rome at the time he wrote it. This is one of many things about the book of Hebrews we simply don't know.

WHEN WAS THE BOOK OF HEBREWS WRITTEN?

The citation of material from the first chapter of Hebrews by Clement in his letter to the Corinthians is clear evidence that the book was in existence and known in Rome by the last decade of the first century, since Clement's letter is dated to about AD 95. Let's see what other clues might help to date this book.

Since the original readers had experienced, and perhaps were experiencing, some degree of persecution, scholars have looked to date the book during a time of persecution in one of the likely destinations. Although the very first Christians to be persecuted were the Jewish Christians in Jerusalem (e.g., Acts 4:3–22; 5:17–42; 6:8–7:60; 8:1–3), the book of Hebrews contains clues that it must have been written later in the first century. Hebrews 2:3 refers to the gospel message that had been announced by the Lord (e.g., Mark 1:14–15) and then confirmed "to us" by "those who heard him." That suggests two degrees of separation between the original audiences of Jesus in Palestine and the author of Hebrews, though the length of time that passed between Jesus' teaching and the writing of Hebrews cannot be estimated from this. Hebrews 5:12 assumes that the original readers had been Christians long enough that they should have been teaching others rather than in need of learning the "elementary truths of God's word all over again." Sufficient time must be allowed for the evange-

The book of Hebrews has been closely associated with Rome.

Did Belief in Jesus Christ Stir Trouble in Rome?

"Since the Jews constantly made disturbances at the instigation of Chrestus, he [Emperor Claudius] expelled them from Rome."

Suetonius, *Claudius* 25.4

Is *Chrestus* an alternate spelling of the Latin *Christus*? The interchange of *e* and *i* is attested elsewhere; the *-us* ending Latinizes the title, which may be a reference to Christ.

lization, growth, previous confiscation of property (10:32–36), and incipient spiritual decline. Most scholars therefore infer that this book was written at least a few decades after Jesus had died, which on that basis would put the book not earlier than AD 60, about the time the Roman emperor Caesar Nero was coming to power.

K. H. Jobes

The Roman Emperor Claudius.

But there was earlier persecution in Rome that might account for the reference to previous persecution in Hebrews 10:32–34. According to the Roman historian Suetonius, Nero's predecessor, the emperor Claudius, had expelled the Jews from Rome sometime around AD 49, possibly because of turmoil caused by preaching about Christ (*Claud.* 25.4). The authorities viewed Christianity in its earliest days as a sect of Judaism because it centered on the worship of a Jewish man who had lived and died in Palestine. Claudius may not have differentiated between Christians and Jews in the expulsion. Or perhaps Suetonius, who records this expulsion, may have referred to Christians as Jews.

Following Claudius, the emperor Nero went on to horrifically martyr Christians in Rome by burning them and by throwing them to wild animals in the Colosseum. When a fire destroyed a large section of the city, a rumor circulated that Nero may have ordered it set. To deflect suspicions, he blamed the Christians of the city, and a period of martyrdom ensued.

> To scotch the rumor, Nero substituted as culprits, and punished with the utmost refinements of cruelty, a class of men, loathed for their vices, whom the crowd styled Christians. Christus, the founder of the name, had undergone the death penalty in the reign of Tiberius, by sentence of the procurator Pontius Pilatus, and the pernicious superstition was checked for a moment, only to break out once more, not merely in Judaea, the home of the disease, but in the capital itself, where all things horrible or shameful in the world collect and find a vogue. First, then, the confessed members of the sect were arrested; next, on their disclosures, vast numbers were convicted, not so much on the count of arson as for hatred of the human race. And derision accompanied their end: they were covered with wild beasts' skins and torn to death by dogs; or they were fastened on crosses, and, when daylight failed were burned to serve as lamps by night. Nero had offered his Gardens for the spectacle, and gave an exhibition in

"Punishment was inflicted [by Emperor Nero] on the Christians, a class of men given to a new and mischievous superstition."

Suetonius, *Nero* 16.57

© Anne Marie Clarke

Nero being crowned by Agrippina.

his Circus, mixing with the crowd in the habit of a charioteer, or mounted on his car. Hence, in spite of a guilt which had earned the most exemplary punishment, there arose a sentiment of pity, due to the impression that they [the Christians] were being sacrificed not for the welfare of the state but to the ferocity of a single man [i.e., Nero]. (Tacitus, *Ann.* 15.54)

In light of this persecution, the book of Hebrews was addressed to Christians who "have *not yet* resisted to the point of shedding your blood" (12:4, emphasis added). If addressed to Christians living in Rome, this statement would sit best before Nero began to kill Christians. With the storm clouds of Nero's hostility to Christians on the horizon, some may have attempted to escape persecution by withdrawing from their Christian commitment. Such a scenario would motivate the warnings in Hebrews against apostasy (6:4–8; 10:26–39) and the exhortations to continue meeting together despite the risk (10:19–25).

A further consideration in regard to the date Hebrews was written is the destruction of the Jerusalem temple in AD 70. The author of Hebrews speaks of the sacrificial rituals in the present tense, and some infer that the temple must have been in operation at that time. Certainly the author's argument that Jesus is the unique and final sacrifice after which no further sacrifices are necessary would have been strongly supported by pointing out the fact that the Jerusalem temple had been destroyed, were that the case. However, the grammatical present tense itself is not sufficient grounds for arguing a date of writing, for the present tense in Greek has other relationships to time.

To complicate matters, the author of Hebrews does not actually refer to the "temple" at all. Whenever the author refers to the sacred place where sacrifice was made under the old covenant, he uses the word *tabernacle*, a portable tent used for worship by ancient Israel (8:2, 5; 9:1, 2, 8, 11, 21; 13:10). In fact, the Greek words for "temple" (*hieron* and *naos*) don't occur at all in Hebrews. This point has been used to argue that Hebrews was written *after* the

Left: Interior of Colosseum *Right:* The Colosseum of Rome, built in 75-80 CE under the Flavian Emperors Vespasian and Titus.

Todd Bolen/www.BiblePlaces.com

© Alexey Arkhipov/www.BigStockPhoto.com

Ariely/Wikimedia Commons

© 1995 Phoenix Data Systems

Left: A model of the Jerusalem Temple as it appeared in the first century. *Right:* A view of the temple mount today.

destruction of the Jerusalem temple, "from the point of view of a generation which had now lost that sacred shrine and, in this sense, was once more back in the wilderness situation."[8]

The choice of *tabernacle* (Gk. *skēnē*) over *temple* was perhaps to distance the priestly work of Jesus from the first-century temple in Jerusalem, with all its politics and corruption. Or perhaps it was to draw the readers' thoughts to that period early in Israel's history when the old covenant had first been established and the tabernacle was set up by the Levites wherever Israel camped during their wilderness journey. Because the author's concern is to contrast the old covenant as ordained by God and the new covenant recently established by Jesus Christ, he focuses his thought on the inception of the old covenant during the time of Moses millennia before Jesus.[9] In this way, the founding events of the old covenant are compared to the founding events of the new, showing how the new grows out of and fulfills the old. And so perhaps for the author's purpose, it was a moot point whether the Jerusalem temple actually existed or not at the time of writing.

On the other hand, the statement and question in Hebrews 10:1–3 would be emptied of its effect if the sacrifices had in fact stopped because of the temple's destruction:

> The law is only a shadow of the good things that are coming—not the realities themselves. For this reason it can never, by the same sacrifices repeated endlessly year after year, make perfect those who draw near to worship. *Otherwise, would they not have stopped being offered?* For the worshipers would have been cleansed once for all, and would no longer have felt guilty for their sins. But those sacrifices are an annual reminder of sins. It is impossible for the blood of bulls and goats to take away sins. . . .
>
> *Day after day every priest stands and performs his religious duties*; again and again he offers the same sacrifices, which can never take away sins. But when this priest [Jesus

8. Isaacs, *Sacred Space*, 77.

9. The use of *tabernacle* or *tent* may also be related to an eschatological understanding of Balaam's oracles in Num. 24. See Philip A. F. Church, "'The True Tent Which the Lord Has Pitched': Balaam's Oracles in Second Temple Judaism and in Hebrews," in *A Cloud of Witnesses: The Theology of Hebrews in Its Ancient Contexts*, ed. Richard Bauckham et al. (London: T&T Clark, 2008), 145–57.

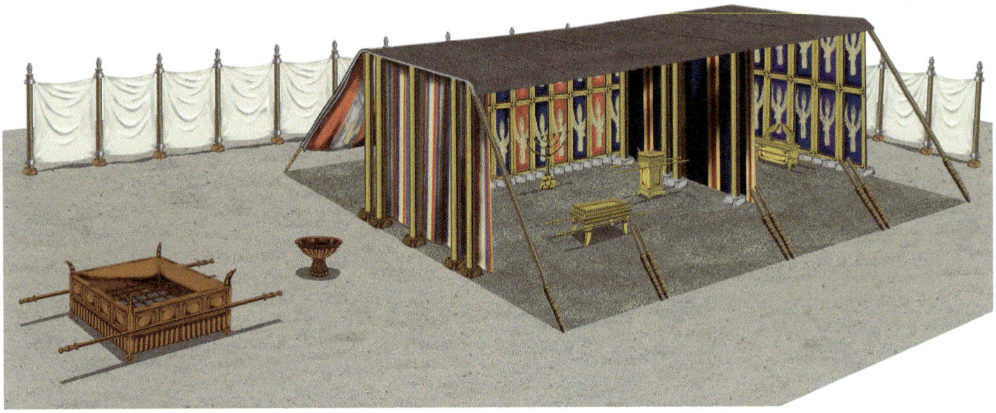

Hebrews interprets the Tabernacle to foreshadow Jesus' atonement.

> Christ] had offered for all time one sacrifice for sins ... he ... made perfect forever those who are being made holy. (vv. 1–4, 11–12, 14, emphasis added)

The author of Hebrews declared the priesthood and animal sacrifices that were centered in the temple in Jerusalem to be obsolete now that Jesus had died on the cross. Had Hebrews been written after AD 70, it would seem odd that the author didn't capitalize on the destruction of the temple to show that the sacrifices that could no longer be offered were in fact no longer needed. When Hebrews 8:13 pronounces the old covenant obsolete, it goes on to predict that "what is obsolete and outdated will soon disappear." While not necessarily a direct prophecy specifically about the temple, it rings truer if in fact the temple was still standing as the centerpiece of the old covenant.

One further clue about the date of the book is found in Hebrews 13:23, which mentions that "our brother Timothy has been released," presumably from prison. The book of Acts mentions Timothy as a traveling companion of the apostle Paul (Acts 16:1–4; 17:14–15; 18:5; 19:22; 20:4) and two books of the New Testament were originally written from Paul to Timothy (1 and 2 Timothy). But none of this material mentions that Timothy was imprisoned. Although this silence doesn't necessarily mean the imprisonment happened after these books were written, most infer that Timothy was imprisoned sometime during Nero's reign. If so, this would pin the date of the book rather precisely to the mid- to late sixties. But Timothy seems to have been a very young man when Paul first met him; he probably could have lived into the eighties and have been imprisoned at other later times. Or, the Timothy mentioned in Hebrews 13:23 could be a completely different person, though this seems unlikely.

Therefore, the best one can infer from clues within the book itself and references to the book by other authors is that it was written sometime in the last forty years of the first century, with good reason to suggest between AD 60 and 70.

WHO WROTE THE BOOK OF HEBREWS?

The question of who wrote this book is, of course, closely tied to the previous questions about its origin. In the earliest manuscript editions of the New Testament books, Hebrews

Titus' arch in Rome commemorates the destruction of Jerusalem by Titus and his Roman army in AD 70. The spoils plundered from Jerusalem are displayed on the arch.

is included after Romans among the books written by the apostle Paul. This was taken as evidence that Paul had written it, and some Eastern churches accepted Hebrews as canonical earlier than in the West. Both Clement of Alexandria (c. AD 150–215) and Origen (AD 185–253) claimed a Pauline association for the book but recognized that Paul himself probably did not put pen to paper for this book, even though they did not know the author's name.[10] Clement of Alexandria suggests that Paul wrote the book originally in Hebrew and that Luke translated it into Greek, though the Greek of Hebrews bears no resemblance to translation Greek (e.g., that of the Septuagint); Origen does not venture a guess at the author's identity, commenting only, "But who wrote the epistle, in truth only God knows."[11]

> "This passage [Heb. 2:3] indicates that this epistle was not written by Paul."
>
> John Calvin, *Commentary on Hebrews*

The nuanced position on the authorship question by the Alexandrian fathers was obscured by later church tradition that mistook Pauline association for Pauline authorship. The enormously influential King James Bible took its cue from this tradition as reflected in the title translated from that found in some manuscripts, "The Epistle of Paul the Apostle to the Hebrews." In spite of this, the careful reader of the epistle will note that the book of Hebrews is in fact anonymous. Few New Testament scholars today believe that Paul wrote it, and both John Calvin and Martin Luther as far back as the sixteenth century also shared that judgment. Even centuries earlier in the fourth century, the church of Rome did not believe Paul wrote Hebrews, possibly retaining a latent memory of the actual author (Eusebius, *Hist. eccl.* 3.3.5; 6.20.3). And so the rejection of Pauline authorship of Hebrews is a long-standing position in the church.

10. Cited by Eusebius in *Hist. eccl.* 6.14.2 and 6.25.12, respectively.
11. Cited by Eusebius in *Hist. eccl.* 6.25.14.

But many of the thoughts of Hebrews are similar to those found in Paul's writings:

Hebrews 1:3 "The Son is the radiance of God's glory and the exact representation of his being, sustaining all things by his powerful word."	Colossians 1:15–17 "The Son is the image of the invisible God.... For in him all things were created ... and in him all things hold together."
Hebrews 2:4 "God also testified to it by signs, wonders and various miracles, and by gifts of the Holy Spirit distributed according to his will."	1 Corinthians 12:11 "All these are the work of one and the same Spirit, and he distributes them to each one, just as he determines."
Hebrews 2:14(–17) "Since the children have flesh and blood, he too shared in their humanity so that by his death he might break the power of him who holds the power of death...."	Philippians 2:7–8 "Being made in human likeness. And being found in appearance as a human being, he humbled himself by becoming obedient to death— even death on a cross!"
Hebrews 8:6 "But in fact the ministry Jesus has received is as superior to theirs as the covenant of which he is mediator is superior to the old one, since the new covenant is established on better promises."	2 Corinthians 3:6 "He has made us competent as ministers of a new covenant—not of the letter but of the Spirit; for the letter kills, but the Spirit gives life."
Hebrews 10:14 "For by one sacrifice he has made perfect forever those who are being made holy."	Romans 5:9; 12:1 "Since we have now been justified by his blood"; "offer your bodies as a living sacrifice, holy and pleasing to God."

The internal evidence presented by the book of Hebrews itself indicates an author other than Paul. The style of Hebrews, except in the closing verses (13:18–25), is quite unlike any other writing of Paul's that has survived, the author does not introduce himself as Paul typically did (cf. 2 Cor. 1:1; Gal 1:1; Eph. 1:1; Col. 1:1; 1 Tim. 1:1; and 2 Tim. 1:1), and its theology, though very compatible with that of the Pauline letters, is very distinctive.[12] The apostle Paul, for instance, never alludes to Jesus as a priest, which is the major motif of Hebrews. In fact, Hebrews is the only New Testament writing to expound on Jesus as the Great High Priest and final sacrifice.

12. For a discussion of the relationship of Hebrews to Paul's writings, as well as to Stephen's speech in Acts 7 and to 1 Peter, see L. D. Hurst, *The Epistle to the Hebrews: Its Background of Thought*, SNTSMS (Cambridge: Cambridge University Press, 1990).

In keeping with the style of a person well educated in formal rhetoric, the Greek of Hebrews is highly literary and very ornate. The vocabulary is sophisticated, and it includes 150 words that are not found elsewhere in the New Testament and 10 that do not occur in any other Greek writings that have survived for our study. The structure of the epistle conforms to conventions found in Greek rhetoric used when a speech was designed to persuade its audience to action. Much of this rhetorical achievement is lost when the original Greek of Hebrews is translated into modern language, but in the original it is elegant and euphonious Greek prose. The high rhetorical quality of Hebrews indicates that its author most likely had the most advanced literary education of any of the New Testament writers.

An even more persuasive argument that the apostle Paul was not the author of Hebrews is the way the author alludes to himself in Hebrews 2:3, stating that the gospel was confirmed "to us" by those who heard the Lord announce salvation. The apostle Paul always made the point that, even though he wasn't one of the twelve original disciples who walked with Jesus during his earthly life, he was nonetheless an apostle of Jesus Christ, and usually identifies himself as such in his letters. It seems unlikely that Paul here in 2:3 would refer to himself as simply someone who received the gospel from those who had heard the Lord. Nevertheless, the **soteriology** of Hebrews is quite consistent with Paul's own teaching. For instance, the statement in Hebrews 10:14 that those who have been "made perfect" are in the process of being "made holy" sounds very much like Paul's teaching on justification (e.g., Rom. 3:21–5:9) and sanctification (e.g., Rom. 8:1–17). Moreover, both Paul and the author of Hebrews thought of Abraham as the spiritual father of Christians in similar ways.

All this adds up to the inference that someone other than Paul wrote the epistle, though the author was likely a close associate of Paul; the author was able to write in a rhetorically ornate Greek style, had become a Christian out of Judaism, and his soteriology (doctrine of salvation) was highly compatible with what the apostle Paul taught, though creatively distinctive.

Although Alexandria, Egypt, does not seem to have been the original destination of Hebrews, its high rhetorical style, use of the Septuagint, and possible conceptual constructs are suggestive of what scholars know about Alexandria in the first century. This may be explained if the author was from the Alexandrian church, regardless of where he was when

The High Rhetoric of Hebrews

"The Epistle to the Hebrews has not its like among the epistles of the New Testament, resembling in this uniqueness of position, as well as in tone and spirit, the great prophetic exhortation of Isaiah 40–66, which in like manner stands alone among the prophetic writings of the Old Testament.... No other book of the New Testament is distinguished by such brilliant eloquence and euphonious rhythm.... It is characterized throughout by conscious repose, dignified solemnity, and majestic quietude."*

*Franz Delitzsch, *Commentary on the Epistle to the Hebrews*, trans. Thomas L. Kingsbury, 2 vols., Clark's Foreign Theological Library (Grand Rapids: Eerdmans, 1952), 1:3.

he penned the letter or to whom it was originally sent, and raises Apollos, a native of Alexandria, as a strong possibility (Acts 18:24). The missionary impetus of the Christian gospel arose in Jerusalem following the stoning of Stephen when a great persecution broke out and Christians began to scatter (Acts 8). When Acts 6:1 mentions both Hellenistic and Hebraic Jews, the phrase *pros tous hebraious* is used in that context, the exact phrase by which Hebrews is later known. One twentieth-century scholar suggested that Christians who were of the same mind as Stephen brought the Christian message to Alexandria, noting several elements common to Stephen's speech in Acts 7 that are also shared by the book of Hebrews.[13] John Mark, a young Christian man from Jerusalem whose name titles the second gospel, is said by Eusebius to have begun the church in Alexandria after separating from Paul and Barnabas (*Hist, eccl.* 2.16). Could it be that the author of Hebrews first heard the gospel in Alexandria? This would make good sense of Hebrews 2:3, for the author would have heard the gospel from someone who had heard Jesus (possibly John Mark).

> "Mark preached the gospel in Egypt ... and was the first to establish churches in Alexandria itself."
>
> EUSEBIUS, *HIST. ECCL.* 2.16

An Alexandrian association was once claimed based on reading the **dualism** within Hebrews as an expression of **Neoplatonism** so prevalent in other Alexandrian authors, such as Philo. Scholarship has largely disproved the direct influence of Philo of Alexandria on Hebrews, and the dualism is best explained in its own terms as eschatological, not Platonic (see discussion below). But it does not follow that because Hebrews is not a Platonic document, it had no connection to Alexandria.

Apollos was from Alexandria and traveled in the apostle Paul's orbit (Acts 18:24). He was taught by Paul's companions, Priscilla and Aquila (Acts 18:24–28), and personally known by Paul, who encouraged his ministry (1 Cor. 16:12). He was a highly educated Alexandrian who would have been schooled in the literary style exemplified by Hebrews. Moreover, as a Jewish believer (Acts 18:24), he had the thorough knowledge of the Old Testament Scriptures in their Greek version that the book of Hebrews exclusively uses. Apollos was a great defender of the Christian faith, vigorously refuting the opposing Jews in public debate and proving from the Old Testament that Jesus was the Messiah (Acts 18:28). He eventually became as influential as the apostles Paul and Peter (1 Cor. 1:12; 3:4–6, 22; 4:6; 16:12). Apollos would also fit the memory handed down to both Clement of Alexandria (c. AD 150–215) and to Origen (AD 185–253), who claimed a Pauline association, while recognizing that Paul himself probably did not put pen to paper for this book.[14] Apollos of Alexandria has been a leading contender for the authorship of Hebrews at least as far back as the great Protestant Reformer, Martin Luther, but he has not been the only contender.

> "The author of the Epistle to the Hebrews—whoever he is, whether Paul or, as I think, Apollos—quotes this passage [Gen. 48:20] most learnedly."
>
> MARTIN LUTHER, *LECTURES ON GENESIS*

Eusebius recognizes that the letter Clement wrote from Rome to the Corinthian church in the late first century contained many allusions to and quotations from Hebrews and notes that on that

13. William Manson, *The Epistle to the Hebrews: An Historical and Theological Reconsideration*, Baird Lecture, 1949 (London: Hodder and Stoughton, 1951), 36–39.

14. Cited by Eusebius in *Hist. eccl.* 6.14.2 and 6.25.12, respectively.

basis some believed that Clement himself was the translator or author of Hebrews (*Hist. eccl.* 3.38.2). However, scholarly examination shows that the Greek text of Hebrews could not be a translation of a Semitic text—at least as we understand "translation" today—because its rhetorical features would be possible only when composed in Greek. And so if either Clement or Luke were involved in the production of the extant book of Hebrews, he would have had a very free hand in working with Paul's material, to the point that he would be an author, not a translator by any modern definition.

The church father Tertullian (AD 160?–220?) mentioned that Barnabas, Paul's traveling companion on his first mission to the Gentiles, authored Hebrews (*Pud.* 20). The association of Barnabas with the book of Hebrews may be because he was described as a "son of encouragement" (Acts 4:36), and Hebrews 13:22 describes the letter as a word of encouragement (or exhortation). Moreover, Barnabas is referred to as an "apostle" (Acts 14:14) and, being a Levite (Acts 4:36), would have had the interest in and knowledge about the priesthood that forms such a dominant theme in Hebrews.

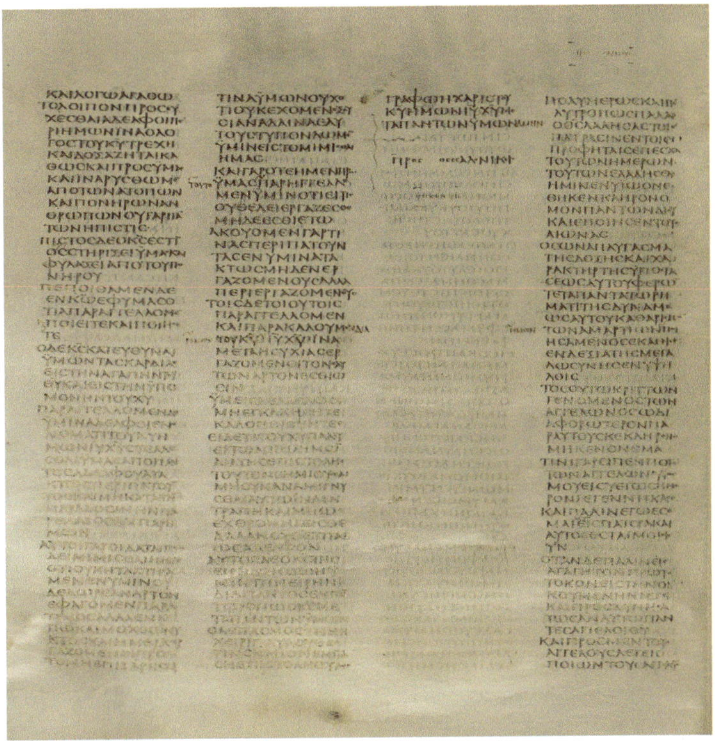

Hebrews in Codex Sinaiticus begins in the fourth column.

A recent theory suggests that Timothy wrote Hebrews, except for the closing verses that Paul appended himself where Timothy is mentioned by name.[15] While Timothy was a close associate of Paul, he was from Lystra, a small town in Asia Minor where it is unlikely he could have received the formal rhetorical training reflected in Hebrews. Furthermore, it is doubtful that Timothy had any connection to Alexandria, though that connection may not be necessary. What we know of Apollos matches more closely what we see in Hebrews than does what we know of Timothy.

The intriguing theory presented in more modern times by the German biblical scholar Adolf Harnack argued that Hebrews was written by Priscilla, the woman who, together with her husband, Aquila, was a close associate of Paul's. Although Harnack's idea generated much discussion in its day, the author refers to *him*self in Hebrews 11:32, using a masculine participle in the Greek original, and there is no manuscript evidence for a feminine variant reading. Harnack's argument that Priscilla deliberately disguised her gender by using the masculine gender is sheer speculation, and his theory remains a curiosity of New Testament scholarship.

15. J. Ramsey Michaels, *Hebrews*, ed. Philip W. Comfort, CBC (Carol Stream, Ill.: Tyndale, 2005), 310.

John Calvin's comments on Hebrews 13:23:

"If this Timothy is the noble companion of Paul (as I am inclined to think), it is probable that Luke or Clement is the writer of this epistle. Paul is more accustomed to call him his son, and further, what immediately follows does not fit Paul. It is clear that the writer was free and able to do what he liked, and further that he was more likely elsewhere than in Rome, indeed that he was making a tour through various cities and was then preparing to cross the sea. All these points could suit either Luke or Clement after the death of Paul."*

*John Calvin, *The Epistle of Paul the Apostle to the Hebrews and the First and Second Epistles of St. Peter*, ed. D. W. Torrance and T. F. Torrance, trans. W. B. Johnston, Calvin's Commentaries (Grand Rapids: Eerdmans, 1963), 216.

Clement? Paul? Luke? Timothy? Barnabas? Apollos? In spite of the weight of scholarly inference, the book of Hebrews does not in fact name its author. And so if you were ever asked about the authorship of Hebrews, the correct answer is well expressed by the church father Origen (AD 185?–254?), who said, according to Eusebius, "Who wrote the epistle of Hebrews in truth only God knows!" (*Hist. eccl.* 6.25.14).

IS HEBREWS REALLY A LETTER?

To understand a text rightly, a good reader always asks, at least subconsciously, *What type of writing is this I'm reading?* You are probably not reading this textbook in the same way or in the same setting that you might read a book that starts out "Once upon a time...." Authors, whether ancient or modern, choose to write in a particular **literary genre** that is familiar in the given culture and that has a particular function and purpose in that society. The author of Hebrews himself describes his work as a "word of **exhortation**" (13:22). That describes the purpose and intended function of the book, but not necessarily the literary genre (type of writing) of the work. An exhortation could be delivered in any of a variety of literary genres—as a parable, a narrative story, a straightforward discourse of propositions, or a sermon.

Origen on the Authorship of Hebrews

"If I gave my opinion, I should say that the thoughts are those of the apostle, but the diction and phraseology are those of someone who remembered the apostolic teachings, and wrote down at his leisure what had been said by his teacher. Therefore if any church holds that this epistle is by Paul, let it be commended for this. For not without reason have the ancients handed it down as Paul's. But who wrote the epistle, in truth, God knows. The statement of some who have gone before us is that Clement, bishop of the Romans, wrote the epistle, and of others that Luke, the author of the gospel and the Acts, wrote it."

Origen, cited by Eusebius,
Hist. eccl. 6.25

Every culture has literary genres that are indigenous to it. Our culture shares some of the literary genres that were common in the first century, but not all of them. Even those we do share may not have functioned in ancient society in the same way they do in ours. We live in a culture that is very visually oriented because our technology allows that. For entertainment and for information, we watch movies, videos, and computer screens. But in the first century, entertainment was limited to watching live performances at the theaters or listening to someone read from the written page. And so to rightly understand the book of Hebrews, a careful reader will want to know something about the literary genre of Hebrews and how that genre functioned in first-century society.

The Roman world had celebrities just as our society does today. Gladiators who were renowned for their strength and endurance were celebrities. The great orators of the Roman world, such as Seneca and Cicero, were another type of celebrity who made powerful speeches before crowds of people who were delighted by a skillful turn of phrase. In fact, a Roman education included training in formal rhetoric, or speech-making, that included mastery of the principles of rhetoric that have been preserved in the writings of Aristotle and Quintillian.

exhortation: an address or communication emphatically urging someone to do something.

OXFORD AMERICAN COLLEGE DICTIONARY

The book of Hebrews is unique among the New Testament books for displaying so many of the conventions of formal Greek rhetoric, suggesting that Hebrews originally was to be delivered orally as a persuasive sermon intended to fire the passion of its hearers for their faith in Jesus Christ. Its many rhetorical features include the use of alliteration (the repetition of initial consonants), paronomasia (the phonetic resemblance, equality, or contrast of words), ellipsis (the omission of words for rhetorical effect), chiasm (reverse occurrence of similar elements in successive clauses), hendiadys (the expression of one concept in two terms), isocolons (equally balanced clauses in cadence and length), and litotes (a positive idea expressed by the negation of its opposite). The epistle also uses metaphors and formulas conventional to formal rhetoric.[16]

While Hebrews was quite likely penned to be delivered orally as a sermon, the text of Hebrews as we have it suggests that it was sent in written form to its original readers, for its author mentions that he has written the exhortation only "briefly" (13:22). Furthermore, Hebrews 13:18–25 contains many personal references in a section that is quite different in style than the rest of the book. The author requests prayer from the recipients of the writing (v. 18), especially that he might be restored to them soon (v. 19), indicating that the author of these words personally knew those to whom he wrote. He refers to Timothy's release (v. 23), indicating that the original readers also knew Timothy. It is likely, but unproven, that Timothy is the same man who traveled with the apostle Paul and to whom 1 and 2 Timothy are addressed, bringing the author of Hebrews into the same circle of associates as Paul. The author of Hebrews is waiting for Timothy so that together they can visit the original readers of the letter.

---

16. See Andrew H. Trotter, *Interpreting the Epistle to the Hebrews*, Guides to New Testament Exegesis (Grand Rapids: Baker, 1997), 67, for a listing of the various rhetorical conventions in Hebrews.

The apparent difference in genre between most of Hebrews and these final verses has led to some debate about whether Hebrews is a literary epistle or a nonliterary letter, but this dichotomy is a false one. In its extant form, the last chapter is clear indication that it was sent as personal correspondence to a specific group of people the author had in mind. And yet the previous chapters comprise a highly literary document. Some scholars speculate that these personal references were added by a different person to the highly rhetorical sermon that was already circulating in written form (like forwarding an email to a friend for whom it was not originally composed and adding your own personal note). But it is just as likely that the author of the powerful sermon sent a copy to a certain group of Christians he knew and, of course, switched style when including the personal references. Even so, the book does not have the standard Hellenistic letter opening that we would expect to find in personal correspondence (as we find in Paul's letters; for instance, "Paul, called to be an apostle of Christ Jesus ... To the church of God in Corinth"). Although some speculate that the opening of Hebrews once contained the name of the church to which the text was first sent, there is no manuscript evidence that such a letter opening was ever a part of Hebrews. This supports the theory that the text was originally composed as a sermon and later sent to a more distant congregation. There would not have been a Hellenistic letter opening originally, and the text was simply preserved that way, unfortunately losing forever the name of the author. Who composed the oration, where it was originally delivered, and to whom it was sent must remain open questions.

AN OVERVIEW OF THE THEOLOGY OF THE BOOK OF HEBREWS

Christology in Hebrews

It is fair to say that every book of the New Testament is Christocentric, that is, it is centrally and substantially about Jesus Christ. (This is true even for a book like Philemon, where its Christocentric nature may not be evident at first glance.) And every book of the New Testament contributes something to our understanding of who Jesus is, what he accomplished in his earthly life, and the relevance of his death and resurrection for all of humanity for all time.

The book of Hebrews underscores the unique and permanent significance of Jesus Christ in a world full of religious claims about God. It presents Jesus as Son of God and elaborates on what that title entails. Hebrews is the only book of the New Testament to present Jesus both as our Great High Priest and as the perfect and final sacrifice for sin. It also refers to Jesus with titles of mediator (8:6; 9:15; 12:24), forerunner (6:20), Shepherd (13:20), heir (1:2; cf. Rom. 4:13), firstborn (1:6 cf. Rom. 8:29; Col. 1:15, 18), and apostle (3:1). The epistle shows the full significance of Jesus' identity not only for redemptive history, but for living with peace of mind today. Because its rich Christology is the major theological theme of Hebrews, chapters 2 and 3 are devoted to a fuller discussion.

God the Father

God is introduced in Hebrews as the God who speaks and reveals himself to humanity (1:1). In the past, he spoke at various times and in various ways through the prophets, but now he speaks fully and finally in the Son, Jesus Christ. It is God the Father who has appointed the eternal reign of God the Son and pronounces the inauguration of that eternal reign at the resurrection of Jesus (1:5, 8). God announced salvation through the Lord Jesus and testified to the truth of the gospel message by "signs, wonders, and various miracles" (2:4). God is gathering a people for himself (3:4) over which the Son presides (10:21). He views these people as his own children (12:7). Hebrews warns not to turn away from the living God who is the source of life (3:12; 10:31). God has opened the way to himself through the sacrifice of Jesus Christ (2:9, 17; 5:10; 6:18; 7:19, 25). We come to him through faith in his redemption that he offers in Christ (11:6). We worship God through Christ (13:15), whom he has brought back from the dead (13:20).

In Hebrews God is presented as the just judge of all people and reveals his will for how we are to live (4:12; 6:10; 9:20; 10:31, 36; 11:40; 12:29; 13:4, 16). He is the creator and ruler of the universe (11:3; 12:2). He is the same God of the Old Testament, the God of Abel (11:4), of Enoch (11:5), of Abraham (11:19), of Moses (11:24–29), and all the believers of the Old Testament times.

The Holy Spirit

The Holy Spirit is integrally involved in the work of the Father and the Son in Hebrews. It is through gifts of the Holy Spirit that God accredits the claims of the gospel announced by the Lord Jesus (2:4 cf. 1 Cor. 12:4). The Spirit is the speaker who enlivens the Word of God to us (3:7; 10:15). And the Spirit teaches the significance of the priestly ministry in the tabernacle (9:8). The Lord Jesus offered himself up to the purposes of God through the Spirit (9:14), who is said to be eternal, like the Father and the Son. Those who turn away from the new covenant in Christ's blood insult the Spirit of grace (10:29).

The New Covenant

The relationship of the new covenant established by the blood of Jesus Christ to the "first covenant" (Heb. 9:15; 13:20) is an overarching theological theme of the book of Hebrews. Repeatedly the covenant established by Christ is described as "better," "superior," and "new" (7:22; 8:6; 9:15; 12:24), primarily because it frees people from sins committed under the first covenant (9:15) that could not be cleansed by the blood of animal sacrifice (10:4). The fatal flaw in the efficacy of the first covenant is that human beings are unable to live by its terms because their hearts are not reconciled to God (8:8–12). The terms of the first covenant, and the consequences for any violation, were clear. As a professor, I usually express my will and the standards of my evaluation of students in my syllabus—the "law" of the class, so to speak. And because I passionately want my students to learn and love the New Testament, I may stipulate that attendance in my classes is mandatory. Most students do comply, but there is no "law" I could write in my syllabus that would give my students a love for the New Testament and an eagerness to learn it such that attendance rules would be moot. That is a heart matter beyond which any professor or syllabus has control. Similarly, when God said "Thou shalt not commit adultery," Jesus tells us that what he meant was, to paraphrase, "Thou shalt not even have impure thoughts" (Matt. 5:27–28). While many might be able to refrain from the actual acts prohibited by the Law under the first covenant, no one is able to be pure in both behavior and heart all the time, without even one violation. God faults his people for their inability to keep the first covenant (Heb. 8:8) and promises them a new covenant that will be in their hearts and minds (Heb. 8:10, quoting Jer. 31:31 – 34). The first covenant was set in place by God to be a shadow of the reality that would come in Christ (Heb. 10:1).

The achievement of that new covenant came at a horrible cost: the violent execution of Jesus Christ, the Son incarnate, who actually was pure in both behavior and heart at all times throughout his earthly life. Hebrews 9 and 10 explain the death of Jesus in terms of a new kind of priest offering a new kind of sacrifice that would ratify the new covenant and allow those who live under it to be transformed in heart and mind (10:15 – 16). Because the new covenant is based on the better promise, the eternal efficacy of Jesus' priesthood, Jesus guarantees a better covenant that saves completely and eternally (Heb. 7:20 – 25). Because of this, Jesus can say that he did not come to abolish the Law, but to fulfill it (Matt. 5:17). And because the new covenant provides for the transformation of the human heart, the Lord expects those who claim the new covenant in Christ to live in accordance with that covenant, in both external behavior and inner life.

Jesus himself introduces this theme of the new covenant at the Last Supper, when he takes the cup and declares, "This cup is the new covenant in my blood, which is poured out for you" (Luke 22:20; parallels Matt. 26:28; Mark 14:24). But without the book of Hebrews, we would not as fully understand the significance of Jesus' statement, nor be able to as deeply appreciate the commemoration of the new covenant when we take Holy Communion at church.

The Reality of Heaven

The book of Hebrews speaks often of heaven. It is the place where God's throne is located (8:1). To be in heaven is to be in the very presence of God himself (9:24). Heaven is where the names are written of those whom God has claimed as his own (12:23 cf. Rev. 3:12; 13:8; 17:8). Hebrews underscores that heaven is the place of the efficacious **atonement** that could not be achieved in any earthly temple (9:11 – 12). All that God had commanded under the first covenant — the consecration of the priesthood, the building of the tabernacle, the sacrifice of animals — was to teach the need for atonement and obedience to God's plan for atonement, but ultimately it was to become obsolete and to disappear after the sacrifice of Jesus Christ (8:13). It is no coincidence of history that the temple of Jerusalem, that great center of God's atonement under the first covenant, was destroyed in AD 70 and has never been rebuilt. Hebrews explains that such a place on earth is no longer necessary, because the final sacrifice for all people, Jew and Gentile, has been made in the true Most Holy Place (9:11). By this Christ has obtained eternal redemption for all who will accept it (v. 12).

The Dualism of Hebrews

The statements in Hebrews 8:5 that the tabernacle was only a "copy and shadow" of what is in heaven have led some interpreters to see the author of Hebrews as a **Neoplatonist**, whose thought is structured by the ontological dualism of the material world and its correspondences in the truer, invisible world of ideals. If you have taken a course in philosophy, you might have learned that around the fifth century **BC**, Plato proposed that reality was comprised of the material world that we can see and in which we live, but also of an unseen world of "ideals" that were imperishable and therefore superior to the material world. This two-part reality is known as **Platonic dualism**, and by the first century of this era, had greatly influenced virtually all religions. Because Western thought is deeply influenced by the Greek philosophical tradition, many today may see that as the most natural direction in which to read the statement, a direction that is very congenial to many popular concepts of heaven. But is this actually what the author of Hebrews is doing?

In texts of the ancient world, there are three types of dualism: (1) the ontological dualism of Plato and his successors; (2) a moral dualism by which people could be categorized, found primarily in Jewish writings such as John's gospel and the sectarian texts produced at Qumran; and (3) a temporal dualism, especially the eschatological dualism of **apocalyptic** writings, again a primarily Jewish concept. The author of Hebrews was clearly profoundly steeped in Judaism, but the literary style of Hebrews shows that it was Hellenistic Judaism, making it more plausible that Greek philosophy shaped his ideas. Even so, Hebrews does not contain the Greek words (*idea* and *eidos*) so prominent in Plato's *Theory of Ideas* to differentiate his ontological dualism. Neither does the author of Hebrews employ the typical method followed by Jewish exegetes who embraced Platonism. Philo, for instance, interpreted Melchizedek to be an image (*eidos*) of the ideal (*idea*) of Reason (*Alleg. Interp.* 3.82).

Second, there is no strong moral dualism in Hebrews such as we find in the **Johannine** writings ("light" versus "darkness"). In fact, the warnings on apostasy are so ambiguous that they have led to centuries of debate about whether the people in view are genuine Christians or not.

The incarnation of Jesus Christ, not the Platonic dualism, is the greatest influence in Hebrews, being the fulcrum of the entire book (1:1–2). As such, the dualism presented in Hebrews is not driven by Greek philosophy or by strictly Jewish categories; rather, the point made by the author of Hebrews is that a new epoch has been inaugurated with the incarnation of Jesus Christ. The fundamental dualism in Hebrews is temporal and eschatological, the "before" and "after" of Christ's sacrifice on the cross.

The Greek word *hypodeigma* in Hebrews 8:5 is typically translated "copy" in English versions, although in its several other occurrences in the New Testament, including Hebrews 4:11, it is usually translated as "example." For instance, in John 13:15, Jesus washes his disciples feet, giving them a *hypodeigma*, which is clearly an example not a copy. In Josephus we find other occurrences of the word where it means "example" (*J.W.* 1.208, 507). Therefore, in Hebrews 8:5 and 9:23, the thought is that the earthly tabernacle was an example, that is, model, of the heavenly reality. By translating *hypodeigma* as "copy," it seems that the English translations tilt the reader's mind in a Platonic direction where it was not intended. Hebrews 8:5 can then be read as saying the tabernacle was "an example and shadow" (KJV) of the heavenly things (i.e., the efficacy of Christ), just as in Hebrews 10:1 the Law was only a "shadow" of the good things to come in Christ.

Understood this way, why was it necessary that the tabernacle had to be built in every detail according to the plan God revealed, as Hebrews 8:5 goes on to say? It was not because the earthly tabernacle was a model of the heavenly place that God saw and revealed to Moses; rather, the tabernacle had to conform to the design that God had revealed in order to fulfill its didactic and prophetic role as an example pointing to the things that would later be accomplished by Jesus Christ.

This distinctively christological understanding of the dualism in Hebrews shows that the author employed a typological method of interpreting the Old Testament. **Typology** functions within the plane of human history, not above or beyond it. Earlier persons, events, and institutions in biblical history are seen as "**types**" that anticipate later persons, events, and institutions that are their "**antitypes**" or "**archtypes**." Melchizedek is a type of Jesus, who is the antitype or archtype. This stands in sharp contrast to Philo's allegorical approach, which, driven by Platonic philosophy, took all material things and persons to represent eternal ideals with no concern for the historical reality.

The author of Hebrews employs many such types as he interprets the significance of Christ:

- Esau is a type of the apostate for whom no repentance is possible.
- Enoch, Noah, and Abel are types of the person who pleases God.
- The Sinai theophany is a type of God's revelation on Mount Zion.
- Israel's wilderness wanderings are a type of the Christian journey.
- The Levitical priesthood, sacrifice, and tabernacle are all types of Christ's crucifixion and ascension.

The distinctive dualism created by such typology indicates a thoroughly eschatological framework (as opposed to an allegorical framework generated by a Platonic dualism) for the thought world of Hebrews, and is based on at least three assumptions:

1. God is unchanging in his purposes throughout human history.
2. God is able to shape history, even in its details.
3. The coming of Christ introduces such a discontinuity that all things before him in the religion of ancient Israel are mere shadows of the reality he inaugurates.

The Definition and Practice of Faith

The New Testament often mentions "faith"—well over two hundred times in the Greek (*pistis*). But nowhere is there a better explanation of what it means to have saving faith than in Hebrews 11: "Now faith is being sure of what we hope for and certain of what we do not see" (v. 1). This definition is quite the opposite of the old saying "Faith is believin' what you know ain't so." Biblical faith can claim a confidence beyond one's own experience because it rests in the character of God, of which there is nothing more certain and constant. All of us exercise the confidence of faith when we believe and act on information we get from someone else whose experience we trust. And so if we have a friend who has been to Paris and we haven't been, we might make plans based on what that person has told us. We trust our friend, and therefore we are confident of what we hope for about Paris and assured of what we haven't yet seen for ourselves. Faith in Christ is very similar. Because of God's trustworthy character, we can live our lives today acting on the promises he gives us in his Word. After defining what he means by faith in Hebrews 11:1, the author makes a long list of people whose actions exemplified the kind of faith it takes to please God, which is simply living as if we believe what God says. A quick scan of the activities of the people in this list reveals many action verbs: *brought, built, went, offered, blessed, gave instructions, hid, chose, kept, passed through, conquered, administered, quenched, escaped.* Clearly the faith in view is not a mere intellectual assent to a set of doctrines, but a complete trust in God that energizes one's actions and decisions in life.

"Now faith is confidence in what we hope for and assurance about what we do not see."

HEBREWS 11:1

Angelology

Our culture adores angels. They adorn greeting cards, are worn as little lapel pins, and have even made it to at least a couple of TV shows and some major motion pictures. But angels as portrayed in our culture have been domesticated and trivialized by their popularity. It is probably natural to have such a fascination with sentient beings who exist outside of our normal sphere of life, but Scripture is the place to go to learn about these wondrous creatures of God.

The book of Hebrews underscores that the Son of God became a human being; the necessity of Christ's humanity is one of the major theological themes of the book. But most of us would consider human beings to be somewhat lower than angels. We are not as powerful and don't have the supernatural abilities of angels. Because of this, Hebrews goes to great lengths to explain that even though Jesus Christ was fully human, he was nevertheless superior to the angels in unique ways. None of the angels can claim to be a son of God, even though God created them all (1:5). Furthermore, it was precisely when the Son took on human form ("when God brings his firstborn into the world," v. 6) that the angels were commanded to worship him, even though he was "made lower than the angels for a little while" by his incarnation (2:9). Imagine the angels worshiping a human being! Moreover, as mighty as the angels may be, none of them will rule over the universe (1:7–8, 13; 2:5); that is the role the Son took on when he ascended after his death and resurrection to the throne of God. Satan, a fallen angel, believed he could usurp that place and does rule those who are willing to follow him, whether angel or human, but only for a time until God vanquishes all of Christ's enemies (1:13). As majestic and powerful as angels may be, they have a supporting role in God's administration of the universe. They are "ministering spirits" sent to serve those whom God saves through Christ (1:14).

Although angels are mentioned frequently, the Bible does not tell us everything we would wish to know about angels. Their description in Hebrews 1:7 as "spirits" (or "winds" since the same Greek word, *pneuma*, can denote either) and as "flames of fire" suggests both the immaterial and transitory nature, yet powerful effect, of angels on earth. Elsewhere in Hebrews we see that there are thousands upon thousands of angels gathered in joyful assembly at "Mount Zion ... the city of the living God, the heavenly Jerusalem," which is where believers in Christ have come (Heb. 12:22). In Hebrews 13:2 we find the enigmatic statement that some "have shown hospitality to angels without knowing it," which is often taken to support the idea made popular by TV shows that angels can take on human form and walk among us.

And so the book of Hebrews attests to the reality of angels, their subordinate place under the Son's authority, their incorporeal nature relative to human flesh and blood, and their role in ministering in unspecified ways to those whom God saves.

THE TEXT AND CANONICITY OF HEBREWS

The Greek Text of Hebrews

The Greek text of Hebrews is quite well preserved in the manuscripts. The major witnesses present an Alexandrian text type, with the Western text of Hebrews preserved in D (**Codex** Claromontanus) in both the Greek and Old Latin texts therein. A Byzantine text of Hebrews is preserved in K (Codex Mosquensis, ninth century) and L (Codex Angelicus, ninth century), and in many minuscules. All of the extant witnesses contain readings from all three text types. Ancient translations of Hebrews into Coptic (both Sahidic and Bohairic) and Syriac are extant. Although well preserved, a few verses require difficult textual critical decisions (e.g., 1:8; 11:17, 37; 12:3, 7).[17]

Significant Manuscripts Containing at Least a Portion of Hebrews* (Listed by Age)

Siglum	MS Name	Date	Contents
𝔓46	P. Chester Beatty II	(c. AD 200)	1:1–9:16; 9:18–10:20, 22–30; 10:32–13:25
𝔓12	P.Amh.3b	(3rd cent.)	1:1
𝔓13	P.Oxy.657	(3rd–4th cent.)	2:14–5:5; 10:8–22; 10:29–11:13; 11:28–12:17
𝔓17	P.Oxy.1078	(4th cent.)	9:12–19
Uncials	**MS Name**	**Date**	**Contents**
ℵ (01)	Codex Sinaiticus	(4th cent.)	complete text
B (03)	Codex Vaticanus	(4th cent.)	verses 1:1–9:13
A (02)	Codex Alexandrinus	(5th cent.)	complete text
C (04)	Codex Ephraemi	(5th cent.)	2:4–7:26; 9:15–10:24; 12:16–13:25
D (06)	Codex Claromontanus	(6th cent.)	1:1–13:20 in both Greek and Old Latin

* Adapted from Harold W. Attridge, *The Epistle to the Hebrews*, Hermeneia (Philadelphia: Fortress, 1989), 31–32.

17. If you read Greek and are interested in textual criticism of Hebrews, see the list of important textual variants in Hebrews in ibid., 95–113. For a discussion of the Greek vocabulary, grammar, and style of Hebrews, see ibid., 117–84.

Canonicity

In the earliest witnesses extant, the book of Hebrews circulated with letters written by the apostle Paul, which is probably how the idea began that Paul was the author, internal evidence to the contrary. If Hebrews was originally sent to the Roman church, it seems odd that its canonical status there was resisted until the fourth century, though perhaps its author was known in Rome and his apostolic status was in question. For the book was clearly known and widely cited by the early Western fathers, such as Clement of Rome (*1 Clement* 36.1–6), Ignatius (*Phld.* 9:1), *Shepherd of Hermas* 2.3.2, and Justin Martyr (*Dial.* 116.1). In spite of this, the **Muratorian Canon** list (c. AD 170–80) does not include Hebrews.

In the eastern Mediterranean churches, Hebrews was accepted as canonical at least as early as the second century, by virtue of the evidence of $\mathfrak{P}^{46}$, where it is placed in the middle of Paul's letters, following Romans. This placement may indicate, rather than authorship, that it too was a letter known to have been originally written to the Roman church. Although Hebrews circulated with some collections of Paul's letters, there are collections in which it is absent or where it follows 2 Thessalonians or is at the end of the collection.[18] Moreover, Hebrews is not found within other collections of non-Pauline material, such as the **Catholic** Epistles. And so there seems to have been a consistent association of Hebrews with the Pauline corpus. There is some evidence that Romans, Hebrews, 1 Corinthians, and Ephesians were collected and circulated together as general letters for the universal church, perhaps even within Paul's lifetime.[19]

The anonymity of Hebrews may be a great mystery, but that knowledge has not been so important for the church's subsequent understanding of its message. There are many questions in biblical studies that will probably remain unanswerable, but that should not detract from or derail taking the message of Scripture to heart, for as Hebrews 1:1 so unequivocally states, God has spoken. What more do we need to know?

OUTLINE OF THE BOOK OF HEBREWS

- I. Jesus as God's Final Word (1:1–4:13)
  - A. Jesus Christ Is God's Final and Fullest Revelation of Himself (1:1–3)
  - B. Christological Claim: The Son Is Greater Than the Angels (1:4–14)
    1. God is his Father (1:5)
    2. The angels worship the Son (1:6)
    3. The Son rules forever (1:7–9)
    4. The Son is eternally sovereign over the universe (1:10–12)
    5. The Son will be victorious over all who oppose him (1:13)
    6. Angels serve God's children (1:14)
  - C. The First Warning (2:1–4)

18. Pamela M. Eisenbaum, "Locating Hebrews within the Literary Landscape of Christian Origins," in *Hebrews: Contemporary Methods—New Insights*, ed. Gabriella Gelardini, Biblical Interpretation Series 75 (Leiden: Brill, 2005), 218–19.

19. David Trobisch, *Paul's Letter Collection: Tracing the Origins* (Bolivar, Mo.: Quiet Waters, 2001).

D. Christological Claim: The Full Humanity of the Son (2:5 – 18)
    1. Jesus, the paradigmatic human being (2:5 – 9)
    2. Jesus is our brother (2:10 – 13)
    3. The benefits of Jesus' humanity (2:14 – 18)
        a. His death breaks the power of death (2:14)
        b. His death frees us from fear of death (2:15)
        c. His humanity qualifies him to be High Priest (2:16 – 18)

E. Christological Claim: The Son, Though Human, Is Greater Even Than Moses (3:1 – 6)

F. Warning against Refusing the Ultimate Sabbath Rest (3:7 – 4:13)
    1. The failure of Moses' generation (3:7 – 11)
    2. Another warning (3:12 – 15)
    3. God did not spare Moses' generation (3:16 – 19)
    4. The Sabbath of the new covenant (4:1 – 11)
    5. Warning that nothing is hidden from God, our Judge (4:12 – 13)

II. Jesus as High Priest (4:14 – 10:18)

A. Christological Claim: The Son Is Our Great High Priest (4:14 – 5:10)
    1. Exhortation to approach God's throne with confidence (4:14 – 16)
    2. The appointment of the High Priest (5:1 – 6)
    3. The Son is the source of eternal salvation (5:7 – 10)

B. Second Warning against Falling Away (5:11 – 6:19)
    1. Need for elementary teaching again (5:11 – 14)
    2. A hard teaching about apostasy (6:1 – 8)
    3. Confidence in God's oath (6:9 – 19)
        a. Exhortation to be diligent to the end (6:9 – 12)
        b. Our hope is based on God's oath (6:13 – 19)

C. Melchizedek and Jesus (6:20 – 7:28)
    1. Jesus' priesthood in the order of Melchizedek (6:20)
    2. About Melchizedek (7:1 – 10)
    3. The new priesthood (7:11 – 22)
    4. The Son is the final, perfect Priest (7:23 – 28)

D. A New Priesthood Means a New Covenant (8:1 – 13)
    1. Our High Priest ministers in heaven itself (8:1 – 2)
    2. The ministry of Jesus is superior to the priesthood of the old covenant (8:3 – 13)
        a. The new covenant is based on better promises (8:3 – 6)
        b. The new covenant is written on hearts (8:7 – 12)
        c. The old covenant is obsolete and will disappear (8:13)

E. Sacrifices of the Covenants (9:1 – 10:18)
    1. Priests offer sacrifices under the old covenant (9:1 – 10)

2. Jesus offered himself to establish the new covenant (9:11–28)
3. The finality of Christ's sacrifice and the new covenant (10:1–18)

III. Living It Out (10:19–13:25)
- A. Exhortation to Persevere (10:19–39)
  1. Let us draw near to God (10:19–22)
  2. Let us hold unswervingly to hope (10:23)
  3. Let us spur one another on (10:24–25)
  4. Warning against deliberate sin (10:26–31)
  5. Remember your past faithfulness (10:32–39)
- B. The Examples of Those Who Persevered before Us (11:1–40)
  1. A definition of faith (11:1)
  2. The examples of the Old Testament believers (11:2–38)
  3. Their faith commended, but the promise deferred (11:39–40)
- C. Another Exhortation to Persevere (12:1–28)
  1. The example of Jesus (12:1–3)
  2. The discipline of the Father (12:4–13)
  3. Warning not to refuse the Father's discipline (12:14–17)
  4. Warning not to refuse the new covenant (12:18–28)
- D. Concluding Exhortations (13:1–19)
  1. Love one another (13:1)
     - a. With hospitality (13:2–3)
     - b. In sexual purity (13:4)
     - c. In contentment (13:5–6)
     - d. In imitation of leaders (13:7)
  2. What Christ's immutability means for Christian living (13:8–19)
- E. Benediction and Greetings (13:20–25)
  1. A new covenant benediction (13:20–21)
  2. Personal greetings (13:22–25)

CHAPTER SUMMARY

This elegant piece of Greek rhetorical prose from the first century comes to us with many unanswered questions about its author, about the original audience, and about the events that surrounded its writing. As interesting as these questions may be, the lack of certain answers does not impede an understanding of the book's timeless message. As Scripture, it is meant to be read by people in all places and ages. Hebrews presents who Jesus is and how he is the fulfillment of what God began to do through the nation of ancient Israel. It explains why Jesus Christ remains forever at the center of God's relationship to humankind.

KEY TERMS AND DATES

AD 70
Alexandria
Apollos
first covenant
genre
high priest
Jerusalem
Melchizedek
Nero
new covenant
papyrus 𝔓[46]
priesthood
redemption
Rome
sacrifice
type/antitype
typology

QUESTIONS FOR REVIEW OR DISCUSSION

1. List what you can infer about the people to whom Hebrews was originally addressed from the text of Hebrews itself.
2. To what might the title "Hebrews" refer?
3. What historical evidence external to the book helps to date when it was written? What internal evidence might indicate the date it was written?
4. What are the prominent characteristics of the author of Hebrews? Who are the primary candidates and why?
5. Describe the sociopolitical situation of the people to whom the book is addressed.
6. What is the major purpose of the book of Hebrews?
7. List the distinctive theological themes of Hebrews. Reflect on those with which you are least familiar.
8. What factors were apparently involved in the acceptance of Hebrews into the canon?

GOING FURTHER

Donelson, Lewis R. *From Hebrews to Revelation: A Theological Introduction.* Louisville: Westminster John Knox, 2001.

Hurst, L. D. *The Epistle to the Hebrews: Its Background of Thought.* Society for New Testament Studies Monograph Series 65. Cambridge: Cambridge University Press, 1990.

Kistemaker, Simon. *The Psalm Citations in the Epistle to the Hebrews.* Amsterdam: Van Soest, 1961.

Lindars, Barnabas. *The Theology of the Letter to the Hebrews.* New Testament Theology. Cambridge: Cambridge University Press, 1991.

Trotter, Andrew H. *Interpreting the Epistle to the Hebrews.* Guides to New Testament Exegesis. Grand Rapids: Baker, 1997.

Vos, Geerhardus. *The Teaching of the Epistle to the Hebrews.* Phillipsburg, N.J.: Presbyterian and Reformed, 1956.

Westfall, Cynthia Long. *A Discourse Analysis of the Letter to the Hebrews: The Relationship between Form and Meaning.* Library of New Testament Studies 297. Studies in New Testament Greek II. London: T&T Clark, 2005.

Commentaries

Attridge, Harold W. *The Epistle to the Hebrews.* Hermeneia. Philadelphia: Fortress, 1989.

Buchanan, George W. *The Book of Hebrews: Its Challenge from Zion.* Eugene, Ore.: Wipf & Stock, 2006.

DeSilva, David A. *Perseverance in Gratitude: A Socio-Rhetorical Commentary on the Epistle "to the Hebrews."* Grand Rapids: Eerdmans, 2000.

Fleer, David, and Dave Bland, eds. *Preaching Hebrews.* Rochester College Lectures on Preaching 4. Abilene, Tex.: A.C.U. Press, 2003.

France, R. T. "Hebrews." Pages 18–195 in *Hebrews–Revelation. Expositor's Bible Commentary.* Vol. 13. Edited by Tremper Longman III and David E. Garland. Rev. ed. Grand Rapids: Zondervan, 2006.

Gordon, Robert P. *Hebrews.* Readings: A New Biblical Commentary. Sheffield: Sheffield Academic, 2000.

Guthrie, George. "Hebrews." Pages 2–85 in *ZIBBC.* Vol. 4. Edited by Clinton E. Arnold. Grand Rapids: Zondervan, 2002.

Isaacs, Marie E. *Reading Hebrews and James: A Literary and Theological Commentary.* Reading the New Testament. Macon, Ga.: Smyth & Helwys, 2002.

Johnson, Luke Timothy. *Hebrews: A Commentary.* New Testament Library. Louisville: Westminster John Knox, 2006.

Koester, Craig R. *Hebrews: A New Translation with Introduction and Commentary.* AB 36. New York: Doubleday, 2001.

Lane, William L. *Hebrews.* 2 vols. Word Biblical Commentary 47A–B. Dallas: Word, 1991.

Lea, Thomas D. *Hebrews and James.* Holman New Testament Commentary 10. Nashville: Holman Reference, 1999.

Lincoln, Andrew T. *Hebrews: A Guide.* London: T&T Clark, 2006.

McKnight, Edgar V., and Christopher Church. *Hebrews–James.* Smyth & Helwys Bible Commentary. Macon, Ga.: Smyth & Helwys, 2004.

Witherington, Ben, III. *Letters and Homilies for Jewish Christians: A Socio-Rhetorical Commentary on Hebrews, James and Jude.* Downers Grove, Ill.: IVP Academic, 2007.

CHAPTER 2

Famous Last Words

DIVINE REVELATION IN HEBREWS

Your Goals for This Chapter

- To understand the contrasts of continuity and discontinuity inherent in God's progressive revelation.
- To articulate the nature of divine revelation and the problem it presents to modern understanding.
- To recognize the use of the **Septuagint** as Scripture by the author of Hebrews.
- To understand how the Old Testament, though remaining God's word to Christians today, has been superseded by the New Testament because the old covenant has culminated in the new.

WHY THIS CHAPTER IS IMPORTANT TO YOU

Have you ever heard someone say, "God told me ..." and wondered how they knew it was God? Have you ever wondered how Islam can claim the Koran as the word of God, Judaism the Hebrew Bible, and Christians the Old and New Testaments? There seems to be a persistent quest to hear what God has to say to us. Of course, some would attribute this to nothing more than the needs of the human psyche being projected as a theological abstraction. On what basis should we accept the claim that God has spoken?

The book of Hebrews addresses this very question in no uncertain terms. Jesus is God's Word spoken into the chaos and confusion of humanity's quest for God. From the perspective of Hebrews, it is not what Jesus *said* that constitutes this message from God, but who Jesus *is* and what he did. On this basis, we can have confidence that we are able to hear what God is saying to us.

The author of Hebrews was a true theologian of the Old Testament, well acquainted with the story it told of God's work on earth that led up to the incarnation of the Son. In distinctive fashion, he introduces quotations from the Greek Old Testament with phrases such as "the Holy Spirit says" (3:7), "just as God has said" (4:3), "But about the Son he [God] says" (1:8). For the author of Hebrews, the words of Scripture *are* the words God speaks, and they are all about Jesus.

This chapter discusses the distinctive understanding of divine revelation as the person of Jesus Christ himself (Heb. 1:1–3) and the extensive and interesting use of the Old Testament throughout Hebrews.

Key Verses

1:1–3: In the past God spoke to our ancestors through the prophets at many times and in various ways, but in these last days he has spoken to us by his Son, whom he appointed heir of all things, and through whom also he made the universe. The Son is the radiance of God's glory and the exact representation of his being, sustaining all things by his powerful word. After he had provided purification for sins, he sat down at the right hand of the Majesty in heaven.

3:1: Therefore, holy brothers and sisters, who share in the heavenly calling, fix your thoughts on Jesus, whom we acknowledge as our apostle and high priest.

10:1a: The law is only a shadow of the good things that are coming—not the realities themselves.

CHAPTER OUTLINE

I. God Has Spoken
   A. Two Times at Which God Has Spoken
   B. Two Peoples to Whom God Has Spoken
   C. Two Modes by Which God Has Spoken

II. Satan's Challenge: "Has God Really Said...?"
   A. Has God Spoken?
   B. Have We Understood God?

III. The Use of the Old Testament in Hebrews
   A. Hebrews Uses the Septuagint
   B. Trinitarian Attribution of the Old Testament Quotations
   C. Relativizing the Old Testament

IV. Christ Himself Is God's Final Revelation

GOD HAS SPOKEN

Because the book of Hebrews does not open with the standard Hellenistic letter opening, the material presented does not appear to have originated as personal correspondence (1:1–3). It is only the last chapter that closes with what seem to be personal greetings (13:17–25), and some argue that this was added after the original sermon had already been in circulation. As the book stands, it appears to be a sermon sent to a group of people who were known to the author. Whether the sermon was delivered orally prior to being sent, or composed for the purpose of being sent and then delivered orally, is unknown. Hebrews 1:1–2 constitutes the opening of the powerful sermon and is foundational for understanding the message of the book:

> In the past God spoke to our ancestors through the prophets at many times and in various ways, but in these last days he has spoken to us by his Son, whom he appointed heir of all things and through whom also he made the universe.

Two Times at Which God Has Spoken

Several contrasting thoughts appear in this opening statement that echo throughout the book. "In the past" contrasts with "in these last days," creating a contrast of time defining two ages that underlies the entire message of the book. (See the discussion of **dualism** in chapter 1.) "In these last days" should not be understood as "God has spoken lately" but rather is a phrase that signals the final revelation of God: "In these days, which are the last days, God has spoken to us." For the author of Hebrews, the final age of time, referred to as "these last days," is defined by the appearance of the Son. In other words, there is no further communication from God to be expected that will supersede the Son. Note the perfect tense of the verb: God *has spoken* (not present, which would mean he currently is speaking), reinforcing the idea of finality.

The fact that God revealed his ultimate and final message to humankind in the person of Jesus some two thousand years ago does not deny or make unnecessary the ongoing

That Was Then . . . This Is Now		
Contrasts in Hebrews		
Contrast of times:	"in the past"	"in these last days"
Contrast of audience:	"to our ancestors"	"to us"
Contrast of mode of revelation:	"through the prophets at many times and in various ways"	"by his Son"

work of the Holy Spirit speaking to human hearts throughout the ages. But the work of the Holy Spirit now is to make clear the significance of the Son, Jesus Christ, as people take God's message of salvation to heart. The Spirit's work is to transform our fallen human nature into people who think and speak and behave more and more like God's Son, Jesus, the perfect human being.

The author of Hebrews gives no room for the idea that another prophet sent from God will come into the world bringing news of a new way of salvation and relationship to God. Such is the claim of the prophet Mohammed and of the religion he founded, Islam, which honors Jesus as just one of the many prophets who spoke at many times and various ways in the past. The powerful message of Hebrews also speaks against forms of spirituality that reject God's revelation in Jesus Christ, whether they are ancient pagan practices or New Age ideas. In other words, the opening verses of Hebrews make a bold claim that Jesus Christ, Son of God, is the full and final way in which God has spoken to humankind. The rest of the book of Hebrews through chapter 10 supports and argues for this claim.

Two Peoples to Whom God Has Spoken

The opening verses also present a contrast between two groups of people God has addressed. In the past it was "our ancestors" to whom God spoke through the prophets. The author of Hebrews considers those who received the word of the prophets in the past to be the ancestors of both himself and of those to whom he writes. In the past God spoke "to our ancestors"; in these last days it is "to us" that God has spoken. If the prophets of ancient Israel were the ethnic and biological ancestors of the "us" to whom God has spoken in the Son, then Hebrews was originally written, at least primarily, to Christian converts from Judaism. In its historical context, the "us" would be those Jewish people in the first century who had come to know and believe in Jesus Christ as the Son. This is certainly a possibility, but the New Testament often extends the spiritual identity and heritage of ancient Israel to all Christians, whether of Jewish or **Gentile** ethnicity, making such evidence less certain for identifying the ethnic identity of the original readers.

Because Hebrews continues to be read by people who have come to know and believe in Jesus Christ, Christians today are also among those to whom God has spoken in the Son. The revelation of God in Jesus Christ unites all who put their faith in him. And so although there is a people proper to each of the two ages defined by these opening verses of

Hebrews, there is not a complete discontinuity between them, for the groups are spiritual relatives. Though differentiated, these two peoples are nevertheless unified because they both have been the recipients of God's word throughout redemptive history. Together they comprise the people to whom God has spoken, albeit at different times and in different ways. "Our ancestors" and "us" are an entity constituted and unified by the reception of God's revelation.

The author of Hebrews develops the theme that because God has spoken to us, it is necessary to respond to God's word in obedience and faith. He holds up examples from ancient Israel where God spoke but the people did not obey because they lacked faith (e.g., 3:16–19; 4:6–11). It is a great privilege to be among those people to whom God has revealed himself, first through the prophets and now through the Son, but it also demands a response. It calls those who hear God speak to respond with faith through obedience, realizing that even no response is a response. This response of faith and obedience is not a simple one-time event; rather, the author of Hebrews wants his readers to continue to respond to what God has said in Christ by a continuous, lifelong obedience, and even when doing so will cause trouble and hardship. And so a major theme of Hebrews is the call to perseverance because of the fact that God has spoken.

Two Modes by Which God Has Spoken

The modes by which God has spoken in these two ages are also contrasted: in the past it was "through the prophets at many times and in various ways," but in the age described as "these last days," God has spoken "by the Son." The plurality and diversity of the many prophets speaking throughout the ages, each in his own time and in various modes of prophecy, is contrasted with the singularity of "Son," which designates both a unique and a more intimate relationship between God and the Son-Word than when he spoke through the lips of the many prophets.

What were some of the ways God's prophets brought his word in the past? We think of Isaiah, who in the year that King Uzziah died, saw the Lord seated on a throne, high and exalted (Isa. 6:1–13). His writings became the most frequently quoted words in the New Testament. There was Jeremiah, who in faith bought a field just as the Babylonians were besieging Jerusalem in order to declare that, despite the destruction and deportation that was at hand, the Lord would bring a remnant of his people back to dwell in the land (Jer. 32:1–15). Jeremiah acted in such a way as to show faith that God's promise would be fulfilled in the future. We think of Ezekiel, the only prophet who spent his entire prophetic ministry in exile, and that master of the

Torah Scroll written on parchment dating from 19th century.

Scala/Art Resource, NY

Painting of the Prophets by Fra Angelico, 15th – century Italian painter.

prophetic performance who shaved off his hair and divided it into thirds, each third representing the judgment coming upon Israel — burning, scattering, and the sword. But God told him to tuck just a few hairs into the folds of his garment to symbolize that a remnant would be enfolded by God's mercy (Ezek. 5:1 – 4). We recall Elijah who stood against kings (1 Kings 21) and Elisha who raised the dead (2 Kings 4:8 – 37). And then there were the twelve "minor" prophets, such as Hosea, Jonah, Amos, Habakkuk, and Haggai, men who spoke brief but powerful messages from God.

Jewish tradition considers the greatest of all the prophets to have been Moses, whose staff split the Red Sea and who carried the tablets of the covenant down from his mountaintop meeting with God (Exod. 19 – 20). All of these prophets were mightily used by God in the many and long generations before the Messiah came, pointing the way, revealing the nature of the covenant relationship that God wanted his people to have with him.

In Hebrews we learn that Moses, the greatest of the prophets representing them all, was just a faithful servant in God's house, bearing witness to what would be spoken by God in the future (3:1 – 6). Jesus, however, is the faithful Son over God's house. And, the writer of Hebrews declares, "We are his house" (3:6), attesting to the unity of the Christian church and the faithful people of God who lived before Christ. Jesus, the Son, is therefore superior to even the greatest of the prophets and, consequently, to all the prophets of the Old Testament era.

In the Greek of Hebrews 1:2, the word translated "Son" is not preceded by the definite article ("the"), though English idiom requires it. Literally, the Greek reads, "God has spoken to us by Son." This signals that the author of Hebrews is concerned with the *quality* or *kind* of revelation brought by the Son and not just the identity of *the* Son. The revelation of God brought by the Son is *qualitatively* different than that previously

Moses, Guercino (Giovanni Francesco Barbieri)/Palazzo Pitti, Florence, Italy/ The Bridgeman Art Library

Left: Moses by Giovanni Francesco Barbieri (1591-1666) / Palazzo Pitti, Florence, Italy.

Attributes of the Son (Heb. 1:1 – 5)

- Heir of all things
- Agent of creation
- Radiance of God's glory
- Exact representation of God's being
- Sustainer of all things by his powerful word
- Provider of purification for sins
- Seated at the right hand of the Majesty in heaven
- Superior to the angels

brought by the prophets. Son-revelation is of a qualitatively different kind than prophet-revelation. The nature of that profound difference is laid out in Hebrews 3 – 10.

The writer of Hebrews goes on immediately in 1:3 – 4 to describe the attributes of the Son, even before the identity of the Son is given in 2:9 as Jesus. This Son through whom God has spoken is the heir of all things, the agent through whom God made the universe, the radiance of God's glory, and the exact representation of God's being; he sustains all things by his word, provided purification for sins, sat down at the right hand of the Majesty in heaven, and became superior to the angels (1:2 – 4). We will look at these statements more carefully in chapter 3 on the **Christology** of Hebrews. But clearly this Son is a superhuman being whose activities far exceed those of even Israel's greatest prophets. The attributes of the Son immediately demolish the thought that Jesus is just another human prophet in a long line. It is because of the nature of Jesus Christ that Hebrews can say with confidence that he is the final word from God. Why? Because Hebrews (as well as the rest of the New Testament) presents the Son as God himself. This claim has far-reaching implications for modern Christianity in an increasingly pluralistic world that would like to see Jesus as just another of God's many and diverse messengers.

These opening verses of Hebrews invite its readers to reflect on continuities and discontinuities between the old covenant of past days when God spoke by the prophets and the new covenant of these last days when God has spoken by Jesus the Son. That was then; this is now. Throughout the **epistle**, the author of Hebrews builds on both the continuities and the discontinuities to explain the relationship of what God had done in Jesus Christ to what God had done in all previous ages. But this also leads to an interesting problem for the author of Hebrews. He wants to affirm that it was God speaking through the prophets in Israel's past, yet he will also need to relativize the divine authority of the prophets of the old covenant in order to claim that God has established a new covenant in Jesus Christ, superseding his preliminary work in the past. It is interesting to watch how the author does this in his discussion of what kind of priest Jesus is, a topic we will take up in the next chapter.

The contrast between the ages ("in the past" versus "these last days"), the audience ("our ancestors" versus "us"), and the mode of revelation ("prophets" versus "the Son") highlights the one concept that has remained the same through all time: *God has spoken to humankind.* The author of Hebrews opens his sermon with the bedrock of all biblical thought. *God has revealed himself to us.* The reality of divine revelation—an idea viewed so skeptically in modern times—is the opening proposition upon which the entire message of Hebrews is built.

SATAN'S CHALLENGE: "HAS GOD REALLY SAID...?"

Please read Genesis 1–3. These opening verses of Hebrews present a challenge to modern sensibilities about the possibility of divine revelation and about the value of other religions that claim true knowledge of God. Why does the author of Hebrews start his sermon with these claims? The emphasis in the opening verses of Hebrews on the fact that God has spoken responds to the serpent's challenge that led Adam and Eve to the fall. In the Genesis story of human origins, God creates a beautiful world full of good things for Adam and Eve to enjoy by speaking it into existence (Gen. 1). The Genesis account shows that God's word is the foundation of the universe's existence and the natural order. After God creates Adam, and from Adam, Eve, God himself is present with them in some very personal way that Genesis 3:8 describes as walking together in the garden. God's interaction with his human creatures is described as verbal, as he blessed and instructed them (Gen. 1:28–30). But to make clear the basic principle of Theology 101—that God is God and we're not—God gave Adam and Even one command: they must not eat the fruit of a certain tree or they would die (Gen. 2:16–17). God didn't command ten things, as he found it necessary to do later in the covenant at Sinai, nor 630 things as the Pharisees of Jesus' time had demanded in God's name. God gave only one command.

Z. Radovan/www.BibleLandPictures.com

An illustration of the tree of forbidden fruit from the Sarajevo Hagada, a 14th-century Hebrew manuscript from Spain.

The catastrophic disobedience of Adam and Eve that plunged humankind into death and darkness began with the serpent's challenge, "Did God really say...?" (Gen. 3:1). The first statement in the Bible about God in the third person casts him as an object to be assessed, questioned, and perhaps rejected, rather than as an authority to be obeyed. The craftiest of creatures attacked God's relationship to human beings at its jugular vein in a challenge that we have never fully put behind us. A later biblical writer identifies the ancient serpent as the devil, Satan (Rev. 20:2). Satan's challenge to the first human beings, "Did God really *say*...?" strikes two chords. First, has God actually spoken at all? Has he really revealed himself? And second, have we really understood what God said? Did God really mean that Adam and Eve would die if they ate that certain fruit? The serpent contradicts God's word and brazenly impugns God's motives (Gen. 3:4). He invites Adam and Eve to use their senses and their reasoning to do the same (v. 6). These two primeval challenges to humankind's relationship to God—the possibility of divine revelation (a topic of philosophy), and the interpretation of divine revelation (the topic of **hermeneutics**)—have been at issue ever since. Therefore, because God's verbal revelation was at the heart of the fall, God's verbal revelation is also at the heart of redemption.

Has God Spoken?

Since the time of the Enlightenment, many people have been persuaded that even if God exists, he cannot interact with or intervene in the things of this world. When science advanced the ability to explain natural phenomena previously attributed to God or the spiritual world, the effect was to reduce if not eliminate God's presence in human life. The

"Has God really said...?"

Much modern thought rejects the Bible as divine revelation:

> If we would destroy the Christian religion, we must first of all destroy man's belief in the Bible.
>
> Voltaire, French Enlightenment philosopher (1694 – 1778)

> It would be more consistent that we called it [the Bible] the word of a demon, than the word of God. It is a history of wickedness, that has served to corrupt and brutalize mankind.
>
> Thomas Paine, author and founding father of the United States (1737 – 1809)

> The inspiration of the Bible depends upon the ignorance of the gentleman who reads it.... I insist that the Bible is *not* the word of God.... The Bible is a sacred record of humanity's childhood.... The Bible is not free from errors, nor is any work of man and time. It abounds in childish views and offensive matters.
>
> Robert Ingersoll, American political leader and orator (1833 – 99)

> One had better put on gloves before reading the New Testament. The presence of so much filth makes it very advisable.... Everything in it is cowardice ... a self – deception.
>
> Friedrich Nietzsche, German philosopher and classical philologist (1844 – 1900)

> The Bible, with its fables, allegories and endless contradictions, has been the great block in the way of civilization.
>
> Elizabeth Cady Stanton, abolitionist and suffragette (1898)*

*Voltaire, quoted in Charles L. Wallis, *A Treasury of Sermon Illustrations* (New York: Abingdon-Cokesbury, 1950), 23; Thomas Paine, *Age of Reason Being an Investigation of True and Fabulous Theology* (London: Eaton, 1794; repr., New York: Wiley, 1942), 24; Robert. G. Ingersoll, *Complete Lectures of Col. R. G. Ingersoll* (Chicago: M. A. Donohue, n.d.), 122, 129, 130; Friedrich W. Nietzsche, *The Antichrist*, trans. H. L. Mencken (New York: Knopf, 1918), 132; Elizabeth Cady Stanton, *The Woman's Bible* (New York: European Publishing, 1895 – 98; repr., Boston: Northeastern University Press, 1993), 2:7.

belief that everything had a natural cause (as opposed to a supernatural cause, such as God) led to the conclusion that God has not spoken and that belief in him can be fully explained psychologically or through other natural phenomena. Therefore, the Bible became not the word of God to humanity, but simply the religious reflections and fictions created by the human minds of its authors. Religion became not about God but all about us.

People today realize that as powerful as science is for explaining natural causes, there is much to human existence that is beyond the reach of its calculations and experiments. But although people now seem more open to the spiritual dimension of human life, the postmodern thought that has succeeded modernist Enlightenment ideas rejects the concept of any truth that is universal for all humankind. Contemporary thought observes the many atrocities committed by religious zealots who believed God was on their side and concludes that any claim to absolute truth is, at bottom, a power play that puts the claimant in a self-serving position of superiority that has motivated the kind of violence perpetrated in God's name throughout history. One answer often offered to this problem is for all people to affirm the validity of others' religious ideas and not to impose on anyone the idea that one concept of God is true and others are false.

Have We Understood God?

The second question raised by the serpent's challenge in the garden of Eden—whether we have correctly understood what God has said—is also reflected in debates about hermeneutics today. Hermeneutics is the theory and practice of interpreting language, especially written texts. Many believe that human language is so ambiguous that religious texts, such as the Bible, really have many meanings over time. Who gets to decide which is the correct one? Well, if there is no single truth about God and his relationship to humankind, then the motivation for determining any single correct interpretation is eliminated. Each person gets to determine the meaning and truthfulness of what he or she reads, apart from any reference to an authority other than his or her own fallen nature. This replay of the error of Adam and Eve has been repeated through all ages. During the time of the Reformation (sixteenth century), Martin Luther observed, "It is exceedingly godless temerity that, where God has humiliated Himself in order to become recognizable, man seeks for himself another way by following the counsels of his own natural capacity."[1]

"It is exceedingly godless temerity that, where God has humiliated Himself in order to become recognizable, man seeks for himself another way by following the counsels of his own natural capacity."

Martin Luther

The fall into sin was constituted by the rejection of God's word for the somehow more appealing, but fatal, word of the serpent. The rejection of God's word in favor of autonomy from him is the crux of sin. Many of the intellectual currents in modern culture are counter to what the author of Hebrews presents as the fundamental truth: God not only exists; God has spoken to humankind. And how one responds to this word that God has spoken is life's most fundamental issue.

1. Martin Luther, *Lectures on Titus, Philemon, and Hebrews*, ed. Jaroslav Pelikan, LW, 29:111.

THE USE OF THE OLD TESTAMENT IN HEBREWS

When the author of Hebrews began his sermon with the claim that God has spoken in the past through the prophets, what specifically did he have in mind? The answer to that question is found by observing that the book of Hebrews quotes and alludes to the Scriptures of ancient Israel, or what Christians call the Old Testament. He doesn't include the wisdom of the Egyptians or the divinations of the Babylonians or the Sibylline oracles of the Greeks. The author of Hebrews is not interested in claiming God's authority for *any* prophetic voice known at his time. He limits his claim that God has spoken specifically and exclusively through the writings of the Old Testament.

Hebrews Uses the Septuagint

There is no other book of the New Testament that contains so many quotations and allusions to the Old Testament as the book of Hebrews. This is not surprising in a discourse that takes as its major topic the relationship between Jesus Christ and the covenant God previously made with Israel. As we have discussed, the author of Hebrews was a highly skilled orator who wrote in the Greek language and addressed people who spoke Greek (as did all the New Testament writers). But the Old Testament prophets of Yahweh spoke and wrote in Hebrew and Aramaic. Just as English-speaking people today read the Old Testament in translations made from the original languages of Hebrew and Aramaic, so the Old Testament used by the Greek-speaking people of the first century was a Greek translation of the Hebrew Bible that is known as the Septuagint and is often abbreviated LXX.[2] The Septuagint, or **Old Greek** (OG), was the first translation to be made of the Hebrew Scriptures, starting in the third century before Christ with the translation of the Pentateuch, most likely in Alexandria. All the other Old Testament books were translated sometime before the end of the first century **BC**, though we don't know by whom, when, or where. Soon after the first Greek translation was made, various revisions and perhaps even other new translations, began to appear. By the time Jesus was born, at least one Greek version of the Old Testament was widely available throughout the Roman Empire wherever Jewish synagogues of Greek-speaking people were found.

It is clear that the New Testament writers often used the Septuagint instead of the Hebrew Bible, because the New Testament rendering of an Old Testament verse often agrees with the Septuagint rather than with the corresponding Hebrew verse. This is why sometimes in our English Bible a quotation of the Old Testament in the New actually might not match the corresponding Old Testament verse when we flip back to it. The New Testament writer is quoting an ancient Greek translation of the Old Testament, and our English Old Testament is translated from the Hebrew. There is a whole field of study called Septuagint studies that examines and debates why the ancient Greek translation appears somewhat different in places from the Hebrew Scriptures we know today. But the point for our purposes is that the writer of Hebrews is clearly using a Greek translation, not the original Hebrew, when he quotes Scripture. The syntax and style of the Greek found in

2. For an introduction to the Septuagint, see Karen H. Jobes and Moisés Silva, *Invitation to the Septuagint* (Grand Rapids: Baker Academic, 2000).

the book of Hebrews is highly literate and shows no traces of bilingual interference from a Semitic language.[3] This means that the author of Hebrews almost certainly was not a native speaker of Aramaic or Hebrew (which counts heavily against Paul's authorship). In fact, if the author was Apollos or someone whose first language was Greek, it isn't certain that he even could have read Hebrew and Aramaic very proficiently, if at all.

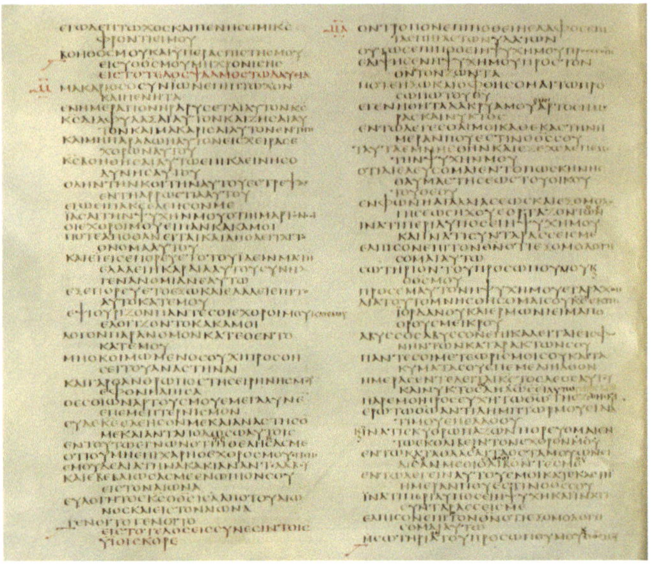

The Greek Psalm 40.

The use of the Greek Old Testament by the author of Hebrews leads to some interesting insights. Psalms is the book most quoted or alluded to in Hebrews, with almost fifty references. Eleven different psalms are quoted, all from their ancient Greek translation. Although one might think that the Greek translation would say the same thing as the Hebrew text it supposedly translates, there are many places where the Greek and Hebrew do not agree. One of these is in the quotation of Psalm 104:4, which is translated in the English version as "He [the Lord God] makes winds his messengers, flames of fire his servants." This suggests that the natural elements of wind and fire are at God's command to achieve his purposes. But the words *mal'ak* in Hebrew and *angelos* in Greek both have two senses, either "messenger" or "angel"; similarly, *rûaḥ* in Hebrew and *pneuma* in Greek can mean either "wind" or "spirit." The ancient Greek translators have interpreted the Hebrew syntax to translate, "He makes his *angelous* ["messengers" or "angels"] *pneumata* ["winds" or "spirits"] and his servants flames of fire." Clearly, the author of Hebrews interprets Psalm 104:4 to be speaking of angels, because that is his topic in Hebrews 1:5–7. The value of the Greek version of Psalm 104:4 is that its parallelism makes the point that the Lord's angels are servants, a point picked up in Hebrews that could not have been as easily made using the Hebrew of the verse. Of course, it is likely that the author of Hebrews could not even read the Hebrew text, and therefore his use of the Greek Psalm 104 may not reflect a deliberate decision; he simply may have used the text available to him.

Trinitarian Attribution of the Old Testament Quotations

Perhaps the most interesting theological point about the way the author of Hebrews uses the Old Testament is that every quotation is attributed to a member of the Trinity regardless of who the human author was. Although the word *Trinity* does not occur in the New Testament, there are ample attestations of the idea. Scan through the book of Hebrews looking at the quotations from the Old Testament (which are set off in most Bibles by

3. For an explanation of this kind of syntactic analysis applied to a different book, see Karen H. Jobes, "The Syntax of 1 Peter: Just How Good Is the Greek?" *BBR* 13 (2003): 159–73.

indentation or sometimes italics). All of the quotations in chapter 1 are attributed to God (as well as those in 4:3, 5, 7; 5:5, 6; 7:21; 8:8; and 13:5). The quotation in Hebrews 2:12 (quoting Ps. 22:22) is attributed to Jesus even though it was first spoken by Israel's King David many centuries before Jesus was born! Similarly, some of David's words are said to have been spoken by Christ *when he came into the world* (Heb. 10:5, quoting Ps. 40:6–8), which shows that the author of Hebrews had the incarnate Jesus specifically in mind and not the preexistent Christ speaking through David (cf. 1 Peter 1:10–12).[4] It is as if Psalm 40 had never previously existed; as if these words originated in Christ's mouth in the first century of this era and not in the psalmist's, some thousand years earlier. This idea of two speakings—one in the distant past and one in more recent history—is, of course, the very idea with which the book of Hebrews opens in 1:1–2. The identification of the words of Psalm 40 with the incarnate Jesus Christ is an expression of the dynastic continuity of Jesus with King David. The seemingly minor differences between the Greek of Psalm 40 in the Septuagint and the way Hebrews quotes it in 10:5–7 express the discontinuity. For instance, in Psalm 40:8, David expresses his desire to do the will of God ("I desire to do your will, my God"). But in Hebrews 10:7, when the words are in the incarnate Christ's mouth, the quote is truncated to read, "I have come to do your will, my God." What David could only desire, Jesus Christ did fully and perfectly.

F. C. Jobes

A modern edition of the Septuagint.

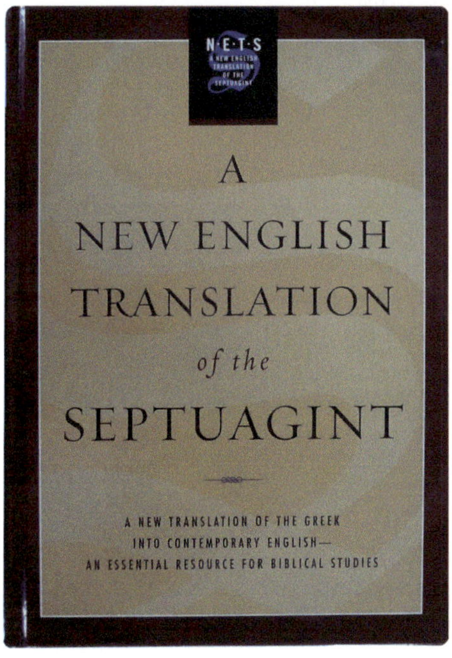

F. C. Jobes

A modern English translation of the Septuagint.

Putting the words of David into the mouth of Jesus helps us to understand why the author of Hebrews does not quote any of the teachings Jesus spoke during his earthly ministry. But it is all the more curious that when God speaks by the Son to us, something more than and other than Jesus' teachings are meant. When the author of Hebrews speaks of what Christ said "when he came into the world," we might expect to hear the Beatitudes or some of Jesus' parables. Oddly, we are presented with Christ speaking the Psalms (Heb. 2:12; 10:5) and Isaiah (Heb. 2:13). This is not to say that the author of Hebrews was unconcerned with what Jesus preached during his earthly ministry. Rather, it shows that Hebrews is concerned to show the organic connection between Jesus Christ as the Word of God and the word of God spoken through the prophets; it was the incarnate Jesus Christ who could most aptly voice those prophetic words in their final and fullest sense. But more important for the author of Hebrews, it was not Jesus' teaching that brought an end to the sacrificial

4. For a fuller discussion of the theology to be found in this very interesting quotation, see Karen H. Jobes, "The Use of Paronomasia in Hebrews 10:5–7," *TJ* 13 (1992): 181–91.

Continuity and Discontinuity Expressed in the "Misquotes" of Hebrews

David says:	"I desire to do your will, my God."
Jesus says:	"I have come to do your will, my God."

system and established a new covenant; it was the obedient sacrifice of his body in death on the cross. And so the words of Psalms 22 and 40 and those of Isaiah 8, which the author of Hebrews puts into the mouth of Jesus, are words that point to the act and result of redemption that Jesus will accomplish. It is within that context that the preaching and teaching of Jesus Christ can be fully appreciated. Otherwise, Jesus would be just another prophet or religious teacher.

It is instructive to observe which quotations of the Old Testament are ascribed to the Holy Spirit. The Holy Spirit is understood as the speaker in Hebrews 3:7 of the warning found in Psalm 95. And in Hebrews 10:15–16 (quoting Jer. 31:33–34), "The Holy Spirit ... says, 'This is the covenant I will make with them after that time,' says the Lord. 'I will put my laws in their hearts, and I will write them on their minds.'" This shows that the author of Hebrews understood the Holy Spirit to be the one who warns against refusing to accept the grace God extends in Christ, and it is the Holy Spirit who makes the new covenant promised by God effective as he writes God's law within us, transforming our hearts and minds.

The Koran, the Scripture of Islam.

The author of Hebrews, like other New Testament writers, clearly believed in the divine inspiration of the Old Testament, but he was not hesitant to refer to a translation of Scripture as God's Word. This notably stands in contrast to the Islamic doctrine of Scripture that claims the Koran as God's word must be read in the original Arabic and cannot be translated. Furthermore, when the biblical sources of the quotations attributed to a member of the Trinity are examined, we find that these quotations were originally words spoken by Moses, David, Nathan, and Jeremiah, providing specific examples of who the prophets were "who spoke at many times and in various ways." In fact, references to all three parts of the Hebrew Bible—the Pentateuch, the Prophets, and the Writings—show that the author of Hebrews probably considered all of what Christians call the Old Testament to be God's word spoken in the past. Clearly the author of Hebrews believed the Old Testament writers to be divinely inspired, for the divine authority of the Trinity stands behind the Old Testament quotations in Hebrews. The human speaker is recognized but is apparently incidental for the purposes of Hebrews.

One of the most interesting uses of Scripture in Hebrews is that passages originally addressed to Yahweh in the Old Testament are now understood as addressed to Jesus. For instance, in Hebrews 1:5–12 we find a series of quotations from the Old Testament attributed directly to God. The quotation in verse 1:8 is prefaced with the statement, "But about the Son he [God] says, 'Your throne, O God, will last for ever and ever,'" which is a quote from Psalm 45:6–7. When that psalm was originally written, the reference to God reigning forever would have been understood as Yahweh, the Creator God of Israel. But as presented by the writer of Hebrews, God the Father is speaking these words *to the Son*, resulting in the claim that God considers the Son himself to be God who will rule forever. In other words, God the Father himself announces the deity of Christ in Hebrews.

Quotations of the Old Testament in Hebrews attributed to...					
God		**Jesus Christ**		**the Holy Spirit**	
1:5	Ps. 2:7	2:12	Ps. 22:22	3:7	Ps. 95:7–11
1:5	2 Sam. 7:14	2:13	Isa. 8:17	10:16	Jer. 31:33
1:6	Deut. 32:43	2:13	Isa. 8:18	10:17	Jer. 31:34
1:7	Ps. 104:4	10:5	Ps. 40:6–8		
1:8	Ps. 45:6–7				
1:10	Ps. 102:25–27				
1:13	Ps. 110:1				
4:3	Ps. 95:11				
4:5	Ps. 95:11				
4:7	Ps. 95:7–8				
5:5	Ps. 2:7				
5:6	Ps. 110:4				
6:13	Gen. 22:17				
7:20	Ps. 110:4				
8:8	Jer. 31:31–34				
13:5	Deut. 31:6				

The way the author of Hebrews chooses to use the Old Testament therefore underscores three points for his Christian readers: (1) the word of God that was spoken in the past to "our ancestors" is found uniquely in the Old Testament; (2) the Old Testament

Psalm 95 in Hebrews

The Psalms are very important in Hebrews and are often quoted. This is especially true of Psalm 95:

Heb. 3:7 – 11	first quotation of Ps. 95:7b – 11
Heb. 3:15	quotes Ps. 95:7 – 8a
Heb. 4:3	quotes Ps. 95:11
Heb. 4:5	quotes Ps. 95:11b
Heb. 4:7	quotes Ps. 95:7b – 8a

"word" was spoken by Father, Son, and Holy Spirit; and (3) all three members of what would later be called the Trinity speak with the same divine authority. Consequently, the Old Testament is to be understood not only as God's words to a past people of the old covenant but also as God's word to Christians after the coming of Jesus.

The author of Hebrews goes to great lengths to press this point of the importance of the Old Testament for his Christian readers. And yet the Old Testament often is overlooked and neglected by Christians today. When was the last time you had your devotions from the Old Testament? When was the last sermon you heard on the Old Testament? Can you trace the contours of Old Testament history? Do you know what the major message of Jonah or of Isaiah is? The Old Testament was the Bible to Jesus, his earliest followers, and to the New Testament writers. If we neglect to read and study it, our understanding of Jesus and the gospel he proclaims will be impoverished.

> "The New within the Old is concealed; the Old within the New is revealed." Several Latin fathers repeat this saying that probably goes back to St. Augustine: "*Novum Testamentum in Vetere latet, Vetus in Novo patet.*"
>
> Augustine, *Quaestiones in Heptateuchum* 2.73

And yet, in the very same sermon, the writer of Hebrews dismisses the old covenant as insufficient — even though it was based on God's word through the prophets — in light of the new covenant established by Jesus' death. This is quite an interesting problem that is of relevance for Christians today who wonder about the authority of the Old Testament. If the Old Testament is the word of God no less than the New Testament, how can the author of Hebrews so clearly highlight the divine inspiration of the Old Testament even while setting it aside as obsolete? Again, the issue of continuity and discontinuity between the old and new in the theology of Hebrews is apparent. Let's see how our theologically astute author of Hebrews, who is himself inspired by God's authority, accomplishes this.

Relativizing the Old Testament

The author of Hebrews affirms that the Old Testament is God's word but relativizes it with respect to the gospel of Jesus Christ. That is, the author of Hebrews wishes to show that even though the Old Testament covenant needed to be obeyed by those who lived in its day, the coming of the Son has changed the relevance of that covenant and the Old Testament forevermore. Even though the Old Testament is God's word to Christians, its **illocutionary force** has changed, to use a term from **speech act theory**.[5] Simply put, a **locution** is a statement, which can be one sentence or an entire discourse. The speaker or author of every locution intends an effect, its illocutionary force. The book of Hebrews, and indeed the entire Bible, can be thought of as a locution originating with its human authors, but more ultimately as a locution spoken by God. The Old Testament is a divine locution whose illocutionary intent changed once Jesus Christ had come. The words of the Old Testament (the locution) remain the same, but their illocutionary force, that is, what God intends to accomplish by those words, has changed with the coming of Christ according to the book of Hebrews. And so while the Old Testament is no less God's word than when its books were first written, its purpose in the context of God's progressive revelation has changed. The author of Hebrews took on the challenge of explaining that change, of relativizing the word of God given under the old covenant. The effect of God's discourse is either the transformation of hearts in covenant obedience or the hardening of hearts in rebellion against God. Any appearance of neutral ground is a delusion.

Todd Bolen/www.BiblePlaces.com

Altar of the Tabernacle in which burnt sacrifices were offered.

Why do Christians no longer offer animals in a temple for our sins even though God commanded it? That command was in effect until the perfect sacrifice, the Lamb of God who takes away the sin of the world once and for all, was offered on the cross. Hebrews, therefore, argues that God himself in the Old Testament had revealed that the old covenant was preparatory for a superior covenant that would be based on a superior sacrifice. Let's see how he explains this.

Please read Hebrews 10:1–18. Hebrews 10:1–18 quotes Psalm 40:6–8, which says that God did not desire "sacrifice and offering" and that he was not pleased with "burnt offerings and sin offerings" (Heb. 10:5–6). Then immediately the author of Hebrews acknowledges that God did in fact command these very things in the Law (v. 8). But now that Christ has come in a body (v. 5), the true desire of God has been fulfilled in the only sacrifice that is truly "pleasing" to him—that is, the only one that truly satisfies God's just requirements—the crucifixion of Jesus Christ. The psalm that said that God was dissatisfied with animal sacrifice was written during the period of time when people were making them in obedience to God's law. Therefore, even at the time the old covenant was being

5. See Kevin Vanhoozer, "From Speech Acts to Scripture Acts: The Covenant of Discourse and the Discourse of the Covenant," in *After Pentecost Language and Biblical Interpretation*, ed. Craig Bartholomew, Calvin Greene, and Karl Möller, Scripture and Hermeneutics Series 2 (Grand Rapids: Zondervan, 2001), 1–49.

practiced in obedience to God, God was hinting through the psalmist that a better sacrifice was needed.

Hebrews goes on to explain that the very fact the priests of the Old Testament covenant had to offer animal sacrifices again and again, day after day, indicated that those sacrifices could “never take away sins” (10:11). And so not only are we told that a new, superior sacrifice was needed, but also, by implication, that the work of the priesthood would someday end. In fact, the superior sacrifice would be offered by a superior priesthood, a priesthood in the order of Melchizedek, not in the order of Aaron (more on this in the next chapter when we discuss that mysterious Melchizedek). The point for now is that, according to the author of Hebrews, the Old Testament priesthood itself implied that a better way than itself was needed.

And then Hebrews 10:15–17 quotes another of the many prophets through whom God spoke in times past, the prophet Jeremiah, who said that a time would come when the Lord would make a new covenant with his people. This new covenant would not be written on tablets of stone like the first one was, when God gave it to Moses on the mountaintop. The new covenant would be written in the hearts and minds of God’s people. The old covenant was written on tablets of stone external to a person, who had no internal power to keep it. Yet God had promised through the prophet Jeremiah that the new covenant would somehow be able to transform people into those whose obedience to God would flow from deep within them. The new covenant would be not external religious practice but a heart-transformed relationship to God.

Representation of the old covenant on stone tablets.

An analogy between the external code of the old covenant and the transforming power of the new covenant might be the difference between a student who comes to class and does all the assignments in compliance with the “law” of the syllabus but hates the subject compared to the student who comes to class because she loves the subject and is eager to learn. As a professor I can write all the “laws” I want into my syllabus, but there is no “law” I can write to make a student love to study the New Testament. That is similar to the difference between the law of the old covenant and the transforming power of the new covenant. It is probably not accidental that the writer of Hebrews introduces the quotation from Jeremiah by attributing it to the Holy Spirit (10:15), for it is the Spirit’s work after Pentecost that applies God’s transforming power to his people in a way that could not have happened before Jesus’ resurrection and ascension.

And so we see that even though the author of Hebrews affirms completely the Old Testament as God’s Word, and acknowledges that worshipers were right to sacrifice animals and to follow the old covenant in its day, the death, resurrection, and ascension of Jesus

Christ have changed all that by making the old covenant obsolete. Hebrews shows more clearly than any other New Testament book that the new covenant in Christ was never God's plan B; it was God's plan *even when he gave the first covenant* to someday establish a new one. So sharp is the difference between these two covenants that they define two distinct periods of time ("in the past" versus "these last days"). Much of the book of Hebrews is taken up with describing how Jesus and the new covenant he establishes relates to the old covenant and why, now that Jesus has come, obedience to the old covenant is really disobedience to God! Furthermore, Hebrews argues that the covenant established by Jesus Christ is God's final word. The new covenant is the final, ultimate deal that God offers; there will be no other, because God has told us so.

CHRIST HIMSELF IS GOD'S FINAL REVELATION

We have been discussing some of the implications of the opening verses of Hebrews (1:1–5) with their claim that in the past God spoke through the prophets in many ways at many times, but that now he has spoken by the Son. It might be natural, therefore, to think of the Son as the final and greatest prophet, who relativizes all who have gone before him. When we look at the Old Testament we find the words and oracles of the prophets in books titled with names like Isaiah, Jeremiah, and Ezekiel. But another clue that God's revelation in Jesus is qualitatively different from these holy men of the past is that there isn't a book in the Bible titled Jesus. It is true that in the four gospels we find many of the words of Jesus preserved for us and that these words are a great treasure. But in many ways, during his earthly life, Jesus did not teach a different message from what had already been taught in the Old Testament. He said that he didn't come to abolish the Law or the Prophets but to fulfill them (Matt. 5:17). He pressed this point by further saying that until heaven and earth disappear, not the smallest part of the Law will by any means disappear (Matt. 5:18). And so the new age ushered in by Jesus should be seen as a fulfillment of the old covenant that leaves the Law still standing. And yet there is much of the Old Testament law that Christians simply don't obey. For instance, have you ever heard of anyone going to the priest when he finds mold in his house (see Lev. 14:33–53)? And yet isn't Leviticus 14:33–53 nevertheless God's inspired word? And so again we are confronted with the issue of continuity and discontinuity. What remains of the old covenant under the new (i.e., continuity), and what does not (i.e., discontinuity)? The answer to that must wait until we discuss in the next chapter what it means that Jesus is a priest in the order of Melchizedek.

As we discussed above, although the four gospels are full of Jesus' words, there is not one of them in the book of Hebrews. This seems rather strange for a book that so confidently states that God has spoken to us by the Son. Wouldn't this mean that Jesus' words are God's words? And if so, shouldn't the author of Hebrews be quoting Jesus right and left to make his case? The fact that the book of Hebrews doesn't *once* quote words from Jesus' teaching is a big clue about another qualitative difference between the revelation given by many prophets of the past and the revelation given by the Son. Where the words of the prophets were the message from God in the past, the Son *himself* is God's final revelation. This is not to say that what Jesus said isn't important. It is to say that the *identity* of Jesus as the divine Son of God is what makes him the perfect and final revelation of God. And so no matter how many other people may come along claiming to be prophets with a word from God, if their message doesn't point to Jesus Christ as God's clearest revelation, their message is worthless for understanding God. If you want to know God, look at Jesus, who is the "exact representation" of God's nature (Heb. 1:3). In other words, Jesus doesn't just speak God's words (that is what the prophets did), he *is* God's word (as John's gospel makes so beautifully clear). With this important distinction in mind, we turn next to see what the book of Hebrews says about who Jesus is — that is, the Christology of Hebrews.

CHAPTER SUMMARY

The theology of the book of Hebrews finds its bedrock in the fact of God's revelation, which God initiated through many prophets early in redemptive history and which culminated in his last word, Jesus Christ, the Son of God. The incarnation is the historical event that creates a temporal dualism between "in the past" and "in these last days" and provides the framework throughout the book by which the author considers both the continuity and the discontinuity of these two ages. The Old Testament was God's word, but Christians no longer follow its letter, for that is what God now intends. God commanded sacrifices in the Old Testament, but Christians no longer offer them, because Jesus' death was the full and final sacrifice. Hebrews both affirms the authority of the Old Testament and shows how it has been relativized by the death and resurrection of Jesus Christ. According to Hebrews, the person of Jesus Christ, not the words that Jesus spoke during his earthly ministry, is himself God's final revelation. It was Christ's death and resurrection that established the new covenant, not his ethical teachings, as important as those teachings are for living righteously. This truth raises Jesus Christ above the level of a mere prophet and shows the error of those religions that acknowledge Jesus as one in a continuing line of prophets.

KEY TERMS

illocution
locution
prophet
revelation
Septuagint
Son
speech act theory

QUESTIONS FOR REVIEW OR DISCUSSION

1. What three contrasts does Hebrews make as it presents Jesus as the final revelation of God?
2. What is the Septuagint? Why is it significant for understanding the book of Hebrews and other New Testament books?
3. Using the book of Hebrews, how would you answer the claim that Jesus was merely a great ethical teacher and a true prophet of God?
4. What is theologically notable about the quotations of the Old Testament books in Hebrews? How does this inform Christian doctrine of Scripture concerning the Old Testament?
5. How does the author of Hebrews both uphold the divine authority of the Old Testament and yet also relativize it?

GOING FURTHER

Frame, John M. "God and Biblical Language: Transcendence and Immanence." In *God's Inerrant Word.* Edited by J. W. Montgomery. Minneapolis: Bethany Fellowship, 1974.

Gheorghita, Radu. *The Role of the Septuagint in Hebrews.* WUNT 160. Tübingen: Mohr Siebeck, 2003.

Jobes, Karen H. "The Use of Paronomasia in Hebrews 10:5–7." *Trinity Journal* 13 (1992): 181–91.

Jobes, Karen H., and Moisés Silva. *Invitation to the Septuagint.* Grand Rapids: Baker Academic, 2000.

Packer, James I. "The Adequacy of Human Language." Pages 197–226 in *Inerrancy.* Edited by Norman L. Geisler. Grand Rapids: Zondervan, 1980.

Pietersma, Albert, and Benjamin G. Wright, eds. *A New English Translation of the Septuagint.* New York and Oxford: Oxford University Press, 2007.

Treier, Daniel J. "Speech Acts, Hearing Hearts, and Other Senses: The Doctrine of Scripture Practiced in Hebrews." Pages 337–50 in *The Epistle to the Hebrews and Christian Theology.* Edited by Richard Bauckham et al. Grand Rapids: Eerdmans, 2009.

Vanhoozer, Kevin. "From Speech Acts to Scripture Acts. The Covenant of Discourse and the Discourse of the Covenant." Pages 1–49 in *After Pentecost: Language and Biblical Interpretation.* Edited by Craig Bartholomew, Calvin Greene, and Karl Möller. Grand Rapids: Zondervan, 2001.

Vos, Geerhardus. *The Teaching of the Epistle to the Hebrews.* Phillipsburg, N.J.: Presbyterian and Reformed, 1956; esp. pp. 49–87.

Wolterstorff, Nicholas. *Divine Discourse: Philosophical Reflections on the Claim That God Speaks.* Cambridge: Cambridge University Press, 1995.

CHAPTER 3

The Son Is Our Great High Priest

THE CHRISTOLOGY OF HEBREWS

Your Goals for This Chapter

- To understand how Hebrews explains the significance of Jesus Christ.
- To be able to explain the relationship of the Son both to God and to the prophets who previously spoke for God.
- To appreciate what the term "Son of God" meant in the first century.
- To understand why the Son is superior to Moses and the angels.
- To be able to articulate why the incarnation of the Son was necessary.
- To learn who Melchizedek was and why Hebrews compares Jesus' priesthood to his.
- To comprehend how the roles of Jesus as Son of God and as High Priest come together in his ascension.

WHY THIS CHAPTER IS IMPORTANT TO YOU

What responsibility do Christians have to the Old Testament? Did God just change his mind about the priests and sacrifices of ancient Israel? Jesus couldn't even go into the temple in Jerusalem; doesn't that matter? Who is Melchizedek and what do we know about him? If you have pondered such questions, the book of Hebrews will answer them. In this chapter we will discuss how Hebrews presents who Jesus is and what he has done in relation to the priesthood and sacrifices established in the Old Testament. The author of Hebrews presents two focal points in his discussion: (1) the sonship of Christ (Heb. 1:1–13), and (2) the eternal priesthood of Christ (Heb. 4:14–5:10; 7:1–28). In order to understand this, we will look at the historical background of these terms. Hebrews also draws an interesting relationship between Jesus as Son and Jesus as priest. Here the mysteries of Melchizedek will be presented with an explanation of why his priesthood is an appropriate paradigm for the role of Jesus Christ as High Priest of a new covenant (Heb. 5:5–6; 6:20; 7:3).

Key Verses

1:1–3: In the past God spoke to our ancestors through the prophets at many times and in various ways, but in these last days he has spoken to us by his Son, whom he appointed heir of all things, and through whom also he made the universe. The Son is the radiance of God's glory and the exact representation of his being, sustaining all things by his powerful word. After he had provided purification for sins, he sat down at the right hand of the Majesty in heaven.

1:5; 5:5: For to which of the angels did God ever say,

> "You are my Son;
> today I have become your Father"?...

In the same way, Christ did not take on himself the glory of becoming a high priest. But God said to him,

> "You are my Son;
> today I have become your Father."

2:8b–9: In putting everything under them, God left nothing that is not subject to them. Yet at present we do not see everything subject to them. But we do see Jesus, who was made lower than the angels for a little while, now crowned with glory and honor because he suffered death, so that by the grace of God he might taste death for everyone.

2:17: For this reason he had to be made like them fully human in every way, in order that he might become a merciful and faithful high priest in service to God, and that he might make atonement for the sins of the people.

4:15: For we do not have a high priest who is unable to empathize with our weaknesses, but we have one who has been tempted in every way, just as we are—yet he did not sin.

5:1, 5–6: Every high priest is selected from among the people and is appointed to represent the people in matters related to God, to offer gifts and sacrifices for sins.... Christ did not take on himself the glory of becoming a high priest. But God said to him,...

> "You are a priest forever,
> in the order of Melchizedek."

7:22(–28): Because of this oath, Jesus has become the guarantor of a better covenant.

9:11(–14): But when Christ came as high priest of the good things that are now already here, he went through the greater and more perfect tabernacle that is not made with human hands, that is to say, not a part of this creation.

10:(11–)14: For by one sacrifice he has made perfect forever those who are being made holy.

10:16(–18):

> "This is the covenant I will make with them
> after that time, says the Lord.
> I will put my laws in their hearts,
> and I will write them on their minds."

CHAPTER OUTLINE

I. Jesus as Son of God
   A. The Nature of the Son
      1. The Son is the appointed heir of all things (v. 2)
      2. The Son is the radiance of God's glory (v. 3).
      3. The Son is the exact representation of God's being (v. 3)
   B. What the Son Has Done
      1. God has spoken by his Son (v. 1)
      2. The Son was the agent of creation through whom God made the universe (v. 2)
      3. The Son sustains all things by his powerful word (v. 3)
      4. The Son provided purification for sins (v. 3)
      5. The Son sat down at the right hand of God (v. 3)
   C. What Did It Mean That Jesus Is "Son of God"?
   D. The Superiority of Jesus Christ over All Others

II. The Son as Priest of God

A. The Incarnation of the Son Was Necessary for His Priesthood
B. Jesus Christ as High Priest of a New Covenant
C. The Priesthood of Melchizedek
1. How is the order of Melchizedek an appropriate analogy for what Jesus has done?
2. Why the emphasis on Jesus being a priest for Christians?

III. The Relationship between Sonship and High Priesthood

A. The Ascension as the Entrance of the High Priest into the Holy of Holies
B. The Ascension as the Coronation of the Kingly Son of God

There is no other book of the New Testament that better explains how Jesus' identity and death relate to the Old Testament concepts that shaped ancient Israel's faith. Any convert to the Christian faith from Judaism in the first century would be vitally interested to know how Jesus fits into the big picture of God's work as it had been revealed through Abraham, Moses, and David and how the gospel relates to the religion based on animal sacrifices offered in the temple in Jerusalem. And converts from **Gentile** paganism would need to be instructed in the fundamentals of Israel's religion from which Christianity emerged to understand the significance of God's redemptive work accomplished by Christ.

> Christology:
> 1. the branch of theology dealing with the nature, person, and deeds of Jesus Christ. 2. an interpretation of the nature, person, and deeds of Jesus Christ.
>
> *Random House Dictionary of the English Language*

The author of Hebrews presents Jesus in two roles that would have been familiar to people living in the first century: his role as "Son" of God and his role as High Priest.

Son and Priest are the two points on which Hebrews focuses our attention in its **Christology**, the term used by systematic theologians to refer to Christian doctrine that describes Jesus Christ.

The author of Hebrews introduces Jesus as both "Son" of God and as Priest in the very opening verses of the book by referring to him first as "Son" and by explaining that he "provided purification for sins," which was the task of a priest as priests were understood in the first century:

> In the past God spoke to our ancestors through the prophets at many times and in various ways, but in these last days he has spoken to us by *his Son*, whom he appointed heir of all things, and through whom also he made the universe. The Son is the radiance of God's glory and the exact representation of his being, sustaining all things by his powerful word. After *he had provided purification for sins*, he sat down at the right hand of the Majesty in heaven. (1:1–3, emphasis added)

The Two Foci of Christology in Hebrews

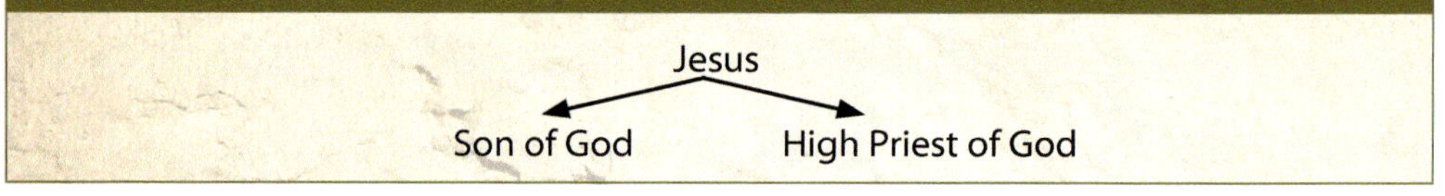

JESUS AS SON OF GOD

After two thousand years of the development of Christian theology, our first thought of Jesus as Son of God is his identity as the second member of the divine Trinity. Sometimes that understanding obscures the finer points of how the New Testament writers use the term and how that title would have been understood in the first century.

Z. Radovan/www.BibleLandPictures.com

Hebrews teaches that Israel's high priest was a foreshadow of Jesus Christ, the final and true Great High Priest.

The Nature of the Son

The book of Hebrews opens with a distinctively Christocentric focus, drawing the reader's mind immediately to the "Son." What that meant to the author of Hebrews is seen in the description of Jesus in these four opening verses, which can be divided into descriptions of the nature of the Son himself and descriptions of what the Son does or did:

The Son is the appointed heir of all things (v. 2).

Here the author of Hebrews employs the concept of an heir to describe the role of the Son and his relationship to God the Father. It is natural to understand this reference in the cultural terms with which we are familiar. In our culture it is typical for parents or other relatives to leave an inheritance to the children of the next generation when they die. The death of the parent or relative is necessary for one to become an heir in our system. Moreover, it is simple to change one's will and thereby rename one's heir, so at any given time an heir is only an heir apparent until the actual death of the parent or relative.

When the identification of the Son as the appointed heir is understood in these terms, it leads to the conundrum of thinking that the death of the Father would be necessary for the Son's role as heir to be actualized, which is of course theologically problematic. This is a good example of how interpreting the Bible must be done within the historical context of its writing, for when Roman law is considered, the conundrum disappears.

Justinian's *Institutes* preserves a digest of Roman law that informs our understanding of legal terms and metaphors in the New Testament.[1] In Roman law the heir was defined in reference to the patriarchal system and the family cult. The heir continued the persona of the ancestor as the family priest and was, as such, the personification of the family that made the ancestor present. This idea of the continuity of the persona of the ancestor and the heir was taken to imply that the legal representation of the heir and his ancestor existed before the latter's death so that the heir was not independent of his father in the eyes of Roman law.[2] The heir became heir not upon the death of his father, but *by virtue of being the first male born to or adopted by the father.* The heir's acquisitions belonged to his father. The heir's actions made his father legally liable, such that the heir did not

1. Justinian, *Institutes*, trans. Peter Birks and Grant McLeod (Ithaca, N.Y.: Cornell University Press, 1987).
2. See Francis Lyall, *Slaves, Citizens, Sons: Legal Metaphors in the Epistles* (Grand Rapids: Zondervan, 1984), 106–17.

have independent legal standing from the father. In other words, being the "heir" did not depend on the death of the father, because in Roman law the status as heir existed by virtue of the relationship between the father and the son. The context of Roman law as it defined and governed the heir provides a fitting way to understand Hebrews 1:2, as it has points of contact both with the priestly motif of Hebrews and it is a way of explaining the congruence between the Son's nature and actions and the Father's. It is a powerful statement that, as in Roman thought, the heir makes the ancestor present in this world; similarly, God the Father is made present by the Son's incarnation.

The Son is the radiance of God's glory (v. 3).

The Son is here described using a Greek word (Gk. *apaugasma*) rare in the biblical text that can mean either "radiance" or "reflection," depending on the context in which the word is used. In Wisdom 7:26 (a book found in the **apocryphal** or **deuterocanonical** books), personified wisdom is described as an *apaugasma* "of eternal light, a spotless mirror of the working of God" (NRSV), where the sense is clearly "reflection" because of the reference to a mirror. In other contexts, such as here in Hebrews 1:3, *apaugasma* refers to a radiance from a source. Just as we know the sun from the radiant energy it provides through heat and light, the Son embodies and radiates the glory of God, which otherwise without him would remain unrevealed.

The Son is the exact representation of God's being (v. 3).

The saying "Like father, like son" is never truer than when applied to Jesus as Son of God. Nature teaches us that the offspring is of the same species and has the same nature as the parent. Genetics teaches us that the offspring share salient traits with the parent. But the author of Hebrews pushes the idea of family likeness to a degree that we don't find in nature (except perhaps in cloning). Hebrews describes the Son with the Greek word *charactēr* of God, translated "exact representation." The Greek word in transliteration looks like the English word *charactēr* (and there probably is an etymological relationship); it was used to refer to something that was an exact representation of its source, bearing all of its distinctive traits. The word was used to refer to the imprint made by a stamp (like our "rubber stamp" today). The *charactēr* was the identical imprint made in clay or ink by the mold. The *charactēr* wasn't just similar to the mold from which it was stamped; it was identical except it existed in a separate medium (e.g., clay or ink) from the mold. This is one of the strongest statements in the New Testament of the relationship between Jesus and God. If you want to know what God is like, look at Jesus. He is the exact representation of God's being.

What the Son Has Done

The opening verses of Hebrews describe not only who the Son is in relation to God but also what he has done:

God has spoken by his Son (v. 1).

One of the ways the gospel of Jesus Christ is distinctively different from pagan religions of the first century is that the God of the gospel has revealed himself. In the worldview of polytheism that was prevalent in biblical times, the desires and intentions of the gods were read from circumstances. If nature wreaked havoc, the inference was that the corresponding god or goddess must be angry about something the people who lived in the region suffering the havoc had done. Abundant rain and plentiful crops were taken as a sign of the gods' favor. (This kind of religious worldview still operates today, even among some Christian believers, even though Jesus himself says in Luke 13:4 that tragedy doesn't necessarily imply guilt.)

The trouble was that the gods and goddesses never actually specified what they wanted. And so ancient polytheistic religion had to second-guess the gods by trying one thing after another to placate them and assure the good life. Because both good and bad things happen, the gods and goddesses were thought to be capricious and unpredictable. It was the job of the priest or priestess to figure out what the gods wanted and stand between their wrath and the people. In the ancient world, this fulfilled a very important role in society, and it almost always involved killing animals. The idea was that if the anger of the gods demanded death, then hopefully they would be satisfied with the death of animals instead of people. Some religions actually practiced human sacrifice of children or virgin girls with the hope that it would spare more widespread suffering and death. The writer of Hebrews introduces the startling idea that the supreme God, the creator of the universe, has in fact revealed what he wants with respect to the problem of sin and that his last word is Jesus (cf. John 1:1–18).

The Son was the agent of creation through whom God made the universe (v. 2).

There is a good theological reason why Genesis 1 describes the creation of the universe in terms of God *speaking* it into existence ("And God *said* ... and it was") and why Jesus is later referred to as the "Word" (Gk. *logos*) of God in John 1:1–2. The author of Hebrews also presents this idea here in describing the Son as the one through whom God made the universe. This role of the Son reveals three essential aspects:

1. The Son eternally existed before he was incarnated as Jesus of Nazareth in the first century.
2. The Son shares the creative power of God the Father because the Son shares the nature of his Father. Remember, "like Father, like Son."
3. The Son shares the Father's creative purposes. In contrast to the Greek pantheon of gods, there are no cross-purposes between the Father and the Son. This contrasts sharply with ancient creation myths such as the Babylonian *Enuma Elish*, which presents the creation of the universe as the result of a cosmic battle between the goddess Tiamat and her descendent, the god Marduk. In the Christian worldview, the universe does not rest fundamentally on conflict, war, and violence but in the peaceful, harmonious relationship within the Godhead of Father, Son, and Spirit. Humankind was created in that image of the Godhead in its perfect order. This is a reason to understand conflict, war, and violence as a disruption of the created order and not as part of the fabric of creation.

The New Testament never presents God the Father and God the Son as two Gods, but always describes them in such a way that preserves both the closest identity possible while

The Son's Relationship to the Father

The following excerpt from the Nicene Creed articulates the orthodox understanding of the relationship between the Father and the Son:

> We believe in one God the Father all-powerful, Maker of heaven and earth, and of all things both seen and unseen.
>
> And in one Lord Jesus Christ, the only-begotten Son of God, begotten from the Father before all the ages, light from light, true God from God, begotten, not made, being of one substance with the Father, through whom all things came to be.*

*Jaroslav Pelikan and Valerie Hotchkiss, *Creeds and Confessions of Faith in the Christian Tradition*, 4 vols. (New Haven, Conn.: Yale University Press, 2003), 1:163.

yet distinguishing them from one another. The church in subsequent centuries produced the great creedal statements about the nature and relationships of the Trinity by fleshing out such statements from the New Testament in theological doctrine.

The Son sustains all things by his powerful word (v. 3).

One of the more intriguing roles of the Son is his ongoing work to sustain the universe by *his* powerful word. We might have the impression that the universe is so established in its material reality that it can exist quite apart from the Creator who made it. This concept was formalized in the theology of deism and is often referred to with the analogy of the watch and the watchmaker. But the New Testament teaches that the creative role of the Son did not end when creation was complete (if, in fact, it is correct to think of a completed creation). The Son has an ongoing role in sustaining all things by his powerful word. As J. B. Lightfoot commented on a similar thought in Colossians 1:17, "He [Christ] is the principle of cohesion in the Universe. He impresses upon creation that unity and solidarity which makes it a cosmos instead of a chaos."[3] For those students interested in physics, reflection on the quest for the unified field theory in relation to Christ's sustaining role of the universe might be a fruitful meditation.

The Son provided purification for sins (v. 3).

Although the writer of Hebrews does not use the word *priest* here, he ascribes to the Son the role that the ancients immediately would have recognized as that of a priest. As discussed above, priests had the unenviable role of trying to discern what would satisfy the gods so they could avert the wrath of the god from the people they represented and served. The writer of Hebrews agrees with the pagan worldview that people have committed sins in the eyes of a higher power. However, what makes the Christian gospel distinctive is first, the knowledge of what God wants in light of human sinfulness, and furthermore, that

3. J. B. Lightfoot, *Saint Paul's Epistles to the Colossians and to Philemon*, 5th ed. (London: Macmillan, 1880), 156.

what God wants has been provided for in his Son, Jesus Christ. In subsequent chapters the author of Hebrews explains in considerable detail how the purification for sins that Jesus provides is both similar to the Old Testament priesthood and sacrificial system and at the same time completely different from it.

The Son sat down at the right hand of God (v. 3).

In Exodus 25–40, we find a very detailed description of the **tabernacle**, which was the place God commanded ancient Israel to make animal sacrifices, and a description of its furniture and accessories used by the priests to make their offerings. The tabernacle was a portable tent so that God's people could take it with them as they journeyed to the land he had promised to them. The design of the tabernacle will find an important place later in Hebrews when the work of the Son as High Priest is described.

When the tabernacle, and later the temple, was built as the earthly place of God's habitation, it was designed "according to the pattern shown you on the mountain" (Heb. 8:5). It was a model of the cosmos as God's dwelling place whose function foreshadowed the **atonement** of Jesus Christ. (See Sabbath Rest in chapter 4.) As the first-century Jewish historian Josephus notes, the tabernacle and everything in it were "made in way of imitation and representation of the universe" (*Ant.* 3.7.7.180). The three-part structure represented the sea (with the water basin), the land (by the bronze pillars of the earth), and heaven (by the ark of the covenant, God's footstool), with the first two parts generally accessible,

The Erection of the Tabernacle by the Children of Israel in the Wilderness, English School, (19th century)/ Private Collection/The Bridgeman Art Library

The tabernacle is an important symbol in Hebrews.

but the third, the place of God's dwelling, restricted only to the high priest. The golden lampstand and the bread of the Presence represent light and food provided by God. The massive curtain separated the Holy of Holies from the place of human dwelling.[4] This was the curtain that was "torn in two from top to bottom" when Jesus died (Matt. 27:51). Hebrews explains that this opened "a new and living way" for us into the very presence of God (10:20).

The instruction that the tabernacle must be built exactly according to the pattern that God revealed is prefaced by the statement that the earthly tabernacle is only a "copy" and shadow of the heavenly (Heb. 8:5). Given the influence of Greek philosophy in Western thinking, it may be natural to read this as an ontological **dualism** similar to that of Plato's parallel worlds of ideals and their material correspondences. Philo understood the earthly tabernacle in all its detail to be a mirror image of the heavenly tabernacle. But rather than representing a Platonic ideal, adherence to the details of the revealed plan for the tabernacle was necessary in order that it would fulfill its role as a prophetic **type** of the person and work of Jesus Christ that would come later in history. (See The Dualism of Hebrews in chapter 1.)

The design of the tabernacle was used much later in Israel's history as the pattern for the temple designed by King David (2 Sam. 7; 1 Chron. 22–29) and built by his son King Solomon (1 Kings 5–8; 2 Chron. 2–7) in the city of Jerusalem when Israel settled in the land to which God had led them. The temple furnishings included a golden altar, tables, lampstands, lamps and tongs, wick trimmers, bowls, dishes, and censors (2 Chron. 4:19–22). Notably, there were no chairs in the temple, because during his cultic work a priest never sat down and the work of offering sacrifices was never done. In sharp contrast, after making purification for sins, the Son not only *sits down*, but he sits down next to God the Father at his right hand on the throne in heaven. In other words, the priestly work required by the Father has been completed. This introduces the idea of the finality of Christ's work as High Priest, which is greatly expanded on later in Hebrews.

---

4. John H. Walton, *The Lost World of Genesis One: Ancient Cosmology and the Origins Debate* (Downers Grove, Ill.: IVP Academic, 2009), 81–82.

Josephus on the Tabernacle as Model of the Cosmos

"For if anyone does but consider the fabric of the tabernacle, and take a view of the garments of the high priest, and of those vessels which we make use of in our sacred ministration, he will find that our legislator was a divine man, and that we are unjustly reproached by others: for if anyone does without prejudice, and with judgment, look upon these things, he will find they were every one made in way of imitation and representation of the universe. When Moses distinguished the tabernacle into three parts, and allowed two of them to the priests, as a place accessible and common, he denoted the land and the sea, these being of general access to all; but he set apart the third division for God, because heaven is inaccessible to men."

Josephus, *Antiquities* 2.3.3.180

Notice that of these five ideas listed in Hebrews 1:1–3, it would seem that Jesus performed only one during his earthly life, and that is the purification for sins when he died on the cross. However, the efficacy of this sacrifice of himself in Jerusalem is described in Hebrews as also located outside the earthly realm, in heaven itself (Heb. 9:11, 24). The Son as the agent of creation obviously refers to acts of the preexistent Son before the world began. Similarly, the Son's action in sustaining all things is a work that transcends the man Jesus' existence in the first century on planet Earth. The Son's seating at God's right hand also took place in the heavenly realm apart from his life on earth, though it was apparently the very first thing Jesus did after he left this world (if it is correct to talk about chronology of events in eternity).

As Hebrews goes on to say in subsequent chapters, it was through the crucifixion of Jesus on a cross in Jerusalem that the Son offered the sacrifice that purified sins. This was the only function of the incarnation that the author of Hebrews wanted to stress—not the ethical teachings of Jesus (as in the Sermon on the Mount in Matt. 5–7), not his healings or his other miracles. God had formerly used the prophets to speak his words, to heal, and even to raise the dead. Jesus did these things as well, but the author of Hebrews wished to focus on Jesus' unique role as High Priest of the new covenant. So even though God has spoken by his Son, the medium of God's message to us is not in Jesus' earthly words (as red letter Bibles might lead us incorrectly to infer) but in his very person as revealed by the incarnation. God's speaking to us in Son-revelation is uniquely distinguished from God's speaking through the merely human agents of the past. This is not to say that the words Jesus spoke during his earthly life are not divine or that they are not essential to the gospel. In fact, because of Jesus' divine identity, his teaching carries the ultimate authority that exceeds any other religious teacher (see Matt. 7:29; Mark 1:22; Luke 4:32). It is simply that for his purposes, the author of Hebrews wanted to point out that the focus of God's revelation to us is on what the incarnate Son did that could not have been achieved by even the greatest of God's servants in the past, such as Abraham, Moses, and David, namely, to **atone** for sin.

atone: to make amends or reparation; in Christian theology, to reconcile God and humankind through Jesus.

ADAPTED FROM *OXFORD AMERICAN COLLEGE DICTIONARY*, 2002

What Did It Mean That Jesus Is "Son of God"?

We see in these opening verses of Hebrews that the author was agreeing with two other New Testament writers, the apostles John (cf. John 1:1–18) and Paul (cf. Col. 1:15–18), about the Son's relationship to creation and (cf. Col. 1:19–20) about the Son's role in reconciling sinful people to a holy God (although Paul never refers to Jesus as a priest). This again highlights that New Testament Christology centers not on the ethical teachings of Jesus of Nazareth, as important as they may be for Christian living, but on his divinity as both the agent of creation and the means of reconciliation with God. When readers today see Jesus' title Son of God, they immediately recognize his place in the Trinitarian Godhead and all that has been inferred from two thousand years of Christian theology. But what would it have meant to the original readers who did not have the benefit of the great creeds that the church later developed?

Titles for Jesus in Hebrews		
Title	***Greek word***	***Verses***
High Priest	*archiereus*	2:17; 3:1; 4:14–15; 5:1, 5, 10; 6:20; 7:26–8:1; 8:3; 9:7, 11, 25; 13:11
Christ	*Christos*	3:6, 14; 5:5; 6:1; 9:11, 14, 24, 28; 10:10; 11:26; 13:8, 21
Son	*huios*	1:2, 5, 8; 2:6, 10; 3:6; 4:14; 5:5, 8; 6:6; 7:3, 28; 10:29
Lord	*kurios*	1:10; 2:3; 7:14; 13:20
Mediator	*mesitēs*	8:6; 9:1; 12:24
Firstborn	*prōtotokos*	1:6; 12:23
Heir	*klēronomos*	1:2; 11:7
Pioneer	*archēgos*	2:10; 12:2
God	*theos*	1:8
Forerunner	*prodromos*	6:20
Shepherd	*poimēn*	13:20
Apostle	*apostolos*	3:1

The title Son of God was already in use long before Jesus came into the world and was applied to many other men before it was applied to Jesus. That means that the people who first heard Jesus called Son of God would have thought first of what the title meant then, not that Jesus was a member of the Trinity. This is the reason the author of Hebrews must describe this "Son of God," and he does it in terms that would have been shocking to people in the first century (and that would shock us today if we weren't so familiar with the idea).

The term *son of god* was used in the ancient world to refer to a ruler, since rulers were assumed to rule only by the power and protection of the god of their kingdom. It was not a term of deity, but it was understood that the human ruler was empowered or endowed by the god with powers appropriate to the scope of his rule. In order to sustain his kingdom, a king must be able to stave off invaders and win wars. Such victory was understood to indicate that the god of the victorious king was greater and more powerful than the god of the conquered king. And so when applied to Jesus, the implication of the title Son of God would have been that he is a ruler of some kind. In fact, Jesus is the human ruler of the kingdom of God, and it was in this sense that Jesus as Son of God would have been understood, fueling typical messianic expectations. But because Jesus did not function as an earthly ruler over a geopolitical kingdom, most who heard it would have puzzled over what would have seemed such an inept title at the time. And so the New Testament writers must explain in what sense Jesus is a ruler.

It can be very startling to realize that Jesus was neither the first nor the only man to be called "son of god" until we realize that Jesus was Son of God in a much greater and

Caesar Augustus as a Divine Savior

Whereas the Providence which has guided our whole existence and which has shown such care and liberality, has brought our life to the peak of perfection in giving to us Augustus, whom Providence filled with virtue for the welfare of mankind, and who, being sent to us and to our descendants as a savior, has put an end to war and has set all things in order; and whereas, having become visible . . . and whereas, finally that the birthday of the god has been for the whole world the beginning of the gospel concerning him, therefore, let all reckon a new era from the beginning of the date of his birth.*

A resolution passed by the Provincial Assembly of Asia Minor in honor of Caesar Augustus a few years before the birth of Jesus Christ

* As quoted in Werner Georg Kümmel, Paul Feine, and Johannes Behm, *Introduction to the New Testament*, rev. ed., trans. Howard Clark Kee (Nashville: Abingdon, 1975), 35. Original inscription in Peter Stuhlmacher, *Das paulinische Evangelium I. Vorgeschichte*, FRLANT 95, 186.

real sense than the title had previously connoted. First-century inscriptions and coins show that the Roman emperors, such as Caesar Augustus and Caesar Caligula, were referred to as "son of god" where the god in mind was one of the gods of the Greco-Roman pantheon. Because Caesar had achieved rule over such an immense area of the world and so many different nations and people groups, it was understood that his god was more powerful than any of the lesser, local deities. Therefore, he must be "son" of the most powerful god who was demonstrating his supremacy through the emperor.

This inscription from Asia Minor dedicated to Caesar Augustus contains several other striking words that in our times are associated uniquely with Jesus, such as "savior" and "gospel," and the fact that the birth of this one was so significant that the calendar was changed to mark time before and after his appearing. (In the case of Christ, the ascriptions **BC** and **AD** in our calendar system refer to before and after his birth.)[5] Rather than construing this as diminishing Jesus Christ in some way, it should be viewed as one of history's great ironies. Just as the most powerful ruler of the world at that time was being hailed as a divine "savior" and "son of god" sent by the gods to bring peace (the *pax Romana*, or Roman peace, of Augustus is meant), the true Son of God and King of the universe stepped into human history to set the record straight.

The gospel writers undoubtedly invited their first-century readers to contrast and compare the kingdom of Caesar with the kingdom of God. In fact, Mark's story of Jesus starts with the same phrase—"the beginning of the gospel"—that is found in the inscription about Augustus. Like the title "son of god," the word *euangelion* (translated into English as "gospel") was already in use in the Greek language to mean "good news" well before Jesus was born. Many people in the Greco-Roman world welcomed the good news of the rule of Caesar Augustus and the benefits of peace and stability his iron-fisted rule brought. In the New Testament, Mark invites his readers to compare the good news of Caesar's kingdom with the good news of God's kingdom as announced by Jesus.

5. AD abbreviates the Latin phrase *Anno Domini*, or "Year of our Lord."

An Inscription to Emperor Caligula Set Up around AD 38 in Ephesus

"The council and the people of the [Ephesians and other Greek] cities, which dwell in Asia and the nations [acknowledge] Gaius Julius, the son of Gaius Caesar, as High Priest and Absolute Ruler ... the God visible who is born of [the gods] Ares and Aphrodite, the shared Savior of human life."

Corpus Inscriptionum Graecarum #2957, 2.602

The region of Asia Minor was especially susceptible to the worship of the Roman emperors as divine "sons of god." But the expression is also found in ancient cultures long before the Greco-Roman period. For instance, the Egyptian pharaohs had for many centuries been called "sons of the Sun God." (The phonetic similarity of "son" and "sun" is a happenstance of English and not of the original language.) By definition in the ancient world, to be a king meant to be one whose authority is representative of the divine, to be chosen by the divine to rule as the god's earthly agent.

K. H. Jobes

Caesar Augustus was called "son of God."

This ancient custom of thinking of a king as a "son of god" is found also in the writings of ancient Israel to describe the Messiah. Among the Dead Sea Scrolls (e.g., 4Q246) are references to a messianic figure who is "son of the Most High" and "son of God" whose kingdom will be everlasting. Messianic texts in the Old Testament move along similar lines. For instance, Psalm 2:7, which is quoted in Hebrews 1:5 and again in Hebrews 5:5, says, "You are my son; today I have become your father" (Ps. 2:7). When this statement is considered in its context in Psalm 2, it is clear that it is a reference to the king of Israel. The Psalms originated from the period of Israel's history when King David ruled from Jerusalem, the city built on Mount Zion. The God enthroned in heaven says, "I have installed my king on Zion, my holy mountain" (Ps. 2:6). God is asserting his rule through his earthly king whom he has brought to power in Jerusalem. The earthly king then proclaims what God has decreed: "He [God] said to me, 'You are my son; today I have become your father'" (Ps. 2:7). "Today" was a reference to the coronation of Israel's king. On the day the king took up his rule, he became "son of God," ruling a theocracy in Jerusalem.

The Lord's decree proclaimed by this king goes on to say that God will "make the nations your inheritance and the ends of the earth your possession" (Ps. 2: 8). Of course, this promise was not fulfilled through ancient Israel's monarchy, but it was expected that the coming Messiah, of whom King David was ancestor and forerunner, would fulfill it. In the sense that the Messiah would be a king of Israel, the title "Son of God" was given to him. The thrust of Psalm 2 is to assert that Israel's king would be victorious over the nations, and therefore that Israel's God, Yahweh, is the most powerful God and deserves the worship of the nations. Because of claims like this found throughout the Old Testament, it is no wonder that, by the time of the first-century Roman occupation of Palestine, the Messiah was expected to be a warrior and king great enough in power to throw off the rule of Caesar over Yahweh's people and land.

Immediately after speaking of the Son as the preexistent agent of creation, Hebrews quotes Psalm 2:7, showing that God said to this Son, "You are my son; today I have become your Father." Well, if the Son existed at the time the universe was created, how could he become the Son "today"? What could this possibly mean? Taking our interpretive clue from Psalm 2 would suggest that Jesus became God's "Son" in the way the term was previously used, referring to the time of his coronation. When could that have been? Hebrews has already explained that the Son, *after* performing as a priest, has sat down on the throne of God. It appears that Hebrews understands the ascension of the resurrected Jesus to be his coronation as the Messiah. And so the title "Son of God," as applied to Jesus, merges his messianic role as the human king of God's kingdom with his preexistent nature as a member of the Trinity. Because the phrase "son of god" has not for centuries been used to refer to geopolitical rulers, modern Christian understanding has lost sight of that very important messianic connotation, which has been eclipsed by the doctrinal concept of Jesus' deity. However, both concepts are represented by the author of Hebrews and are important to his Christology.

The concept of the Son as the great ruler of God's kingdom and the Son as a member of the Godhead are brought together in the most striking way in Hebrews 1:8, which is one of the many Old Testament quotations put directly on the lips of God as divine speech. The author of Hebrews writes, "But about the Son he [God] says, 'Your throne, O God, will last forever and ever.'" The words of the psalmist in Psalm 45:6–7 that speak of the eternal rule of Yahweh are here presented as if Yahweh himself is speaking them about the Son. This move is astounding! The Son as Messiah is here proclaimed not only to have an eternal rule, but is proclaimed by God to be God! The greatest surprise of history is that Israel's Messiah was none other than God become man!

The Superiority of Jesus Christ over All Others

This announcement that the Son is God who will corule with the Father forever is presented in contrast to the power of the angels to show their inferiority to the Son. Hebrews describes the Son as the heir of all things (cf. Ps. 2:8), the agent and sustainer of creation, the radiance of God's glory, and the exact representation of his nature in order to argue that the Son is superior first to the angels (1:5–14) and second to Israel's greatest prophet, Moses (3:1–6). What is said of the Son in Hebrews 1 could not be said of any of the angels, who are but servants of God who worship the Son (v. 6) and minister to those who will inherit salvation (v. 14).

Many in the ancient world, and not a few in our modern times, might argue that because Jesus was a man, he must be inferior to the angels, because human beings are inferior to angels in power, position, and access to God's presence. This was certainly the view based on **Neoplatonism** that later developed into **Gnosticism**. In that worldview, God was purely spirit and could not involve himself directly in the material world, which was believed to be inferior to the spiritual world at best and evil at worst (contra Gen. 1:31, in which God proclaims the material creation good). In this worldview, the angels would have

The Son's Superiority over the Angels	
The Son	*The Angels*
• God is his Father	• God is their creator
• Object of angels' worship	• Are to worship the Son
• Is God's eternal king	• Are servants of God
• Co-occupies God's throne	• Serve those people who will inherit salvation

been considered far superior both in power and purity in comparison to the human being Jesus. The author of Hebrews corrects this falsehood firstly by revealing the true nature of the Son (1:1–14). He then explains that, despite their power and position, the angels are not to rule the world to come (2:5); rather, the ruler will be from the race of human beings, who, despite being "made a little lower" than the angels, have "everything under their feet" (2:7). Yet at the present time, the author of Hebrews concedes, it sure looks like angels are superior, because "we do not see everything subject" to humankind. But what do we see? Praise God, "we ... see Jesus, who was made lower than the angels for a little while" (i.e., made human) but who is now "crowned with glory and honor because he suffered death" (2:8–9). The human incarnation of the Son does not make him inferior to the angels; rather, it makes him uniquely qualified to accomplish God's plan to redeem humanity from the curse of death on humankind because of their sin (Gen. 2:17; 3:11–19). The incarnate Son did what no angel could ever do—he died. And because of that he is in fact superior to the angels despite being fully human.

In Jewish tradition Moses is the greatest and most significant human person in Israel's history, for it was Moses to whom God revealed himself in the burning bush, who led the Israelites from bondage in Egypt, and who delivered God's holy covenant to the people at Mount Sinai. And so it follows that the author of Hebrews needed also to explain Jesus' relationship to Moses, the founder of the old covenant. God appointed both Jesus and Moses to their respective roles, and both were faithful to what that role entailed (3:2–6). But Moses was faithful as a servant in God's house and bore witness as a prophet to what God would speak in the future (3:5), which was the Son (1:1–2). Christ, however, is God's faithful Son, who is over God's house, and therefore Jesus is worthy of greater honor than even Moses (3:3, 6). Hebrews understands "house" to be a metaphor for God's people ("we are his house," 3:6), which Moses served but which bows in worship of Jesus Christ. It is with this comparison of Jesus and Moses that Hebrews begins to explain both the continuity and the discontinuity of the Christian gospel with the Sinai covenant. The author of Hebrews continues to explain the relationship of Christ to the priesthood and sacrificial system of the Old Testament covenant by expounding on the priestly role of Jesus.

THE SON AS PRIEST OF GOD

In the ancient world, it was the priest who stood as an intermediary between the people and God. In ancient Israel there were many priests, but only one high priest at any time.

The crucifixion of Jesus Christ put an end to animal sacrifice.

"Every high priest is selected from among the people and is appointed to represent the people in matters related to God, to offer gifts and sacrifices for sins" (Heb. 5:1). Prophet, priest, and king were together the conduit of dealings between God and his people. To represent the people before God meant primarily to present an atoning sacrifice for the sins of the people in God's presence. This representation brought the people symbolically into the presence of God and involved elaborate rituals through which the priest first atoned for his own sin, purified himself, and then presented the blood of the sacrificed animal in the temple. The Old Testament book of Leviticus is largely a description of the rituals involved and the types of sacrifices needed for various kinds of transgressions.

In the temple of God in Jerusalem, many animal sacrifices were offered daily, and so many priests were needed. To service the highest holy days, such as Passover, it is estimated there would have been about 17,000 priests and Levites, with about 200 serving as chief priests and 7,200 as ordinary priests, and about 9,600 Levites (those who assisted the priests with slaughtering the sacrificial animals).[6]

But in ancient Israel's priesthood there was but one high priest whose privilege and responsibility it was to enter the Most Holy Place on just one most holy day each year, Yom Kippur, and to offer the blood of a sacrifice that would atone for the sins of all Israel.

Animals were tied to the horns of the altar and sacrificed.

6. K. Ward, ed., *Jesus and His Times* (Pleasantville, N.Y.: Reader's Digest, 1987), 140.

The Incarnation of the Son Was Necessary for His Priesthood

As a representative of the people, the high priest obviously was human himself. It was the eternally preexistent Son's role as High Priest that required his incarnation into the human race: "Since the children have flesh and blood, he too shared in their humanity so that by his death he might break the power of him who holds the power of death — that is, the devil — and free those who all their lives were held in slavery by their fear of death" (Heb. 2:14–15). Jesus was not a high priest of the angels but of the human race, which was alienated from God by sin, and he therefore had to be made like those he represented before God. "Both the one who makes people holy and those who are made holy are of the same family. So Jesus is not ashamed to call them brothers and sisters" (2:11). In other words, the Son had to become human to function as a high priest for us by atoning for the sins of the human race (2:17).

The Incarnation Was Necessary for the Son to Be a Priest

"Since the children have flesh and blood, he too shared in their humanity.... For this reason he had to be made like his brothers and sisters in every way, in order that he might become a merciful and faithful high priest."

Hebrews 2:14, 17

The necessity of the incarnation means that the Son had to experience all that it means to be a human being and yet not sin. Jesus was repeatedly tempted by Satan to deny his mission and to disobey God. Although he went willingly to his crucifixion, his death in Jerusalem was not a surprise to those closest to him (Mark 8:31–32; John 11:16). In the garden of Gethsemane, he suffered all the psychological pain any human being would who knew what physical suffering lay ahead when the Jewish leaders seized him and the Romans executed him.

Therefore, through Jesus, God knows all that we experience in our humanness, most particularly the fear of death and the temptation to disobey him in order to avoid suffering (Heb. 2:14–15, 18). It is in this context of Jesus' full humanity that it was necessary for him to be "made perfect" through what he suffered as a human being (2:10). In other words, the temptations and pain that Jesus suffered on earth were real, and he had to overcome them as a human being in order to fulfill his role as priest and, what's more, as sacrifice. And as Hebrews says, "Because he himself suffered when he was tempted, he is able to help those who are being tempted" (2:18). And so, like all previous high priests, Jesus was tempted in all ways as we are. But unlike previous high priests, Jesus did not have to offer sacrifice for his own sins, because through all his temptation and suffering he was without sin (4:15).

The Son had to become human so he could be the Great High Priest of the ultimate atonement. And it is because Jesus became human that the author of Hebrews has to defend Jesus' superiority over the angels. Even today angels are thought of as more powerful than human beings, but in the first century this idea was part of a worldview formed by the philosophy of **Neoplatonism**. Around the fifth century BC, Plato, as you may recall from your philosophy class, proposed that reality was comprised of the material world that we can see and in which we live, but also of an unseen world of "ideals" that were imperishable and therefore superior to the material world (known as the **Platonic dualism**). By the first century, Plato's thought had been developed to teach that the material world was not only metaphysically inferior to the world of ideals but morally inferior as well. That belief led to a cosmology that understood God to dwell in the highest heaven, which was the world of

Jesus in Gethsemane by El Greco.

ideals, and the angels somewhere between the material universe and this ideal world. That meant first, that the Christian doctrine of the incarnation of God was absurd to Neoplatonists, and second, that angels were vastly superior to human beings. According to this worldview, if Jesus was fully human, he could be neither divine nor superior to the angels.

The early church had to explain Jesus in light of such philosophical concepts. The author of Hebrews defends Jesus' superiority to the angels because (1) he shared the nature of God (1:1–5) and (2) by being fully human he accomplished something that no angel was qualified to accomplish—the redemption of the human race. And so we see that even though the Son became human, he is nevertheless greater than the angels, because in his incarnation he became the perfect mediator between humankind and God. The Son is the perfect and final speaking of God, replacing all merely human prophets; and the Son is the perfect and final High Priest of God, replacing all merely human priests. The Son accomplishes what no angel ever could, atonement for the sins of the human race—and that is God's final message to us.

The author of Hebrews notes that Israel had many high priests throughout its history, because death prevented them from continuing their office. But because Jesus was resurrected, he lives forever and his priesthood is therefore permanent (7:23–28). Because Jesus is now alive forever, he will always continue in office, always be our High Priest, always represent us to God and intercede on our behalf. For this reason, Christ's priesthood is better than and greater than that of the priests of the old covenant.

Jesus Christ as High Priest of a New Covenant

Perhaps the most startling concept that Hebrews presents concerning Jesus' relationship to the old covenant is not his high priesthood, as intriguing as that may be. The writer of Hebrews explains that Jesus was not only the final and ultimate High Priest, but that he also was the perfect, ultimate, and final sacrifice as well![7] After two thousand years of Christian theology, this idea is not new, but for those reading Hebrews for the first time in the cultural context of the first century, it would have been a staggering idea.

The author of Hebrews explains that Jesus did not enter the temple in Jerusalem with the blood of an animal but entered into the Most Holy Place of heaven itself by his own blood (9:11–14). "For this reason Christ is the mediator of a new covenant, that those who are called may receive the promised eternal inheritance—now that he has died as a ransom to set them free from the sins committed under the first covenant" (v. 15). Although it is common for Christians to speak of Jesus Christ as fulfilling the old covenant—and that is true—Hebrews presents Jesus as the mediator of a new and better covenant that supersedes the old. God's dealings with his people under the old covenant were comprised of a priesthood and a sacrificial system administered by that priesthood that was centered in the Jerusalem temple. By definition, when that priesthood was replaced (by Jesus the High Priest) and the sacrifice was replaced (by the blood of Jesus), a new covenant was established that replaced the old. This is the primary theological point of the book of Hebrews. The connection between the old and new covenants is that the old covenant indicted people for their sins, but the priestly work of the Son, as he offers the blood of his own incarnation, releases people from the condemnation of the old and into a new covenant with God based

7. For a response to those who find the idea of sacrifice offensive to modern sensibilities, see Andrew T. Lincoln, *Hebrews: A Guide* (London: T&T Clark, 2006), 110–14.

Todd Bolen/www.BiblePlaces.com

The author of Hebrews interpreted the Tabernacle as foreshadowing Jesus' atoning sacrifice.

not on more animal blood but on the blood of the incarnate Son. Because Christ is a superior priest and a superior sacrifice, the covenant he mediates between God and humankind is a covenant superior to that of the Old Testament.

Christ's sacrifice is the last one, in contrast to the unending work of the temple priests. The temple in Jerusalem, and the tabernacle before it, had some splendid furnishings, but there were no chairs. Day after day the priests performed their duties in the temple; year after year the high priest presented blood in the Holy of Holies. "But when this priest [Jesus] had offered for all time one sacrifice for sins, he *sat down* at the right hand of God" (Heb. 10:12, emphasis added). The priestly work that God required was finished. The High Priest took his seat, having completed the act of atonement for the sins of humankind.

The Qualities of Jesus as High Priest*

As High Priest, Jesus exhibits many very impressive qualities. The following list from Hebrews is representative.

"merciful and faithful"	2:17
"able to help those who are being tempted"	2:18
"who has ascended into heaven"	4:14
"not ... unable to empathize with our weaknesses"	4:15
"tempted ... as we are—yet he did not sin"	4:15
appointed by God	5:5
"[a] forerunner ... on our behalf"	6:20
"holy, blameless, pure, set apart from sinners"	7:26
"exalted above the heavens"	7:26
"made perfect forever"	7:28
"[seated] at the right hand of the throne of the Majesty in heaven"	8:1
a minister "in the sanctuary, the true tabernacle"	8:2
"high priest of the good things that are now already here"	9:11
"entered the Most Holy Place once for all by his own blood"	9:12
"obtaining eternal redemption"	9:12

*Adapted from Donald A. Hagner, *Encountering the Book of Hebrews* (Grand Rapids: Baker, 2002), 104.

By that one sacrifice, Christ has made *perfect* forever those who are *being made holy* (Heb. 10:14). (See chapter 4 for more discussion of this.) The wording of this description of the efficacy of Christ's sacrifice is interesting. It speaks of those who by Christ's sacrifice *have been made perfect* (*teteleiōken*, in the Greek perfect tense) and who are in the process of *being made holy* (a present tense, passive voice verb form in the Greek). This is congruent with the Pauline doctrines of justification and sanctification, respectively. The Christian's standing before God is justified once for all by Christ's sacrifice. But the ongoing life of the Christian continues to be brought into conformity with God's standard for a righteous human being as exemplified by Jesus. In this way, too, the new covenant is superior to the old because the Holy Spirit writes the stipulations of the new covenant on the heart as God once predicted through the words of the prophet Jeremiah, which Hebrews quotes: "'This is the covenant I will make with them after that time, says the Lord. I will put my laws in their hearts, and I will write them on their minds.' Then he adds: 'Their sins and lawless acts I will remember no more.' And where these have been forgiven, sacrifice for sins is no longer necessary" (Jer. 31:33, quoted in Heb. 10:16–18). The old covenant was written on tablets of stone external to the human heart; it stipulated God's just requirements but provided no life-transforming power. The Holy Spirit writes the new covenant internally on human hearts, which is a way of saying that the new covenant transforms human hearts to conform to God's standards. This is the lifelong process of sanctification.

Courtesy of the Pitts Theology Library, Candler School of Theology, Emory University

A woodcut showing Christ as high priest in Hebrews. By Johann Christoph Weigel, 1695.

The Priesthood of Melchizedek

The main christological point in Hebrews is that Jesus Christ is the Great High Priest of the new covenant promised by the old: "Therefore, since we have a great high priest who has ascended into heaven, Jesus the Son of God, let us hold firmly to the faith we profess" (Heb. 4:14). This would have been a provocative statement to converts from Judaism

The Two Priesthoods*

Levitical	*Jesus Christ*
Based on genealogical descent	Based on the promise of God
Temporary and weak	Eternal and most efficacious
Human priests in succession	One eternal Priest, no succession
Was for one nation	Was for all nations, all people
Priest offered for his own sins	Christ had no sin
Did not clear the conscience	Cleanses the conscience

*Adapted from Marshall Neal, "Melchizedek and Christ: Hebrews 7," *BV* 24 (1990): 57.

because it would have been well known that Jesus had not even been born into the priestly tribe (Levi), nor was he a descendant of either of the priestly lines disputed in the first century from which high priests came. Jesus' lineage was from the tribe of Judah, and no one from that tribe was allowed to minister in the temple, much less become high priest (Heb. 7:14). Ironically, Jesus could not even have entered the inner temple precincts during his earthly life. And this was by God's design. Yet the author of Hebrews claims that Jesus Christ is the great and final High Priest. But he is not a priest like Aaron (see Lev. 8 and 9).

Jesus is presented in Hebrews as the High Priest of a different and better covenant than that which God had established previously. And so the author of Hebrews must relativize the old covenant with respect to the new and explain how the new covenant, though new in time, was actually a part of God's redemptive plan all along. In fact, Hebrews shows that the old covenant itself promised and predicted a new covenant based on a different priesthood, the priesthood of Melchizedek:

> Every high priest is selected among the people and is appointed to represent the people in matters related to God, to offer gifts and sacrifices for sins.... In the same way, Christ did not take on himself the glory of becoming a high priest. But God said to him,
>
> "You are my Son;
> today I have become your Father."
>
> And he [God] says in another place,
>
> "You are a priest forever,
> in the order of Melchizedek." (5:1, 5–6)

Jeremiah mourning over the Destruction of Jerusalem, Rembrandt Harmensz. van Rijn/Rijksmuseum, Amsterdam, The Netherlands/The Bridgeman Art Library

The prophet Jeremiah laments the destruction of Jerusalem. Painting by Rembrandt van Rijn (1606-1669).

The author of Hebrews affirms that the Levitical priesthood was in fact established by God, but that does not mean that it was an eternal priesthood. The law was God's word, but it wasn't God's *last* word, which is found only in the Son (1:1). Quoting Psalm 110:4, Hebrews points out that God had said even during the time of the old covenant that his Messiah would be a priest, not like Aaron and his descendants, but like Melchizedek. Who is this mysterious Melchizedek?

Melchizedek appears in the narrative of Israel's history only once, in Genesis 14:17–20:

> After Abram returned from defeating Kedorlaomer and the kings allied with him, the king of Sodom came out to meet him in the Valley of Shaveh (that is, the King's Valley). Then Melchizedek king of Salem brought out bread and wine. He was priest of God Most High, and he blessed Abram, saying,
>
> "Blessed be Abram by God Most High,
> Creator of heaven and earth.
> And praise be to God Most High,
> who delivered your enemies into your hand."
>
> Then Abram gave him a tenth of everything.

Abraham and Melchizedek, Rubens, Peter Paul/Musee des Beaux-Arts, Caen, France/Giraudon/The Bridgeman Art Library

The Meeting of Abraham and Melchizedek, c. 1626 by Sir Peter Paul Rubens.

This meeting of Abraham and Melchizedek happened almost as long before the time of Christ as we today live after—about two thousand years in round numbers. Abram (Abraham) and his wife Sarai (Sarah) were the couple God chose to be the ancestors of the ancient nation of Israel through whom God would redeem humankind. Melchizedek was king of a town called Salem (Gen. 14:18), which about one thousand years later became the city of Jerusalem, the capital city of God's chosen people. But Melchizedek was also a priest "of God Most High" and brought out bread and wine to refresh Abram after battle. Notice that Melchizedek blesses Abram (v. 19), not vice versa. The question of who tithes to whom is ambiguous in the Hebrew of Genesis 14:20, which literally reads, "And he gave him a tithe of everything." The view that Abram acknowledged Melchizedek to be his priest by offering a tenth (tithe) of his plunder to God through Melchizedek's priestly ministry is long-standing by both Jewish and Christian interpreters (e.g., Josephus, *Ant.* 1.10.2; *Targum Pseudo-Jonathan*; and of course, the author of Heb. 7:2). Long before ancient Israel's priesthood was established in the Jerusalem temple, God was pleased to allow Melchizedek to minister to the father of the future nation of Israel. This episode relativizes the later priesthood of Aaron by showing that it is not the only priesthood God honored, even though God had established the **Aaronic priesthood** through the Sinai covenant.

About a thousand years after Abram, Israel's King David conquered what had been the town of Salem previously ruled by pagan Melchizedek and called it Jerusalem. It was David's son Solomon who built a grand temple in Jerusalem where the priests of Israel's religion could offer animal sacrifices to God. Under Israel's law, given by God through Moses, the king and the high priest could not be the same person. Nevertheless, one of the psalms of David speaks of Israel's coming king, the Messiah, as a priest. The Messiah would be a priest-king.[8] God swears that the coming Messiah will be a priest forever, and not in the priesthood of Aaron, but in the priestly order of Melchizedek (Ps. 110:4). Apparently it was understood even at the time of David that the ultimate objective of God could not be attained under the Levitical priesthood, or he would not have promised a new one with the Messiah (Heb. 7:11). The writer of Hebrews notes that the priest-king God himself promised with an oath *under the old covenant* was his Son, whom the author further identifies as Jesus (7:20–21). In this way, the author of Hebrews could both affirm that the priesthood of Aaron, based on the covenant made with Moses, was indeed God's will for Israel, and yet also show that God had planned a new covenant based on a different priesthood someday. When God changed to this priesthood, his doing so would inaugurate a new law and covenant as well (7:12)—the covenant that would be written on hearts instead of on stone, as the prophet Jeremiah predicted (Jer. 31:31–34, quoted in Heb. 8:8–12).

Melchizedek in the Bible

The mysterious Melchizedek is mentioned only ten times in the Bible, and eight of those times are in Hebrews where he is presented as an analogy for the priesthood of Jesus Christ (Gen. 14:18; Ps. 110:4; Heb. 5:6, 10; 6:20; 7:1, 10, 11, 15, 17).

How is the order of Melchizedek an appropriate analogy for what Jesus has done?

The author of Hebrews says that God designated his Son to be High Priest in the order of Melchizedek (Heb. 5:10). Since Melchizedek was a "Gentile" (not an Israelite),[9] this raises the question of how his priesthood is an appropriate way for understanding what Jesus has done on the cross. Hebrews draws on information about Melchizedek found in Genesis 14:17–20.

The book of Hebrews points out some interesting facts about Melchizedek's name and title (7:2). In Hebrew, the consonants in the name Melchizedek can be pointed as *melchi*

8. Various views were held about the role of the Messiah and whether there would be one or more persons who would fulfill the messianic expectations. See Richard S. Hess and M. Daniel Carroll R., eds., *Israel's Messiah in the Bible and the Dead Sea Scrolls* (Grand Rapids: Baker Academic, 2003).

9. It is, of course, anachronistic to refer to someone as a "Gentile" or an "Israelite" at the time of Abraham and Melchizedek, because the nation of ancient Israel did not yet exist.

The Meaning of Melchizedek's Name and Title

מַלְכִּי־צֶדֶק Μελχισέδεκ

1. מַלְכִּי read as *melki* ("my king") + *zedek* ("of righteousness").
2. Melchizedek was king of the town of Salem, where the consonants of "Salem" (*slm*) are the same consonants in the Hebrew word for "peace"; (*shalom*) = "king of peace."

("my king") + *zedek* ("of righteousness"), which is how the **Septuagint** translator read the Hebrew. Furthermore, the "king of righteousness" ruled as king of the town of Salem (Gen. 14:18), and the word "Salem" can be construed from its consonants in Hebrew as the word for "peace," so Melchizedek was "king of peace" (Heb. 7:2). In other words, Melchizedek's name foreshadowed the role of the Messiah.

Hebrews also points out that Abraham (previously called Abram) tithed to God through Melchizedek and received God's blessing through Melchizedek (7:4, 6). This demonstrates that the father of God's chosen people tithed and worshiped Yahweh through a priest who was not of the tribe of Levi, because that tribe wouldn't come into existence until hundreds of years later (7:6). Because all of the priests of the tribe of Levi who would later minister in the temple in Jerusalem were descendants of Levi, who was "still in the body of his ancestor [Abraham]" (7:10), one could reason that all of the tithes of ancient Israel collected under the old covenant established by Moses were symbolically offered to God by their ancestor Abraham through the priest Melchizedek (7:9). This would allow the original readers of Hebrews to see that God could be appropriately worshiped outside of the ritual structures of Judaism, specifically through Jesus Christ.

The next point of analogy is a bit mystifying, when Hebrews says that Melchizedek was "without father or mother, without genealogy, without beginning of days or end of life" (7:3). It is certainly true that the Genesis account of Melchizedek does not mention the kingly dynasty in which Melchizedek stood and does not mention when he was born or died. In contrast, the ancestry of Aaron, the first high priest of the Levitical priesthood, is given; his birth as a descendant of Levi, the son of the patriarch Jacob, is recorded, and his parents' names are given as Amram and Jochebed (Ex. 6:16–20). Aaron's death is also recorded in Numbers 20:24–28. But in Genesis 14 there is no mention of the ancestry or death of Melchizedek, a silence that invited speculation about the origin and nature of Melchizedek.

In the ancient world, there was a Jewish exegetical technique referred to as *non in thora non in mundo* ("not in the Torah, not in the world"). This Latin phrase refers to the interpretive technique—which may seem very odd to our modern sensibilities—that was based on the idea that if the Torah (in this case, Genesis) was silent about something (in this case, the birth and death

Courtesy Israel Antiquities Authority

Fragments from the Dead Sea Scroll, Melchizedek (11QMelch).

Melchizedek in the Dead Sea Scrolls

"And the Day of Atonement is the end of the tenth Jubilee, when all the Sons of Light and the men of the lot of Melchizedek will be atoned for.... For this is the moment of the Year of Grace for Melchizedek.... And Melchizedek will avenge the vengeance of the judgments of God.... And your *elohim* is Melchizedek, who will save them from the hand of Belial."*

11Q13, first century BC

*Geza Vermes, *The Complete Dead Sea Scrolls in English*, 3rd ed. (New York: Penguin, 1997), 501 – 2.

of Melchizedek), then that "thing" could be understood not to exist (in this case, that Melchizedek hadn't been born or died) for interpretive purposes.[10]

Apparently, by using this technique, some interpreters throughout Jewish history have understood Melchizedek to be a supernatural angelic being (e.g., the Dead Sea Scrolls, 2 Enoch, and some rabbinic writings). For example, one of the Dead Sea Scrolls (11Q13) speaks of Melchizedek as an angel who will carry out the judgments of God and save a segment of humanity from the hand of Satan. The idea that Melchizedek was a supernatural being has come into Christian tradition with speculation that perhaps he was a preincarnation appearance of the Son of God. Most New Testament interpreters today do not follow that reasoning; they acknowledge that the silence of Genesis 14 about Melchizedek's birth and death was the cause of such traditions, and rather than concluding that he was supernatural, simply believe that he was a human priest-king whose lineage had been lost or considered unimportant at the time Genesis was written. The later Jewish Targums supply a genealogy for Melchizedek by identifying him with Shem ("the Great"), the son of Noah (Gen. 9:18; 11:10–26) and making him one of Abram's own ancestors. Jerome (*Epist.* 73.5) preserves the Jewish tradition that, at the time of Abram's birth, Shem (Melchizedek) was 390 years old. Taking the ages given in Genesis 11 literally (500 years for Shem) and applying (probably incorrect) numeric assumptions about the number of years represented by a generation to the genealogy of Genesis 11, Shem (Melchizedek) was believed to have outlived Abram by 35 years.[11] Since Jewish tradition held that sons of Noah were priests of God before the Levitical priesthood began, and since Shem was believed to have been alive during Abram's lifetime, it was an easy step to identify Melchizedek as Shem.

Some scholars see close parallels between Hebrews and texts from Qumran, particularly relating to concepts of "a heavenly priesthood and an angelic understanding of Melchizedek."[12] In the mid-twentieth century, shortly after the Dead Sea Scrolls were discovered, some saw such a strong connection that they proposed Essenes or former Essenes

10. Kenneth Schenck, *Understanding the Book of Hebrews: The Story behind the Sermon* (Louisville: Westminster John Knox, 2003), 78.

11. Martin McNamara, "Melchizedek: Gen 14, 17–20 in the Targums, in Rabbinic and Early Christian Literature," *Biblica* 81 (2000): 12–13.

12. Eric F. Mason, *"You Are a Priest Forever": Second Temple Jewish Messianism and the Priestly Christology of the Epistles to the Hebrews*, STDJ 75 (Leiden: Brill, 2008).

Comparing the Old and the New Covenants*	
New	*Old*
Present realities (9:11, 23–24; 10:1)	Shadows, copies (8:5; 9:23; 10:1)
Greater and more perfect tabernacle (9:11, 24)	Human built, earthly sanctuary (9:1, 11, 24)
Christ enters once for all (9:12, 25–28; 10:1–3, 10–14)	Priests enter every day; high priest annually (7:27; 9:7; 10:1)
Christ's own blood (9:12; 10:4–10)	Blood of animals (9:12, 18–22)
Brings eternal salvation (9:12; 10:14)	Brings temporary cleansing (9:9; 10:2, 11)
Purifies the conscience (9:14–15)	Achieves ritual purity (9:13)
Consummation of God's plan (9:26)	Until the new order came (9:10)

*Adapted from Donald A. Hagner, *Encountering the Book of Hebrews* (Grand Rapids: Baker, 2002), 122.

as the original readers of Hebrews, but later scholarship has disproved this idea.[13] The parallels are more likely indications of the ubiquity of the Melchizedek tradition.

While speculation about Melchizedek's identity and nature may be fascinating, the Christology of Hebrews is not compromised, because Hebrews does not say that Jesus is like Melchizedek (much less that he *is* Melchizedek!), but rather that Melchizedek, who appears to have remained a priest forever, resembles the Son of God (7:3), who *is* a priest forever because of the resurrection (7:16). Therefore, it is the eternality of Jesus' priesthood by virtue of his preexistent sonship and his resurrection into eternal life that is the major point of analogy with Melchizedek. Jesus has become the final Great High Priest based on the power of his indestructible life (7:16).

The priesthood of Melchizedek is an apt analogy for explaining the priesthood of Jesus Christ for at least two reasons: (1) it was a priesthood that predated, and therefore relativized, the Levitical priesthood that was established and governed by the covenant made much later with Moses, and (2) it pictured an eternal priesthood, which relativized the Levitical priesthood by showing that it would one day be superseded when the Priest-King Messiah came. By showing that the God-given old covenant itself promised a new covenant based on a different priesthood of the Messiah, the author of Hebrews can fully affirm divine authority in the old covenant while yet arguing that it has been replaced by a new covenant based on a better priesthood and a better sacrifice. The new covenant in Christ's blood is therefore a better covenant (Heb. 7:22).

Why the emphasis on Jesus being a priest for Christians?

The book of Hebrews is the only book in the New Testament that describes Jesus as High Priest and explains his death on the cross in such an extended and detailed discussion of the sacrificial system of ancient Israel. In fact, this presentation of the person and work

13. Yigael Yadin, "The Dead Sea Scrolls and the Epistle to the Hebrews," in *Aspects of the Dead Sea Scrolls*, ed. Chaim Rabin and Yigael Yadin, ScrHier 4 (Jerusalem: Magnes, 1958), 36–55; Ceslas Spicq, "L'Épître aux Hébreux, Apollos, Jean-Baptiste, les Hellénistes et Qumran," *RevQ* 1 (1958–59): 365–90.

of Jesus would have been of greatest interest and have made the most sense to a Jewish audience, who would have understood the temple, priesthood, and animal sacrifice to be the center of their religious identity. Since within thirty to forty years of the death of Jesus the demographic of the Christian church was predominantly Gentile, most books of the New Testament were written to that audience and not to the relatively few Jews who had come to recognize Jesus as Messiah and to worship him as God in the flesh.

And so while it is understandable that a presentation of Jesus as High Priest would have been very appropriate originally for Christians coming from a Jewish background, it is nonetheless a rich theological foundation on which all Christians, regardless of ethnicity, may understand the atonement. The New Testament books are not simply treatises on interesting subjects but were written to motivate Christian living. Was there a particular reason the original readers for whom Hebrews was written needed this understanding of Jesus in order to live as Christians?

If the high priesthood of Jesus is one of the two major themes in the Christology of Hebrews (the other being Jesus as Son of God), and if the priesthood of Melchizedek is of central importance for understanding the nature of Jesus' priesthood, then it is instructive to consider the context in which this idea is introduced. The ministry of Jesus as Priest is introduced and repeated in the context of exhortations to remain faithful: "Therefore, since we have a great high priest who has ascended into heaven, Jesus the Son of God, *let us hold firmly to the faith we profess*" (4:14, emphasis added). And the first time Melchizedek is mentioned (5:6, 10) occurs immediately before a stern warning about falling away from Christian faith in Hebrews 5:11–6:12. How would understanding Jesus as High Priest address the concerns of the original readers and dissuade them from turning away from the faith?

It is clear that the Christians who first read Hebrews had been subject to the threat of persecution (2:18; 10:32–35), a common experience of Christians in those earliest days of the church. The Christians to whom Hebrews was originally written had endured great conflict that had caused them to suffer public insult and persecution, and they had also stood with other Christians who were persecuted and imprisoned (10:34). They even had had property confiscated because of their faith in Christ. These were no weaklings in the faith, and yet they had reached a point in their journey with Christ where they apparently needed a very strong exhortation to continue in the faith. What might they be thinking that called for a better understanding of Jesus as High Priest?

It is true that if people reject Christ, they are turning away from the only source of atonement for their sin, as the author of Hebrews makes abundantly clear. But that point could have been made without the extensive and elaborate descriptions of the tabernacle and comparisons with the Levitical priesthood. One interpreter has suggested that, as former Jews, these Christians were used to going routinely to the temple, either in person or vicariously, and offering an animal for their sins.[14] Now that they were Christians, they understood that Jesus had made purification for sin, but how did that relate to the system of atonement that Israel had practiced for centuries? And what about sins that were committed

---

14. Barnabas Lindars, *The Theology of the Letter to the Hebrews*, New Testament Theology (Cambridge: Cambridge University Press, 1991), 59.

after they became Christians? Perhaps Christian life and practice, as they apparently knew it, did not offer a tangible rite by which one might deal with a troubled conscience—at least not in the same way their past Jewish rituals had. Perhaps they were either not taking Holy Communion or not understanding that by doing so they were partaking of the sacrificed body and blood of Jesus. Even though they had been firm in their faith at the beginning, even in the face of persecution, a more troubled state of mind may have developed over time because of temptation that pressured them to abandon the Christian faith and to return to the solace of the Jewish purification rites and the way of dealing with sin that previously had been the center of their relationship with God. Of course, we can never be certain what they were thinking or feeling, but it is also too easy for us today to read the New Testament books not mindful of what a momentous change to religious thought and practice Christian faith must have been to its first converts.

The writer of Hebrews wants to make it clear that sacrifices repeated year after year, whatever comforting psychological value they may have had, can never make perfect those on whose behalf the sacrifices are made (10:1). In fact, Hebrews points out that the very fact that the sacrifices have not ceased to be offered proves that none of them was once and for all efficacious for atonement (10:2). What readers of Hebrews need to know is that, because Christ came into the world and inaugurated the new covenant in the once-for-all-time offering of himself on the cross for their sins, God doesn't keep a tally of sins committed after conversion (10:17–18). In Christ, God has forgiven all of each believer's sin, whether committed before or after coming to faith, "and where these have been forgiven, sacrifice for sin is no longer necessary" (10:18). Hebrews acknowledges that believers continue to sin when it says, "by one sacrifice he [God] has made perfect forever those who are being made holy" (10:14). Christians are those who *have been made perfect* in God's reckoning once for all because of the death of Jesus, but who *are also being made holy* (i.e., continue to sin, but with the expectation of increasing holiness). Hebrews also warns, however, that this does not give license for any thought that willful and deliberate sinning is acceptable after coming to faith in Christ. In fact, if Christ's death is taken so lightly as not to motivate a change in living that turns from sin when it comes to light, then there is no other avenue of forgiveness (10:26).

As the author of Hebrews argues, it makes no sense to return to offering animals again and again, which cannot atone for sin, even though God had once commanded them (10:8). The solution to the troubled consciences of these Christians was to understand the death of Jesus in the familiar and comforting categories of priesthood and sacrifice so that they would not return to the Jewish religion and its practice of animal sacrifice but would remain faithful to Christ, the promised Priest-King.

THE RELATIONSHIP BETWEEN SONSHIP AND HIGH PRIESTHOOD

The book of Hebrews presents a Christology that has two focal points: Jesus as Son of God (understood in its first-century sense) and Jesus as the great and final High Priest of a new covenant based on his death. This leaves us with the question of how the author of Hebrews relates Jesus in his identity as Son of God with his identity as High Priest. These two roles come together in Hebrews at the ascension. Although Ascension Day is not a major holiday on the Christian calendar—at least not for Protestants—the New Testament presents the ascension as a major component of what Jesus Christ accomplished, without which the atonement would be incomplete.

The Ascension as the Entrance of the High Priest into the Holy of Holies

The author of Hebrews makes it clear that the priestly ministry of Jesus did not involve the Jerusalem temple, with all its priestly workers and rituals as they existed in the first century. He writes, "But when Christ came as high priest of the good things that are now already here, he went through the greater and more perfect tabernacle that is not made with human hands, that is to say, is not a part of this creation" (9:11). During his earthly life, Jesus was not permitted to enter the temple any further than was the general male population, and he often taught in its *outer* courts. Perhaps to distance the priestly work of Jesus from the first-century temple in Jerusalem, with all its politics and corruption, the writer of Hebrews compares the place of Jesus' ministry not to the temple at all, but to the tabernacle, which was the place of worship and sacrifice instituted by God through Moses in the earliest days of the nation of Israel (Ex. 25–31).

The tabernacle, as the first instance of the Holy Place where God would teach his people that the death of a sacrifice is necessary for the forgiveness of sin, becomes representative of that whole system of atonement under the old covenant, even though the tabernacle itself had been succeeded in Jerusalem first by Solomon's temple and then, by the time of Jesus, by Herod's temple. Hebrews 9:1–7 summarizes the operation of the priestly ministry in its old covenant setting and then interprets its practice over long centuries by explaining that, as long as the sacrificial system of the old covenant was functioning, the Holy Spirit was showing that the way into the Most Holy Place had not yet been disclosed, in spite of the fact that the Most Holy Place of the tabernacle (and later the temple) was entered once a year by the Levitical high priest (v. 8). The author of Hebrews understands the entire sacrificial system to have been an illustration pointing to the ultimate sacrifice of Christ. It showed that those gifts and offerings were not efficacious in and of themselves but were necessary until the time of the new covenant that God had promised (vv. 9–10). God could promise atonement through ancient Israel's sacrificial system only because one day the ultimate sacrifice that system foreshadowed would be made on the cross of the Son, Jesus Christ.

The Ascension, West, Benjamin/Private Collection/Photo © Rafael Valls Gallery, London, UK/The Bridgeman Art Library

Benjamin West's painting of the Ascension (1738–1820).

Christ did not enter the Holy Place in Jerusalem bearing the blood of calves and goats; he entered heaven itself bearing his own blood as the sacrifice (Heb. 9:12, 24). And so the question is, when did Jesus enter heaven itself? That is, when did he fulfill his ministry as the final and greatest High Priest? According to the gospel of Luke and its sequel, the book of Acts, the resurrected Jesus ascended to heaven forty days after his resurrection (Luke 24:50–53; Acts 1:3). Before leaving, he told his disciples to wait in Jerusalem to receive the promise of the Father that would be poured out when the new covenant had been ratified (Acts 1:4–5). Ten days later the promise was received on the day of Pentecost when the Holy Spirit first came to indwell the believers in Jesus (Acts 2), affirming that Jesus had ascended as promised and that the work of his incarnation was complete.

When Hebrews introduces the Son of God in its opening verses, this completion of the work of Jesus is presented as having "provided purification for sins" (1:3). Therefore, "we have a great high priest who has ascended into heaven" (4:14). Hebrews 4:14 further mentions that our great high priest is "Jesus the Son of God." The author of Hebrews joins together the priestly role of Jesus and his coronation as the kingly Son of God in the ascension.

The Ascension as the Coronation of the Kingly Son of God

Recall the discussion above that the phrase "son of God" was in use before Jesus was born to refer to a king. Psalm 2 is an example of this where the Lord's Anointed, the Messiah, is installed on Mount Zion and declared to be Son of God (vv. 6–7). Psalm 2 is describing the coronation of God's King who would rule his people, and is used to argue for the superiority of the Son over the angels (Heb. 1:5). The coronation of the Son is implied in Hebrews 1:3, where the Son sits down at the right hand of the Majesty in heaven *after* having provided purification for sins. Although the eternality of the Son of God is clearly taught in the New Testament, the author of Hebrews is thinking of Jesus as a King whose title "Son of God" is declared at some point in time, namely, "*today* I have become your Father" (Heb. 5:5, emphasis added). Furthermore, the point of time at which Jesus is declared to have become Son of God happens *after* he provides purification for sin, which is when he enters the Most Holy Place, heaven itself. Combining these points with the reference to Jesus taking his seat at the throne of God (a coronation image) in Hebrews 1:3 shows that Jesus' coronation and declaration to be the King of God's kingdom also happen at the ascension. The thought that the incarnate Christ "becomes" the Son of God at some point in his redemptive work does not deny or diminish the eternal existence of the second member of the Godhead, but rather shows how Jesus is Son of God in a fuller and more profound sense than any other man to whom the term had previously been applied.

> Ascension Day is celebrated forty days after Easter on the church calendar and ten days before Pentecost. Although the elaborate celebration of Easter in the churches eclipses these two subsequent holy days, the church should commemorate their significance.

And so we see that the book of Hebrews centers its Christology on all that was achieved in the ascension of Jesus Christ. This convergence of the sonship and high priesthood of

Handel's "Hallelujah Chorus"

Composed by George Frideric Handel in 1741 as part of *The Messiah*, the "Hallelujah Chorus" takes its words from the book of Revelation. It captures the glory of Christ's ascension to the throne of God to reign forever.

> Hallelujah, for the Lord God omnipotent reigneth.
> The kingdom of this world is become the kingdom of our Lord and of his Christ;
> and he shall reign for ever and ever.
> King of Kings, and Lord of Lords. Hallelujah!

Christ in the ascension perhaps explains why the author of Hebrews assumes the resurrection but mentions it only once (13:20). The ascension is often thought of as one and the same as the resurrection of Christ, even though the two events happened forty days apart and are clearly distinguished in the Gospels and Acts. Theologically, the three events of Jesus' crucifixion, resurrection, and ascension cannot be separated. However, the author of Hebrews reveals what happened in the unseen presence of God that completed Christ's work and freed the Holy Spirit to be poured out on Pentecost. Even though the ascension is eclipsed by the celebration of the resurrection in the church year, it is of paramount importance in our theological understanding of what Jesus Christ has achieved.

CHAPTER SUMMARY

The book of Hebrews presents a unique portrait of Jesus and what he has accomplished. Centered on the two focal points of Son and High Priest, Hebrews shows that as Son, Jesus embodies the nature of God the Father and is in this way God's fullest possible revelation to us. But at the time of Jesus, the title "son of god" was in general usage as a reference to a ruler who enjoyed the special empowerment of his god. Applied to Jesus, it would have struck a messianic tone, which makes the crowd's mockery while Jesus was on the cross poignantly ironic: "Come down from the cross, if you are the Son of God!" (Matt. 27:40). As High Priest, Jesus completes God's sacrificial system by offering himself to die for sin, providing the complete and final sacrifice that animal sacrifice under the old covenant merely foreshadowed. To relativize the old covenant with respect to the new, Hebrews affirms that the sacrifices of the old had been commanded by God but also that God himself had hinted that a better covenant was coming that would be based not on the priesthood of ancient Israel but on a priesthood like that of Melchizedek.

These two foci of Hebrews' Christology—Jesus as Son of God and Jesus as Priest—come together for the author of Hebrews in the ascension, where Christ is both crowned as the King of the universe at God's right hand and where he presents the final sacrifice of his own blood to God in the true Holy of Holies. After the mission of his earthly life is done, the resurrected Jesus ascends as the Lord and Savior of all creation.

KEY TERMS

ascension
Caesar Augustus
Christology
Dead Sea Scrolls
incarnation
Melchizedek
Son of God (first-century sense)
tabernacle

QUESTIONS FOR REVIEW OR DISCUSSION

1. Which two distinctive roles of Jesus does Hebrews present, and how are they related?
2. How is Jesus related to God the Father as described in the opening verses?
3. What did the title "son of god" mean in Greco-Roman thought before Jesus came? Consequently, how would the Roman occupation of Palestine and Jesus' execution have been construed by Romans?
4. In what sense has God spoken in his Son?
5. What was the function of a priest in ancient society?
6. Who is Melchizedek? What was his relationship to the priesthood of the old covenant?
7. Why is Melchizedek an appropriate analogy for the priesthood of Jesus?
8. At what point and in what ways do the two roles of Jesus come together?

GOING FURTHER

Barrett C. K. "The Christology of Hebrews." Pages 110–27 in *"Who Do You Say That I Am?" Essays on Christology in Honor of Jack Dean Kingsbury*. Edited by Mark Allan Powell and David R. Bauer. Louisville: Westminster John Knox, 1999.

Beale, Gregory K. *The Temple and the Church's Mission: A Biblical Theology of the Temple*. New Studies in Biblical Theology 17. Downers Grove, Ill.: InterVarsity, 2004.

Evans, Craig A., and Stanley E. Porter. *Dictionary of New Testament Background*. Downers Grove, Ill.: InterVarsity, 2000.

Fitzmyer, Joseph A. "Further Light on Melchizedek from Qumran Cave 11." *JBL* 86 (1967): 25–41.

Horton, F. L. *The Melchizedek Tradition: A Critical Examination of the Sources to the Fifth Century A.D. and in the Epistle to the Hebrews*. SNTSMS 30. Cambridge: Cambridge University Press, 2005.

Mason, Eric F. *"You Are a Priest Forever": Second Temple Jewish Messianism and the Priestly Christology of the Epistle to the Hebrews*. STDJ 74. Leiden: Brill, 2008.

Robertson, O. Palmer. *The Christ of the Covenants.* Phillipsburg, N.J.: Presbyterian and Reformed, 1980.

Schenck, Kenneth. *Understanding the Book of Hebrews: The Story behind the Sermon.* Louisville: Westminster John Knox, 2003.

Vos, Geerhardus. *The Teaching of the Epistle to the Hebrews.* Phillipsburg, N.J.: Presbyterian and Reformed, 1956.

Williamson, Paul R. *Sealed with an Oath: Covenant in God's Unfolding Purpose.* New Studies in Biblical Theology 23. Downers Grove, Ill.: InterVarsity, 2007.

CHAPTER 4

"How Shall We Escape?"

THE SOTERIOLOGY OF HEBREWS

Your Goals for This Chapter

- To relate the **soteriology** presented in Hebrews to that in the rest of the New Testament.
- To understand how Israel's ancient priesthood foreshadowed the **atonement** that Christ achieved.
- To explain what the author of Hebrews means about "perfection."
- To articulate the main views about **apostasy**.
- To identify and explain the distinctive images Hebrews uses for salvation.

WHY THIS CHAPTER IS IMPORTANT TO YOU

The most important issue a human being faces is his or her relationship to the God who created all things. Both the existential human condition we experience and the Scriptures tell us that human beings are alienated from God. The story line of the Bible from Genesis to Revelation is how God has taken the initiative to reconcile his human creatures to himself and redeem the universe from its fallen state. This chapter discusses the distinctive message of salvation as told by the author of Hebrews, raising some disturbing questions for those who profess to believe in Jesus Christ.

Have you ever felt as if you have done something so bad that maybe you have lost your salvation? *Can* a Christian lose his or her salvation? And then get saved again? The theology of the book of Hebrews is second only to Paul's letter to the Romans, with its clear exposition of the gospel and its emphasis on justification by faith alone. But in Hebrews we find some of the most terrifying statements about the loss of faith and the possibility of apostasy. Hebrews is distinctive in its blunt statements that one can "fall away" (6:6) and lose the benefit of Christ's sacrifice (10:26).

The disturbing statements we find in Hebrews must be understood within the context of the letter's presentation of salvation, or what theologians would call its soteriology. What does Hebrews say about salvation? How are Christians saved according to Hebrews? Within that context of how Hebrews understands salvation, can Christians lose their salvation? How do the distinctive images of salvation that Hebrews presents, such as the Sabbath rest, inform Christian life and practice today? Those are the questions to which this chapter is addressed.

Key Verses

1:3:	The Son is the radiance of God's glory and the exact representation of his being, sustaining all things by his powerful word. After he had provided purification for sins, he sat down at the right hand of the Majesty in heaven.
2:2–3a:	For since the message spoken through angels was binding, and every violation and disobedience received its just punishment, how shall we escape if we ignore so great a salvation?
2:10:	In bringing many sons and daughters to glory, it was fitting that God, for whom and through whom everything exists, should make the pioneer of their salvation perfect through what he suffered.
4:3a:	Now we who have believed enter that rest....
5:8–9:	Son though he was, he learned obedience from what he suffered and, once made perfect, he became the source of eternal salvation for all who obey him....
6:4–6:	It is impossible for those who have once been enlightened, who have tasted the heavenly gift, who have shared in the Holy Spirit,

	who have tasted the goodness of the word of God and the powers of the coming age and who have fallen away, to be brought back to repentance. To their loss they are crucifying the Son of God all over again and subjecting him to public disgrace.
10:14:	For by one sacrifice he has made perfect forever those who are being made holy.
10:26–27:	If we deliberately keep on sinning after we have received the knowledge of the truth, no sacrifice for sins is left, but only a fearful expectation of judgment and of raging fire that will consume the enemies of God.
12:22:	But you have come to Mount Zion, to the city of the living God, the heavenly Jerusalem.

CHAPTER OUTLINE

- I. Hebrews' Theology of Salvation
  - A. The Covenants
  - B. Escape from the Consequence of Sin
  - C. Salvation in Hebrews
  - D. Eternal Life
- II. The Call to Obedient Perseverance
  - A. "Perfection" in Hebrews
  - B. Sabbath Rest
  - C. Perseverance and Apostasy
    1. Views on the warning passages
       - a. Are the people described genuine Christian believers?
       - b. Is the consequence described eternal damnation or something less?
    2. Dealing with the fear of apostasy
    3. The great cloud of witnesses

HEBREWS' THEOLOGY OF SALVATION

The message about salvation in the book of Hebrews is very consistent with that found throughout the New Testament. For many Bible readers, Paul's letters to the Romans and Galatians are the touchstones concerning this issue with his message of justification and sanctification by grace through faith in Christ alone. Hebrews 10:14 reflects these Pauline categories: "For by one sacrifice he [Jesus Christ] *has made perfect* forever those who are *being made holy*" (emphasis added). The reference to "has made perfect" reflects the status of justification; "being made holy" refers to ongoing sanctification, an especially important topic in the soteriology of Hebrews. Notice that the phrase "those who are being made holy," that is, those whose lives exemplify the process of sanctification, defines those whom the sacrifice of Jesus "has made perfect." This also helps to define the terms *perfect* and *perfection* that are used so frequently to describe believers in Hebrews. (See further discussion of this distinctive characteristic of Hebrews below.)

The overarching message of the book of Hebrews is that God has spoken to the people of planet Earth. And God's word to us is that the life, death, and resurrection of his Son in the first century is his fullest and final message to humanity. All of the book's soteriology takes as its starting point the necessity of a response to what God has spoken, for neglect or rejection of the message has dire and eternal consequences. Hebrews 1:1 – 4 clearly states that God has spoken most recently by the Son, who is identified in 2:9 as the man we know as Jesus. But as we noted in chapter 2, the writer of Hebrews does not then present the teaching and preaching of Jesus, as if Jesus' words are the primary message in view. In fact, the book of Hebrews is conspicuously devoid of the words spoken during Jesus' earthly ministry. Instead, Hebrews presents God's message as the Son *himself*; the message God has spoken is in the identity of Jesus and what he accomplished, namely, the purification for sins (1:3b). This incarnate Word of God (cf. John 1:1 – 18), rather than the verbal words of God, moves the Creator's message to humanity beyond the realm of moral, ethical, and religious teaching. It precludes the mistaken idea that Jesus is just another good teacher of religion and morality, allowing him to be viewed, as so many seem to do, as just another teacher of the world's great religions. The author of Hebrews wants to underscore the point that Jesus, and *only* Jesus, provided purification for sins and now sits enthroned in heaven as Lord of the universe. What do *you* say to that? The entire soteriology of Hebrews is grounded in the necessity of a response to that message from God.

"For by one sacrifice he [Jesus Christ] has made perfect forever [i.e., justified] those who are being made holy [i.e., sanctified]."

Hebrews 10:14

The Covenants

The need for purification from our sins is the root problem of humanity with which God seeks to get our attention and toward which God has worked throughout human history. In the garden of Eden, when humanity was new, God permitted Adam and Eve to freely enjoy all that God created, as well as personal fellowship with the Lord himself. He required only one thing of them to preserve his rightful rule as God over the human race he had created. His request was seemingly a simple one: that they abstain from eating the fruit from just one of the trees in the middle of the garden, the tree of the knowledge of good and evil (Gen. 2:16 – 17). As long as they obeyed, they could have no knowledge of good and evil, because by definition of their obedience, they had not experienced evil. Tragically, Adam and Eve chose not to obey God, but instead to live their lives by the false and deceitful word of the serpent, Satan, who had made himself an enemy of God by rebelling against God's rule (Gen. 3). Ever since that time, human beings have been faced with the same choice as Adam and Eve — to listen to God and obey him or to follow the fatal temptations of God's enemy. Because Adam and Eve failed when God first spoke to humankind, it became necessary for God to "speak" once more to purify sin and extend God's forgiving grace. This God did throughout history in words that have come down to us as the Bible.

But the consummation of that message was the coming of the Son himself to achieve the promised purification for what humanity had done. And so for the author of Hebrews, one's relationship with God hangs upon one's response to that Son, Jesus Christ.

God began working in human history toward the one final sacrifice by first choosing for himself a portion of humankind whom he would school in the problem of sin and the need for sacrifice to atone for it. He chose Abraham and Sarah (Gen. 12–23), whose family would grow into a select (i.e., chosen) nation to whom God would reveal himself through redemptive deeds (e.g., the parting of the Red Sea) and words (e.g., the giving of the covenant at Sinai). God's relationship with this select people was governed by the covenant he made with them through Moses at Mount Sinai when he led them out of slavery. That covenant had both stipulations governing the purification of sins by the priesthood and sacrificial system and stipulations governing the moral quality of human life. The people God chose were eager to obey him, for when Moses read the book of the covenant to them, they responded by saying, "We will do everything the Lord has said; we will obey" (Ex. 24:7). The rest of the Old Testament documents their sad failure; the human spirit may willingly reach toward God, but the flesh is indeed weak. The failure of the Israelites to keep the covenant with its moral demands was not peculiar to them; they simply represent the failure of all human beings to keep God's law despite the best of intentions. This came as no surprise to God, but the failure of Israel to keep the covenant revealed to all humankind our inability to obey God, even when we want to. But there was another lesson to come. Even during that first covenant, God promised a time when a new covenant would come, a time when his law would be written on the hearts and minds of people (Jer. 31:33), indicating an empowerment to obey what was previously unattainable.

atone: v. [intrans.] make amends or reparation.

Oxford American College Dictionary, 2002

Hebrews interprets the life and death of Jesus as the inauguration of that promised covenant, that better covenant with its better promises, better priesthood, and better sacrifice. (See chapter 3.)

Escape from the Consequence of Sin

When God commanded Adam and Eve not to eat the fruit from the tree of the knowledge of good and evil, he also told them the consequences of disobedience, "for when you eat of it you will certainly die" (Gen. 2:17). Notice that God did not say, "for when you eat of it I will kill you." Death is not a punishment; it is the inevitable consequence of turning away from the source of life, which is God himself (cf. Rom. 6:23, "For the wages of sin is death, but the gift of God is eternal life in Christ Jesus our Lord"). The punishment for sin is listed in the curses that God imposed on human life in our fallen state, that life would be difficult and painful for people and then their bodies would return to the ground (Gen. 3:14–19).

The covenant God gave to his people at Sinai provided a substitutionary death, with animals as the substitute. These animal sacrifices under the old covenant taught that people could escape the consequence of sin—that is, death—and be reconciled to God because a substitute died in their place. These animal sacrifices only anticipated the ultimate sacrificial death, when God himself would take on a human body and die as the final substitute sacrifice, so that there would be a way to escape the consequence of being eternally separated from the source of life. The book of Hebrews explains that Jesus was God incarnate and that his death on the cross was the full and final substitution, making him both the priest and sacrifice of the new, and better, covenant. This is God's final word to humankind — so that people who respond can come into the new covenant relationship with God through Jesus Christ and escape the judgment of death.

Salvation in Hebrews

The opportunity to disobey God was not unique to Adam and Eve. In fact, all human beings are born with an innate urge to yield to evil impulses that Scripture defines as disobedience to God, and we inevitably begin to act upon them early in life. Hebrews refers to the escape from the consequence of disobedience to God as "salvation," a word used by many Christians today, especially evangelicals. The Greek noun *sōtēria* and its cognate verb *sōdzō* occur nine times in Hebrews (1:14; 2:3, 10; 5:7, 9; 6:9; 7:25; 9:28; 11:7).

The first time salvation is mentioned in Hebrews, it is in a statement about angels, who are "ministering spirits sent to serve those who *will* inherit salvation" (1:14, emphasis added). Today many Christians might say, "I was saved" and speak of salvation as a past event, sometimes giving a testimony that recounts a time in their life when they repented of their sins, accepted Christ, and became "saved." Modern evangelicalism puts the emphasis on a past, personal conversion. But the author of Hebrews agrees with other New Testament writers in seeing salvation not simply as a past event, but as a yet future event that will be fully realized only at the consummation when Christ returns (Heb. 9:28) and all humanity stands before God to be judged. This does not mean that Christians today need be unsure of their personal salvation. Because salvation rests on the *past* event of Jesus' substitutionary death on the cross, it is a done deal that is as certain as anything can be. This is why, even though salvation is viewed as a yet future event, the New Testament speaks of believers in Christ as "those who *will* inherit salvation" (Heb. 1:14). Salvation has been secured, and it is certain that followers of Christ will inherit it.

The major concern of the author of Hebrews is the possibility of his readers rejecting the salvation that God offers through Jesus Christ, especially after professing faith in him. Immediately after the reference to "those who will inherit salvation" in Hebrews 1:14, comes the stern warning of Hebrews 2:1 – 4, the first of several warnings that are a distinctive characteristic of the book of Hebrews. It calls those who are heirs apparent to salvation to pay careful attention so that they will not drift away. Hebrews 2:2 reminds its readers that the "message spoken through angels was binding," a reference to the Sinai covenant made with Moses. Even though that covenant was anticipatory and temporary, it was still God's word to those people who lived under it and, therefore, binding upon them with consequences for disobedience. But, the author of Hebrews says, Jesus Christ is greater than both the angels (1:5 – 14) and Moses (3:1 – 6). If disobedience to *that* covenant was a fearful thing, how much greater the consequences of ignoring the salvation offered by Jesus Christ? There is no escape, no salvation, for anyone who ignores the salvation offered by God in Christ (2:3).

Note that the warning is to pay careful attention "to what we have heard" (Heb. 2:1). In the immediate context of the letter, this can refer only to what the author has previously mentioned, that God has spoken by the Son (1:2). Salvation for Hebrews is, as noted above, based on the appropriate response to the Son, Jesus Christ, who is greater than any other source of knowledge of God. Pay careful attention to the gospel, and do not drift away from it. If left uncorrected, drifting amounts to ignoring salvation, and those who ignore it, by definition, cannot inherit it.

Eternal Life

One of the perhaps most perplexing thoughts about sin, and salvation from its consequences, concerns death. God warned Adam and Eve that if they ate fruit from the tree of the knowledge of good and evil, they would die. Their disobedience to God would separate them from him, and the only source of life. Therefore, the natural consequence of turning away from God is to turn to death. But apparently Adam and Eve did not drop dead immediately, as if from food poisoning. Instead, they were cast out of the garden (a truly redemptive act), had children, and died at a very ripe old age. And even though Christian believers today are saved from the consequence of sin, which is death, still everyone dies, believer and unbeliever alike.

Planet Art

Adam and Eve cast from Eden, painting by Gustave Dore (1832 – 83).

Death, and all that attends it, is the most profound of life's mysteries, made even more so by the death of Jesus himself. The eternal God incarnate for some reason had to experience human death in order to make human redemption possible. Hebrews 2:10 states this mystery: "In bringing many sons and daughters to glory, it was fitting that God, for whom and through whom everything exists, should make the pioneer of their salvation perfect through what *he* suffered" (emphasis added). Salvation is attained not through what *we* suffer but through what *God* suffered. God in Christ is called the "pioneer" of salvation (Gk. *archēgos*).

Hebrews 5:7–9 elaborates, "During the days of Jesus' life on earth, he offered up prayers and petitions with fervent cries and tears *to the one who could save him from death*, and he was heard because of his reverent submission. *Son though he was*, he learned obedience from what he suffered and, *once made perfect*, he became *the source of eternal salvation for all who obey him*" (emphasis added). The thought of death made Jesus offer fervent cries and tears! This is most poignantly seen in the garden of Gethsemane, when his death was imminent. Jesus cried out to the one who could *save* (Gk. *sōdzō*) him from death, and God heard Jesus' cries. Even so, God did not save Jesus from the experience of death, for to save Jesus from death would have meant to lose salvation for the human race. Jesus was "made perfect" through facing and experiencing death, and because of that experience he became the source of eternal salvation. *As a human being,* Jesus went through death and was resurrected to show us that physical death is not the final judgment on a human life. Jesus brings sinful human beings, who were dead in their separation from the source of life, back to God. As a human being, Jesus opens the way for us back to God and frees us from our fear of death. Rather than death being the door to eternal separation from God, Jesus has made death the pathway of following him into the presence of God where there awaits a welcome and not a judgment.

Jesus in the Garden of Gethsemane, from the Trebon Altarpiece, Master of the Trebon Altarpiece/Narodni Galerie, Prague, Czech Republic/Giraudon/The Bridgeman Art Library

Even though Jesus was God incarnate, he experienced human life as all people do. Knowledge of his impending death created within him all the emotional agony that every person faces.

Perhaps you are wondering, *Why didn't God just let people live forever in our earthly lives because of Jesus? Why doesn't salvation mean that we need not physically die?* Even though Jesus raised Lazarus from the grave (John 11:38–53), Lazarus died again. He is not still living in Bethany. And even Jesus himself did not remain on earth in his resurrected body. This shows that this body, this life, this earth are not suitable for eternal life. Why did God cast Adam and Eve out of the garden? Was it to punish them and vent his anger? God tells us why he did it in Genesis 3:22–24:

> And the Lord God said, "The man has now become like one of us, knowing good and evil. *He must not be allowed to reach out his hand and take also from the tree of life and eat, and live forever.*" So the Lord God banished him from the Garden of Eden to work the ground from which he had been taken. After he drove the man out, he placed on the east side of the Garden of Eden cherubim and a flaming sword flashing back and forth to guard the way to *the tree of life.* (emphasis added)

God did not want human beings to live forever separated from him in their fallen state, with all the misery and curses that fallenness brought into this world. Can you imagine growing older and older forever? Experiencing pain in body and in relationships endlessly? Unending life on this earth in our fallen state would be more like hell than heaven. God's expulsion of Adam and Eve from the garden was a gracious and redemptive act, not a punishment. It spoke of a journey to redemption and reconciliation that the human race collectively, and individuals personally, have been on ever since. Jesus came to lead that journey back to glory; to be the first to be "made perfect," to pass through death's door unconquered by it, and to show the way to a place suitable for an endless life.

Hebrews is written to those who have heard the message of salvation "first announced by the Lord" and "confirmed to us by those who heard him" (2:3). And to those who have heard what Jesus has done, he pronounces the sternest warnings of Scripture:[1]

> See to it, brothers and sisters, that none of you has a sinful, unbelieving heart that turns away from the living God. (3:12)
>
> Today, if you hear his voice, do not harden your hearts. (4:7)
>
> But land that produces thorns and thistles is worthless and is in danger of being cursed. In the end it will be burned. (6:8)
>
> If we deliberately keep on sinning after we have received the knowledge of the truth, no sacrifice for sins is left, but only a fearful expectation of judgment and of raging fire that will consume the enemies of God. (10:26–27)
>
> It is a dreadful thing to fall into the hands of the living God. (10:31)

God first revealed his grace and intention to save the fallen human race when he barred Adam and Eve from eating from the tree of life.

Adam and Eve, Voysey, Charles Francis Annesley/Private Collection/The Stapleton Collection/The Bridgeman Art Library

It is not for nothing that people fear death when their consciences are weighed down by the knowledge that they have not heeded the grace of God offered in Christ and have continued to live in disobedience to God. To die without Christ's purification of sin is to be left in that place of separation from God who is the source of life. Not only do these people experience physical death, but they also enter into a place of eternal separation from God that is consistently imaged in the New Testament as a place of burning.

Hebrews 5:9 speaks of Jesus having become the source of eternal salvation, but this salvation is only "for all who obey him." Just as Adam and Eve were personally involved in the decision to eat from the forbidden tree and, by doing so, to turn away from God, so all who would be reconciled to God in Christ must be personally involved in deciding to obey. It is this call to obedience that is of utmost concern to the author of Hebrews as he writes with such passionate words.

THE CALL TO OBEDIENT PERSEVERANCE

"Perfection" in Hebrews

The book of Hebrews is distinctive in its use of a certain Greek word group (Gk., *teleioō*) usually translated "perfect"/"perfected"/"perfection." When this English word is encountered in a religious text, such as a book of the Bible, one's first thought may be moral

1. The question of what happens to people who die without ever having heard the gospel message is important both theologically and pastorally, but it is not the situation addressed by the author of Hebrews. You may wish to read John Hick, Dennis Okholm, and Timothy Phillips, eds., *More Than One Way? Four Views on Salvation in a Pluralistic World* (Grand Rapids: Zondervan, 1996).

perfection or a state of sinlessness. This is not the sense of the Greek word, which generally means "to complete, bring to an end or goal, finish" and can in certain cultic contexts have the derivative meaning "to initiate or consecrate." If used of growing things, the English translation "mature" or "reach maturity" would capture the sense. If used of a plan to reach a goal, "complete or finish" would be the sense.

In the book of Hebrews, the word is used in reference to a range of objects: the Old Testament saints are *perfected* only with "us" (11:40); Christ is the *perfecter* of our faith (12:2); only his blood can *perfect* the conscience (9:9; 10:1, 14); and Christians are called to the *perfection* of maturity (5:14; 6:1). Perhaps most surprisingly, Jesus himself reached *perfection* through his sufferings (2:10; 5:9; 7:28). But wasn't Jesus already perfect by nature in every way, and certainly morally so?

Understanding the sense of *perfection* in Hebrews must begin with how the word is applied to Jesus in 2:10; 5:9; and 7:28 (emphasis added):

> In bringing many sons and daughters to glory, it was fitting that God, for whom and through whom everything exists, should *make the pioneer of their salvation perfect through what he suffered.* (2:10)
>
> ... and, *once made perfect,* he became the source of eternal salvation for all who obey him. (5:9)
>
> ... but the oath, which came after the law, appointed the Son, *who has been made perfect forever.* (7:28)

Hebrews explicitly says that Jesus was without sin and morally perfect (4:15). So in what sense did Jesus become perfect, and how did suffering make him so? The key to understanding his perfection is noting that in Hebrews (and elsewhere in the New Testament, e.g., Rom. 1:4) Jesus Christ *became* the Son in a way that he was not Son previously in his eternally preexistent state as a member of the Trinity (Heb. 1:5; 5:5). As discussed in chapter 3, Jesus' ascension was his coronation in his glorified human body as Son of God and his entrance into the true Holy of Holies as High Priest (and sacrifice). The perfection of Jesus through what he suffered indicates a change effected in his life as a human being, that is, "between two successive stages in his human-messianic existence."[2] Christ was the Messiah before he suffered but came to perfection of that role only through his death, resurrection, and ascension. The eschatological understanding of Hebrews that in the death, resurrection, and ascension of Christ there has been a turn of the ages is clear from the reference to the incarnation in Hebrews 1:2, "*in these last days* he has spoken to us by his Son," and 9:26, "But he [Christ] has appeared once for all *at the culmination of the ages* to do away with sin by the sacrifice of himself." Hebrews sees the *completion* or *fulfillment* of God's redemptive plan to have been accomplished by Jesus Christ. In other words, Jesus has brought God's redemptive plan to its *perfection*—in so doing he *became* the Son in a way he was not previously.

But to attain this fulfillment of redemption, Jesus had to suffer, and it was that suffering that brought *him* to perfection as a human being in the sense that his obedient suf-

2. Moisés Silva, "Perfection and Eschatology in Hebrews," *WTJ* 39 (1976): 64.

fering brought his role as the Messiah to *completion* or *fulfillment*. Jesus is the "perfecter" of faith (Heb. 12:2), in other words, the one who brings faith to its efficacious completion for the salvation of human beings. His role in God's redemptive plan as Messiah was perfected only when he suffered and died on the cross. Moreover, Jesus has been made perfect *forever* (Heb. 7:28); the fulfillment of his role is the full and final completion of God's redemptive plan. From the "perfection" of Jesus, we can see that the words of "perfection" (the *teleō* group in Greek) in Hebrews are used in an eschatological sense. It is not moral perfection that is in view, but the completion of Christ's work to usher in the eschatological age.

Christ Accepting the Office of Redeemer (Illustration to Milton's "Paradise Lost," 1808).

The efficacy of the new covenant confirms this understanding of "perfection." Hebrews 7:11, 19 point out that the Levitical priesthood and the law could not bring God's redemptive plan to "perfection," that is, its completion. Hebrews 9:9 and 10:1 explain that the observances of the old covenant were not able to "perfect" the conscience of the worshiper (though many English versions translate this word as "clear" or "cleanse"). This "is not a reference to forgiveness or fitness to approach God, which Old Testament saints did experience (cf. Ps. 32 and Rom. 4), but to the enjoyment of the time of fulfillment, the new epoch introduced by the Messiah through his exaltation."[3] The old covenant was not able to bring the person who entered into it to the place of final eschatological rest.

This eschatological understanding of perfection then makes good sense of the claims that the Christian believer is "perfect" in Hebrews 10:14; 11:40; and 12:22–23 (emphasis added):

> For *by one sacrifice he has made perfect forever* those who are being made holy. (10:14)
>
> God had planned something better for us so that *only together with us would they be made perfect.* (11:40)
>
> But you have come ... to the church of the firstborn, whose names are written in heaven. You have come to God, the Judge of all, to the *spirits of the righteous made perfect, ...*" (12:22–23)

The human quest for redemption is brought to its completion when people come to faith in Christ. Christians are perfected because, by faith in Christ's sacrifice to purify their sin, they come into a new and final state of reconciliation with God. When the term "perfected" is applied to believers in Hebrews, it is analogous to what "justification" (Gk., *dikaiōsis*) refers to in Romans (emphasis added):

3. Ibid., 67.

> He was delivered over to death for our sins and was raised to life for our *justification*. (Rom. 4:25)

> Consequently, just as one trespass resulted in condemnation for all people, so also one righteous act resulted in *justification* and life for all people. (Rom. 5:18)

When we understand perfection as a reference to the eschatological state into which Christ brings those who believe in him, the statement that "only together with us would [the Old Testament believers] be made perfect" makes sense. Although they believed in the promise of God and were commended for that faith, they did not receive the fulfillment, because that perfection had to await its fulfillment in the final and ultimate sacrifice of Jesus Christ on the cross. This indicates that those who lived before Christ and were faithful to the covenant as God had revealed it are saved only because of Christ's death and resurrection, even though they could not have foreseen it from their historical location.

British Library/HIP/Art Resource, NY

The tree of vices, 14th century. The vices are listed in Latin, spread through the tree in seven groups, corresponding to the deadly sins. From the Psalter of Robert de Lisle.

While it may be of some relief to realize that "perfection" in Hebrews does not mean moral perfection, which most Christians would find an impossible goal, for the author of Hebrews it certainly is related to holiness, which does bring moral virtue into view. Hebrews 10:14 speaks of those who Christ "has made perfect forever" (note the perfect tense) as "those who are being made holy" (note the present tense). For the author of Hebrews, these two categories, though distinct, must nevertheless be inseparable in the life of the Christian. Jesus did not offer himself as the final sacrifice so that people may give him a nod on Sunday and then continue to live in disobedience to God. Hebrews does not speak of the believer as "saved" but as "being made holy." Salvation from judgment, which is assured, still stands in the future. The writer of Hebrews exhorts his readers to "throw off everything that hinders and the sin that so easily entangles" (12:1). It further expects those who have "been perfected" to "make every effort to live in peace with everyone *and to be holy*; without holiness no one will see the Lord" (12:14, emphasis added). It speaks against adultery and all sexual immorality (12:16; 13:4). Like the other New Testament writers, the author of Hebrews encourages believers to love one another (13:1), to show hospitality to strangers (13:2), to be in solidarity with those believers in prison (13:3). Contentment free from a love of money is a mark of holiness (13:5), as is a willingness to follow faithful leaders in the church (13:7, 17). Verbal witness to our faith is a characteristic of those who have been "perfected" in Christ (13:15), accompanied by doing good and sharing with others (13:16). And finally, believing prayer for the circumstances of others marks those who are being made holy (13:18–19).

The Exhortations of Hebrews*		
Let's Hold On	*Let's Draw Near*	*Let's Go Forward*
2:1 We must pay attention to the things we hear.	4:16 Let's draw near to the throne of grace.	4:1 Let's be afraid that one of you may fall short of the [Sabbath] rest.
4:14 Let's hold on to our confession.	10:22 Let's go into the Holy of Holies.	4:11 Let's make every effort to enter that rest.
10:23 Let's hold on to the confession of our hope.	12:28 Let's have grace and let's worship/serve God.	6:1 Let's press on to maturity.
	13:12 Let's go to Jesus outside of the camp.	10:24 Let's consider how to stimulate each other to love and good works.
	13:15–16 Let's offer sacrifices of gratitude, good works, and sharing.	12:1 Let's run the race!

*Adapted from Cynthia Long Westfall, *A Discourse Analysis of the Letter to the Hebrews: The Relationship between Form and Meaning*, Library of New Testament Studies 297, Studies in New Testament Greek (London: T&T Clark, 2005), 298.

Sabbath Rest

Another distinctive element of the book of Hebrews is its exposition of the wilderness wanderings of ancient Israel as a refusal to enter God's rest and an act of disobedience. Just as the priesthood and sacrifices pictured a substitutionary death for sin, so the exodus under the leadership of Moses and the entrance into the Promised Land under the leadership of Joshua pictures the redemptive journey arriving at its destination. In Adam and Eve, the human race was cast out of Eden and into a journey back to reconciliation of our fractured relationship with God. The exodus from Egypt to travel to a promised land where God would dwell with his people pictured that reconciliation. The people had received God's covenant with enthusiasm, saying, "Everything the Lord has said we will do" (Ex. 24:3). But as they stood on the border of the Promised Land, which flourished with food reminiscent of Eden (Num. 13:23), they balked in fear and refused to act on what the Lord had told them (Num. 14; Deut. 1). Because of their rebellion against God's will (Deut. 1:26),

Joshua ⇔ Jesus

"For if Joshua had given them rest, God would not have spoken later about another day."

Hebrews 4:8

Where the Hebrew Old Testament text speaks of "Yehoshua," it was translated in the Greek Old Testament as "*Iēsous*," the name Jesus in English. Mentioning Joshua by name in 4:8 results in two "Jesuses" brought to mind — the "Jesus" of the Old Testament who was unable to bring God's people to rest in the promises of God and Jesus Christ who opens the full and final rest. The contrast would have been apparent to those reading Hebrews in the original Greek.

that generation consequently wandered in the desert wilderness for forty years, dying without ever entering the land. The Lord declared that, except for faithful Joshua and Caleb, not one of them would see the land (Num. 14:22; Deut. 1:34–36).

It is this sad episode in Israel's history that became the paradigmatic example of failing to believe that the Lord God is able to do what he says—another instance of the failure to obey that echoes the sin of Adam and Eve. In spite of all the Lord had done to provide for and protect them as he led them out of Egypt, the wilderness generation did not fully trust him (Deut. 1:32). The author of Hebrews uses this example as an analogy to argue that his readers were in a similar danger (Heb. 3:7–19). Hebrews refers to this story, not as it is found in the Pentateuch, but as it was retold and interpreted in Psalm 95 many centuries later during the Davidic dynasty. In Psalm 95 God declares about that wilderness generation, "They shall never enter *my rest*" (v. 11, emphasis added). The wilderness generation did not enter the Promised Land, which is interpreted in Psalm 95 as not entering God's rest. Because of this, the Promised Land is understood in Hebrews as an image of the destination where God offers rest from the redemptive journey that began when Adam and Eve left Eden.

The Rest God Has Offered*

In the Wilderness	*At the Time of David*	*For the Readers of Hebrews*
(Ex. 17:1–7; Num. 14:20–25)	(Ps. 95:7–11)	(Heb. 3:7–4:11)
Entry into Canaan	"Today" do not harden hearts	As long as it is called "today"
Unable to enter because of disbelief	The rest remains for some	There remains a "Sabbath" rest for the people of God
"They shall never enter"		Invitation to eschatological rest

*Adapted from Donald A. Hagner, *Encountering the Book of Hebrews* (Grand Rapids: Baker Academic, 2002), 72.

The author of Hebrews noted that in Psalm 95:7, written centuries after the wilderness generation refused to enter the land, the Holy Spirit was still extending the invitation to enter God's rest: "*Today*, if you *hear his voice*" (emphasis added). Even during the Davidic dynasty, the Spirit was saying *today* is not too soon or too late to trust and obey God's voice. Although the historical opportunity to enter the land of Canaan was long past, the opportunity to obey where that generation had failed was present wherever and whenever God's voice could be heard. This was the same plea being made by the author of Hebrews. Because God has spoken by the Son (1:1–2), people are called to hear and to trust his message. "Therefore, since the promise of entering his rest still stands, let us be careful that none of you be found to have fallen short of it.... Now we who have believed enter that rest" (4:1, 3). In other words, faith in Christ's purification for our sin brings us to the final destination of our redemptive journey.

The exodus under the leadership of Moses and the entrance into the Promised Land under the leadership of Joshua pictures the redemptive journey arriving at its destination.

The concept invoked by the phrase "God's rest" brings to mind the command to observe the Sabbath, for it is based on the statement in the creation account in Genesis 2:2, which the author of Hebrews quotes in 4:4. The thought that God rested on the seventh day after six days of creation is commonly thought of as a cessation of labor, because the Sabbath was observed by not working. It suggests a time when God put his feet up to rest and relax after all the exertion of creating the universe. But this is far from what it meant that God rested when that phrase is understood in its original context of ancient cosmology. Ancient readers of Genesis 2:2 would understand immediately that "deity *rests* in a temple, and only in a temple."[4] And "rest" in its ancient context "is what results when a crisis has been resolved or when stability has been achieved."[5] Genesis 2:2 is therefore

© benkrut/www.BigStockPhoto.com

4. John H. Walton, *The Lost World of Genesis One: Ancient Cosmology and the Origins Debate* (Downers Grove, Ill.: IVP Academic, 2009), 72 (emphasis added). See also Gregory K. Beale, *The Temple and the Church's Mission: A Biblical Theology of the Dwelling Place of God*, New Studies in Biblical Theology (Downers Grove, Ill.: InterVarsity, 2004).

5. Walton, 73.

a statement that, after creating order and function in the universe, the cosmos becomes God's temple. "When the deity rests in the temple, it means that he is taking command, that he is mounting to his throne to assume his rightful place and his proper role."[6]

This explains why the **tabernacle**, and later the temple, was designed "according to the pattern shown you on the mountain" (Heb. 8:5) as a model of the cosmos. (See The Son Sat Down at the Right Hand of God in chapter 3.) As the first-century Jewish historian Josephus noted, the tabernacle and everything in it was "made in way of imitation and representation of the universe" (*Ant.* 3.7.7.180).

שׁבּת

The Hebrew word for *Sabbath*.

This understanding of God resting by entering his temple explains why it is the reason for the Sabbath he commands of his people in his moral law (Ex. 20:8–11). The deity takes up residence, indicating his sovereign rule of the cosmos. Because he is the sovereign ruler, he commands his people to live in the way intended before the fall. Have you ever noticed that keeping the Sabbath is the fourth of the Ten Commandments (Ex. 20:8; Deut. 5:12)? It's right up there with the commands not to murder, commit adultery, or misuse the Lord's name! Although many of the ritual laws of the Old Testament have been abrogated, such as eating kosher food, Jesus upheld the Ten Commandments and raised their observance to the higher plane of inner obedience, not just external behavior (Matt. 5:17–48). And while Christians still believe it is sin to murder or steal, many Christians don't seem to have any understanding of how they might obey the fourth commandment in our times.

Under the old covenant, the Israelites were to cease their work on the seventh day. This is because on the seventh day God rested from his work; he took up his rightful place as ruler of the universe he had created. But if God's rest on the seventh day is a reference to his rule of what he has created, his people obviously cannot imitate that. Instead, the cessation of work on the seventh day of each week is an acknowledgment of the basic principle of Theology 101—that the Creator God is in control and we are not; that it is he who brings stability and order to our lives. "Sabbath is for recognizing that it is God who provides for us and who is the master of our lives and our world."[7]

6. Ibid., 75.
7. Ibid., 147.

What Does Sabbath Mean for Christians Today?

"Clearly, some Sabbath observance is an appropriate response both to God's sovereignty and to the fulfillment in Christ of his promise to make his people holy. The author of Hebrews exhorts his readers to "not give up meeting together" (Heb. 10:25), and so attendance at worship is one appropriate observance of Sabbath rest. Stepping away from our normal work and routines is another way to acknowledge that the Lord is in control and we aren't. The world will go on without our help for a day or a period of Sabbath rest. 'Do whatever will reflect your love, appreciation, respect and awe of the God of all the cosmos.' "*

*John H. Walton, *The Lost World of Genesis One: Ancient Cosmology and the Origins Debate* (Downers Grove, Ill.: IVP Academic, 2009), 147.

This view of God's rest as the basis of Sabbath explains why Sabbath observance was important enough to be included among the Ten Commandments. It takes on further significance in the context of redemption from sin. "Say to the Israelites, 'You must observe my Sabbaths. This will be a sign between me and you for the generations to come, so you may know that I am the LORD, who makes you holy" (Ex. 31:13). Sabbath observance is an acknowledgment that God is the Lord, an acknowledgment that we cannot make ourselves holy; only the Lord can do that.

The biblical motif of Sabbath rest as the acknowledgment of God's sovereignty and his covenant with his people is prevalent throughout the Old Testament, bringing together the concepts of the Promised Land, the temple, and messianic kingship—in short, all of the covenant blessings promised by God to his people.[8] And it was this promise of rest that believers in the Old Testament lived by, even though they did not receive that promise in their earthly lifetime. Hebrews points out that those who lived under the old covenant would reach that promised destination only "together with us" (11:39–40). The Old Testament promises of a sacred city and a holy land (11:10, 16) would not be attained by any generation of Israel, for the promise would be fulfilled only in Jesus Christ.

As a yoke is used for oxen in plowing, so Christ uses a yoke to represent his Lordship. But unlike the oxen's yoke, Christ's yoke is easy and the burden is light.

It is against this Old Testament background that Jesus' invitation to rest in Matthew 11:28–30 can be understood. Jesus beckons with the invitation, "Come to me, all you who are weary and burdened, and I will give you *rest.* Take my yoke upon you and learn from me, for I am gentle and humble in heart, and you will find *rest* for your souls. For my yoke is easy and my burden is light" (emphasis added). With the image of the yoke representing submission to Christ's lordship,[9] this invitation implies that "the total salvation which God promised his covenant people, in its most far-reaching and inclusive sense, is coming to realization through the person and work of Messiah Jesus."[10]

This invitation to enter rest as the destination of one's spiritual journey through belief in Jesus Christ is reflected in Hebrews 4:3: "Now we who have believed [in Christ] enter that rest." This statement is not an invitation to idleness, spiritual or otherwise. Rather, it is a place of being where the normal routines of a right relationship with God can be established and enjoyed, because Christ has resolved the crisis of humanity's separation from God and an eternal stability has been achieved.[11] To enter the rest that God has

8. For a full discussion of this biblical motif, see Jon Laansma, *"I Will Give You Rest": The Rest Motif in the New Testament with Special Reference to Mt 11 and Heb 3–4,* WUNT 2/98 (Tübingen: Mohr Siebeck, 1997).

9. Leland Ryken, James C. Wilhoit, and Tremper Longman III, eds., *Dictionary of Biblical Imagery* (Downers Grove, Ill.: InterVarsity, 1998), s.v. "yoke."

10. Laansma, *"I Will Give You Rest,"* 251.

11. Adapting Walton's definition of rest to the context of the new covenant (*Lost World*, 73).

Sabbath rest. "He makes me lie down in green pastures."

promised means to live life under God's fullest blessings both here and after death. But in fact the author of Hebrews does not see the promised destination as fully realized here and now even by the Christians to whom he writes, for "here we do not have an enduring city, but we are looking for the city that is to come" (13:14). Because of the still future realization of the final destination that is entered only through belief in Christ, there is also the horrifying possibility of yet missing it through disbelief and, therefore, the need to continue in faith to the very end.

> "See to it that you do not refuse him who speaks. If they did not escape when they refused him who warned them on earth, how much less will we, if we turn away from him who warns us from heaven?"
>
> Hebrews 12:25

The author of Hebrews warns his readers that some of them are facing a situation analogous to the wilderness generation who refused to enter the Promised Land, with its attendant rest, because they did not trust God's word to them (4:6b). And yet "since it still remains for some to enter that rest ... God again set a certain day, calling it 'Today.' ... There remains, then, a Sabbath-rest [Gk. *sabbatismos*] for the people of God.... Let us, therefore, make every effort to enter that rest, so that no one will perish by following their example of disobedience" (4:6–11). This plea is at the heart of Hebrews' central concern to call its readers back from the danger of apostasy so that they may persevere in obedient belief.

Perseverance and Apostasy

If the major theme of the book of Hebrews concerning soteriology could be summed up in one statement, it would have to include the idea that one's initial faith in Jesus Christ for the purification of sins must be the *starting point* of a lifelong commitment of growth toward spiritual maturity and holiness, persevering in faith even through times of temptation to turn away. The exhortation to perseverance runs throughout the book (emphasis added):

> But Christ is faithful as the Son over God's house. And we are his house, *if indeed we hold firmly* to our confidence and the hope in which we glory. (3:6)
>
> See to it, brothers and sisters, that none of you has a sinful, unbelieving heart that *turns away* from the living God. (3:12)
>
> We have come to share in Christ, *if indeed we hold* our original conviction firmly to the very end. (3:14)
>
> Therefore, since the promise of entering his rest still stands, *let us be careful that none of you be found to have fallen short of it.* (4:1)
>
> Let us, therefore, *make every effort to enter that rest,* so that no one will perish by following their example of disobedience. (4:11)
>
> We have much to say about this, but it is hard to make it clear to you because *you no longer try to understand.* In fact, though by this time *you ought to be teachers,* you need someone to teach you the elementary truths of God's word all over again. (5:11 – 12)
>
> We do not want you to become lazy, but to imitate those who *through faith and patience inherit what has been promised.* (6:12)
>
> *Let us hold unswervingly to the hope we profess,* for he who promised is faithful. (10:23)
>
> *You need to persevere* so that when you have done the will of God, you will receive what he has promised. (10:36)
>
> And let us *run with perseverance* the race marked out for us. (12:1b)
>
> See to it that no one falls short of the grace of God. (12:15)

Perseverance

When I was young in my Christian faith, in the emotional excitement of having come to Christ, feeling the relief of sins forgiven and the warmth of fellowship with like-minded believers, I wondered why the book of Hebrews was so adamant about perseverance. What was there to persevere? The Christian life was so exciting, so fun, so fulfilling. But now, decades later, I realize that the various seasons of life as we age bring new challenges to the faith. Even without persecution for being a Christian, there are times when a believer might wonder if the gospel of eternal life in Jesus Christ is true, or perhaps whether it is relevant for life's deepest challenges. Disappointed hopes and dreams, the aging and death of parents, siblings, and spouses with all of dying's attendant indignities, the continued waywardness of a child or loved one, addictions of various kinds, broken relationships, one's own health and mortality — all of these personal circumstances can challenge one's faith in the goodness of God and the reality of his promise in Christ. And then there are the perennial episodes of evil in our world — wars, genocides, horrific crimes, global economic woes, and catastrophes of nature. It is against all the vicissitudes of life that the book of Hebrews encourages believers to keep on in the faith, "fixing our eyes on Jesus, the pioneer and perfecter of faith" (Heb. 12:2), who endured the most unjust torture to free us from the fear of death (Heb. 2:15), and therefore freeing us from our fears of life.

Karen Jobes

The sheer number and weight of these many verses that speak of the necessity of continuing faithfulness to Christ makes it clear that this isn't merely a passing thought but is the overarching purpose for the letter. And therefore, by implication, there must have been a real danger of the original readers giving up on the Christian faith, even if we can't know for certain their specific circumstances. (See the discussion in chapter 1.)

Indeed, the exhortations to persevere in faith become in places warnings that are very disturbing:

> *It is impossible* for those … who have fallen away, *to be brought back to repentance.* (Heb. 6:4, 6)

> *If we deliberately keep on sinning* after we have received the knowledge of the truth, *no sacrifice for sins is left*, but only a fearful expectation of judgment and of raging fire that will consume the enemies of God. (Heb. 10:26–27)

> See to it that you do not refuse him who speaks. If they did not escape …, how much less will we, *if we turn away from him* who warns us from heaven? (Heb. 12:25)

The book of Hebrews contains perhaps the most severe warnings in the New Testament, warnings that raise the question of whether a Christian can lose his or her salvation. Part of the reason this question may come to mind is because many Christians think of salvation as a spiritual transaction that has happened sometime in their past, perhaps at a vacation Bible school or youth group, perhaps at confirmation or water baptism, perhaps at an evangelistic rally. Those types of experiences are evidence of God's grace reconciling one to himself in Christ. Because Christ has ascended and has taken his seat at the right hand of the Father (Heb. 1:3), salvation *is* a done deal and Christians can rest with perfect confidence in God's promise. It is biblically sound to speak of a past conversion in a believer's life ("I was saved"), an ongoing work of grace toward spiritual maturity ("I am being saved"), as well as the future completion of salvation when God's wrath is escaped ("I will be saved").

The Temporal Aspects of Salvation in Life		
Past	***Present***	***Future***
Conversion	Perseverance	Delivery from God's judgment

What the book of Hebrews warns against is thinking of the "sinner's prayer" or going forward at an altar call to be fully and finally constitutive of salvation, as if in such an act one acquires a ticket to heaven that makes the rest of one's life irrelevant to one's salvation. "Christ was sacrificed once to take away the sins of many; and he will appear a second time … to *bring* salvation *to those who are waiting* for him" (9:28, emphasis added). It is possible for people to profess a faith in Christ but later to wander away from the church and away from faith in Christ. The author of Hebrews passionately warns his readers against that danger. But what does he mean that it is "impossible" for those who have "fallen away" to be brought back to repentance? Is there some kind of limit on God's grace? Is God's unconditional love not really unconditional? Is there such a thing as a doctrine of eternal security?

The warnings in Hebrews 6:4 and 10:26–27 are so striking and raise such important questions that they have generated a spectrum of interpretations throughout the church's history.

Views on the warning passages.

It may be helpful to first consider these warning passages in their original historical context before thinking about their significance for modern theology, for instance, the doctrine of eternal security. Although the historical circumstance addressed by Hebrews must be inferred solely from the content of the book itself, it seems clear (1) that the issue(s) must have concerned Jewish theology and ritual as practiced in the priesthood and sacrificial system, evidenced by the elaborate and extensive discussion of Christ superseding both, and (2) that the original readers were in danger of turning away from Christ, quite possibly by returning to the practice of first-century Judaism.

When viewed against this background, the statements that those who turn away are "crucifying the Son of God all over again" (Heb. 6:6) and have "trampled the Son of God underfoot," treating the blood of the new covenant as unholy (Heb. 10:29), are clearer. For Jewish Christians to give up on belief in Christ's atonement and return to the practices of Judaism aligns them with the Jewish leaders and Romans who executed Jesus, rejecting his claim to be the Messiah and Son of God. To (re)turn from Christianity to Judaism is to agree that Jesus' blood has no significance other than that of a common criminal or the untimely death of a good man. This deliberate decision to no longer be a Christian is what theologians call "**apostasy**."

apostasy: (n.) the abandonment of a religious belief.

Oxford American College Dictionary

The consequence of apostasy from Christ is that "it is impossible ... to be brought back to repentance" (Heb. 6:4–6), for "no sacrifice for sins is left, but only a fearful expectation of [God's wrathful] judgment" (10:26–27). In its original historical context, the reference to "deliberately keep on sinning after we have received the knowledge of the truth" (v. 26) likely refers to professing Christians who continued to practice the rituals of sacrifice, such as celebrating the Day of Atonement, when the high priest offered the sacrifice in the Jerusalem temple for all Israel, including those living in **diaspora**. Hebrews explains why such sacrifices in the Jerusalem temple are not only no longer needed but are a denial of the significance and efficacy of Christ's death. And so to continue to practice the sacrificial rituals of Judaism (or of any other religion) while professing to be a Christian is to "keep on sinning." This is not to say that the animal sacrifices under the old covenant were innately sinful. God had commanded them. But once Christ died as the full and final sacrifice, any practice of animal sacrifice would be a denial of what God had revealed in Christ and consequently sinful for those living in the Christian era. The author of Hebrews was putting his original readers on notice that such syncretism can no longer be tolerated.

The danger of apostasy from faith in Christ begins with "drifting," which in Hebrews 2:1 is described as not paying due attention to the message of who Jesus Christ is and what he has achieved. It seems to involve a spiritual laziness or malaise that has set in, stunting the spiritual growth and maturity of these believers. They apparently have not grown in their understanding beyond the fundamentals of the Christian faith (6:1–3) and are therefore in danger of falling away. A deeper understanding of God's redemptive work in Christ, namely, that it supersedes all of the previous practice of Judaism, is necessary to face up to the challenging circumstances in which the readers find themselves. Without greater spiritual maturity, the risk of falling away becomes great—and without the possibility of a second repentance and return to Christ. Note, however, that the author of Hebrews expects his original readers to respond to his explanation of Christ's superiority and to press on in their spiritual growth (6:11–12). He does not want them "to become lazy" in their faith. In other words, after enthusiastically professing Christ and even enduring some hardship for the gospel, these people need to avoid spiritual laziness and complacency by persevering in their spiritual growth. They need to be diligent "to the very end" in order to inherit what is promised in Christ, eternal life (6:11–12).

Mary Evans Picture Library

The book of Hebrews identifies Jesus as both the true and final high priest and sacrifice, whose redemptive work was foreshadowed by Israel's high priests and sacrificial system.

All of this can, and should, be applied to Christian believers today. When life's challenges press in, knowledge of Christ that goes beyond the fundamentals is called for. It takes a maturing Christian who is diligent for spiritual growth to deal with such questions as, Why is there so much evil in the world? Why do horrific things happen to good people? How do I deal with my ongoing temptations and yielding to sin? It would be untrue to the New Testament to tell someone who has just prayed the sinner's prayer that no further involvement on their part is needed. To make a decision for Christ means to adopt an ongoing stance of faith throughout one's life, not just for a momentary utterance.

Does a Christian ever become so mature that the danger of apostasy is past? The warnings in Hebrews seem to suggest not, for the journey toward realized salvation is pictured as a lifelong race stretched before the believer. Salvation from God's wrath is fully realized by definition only after God has judged, which is an event that occurs in the afterlife.

Does this mean that Hebrews teaches that a Christian can lose his or her salvation at some point along the way? Is there no such thing as the eternal security of the believer? These are theological questions not directly or unambiguously answered by the book of Hebrews. And accordingly, from the earliest days of the church, interpreters have debated the answers to those questions. During times of harsh persecution and martyrdom in the ancient church, many professing Christians recanted their faith to avoid suffering or death. Later the church had to decide whether such people could be received back into the fellowship of the church, which led to the Donatist schism. Even where reinstatement was permitted, it often involved a long process for full reinstatement that could take many years. The lapsed Christian would first be allowed to beg for the prayers of those going into the church assembly; eventually he could kneel inside the church building during services, and then sometime later stand with the congregation. Only after such a long process could he take Holy Communion and be fully reinstated. But the Donatists believed that the church was responsible for enforcing the warnings against apostasy and should permanently bar lapsed Christians from reinstatement. (See Augustine, *On the Correction of the Donatists.*) This, of course, led to great controversy.

View of a gold/silver crown of laurel wreaths that was given to a victor. It dates to the Classical Period — fourth century B.C. In ancient Greece, a laurel wreath — not of gold(!) — was given to winners of athletic contests.

Laurel wreath, Mycenaean/National Archaeological Museum, Athens, Greece/The Bridgeman Art Library

After two thousand years of reflection on such issues, different theological traditions have arrived at somewhat different conclusions about the warnings in Hebrews. This is one topic about which your instructor may wish to provide additional material on those distinctives of the denomination or tradition in which you are studying. Or you may wish to consult commentaries on these verses for a deeper understanding of the issues involved (see Going Further at the end of chapter 1). What follows is a summary of core questions raised by these passages in Hebrews and the general answers given by different traditions.[12]

Are the people described genuine Christian believers?

The question of whether Hebrews teaches that Christians can lose salvation depends on whether those described truly are Christians. Hebrews 6:4–5 describes those at risk of falling away without possibility of repentance as those who have:

- once been enlightened
- tasted the heavenly gift
- shared in the Holy Spirit
- tasted the goodness of the word of God and the powers of the coming age

The question is whether such people are genuine Christian believers. Or, to put it differently, does God, who can see the heart, know these are people who have truly believed and have his Spirit within them (ontological perspective)? Or are they professing believers who from every outward appearance would be judged by other people to be Christian (phenomenological perspective)? The answer to this question generally differs between Arminian interpreters and Calvinist/Reformed interpreters. Some interpreters, typically in the Arminian tradition, see this as a description of true, genuine believers whose salvation is based primarily on the freedom of the human will. If they decide to leave the faith, their freely chosen decision disqualifies them from God's grace. Those in the Calvinist/Reformed tradition generally see a greater role for God's sovereign election of those who

12. For an in depth discussion of these passages from the perspectives of a classical Arminian view, a classical Reformed view, a Wesleyan Arminian view, and a "moderate" Reformed view, see Herbert W. Bateman, ed., *Four Views on the Warning Passages in Hebrews* (Grand Rapids: Kregel, 2007). As this book shows, even within a given theological tradition, there are a number of variations on the same theme.

will be saved and hold to the doctrine of the perseverance of true believers who constitute the elect, defined as those who will be saved at the final judgment.[13] Such Reformed interpreters, and others who believe in the doctrine of eternal security, see this as a description of the outward appearance of all professing Christians, some of whom may turn out eventually to be apostates. And so the question becomes whether an apostate was a true, regenerated believer who then lost his salvation or was not ever saved but only participated, even if sincere at the time, in the life of the church.

There is good biblical warrant to believe in the eternal security of the true believer (e.g., Rom. 8:28, 39). But a biblical understanding of eternal security must be based on the principle of perseverance *in holiness*, not on a delusion that salvation is a ticket to heaven despite one's ongoing attitudes and behaviors. The Reformed doctrine speaks of the perseverance of the saints in holiness. In other words, only those who persevere in holiness show themselves to be truly regenerate.

How can the description be phenomenological if the author of Hebrews addresses his readers as "brothers and sisters"? Wouldn't the inerrancy and infallibility of Scripture mean that they must be true believers? Not necessarily. The author addresses them as "brothers and sisters" and ascribes to them the experiences of a true believer because he is presenting a sermon that treats his audience according to their self-profession as Christians without being able to truly see their hearts, just as preachers must do today.

13. Perseverance of the saints is the *P* in the TULIP acronym often used to describe the five points of Calvinism.

Chapter XVII of the Westminster Confession of Faith

Of the Perseverance of the Saints

I. They, whom God has accepted in His Beloved, effectually called, and sanctified by His Spirit, can neither totally nor finally fall away from the state of grace, but shall certainly persevere therein to the end, and be eternally saved.

II. This perseverance of the saints depends not upon their own free will, but upon the immutability of the decree of election, flowing from the free and unchangeable love of God the Father; upon the efficacy of the merit and intercession of Jesus Christ, the abiding of the Spirit, and of the seed of God within them, and the nature of the covenant of grace: from all which arises also the certainty and infallibility thereof.

III. Nevertheless, they may, through the temptations of Satan and of the world, the prevalency of corruption remaining in them, and the neglect of the means of their preservation, fall into grievous sins; and, for a time, continue therein: whereby they incur God's displeasure, and grieve His Holy Spirit, come to be deprived of some measure of their graces and comforts, have their hearts hardened, and their consciences wounded; hurt and scandalize others, and bring temporal judgments upon themselves.*

*www.reformed.org/documents/wcf_with_proofs/ (accessed August 6, 2009)

Both the Reformed and Arminian perspectives take into account the observable experience that sometimes even those who seem to be true believers do in fact leave the Christian church, sometimes drawn away by a sinful lifestyle, sometimes to other religions. And sometimes after a season of unbelief and sin or a sojourn in another religion, people do return to the church. Should we think of them as saved, then not saved, then saved again? Or as true believers who "fall into grievous sins" for a time? Or as not truly saved until they sustain a lifetime of perseverance in holiness?

Such unanswerable questions show that one human being cannot know the heart of another as only God can. Only God knows if someone is truly and eternally lost. Therefore, Hebrews teaches that professing Christians must "encourage one another daily, as long as it is called 'Today,' so that none of you may be hardened by sin's deceitfulness" (3:13).

In both the Arminian and Calvinist/Reformed views, Jesus knew some people would profess faith at one point in their lives but later recant. He speaks of them being like the seed that falls on rocky ground or is choked out by thorns (Matt. 13:20–22; Mark 4:16–19; Luke 8:13–14). Despite promising appearances at first profession of faith, they do not come to their fullest end and at some time fall away from Christian faith.

Jesus taught about the kingdom of God in parables of images that would have been familiar to his first-century listeners. The preaching of the gospel is likened to the scattering of seed by a sower.

Is the consequence described eternal damnation or something less?

The statement that it is "impossible" for such people "to be brought back to repentance" (Heb. 6:6) and that "no sacrifice for sins is left" but only fearful expectation of judgment (10:26), also raises questions. A minority position interprets these consequences to be during the earthly life only and not referring to eternal separation from God. This view is based primarily on the analogy with the disobedient wilderness generation (3:7–4:11), who were condemned to wander until they died without entering the Promised Land. Those who hold this view assume that the wilderness generation was fully punished in its earthly wanderings and went on to enjoy an afterlife with God, even though this point is not addressed in the relevant texts and rests on other theological assumptions.

Some of the earliest interpreters in the ancient church took Hebrews 6:4 to mean that any sins committed after one was baptized could not receive forgiveness.[14] This motivated many believers to delay baptism until as close to death as possible. Eventually, this line of interpretation developed into the understanding that baptism is a one-time ritual that must not be repeated, a view that is still held today especially in the Orthodox church.[15] Therefore, even following a season of sin, a Christian cannot be rebaptized as readmission to fellowship.

14. Erik M. Heen and Philip D. W. Krey, eds., *Hebrews*, ACCS 10 (Downers Grove, Ill.: InterVarsity, 2005), 83.

15. Dmitri Royster, *The Epistle to the Hebrews: A Commentary* (Crestwood, N.Y.: St. Vladimir's Seminary Press, 2003), 89.

© PhotoStock-Israel/Alamy

Baptism in water has been an important ritual for Christians from the very beginning, but the mode of baptism and its significance has been understood in different ways by various groups of Christians throughout church history.

Most interpreters of the Protestant tradition do take these statements to refer to eternal separation from God based on their context within Hebrews. The point is that God has given his last word to humankind in the Son, Jesus Christ, and that there is no salvation apart from Christ. Therefore, those who wander from the faith to the point of repudiating their Christian belief are in no better place than people who have never professed Christ and therefore remain under God's judgment for sin. The difference between them is that previously professing Christians cannot be brought back to "repentance" and presumably will not be among those who escape God's judgment. This may be perhaps because they have believed just enough, just long enough, to be inoculated, so to speak, against the gospel, and tragically will never again desire to be reconciled to God in Christ. Or putting this in a different perspective, it may be that God's Spirit will not again convict them of their sin, so that they will find no opportunity before death to be reconciled with God. It is especially dangerous for individuals to realize they are not right with God but to believe that they can repent and be reconciled whenever they wish to be at some future time. Circumstances might work against them; perhaps they will meet a sudden and untimely death that doesn't afford an opportunity for repentance. The sad case of Esau is given as an example of someone who despised his covenant birthright and later came to the hard realization that "he could not change what he had done" (Heb. 12:17, referring to Gen. 25:29–34). Whether Esau suffered eternal or just earthly consequences, the point Hebrews makes is that once we do something it cannot be undone and consequences will follow.

> "It is out of the question, he is saying, for those who have approached all-holy baptism … to make their approach again and be granted another baptism."
>
> Theodoret of Cyr (c. AD 393–c. 457)

Dealing with the fear of apostasy.

Apostasy is akin to "the unforgivable sin," which in the **Synoptic Gospels** Jesus calls "blasphemy against the Holy Spirit" (Matt. 12:31; cf. Heb. 10:29). The reason the unforgivable sin is unforgivable is that by rejecting the work of Christ as something other than the gracious work of God, one cuts oneself off from the only means of forgiveness and the only salvation that God offers. It is, therefore, the only sin that cannot be forgiven, at least as long as one continues to reject Christ. Saul's conversion in Acts 9 is sometimes given as evidence that people who reject Christ for a time and even murder his followers can nevertheless repent and even become, as in Saul's case, a great leader of the Christian church. Apostasy as presented in Hebrews is different only in that the apostate will never be reconciled to God.

Readers of this book might be preparing for the ministry, where inevitably some worried person will come asking if they have committed the unforgivable sin. Or perhaps you are thinking of a terrible sin you have committed and are wondering if you have become apostate. The first point in answer to such questions is that anyone worried about committing the unforgivable sin or becoming apostate hasn't done so. Apostates are by definition hardened to God and arrogant toward what he has said by the Son. Whether they will persist and die in that state only the Lord knows for sure, and so it is the job of the pastor or teacher to continue to present opportunities for repentance without giving up on someone.

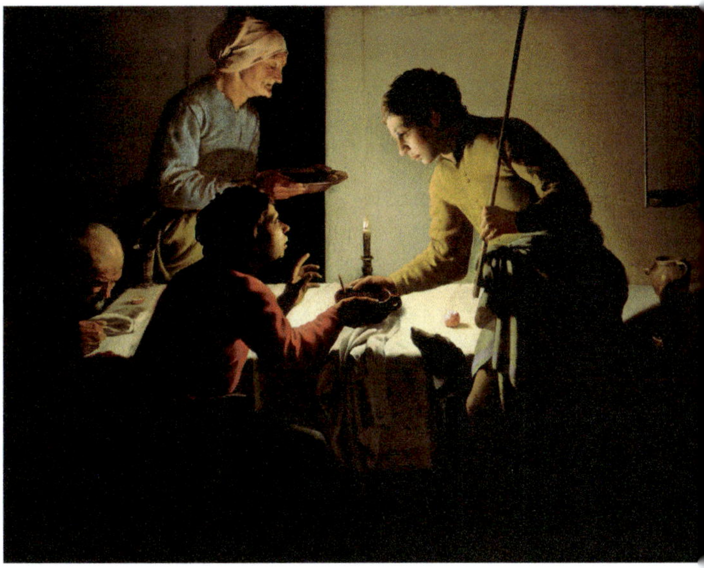

Bildarchiv Preussischer Kulturbesitz/Art Resource, NY

Esau selling his birthright, by Hendrik Terbrugghen (1588–1629).

The book of Hebrews is an exhortation to Christian believers to pay attention to their own spiritual state. There should be no presumption on the grace of God — no thought that, because I'm saved, a little sin is okay. There is a difference between the temptations and sins that every believer struggles with throughout life and apostasy, but an uncaring attitude about one's sin is a first step toward apostasy. The warnings seem to progress in their intensity, beginning with a warning against "drifting" (2:1), then to a warning against "falling away" (6:6), and finally to a state where only judgment is expected (10:27). There is a difference between "backsliding" and apostasy, but everyone who apostatizes starts in that direction by backsliding (though the converse is not true; not everyone who backslides will inevitably apostatize). But there can be no assurance of one's salvation as long as one is sinning. The nagging potential for apostasy will always haunt as long as one is knowingly committing sin.

The book of Hebrews warns that it is a grave mistake to see how close to a sinful life one can live and still be a Christian. The ambiguity present in these warnings that has led to long debates throughout church history is no doubt intentional. The call is for believers to throw off the sin that so easily entangles and to run the race marked out with perseverance. To stay in a spiritually immature state under the delusion that it is okay to sin is like walking backward in the dark toward the cliff of apostasy. The author of Hebrews, both God himself as the ultimate author and the human author, whoever that may be, want Christians to be warned in terms that do not permit either an easy legalism or a cheap grace. Believers are called to nothing less than living with eyes fixed on Christ from conversion to death.

The great cloud of witnesses.

Hebrews 12:1 – 3 is a key verse for this theme of perseverance in holiness. Following on chapter 11, which is a long list of Old Testament believers commended for their faith, verse 12:1 begins by mentioning that "great cloud of witnesses."

> Therefore, since we are surrounded by such a great cloud of witnesses, let us throw off everything that hinders and the sin that so easily entangles. And let us run with perseverance the race marked out for us, fixing our eyes on Jesus, the pioneer and perfecter of faith. For the joy set before him he endured the cross, scorning its shame, and sat down at the right hand of the throne of God. Consider him who endured such opposition from sinners, so that you will not grow weary and lose heart. (vv. 1–3)

This description might bring to mind the image of a stadium filled with those believers who have passed on to glory observing and cheering on the "race" of Christians alive today. "Cloud" is a literal translation of a classical idiom in literary Greek that simply meant a large number of witnesses and so should not be taken as an image of people hovering around or above us in their heavenly existence.[16] Scripture does not teach that those who are now with the Lord in glory can see back into the affairs of people on earth. It is not because your late grandmother in heaven might see you sinning that you should run with perseverance in faith. No, the great cloud of witnesses refers to the testimony by example that those Old Testament believers mentioned in Hebrews 11 have left for us. They have witnessed by their actions throughout their lives to their faith in the great promises of God, giving us hope that it is possible for human beings to finish the race and on that great day to be made perfect with all the saints (Heb. 11:40).

CHAPTER SUMMARY

The book of Hebrews is at once a great assurance of the certainty of salvation for those whose faith is in Jesus Christ and the greatest of warnings about not taking that salvation for granted. As in other books of the New Testament, soteriology in Hebrews is based on the objective, historical death and resurrection of Jesus and presents the theological significance of that objective reality. It then underscores the subjective and individual role of the believer's faith in what Jesus Christ has already done and calls Christians to obediently live out that faith for their whole lives, in every season and circumstance. Though at times the faithful Christian life may seem easy, and at other times impossible, the book of Hebrews lists many who, without benefit of the completed revelation of God, nevertheless ran the race and kept the faith. People living in the Christian era have the advantage of the full story, which is also the final story. How one responds to what God has spoken by the Son determines one's eternal destiny.

---

16. F. F. Bruce, *The Epistle to the Hebrews*, rev. ed., NICNT (Grand Rapids: Eerdmans, 1990), 333.

KEY TERMS

apostasy	Calvinism	Reformed
Arminianism	eschatological	sanctification
atonement	justification	soteriology
backsliding	perfect/perfection	

QUESTIONS FOR REVIEW OR DISCUSSION

1. Why does everyone die?
2. On what basic concept is soteriology in Hebrews grounded?
3. What does it mean that Jesus became "perfect" through what he suffered?
4. Should Christians observe a Sabbath day? Give reasons why and why not.
5. What is apostasy? What are the questions concerning the warnings in Hebrews that are answered differently by the theological traditions?
6. From a pastoral perspective, how would you minister to someone who fears he or she has become apostate?

GOING FURTHER

Attridge, Harold W. *The Epistle to the Hebrews*. Hermeneia. Philadelphia: Fortress Press, 1989.

Bateman, Herbert W. *Four Views on the Warning Passages in Hebrews*. Grand Rapids: Kregel, 2007.

Bruce, F. F. *The Epistle to the Hebrews*. Rev. ed. NICNT. Grand Rapids: Eerdmans, 1990.

Laansma, Jon. *"I Will Give You Rest": The Rest Motif in the New Testament with Special Reference to Mt 11 and Heb 3–4*. WUNT. Tübingen: Mohr Siebeck, 1997.

Lindars, Barnabas. *The Theology of the Letter to the Hebrews*. New Testament Theology. Cambridge: Cambridge University Press, 1991.

McKnight, Scot. "The Warning Passages of Hebrews: A Formal Analysis and Theological Conclusions." *TJ* 13 (1992): 21–59.

Rhee, Victor (Sung-Yul). *Faith in Hebrews: Analysis within the Context of Christology, Eschatology, and Ethics*. Studies in Biblical Literature 19. New York: Peter Lang, 2001.

Schenck, Kenneth. *Understanding the Book of Hebrews: The Story behind the Sermon*. Louisville: Westminster John Knox, 2003.

Silva, Moisés. "Perfection and Eschatology in Hebrews." *WTJ* 39 (1976): 60–71.

Thomas, C. Adrian. *A Case for Mixed-Audience with Reference to the Warning Passages in the Book of Hebrews*. New York: Peter Lang, 2008.

Vos, Geerhardus. *The Teaching of the Epistle to the Hebrews*. Phillipsburg, N.J.: Presbyterian and Reformed, 1956.

PART 2

Letters from Jesus' Brothers

CHAPTER 5

Introducing the Letter from James

PROPHET AND SAGE OF THE KINGDOM OF GOD

Your Goals for This Chapter

- To be able to evaluate the evidence for the authorship of the **epistle** known as James.
- To discuss how the evidence relates to the issues of when and to whom the letter was written.
- To identify the major themes of the book.
- To reflect on how this letter to Christians who lived so long ago still speaks into the lives of believers today.

WHY THE BOOK OF JAMES IS IMPORTANT TO YOU

Jesus himself wrote no books of the New Testament, but the letters from James and Jude are likely to have come from Jesus' own half brothers. That alone should make this book of special interest to Christians. This letter provides a glimpse into how a brother of Jesus came to understand the significance of Jesus' life and the role Jesus' family played in the early church. And a recent find by an antiquities dealer in Israel has put the brother of Jesus into the center of an international controversy over the authenticity of the **ossuary** that bears the inscription "James, son of Joseph, brother of Jesus."

Beyond its historical interest, the letter from James indicates the wrestling that occurred as the apostles came to understand the relationship of the new covenant of Christ's blood to the old covenant of Sinai as expressed in the Ten Commandments and applied by the Old Testament prophets. This is perhaps its greatest importance for Christians today—to understand the ethical basis for Christian living, especially the role of the Old Testament. Its controversial statement "You see that a person is considered righteous by what they do and not by faith alone" (James 2:24) seems to contradict not only the great Reformation principle of salvation by faith alone, but the apostle Paul's teaching on justification by faith alone (e.g., Rom. 3:28, "For we maintain that a person is justified by faith apart from the works of the law"). Moreover, the action James has in mind is largely concerned with issues of social justice, an agenda that has historically been a defining characteristic of liberal Protestantism. It is safe to say that no Christian who is serious about living out his or her faith can ignore this intriguing and challenging letter.

Key Verses

1:1: James, a servant of God and of the Lord Jesus Christ, To the twelve tribes scattered among the nations: Greetings.

1:5: If any of you lacks wisdom, you should ask God, who gives generously to all without finding fault, and it will be given to you.

1:22–25: Do not merely listen to the word, and so deceive yourselves. Do what it says. Anyone who listens to the word but does not do what it says is like someone who looks at his face in a mirror and, after looking at himself, goes away and immediately forgets what he looks like. But whoever looks intently into the perfect law that gives freedom, and continues in it—not forgetting what they have heard, but doing it—they will be blessed in what they do.

2:24: You see that a person is considered righteous by what they do and not by faith alone.

3:13: Who is wise and understanding among you? Let them show it by their good life, by deeds done in the humility that comes from wisdom.

Challenges Presented by the Book of James

- Its paucity of references to Jesus.
- The prima facie lack of a unifying theme.
- The relationship of James's view of saving faith to that of the apostle Paul.
- Its convicting message about the rich and the poor.

CHAPTER OUTLINE

I. Who Wrote the Epistle of James?
   A. "James" in the New Testament
   B. Internal Evidence That the Letter Was Written by James the Just
   C. James as a **Pseudonymous** Writing
   D. Evidence of Authorship outside the Letter
      1. From the New Testament
      2. Beyond the New Testament
   E. The Date of James
II. The Genre, Original Recipients, and Purpose of the Letter of James
   A. Genre
   B. Original Recipients
   C. Purpose of the Letter of James
III. The Major Themes of James
   A. Testing and Trials
   B. Poverty and Oppression
   C. Favoritism
   D. Godly Speech
   E. Faith and Good Deeds
   F. The Law
IV. The Text and Canonicity of James
   A. The Greek Text of James
   B. The Canonicity of James
V. Structure and Outline of the Book of James

Please read the book of James in one sitting before reading this chapter.

The book of the New Testament that comes to us as a letter from James is intriguing. Tradition holds that it was written by the half brother (or cousin) of Jesus, and yet it mentions Jesus only twice (James 1:1 and 2:1). For this reason, the great Protestant Reformer Martin Luther discounted the value of James's letter for the church. Furthermore, instead of being written to a Christian church in a certain city, as the apostle Paul's letters were, it is addressed "To the twelve tribes scattered among the nations" (James 1:1), raising questions about the ethnicity of the original recipients of the letter. The letter is concerned with how to live wisely under the new covenant, especially when facing trials and temptations. In this chapter we will consider the introductory issues of author, date, original audience, purpose, and genre, as well as introduce the major themes and issues concerning the book of James.

WHO WROTE THE EPISTLE OF JAMES?

The first verse of the book of James is in the form of the standard Hellenistic letter address:

> James, a servant of God and of the Lord Jesus Christ,
> To the twelve tribes scattered among the nations:
> Greetings.

The book of James is clearly a letter that presents itself as being written from a man named James who considers himself to be a "servant" of God (Gk. *doulous tou theou*) and of the Lord Jesus Christ. In its historical context, such a descriptor would have been understood as a reference to the prophetic role, for beginning with Moses the prophets were called "servants of God/the Lord." The content of the letter is consistent with that self-designation as a prophet of both God and of Jesus Christ.

The Anglicized name "James," which is *Iakōbos* in the Greek text, obscures an interesting connection to the Old Testament. *Iakōbos* is the Greek spelling of the Hebrew name Jacob, which is of course the name of Israel's great patriarch whose twelve sons became the tribes of ancient Israel. Because of the celebrity of the patriarch Jacob, many Jewish men bore that name throughout history.

Because the letter is from "Jacob" to "the twelve tribes," the idea arose that the book of James might have begun as a pre-Christian, Jewish **pseudepigraphal** writing that was then picked up and Christianized by the insertion of two references to Jesus. But this view fails to recognize the underlying teaching of Jesus that informs the letter throughout. (See chapter 7.) Others have looked for an analogy between the structure and content of James with Genesis 49, where the patriarch Jacob addressed each of the twelve tribes, or to the pseudepigraphal text, *Testaments of the Twelve Patriarchs*, that more fully developed the biblical material. However, attempts to segment James into twelve parts and relate each of them to some idea in the corresponding passage of the *Testaments* or Genesis 49 have yielded only isolated lexical parallels that have not been convincing. Rather, the reference to the twelve tribes of Israel in a Christian text reflects the belief of its author that the eschatological hope for the regathering of Israel's tribes was now taking place in those who had believed in Jesus as the promised Messiah. This message of eschatological fulfillment corroborates James's self-designation as a "servant," or prophet, of God and of Jesus Christ.

"James" in the New Testament

The name occurs forty-two times in the New Testament, apparently referring to several different men:

- James, one of the twelve disciples of Jesus and a son of Alphaeus (Matt. 10:3; Mark 3:18; Luke 6:15; Acts 1:13)
- James the "Younger," whose mother's name was Mary (Matt. 27:56; Mark 15:40; 16:1; Luke 24:10). He may have been the same James who is elsewhere called the son of Alphaeus.
- James, whose son Judas (not Judas Iscariot) was among Jesus' twelve disciples (Luke 6:16; Acts 1:13)
- James, son of Zebedee and brother of John. Both John and James, sons of Zebedee, were in the innermost circle of Jesus' disciples (Matt. 4:21; 10:2; 17:1; Mark 1:19, 29; 3:17; 5:37; 9:2; 10:35, 41; 13:3; 14:33; Luke 5:10; 6:15; 8:51; 9:28, 54; Acts 1:13; 12:2). This James died a martyr's death at the hands of Herod Agrippa I about **AD** 44, according to Acts 12:2.
- James, the brother of the New Testament writer Jude (Jude 1:1), who may also be the half brother of Jesus. He may also be the James who came to be known as "the Just," whom the apostle Paul identifies as the (half) brother of Jesus (Gal. 1:19) and possibly brother of Jude (Matt. 13:55; Mark 6:3; Acts 12:17; 15:13; 21:18; 1 Cor. 15:7; Gal. 1:19; 2:9, 12). James the Just became the leader of the church in Jerusalem after the apostle Peter was miraculously rescued from prison and "left for another place" (Acts 12:17–19). According to Josephus, this James who was the leader of the Jerusalem church was martyred before AD 62 (*Ant.* 10.9.200).

Given the evidence of the New Testament, it is difficult to say to how many different men named James it refers. But because of the number of possibilities, any theory that this letter is attributed to some other man named James who is otherwise unknown seems highly implausible. The author was evidently well known to the original recipients of the letter; his authority stood even without elaboration of who he was beyond his personal name.

In the excitement that followed the discovery of the Dead Sea Scrolls in the mid-twentieth century, scholars looked for connections between the scrolls and early Christianity. The idea that some of the scrolls actually came from the early Christian community

Josephus on the Death of James, Brother of Jesus

"Festus was now dead ... so Ananus, the High-Priest, assembled the Sanhedrin ... and brought before them the brother of Jesus, who was called Christ, whose name was James, and some others; and when he had formed an accusation against them as breakers of the law, he delivered them to be stoned."

Josephus, *Antiquities* 20.9.1

Jerome's Version of the Death of James

The fifth-century church father Jerome gave a detailed description of the death of James, leader of the Jerusalem church.

Ananus the high priest, the youthful son of Ananus of the priestly class,... assembled a council and publicly tried to force James to deny that Christ is the Son of God. When he refused, Ananus ordered him to be stoned. Cast down from a pinnacle of the temple, his legs broken, but still half alive, raising his hands to heaven, he said, "Lord, forgive them for they know not what they do." Then, struck on the head by a club,... he died.

St. Jerome, *De viris illustribus* (*On Illustrious Men*) 2.7 – 8

led by James the Just, and that James may actually have been the Teacher of Righteousness mentioned in the sectarian Qumran documents, has not enjoyed a wide following.[1]

Internal Evidence That the Letter Was Written by James the Just

Since in 1:1 the author of this epistle identifies himself simply as "James" with no further identification (e.g., James of Jerusalem or James, one of the Twelve, et al.), only James, the son of Zebedee who was one of the Twelve, or James, the leader of the Jerusalem church, would have been sufficiently well known to the early church. Because of the concerns of the letter, most scholars do not believe it could have been written before AD 44, which was the year James, son of Zebedee, was killed. Although certainty eludes us, it seems more likely that this letter was written by James the leader of the church in Jerusalem, who was the half brother of Jesus, martyred about AD 62. He likely succeeded Peter as leader of the Jerusalem church about AD 44 when, after James, son of Zebedee, was martyred, Peter "left for another place" (Acts 12:17). As the first twelve chapters of the book of Acts presents him, Peter seems to have emerged as the spokesman for Jesus' followers in the days following the crucifixion (e.g., Acts 1:15 – 22; 2:14 – 41). But James, brother of Jesus, was considered the first "bishop" of the Jerusalem church according to the list given by Eusebius (*Hist. eccl.* 4.5.1 – 4; Eusebius anachronistically applied the title *bishop*, which was current at his time, to the context of the earliest church).[2] Acts 12:17 suggests that Peter recognized James's leadership, whether actual or potential, when he singled him out before leaving Jerusalem.[3]

Some Christians believe that Jesus' mother, Mary, remained a virgin for life, and therefore Jesus could not have had siblings. The Protestant church has no such doctrine

1. See Robert Eisenman, *James the Brother of Jesus: The Key to Unlocking the Secrets of Early Christianity and the Dead Sea Scrolls* (New York: Penguin, 1997). For a critique of Eisenman, see Philip R. Davies, "James in the Qumran Scrolls," in *James the Just and Christian Origins*, ed. Bruce Chilton and Craig A. Evans, NovTsup 98 (Leiden: Brill, 1999); John Painter, *Just James: The Brother of Jesus in History and Tradition*, Studies on Personalities of the New Testament (Columbia: University of South Carolina Press, 1997).

2. In fact, the family of Jesus may have had a continuing role in the leadership of the church in Judea. See Richard Bauckham, *Jude and the Relatives of Jesus in the Early Church* (Edinburgh: T&T Clark, 1990).

3. See John Painter, "James and Peter: Models of Leadership," in *The Mission of James, Peter, and Paul: Tensions in Early Christianity*, ed. Bruce Chilton and Craig Evans; NovTSup 115 (Leiden: Brill, 2005), 143 – 209, who argues that James was the first leader of the Jerusalem church and that Peter was pioneer missionary of the Jerusalem church.

of Mary's perpetual virginity.[4] There is no reason to think that after Jesus was born, she did not have normal relations with Joseph that would have led to the birth of other children. In that scenario, James would have been legally a full brother of Jesus, though a half brother biologically. Interpreters in Christian traditions believing Mary remained a virgin after Jesus' birth seek a different understanding of the brothers (Gk. *adelphoi*) and sisters (Gk. *adelphai*) mentioned in Matthew 12:46–47; 13:55–56; Mark 3:32; 6:3; and Luke 8:19–20. The discussion is ancient. Some follow Jerome, who argued in *Against Helvidius* (*Helv.*) that the reference should be understood more loosely as relatives such as cousins, though there is no justification for this view in the usage of the Greek word.[5] Helvidius had argued along the line of what Protestants later believed, that Mary had other children with Joseph after Jesus was born. Another ancient understanding is represented by Epiphanius, who understood Jesus' siblings to be Joseph's children by a previous marriage. If Helvidius was correct, then James was a younger brother of Jesus; if Epiphanius was correct, then James was an older stepbrother.[6] Since James the Just lived for about thirty years after Jesus died, if he is Jesus' brother, it might be more plausible that he was younger than Jesus.

The identification of James the Just as author of this letter also fits with what we know of him from the book of Acts, though this depends on one's view of the historical reliability of that book. James's language in this epistle has several parallels with the speech of James as found in Acts 15:23–29:[7]

- The unusual collocation of the Greek words *epikaleō* and *onoma* ("the name called over you/them") is found both in James 2:7 and Acts 15:17.
- The expression "listen, my brothers" occurs both in James 2:5 and Acts 15:13.
- Several individual Greek words occur in both the epistle and James's speech in Acts 15, though some occur in other parts of Acts as well:

  chairein ("greetings") in James 1:1 and Acts 15:23
  episkeptomai ("to visit, to care for") in James 1:27 and Acts 15:14
  epistrephō ("to turn to") in James 5:19–20 and Acts 15:19
  tērein heauton ("keep yourselves/yourself") in James 1:27 and Acts 15:29
  agapētos ("beloved") in James 1:16, 19 and Acts 15:25

Furthermore, James 5:7 refers to the autumn and spring rains that characterize Palestine's climate, making the reference most apt for one, such as James the Just, who would have been familiar with life in Palestine.

In addition, the book of James assumes a great deal of Jesus' teaching that is found in the **Synoptic Gospels**, especially Matthew, but not in the *form* the teaching is found there.

4. For a survey on how this issue has been handled in the history of the wider church, see William Barclay, *The Letters of James and Peter*, rev. ed. (Philadelphia: Westminster, 1976), 14–20.

5. See Bruce Chilton, "James, Jesus' Brother," in *The Face of New Testament Studies*, ed. Scot McKnight and Grant R. Osborne (Grand Rapids: Baker Academic, 2004), 254–55.

6. For a more extensive discussion of these three views, see John Painter, "Who Was James?" in *The Brother of Jesus: James the Just and His Mission*, ed. Bruce Chilton and Jacob Neusner (Louisville: Westminster John Knox, 2001), 13–23.

7. Donald Guthrie, *New Testament Introduction*, 4th ed. (Downers Grove, Ill.: InterVarsity, 1990), 729.

(See chapter 6.) This suggests that James was knowledgeable of the early oral tradition of Jesus, suggesting a date earlier than when the Gospels were composed in the second half of the first century. This evidence is consistent with a date in the late 40s or 50s.

Beyond this internal evidence, we know that the church in Jerusalem suffered through great famine and poverty in the 50s. The apostle Paul gathered financial assistance for the church in Jerusalem (1 Cor. 16:1 – 3). This historical setting accords well with the concerns for social justice within the church communities that is of great importance in the book of James.

James as a Pseudonymous Writing

In the mid-nineteenth century, New Testament scholarship led by F. C. Baur and the Tübingen school tended to date the books of the New Testament well after the lifetimes of the apostles. On such a late dating of James and other New Testament epistles, the only explanation for authorship was that someone in the second century wrote a pseudonymous letter using the name of James. A case for pseudonymous authorship of James (and other New Testament books as well) was built on the claims that (1) the Greek of the epistle was too good to have been written by a Palestinian Jew for whom Greek would have been a second language; (2) that the author of James doesn't identify himself as Jesus' brother (cf. Jude 1:1a); (3) that certain words found in James are terms that **Gnostics** used in the second century; (4) that the book was slow to be accepted into the canon; (5) that what the epistle says about faith and works is a correction to what the apostle Paul says and therefore must have been written after Paul's letters were in circulation, which as some argue, would have been after the death of James in AD 62. In fact, one scholar has recently argued that the book of James (and 2 Peter) was actually composed by an anonymous second-century author (at the time the canonical books were being bound together) to counterbalance Paul's writings.[8]

First, the claim that the Greek is too good rests on assumptions about how well Palestinian Jews could master Greek as a second language. Archaeological evidence has shown that Greek was widely used not only in Galilee, but even in Jerusalem. The Council of Jerusalem (Acts 15) involved residents of Antioch who probably could not speak Aramaic or Hebrew, suggesting that the proceedings James oversaw were conducted in Greek. Because of the dominance of the Greek language and culture for the preceding two centuries, the New Testament writers were aware of and probably influenced by Hellenistic literature. Moreover, the use of an **amanuensis**, someone employed as a scribe to put an author's thoughts into writing, was widely practiced. It is possible that James or other New Testament authors dictated their letters to someone with better mastery of the Greek language. Therefore, the quality of the Greek of the epistle is not compelling evidence that it could not have originated with James the Just. However, the presence of Greek wordplays, alliteration, and catchwords are elements that would argue against this being a translation from a Semitic source.

---

8. David R. Nienhuis, *Not by Paul Alone: The Formation of the Catholic Epistle Collection and the Christian Canon* (Waco, Tex.: Baylor University Press, 2007).

Second, the fact that the author of James does not identify himself as a brother of Jesus actually argues against pseudonymous authorship. If James were the author, he would know that everyone to whom he was writing already knew of his family relationship to Jesus and would have no reason to assert it. But a pseudonymous author would more likely have stressed that fact to give added exceptional authority to his writing.

Third, the theory that words such as "the implanted word" (James 1:21, Gk. *ton emphuton logon*) and "perfect" (1:25, Gk. *teleion*) are Gnostic terms that would entail a second-century date for the letter should be rejected. Such slim lexical evidence based on words that had a much wider use through time do not indicate a distinctively Gnostic perspective and cannot bear the weight of such a theory.

Fourth, the slow acceptance of the letter into the canon of the universal church does not necessarily support the pseudonymous authorship of James, for that fact can be explained otherwise. While confusion about *which* James wrote the book would be understandable, there is no evidence that the early church thought that it was pseudonymous; if it had been known to be pseudonymous, it almost certainly would not be in the canon that has come down to us. (See the discussion of pseudonymity in the introduction.) A more likely explanation of its relatively slow acceptance into the canon of the universal church is that it was originally written to a minority population, Jewish Christians of the eastern Mediterranean regions, in the infancy of Christianity. Its relatively narrow focus and limited circulation prevented it from being widely read throughout the Greco-Roman world.

St. James the Greater, Garofalo, Benvenuto Tisi da/Palazzo Pitti, Florence, Italy/The Bridgeman Art Library

James by Garofalo, Benvenuto Tisi (1481-1559), Florence, Italy.

Fifth, to read James in engagement with the writings of the apostle Paul *assumes* that James was written later and knew of Paul's writings, especially of Galatians and/or Romans, and is, therefore, a somewhat circular argument. This argument would be compelling only if it could be established on other grounds that James must date later than AD 62. But if that dating can be discounted, then there is no reason to believe that what James says about faith and works was necessarily written in direct engagement with Paul's writings. The relationship between faith in Christ and the works of the law as they had been practiced in Jewish tradition would have been a relevant topic for any Jewish Christian from immediately after the resurrection of Jesus onward. The apostle Paul had to address the problem of Gentiles entering the Christian church, a topic not addressed in James at all. This suggests that James was written either before the issue arose or after it had been resolved. Specifically, Paul had to deal with the **Judaizers**, those Christian Jews who taught that **Gentile** Christians must be circumcised and obey the law (Acts 15:5). James does not mention **circumcision** at all.

Most recently a prominent New Testament scholar has forcefully presented evidence that James 2:14–26 exhibits a literary dependence on Galatians 2:16–3:29 and wording within 1 Corinthians, concluding that James was pseudonymously authored by someone within the Pauline community.[9] The evidence is not compelling, resting on brief **locutions** such as "Don't be deceived!" (Gk. *mēplanasthe* in James 1:16 and 1 Cor. 15:33), "the Lord of glory" (Gk. *ho kurios tēs doxēs* in James 2:1 and 1 Cor. 2:8), and the prepositional phrase "by faith alone" (Gk. *ek pisteōs monon* in James 2:24, but contrary to the argument, *ek pisteōs* occurs not only many times in Paul's writings, but also in Heb. 10:38 and the **Septuagint** of Hab. 2:4). Such parallels are not distinctive enough to conclude a literary relationship between James and the Pauline texts. Furthermore, the argument presumes that Paul's letters never circulated except as much later collections, and it confuses reception history with exegetical issues. Only after both James and Paul's writings were known to a given readership could they be read in light of each other. That question must be distinguished from the original intent and meaning of James for the original readers.

There is no compelling exegetical evidence that James wrote specifically to engage or correct Paul's teaching of justification by faith alone. (See discussion in chapter 7 about Christian wisdom and ethics in James.) More likely, he seems to have written on the topic of faith and law quite independently of the apostle Paul, whether Paul's writings were known to him or not. The theological and ethical issues faced by Jews coming to faith in Jesus as their Messiah were pressing in the earliest decades of Christianity. As the church became predominantly Gentile in later decades, and as the apostles hammered out resolutions to such issues, these concerns diminished.

But the church now has both James's and Paul's writings in the completed canon and must of course consider whether these two apostolic writers held differing or even contradictory views and how these two can be understood in relation to one another. That important question is pursued in chapter 7.

9. Margaret M. Mitchell, "The Letter of James as a Document of Paulinism?" in *Reading James with New Eyes: Methodological Reassessments of the Letter of James*, ed. Robert L. Webb and John S. Kloppenborg, Library of New Testament Studies 342 (London: T&T Clark, 2007), 75–98.

Parallels between James and 1 Peter*

James	*1 Peter*	
1:1	1:1	to the Diaspora people
1:2	1:6	trials of various kinds (Gk., *poikilois peirasmois*)
1:12	5:4	crown of life/glory promised as reward for perseverance
1:18	1:23	new birth through the word of truth/God
1:21	2:1	exhortation to be rid of evil
3:13	3:2, 4	live a good life in humility
4:1	2:11	sinful desires battle within
4:6	5:5	God opposes the proud (both quoting Prov. 3:34)
4:10	5:6	humble yourselves that God might lift you up

*With special thanks to Brandon Holiski, a graduate student in my class on James at Wheaton Graduate School in spring 2007, who compiled these parallels.

A variation on the theory of pseudonymous authorship is that most of the book of James already existed before the time of Christ as a pseudonymous Jewish text allegedly written from Jacob to the twelve tribes who descended from his twelve sons. A later believer "Christianized" it by inserting Jesus' name a couple of times, and it was eventually mistaken to be a letter from a Christian leader named James. (Remember that James is the English form of the name Jacob.) This theory is unlikely because James presents distinctively Christian teaching (see chapter 6) and has affinities with other distinctly Christian literature (e.g. 1 Peter). James refers to God, Lord, and Jesus interchangeably (an implicit **Christology**), and extensively alludes to the teachings of Jesus, especially the Sermon on the Mount, in a form that apparently predates the Synoptic Gospels.[10] (See chapter 6.) This would be more difficult to explain if James were written pseudonymously in the second century, when its author would more likely have had access to at least one of the four gospels and when the pre-gospel forms of Jesus' teaching would be less accessible.

Evidence of Authorship outside the Letter

From the New Testament.

The content of James fits well with a historical setting known from the book of Acts. Notice that the epistle was written from James "to the twelve tribes scattered [Gk. *diaspora*] among the nations" (1:1), an allusion to the **Diaspora** of the Jews that first began many centuries earlier. (See discussion of Original Recipients below.) The book of Acts describes a great persecution that broke out against the Christians in Jerusalem (8:1) that scattered (Gk. *diaspeirō*) them as far as Phoenicia, Cyprus, and Antioch (11:19). This historical setting fits the book of James aptly, for the leader of the persecuted church who remained in Jerusalem would have every reason to write to those of his flock who had been scattered by persecution. Because they had not all fled to one place, he could not write "to the church at such-and-such a place." Instead, he must address them as those who had been "scattered."

Furthermore, as mentioned above, the eastern Mediterranean regions were gripped by famine in the 50s of the first century, leading to poverty and a greater socioeconomic separation between the rich and poor. The issues of social justice concerning the needs fellow Christians had for food and clothing and the oppression of the poor by the rich would have been especially relevant given the circumstances in the last decade of James's life as leader of the impoverished Jerusalem church.

Beyond the New Testament.

The ancient books of *1 Clement* and *Shepherd of Hermas* seem to allude to the letter of James in the late first/early second century, bringing its plausible date within the lifetime of James the Just. (Of course, those who date the letter of James to the second century might claim that perhaps James is using Clement.)

Origen was the first to make clear reference to the epistle as Scripture and to the tradition that James, the brother of Jesus, is its author, though he notes that some find that

10. See Patrick J. Hartin, *James and the Q Sayings of Jesus*, JSNTSup 47 (Sheffield: Sheffield Academic, 1991), 161.

Clement of Rome Used James?

1 Clement 10.1: "Abraham, who was called 'the friend,' was found faithful when he became obedient to the words of God" (also 17:2).	James 2:23: "And the scripture was fulfilled that says, 'Abraham believed God…,' and he was called God's friend."
1 Clement 11.2: "As a result she became a pillar of salt to this day, that it might be known to all that those who are double-minded …"	James 1:8: "Such a person [the doubter blown and tossed by the wind] is double-minded and unstable in all they do" (also 4:8).
1 Clement 12.1: "Because of her faith and hospitality, Rahab the harlot was saved" (12.2–7 proceeds to tell the story of Rahab).	James 2:25: "In the same way, was not even Rahab the prostitute considered righteous for what she did when she gave lodging to the spies and sent them off in a different direction?"
1 Clement 30.2: "'For God,' it says, 'resists the proud, but gives grace to the humble.'"	James 4:6: "That is why Scripture says: 'God opposes the proud but shows favor to the humble'" (citing Prov. 3:34).
1 Clement 46.5: "Why is there strife and angry outbursts and dissension and schisms and conflict among you?"	James 4:1: "What causes fights and quarrels among you? Don't they come from your desires that battle within you?"

suspect.[11] Other earlier Christian works may have known of the epistle of James (e.g., *Hermas* and *1 Clement*), but the allusions are not substantial enough to be conclusive. Other attestations are late and sparse, which could be explained if the epistle had a late nonapostolic origin by an unknown author or if the epistle was an apostolic first-century letter but didn't circulate very widely beyond its original recipients. Because of its strongly Jewish nature and the relative minority of Jewish Christians in the church after the mid-first century, it is understandable that the letter may not have enjoyed a wide circulation.

When all the evidence is weighed, and in keeping with the tradition of the church, it seems most plausible that the epistle known as James was written by James the Just, half brother of Jesus and leader of the Jerusalem church who died about AD 62.

The Date of James

Ironically, James the Just apparently did not believe his brother Jesus was the Messiah until after Jesus' death, when he appeared to James as the resurrected Christ (1 Cor. 15:7). If the book of James was written between AD 33 and 62 (the death of Jesus and the death of James the Just, respectively), then can it be dated more exactly? As mentioned above, the

11. Brooke F. Westcott, *A General Survey of the History of the Canon of the New Testament*, 7th ed. (New York: Macmillan, 1896), 369n3; Joseph B. Mayor, *The Epistle of St. James*, Classic Commentary Library (Grand Rapids: Zondervan, 1954), lxvi–lxix.

book contains extensive allusions to the teachings of Jesus but does not quote the Synoptic Gospels, suggesting perhaps that the Gospels were not yet in circulation, or at least that they were not known to the author of James. If the **Q-document** served as a pre-Synoptic source of Jesus' teaching for James, scholars estimate it first emerged in written form in Greek around the middle of the first century.[12] However, James may have had access to an Aramaic version of the sayings of Jesus. Furthermore, there are no references to Jesus' public ministry, in which the half brother of Jesus had not personally participated. Moreover, if we allow that James was written independently of the apostle Paul's writings, it could have been written as early as the mid-40s when James the Just assumed leadership of the Jerusalem church, just before or after the Council of Jerusalem in AD 49, or any time up to his death in AD 62. If dating from the 40s, this letter from James would be the first of the New Testament books to come into existence.

12. Hartin, *James and the Q Sayings*, 226; however, see critique of Hartin by Richard Bauckham, *JTS* 44 (1993): 298–301.

Excursus: Has James's Ossuary Been Found?

In October 2002 the news headlines announced that an ancient inscription found in or near Jerusalem read in Aramaic, "James, son of Joseph, brother of Jesus." The inscription was on an ossuary, a limestone burial box that once held the bones of a person long deceased. Ossuaries were used inside tombs cut into rock to hold the bones of a previous burial so the tomb could be reused again and again by the family throughout the generations.* Since only wealthier families could afford rock-cut tombs, an authentic ossuary of James, brother of Jesus, would indicate either that James had attained sufficient wealth or that he was the beneficiary of a burial beyond his personal means, not unlike the provision of a tomb for Jesus by Joseph of Arimathea (Mark 15:43; John 19:38).

The *New York Times* reported, "If the inscription is authentic and indeed refers to Jesus of Nazareth, it would be the earliest known documentation of Jesus outside the Bible."† Although all three names were common among Jewish men of the first century, to have them appear together in this kinship order would be very strong circumstantial evidence that the box once held the bones of James the Just who

Ossuaries were used to deposit bones and so clear tombs for repeated use.

*For an excellent survey of Jewish burial practices, see Jodi Magness, "Ossuaries and the Burials of Jesus and James," *JBL* 124 (2005): 121–54. Magness argues that the James ossuary would not have held the bones of James, because the Jerusalem church was too poor to provide such a burial and because James himself was an opponent of the rich and would have been displeased with such a show of wealth.

†John Noble Wilford, "'Jesus' Inscription on Stone May Be Earliest Ever Found," *New York Times*, October 22, 2002.

continued on next page...

was martyred in Jerusalem about AD 62. The discovery has set off a long and heated debate about whether the inscription is authentic or a fraud. Paleographic analysis supported the antiquity of the inscription, concluding the fact that the writing style of the Aramaic letters was that used in the mid- to late first century. But the Israeli Antiquities Authority (IAA) declared the inscription a forgery less than a year later and arrested the antiquities dealer, Oded Golan, who first brought the box to the public's attention, charging him with the forgery of antiquities.‡

Is this the first archaeological link to Jesus and his family?

After four years of investigation, the case against Oded Golan has crumbled due to the prosecution's inability to prove that the ossuary is a fake. While the failure of the prosecution is indicative of the shortcomings of the IAA's findings, it does not prove that the inscription is not a forgery, merely that the prosecution was not able to prove beyond a reasonable doubt that it is a forgery. However, scholarly consensus at this time seems to conclude that the ossuary is authentic, ultimately because there is no counterevidence to suggest otherwise. Yet even if the inscription is authentic, dating to the first century, it is impossible to prove that "Jacob, son of Joseph, brother of Jesus" would have been an inscription unique to the family of Jesus of Nazareth.§

The inscription on this ossuary is very controversial.

An interesting footnote to the discovery of the ossuary is the damage it sustained when being shipped to the Royal Ontario Museum in November 2002, to be displayed during the annual meetings of the Society for Biblical Literature. It arrived in Toronto cracked into five pieces, with one crack running directly through the inscription!** A skilled curator at the museum was authorized to repair it for its exhibition, and I was able to see it on display at that time.

While it would be quite exciting if this ossuary were authentic, physical evidence from the life of James, brother of Jesus, it neither adds nor detracts from anything we know about Jesus or James from other sources.††

---

‡Greg Myre, "Israelis Say Burial Box of Jesus' Brother Is Fake," *New York Times*, June 19, 2003; "Israel: Burial Box Owner Arrested," *New York Times*, July 23, 2003.

§For a critique of the theory, see Magness, "Ossuaries and the Burials of Jesus and James," 121 – 54.

**For the interesting story of the discovery of the ossuary, see Hershel Shanks and Ben Witherington III, *The Brother of Jesus: The Dramatic Story and Meaning of the First Archaeological Link to Jesus and His Family* (New York: HarperSanFrancisco, 2003).

††For an assessment of this and other relevant artifacts, see Craig A. Evans, "A Fishing Boat, a House, and an Ossuary: What Can We Learn from the Artifacts?" in *The Missions of James, Peter, and Paul: Tensions in Early Christianity*, ed. Bruce Chilton and Craig Evans, NovTSup 115 (Leiden: Brill, 2005), 211 – 31.

THE GENRE, ORIGINAL RECIPIENTS, AND PURPOSE OF THE LETTER OF JAMES

Genre

The question of the genre of biblical books is seldom a simple issue, but genre is nevertheless important to ensure that we read the book as it was intended by its author as best we can. The book of James opens with a typical Hellenistic letter form, but it was not sent to an individual (cf. Philemon) or to a specific church (cf. Romans) as other letters in the New Testament. Its addressees are broadly identified as "the twelve tribes scattered among the nations" (1:1). Furthermore, the contents of the book aren't as personal as, for instance, the greetings in letters from the apostle Paul, nor do they inform readers of a specific event or other information, as many Hellenistic letters did. Moreover, the letter does not end with any closing greetings to personal acquaintances. On the other hand, the book of James is nevertheless full of first and second person pronouns (e.g., "me" and "you"), suggesting a personal connection of some type between the author and the original readers. Although it isn't a personal note in form (compared, for instance, with Philemon), it is clearly some kind of letter meant for a relatively broad audience.

One of the issues in genre identification is whether a text's genre should be determined by formal markers of structure found within the text or by its content. Formal markers are often considered determinative; for instance, stories that begin with the formal marker "Once upon a time ..." are categorized in the modern genre of fairy tale regardless of their specific stories. The genre marker functions to signal to the reader *how* the contents are to be taken. But almost any kind of text can be turned into a letter by simply adding an address. And so to say that the book of James is a letter does not completely specify its genre.

When its contents are examined, the book of James moves from one moral exhortation to another with few discourse markers or strong connections to structure its logical flow of thought. Furthermore, the reader is given no clue about what specific situation prompted James to write, which suggests that perhaps James was addressing the broad and general situation of his readers at that moment rather than a particular local crisis or event. That situation involved poverty, persecution, strained relationships—especially between the rich and poor—and questions about the nature of faith and its relationship to good deeds.

The content is clearly meant to exhort, inspire, and be taken to heart by the reader, for the book of James has a greater frequency of imperatives than any other book in the New Testament, considering its length. Some see in James's succinct statements of moral truth a similarity to Greco-Roman **paraenesis** (Lat.), a genre written by the Greek moral philosophers that takes its name from the Greek word *parainesis*, meaning "exhortation" or "advice" that warns of impending evil. Of course, paraenesis could be included in the form of a letter. And James's conversation with a hypothetical opponent in 2:18–24 is similar to the Greek diatribe, which through rhetorical questions seeks to argue a point by the personal conviction of the reader rather than by strict logic. The similarities of the letter to forms of Greco-Roman rhetoric taught in higher education have led some to reject authorship by a Palestinian, who almost certainly was not formally trained. But even those not formally trained lived in a world where familiarity with such forms was part of the oral and written culture. Therefore, such similarities do not make James distinctively Greco-Roman, and its other qualities put it soundly in the Jewish, and probably Palestinian Jewish, tradition.

It has become popular to categorize the genre of James as a wisdom book in the tradition of Jewish wisdom literature. But Jewish wisdom literature exhibits a variety of literary forms ranging from the Old Testament book of Job, to the pithy sayings of Proverbs, to the autobiography of Ecclesiastes, as well as to the apocryphal wisdom books of Sirach (also known as Ecclesiasticus) and the Wisdom of Solomon. Wisdom literature seems less like a category of genre than a way of describing the purpose for which a number of different kinds of texts were written: to instruct their readers on how to live wisely in the moral universe. Wisdom, defined as living toward life's highest good, was especially important to the Greeks, but the ancient Near East also had a rich corpus of wisdom literature. When Judaism had to interact with Greek culture, especially in the Diaspora, its wisdom literature offered another definition of life's highest good: living one's life in covenant with the creator God of Israel by being obedient to his law.

The book of James stands squarely in this tradition of Jewish wisdom literature, for it is clearly concerned with living wisely in God's kingdom announced by Jesus Christ, which emerged as a fulfillment of Old Testament prophecy. James begins his letter by inviting those who lack wisdom when facing trials to seek it from God (James 1:5), for in James's conceptual universe, only God is the source of true wisdom. He goes on in 3:13 to ask, "Who is wise and understanding among you? Let them show it by their good life, by deeds done in the humility that comes from wisdom." This question echoes the closing rhetorical question of Hosea 14:9, which is in turn an echo of Deut. 4:6.[13] And so James is indeed thinking in the same theological framework of the Jewish wisdom tradition that identified wisdom as listening to and obeying God's Torah, or Law. For this reason, the law is important to James also (1:25; 2:8–12; 4:11), but he defines the law as "the perfect law that gives freedom" and "the royal law found in Scripture" that is important. In other words, it is the Old Testament law as taught by Jesus that has become wisdom for James. (See further discussion in chapter 7.)

The book of James reads like the genre we might recognize as a sermon, preached to call its hearers to a way of life that is faithful to Christ's teaching on law, especially as found in the Sermon on the Mount (Matt. 5). Some interpreters have suggested the letter is comprised of one or more sermons that James preached, which were later written down and circulated by a subsequent redactor who was better at Greek than James is presumed to have been.

The situations James addresses are typical kinds of situations that may happen anywhere, as opposed to specific situations within a given congregation, such as the apostle Paul addresses in his letters to the Corinthians or the Thessalonians. James begins, "Consider it pure joy ... *whenever* you face trials" (1:2, emphasis added), and continues with a hypothetical tone that suggests the generality of his exhortations. "*Suppose* a man comes

13. See Karen H. Jobes, "The Minor Prophets in James, 1 & 2 Peter and Jude," in *The Minor Prophets in the New Testament*, ed. Steve Moyise and M. J. J. Menken, Library of New Testament Studies 377 (London: T&T Clark, 2009), 135–53.

into your meeting" (2:2, emphasis added); "*If* you really keep the royal law" (2:8, emphasis added); "What good is it ... *if* someone claims to have faith" (2:14, emphasis added); "Now listen, *you who say*" (4:13, emphasis added). Expressions like this suggest that James is preaching about typical circumstances that his readers may sometime face or may be experiencing at the moment. In other words, if the shoe fits, wear it.

Scholars have struggled to identify a unifying theme to these various topics James addresses, which include a call to wisdom, an exhortation to perseverance in trials, relationships between rich and poor, favoritism, the place of deeds in the life of faith, proper restraint of one's speech, discord in the community, the illusion of being in control, swearing, and prayer for healing. Broadly speaking, these topics comprise the theme of living under the new covenant, and James alludes often to both old covenant law and to the teachings of Jesus. This writer suggests that the "royal law" of wholehearted love for God and love for neighbor as oneself is the unifying theme under which all elements of James's teaching can be subsumed.

The tone of James gets stronger as the letter gets longer. By verse 4:4, it reaches an almost thunderous tone as James shouts, "You adulteresses!" (NIV, "adulterous people"). The feminine form of this word in the Greek is key to recognizing an allusion to the spiritual unfaithfulness condemned by the prophet Hosea. Moreover, James's ethical concerns echo those found in Malachi 3:5.[14] Sometimes James sounds more like the Old Testament prophets who thundered against faithless Israel and Judah, calling them to repent and turn back to God, than like a Christian preacher of the gospel of grace. But the voice of James is important for rightly understanding the Christian's responsibility to God's moral demands in the Old Testament now that Christ has come. And if this text was originally preached, even if only in the mind of the author as he wrote, it is not surprising to find within it rhetorical forms that would effectively deliver its message when heard aloud. But unlike most sermons that focus on one topic, the book of James ranges widely from topic to topic (see below). This particular quality of the book may be explained by thinking further about for whom it was originally created.

Original Recipients

Christians today who frequently read the Bible sometimes forget that each of its books was originally written to specific recipients. James addresses his thoughts to "the twelve tribes scattered among the nations" (James 1:1). What would this have meant in its original historical context? The Jewish people had been scattered away from their homeland beginning at least as far back as 722 **BC** when the Assyrians conquered the ten northern tribes of Israel and deported them to other places in the Assyrian Empire. The Babylonians later conquered Judah and Jerusalem in 586 BC, destroying the temple and carrying the people into exile. The word *diaspora* derives from the Greek verb that means "to scatter" (*diaspeirein*) and was used to refer to those Jews living, not in the Promised Land, but scattered among the nations. Nevertheless, because the temple was in Jerusalem, where God had placed his name (Deut. 12:5, 11), the holy city remained the heart of Judaism and the center of spiritual authority until it was destroyed for the last time by the Romans in AD

14. See ibid.

The eastern Mediterranean regions were the likely location of the original readers of James, though the exact destination(s) is unknown.

70 (though Jewish leaders in Egypt and in Babylon had sometimes disputed the authority of Jerusalem).

Throughout the centuries after the return from the Babylonian exile, letters from the Jewish authorities in Jerusalem were written to the Jewish communities in the Diaspora to provide spiritual guidance. James, the leader of the Jewish Christian congregation in Jerusalem, would naturally be viewed as having a similar authority for Jewish Christians living in other places. In this letter that bears his name, James is writing out of a concern for Jewish Christians scattered throughout the eastern Mediterranean world, perhaps especially those who left Jerusalem following the persecution there (Acts 8:1). Only later when James (and 1 Peter with its similar address) was read by Christians who had not been physically displaced did the metaphorical sense of being scattered around the world away from our heavenly home develop.

James addresses his thoughts to "the twelve tribes" in order to include all Jewish Christians wherever they may be living and from wherever they may have come, calling attention to the fulfillment of the promised eschatological regathering of Israel's tribes around faith in Jesus Christ. If James is centered in the Jerusalem church, the people he originally addressed were most likely ethnically Jewish converts to faith in Jesus as the promised Messiah (Christ). But the denotation of the twelve tribes also came to refer to the true remnant of Israel who would enjoy eschatological salvation and to whom Gentile believers in Christ would be grafted (Rom. 11).

Scholars have speculated that Antioch in Syria may have been the major destination of James's letter, though there is nothing to suggest that its original circulation was limited to just that city. James has apparent associations with Matthew's gospel, which is also thought to have been written to or for a Jewish Christian community in Antioch.[15]

The content of the letter of James further supports the theory of an original audience comprised of Jewish converts to Christianity:[16]

15. See Raymond E. Brown and John P. Meier, *Antioch and Rome*, New Testament Cradles of Catholic Christianity (New York: Paulist, 1983).

16. With thanks to Brandon Holiski, a graduate student in my class on James at Wheaton College in spring 2007, for itemizing these.

- Several passages in James assume the centrality of the law in God's dealings with people (James 1:21, 24–25; 2:8–13; 4:11–12), a concept that would have been largely meaningless to Gentile Christians.
- James 4:4 is a strong allusion to the Old Testament metaphor of Israel's marriage to Yahweh as found in the prophet Hosea. For a Christian to be "friends with the world" is by definition, according to James, to be spiritually unfaithful to God.
- In 5:4 James uses a title for God, "Lord Almighty" (Gk. *kuriou sabaoth*), commonly found in the Old Testament, which literally means Lord of the hosts (armies) of heaven. The only other occurrence of this title in the New Testament is in a quotation of Isaiah 1:9 in Romans 9:29.
- James assumes Old Testament beliefs, for instance, monotheism in 2:19.
- People from Israel's history, such as Abraham (2:21), Rahab (2:25), and Elijah (5:17) are mentioned as if familiar to the readers.

The Sacrifice of Abraham, Rembrandt Harmensz, van Rijn/Hermitage, St. Petersburg, Russia/The Bridgeman Art Library

Painting of Abraham sacrificing Isaac by Rembrandt Harmensz van Rijn (1606-1669). "Was not our father Abraham considered righteous for what he did when he offered his son Isaac on the altar?" (James 2:21).

Standing in the prophetic tradition of Judaism, James is authoritatively addressing various situations in which all Christians of that time—and yet today—might find themselves.

Purpose of the Letter of James

The question of its genre, original readers, and the purpose of the letter cannot be neatly separated, and so the following discussion may seem to circle back at times. Although in the form of a letter, the book of James reads more like a sermon that covers a multitude of topics assumed to be relevant to the original readers and cast in language that would make the most sense to Jewish Christians previously familiar with the Old Testament. Taking all this into consideration, perhaps the best genre identification of James is that of a *diaspora letter*, such as those written by the leaders of ancient Judaism. The prophets identified diaspora as the place of divine judgment for covenantal disobedience. For this reason they called God's people to repentance while also offering the promise of divine deliverance from judgment.[17] Examples of Diaspora letters include Jeremiah 29:1–23; *The Epistle of Jeremiah*; 2 Maccabees 1:1–9; 1:10–2:18; and *2 Apocalypse of Baruch* 78–86. Diaspora letters have strong associations with the covenant blessings and curses of Deuteronomy, often as mediated through the prophets. They offered consolation and hope to God's people while in diaspora and exhorted covenant faithfulness. James shares this same character, consoling his readers in their many trials

17. Donald J. Verseput, "Genre and Story: The Community Setting of the Epistle of James," *CBQ* 62 (2000): 101.

and exhorting them to live in obedience to the royal law as an expression of new covenant faithfulness.

Reading James as a covenantal diaspora letter may explain why he expresses himself with the rhetoric of persuasion and the authority of a prophet while invoking new covenant principles for faithfulness. He may have been one of the first Christian leaders to write such a letter, but certainly not the last. The apostle Paul apparently wrote the book we know as Ephesians as a circular letter to the churches in Ephesus and its outlying towns. In the history of the Christian church, such an authoritative letter coming from a spiritual leader (such as the Roman Catholic pope) has been called an encyclical letter.

If the book of James was originally written as a diaspora letter to Jewish Christians from the leader of the church in Jerusalem, its purpose was to provide spiritual instruction and exhortation on matters critical to the unity and life of the Christian community (see discussion below on major themes). James chooses to do this by arguing that Christian wisdom is a life lived in obedience to God's law as revealed by Israel's prophets (starting with Moses) but as that law has been transposed by the life and teachings of Jesus Christ. Faith in Christ does not eliminate the need to actively live out covenant obedience to God. While many Christians read Scripture as private instructions to oneself, the communal nature of the teaching in James should be taken seriously.[18]

According to James, wisdom — that is, living toward life's highest good — is to become "perfect," that is, a spiritually mature Christian. James, as other New Testament writers, sees the mature Christian as one living well with others in the Christian community. The instruction James gives toward that end links faith in Christ to the wisdom tradition of the Old Testament by showing Jesus to be a teacher of wisdom who reveals "the perfect law that gives freedom" (1:25; 2:12). (See chapter 6.) To live by *that* law is James's definition of life's highest good, for it allows one to stand in the final judgment of God without condemnation. James's letter, written early in the Christian church, is a creative synthesis of the old covenant law with new covenant faith in Christ, of the relationship of Israel's wisdom tradition with the prophetic mantle that James assumes, and all of this toward the eschatological endpoint of deliverance from God's judgment. Simply put, the purpose of the letter was to instruct Jewish Christians how to live faithfully to Christ within their heritage as Jews.

Something of James's approach to this synthesis is revealed in his leadership at the Jerusalem Council as portrayed in Acts 15. James did not side with the Judaizers who argued that the Gentile Christians must be circumcised and required to keep the law of Moses (Acts 15:5). Instead, after listening to the apostles Peter and Paul, he affirmed their mission to and experience with the Gentiles as a fulfillment of prophecy (Acts 15:15–18). Acting in his office of leader of the church of Jerusalem, James sided with Peter and Paul but also stated a mediating position concerning the behavior of Gentile Christians that would allow them to have fellowship with Jewish believers (Acts 15:20). James, the brother of Jesus, is a creative pastoral leader at the intersection of ancient Judaism and nascent Christianity.

However, the purpose of the diaspora letter from James is not fully realized when received by its original recipients. By virtue of its being in the canon of the New Testament,

18. See ibid., 96–110.

the book of James has relevance and application for the whole church in all places and at all times. Because Gentile believers have been grafted into God's people, all believers in Christ are called to adopt the moral worldview and eschatological expectation that the brother of Jesus presents.

THE MAJOR THEMES OF JAMES

The Greek word for wisdom (*sophia*) occurs four times in the letter of James (1:5; 3:13, 15, 17). Wisdom is not a topic or theme of the book of James, but it is an assumed value essential for Christian living and under which all the various topics of the book are subsumed. James applied Jewish wisdom as it was developed and controlled by the teachings of Jesus to all these practical topics for the wise Christian believer to take to heart in his or her life. (See chapter 7 for a fuller discussion.)

James recognized that wisdom is called for in many trying situations where one might feel a lack of it, and that ultimately God is the source of all true wisdom (1:5). The wise and understanding Israelite was one who hearkened to the prophetic warning (Hos. 14:9) that called for covenant faithfulness (Deut. 4:5–6 LXX):

> See, I have shown you statutes and ordinances, as the Lord has commanded me, to do so in the land into which you are entering there to inherit it. And you shall keep and do them, because this is your wisdom and discernment before all the nations, as many as might hear all these statutes, and they will say, "Look, this great nation is *a wise and understanding people*!" (emphasis added)

By the time James wrote, there was already a well-developed corpus of Jewish wisdom literature that related keeping the Torah to the practical situations of life in diaspora. James seems particularly familiar with the apocryphal book we know as the Wisdom of Ben Sira (also referred to simply as Sirach or Ecclesiasticus; see chapter 7 for a more in-depth discussion of this). James also considers the teachings of Jesus, which took the understanding of the law to a new level (see Matt. 5, esp. vv. 17–20), as essential to living wisely as a Christian. James brings this rich tradition as transposed by Jesus to the issues he felt were pressing at that moment, and which retain their significance for life as a Christian today. Those issues include:

Testing and Trials (1:2–4, 12)

James "is a book written for readers whose faith in God is threatened by a daily struggle with hardship. This 'testing of faith' is provoked by a variety of external and historical circumstances or 'trials.' Yet more importantly, every test occasions a theological crisis, when the believer is more easily deceived or confused about who God is and how God acts."[19] James understands the true goal of such trials to be perseverance, a theme that is common to the General Epistles. And perseverance works toward spiritual maturity and wholeness, presented implicitly as a worthy goal in the life of the Christian. One's lifetime in its entirety seems to be in view as the period of potential testing and trials, for verse 12

19. Robert W. Wall, *Community of the Wise: The Letter of James*, New Testament in Context (Valley Forge, Pa.: Trinity Press International, 1997), 273.

suggests that promised eternal life ("the crown which is life," reading the Greek genitive as appositional) will be the blessed reward of those who persevere under trial.

The two obstacles to perseverance are double-mindedness (1:6–7) and the pitfalls of one's socioeconomic status (1:9–11). The double-mindedness of those who doubt God echoes the "divided hearts" of covenant breakers who were lured from faithfulness by the prosperity of the land (cf. Hos. 10:1–2). To doubt God is to be unstable in all one's ways, like the wind-tossed sea. No stability for perseverance can be found there.

Instead of double-mindedness, James calls his readers to wholeheartedness toward God, a quality entailed in Jesus' command to love God with all one's being (Matt. 22:37; Mark 12:30; Luke 10:27). Such wholeheartedness produces perseverance through patience while waiting for the Lord's coming (James 5:7–11). During that time of patient perseverance, anyone in trouble should pray, and the sick should call for the anointing and prayer of the church elders (5:13–18).

James introduces the topic of "the rich" (1:10) immediately after warning against double-mindedness (1:8), suggesting that the pursuit of socioeconomic gain might well

Todd Bolen/www.BiblePlaces.com

Storm on the eastern shore of the Sea of Galilee. "But when you ask, you must believe and not doubt, because the one who doubts is like a wave of the sea, blown and tossed by the wind" (James 1:6).

encourage double-mindedness. To be well fed and even moderately prosperous in the first-century Greco-Roman world would mean complicity with Roman ways to at least some extent. According to James, some of those practices amounted to a friendship with the world that was enmity with God comparable to the spiritual adultery that had sent Israel into exile.

The one who successfully perseveres under testing is the one who does not let their own evil desire drag them into the downward spiral of sin and death (1:13–15). Those desires for evil are contrary to every good and perfect gift, which comes from the Father who gives life through the word of truth (1:16–17). James invites his readers to live wisely by choosing life rather than death.

THE DOWNWARD SPIRALING CYCLE OF SIN

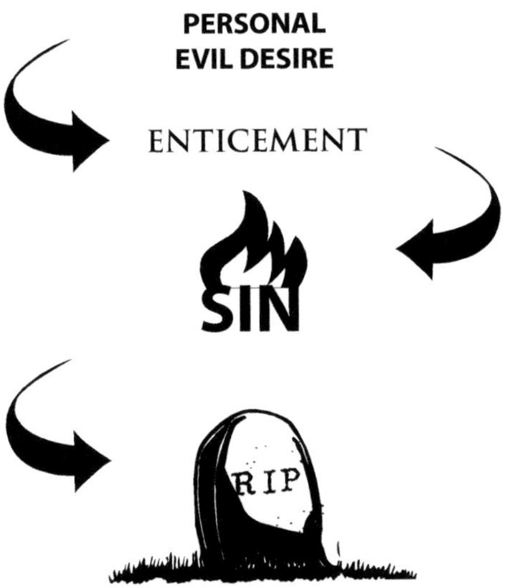

Poverty and Oppression (1:9–11; 2:1–13; 5:1–6)

Socioeconomic disparity, both in society and in the church, seems to have been a major concern in James's mind as he wrote this letter. He introduces the topic by leveling the differences between the "humble" and the rich when viewed from the perspective of spiritual realities (1:9–11). Though dismissed and disdained in the eyes of society, the humble believer has received every privilege from God, who gives without consideration of one's material resources. Rich believers have been humbled, because no amount of wealth could buy what they have received from God in Christ; therefore, their resources are worthless in view of the gospel and can be no source of pride within the Christian community. The poor, without material resources, have also received the riches of God's grace in Christ. Furthermore, the rich and poor are alike in another way—both will pass away. Whatever protection the rich think their wealth will afford against the ups and downs of life, allowing them to live in relative luxury, is fleeting and temporary—their lives are like wildflowers that have a short time of glory and then wither and pass away. In other words, in light of spiritual realities, financial resources or the lack of them are irrelevant to one's standing with God and one's inevitable future. For this reason, they should not be a defining issue in the social dynamic of the Christian church.

Rich people, whether understood as fellow believers or unbelieving visitors, should especially not be shown favoritism in the gatherings of the Christian community (2:1–13). Their show of wealth in the way they dress is not reason to receive more honorable treatment in the community. And the poor person should not be dishonored by less caring treatment because of the poor condition of their clothing. In other words, all believers and visitors should be welcomed alike, without regard for wealth, because to do otherwise is to violate the great command of love for one's neighbor.

James does, however, issue a prophetic denouncement of those rich who have accumulated their wealth by the oppression and exploitation of others (5:1–6). The harsh pronouncement of their coming misery suggests that even self-professing Christians who have so unjustly earned their wealth at the expense of others have missed the point of the gospel and will suffer judgment not different from the unbelieving rich. By putting the accumulation of money above love for others, such people are the "adulterous people" (4:4) who stand in enmity against God because of their friendship with the world. The very wealth on which such people rely will be the witness against them.

All of James's discussion of wealth is intended to put the Christian's resources, no matter how little or how much, under God's sovereignty. To plan to do business and make money apart from recognition of God's control over one's life speaks of an evil arrogance that is incompatible with spiritual maturity (4:13–16). The sequence of James's remarks suggests that a belief that one is in control of one's earning power apart from God's enabling is a presumption that may lead to oppressing others in one's pursuit of wealth.

Prosperity has always been a great danger to God's people in ancient times, even back when God first gave the covenant at Sinai:

> When you have eaten and are satisfied, praise the LORD your God for the good land he has given you. Be careful that you do not forget the LORD your God, failing to observe his commands, his laws and his decrees that I am giving you this day. Otherwise, when you eat and are satisfied, when you build fine houses and settle down, and when your herds and flocks grow large and your silver and gold increase and all you have is multiplied, then your heart will become proud and you will forget the LORD your God, who brought you out of Egypt, out of the land of slavery. (Deut. 8:10–14)

The self-righteous attitude fostered by prosperity is the pride that goes before the fall of covenant violation. The prophets later indicted God's people for idolatry and the social injustice among them, the same refrain that James picks up in his letter.

> The merchant uses dishonest scales
>   and loves to defraud.
> Ephraim boasts,
>   "I am very rich; I have become wealthy.
> With all my wealth they will not find in me
>   any iniquity or sin." (Hos. 12:7–8)

Favoritism Breaks the Royal Law

"Jesus said, 'Love the Lord your God with all your heart and with all your soul and with all your mind.' This is the first and greatest commandment. And the second is like it: 'Love your neighbor as yourself.' All the Law and the Prophets hang on these two commandments.'"

Matthew 22:37–40

Prosperity throughout redemptive history has led people to forget God (Hos. 2:13; 13:6). In our times of enormous corporate scandal and financial scams from which certain people have gained extreme wealth, issues of rich and poor continue to entangle the church. James expects those with resources to do more than have pity on others who live in poverty and to do something to provide for their food and shelter (2:14–16). Christians of poor nations indict the North American church for its lack of concern about clean water and adequate food in the poverty-stricken nations.[20] The enticement of wealth is still a great danger to Christians today.

Favoritism (2:1–13)

While favoritism may seem a relatively small infraction to modern sensibilities, James points out that showing favoritism, especially in the Christian community, is breaking the royal law, "Love your neighbor as yourself." This command is second only to loving God wholeheartedly (i.e., undividedly). Recognizing that the "royal law" sums up all of the commandments that govern relationships between people, James points out, "If you show favoritism, you sin and are convicted by the law as lawbreakers. For whoever keeps the whole law and yet stumbles at just one point is guilty of breaking all of it" (2:9–10). Just as adultery and murder violate love for neighbor, so does favoritism. And then, as now, an inordinate valuing of those who possess material riches drove favoritism.

Godly Speech (1:20, 26; 3:1–12; 4:11–12; 5:12)

One of the New Testament's foremost ethical concerns is how people, especially God's people, use words. The expression of ourselves through speech is the primary way in which we interact with others, and it shapes our relationships day by day throughout our lives. James is particularly concerned with godly speech and lays out some principles:

- Be quick to listen, slow to speak, and slow to anger (1:19).
- The religion of those who do not have control over their mouths is worthless (1:26).
- Teachers are held especially accountable for what they say, and for that reason James cautions that not many among his readers should presume to teach (3:1–2).

20. See Elsa Tamez, *The Scandalous Message of James: Faith without Works Is Dead* (New York: Crossroad, 1992), for an interpretation of James from outside the North American church.

- Although the tongue is a small part of the human body, it is the part that steers the course of the whole of one's life (3:3–5). Furthermore, the destruction it can cause is extensive (3:5–8).
- A Christian must not presume to praise the Lord while cursing others (3:9–12). Godly speech is consistently wholesome.
- Those who speak slanderously to accuse someone of violating God's law is breaking the law themselves (4:11–12).
- Christians should not swear, that is, take oaths, by created things. A simple yes or no should be as binding as any oath, for keeping one's word is one's integrity (5:12).

Then, as now, Christians lie, break promises, spread gossip, violate confidences, and use their words to promote themselves and to put down others. James wants his readers to understand that what a person says is an expression of what that person is. This echoes Jesus' teaching in Luke 6:45: "A good man brings good things out of the good stored up in his heart, and an evil man brings evil things out of the evil stored up in his heart. For the mouth speaks what the heart is full of." Spiritually mature people exhibit godly speech that is consistent with who they are becoming in Christ.

Faith and Good Deeds (1:6–8; 2:14–26; 5:14)

The letter of James includes several topics of importance. But the debate over whether James contradicts Paul is perhaps the most famous topic associated with the letter, and our understanding of James is the worse for it. Martin Luther suggested that the statement "a person is considered righteous by what they do and not by faith alone" (2:24) contradicts Paul's theology of salvation by faith alone, especially as it is stated in Galatians 2:16. And ever since, it is that controversy that is most strongly associated with James's letter, overshadowing the rich contribution of the letter to Christian thought. The historical moment in which Martin Luther lived perhaps called for such a rejection of righteousness by works, and he probably could not have foreseen that his attitude toward James would skew the Protestant reading of the epistle for centuries. Yet his perspective is unfortunate, because pitting James against Paul distracts energy away from the force of James's total argument and into a theological debate that easily misses the point of the letter.

There is no compelling reason to believe that James is directly engaging Paul or his writings on the point of justification by faith in Christ. (See further discussion in chapter 7.) It is natural for Christians reading James in light of the complete canon to immediately question how what James says and what Paul says agree, disagree, or mutually enlighten the other, and even in the ancient church, James was used as a corrective to abuses of Paul's teaching. But first each author must be allowed his own voice and the right to be understood for his individual intent. Galatians was among Paul's earliest letters, likely written about the same time James was writing his letter, either shortly before or after the council of Jerusalem. But Paul was writing about observing the law of Moses as it was understood and practiced in the first century, while James is writing about deeds of social justice in a life motivated by faith in Christ. James is very clear that God the Father "chose to give us birth through the word of truth" (1:18) and that it is "the word planted in you" that is the source of salvation (1:21), not any type of deeds.

James was most likely writing very early in the history of the Christian church, while Christianity was still immersed in Judaism and while the apostles were hammering out both its continuity and discontinuity with that ancient revelation of God found in the old covenant. Both James and Paul were Jewish Christian thinkers who had to lead the nascent church into a correct understanding of salvation by faith on the one hand and of ethical living in Christ on the other. James knew Paul during all the years of his missionary activity among the Gentiles and no doubt understood where they agreed and disagreed. Early in Paul's Christian life, three years after his conversion and calling, he went to Jerusalem, staying with the apostle Peter for two weeks and also meeting with James (Gal. 1:18–19). Fourteen years later, Paul again met with James, Peter, and John in Jerusalem, and they affirmed his orthodox understanding of the gospel (Gal. 2:9). Then toward the end of Paul's active ministry when he returned to Jerusalem and was unexpectedly arrested, he met with James once again (Acts 21:18). Paul and James knew each other throughout their years of active leadership in the churches. Moreover, James listened to Paul's accounts of the Gentiles' conversion at the council of Jerusalem and took the lead in adjudicating the dispute stirred by the Judaizers (Acts 15). These meetings suggest substantial agreement between James and Paul on the gospel message and an overarching unity among the first-century apostles of the church.

However, it is unimaginable that issues of such theological importance and practical significance could be worked out without some personal friction, differences of opinion, or points of emphasis. There is a broad range of scholarly opinion about the degree and substance of disagreement among the apostles, especially between Paul and Peter and James.[21] And so it would be unrealistic to expect every New Testament writer to say exactly the same thing, no more, no less. Perhaps we get a glimpse of tensions in Paul's comments in Galatians 2, especially the comment that those Judaizers who caused a change in Peter's behavior toward Gentiles had come from James, that is, from the Jerusalem church to Antioch. Whatever the scenario and precise cause of the tension, James and the authority of the Jerusalem church may have encroached on what Paul viewed as the jurisdiction of the church in Antioch (cf. Acts 11:22; Gal. 2:12), which was Paul's home church (Acts 13). Given that James and Paul, as well as Peter, left the Jerusalem Council in agreement on the epoch-making decision that Gentiles would be received as Christians without becoming Jewish and keeping the law of Moses, it seems unlikely that they disagreed over the fundamental nature of faith and salvation. Rather, the source of the tension was perhaps over jurisdiction and the authority to dictate practice, an unfortunate but inevitable issue as the church expanded rapidly outside the borders of Palestine. Conflict over the view of mission and territory may well have developed in the early church, as the gospel spread beyond the Jewish population into those of the Greek culture who had no previous knowledge of the one, true God.[22]

Instead of seeing James 2:14–26 as in some way undermining or opposing Paul's teaching that works cannot save, we should read James as explaining the nature of the faith that

21. For one scholarly reconstruction of factions within the two missions of the early church (to the circumcised and to the Gentiles), see Painter, *Just James*, esp. 73–82; also idem, "James and Peter," esp. 180–86.

22. See Bruce Chilton and Craig Evans, eds., *The Missions of James, Peter, and Paul: Tensions in Early Christianity*, NovTSup 115 (Leiden: Brill, 2005).

saves. A faith that can look on others in need of food and shelter and pronounce a blessing without doing something to help provide their physical needs is not the kind of faith that saves (vv. 14–17). A faith that consists of mental assent to doctrinal statements but has no outward expression in life is not the kind of faith that saves (vv. 18–19). The kind of faith that saves is a life-transforming faith that changes one's character and behavior by the fruit of the Spirit, as Paul would say it, or by deeds of social justice as James has put it.

James gives two telling examples of faith that was expressed in action: Abraham and Rahab. The kind of faith that Abraham had that was reckoned as saving faith was the kind of faith that motivated his action to obey God even against all human reason (2:21–24). And Rahab's faith motivated her to put her own life at risk as she harbored and protected the spies who were God's people (2:26). James chose two examples of deeds expressing faith that have nothing to do with the law of Moses. Abraham lived centuries before Moses brought the law of the covenant to the people. And Rahab was a Gentile who had most likely not even heard of the law at the time she acted. These examples indicate that James is not directly engaging Paul, who spoke of the impotence of *observing the law of Moses* for salvation. In fact, James may have chosen these examples to avoid being read against Paul's teaching of salvation by faith alone. James would agree that it is faith in Christ that saves; Paul would agree that such faith in Christ must result in behavior (deeds) that expresses the fruit of the Spirit (Gal. 5:13–26). How sad to read these two in opposition when they should be read as both explicating the nature of faith that saves.

Rahab of Jericho (17th century, Italian school). "In the same way was not even Rahab the prostitute considered righteous for what she did when she gave lodging to the spies . . . ?" (James 2:25).

Rahab and the Emissaries of Joshua, Italian School, (17th century)/ Musee des Beaux-Arts, Nimes, France/Giraudon/The Bridgeman Art Library

Moreover, the apostle John also shares James's exhortation that works that are consistent with love for God must accompany faith: "Whoever says, 'I know him,' but does not do what he commands is a liar, and the truth is not in that person. But if anyone obeys his word, love for God is truly made complete in them. This is how we know we are in him: Whoever claims to live in him must live as Jesus did" (1 John 2:4–6).

The Law (1:24; 2:8–13; 4:11–12)

James does not directly refer to the law of Moses. Instead, he speaks of "the perfect law that gives freedom" (1:24; 2:12). In 2:8 he refers to "the royal law found in Scripture, 'Love your neighbor as yourself.'" This is one of the two commands that Jesus said summed up all the Law and Prophets (Matt. 22:39; Mark 12:31; Luke 10:27). James uses this summary statement of the law as given by Jesus as the conceptual basis of his ethical system. Love of neighbor is violated when favoritism is shown to the rich and disdain is shown to the poor (2:9). To James, anything that would violate love of neighbor is as serious as violating any of the Ten Commandments—such as adultery or murder (2:11)—for surely adultery and murder are a serious violation of love for neighbor.

The faith that saves is a faith that motivates deeds of love for neighbor, such as providing for the physical needs of the poor (2:14–17), looking after orphans and widows (1:27), taming the tongue from hurting others (3:1–12; 4:11), desisting from fights and quarrels (4:1–3), and turning others back to the truth (5:19–20). James's vision for Christian morality and ethics moves beyond a legalism that demands compliance with individual commandments to Jesus' teaching that all of the commandments can be summed up in love for neighbor and love for God. (See chapter 7 for further discussion.)

> "James is not opposing faith and works, but living faith and dead faith."
>
> Thomas W. Leahy, "The Epistle of James,"

On this view of fulfilling the law, James shows amazing agreement with Paul in Romans 13:8–10:

> Let no debt remain outstanding, except the continuing debt to love one another, for *whoever loves others has fulfilled the law.*
>
> The commandments, "You shall not commit adultery," "You shall not murder," "You shall not steal," "You shall not covet," and whatever other command there may be, are summed up in this one command: "Love your neighbor as yourself." Love does no harm to its neighbor. Therefore *love is the fulfillment of the law.* (emphasis added)

At the time of Jesus, the Pharisees had taken the Ten Commandments given by God through Moses and teased out of them 613 other "laws" that had to be obeyed (*b. Makkoth* 24a). For instance, a woman must not look in the mirror on the Sabbath, for she might see a gray hair and be tempted to pluck it out, which would count as "working" and constitute a violation of the fourth commandment. On the other hand, the Pharisees were skilled at interpreting the law in such a way as to create loopholes in it for their convenience. For instance, one should not travel more than three-fifths of a mile from one's home on the Sabbath. To technically obey this command when one wanted to travel further, a Pharisee could, prior to the Sabbath, deposit food every three-fifths mile in the direction he wanted to travel. Then each deposit of food became his home away from home, and he could rationalize traveling another three-fifths mile!

As Jewish people came to faith in Jesus as the Messiah and realized that it was his death and resurrection that saved them from their sins, a natural question would be what "laws" they might still need to observe. James, following Jesus' teaching, completely transposes the ethical basis of Christian faith from any form of legalism to the more demanding law of loving one's neighbor as oneself.

THE TEXT AND CANONICITY OF JAMES

The Greek Text of James

The earliest manuscripts of James that have survived date from the third century. 𝔓[20] (Am 4117; P.Oxy. 1171) includes James 2:19–3:9. 𝔓[23] (P.Oxy 1229) contains James 1:10–12 on one side and 15–18 on the other. These manuscripts are dated to the third century based on paleography and were among the finds excavated by Bernard Grenfell and Arthur Hunt at Oxyrhynchus Egypt in 1896. The earliest complete manuscript of James that has survived is found in Sinaiticus, a fourth-century **codex** that contains the entire New Testament as we know it today.[23]

There is no reason to believe that James's letter was originally written in a Semitic language, for it does not read like translation Greek. There is no surviving Western text of this book, which may be a happenstance or may suggest that it circulated primarily in the eastern Mediterranean. It is included in the New Testament of the Syriac Peshitta. Of its 108 verses, only 14 have textual variants that may be of exegetical significance (1:2, 12, 17, 19, 27; 2:3, 20; 3:3, 6, 8, 9; 4:2; 5:7, 11).[24] Its relatively few textual variants may be due to rather limited copying, which would corroborate the idea that the letter had only limited circulation in the early church, and may account for, or result from, its slow acceptance into the universal canon.[25]

Princeton University Library

Recto side of P.Oxy. IX 1171. This earliest manuscript containing the letter of James dates to the 3rd century.

The Canonicity of James

James was universally accepted into the New Testament canon in the fourth century, probably because Jerome accepted and translated it for his Latin Vulgate. But this does not mean that the book was unknown or not used as Scripture prior to that time. Origen's writings contain the first explicit reference to the book of James and the tradition that it was written by the brother of Jesus, but he observes that some were skeptical of that authorship even then. This skepticism is also reported in Eusebius (*Hist. eccl.* 2.25; 3.2), who nonetheless remarks that James (along with Jude, 2 Peter, and 2 and 3 John) were "well-known and recognized by most" (*Hist. eccl.* 3.38). Eusebius's comment reminds us that skepticism on the part of some does not compel the conclusion that a book was not considered canonical Scripture by others, who were perhaps in a better position to know.

The book of James seems to have been known very early in the history of the church. Clement of Rome, a Western writer of the late first century, appears to have had a knowledge of and alluded to the book of James. When discussing justification by faith, Clement invoked the examples of Abraham and Rahab, both used by James in his argument; he comments, "Let us then work from our whole heart the work of righteousness."[26] Not all scholars consider such allusions as compelling evidence, but Clement moves in the same direction as James. Although he knows that not everyone believes the brother of Jesus wrote the letter, Origen, an Eastern father of the church, refers to James authoritatively in his commentary on other parts of Scripture. Although not included in early Syriac canon lists, the book of James was nevertheless translated and appears in the Peshitta, which already by the fourth century was an old and venerable Bible.

---

23. For a more complete listing of the manuscript witnesses to James, see Peter Davids, *The Epistle of James*, NIGTC (Grand Rapids: Eerdmans, 1982), 60.

24. Ben Witherington III, *Letters and Homilies for Jewish Christians* (Downers Grove, Ill.: IVP Academic, 2007), 387.

25. Those readings in *Editio Critica Maior* that vary from NA27 can be found in Peter M. Head, 'Editio Critica Maior: An Introduction and Assessment', *Tyndale Bulletin* 61.1 (2010), 149–152, available online at https://www.academia.edu/3633883/_Editio_Critica_Maior_An_Introduction_and_Assessment_Tyndale_Bulletin_61.1_2010_131-152 (accessed May 2, 2016).

26. *1 Clement* 10, 12, 33.

> **Luther's Canon within the Canon?**
>
> "Saint John's gospel and his first letter, Saint Paul's letters, especially those to the Romans, Galatians, Ephesians, and Saint Peter's first letter — these are the books that show Christ to you and teach you everything needed and blessed for you to know even though you never see or hear any other book or doctrine. Therefore, Saint James's letter is a right strawy epistle in comparison with them, for it has no gospel character to it. Therefore I will not have it in my Bible in the number of the proper chief books, but do not intend by this to forbid anyone to place and exalt it as he pleases, for there is many a good saying in it."
>
> Martin Luther, *Preface to the New Testament*

This evidence shows that James, like many other books of the New Testament, may have been slow to be universally recognized as Scripture, but that it was viewed as authoritative in those places that did know of it. This is consistent with the scenario that James originally wrote in the earliest days of the Christian faith to Jewish Christians who were living in Palestine, Syria, and other regions in the eastern Mediterranean, and who formed an increasingly small population within the growing church. Because James, unlike the apostle Paul, spent his whole life of ministry centered in Jerusalem, he was not personally known to many outside of Palestine, especially if he sent emissaries rather than making personal visits (cf. Gal. 2:12). And he wrote only one brief letter on practical matters that mentions Jesus only twice. Moreover, unlike Peter's relation to the church at Rome and Paul's to the churches of Asia Minor, the church that claimed James as its foundational leader did not survive much past the destruction of Jerusalem in AD 70. Therefore, it is not too surprising that his letter did not enjoy the wide circulation and acceptance of other New Testament books, and that its author's status in the early church has not been fully appreciated by later generations of Christians. Nevertheless, its practical theology for Christian living is a rich and challenging word for Christians living in every age.

STRUCTURE AND OUTLINE OF THE BOOK OF JAMES

Delineating the structure of the book of James is one of the greatest challenges presented by the letter. Topics appear and reappear; there are few discourse markers to indicate a logical flow. Martin Luther, who held a low view of the book of James, wrote that its author simply threw things together chaotically.[27] One scholar in the mid-twentieth century, Dibelius, asserted that there is nothing that can be described as a structure to James; rather, its paragraphs are like pearls on a string, unrelated except in textual proximity. Others have detected a chiastic arrangement within the body of the letter (2:1 – 5:6), with the theme of "Righteous vs. Worldly Wisdom" (3:13 – 18) at its center.[28] While every outline of James

27. Martin Luther, "Preface to the New Testament" (1522), ed. J. Pelikan and W. A. Hanson, trans. P. D. Pahl, LW, 35:397.

28. See George H. Guthrie, "James," in "Hebrews – Revelation," ed. Tremper Longman III and David E. Garland, *The Expositor's Bible Commentary*, vol. 13, rev. ed. (Grand Rapids: Zondervan, 2006), 206.

seems to be imposing structure on a text that does not emerge naturally, there do appear to be recurring themes under the broad call to new covenant living: coping with trials and testing, living wisely, riches and poverty, and the ethical use of speech. All of these can be subsumed under the concern that Christians live according to the "royal law" that Jesus taught: love for God and love for neighbor (see chapter 7).

I. Address and Salutation (1:1)

II. A Call to New Covenant Living (1:2–5:20)

   A. Trials and Temptations (1:2–18)
      1. The testing of faith (1:2–4)
      2. The need for wisdom (1:5–8)
      3. Poverty and riches (1:9–11)
      4. The blessing of perseverance (1:12–18)

   B. A Call to Action (1:19–2:13)
      1. Be slow to speak and to anger (1:19–20)
      2. Be doers of the Word (1:21–25)
      3. Pure and faultless religion (1:26–27)
      4. Do not show favoritism (2:1–7)
      5. Keeping the royal law (2:8–13)

   C. The Relationship between Faith and Action (2:14–26)

   D. A Call to Control One's Speech (3:1–12)
      1. A caution about being teachers (3:1–2)
      2. The power of speech (3:3–4)
      3. The destructive power of speech (3:5–8)
      4. A call to pure speech (3:9–12)

   E. A Reminder of Covenant Wisdom (3:13–18)

   F. A Prophetic Rebuke (4:1–5:6)
      1. The source of discord (4:1–3)
      2. Spiritual adultery (4:4–10)
      3. Slander (4:11–12)
      4. Failure to recognize the Lord's control (4:13–17)
      5. Warning to rich oppressors (5:1–6)

   G. A Call to Patience and Prayer (5:7–18)
      1. A call to patience (5:7–11)
      2. Do not swear (5:12)
      3. The prayer of faith (5:13–18)

   H. A Call to Restoration (5:19–20)

CHAPTER SUMMARY

The book of James has often wrongly been treated as merely a footnote to Pauline theology. While it explicitly mentions Jesus only twice, as the next chapter will show, it is a thoroughly Christian book that deserves the devoted attention of all Christians. Likely written by someone from Jesus' own immediate family, its practical theology provides a necessary framework in which to consider ethical questions today about the integrity of one's speech, poverty, and wealth, and the important issue of how a Christian's deeds and behavior relate to his or her faith in Jesus.

KEY TERMS AND DATES

- AD 33
- AD 44
- AD 49
- AD 62
- AD 70
- diaspora letter
- faith and works
- Luther's opinion on James
- ossuary
- papyrus $\mathfrak{P}^{20}$, $\mathfrak{P}^{23}$
- Q-document
- royal law

QUESTIONS FOR REVIEW

1. Use a concordance to look up the verses that mention a man named James and determine for yourself how many different men are referred to.
2. What are the arguments for pseudonymous authorship of the book of James?
3. What would be at stake for you if the book of James were pseudonymous?
4. What is the evidence that James the Just wrote it?
5. What role should archaeological evidence play in Christian faith?
6. List the evidence that this letter was probably originally written to Jewish converts to Christianity.
7. What are the major themes of this letter? Which seem particularly relevant to you today? Why?

GOING FURTHER

Adamson, James B. *James: The Man and His Message*. Grand Rapids: Eerdmans, 1989.

Bauckham, Richard. *James: Wisdom of James, Disciple of Jesus the Sage*. New Testament Readings. London and New York: Routledge, 1999.

Cargal, Timothy B. *Restoring the Diaspora: Discursive Structure and Purpose in the Epistle of James*. SBLDS 144. Atlanta: Scholars, 1993.

Chester, Andrew, and Ralph P. Martin. *The Theology of the Letters of James, Peter, and Jude*. New Testament Theology. Cambridge: Cambridge University Press, 1994.

Chilton, Bruce, and Craig A. Evans, eds. *James the Just and Christian Origins*. Supplements to Novum Testamentum 98. Leiden: Brill, 1999.

———. *The Missions of James, Peter, and Paul: Tensions in Early Christianity*. Supplements to Novum Testamentum 115. Leiden: Brill, 2005.

Chilton, Bruce, and Jacob Neusner, eds. *The Brother of Jesus: James the Just and His Mission*. Louisville: Westminster John Knox, 2001.

Doering, Lutz. "Jeremiah and the 'Diaspora Letters' in Ancient Judaism: Epistolary Communication with the Golah as Medium for Dealing with the Present." Pages 43–72 in *Reading the Present in the Qumran Library: The Perception of the Contemporary by Means of Scriptural Interpretation*. Edited by Kristin De Troyer and Armin Lang. SBLSymS 30. Atlanta: Society of Biblical Literature, 2005.

Donelson, Lewis R. *From Hebrews to Revelation: A Theological Introduction*. Louisville: Westminster John Knox, 2001.

Harner, Philip B. *What Are They Saying about the Catholic Epistles?* What Are They Saying Series. New York: Paulist, 2004.

Hart, George, and Helen Hart. *A Semantic and Structural Analysis of James*. Dallas, Tex.: SIL International, 2001.

Johnson, Luke Timothy. *Brother of Jesus, Friend of God: Studies in the Letter of James*. Grand Rapids: Eerdmans, 2004.

Painter, John. *Just James: The Brother of Jesus in History and Tradition*. Studies on Personalities of the New Testament. Columbia: University of South Carolina Press, 1997.

Shanks, Hershel, and Ben Witherington III. *The Brother of Jesus: The Dramatic Story and Meaning of the First Archaeological Link to Jesus and His Family*. New York: Harper: 2003.

Tamez, Elsa. *The Scandalous Message of James: Faith without Works Is Dead*. New York: Crossroad, 1992.

Commentaries

Adamson, James B. *The Epistle of James*. NICNT. Grand Rapids: Eerdmans, 1976.

Blomberg, Craig L., and Marian J. Kamell. *James*. ZECNT. Grand Rapids: Zondervan, 2008.

Brosend, William F., II. *James and Jude*. New Cambridge Bible Commentary. Cambridge: Cambridge University Press, 2004.

Cheung, Luke. *The Genre, Composition and Hermeneutics of the Epistle of James*. Paternoster Biblical and Theological Monographs. Waynesboro, Ga.: Paternoster, 2003.

Davids, Peter H. *The Epistle of James*. NIGTC. Grand Rapids: Eerdmans, 1982.

Guthrie, George. "James." Pages 199–273 in *The Expositor's Bible Commentary*. Vol. 13: *Hebrews–Revelation*. Rev. ed. Edited by Tremper Longman III and David E. Garland. Grand Rapids: Zondervan, 2006.

Hartin, P. J. *James, First Peter, Jude, Second Peter.* New Collegeville Bible Commentary. Collegeville, Minn.: Liturgical Press, 2006.
Johnson, Luke Timothy. *The Letter of James.* AB 37A. New York: Doubleday, 1995.
Martin, Ralph P. *James.* Word Biblical Commentary 48. Waco, Tex.: Thomas Nelson, 1988.
Mayor, Joseph B. *The Epistle of St James.* Classic Commentary Library. Grand Rapids: Zondervan, 1954.
McCartney, Dan G. *James.* BECNT. Grand Rapids: Baker Academic, 2009.
Moo, Douglas J. "James." Pages 86–119 in *ZIBBC.* Vol. 4. Edited by Clinton E. Arnold. Grand Rapids: Zondervan, 2002.
———. *The Letter of James.* Pillar New Testament Commentary. Grand Rapids: Eerdmans, 2000.
Nystrom, David P. *James.* NIV Application Commentary. Grand Rapids: Zondervan, 1997.
Wall, Robert W. *Community of the Wise: The Letter of James.* The New Testament in Context. Valley Forge, Pa.: Trinity Press International, 1997.

CHAPTER 6

A Christian Letter?

CHRISTOLOGY IN JAMES

Your Goals for This Chapter

- To understand the implicit **Christology** that undergirds James's letter.
- To identify aspects of the letter that comprise the Christology of James.
- To see how the material in James relates to similar material in the **Synoptic Gospels** and the **Q**-document.
- To better understand how Jesus was viewed in the earliest days of the church.

WHY THIS CHAPTER IS IMPORTANT TO YOU

Is there any book of the Bible that we can safely ignore? Throughout much of Protestant history, beginning with Martin Luther, the book of James has been viewed as somewhat sub-Christian because Jesus Christ does not seem to have a central place. And because the apostle Paul's writings spoke so forcefully to Luther at a historical moment when the essential truth of salvation by faith in Christ alone had become obscured, the Protestant Reformation that ignited from Luther's insight has largely formed its doctrine from the writings of Paul. But God has given us not only the writings of the great apostle Paul but of other inspired writers as well, whose voices must be heard by the church in every generation.

The New Testament's teaching about Jesus Christ is rightly at the heart of the Christian religion, and judged by a Christocentric criterion, the book of James has not fared well. Because it mentions Jesus Christ only twice in the entire letter, and then only incidentally, Martin Luther and many of those after him have questioned even the place of James in the Christian canon. And James doesn't mention the Holy Spirit, even once, making him additionally suspect. Moreover, the book's emphasis on issues of social justice further alienated some who saw such issues as the hallmark of the liberal Protestant agenda for an antisupernatural modern age.

Readers of a book such as this, perhaps preparing for ministry in the church or advanced work in biblical studies, especially need to understand just how Christocentric the book of James actually is. And a study of James's Christology gives a fresh infusion of what it means to live out the Christian faith in a way pleasing to God.

Key Verses

1:1: James, a servant of God and of the Lord Jesus Christ, To the twelve tribes scattered among the nations: Greetings.

2:1: My brothers and sisters, believers in our glorious Lord Jesus Christ must not show favoritism.

2:8: If you really keep the royal law found in Scripture, "Love your neighbor as yourself," you are doing right.

5:8–9: You too, be patient and stand firm, because the Lord's coming is near. Don't grumble against one another, brothers and sisters, or you will be judged. The Judge is standing at the door!

CHAPTER OUTLINE

I. Explicit References to Jesus Christ

II. The Implicit Christology of James

  A. James's Use of *Lord*

  B. Both God and Jesus Christ Are "Judge"

C. Echoes of the Teaching of Jesus
    1. The Sermon on the Mount
    2. The "royal law" (James 2:8)
D. The Ongoing Existence and Return of Jesus
III. The Distinctly Christian Nature of James's Letter

It may seem bold beyond reason to include a whole chapter here about the Christology of James when Jesus Christ is mentioned only twice in the letter, and then only incidentally. One might expect a very short chapter! But because all writers assume shared knowledge with their readers, and often shared values and concepts as well, one can look at what James implies about his knowledge and beliefs concerning Jesus that he presumably shared with the original readers of his letter. But before addressing James's implicit Christology, we ought to examine the two places where he does explicitly mention Jesus, because those references will most unambiguously inform our understanding of James's Christology.

EXPLICIT REFERENCES TO JESUS CHRIST

The only explicit references to Jesus are found in James 1:1 and 2:1, and neither of them is the main point of the sentence. But does this really diminish the Christology of James, as some would claim? Is it evidence that someone took the text of James from a previously existing Jewish work and "Christianized" it by adding Jesus' name here and there?

> "James represents not teaching about Jesus but the teaching of Jesus applied to a new situation."
>
> David P. Nystrom, *James*

James 1:1 is the typical Hellenistic letter formula that states the sender and recipients. In this case, James identifies himself as the author who is "a servant of God and of the Lord Jesus Christ." Because all of the nouns in the Greek are anarthrous (do not have a definite article), one cannot argue from the syntax that "God" and "Lord Jesus Christ" refer to the same entity. But even so, James certainly is presenting a high Christology. By stating that he is first a servant (or slave) of God, he accredits Jesus as a legitimate master (Lord) for those who worship God, a point that would have impressed monotheistic Jews. James is declaring himself to be in the same relationship of submission to Jesus that he is to God, and by this analogy, he gives Jesus a remarkably high authority. James considers himself a servant of both God and of Jesus Christ, expressing no tension or competition between his two masters. This is especially remarkable, humanly speaking, if James is the half brother of Jesus, given the psychological dynamics between siblings. (Can you imagine giving your sibling such authority over your life?) Second, the word "Christ" translates the Greek word *christos*, which is the equivalent for the Hebrew word *Messiah*. James recognizes Jesus as God's Messiah with all of the authority and power associated with that title and role.

In the greeting of 1:1 there is apparently no need for James to claim apostolic authority, which his readers would already recognize in a letter coming from a widely known leader of the Jerusalem church. Nor does he make a point of his familial relationship to Jesus, for

Jesus Is Mentioned Only Twice in James

James 1:1:	"James, a servant of God and of the Lord Jesus Christ, To the twelve tribes scattered among the nations: Greetings."
James 2:1:	"My brothers and sisters, believers in our glorious Lord Jesus Christ must not show favoritism."

that, too, would be well known. Moreover, the fact that he grew up with Jesus is apparently incidental to his relationship to Jesus as God's Messiah. A pseudepigrapher would almost certainly have made an explicit claim to the apostolic authority of James, especially if written outside of the provenance of the historical James.

The second explicit reference to Jesus in 2:1 is in a clause that defines "brothers and sisters" (Gk. *adelphoi*) as "believers in our glorious Lord Jesus Christ," and as such they are not to practice favoritism. Clearly James is writing as someone who identifies himself as such a believer in Christ. The syntax of the Greek, especially the genitive *doxēs* ("glory") that is most relevant to Christology, can be understood in more than one way.

It is grammatically possible to take "glory" to be in apposition to "our Lord Jesus Christ," thereby providing a further definition of Jesus as "the Glory." Those who are inclined to read *doxēs* this way associate it with *shekinah* glory of God. The word *shekinah*, a Hebrew form meaning "dwelling," is found in postbiblical writings of Palestinian and Babylonian Judaism to refer to the divine manifestation of the presence of God in the world. For instance, in 2 Chronicles 7:1–2, at the dedication of Solomon's temple, God's glory (Heb., *kābōd*; LXX/OG, *doxēs*) filled the place with a manifestation of God's presence. Later Jewish writings refer to that manifestation of God's dwelling as the *shekinah*. If that is James's sense of *doxēs* in 2:1, it would express a very high Christology indeed, making Jesus the visible presence of God.

If *doxēs* is construed as a genitive of place or sphere, it would be an allusion to the state of the resurrected Jesus and his ascension to the right hand of God ("our Lord Jesus Christ in/of glory"), which also communicates a high Christology. This idea is supported by other uses of the word "glory" to refer to the eschatological state of being present with God (e.g., Luke 24:26; John 17:5; 1 Cor. 15:43; Phil. 3:21), though in most of those cases a preposition clarifies the sense.

How to Understand the Genitive?

τοῦ κυρίου ἡμῶν Ἰησοῦ Χριστοῦ τῆς δόξης

Appositional genitive:	"our Lord Jesus Christ, the Glory"
Attributive genitive:	"our glorious Lord Jesus Christ"
Genitive of place:	"our Lord Jesus Christ in/of glory"

Most English translations take "glory" to be an attributive genitive, expressing an attribute of Jesus Christ and translating it with the English adjective "glorious." This still requires that the sense of "glorious" in reference to Jesus Christ be understood by its other biblical uses. So understood, James may be thinking of Jesus Christ as the revelation of God's glory, as having been resurrected into God's glory, or as having more generalized characteristics associated with the eschatological glory of the Messiah. Regardless of how the genitive is construed, James's point is to affirm that Christians ought to believe in this glorious Jesus Christ, a concept that when used elsewhere in Scripture means to believe in God's covenant promises.[1]

At the dedication of Solomon's temple, God's glory was a manifestation of God's presence.

In any case, the way that James is able to refer to Jesus in these exalted terms in a passing reference shows that both James and his readers shared a high view of Jesus Christ on which he could assume and for which he did not need to argue. This means that James's Christology is the assumed and implicit perspective from which he writes. Christians today may speak or write from a thoroughly orthodox and high Christology, but that does not mean that every sentence, writing, or conversation contains explicit references to Jesus Christ. It is therefore a fallacious conclusion to judge that James is a sub-Christian writer simply because he mentions Jesus only twice. In fact, when the content of James's message is carefully examined, it is clear that his letter is a thoroughly Christian document.

THE IMPLICIT CHRISTOLOGY OF JAMES

Although James explicitly refers only twice to Jesus Christ, there are a number of implicit references and allusions to him that also inform the Christology of James. Because the Christology that undergirds these references must be inferred, it points to an implicit Christology that James does not teach but assumes.

James's Use of *Lord*

In both occurrences of "Jesus Christ" in James (1:1; 2:1), Jesus is described as "Lord." These are only two of the fourteen times "Lord" (Gk. *kurios*) is used in James's letter.

1. For a discussion of whether the phrase *tou kuriou . . . Iēsou Christou* should be construed as an objective or subjective genitive, see the commentaries listed in the Going Further section of chapter 5.

Examination of this title in James further illumines his Christology, for Lord is the title he most frequently uses to refer to Jesus. The Greek word *kurios*, translated "Lord," does not necessarily imply divinity. It was a title of deference that could be used to indicate the superior social position of one over another, such as in the English phrase "lord of the estate." When the first translation of the Hebrew Bible into Greek was made centuries before the advent of Jesus, the divine name *Yahweh* was most frequently rendered using the Greek word *kurios*, which either was, or consequently became, a title for God in Greek-speaking Judaism. The title was preserved in English translation using "Lord," which has become one of the most common ways people refer to God.

Important to this discussion is James's statement in 2:19, "there is one God" (or, "God is one," which amounts to the same idea). James is a monotheistic Jew, writing to people who also believe in the one God of Judaism. It is therefore quite remarkable how James uses "Lord" in his letter to refer both to God and to Jesus, and in some cases feeling no need to resolve the ambiguity. Furthermore, Lord is perhaps the most frequent title used in reference to Jesus throughout the New Testament, indicating that all of its writers allowed Jesus to share the Greek title of Yahweh. Given the varied provenance and destinations of the New Testament letters, this view that Jesus is Lord must have been universally held throughout the earliest decades of the church's existence.

There are at least six places in James where most interpreters believe God is called Lord in James:

> . . . the one who doubts. . . That person should not expect to receive anything from the Lord. (1:6–7)

> With the tongue we praise our Lord and Father, and with it we curse human beings, who have been made in God's likeness. (3:9)

> Humble yourselves before the Lord, and he will lift you up. (4:10)

> The cries of the harvesters have reached the ears of the Lord Almighty. (5:4b)

> Brothers and sisters, as an example of patience in the face of suffering, take the prophets who spoke in the name of the Lord. (5:10)

> You have heard of Job's perseverance and have seen what the Lord finally brought about. The Lord is full of compassion and mercy. (5:11b–c)

James also uses the title Lord to refer unambiguously to Jesus (1:1; 2:1; 5:7a–8). In addition to the two occurrences discussed above, James uses Lord when referring to Jesus' second coming:

> Be patient, then, brothers and sisters, until the Lord's coming. (5:7a)

> You too, be patient and stand firm, because the Lord's coming is near. (5:8)

In a few places, the referent of "Lord" is ambiguous:

> Instead, you ought to say, "If it is the Lord's will, we will live and do this or that." (4:15)

> Is anyone among you sick? Let them call the elders of the church to pray over them and anoint them with oil in the name of the Lord. (5:14)

And the prayer offered in faith will make them well; the Lord will raise them up. If they have sinned, they will be forgiven. (5:15)

Our interest here is not to resolve these ambiguities, for which you can refer to the commentaries. The point is that James, a monotheistic, Jewish writer, had no qualms about (1) referring to Jesus as Lord, a title usually applied to God in Jewish tradition, and (2) using it ambiguously to refer either to Jesus or God where he could have been clearer if he so chose.

Given the serious nature of blasphemy in first-century Judaism, James's use of the title Lord is truly extraordinary and indicates an assumed high Christology that elevates Jesus to the status of God.

Jesus brought before Caiaphas and the Council, Hole, William Brassey/Private Collection/© Look and Learn/The Bridgeman Art Library

Jesus was charged with blasphemy and brought to trial by the Jewish leaders.

Both God and Jesus Christ Are "Judge"

In a statement similar to 2:19, "there is one God," James also declares that "There is only one Lawgiver and Judge, the one who is able to save and destroy" (James 4:12). In this second statement of monotheism, James points to God in his role as giver of the law at Sinai, as the Judge who evaluates people in light of that law, and therefore, as one who has the power either to save or destroy. But James also describes Jesus Christ in that same role as the Judge at his return:

> Be patient, then, brothers and sisters, *until the Lord's coming*. See how the farmer waits for the land to yield its valuable crop, patiently waiting for the autumn and spring rains. You too, be patient and stand firm, because *the Lord's coming is near*. Don't grumble against one another, brothers and sisters, or you will be judged. *The Judge is standing at the door*! (5:7–9, emphasis added)

Thus, James views Jesus as united with God in the role of divine judge. James also views Jesus as sharing in God's role as lawgiver, to which we now turn.

Echoes of the Teaching of Jesus

Any reader familiar with Jesus' teachings in the **Synoptic Gospels**, and especially in Matthew's gospel, will recognize echoes of Jesus' voice in James's message. Much of James's instruction comes from the Sermon on the Mount (Matt. 5:1–7:29). Perhaps the clearest parallel is James 5:12 with Matthew 5:34–37, a teaching that forbids swearing an oath. A comparison of these two passages shows that they are clearly the same teaching but that James is not quoting Jesus' teaching as it was finally recorded in Matthew's gospel. This

The Last Judgement, Spranger, Bartholomaeus/Galleria Sabauda, Turin, Italy/Alinari/The Bridgeman Art Library

James views Jesus as united with God in the role of divine judge.

is an important point, for it shows that James didn't copy his material from the published Gospels, which implies at least two significant points: (1) James could have been written earlier than the Synoptic Gospels, since his message wasn't dependent on them; and (2) James is reflecting the teachings of Jesus from a source, either oral or written, that is quite possibly earlier than the sources used in the Synoptic Gospels, yet one that is consistent with the Gospels.

Despite extensive parallels with Matthew's gospel, there are at least three striking similarities between James and Luke's gospel.[2] First, when the vocabulary of James is compared to that of the Synoptic Gospels, 70 percent of its words are in common with Luke-Acts, 15 percent in common with Matthew, and 15 percent with Mark. Second, elements of the **eschatology** of James are similar to that of Luke, most notably that both view Satan as the adversary in this age who makes diligence and perseverance necessary. (The apostle Peter also shares that view as expressed in 1 Peter 5:8–9.) And third, James shares Luke's condemnation of the rich and the dangers of wealth.

The fact that James is similar in different ways to both Matthew's and Luke's gospels suggests that James may have used a source from which both Matthew and Luke also drew,

2. Peter H. Davids, *The Epistle of James*, NIGTC (Grand Rapids: Eerdmans, 1982), 49.

James's Clearest Echo of the Teaching of Jesus

"Above all, my brothers and sisters, *do not swear — not by heaven* or *by earth* or by anything else. *All you need to say is a simple 'Yes' or 'No.'* Otherwise you will be condemned."

James 5:12 (emphasis added)

"But I tell you, *do not swear an oath* at all: *either by heaven*, for it is God's throne; *or by the earth*, for it is his footstool; or by Jerusalem, for it is the city of the Great King. And do not swear by your head, for you cannot make even one hair white or black. *All you need to say is simply 'Yes,' or 'No'*; anything beyond this comes from the evil one."

Matthew 5:34 – 37 (emphasis added)

each writer emphasizing different elements of that pre-Synoptic tradition. This of course immediately brings to mind the **Q-document**.

Because Jesus preached but didn't leave written works, his teachings were initially preserved in oral form. People who heard Jesus told others what he said, who probably told others, and so on. When the twelve apostles began preaching, they of course drew on what they had heard Jesus teach, and the content of that preaching is referred to as the ***kerygma*** (a Greek noun for preaching). The written record of Jesus' words may have begun with his twelve disciples. Matthew may have taken written notes, probably in Aramaic, even as he listened to Jesus, and perhaps they are the *logia* to which Papias referred.[3] Eventually many of the teachings of Jesus were written down, perhaps in several different documents at different places and times, probably in Aramaic as well as Greek. **Q** (likely from the German noun for "source," *Quelle*) is the name scholars have given to what is believed to have been an early written record of some of Jesus' teachings plus a few narratives written in Greek that may have come into existence by the middle of the first century.[4] Because no physical evidence of such a document has survived, it is a purely hypothetical construct that scholars have created to explain how sections of Matthew's gospel and Luke's gospel, primarily the sayings of Jesus, have such verbal similarity. Either one gospel writer copied from the other or both copied from a document that we now call Q.

Q(uelle)

The Q document is a hypothetical source that stands behind the gospels of Matthew and Luke and, in an earlier version, may have been known to James.

Because scholars have reconstructed Q as basically a more primitive form of that material shared by both Matthew and Luke but not found in Mark, studies that compare

3. A thorough discussion of Gospels source criticism lies outside the scope of this work, but it is important that typical readers of this volume understand how the Gospels came into existence. See a good introduction to the New Testament, such as Gary M. Burge, Lynn H. Cohick, and Gene L. Green, *The New Testament in Antiquity* (Grand Rapids: Zondervan, 2009), 112 – 21; Robert H. Gundry, *A Survey of the New Testament*, 4th ed. (Grand Rapids: Zondervan: 2003), 94 – 103; Mark L. Strauss, *Four Portraits, One Jesus: An Introduction to Jesus and the Gospels* (Grand Rapids: Zondervan, 2007), 44 – 55.

4. Patrick J. Hartin, *James and the Q Sayings of Jesus*, JSNTSup 47 (Sheffield: Sheffield Academic, 1991), 226.

Antioch was a center of early Christianity. It has been associated with both the letter of James and Matthew's Gospel.

Ancient Antioch was where believers in Jesus were first called "Christians."

subsequent writings to Q are based on many levels of inference and subjective scholarly judgment about the nature of the development of the oral tradition. Since the echoes of Jesus' teaching in James don't match the words in Matthew or Luke, they have been compared to the reconstructed Q.[5] One study that compares James to Q concludes that James must have been written before Matthew's gospel and reflects an awareness of the Q tradition (in either its oral or written form) as it had begun to develop toward the form it took when later used in that gospel.[6] The more limited similarities of James to Luke's gospel indicate that, while both James and Luke used material from an early form of Q, James did not know the version of Q that had developed and was used as a source of the third gospel.[7] (The development of an oral or written tradition could have continued as it came in contact with other oral or written traditions about Jesus and his teachings and been revised accordingly.)

Of course, since there is no **extant** copy of the Q-document from ancient times, such comparisons contain a degree of scholarly circularity. It does seem clear that James's **epistle** and Matthew's gospel were produced in one or more communities (Jerusalem and Antioch?) that both had access to the same form of Jesus' Sermon on the Mount, since the similarities are predominantly found in that section of Matthew. Whether James was using a form of Q material at particular points and locations of its development—and even whether Q ever actually existed and functioned as Q scholars argue for—remains uncertain. James may have used the *logia* of Matthew himself, since both men lived in proximity. It is clear that, while James drew from the same material as Matthew

5. See ibid., esp. chart on pp. 141–42; also Luke Timothy Johnson and Wesley Wachob, "The Sayings of Jesus in the Letter of James," in *Brother of Jesus, Friend of God: Studies in the Letter of James* (Grand Rapids: Eerdmans, 2004), 136–54.

6. Ibid., 242–43; however, see critique of Hartin by Richard Bauckham, *JTS* 44 (1993): 298–301.

7. Ibid., 171–72.

and possibly Luke, there is no direct literary dependency between James and either of those gospels. James was expressing a form of Jesus' teaching that predates the Gospels and was therefore preserving an important early snapshot of Jesus' teaching.

The Sermon on the Mount.

James never mentions Jesus as the source for his material, but so much of what he teaches sounds very similar to what Jesus taught. If his readers had heard Jesus themselves or had Matthew's gospel available, they surely would have recognized that James was alluding to Jesus' teaching. And what Jesus taught was not completely new and innovative; he was drawing on a highly developed wisdom tradition that had its source in the Torah. (See chapter 7 for a discussion of wisdom in James.) In fact, one of the hallmarks of the

Probable Allusions to Jesus' Teaching in Matthew's Gospel*

James	*Matthew*	*Topic*
1:2	5:10–12	Joy and blessing in the face of trials and suffering
1:4	5:48	Completion/perfection
1:5	7:7–12	Ask (God) and it will be given to you
1:6	21:21	Do not doubt
1:9	5:3	The poor are to be respected in the church
1:12	7:14	Those who persevere receive eternal life
1:17	7:11	Good gifts from the Father
1:20	5:22	Against anger
1:22–23	7:21–27	Put Jesus' words into practice
2:5	5:3	The poor inherit the kingdom
2:8	22:39	"Love your neighbor as yourself"
2:13	5:7; 6:14–15	Mercy for the merciful
2:14–16	7:21–23	Faith without works of no avail
3:6	5:22	Power of ungodly words
3:10–12	7:15–20	Bad trees cannot bear good fruit
3:18	5:9	Peacemakers are blessed
4:4	6:24	One cannot serve two masters
4:8	5:8	Pure of heart
4:10	5:5	The humble are exalted
4:11–12	7:1–5	Do not judge others
5:2–3	6:19–20	Earthly treasures are fleeting
5:9b	24:33	Judgment is near
5:10	5:12	Prophets as examples of suffering and persecution
5:12	5:33–37	Against swearing oaths

*Special thanks to Ben Ribbens for compiling this list from John MacArthur, *James*, MacArthur New Testament Commentary (Chicago: Moody, 1998), 2; Davids, *James*, 729–30; Donald Guthrie, *New Testament Introduction*, 4th ed. (Downers Grove, Ill.: InterVarsity, 1990), 729–30.

Sermon on the Mount is that Jesus invokes the law as it was being taught in his day. He often begins, "You have heard that it was said.... But I tell you" (Matt. 5:21, 27, 33, 38, 43). In his teaching, Jesus presents himself as a teacher with greater authority than that of the teachers of the law and the Pharisees, and this point was not lost on those who heard him (Matt. 7:29). By using Jesus' teaching as the basis of his ethical exhortation, James is submitting to and communicating the authority of Jesus as normative for his Christian readers. Jesus' teaching was so integrated into James's thoughts that his own exhortations are reexpressions of the Lord's words.

"No other book of the New Testament offers as many echoes of the Sermon [on the Mount] as the letter of James."

JEAN CANTINAT, *LES EPITRES DE SAINT JACQUES ET DE SAINT JUDE*

For instance, consider the exhortation in James closest to Jesus' words in Matthew 5:33–35. Jesus first presents the moral law as it was taught in his day: "You have heard that it was said to the people long ago, 'Do not break your oath....' But I tell you, do not swear an oath at all." Without discussion or debate, James simply presents in 5:12 Jesus' teaching as the moral truth by which Christians are to live: "Above all, my brothers and sisters, do not swear."

The way James uses the teachings of Jesus as his moral reference point reveals another aspect of his assumed Christology, that what Jesus taught supersedes the traditional teaching of the religious leaders of first-century Judaism. In implicit agreement with one of the points of Matthew's gospel, James perceived Jesus as a new Lawgiver.

James sees the moral concepts that Jesus taught as the transposition of the law of Moses forming the basis for Christian life under the new covenant, a moral life that through behavior expresses faith in Jesus as the Messiah and new Lawgiver. (See chapter 7.)

Mount of Beatitudes. The probable place Jesus preached the Sermon on the Mount.

The "royal law" (James 2:8).

James takes very seriously Jesus' declaration that he has not come to abolish the Law and the Prophets but to fulfill them (Matt. 5:17). Therefore, James does not repudiate the law of Moses as the basis for the moral life that pleases God, but like the evangelist Matthew, James argues for "the continuing value of a properly interpreted law" in the lives of the Christians to whom he writes.[8] James upholds the familiar points of the law, such as the prohibition against adultery and murder (2:11), which were affirmed by the Lord Jesus. Jesus identified anger toward others as akin to murder and worthy of judgment (Matt. 5:21–25), and it seems to be that broadening of the sixth commandment to encompass the origin of murder in the human heart that James invokes in 4:2 and 5:6.

James values the law, not by fencing it as the Pharisees did and effectively multiplying the number of laws to be kept, but by understanding the principle that Jesus revealed when asked which commandment was the most important one to obey:

> Jesus replied: "'Love the Lord your God with all your heart and with all your soul and with all your mind.' This is the first and greatest commandment. And the second is like it: 'Love your neighbor as yourself.' All the Law and the Prophets hang on these two commandments." (Matt. 22:37–40; Mark 12:29–31)

> "Do not seek revenge or bear a grudge against anyone among your people, but love your neighbor as yourself. I am the LORD."
>
> LEVITICUS 19:18

This understanding of the law allows James to conclude that favoritism, which might be viewed as a natural social dynamic or a relatively minor offense at worst, is in fact an infraction of the law that breaks all of it (2:8–11), for it violates the principle of loving one's neighbor as oneself. The principle of loving one's neighbor as oneself was not new with Jesus' teaching, for it is found in Leviticus 19:18 as one of a long list of social evils to avoid, including not showing favoritism (Lev. 19:15). Jesus points out that the entire law and message of the prophets rests on this principle—to love one's neighbor—which in turn flows from the principle of love for God. For James, this "royal law" is the basis for Christian ethics and morality. More on this in chapter 7.

It is the adjective "royal" (Gk. *basilikon*) that is most telling for James's implicit Christology. This word is the adjectival cognate of the nouns for "king" (*basileus*) and "kingdom"

---

8. Davids, *James*, 49.

A Summary of the Christology in James

- James twice refers to Jesus as "The Lord Jesus Christ" (1:1; 2:1).
- James uses the title Lord for both God and Jesus.
- Jesus shares the role of Judge with God.
- Jesus' teaching has an authoritative, normative character .
- Jesus shares the role of lawgiver with God.
- Jesus continues to exist and will return.

Library of Congress

As an infant, Jesus was honored as a king by the Magi. Laon Cathedral, France.

(*basileia*). The royal law is the law of God's kingdom, a kingdom that Jesus proclaimed as the heart of his message (Matt. 4:17; Mark 1:14–15; Luke 4:43). As Messiah, Jesus is the King of God's kingdom (Ps. 2:6–7), and his Word is its law. (Note that this is congruent with Matthew's gospel, which has as its major theme God's kingdom and Jesus as the Lawgiver for God's kingdom.) For the point of James's implicit Christology, it is clear that James accepts Jesus' view as the true, right, and normative way to understand the continuing value of the law in the kingdom of God.

The Ongoing Existence and Return of Jesus

Perhaps the most telling clue to James's implicit Christology is found in James 5:7–9, where the coming of "the Lord" is mentioned twice using the Greek word ***parousia***. The teaching that Jesus Christ will return is found in even the earliest New Testament writings, 1 and 2 Thessalonians, where it is referred to as the parousia (1 Thess. 2:19; 3:13; 4:15; 5:23; 2 Thess. 2:1, 8, 9). It is the standard word used in the New Testament to refer to the return of Christ (Matt. 24:3, 27, 37, 39; 1 Cor. 15:23; 2 Peter 3:4; 1 John 2:28) and was also used to refer to his glorious appearance on the Mount of Transfiguration (2 Peter 1:16). Notice that the majority of New Testament writers—Matthew, Paul, Peter, James, and John—refer to the return of Christ, so it was a widely taught belief of the earliest Christians. In Acts 1:11, immediately following Jesus' ascension, the angels announce that Jesus will return, though the word *parousia* isn't used there.

James does not teach about the future return of Jesus or give any additional details about this extraordinarily mysterious event. James simply assumes that his readers are acquainted with the belief in the parousia, and he uses it to encourage his readers to persevere. However, James does connect the parousia to Jesus' role as Judge (see above). The doctrine of the parousia as presented in the New Testament necessarily entails the resurrected state of Jesus and his presence with the Father, from where he will come "to judge the living and the dead," as the Apostles' Creeds puts it.

παρουσία

The doctrine of the *parousia*, the return of Christ, is among the earliest and most fundamental beliefs of Christianity.

The theology of Judaism that developed from the Old Testament included belief that God was the final, ultimate Judge and that a day would come, "the day of Lord," when the nations would be judged. This is a major theme of the prophets, who offered it as hope to God's

> **What the Apostles' Creed Says about Jesus**
>
> I believe ... in Jesus Christ, [God the Father's] only Son, our Lord:
> who was conceived by the Holy Spirit,
> born of the Virgin Mary,
> suffered under Pontius Pilate,
> was crucified, dead, and buried;
> he descended into hell;
> the third day he rose again from the dead;
> he ascended into heaven,
> and sits at the right hand of God the Father Almighty;
> from thence he shall come to judge the living and the dead.

ancient people that they would be eternally vindicated when God destroys those who would destroy them. It was also a motivation for God's people not to live as the pagans do but to maintain covenantal faithfulness, so that they would not fall under the same coming judgment. By the time James wrote, the concept of God as Judge was a prominent point of Judaism.

What the New Testament brings to that theology is the concept that Jesus, the Messiah, will be the agent of that judgment at a time referred to as the parousia, or return, of Christ. Even if this idea does not form the major point of James's letter, James clearly believes this doctrine and reminds his readers of it in 5:7–9. The ongoing existence of Jesus Christ until his return implies a very high Christology indeed.

THE DISTINCTLY CHRISTIAN NATURE OF JAMES'S LETTER

Those who believe the two occurrences of "Jesus Christ" in James's letter (1:1; 2:1) can be simply excised and produce a thoroughly Jewish text that may have existed prior to Christ have missed the thoroughly Christian nature of the letter. James was not writing to expound theological doctrine, as the apostle Paul did with such power. James was writing to teach ethical living to Christian communities as Jesus had taught it. In fact, one interpreter has said, "To listen to James ... is to listen to Jesus!"[9]

Now it is true that Jesus was not introducing new concepts when it came to the moral demands of the law, but was transposing the moral standards of first-century Judaism into a new key. As he himself said, he came not to abolish the law and replace it with something new but to fulfill it (Matt. 5:17). And so what Jesus taught in the Sermon on the Mount and elsewhere sounded much like the teachings of first-century Judaism, which was based on ideas about the Law as God's wisdom for living. Jesus' teaching sounds similar to material found in Sirach in the **Apocrypha** and even of texts such as the *Testament of the Twelve*

---

9. Franz Mussner, *Der Jakobusbrief*, HTKNT 13 (Freiburg: Herder, 1964), 52–53, quoted in Harner, *What Are They Saying?* 15.

Patriarchs, because he was standing in the same ethical tradition as the men who wrote those books. More on this in Chapter 7.

Christian theology is the very fiber of James's letter, showing that its author was a thoroughly Christian thinker. He is not reporting the teachings of Jesus, as Matthew's gospel does, and he is not expounding on the great theological themes of Christian belief, as the apostle Paul does. James is not teaching *about* Jesus, but is applying the teaching of Jesus as normative for the Christian life. His "preaching" flows out of a milieu that is concerned not with doctrine, but with Christian living, much as most modern preaching is today. Modern sermons may be solidly based on the doctrines of the incarnation, justification by faith, Scripture as the Word of God, and everlasting life, but those topics are not necessarily mentioned, defended, or taught by any given sermon. They are the assumed theological framework within which the preacher instructs his or her congregation how to live out the Christian faith. The epistle of James may be the earliest application of Christian doctrine to ethical issues that has survived. And so it is that topic of James's ethical instruction for Christian life that we will take up in the next chapter.

"James is as Christological as we should expect the kind of Christian literature he writes to be."

Richard Bauckham, *James: Wisdom of James, Disciple of Jesus the Sage*

CHAPTER SUMMARY

The book of James is quite possibly the earliest Christian writing to have survived, and with good evidence that it was written by a member of Jesus' immediate family in the very epicenter of the gospel, the holy city of Jerusalem. Contrary to conclusions that might be inferred from only a cursory reading of the book, James is a thoroughly Christian thinker who forms an important bridge from the ethical tradition of first-century Judaism to the kingdom ethics preached by Jesus Christ.

While not writing in the same categories addressed by the apostle Paul, James's message rests on a high Christology, which includes the divinity of Christ, the normative authority of Jesus' teaching, his resurrection and ascension, and the expectation of his return. For too long the Protestant church has not appreciated the unique character of the book of James and has been distracted by questions raised when James is read in the canonical context of the Pauline writings on **soteriology**.

KEY TERMS

- day of the Lord
- kerygma
- parousia
- Q(uelle)-document
- royal law
- Sermon on the Mount
- Synoptic Gospels

QUESTIONS FOR REVIEW OR DISCUSSION

1. Why do you think Jesus is mentioned so infrequently in the book of James? Does this diminish the value of James as a distinctively Christian book?
2. What is the difference between explicit Christology and implicit Christology?
3. List the characteristics of the letter of James that contribute to its Christology.
4. Describe the relationship of James's teaching to that of Jesus, especially as found in Matthew's gospel.
5. Describe the relationship of Jesus' teaching to the Old Testament law as it was understood at that time?
6. How would you respond to someone who claims that James is presenting generic moral teaching that is found in many different religions? Is Jesus just another religious teacher of ethics?

GOING FURTHER

Baker, William R. "Christology in the Epistle of James." *EQ* 74 (2002): 47–57.

Bauckham, Richard. *James: Wisdom of James, Disciple of Jesus the Sage.* New Testament Reading. London: Routledge, 1999.

Chester, Andrew. "The Theology of James." Pages 1–62 in *The Theology of the Letters of James, Peter, and Jude.* New Testament Theology. Cambridge: Cambridge University Press, 1996.

Donelson, Lewis R. *From Hebrews to Revelation: A Theological Introduction.* Louisville: Westminster John Knox, 2001.

Hartin, Patrick J. *James and the Q Sayings of Jesus.* JSNTSup 47. Sheffield: Sheffield Academic, 1991.

Johnson, Luke Timothy. *Brother of Jesus, Friend of God: Studies in the Letter of James.* Grand Rapids: Eerdmans, 2004.

Reumann, John. "Christology of James." Pages 128–39 in *Who Do You Say That I Am? Essays on Christology in Honor of Jack Dean Kingsbury.* Edited by Mark Allan Powell and David R. Bauer. Louisville: Westminster John Knox, 1999.

Wachob, Wesley Hiram. *The Voice of Jesus in the Social Rhetoric of James.* Cambridge: Cambridge University Press, 2000.

Wall, Robert W. *Community of the Wise: The Letter of James.* New Testament in Context. Valley Forge, Pa.: Trinity Press International, 1997.

CHAPTER 7

The "Royal Law"

CHRISTIAN WISDOM AND ETHICS IN JAMES

Your Goals for This Chapter

- To learn how the various topics in the letter of James are related to each other and to the gospel of Jesus Christ.
- To understand that the teachings of James, and of Jesus himself, stand in a long tradition of Jewish moral wisdom and yet are the hallmarks of the kingdom of God.
- To examine James's most famous statement, "Faith without works is dead" (James 2:26 KJV) and to understand its relationship to Paul's teaching on justification by faith alone.
- To observe what issues James considers essential to the spiritual growth and maturity of the single-minded Christian.
- To understand the theological basis of the ethical system that James presents.

WHY THIS CHAPTER IS IMPORTANT TO YOU

"Faith without works is dead" (James 2:26 KJV). Christians, and perhaps all humans, have tried to maintain some kind of distance between their deeds and their true selves. We often have a certain disappointment with our acts. We think we could have done better. And we like to imagine that these dreams of a better self are who we really are. We want to believe that we are not fully identical with our acts.[1]

This interesting observation raises the question, Who am I really? What really defines me? Do my beliefs and intentions define me? Or my actions and behavior? We know that Christians should love God with our whole selves—heart, soul, mind, and strength (Mark 12:30). The integration of the self means that one's inner life and one's outward behavior should be consistent, and for the Christian, both should be bound by covenant love for God.

James is presenting the Christian concept of a whole and unified person as the goal of spiritual maturity. The opposite of an integrated Christian is the "double-minded" person who is unstable in all he or she does. The mental resolve and actions of such people are inconsistent and unreliable. Double-minded people waver between obedience to God and friendship with the world. And so the book of James presents an ethical system of thought that is essential to understand, first, for one's own spiritual growth and maturity, and second, as a prerequisite for ministering to the spiritual vitality of others.

In addition, the book of James, while largely overlooked in Protestant doctrine, has often motivated Christian involvement in public policy. Political candidates, such as Hillary Clinton, John Kerry, and Al Gore, have appealed to the book of James.[2] Especially in areas of social justice for the poor, the book of James has been perceived as providing a biblical warrant. Some interpreters claim that James shares an ethical agenda with Judaism and Islam that is congenial to public policy in a religiously pluralistic democracy. With the growing engagement of religion and politics, an understanding of the ethics of James is essential to avoid a misuse of scriptural authority.

CHAPTER OUTLINE

I. The Royal Law as the Basis of James's Ethics

II. Wisdom from Above and Torah

III. James and the Teaching of Jesus

IV. Faith and Works

V. Faith in Action

  A. The *Dipsychos* Person

  B. Godly Speech

  C. Rich and Poor

---

1. Lewis R. Donelson, *From Hebrews to Revelation: A Theological Introduction* (Louisville: Westminster John Knox, 2001), 35.

2. Benedicta Cipolla, "Faith and Works in American Politics," www.pbs.org/wnet/religionandethics/week1140/exclusive.html (accessed November 4, 2009).

Key Verses

1:5 If any of you lacks wisdom, you should ask God, who gives generously to all without finding fault, and it will be given to you.

2:8 If you really keep the royal law found in Scripture, "Love your neighbor as yourself," you are doing right.

2:14 What good is it, my brothers and sisters, if someone claims to have faith but has no deeds? Can such faith save them?

3:13–15 Who is wise and understanding among you? Let them show it by their good life, by deeds done in the humility that comes from wisdom. But if you harbor bitter envy and selfish ambition in your hearts, do not boast about it or deny the truth. Such "wisdom" does not come down from heaven but is earthly, unspiritual, demonic.

3:17 But the wisdom that comes from heaven is first of all pure; then peace-loving, considerate, submissive, full of mercy and good fruit, impartial and sincere.

4:8 Come near to God and he will come near to you. Wash your hands, you sinners, and purify your hearts, you double-minded.

THE ROYAL LAW AS THE BASIS OF JAMES'S ETHICS

The search for a unifying theme in James has been elusive. On a surface reading, the letter seems to jump from topic to topic with little continuity of thought or structure of argument. It covers a variety of ethical issues that address concerns of justice and harmony in the community. Most interpreters see the content of James as motivated by pressing issues that either existed in the congregation(s) or that were plausible in that social context. It might be presumptuous even to attempt to state a unifying theme, but it appears that James is very concerned with applying the "royal law," the "perfect law that gives freedom" (1:25) to the life situations of his readers. And that "royal law," as we discussed in chapter 6, is the summary statement that Jesus gives about the greatest commandment in the Law, "'Love the Lord your God with all your heart and with all your soul and with all your mind.' This is the first and greatest commandment. And the second is like it: 'Love your neighbor as yourself.' All the law and the Prophets hang on these two commandments" (Matt. 22:37–40; Mark 12:28–31; Luke 10:25–28). In what is now sometimes called the Golden Rule, Jesus was not only summing up the moral demands of the old covenant, but because he came to fulfill and not abolish the law, he was establishing the basis of the moral law for the kingdom of God he inaugurated. In the first century there was a close association between the coming of God's kingdom and the land of Palestine. But Jesus' teaching shows that we should understand "kingdom" in the sense of God's reign and rule over human hearts wherever and whenever they live.

The first principle of the kingdom of God is to love God in obedient relationship to him. But just how would one do that? We can't give God a big hug or send a Valentine on

What Is the Difference between Morality and Ethics?

Morals are the fundamental principles that one believes and that consequently define one's character. Ethics are the application of those principles in a given society or community. One's morals might include "Thou shalt not steal." But then that principle has to be applied to given situations, such as making personal phone calls on a company phone or pointing out when a restaurant server forgets to put an item on the check. Those are ethical decisions. Many ethical decisions are defined by the particular social group involved, showing that even shared moral values can be applied in various ways. Consequently, ethical decisions require wisdom.

February 14. God has always told his people that they express love for him by proper worship and by allowing the moral law he has established to govern behavior with one another. That is why the first four of the Ten Commandments govern relationship with God and the rest of them govern relationship with other people. Loving God by loving others is what Jesus was talking about when he said that whatever you do for one of the least in the community, you do for the Lord (Matt. 25:40, 45). Loving our neighbors as ourselves is the summary principle of God's moral demands upon us with respect to our relationships with one another. We cannot truly love God if we deny love to others. And so Jesus added, "There is no commandment greater than these" (Mark 12:31). Furthermore, this is the key to eternal life, for in Luke 10:28, Jesus remarked to the expert in the law that if he loved God and loved his neighbor, he would live—a thought that sounds rather like James's point that a faith that lacks love of neighbor cannot save (James 2:14–17).

It was in Jesus' teaching that James saw the transposition of the law of the Sinai covenant into the royal law that gives freedom for the life of the Christian believer. Jesus, as discussed in chapter 6, was understood to be the Messiah, the King of God's kingdom. He dispelled the misconceptions about the law by showing that it is not a matter of keeping more and more regulations, but of internal transformation into a righteousness "that surpasses that of the Pharisees" with their 613 commandments (Matt. 5:20). Jesus transposed the law by establishing with his blood the new covenant and its promises to write the law

Law in James

- "the perfect law that gives freedom" (James 1:25)
- "the royal law" (James 2:8)
- "the law that gives freedom" (James 2:12)

God's moral will for human beings is disclosed in the Old Testament law, which Jesus the King reinterpreted when he inaugurated the kingdom of God, and which is summed up by the love command. The association of freedom with living in a way that pleases God is expressed also in Psalm 119:32: "I run in the path of your commands, for you have set my heart free" (NIV 1984).

Jesus Transposes the Law

Jesus transposes the Law of Sinai into the Law of God's Kingdom by

1. requiring that it be internalized;
2. refocusing it on moral and ethical issues;
3. intensifying obedience from mere compliance to love for others.*

*From Richard Bauckham, *James: Wisdom of James, Disciple of Jesus the Sage*, New Testament Readings (London: Routledge, 1999), 142–47.

on hearts (Jer. 31:33) and to provide new hearts and spirits (Ezek. 18:31; 36:26). This transposition refocuses the law on its moral and ethical aspects and away from its ritual and cultic practices. Both Jesus, in the Sermon on the Mount, and James, in his letter, focus their teaching on the moral demands of God's law and its application to ethical decisions; in contrast, neither addresses the rituals and customs of first-century Judaism that centered on the temple sacrifices and their purity laws. In addition, Jesus' transposition of the Law intensifies it by shifting the measure of obedience to love rather than mere compliance. The test of a distinctively Christian system of ethics and morality must be judged against the royal law as restated by Jesus in the Golden Rule: "So in everything, do to others what you would have them do to you, for this sums up the Law and the Prophets" (Matt. 7:12; Luke 6:31).

Loving one's neighbor is not a new commandment added to the list. In fact, the Greek word used in James, *nomos*, seldom refers to an individual commandment in the **Septuagint** or New Testament, which is usually referred to with the word *entolē. Nomos* usually refers to the law as a corpus in its entirety and is the Greek word that translates *Torah* in the Septuagint. Therefore, love of neighbor is the overarching moral principle (Gk. *nomos*, Torah) which is expressed in specific commandments (Gk. sg. *entolē*). The individual commandments (Gk. sg. *entolē*) Jesus mentions in Matthew 5, such as the prohibition against murder and adultery, are commandments by which God expects his people to love their neighbors, not only through external behavior but in the inner person that recognizes even anger and lust as unloving acts. In similar fashion, James applies the moral principle of love for neighbor to the ethical problems of favoritism, slander, oppression of the poor, and other topics throughout the letter.

© GodSpeaks, Inc./www.godspeaks.com

Love for God expressed through love for neighbor is the wellspring of the faithful life wisely lived. You might ask, "How can I love a stranger I don't even know?" Or "How can I love someone if I don't even like him?" But the love that Jesus commands is not an emotion, though it may have emotional aspects. Love as Jesus defines it does not have to do with warm fuzzy feelings toward another person, but rather with treating that person rightly. In the parable of the good Samaritan (Luke 10:29–37), the expert in the law wants to selectively love and so asks Jesus, "And who is my neighbor?" In response, Jesus tells a story about a Samaritan, a hated ethnic group at that time, caring for a man of Jerusalem who had fallen into dire need. It is the Samaritan, whom Jews loved to hate, who is the neighbor Jesus wants the expert in the law to love! But Jesus also defines love in the parable not as emotion, but as the considerate response to meet the evident needs of another person, regardless of race, ethnicity, religious affiliation, gender, and so forth.

The Golden Rule Was Part of Jewish Tradition

"What is hateful to you, do not do to your neighbor; that is the whole Torah, while the rest is the commentary thereof."

HILLEL, *B. ŠABBAT* 31A

The law of love addresses the problem of unity and harmony in the churches, and therefore undergirds all New Testament exhortation. Treating each other rightly within a community establishes and preserves unity and harmony. And every one of James's exhortations or prohibitions points toward that goal of loving others as oneself and doing to them only what one would have done to himself or herself. This "royal law," the principal law of the kingdom, is mentioned only in James 2 in the specific context of favoritism, but as we saw in chapter 6, Jesus' teaching in the Sermon on the Mount permeates James's thought. The moral demands taught by the King, referred to by James as "the royal law," constitute the basis for ethical Christian living under God's rule.

But a moral code based on love is more difficult to live out than a system of legalism based on a list of dos and don'ts. And particularly when one is experiencing trials and suffering, it may not always be evident how to live by that royal law. Wisdom from above is needed both to recognize how to live out faithfully the moral demands of Jesus' teaching in each situation and to maintain the motivation to do so (James 1:5).

WISDOM FROM ABOVE AND TORAH

A decade ago it became popular to read James as a sort of Jewish wisdom literature, and many books on James include the word "wisdom" in their titles. The letter of James, however, does not take the form of the wisdom genres of Judaism, such as Proverbs, Ecclesiastes, or the apocryphal books of Ben Sira (also known as Sirach or Ecclesiasticus) and the Wisdom of Solomon, although there are some apparent parallels in content. And although James mentions "wisdom" or "wise" five times (1:5; 3:13, 15, 17), he does not dwell on it as a topic. Like his assumed **Christology**, James *assumes* the wisdom tradition of Judaism, but as it has been transposed by Jesus' teaching.

What Is Wisdom?

wisdom: the quality of having experience, knowledge, and good judgment; the quality of being wise; the soundness of an action or decision with regard to the application of such experience, knowledge, and good judgment.

Oxford American Dictionary

The long tradition of Jewish wisdom developed through the centuries came into contact with Greek ideas about wisdom during the Hellenistic period. In the Greek world, wisdom was the common goal of all the great philosophical schools. In that cultural setting, wisdom was defined as knowing how to live toward life's highest good, and there were several schools of thought about what life's highest good might be. In other words, the wisdom of one's decisions and behavior depends on evaluating it toward the goal of life's highest good. All wisdom is relative toward an end.

In the first century when the New Testament was written, the **Epicureans** believed that the highest ideal for humanity was plea-

A Greater Wisdom from the One Greater than Solomon

"The Queen of the South will rise at the judgment with this generation and condemn it; for she came from the ends of the earth to listen to Solomon's wisdom, and now one greater than Solomon is here."

Jesus, Matthew 12:42

sure, defined not as sensual pleasure but as a well-being that could be attained only through avoiding anything that might disturb the tranquility of the soul. In contrast, another major school was the **Stoics**, rationalists who believed that an impersonal, all-powerful cosmic force, which they referred to as Reason, controls both the physical and moral order of the universe. The highest good in Stoic thought was to live in harmony with nature and the cosmic purpose that controlled the universe, which led to a very fatalistic view of life. Many other philosophical views were current in the Hellenistic age, each offering some definition of life's highest good and of wisdom as living toward that goal.

When Judaism found itself engaging with Greek culture following the conquest of Alexander the Great, it too had its definition of life's highest good and of wisdom. After all, the Greeks sought wisdom, and Israel's King Solomon was reputed to have been the wisest man who ever lived (1 Kings 4:29; 5:12; 10:23; 2 Chron. 1:11–12; 9:22–23). Solomon's wisdom came from Yahweh, the creator of life who defined life's highest good and who created the moral order of the universe. Wisdom in Jewish thought, therefore, was found in obedience to Torah, the covenant law of ancient Israel. But Jesus is greater than Solomon, and it is his teaching that forms the basis of the Christian wisdom tradition.

Jesus transposed the ancient Law represented by the Ten Commandments into the royal law of his kingdom.

In an ancient expression of the idea that all truth is God's truth, Jewish writers living in the Greek culture, such as the authors of Sirach and the Wisdom of Solomon, engaged Greek philosophy and argued that the best of Greek wisdom was actually consistent with the Torah that embodied Israel's wisdom. Life's highest good was to obey God:

> Observe them [God's decrees and laws] carefully, for this will show your *wisdom and understanding* to the nations, who will hear about all these decrees and say, "Surely this great nation is a *wise and understanding* people." (Deut. 4:6, emphasis added)

The failure to observe God's decrees and laws carefully is indicted by the prophets. For instance, Hosea echoes Deuteronomy 4:6 when he asks:

Who is wise? Let them realize these things.
  Who is discerning? Let them understand.
The ways of the LORD are right;
  the righteous walk in them,
but the rebellious stumble in them. (Hos. 14:9, emphasis added)

Recalling the warning of spiritual unfaithfulness in Hosea, James challenges his readers with the same question in 3:13 (emphasis added):

> *Who is wise and understanding among you?* Let them show it by their good life, by deeds done in the humility that comes from wisdom.

Of course, James lived centuries after Hosea, and during that time tremendous historical changes brought about further development of the theological and moral traditions of Judaism. Two developments are most relevant for this discussion: (1) the explicit identification of wisdom with Torah and (2) the idea of an eschatological afterlife following God's judgment. Both of these concepts form the background of James's message of Christian life and ethics.[3]

Hellenistic culture valued wisdom as the way to attain life's highest good. Since Judaism considered the observation of Torah to be the way to life's highest good, wisdom and Torah became more closely identified, building on Deuteronomy 4:6. Over the centuries two traditions of interpreting Torah developed:[4]

---

3. See Peter Davids, *The Epistle of James*, NIGTC (Grand Rapids: Eerdmans, 1982), 51–56.
4. Richard Bauckham, *James: Wisdom of James, Disciple of Jesus the Sage*, New Testament Readings (London: Routledge, 1999), 152.

Wisdom Is Torah Observance

"Wisdom praises herself,
  and tells of her glory in the midst of her people. . . .
All this [wisdom's glory] is the book of the covenant of the Most High God,
  the law that Moses commanded us
  as an inheritance for the congregations of Jacob."

Sirach 24:1, 23 (NRSV)

"She [wisdom] is the book of the commandments of God,
  the law that endures forever.
All who hold her fast will live,
  and those who forsake her will die."

Baruch 4:1

"Wisdom, next, is the knowledge of divine and human matters and the causes of these. This, in turn, is education in the law, by which we learn divine matters reverently and human affairs to our advantage."

4 Maccabees 1:16–17

Related Genres of Jewish Tradition*

Law is the command of God to his covenant people.
Prophecy is a message from God to people at a particular juncture in their history.
Apocalypse is the communication of revelations of divine mysteries.
Wisdom is the teaching of a sage who instructs with the authority of his own experience, observation, insight, and reflection.

*Richard Bauckham, *James: Wisdom of James, Disciple of Jesus the Sage*, New Testament Readings (London: Routledge, 1999), 31.

1. **Halakhah**, which aims to specify what each individual commandment of Torah requires in a given context, as does, for instance, 4QMMT from Qumran, the later **Mishnah**, and the rabbinic literature. This approach tends to multiply the number of commandments, resulting in the 613 commandments noted in the Talmud (*b. Mak.* 24a).
2. Torah as wisdom (e.g., as in Sirach), which seeks to instill the s/Spirit of the Law, to illustrate its demands, and to draw on the law as source of moral formation and advice.

> "Wisdom is the hidden knowledge of God's eschatological plan."
>
> Peter Davids, *The Epistle of James*

James approaches the law in the second way, probably representing how the earliest Jewish Christians understood Jesus' transposition of the law of Sinai into the royal law of the kingdom.

The development of the theme of wisdom during the intertestamental period can be seen best by reading the apocryphal books. Although Protestants reject the apocryphal books as Scripture, they are nevertheless profitable to read because they are an integral part of the literary and theological heritage of first-century Judaism. The development of Christian theology in the New Testament is better understood with some knowledge of the content of the apocryphal books. Because wisdom is personified as a woman in Proverbs 8:22–31, discussions of wisdom in the Hellenistic texts typically sustain that personification, referring to wisdom as "she"; in fact, the grammatically feminine Greek word for wisdom, *sophia*, functions as a female proper name. These developments can be seen in many of the apocryphal texts, such as Sirach 24 (esp. v. 23); Baruch 3:29–4:1; and 1 Maccabees 1:16–17. For the background of James, Sirach (also known as Ben Sira and Ecclesiasticus) is probably of greatest relevance.

K. H. Jobes

Personification of Wisdom (Gk., *Sophia*) at the Celsus library in Ephesus.

During the Hellenistic period, the literature of Qumran and the apocryphal book Wisdom of Solomon began to view Israel's wisdom

Elements in Common with Wisdom Literature

James shares common elements with the wisdom literature of the Old Testament and its later development in the intertestamental period but is distinctively Christian in its viewpoint.

James

- addresses many of the same topics, such as riches, speech, favoritism, future plans, and pride;
- uses images from common life, especially agricultural images;
- presents the two ways of Israel's wisdom tradition (two kinds of wisdom: earthly and from above; friend of the world, enmity with God);
- presumes a theology (and a Christology), just as books like Proverbs do;
- gives instruction for character development; and
- uses rhetorical questions, as found often in Jewish wisdom literature.

tradition from an eschatological perspective. In the Old Testament book of Proverbs, we see that the benefits of wisdom, and the resulting justice, are achieved *in this life*. But in the Qumran texts and in the Wisdom of Solomon, justice is often not achieved in this life. Rather, it occurs in the afterlife following the judgment of the wicked.[5] Life's highest good then becomes acquittal at God's judgment and the attainment of eternal life. Because of this, the wisdom tradition of the intertestamental period also overlaps with the contemporaneous development of **apocalyptic** literature that takes a decidedly eschatological perspective on life.

"Wisdom is the revelation of God's truth that enables the believer to know how to pass the testing of faith; and it is wisdom's way to lead the believer through such testing and ultimately into God's future blessing."

ROBERT WALL, *COMMUNITY OF THE WISE: THE LETTER OF JAMES*

Apocalyptic literature reveals the larger picture of divine mysteries concerning the destiny of God's people, who will ultimately be vindicated, if not in this life, then at the great judgment when their oppressors are destroyed. It is often a response to oppression; for this reason, we see the eschatological wisdom tradition also addressing contexts of oppression. James picks up on this tradition by noting that his readers are facing trials of various kinds, some no doubt a consequence of their faith in Christ. He reminds them that God will give wisdom as they seek it from him, a wisdom that will allow them to persevere (James 1:2–5).

Jewish wisdom literature not only gives practical advice for ethical behavior, but also for character development, which it puts in terms of the antonyms *righteous/wicked* and *wise/fool*, following the precedent set by Proverbs. In the ethical tradition of Judaism, wisdom is a gracious gift from God that cannot be attained apart from him, and it produces virtues such as humility, patience, discernment, charity, goodness, and steadfast faithfulness.[6] These virtues then enable the covenant person to endure testing and trials.

5. See ibid., 29–35.
6. Davids, *James*, 54–55.

In the Old Testament there is only an implicit association of God's Spirit with wisdom, but that idea comes to fullest fruition in the New Testament. The apostle Paul declares that Jesus Christ is the wisdom of God (1 Cor. 1:22–24) and that the fruit of the Holy Spirit are the virtues needed for ethical Christian living (Gal. 5:22–25). In James, wisdom endows the believer much as the Spirit does in Paul's writings. It is graciously given by God, endowing the Christian with virtues that allow a way of life that both sustains one's faithfulness to Christ through the trials of this life and prepares one to stand before God's judgment in the afterlife.

> "Wisdom is the God-given ability of the transformed heart to discern and to practice God's will."
>
> RICHARD BAUCKHAM, *JAMES: WISDOM OF JAMES, DISCIPLE OF JESUS THE SAGE*

JAMES AND THE TEACHING OF JESUS

Although James stands in the same wisdom tradition that has its origin in the Old Testament and that subsequently developed in the intertestamental period, he stands closer to Jesus' teachings than he does to the Old Testament.[7] But Jesus himself also stood in the tradition of Jewish wisdom based on the ancient Torah, and scholars debate how his teaching related to it. Certainly not everything Jesus said was completely innovative, for he came as the culmination of God's dealings with humankind that had been in the works for centuries. One cannot help but to expect Jesus, a Jew and the promised Messiah, to be consistent with the revelation given by God to and through ancient Israel.[8] On the other hand, in fulfilling the ancient promises of God, Jesus transposed the Torah and the old covenant into a new Torah and a new covenant that inaugurates the kingdom of God, and in so doing introduced substantial differences.

It might be disconcerting to realize how much Jesus had in common with the Jewish teachers of wisdom that had come before him. Such a realization might challenge the distinctiveness of Christ, and indeed some scholars have come to see him as merely another Jewish sage. What is distinctive in his message is that he proclaims himself to be the way to life's highest good—the way to eternal life reconciled with God. Jesus said, "I am the way and the truth and the life. No one comes to the Father except through me" (John 14:6). Therefore, belief in Jesus Christ is life's highest good. James follows Jesus' distinctive wisdom more than the Jewish tradition. This is evidenced by the absence in both Jesus' and James's teaching of a number of topics prominent in Jewish wisdom. These include the following:[9]

- exhortations against idleness and to hard work
- advice about friends
- descriptions of good and bad wives
- how to raise children
- how to manage daughters
- how to treat slaves

7. See Bauckham, *James*, 94–108, for a deeper discussion of Jesus' relationship to the conventional wisdom tradition of Judaism.

8. And for this reason, any attempt to use continuity and discontinuity with previous teachings as a criterion for authenticity of Jesus' sayings is deeply flawed.

9. Bauckham, *James*, 95.

Jesus and the Greek Philosophers

The Greek moral philosophers also had some ideas similar to those taught by Jesus:*

> By their fruit you will recognize them. Do people pick grapes from thornbushes, or figs from thistles? Likewise, every good tree bears good fruit, but a bad tree bears bad fruit. A good tree cannot bear bad fruit, and a bad tree cannot bear good fruit.
>
> Jesus, Matthew 7:16 – 18

> We do not expect the vine to bear figs, nor the olive, grapes.
>
> Plutarch, *Moralia* 472F

> Good does not spring from evil any more than figs grow from olive trees.
>
> Seneca, *Epistles* 87.25

> For how can a vine be moved to act, not like a vine, but like an olive, or again, an olive to act, not like an olive, but like a vine? It is impossible, inconceivable.
>
> Epictetus, *Dissertationes* 2.20.18

*Richard Bauckham, *James: Wisdom of James, Disciple of Jesus the Sage*, New Testament Readings (London: Routledge, 1999), 89.

Of course, what is left out of the surviving teachings of Jesus and James is only of limited value in inferring their relationship. But when the distinctive elements of Jesus' message are considered, the extent to which James follows Jesus is clearer:[10]

1. Jesus' ethical demands are more radical than those of the Torah as conventionally interpreted, or of the exhortations of Jewish wisdom. James stands with Jesus in his insistence on a wholehearted and single-minded loyalty to God in his call for perfect integrity in all of one's speech, thereby making oaths unnecessary, and in his view that the heart is the source of words and actions and therefore reveals mixed motives when the heart is divided. The emphasis by both Jesus and James on obedience to the whole law goes beyond a demand that every individual commandment be obeyed to a call for behavior that flows from wholehearted love for God in every situation.
2. Jesus envisages a society under the rule of God that contrasts radically with the hierarchical structures of first-century society. This may be the point at which Jesus differs most from conventional wisdom, which tended to uphold the status quo and gave guidance for successfully navigating its social dynamics. James follows Jesus in his teaching about countercultural community that replaces hierarchy and status with an equality and mutuality that break barriers between the rich and poor, the powerful and the lowly.

10. Summarized from ibid., 97 – 105. For a somewhat different view of the relationship of Jesus and James to the Jewish wisdom tradition, see Ben Witherington III, *Jesus the Sage: The Pilgrimage of Wisdom* (Edinburgh: T&T Clark, 1994).

3. The criterion for discerning right and wrong is God's eschatological action in judgment or vindication, rather than what is socially and culturally accepted. For instance, James shows little or no concern for honor and shame in society, a concern that looms large in Sirach's exhortations. Instead, James adopts a Christocentric **eschatology**, where Jesus, King of God's kingdom and Teacher of its wisdom, is also the coming Judge. With that eschatological perspective always in view, Christians are to live with courageous endurance until Jesus returns, knowing that they will be fully vindicated as Jesus himself was.
4. Jesus came because God loves the world and wishes to redeem it. Because of this mission, Jesus presents a view of God as compassionate, gracious, and generous, taking precedence over God as the dispenser of distributive justice found in Jewish wisdom literature. Because James also assumes a Christ-centered eschatology, he too presents God as the compassionate and merciful one who generously gives good gifts to those who ask without doubting. Because of God's abundant mercy, Christians are to exemplify such mercy to others as they have themselves received.
5. Jesus is concerned with the renewal and reconstitution of Israel as the people of God who live under the rule of God. James envisions the Jewish Christian communities as the nucleus of the messianic renewal of God's people when he writes to them as, literally, "the twelve tribes in the **diaspora**" (James 1:1). Identifying Jesus as the Messiah, James recognizes the redemption that Jesus initiated and the global scope of the messianic mission.

During the intertestamental period, the wisdom tradition itself split into at least two streams, as the Jewish sages decided to harmonize Torah wisdom in different ways with the philosophical traditions of Greek wisdom. The Greek translation of Proverbs is the first of such attempts to present Jewish wisdom in a Greek intellectual milieu. Later Sirach presented a rather conservative understanding of the book of Proverbs reexpressed for the Hellenistic age. In contrast, the Wisdom of Solomon, while maintaining many points of contact with Proverbs, shows the influence of Stoic philosophy and of traditions associated in Greek culture with *Sophia*, who was considered something of a demigod in the Greek context.[11] James has more continuity with the Proverbs-Sirach trajectory, whereas the stream of thinking that produced the Wisdom of Solomon went on in the Christian era to provide an intellectual basis for a form of Jewish and Christian **Gnosticism**. Despite any prima facie similarities to Jewish wisdom literature, the letter of James is thoroughly Christian in its viewpoint, providing an application of the law of the kingdom of God to ethical situations current in the communities to which James writes.

Even a quick look at James compared to prior wisdom literature shows that while the topics are discussed in similar language, James does not precisely quote from it. This is itself a characteristic of wisdom literature, for the role of the sage was not merely to transmit previous wisdom but to reexpress it in terms that suited its contemporary application.

---

11. For a discussion of this bifurcation of wisdom literature, see Karen H. Jobes, "Sophia Christology: The Way of Wisdom?" in *The Way of Wisdom: Essays in Honor of Dr. Bruce K. Waltke*, ed. J. I. Packer and Sven Soderlund (Grand Rapids: Zondervan, 2000), 226–50.

A Selective Comparison of James to Earlier Wisdom Literature			
Proverbs	*Sirach (NRSV)*	*Wisdom of Solomon (NRSV)*	*James*
		7:7 Therefore I prayed, and understanding was given me; I called on God, and the spirit of wisdom came to me.	1:5 If any of you lacks wisdom, you should ask God, who gives generously to all without finding fault, and it will be given to you.
10:19 Sin is not ended by multiplying words, but the prudent hold their tongues. 17:27 The one who has knowledge uses words with restraint, and whoever has understanding is even-tempered.	5:11 Be quick to hear, but deliberate in answering. 32:8 Be brief; say much in few words; be as one who knows and can still hold his tongue.		1:19 My dear brothers and sisters, take note of this: Everyone should be quick to listen, slow to speak and slow to become angry.
15:25 The LORD tears down the house of the proud, but he sets the widow's boundary stones in place. 23:10 Do not move an ancient boundary stone or encroach on the fields of the fatherless.	4:10 Be a father to orphans, and be like a husband to their mother; you will then be like a son of the Most High, and he will love you more than does your mother.		1:27 Religion that God our Father accepts as pure and faultless is this: to look after orphans and widows in their distress and to keep oneself from being polluted by the world.
	29:1 The merciful lend to their neighbors; by holding out a helping hand they keep the commandments.		2:16 (cf. 1:13) If one of you says to them, "Go in peace; keep warm and well fed," but does nothing about their physical needs, what good is it?
	19:16 A person may make a slip without intending it. Who has not sinned with his tongue?		3:2 We all stumble in many ways. Anyone who is never at fault in what they say is perfect, able to keep their whole body in check.

A Selective Comparison of James to Earlier Wisdom Literature			
Proverbs	*Sirach (NRSV)*	*Wisdom of Solomon (NRSV)*	*James*
	22:27 Who will set a guard over my mouth, and an effective seal upon my lips, so that I may not fall because of them, and my tongue may not destroy me?		3:6 The tongue also is . . . a world of evil among the parts of the body. It corrupts the whole body, sets the whole course of one's life on fire.
3:34 He mocks proud mockers but shows favor to the humble and oppressed.	3:18 The greater you are, the more you must humble yourself; so you will find favor in the sight of the Lord.		4:6 "God opposes the proud but shows favor to the humble."
		1:11 Beware then of useless grumbling, and keep your tongue from slander.	4:11 Brothers and sisters, do not slander one another.
	23:9–11 Do not accustom your mouth to oaths, nor habitually utter the name of the Holy One . . . the person who always swears and utters the Name will never be cleansed from sin. The one who swears many oaths is full of iniquity, and the scourge will not leave his house. If he swears in error, his sin remains on him, and if he disregards it, he sins doubly; if he swears a false oath, he will not be justified.		5:12 Above all, my brothers and sisters, do not swear—not by heaven or by earth or by anything else. All you need to say is a simple "Yes" or "No." Otherwise you will be condemned.
	48:1–3 Then Elijah arose, a prophet like fire, and his word burned like a torch. He brought a famine upon them, and by his zeal he made them few in number. By the word of the Lord he shut up the heavens, and also three times brought down fire.		5:17–18 Elijah was a human being, even as we are. He prayed earnestly that it would not rain, and it did not rain on the land for three and a half years. Again he prayed, and the heavens gave rain, and the earth produced its crops.

Tested and Developed through Perseverance

Consider it pure joy, my brothers and sisters, whenever you face trials of many kinds, because you know that the testing of your faith produces perseverance. Let perseverance finish its work so that you may be mature and complete, not lacking anything. If any of you lacks wisdom, you should ask God, who gives generously to all without finding fault, and it will be given to you. But when you ask, you must believe and not doubt, because the one who doubts is like a wave of the sea, blown and tossed by the wind.

James 1:2–6

When we look at James, we see that he has so internalized the teachings of Jesus that he stands in relation to those teachings as Ben Sira did to the Proverbs. Jesus taught in Palestine; James takes that wisdom to the Diaspora. James doesn't quote Jesus, because he has reformulated Jesus' wisdom as his own for the context of his readers. James doesn't simply quote Jesus' teaching; his own teaching is inspired by it. "The wisdom of Jesus functions for James as the focus and guiding principle of his appropriation of Jewish wisdom."[12] James applies the Jewish wisdom tradition to the Christian community of faith as he reflects on the teachings of Jesus.

The values of James's wisdom are the values of the kingdom of God based in Jesus' teaching of the greatest commandment: wholehearted (mind, body, soul, and strength) love for God and love for neighbor as oneself. It is this sense of wholeness toward God that is the basis for the idea of spiritual maturity in James. Wholehearted loyalty to God requires that one cannot be a friend of the world. Wholehearted obedience to God means one can't pick and choose, for instance, not to be an adulterer but to be a murderer (James 2:11). It is the integrity of the wholeness of self in relation to God that results in the wholeness of the community.

Perseverance in trials is the way a believer's wholeheartedness toward God is tested and developed, and any "lack" (incompleteness) revealed in trials can be filled by asking God for wisdom, or in other words, how to live in relationship to others in a trying situation that will please God.

FAITH AND WORKS

Perhaps the most famous, or notorious, passage in the letter of James is 2:14–26, where James discusses the issue of faith and deeds. It is sometimes claimed that James was engaging the apostle Paul's teaching of salvation by faith alone, and some would even say James was contradicting Paul. One theory even suggests that James was composed by an anonymous second-century author as a counterweight to Paul's writings as the canon took shape.[13] For those living after the canonical books were issued in one volume, it is natural

12. Bauckham, *James*, 108.

13. David R. Nienhuis, *Not by Paul Alone: The Formation of the Catholic Epistle Collection and the Christian Canon* (Waco, Tex.: Baylor University Press, 2007).

to read James and Paul in light of the other and to ponder the relationship between them. But to say that James was intentionally engaging Paul implies that James knew of Paul's position, either through personal contact, word of mouth, or Paul's letters, and that James was writing with the intent to clarify, contradict, or otherwise respond to Paul's teaching. This is a good example of how a **historical-grammatical** reading of a book might differ from a **canonical** reading of the same book, and so it is worth understanding the issues.

It is always important to have in mind the frame of reference of a statement. The philosophical law of noncontradiction is so self-evident that most people reason by it even if they can't name it. That is, a statement cannot be both true and not true at the same time. But that logic assumes a frame of reference. When discussing this point, I sometimes ask my students, "Are you moving?" Because they are sitting in their desks in a classroom, the typical answer is "No, we're not moving." And that is true if the frame of reference is the walls of the classroom, with respect to which no one is moving. But if we consider the solar system as the frame of reference, then in fact we are moving at dizzying speeds as the planet Earth rotates on its axis and revolves around the sun. If we take the galaxy as the frame of reference, then the speed of the solar system rotating around the center of the galaxy also must be considered. In other words, the statements "We are not moving" and "We are moving" can be true at the same time if the frame of reference is different. Analogously, James can say that faith without works cannot save (2:14, 26), Paul can say that no one is saved by observing the law (Gal. 2:16), and both can be telling the truth if the conceptual frame of reference is different. So one frame of reference would be the closed New Testament canon, while two additional frames of reference would be the historical situation in which Paul and James each originally wrote.

There are several ways to understand the perceived tension between James and Paul:[14]

1. The apostles Paul and James substantially disagreed about the means of justification.

It would not be surprising that there was some degree of disagreement among the apostles concerning the epoch-making implications of the gospel as Christian theology parted ways with the theological understandings of Judaism. Some interpreters understand the New Testament writings to be nothing more than snapshots of the thought of leaders of the Christian movement at various moments during the emergence of the church. By that way of thinking, disagreement among the apostles, even on substantial theological matters, is not a problem. For other interpreters, the divine authorship of these books implies an essential coherence of the truth about such a central issue as the means of salvation. Even if Paul and James did have different viewpoints on the truths of the gospel, their canonical writings can be expected to have substantial congruence that would eliminate the possibility of outright contradiction of each other.

2. Paul has misunderstood James's teaching, or

3. James has misunderstood Paul's teaching.

The terms of the admission of **Gentiles** into the church generated huge debate, as can be seen from Acts 15 and the apostolic council of Jerusalem. In the midst of this debate, there was ample opportunity for misunderstanding and confusion. Either soon before or

14. Special thanks to Brandon Holiski, a graduate student in my class on James at Wheaton Graduate School in spring 2007, for his organization of the options.

soon after the council, either or both apostles may have written to address a misunderstanding of the other's position. Perhaps the reason that the relationship of James's letter to Paul's writings is so unclear is that neither apostle explicitly mentions the other's teaching. Paul mentions meeting James (and Peter and John) in Jerusalem (Gal. 2:9), but the point seems to be to confirm that they were all substantially on the same page concerning the gospel message (Gal. 2:6–7).

Paul and James do use similar language, and there is no denying that what James says about faith, works, and righteousness stands in stark contrast to what Paul says about those issues, especially on a surface reading. In Galatians 2:16 Paul says that no one will be justified (Gk. *dikaioō*) "from works of [the] law" (Gk. *ex ergōn nomou*). In Romans 3:28 he writes, "For we maintain that a person is justified [Gk. *dikaioō*] by faith apart from works of the law [Gk. *chōris ergōn nomou*]." Without mentioning "law," James 2:24 claims that, "people are justified [Gk. *dikaioō*] by what they do [Gk. *ex ergōn*] and not by faith alone." Both use the word "faith" (Gk. *pistis*); Paul, in Galatians 2:16, says, "a person is not justified by the works of the law, but by faith in Jesus Christ," and James in 2:14, "What good is it, my brothers and sisters, if people claim to have faith but have no deeds? Can *such* faith save them?" Note that James does not argue that works save *instead* of faith; nor does he argue that works must be *added* to faith, which is really the point Paul argues against in Galatians and Romans.

James and Paul on Faith and Works

James:	A person is justified by works and not by faith alone.
Paul:	A person is justified by faith and not by works of the law.

Although one can reduce the tension between Paul and James by defining Paul's "works of the law" as simply identity markers (e.g., **circumcision**) or the observance of ritual acts (e.g., animal sacrifice), the phrase was probably used to refer more broadly to even works of compassion and charity that the law required. It is probably best to picture Paul's view as any acts motivated by the law whether ritual or ethical. James seems to be thinking primarily of only works of compassion, for those are the only kind of works he mentions. So while Paul and James may be emphasizing different kinds of works, the tension cannot be resolved simply in how we define "works."

The word *dikaioō* refers to vindication at the judgment where God is Judge, which is the same concept as being "saved." In the Old Testament the outcome of divine judgment is based on one's conduct with respect to the Torah (e.g., Mic. 6:11), and that same idea is found in James 2:12, except that the Torah has been transposed into "the law that gives freedom." Jesus can say in his exposition of the law in Matthew 12:37, "For by your words you will be acquitted [*dikaioō*, "justified"], and by your words you will be condemned." Is Jesus teaching salvation by (verbal) works? In context, Jesus has just reminded his hearers that what the mouth speaks indicates the condition of the heart (v. 34). In other words, one's words and, in James, one's actions, are indicators of one's true identity. Jesus and James agree that evil speech and deeds, by commission or omission, show one to be something other than the righteous person in good standing with God.

Finally, one must consider how each uses the word "faith" (Gk. *pistis*).

Paul is referring to faith in Christ's **atonement** for sin (Rom. 3:20–28). But is this what James is referring to? Note how James defines his use of the word in setting up his argument of 2:14–26: "What good is it, my brothers and sisters, if someone claims to have faith but has no deeds? Can *such* [a] faith save them?" (emphasis added; note the anaphoric article in the Greek). James specifies that he is using the word "faith" here to refer to a kind of faith that has no outward expression. Can *such* a faith save? Subsequent use of the word "faith" throughout the argument is shorthand for the kind of faith that has no works. In verse 24 he reinforces this by saying "faith alone," that is, a bogus faith.

Moreover, James is writing to *Jewish* Christians who need to understand how the requirements of Judaism have not been abrogated, but transposed, by Jesus who came to fulfill and not abolish the Law. In contrast, Paul is writing Galatians and Romans to Gentile Christians who need to understand that observing the Jewish law will not put anyone—Jew or Gentile—in right standing with God. Only a heart-transforming faith in God's provision for atonement, Jesus Christ, can do that. Faith that does no work doesn't work when we stand before God at the judgment!

> "As Paul contends that we are justified apart from the help of works, so James does not allow those who lack good works to be reckoned righteous."
>
> John Calvin (*Institutes* 3.27.2)

For these reasons, it seems likely that:

4. James and Paul each were writing from a different conceptual frame of reference without any intention of directly engaging the other.

It is clear from Acts and Galatians that James and Paul knew each other, heard each other speak, and were aware of the perspective that the other took on the gospel. But when James penned his letter, he was not necessarily reflecting on Paul's teaching about justification. Each of them appropriated their Jewish heritage to address different circles of concern and debate. If that is true, it is not legitimate to pit them against each other as many have done, most notably, Martin Luther. Every apostolic author is consistent with the truth of the gospel, but that doesn't mean that all said exactly the same thing. To insist that Paul and James say the same thing is just as wrong as insisting that they contradict each other. Every New Testament writer deserves to be heard on his own terms.

James, reflecting on the need for behavior that was consistent with the profession of a Christian, was writing to help Jewish Christians understand how Jesus had transposed the law of Sinai into the royal law of the kingdom, and how to live in community by that new understanding. For example, after questioning whether faith without "works" (Gk. *erga*) can "save" (Gk. *sōzō*) in 2:14, James illustrates his point by an example of providing for the poor as an act of mercy, which is one of the implications of both Jewish law and the "royal law" of 2:8. By choosing this particular example, James further reinforces his exhortation to care for the poor and not to dishonor them through neglect. (See further discussion below on the rich and poor in James.)

In other words, James was not writing in reference to justification but rather to describe the moral responsibilities that flow from saving faith. The absence of acting upon those responsibilities calls into question the presence of saving faith in the life of a professing Christian, since by their fruit God's people will be known. On this point, Paul's teaching concerning the fruit of the Spirit would seem to agree (Gal. 5; also Rom. 1:5; 16:26; 1 Cor. 15:58; 2 Cor. 9:8; Col. 1:10; 1 Thess. 1:3; 2 Thess. 1:11). In other words, James and Paul would agree that "works are not a substitute for faith, but are the evidence of faith."[15]

The fact that James must point out that acts of compassion are central to true religious belief suggests that some whom he has in mind as he writes were neglecting such deeds. These people are the ones who claimed to have faith but didn't see what works had to do with it. They were those who were hearers of the word but not doers. They believed rightly in the one true God (2:19) and apparently felt that belief in such orthodox doctrine was sufficient for being declared righteous when judged by the law of freedom.

5. The solution is some combination of the above.

It is probably impossible to reconstruct the historical situation with sufficient precision to put this debate to rest once and for all. What is clear is that reading Paul and James in the context of the canon raises the question of theological congruence that perhaps had not previously been an issue for the original readers of these texts.

The prominence of the apostle Paul's writings in Christian theology, and most especially in Protestant **soteriology**, has had the unfortunate side effect that what all other New

15. R. A. Martin, "James," in *James, I–II Peter, Jude*, ACNT (Minneapolis: Augsburg, 1982), 31.

The Church Fathers Comment on James and Paul*

"On that which the apostle James said [2:20]. Seeing that the apostle Paul, in preaching that a man is justified by faith without works, is not rightly understood by those who received this statement such that they supposed they could be saved by faith when once they had believed in Christ, even if they were wickedly engaged and lived in a criminal and disgraceful manner, this very passage [2:14–26] of [the apostle James's] letter explains in what way the precise meaning of the apostle Paul is to be understood."

Augustine, *De diversis quaestionibus LXXXIII* 76 (PL vol. 40, cols. 37–38).

"Although the apostle Paul preached that we are justified by faith without works, those who understand by this that it does not matter whether they live evil lives or do wicked and terrible things as long as they believe in Christ, because salvation is through faith, have made a great mistake. James here expounds how Paul's words ought to be understood."†

Bede, *Concerning the Epistle of St. James*

"According to James, someone who thinks that it is possible to believe without acting accordingly is out of his mind."‡

Oecumenius, *Commentary on James*

*See Gerald Bray and Thomas Oden, eds., "James," *in James, 1–2 Peter, 1–3 John*, ACCS (Downers Grove, Ill.: InterVarsity, 2000), 26–34.

†Ibid., 31.

‡Ibid.

Ironically, Luther Agreed with James about the Nature of Saving Faith

"O it is a living, busy active mighty thing, this faith. It is impossible for it not to be doing good things incessantly. It does not ask whether good works are to be done, but before the question is asked, it has already done this, and is constantly doing them. Whoever does not do such works, however, is an unbeliever. He gropes and looks around for faith and good works, but knows neither what faith is nor what good works are. Yet he talks and talks, with many words, about faith and good works."

Preface to Luther's *Commentary on Romans*

Testament writers have said is typically read through the lens of Paul, evaluated in comparison to Paul, and squeezed and bent to make it harmonize with Paul. While Paul is undoubtedly foundational for New Testament theology, should Paul be the normative measure of all other biblical teaching? Are Paul's writings truly the canon within the canon? With all due respect to Martin Luther, who took a very dim view of the book of James, if Paul is the measure of Christian theology, why did God bother to give us other writers: John, Peter, Matthew, Mark, Jude, the author of Hebrews, and James?

Portrait of Martin Luther, 1529 by Lucas Cranach, the Elder (1472–1553) Museo Poldi Pezzoli, Milan, Italy/The Bridgeman Art Library

Martin Luther took a dim view of the book of James.

FAITH IN ACTION

If James was writing anything that could be described as theology, it would be practical theology intended to pastor the diaspora audience to whom he writes. He is not concerned to expound on the atoning efficacy of the crucifixion or to be an apologist for the resurrection of Jesus. He is interested in eschatology, but only as it bears on how his readers should be conducting their lives in the present. His interest is to identify those issues that would destroy community: evil speech, presumptuous oaths, oppressive social status, favoritism, neglect of the less fortunate, failure to persevere under trial. James is a preacher passionately exhorting his readers to be whole people with a single-minded intent to love God and neighbor. Whatever a profession of faith in Jesus Christ might mean, it cannot mean a license to live free of God's moral order. It cannot mean mere cognitive assent that Jesus had lived and died proclaiming himself to be the Messiah. James pushes his readers to see moral imperatives as motivated by authentic faith in Christ and demands that their daily conduct bear the fruit of that commitment. For therein lies the wisdom to live toward life's highest good: eternal life with God in Christ.

"Who is wise and understanding among you? Let them show it by their good life, by deeds done in the humility that comes from wisdom."

James 3:13

Sapiential Theology

"The central theological task is and has always been pastoral, assisting people to know God, and by knowing him to be enabled to strive toward the excellence of his character in their own lives.... Theologians such as the well-known Calvin and the less-known Basil of Caesarea recognized this to be their calling.... Such an enterprise [can be labeled] 'sapiential theology,' or theology which, through understanding Scripture, enables everyday Christians to live wisely and well. It was a marriage of mind and heart, or mind and spirit. So it must be today."*

---

*William R. Baker, "Christology in the Epistle of James," *EQ* 74 (2002): 48, quoting Ellen Charry, *By the Renewing of Your Minds* (New York: Oxford University Press, 1997), 5, 115.

The *Dipsychos* Person

Have you ever known someone who was two-faced? A person who would say one thing to your face but something quite contrary to other people—and you could never figure out what that person honestly thought, which "face" was the true one? James apparently knew professing Christians who couldn't quite make up their minds about what they believed. Twice he refers to those who are not right with God as *dipsychos*, typically translated as "double-minded." If the greatest commandment is to love God with one's whole self—heart, soul, mind, and strength (Matt 22:37; Mark 12:30; Luke 10:27)—then to be double-minded about God is to fail miserably. It is the opposite of living wisely through trust in God.

The word *dipsychos* may have been coined by James, for this book is the oldest **extant** occurrence of the word. But the idea is certainly not an innovation of Christian thought. The opening verses of the Wisdom of Solomon (1:1–2) are an exhortation to seek the Lord with a sincere (undivided) heart:

> Love righteousness, you rulers of the earth,
> think of the Lord in goodness
> and seek him with sincerity of heart;
> because he is found by those who do not put him to the test,
> and manifests himself to those who do not distrust him.

Going farther back into the history of Israel, the prophet Hosea spoke of the danger of a divided heart that made the people ripe for destruction (Hos. 10:2). The author of the

Dipsychos in James

The one who doubts ... that person should not expect to receive anything from the Lord. Such a person is *double-minded* and unstable in all they do.

James 1:7–8, emphasis added

Come near to God and he will come near to you. Wash your hands, you sinners, and purify your hearts, you *double-minded*.

James 4:8, emphasis added

Qumran *Thanksgiving Scroll* speaks of those who enquire of the Lord "with a double heart, and do not stand firm in thy truth."[16] And the idea of the inner person being torn between two desires or loyalties is also found in Greek writers such as Homer, Herodotus, and Xenophon.[17]

The double-minded person is spiritually immature.

The recognition of the conflicting impulses within the human heart are widely recognized, but within the wisdom tradition of Judaism, they represent the "two ways" of the Hebrew *yeṣer ha-tov* (the good impulse) and the *yeṣer ha-ra* (the evil impulse). To live wisely is to allow the good impulse to control one's life, to live in obedience to God. To follow the evil impulse is to live by a "wisdom" that is earthly, unspiritual, and demonic (James 3:15). James speaks of the evil impulse in 1:14–15, when he points out that temptation comes because of the evil desire within that conceives, gives birth to sin, and leads to death. In contrast, the way of wisdom is the way to life.

In 4:1–2 James points to the desires that battle within as the root cause of strife within the community. Yielding to the evil desires within spirals into increasingly greater sin. James sees this conflicted position of not being single-mindedly loyal to God as the overarching problem among his readers. And so he uses the teachings of Jesus to instruct and exhort them to wise living under the reign and rule of God in Christ. Simply knowing the word and counting it as Christian faith is self-deception (1:22). James exhorts his readers to be doers of the word—the perfect law that gives freedom (1:25). James exhorts action on many points, but two major issues that pervade much of his letter concern the wisdom of godly speech and the wisdom of social justice, both being necessary entailments of the royal law of loving neighbor as oneself.

> "Faith without works is dead, but works without faith is too hard."
>
> HILLARY CLINTON

Godly Speech

There is probably no greater self-revealing way we can present ourselves to the world than through what we say. Not only the content of what we say, but also the tone and intent of our speech may reveal more of our heart than intended. Jesus recognized this when he said that out of the heart the mouth speaks (Matt. 12:34; 15:18; Luke 6:45). Although many might wish to distance who they "really" are from the words that come out of their mouths, Jesus and James show the folly of that way of thinking. Because speech is so indicative of the inner person, the wise use of the "tongue," a **metonymy** for speaking, is one of the major themes of Jewish wisdom literature. James goes beyond the wisdom tradition by exhorting Christians to speak as those who profess belief in Christ. Following is a list of what he says concerning the use of speech:

16. Quoted by Oscar J. F. Seitz, "Afterthoughts on the Term *Dipsychos*," *NTS* 4 (1958): 328.
17. See Stanley E. Porter, "Is *dipsuchos* (James 1, 8; 4, 8) a 'Christian' Word?" *Bib* 71 (1990): 470–71.

- Be slow to speak, and then only after listening (1:19).
- Control the tongue or one's religion is useless (1:26).
- Realize that both speech and actions will be judged (2:12).
- Understand that those who teach, that is, use words to instruct others, will be judged more strictly (3:1).
- Recognize that the size of the tongue is disproportionate to the trouble it can cause (3:5).
- Realize that the tongue is most difficult to control for good (3:8).
- Understand that the tongue bears witness of double-mindedness (3:9 – 10).
- Must not slander one another (4:11).
- Must not speak presumptuously (4:13).
- Must not grumble against one another (5:9).
- Must not swear (5:12).
- Should pray, sing praise, call for elders when sick (5:13 – 14).

James condemns slander for its destructive effect in a community.

A quick perusal of the list shows that James believes Christians must be concerned with the integrity of what they say. Jesus and James stand apart from Jewish wisdom literature in forbidding oaths. Their point is that *everything* a Christian says should be as truthful and trustworthy as if they were under oath. Let your "yes" mean yes, and your "no" mean no. Personal integrity is built on telling the truth and standing by one's word. One cannot be two-faced about it, saying one thing here and another there. The stability of a community (or a nation) rests on the integrity of its people.

Although the children's ditty says, "Sticks and stones may break my bones, but words can never hurt me," we have all seen and experienced the hurt and damage that comes from lies, slander, and grumbling. Often those who are criticized by the speech of others feel they have been judged unfairly and misunderstood. If their critic had known only one more thing about the situation, they would not have thought the worst. Personal relationships can be easily damaged or broken when someone speaks before listening (James 1:19), speaks in anger (1:20), or slanders others. Consequently, their community can also be damaged.

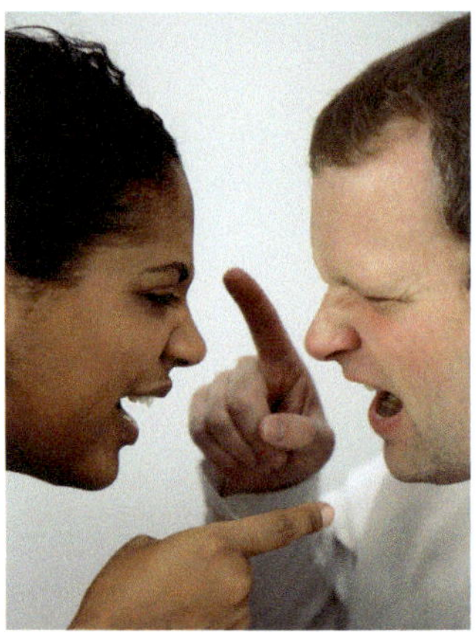

Angry words do not produce righteousness (James 1:19-20).

And once said, words cannot be taken back, but have the power to change the whole course of one's life. How many of us have thought, *If only I could take that back!* Words, though as intangible as flames of fire, can take on a life of their own. How especially true this is in our age of instant messaging, YouTube, and tweeting. How many regret a hasty word that reached far beyond the ears or eyes intended.

James also points out that speech can reveal a presumptuous spirit that doesn't recognize God's sovereignty over life. Announcing plans for self-profit under the delusion that one is in control of one's life contradicts a trusting dependence on the Lord required for wise living. People sometimes speak and consider it done, without recognizing that only God can speak reality into existence. Boastful, arrogant words characterize sin (James 4:16–17).

Because the unreined tongue is characteristic of the natural, fallen state of humanity, James recognizes the difficulty even Christians have in speaking from the wisdom that faith in God imparts. The goal is never to be at fault in what we say (James 3:2) and have the self-control to keep one's whole body in check. Those who teach use words to instruct others, and so they must be characterized by integrity and have mastered the impulse to gossip, slander, and talk arrogantly. Because of the influence teachers have on so many others, both in the content of their speech and as role models, not many among James's readers should "presume" to be teachers. It is a sobering responsibility, for words constantly pour out of the heart day after day everywhere one goes and in every situation one encounters.

Double-minded people cannot speak consistently with the wisdom of God and are therefore unstable in their ways, introducing instability into the community. James points out to his readers that something as common as the way they talk is foundational to the stability of their congregations. It is a primary way of loving others as we love ourselves, of doing to others as we would have done to ourselves. Keeping one's word with integrity, praying, and honoring the Lord with one's speech are foundational for life in the kingdom.

Chris Lombardi/Getty Images

The tongue is a fire . . . setting the whole course of one's life on fire. (James 3:6)

Rich and Poor

The topic of the "rich" and the "poor/lowly" is a major theme in the message of James and is the key to understanding James's ethical system, for it is here that we see most clearly the relationship between his ethics and his eschatology. Many Christians today think of eschatology as pertaining to future headlines of events that fulfill biblical prophecy and usher in the end times and return of Christ. But eschatology is a much more sweeping concept in the biblical writings, intended not to predict the future but to motivate right living in the present. For how we live today depends largely on what we believe about the future, for those beliefs shape our priorities and motivations. Most people have a very shortsighted view of the future that might extend to living now in a way that will afford a comfortable retirement, but the biblical writers want us to see that how we live now is related to our afterlife and to choose to live accordingly.

"How hard it is for the rich to enter the kingdom of God!"

Jesus, Mark 10:23; Luke 18:24

Christian eschatology obtained from its Jewish heritage a **dualism** that understood this fallen world and its powers to be arrayed against God and his people. When the Messiah comes and establishes the kingdom of God, only then will the injustices, oppression, and evils of this world be fully and finally judged and destroyed, and only then will God's people in their glorified form live in a world of peace and justice. The point of this apocalyptic viewpoint is that what one believes today and how one lives in this life will determine which side of that judgment one will experience. Obviously, given knowledge of a future afterlife, the biblical writers expect the wise person to choose to live for God and his Messiah, Jesus Christ, in this life, for Jesus is the gateway to eternal life in the kingdom of God.

James presents the categories of rich and poor not as simple socioeconomic classes in conflict but as representing the two sides of the eschatological dualism. Historically throughout human history, and all too evident in our own times, the rich have exploited the poor, often through legally sanctioned opportunities, and have been unconcerned with the effects that oppression has. Sometimes that oppression leads to death through extreme poverty, such that the poor cannot sustain a living or receive life-extending medical treatment for their illnesses. Sometimes oppression causes a suicidal hopelessness. In the ancient world, as is the same today, the resources available to the rich are not within reach of the poor, and so God's help was the only recourse of the impoverished. For this reason, the poor were typically understood to be pious and closer to God, because he was their only help. God's particular concern for the poor of this world is a constant theme throughout Scripture.

> For the LORD your God is God of gods and Lord of lords, the great God, mighty and awesome, who shows no partiality and accepts no bribes. He defends the cause of the fatherless and the widow, and loves the foreigners residing among you, giving them food and clothing. (Deut. 10:17–18)

> For he will deliver the needy who cry out,
> the afflicted who have no one to help.
> He will take pity on the weak and the needy
> and save the needy from death. (Ps. 72:12–13)

Job's Compassion on the Poor

"If I have denied the desires of the poor
or let the eyes of the widow grow weary,
if I have kept my bread to myself,
not sharing it with the fatherless—
but from my youth I reared them as a father would,
and from my birth I guided the widow—
if I have seen anyone perishing for lack of clothing,
or the needy without garments,
and their hearts did not bless me
for warming them with the fleece from my sheep,
if I have raised my hand against the fatherless,
knowing that I had influence in court,
then let my arm fall from the shoulder,
let it be broken off at the joint.
For I dreaded destruction from God,
and for fear of his splendor I could not do such things."

Job 31:16–23

"He saves the needy from the sword in their mouth;
  he saves them from the clutches of the powerful.
So the poor have hope,
  and injustice shuts its mouth." (Job 5:15–16)

This is what the LORD says:
"For three sins of Israel,
  even for four, I will not turn back my wrath.
They sell the innocent for silver,
  and the needy for a pair of sandals.
They trample on the heads of the poor
  as on the dust of the ground
  and deny justice to the oppressed." (Amos 2:6–7a)

"Blessed are you who are poor for yours is the kingdom of God." (Luke 6:20)

God's concern and care for the poor and his condemnation of the rich are ancient and integral elements of biblical ethics. In the intertestamental period, three concepts developed that inform our understanding of this subject matter in the New Testament:[18] (1) The need of pious people to care for the poor became a traditional religious duty within Judaism. (2) The rich were viewed as unlikely to be pious and carry out that responsibility to the poor, and therefore stood under God's judgment. (3) "The poor" became a designation of pious groups who felt oppressed.

Job was known for his compassion on the poor (Job 31:16–23), which did not save him from great misfortune himself. Andrea Sacchi (1599–1661).

The biblical teaching on the rich and poor is upheld by Jesus and consequently adopted by the New Testament writers. Care for the poor would be viewed as part of the "royal law" that commands love for God and love for neighbor as oneself. It appears that the disparity between rich and poor in the social world of James's original readers was the most glaring violation of the royal law and the issue that most needed correction in the Christian communities to whom James wrote. "James objects to far more than simple acts of exploitation" of the poor by the rich. James interprets "Jesus' teaching within the context of an apocalyptic construction of reality," creating a powerful social critique. "He objects to a whole cosmic structure that is in open conflict with God and that determines the false social structure in which humans live."[19] And his message still rings loud and clear on similar disparities in our society today.

The definition of "rich" and "poor" measured in dollars varies widely throughout history and from society to society. Needless to say, there have always been those who have more and those who have less, so no strict definition of the economic resources of the rich

18. Davids, *James*, 43.

19. Patrick A. Tiller, "The Rich and Poor in James: An Apocalyptic Ethic," in *Conflicted Boundaries in Wisdom and Apocalypticism*, ed. Benjamin G. Wright III and Lawrence M. Wills, SBLSymS 35 (Atlanta: Society of Biblical Literature, 2005), 176, 179.

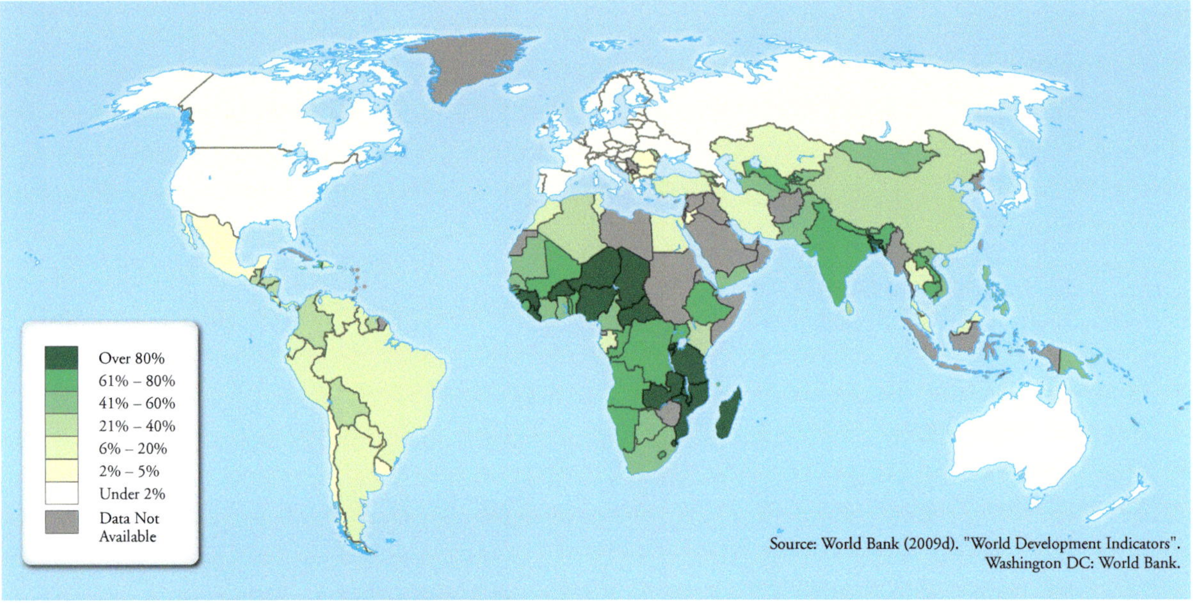

Vast numbers of people subsist on income of less than $2 per day.

and the poor are needed. Ubiquitously, those who have more in any society are "the rich," and their resources give them social power, prestige, and status. Others in society look up to them, desire to emulate them, and covet their possessions. Wealth per se is not evil, and the Bible does not condemn having wealth. But because of the evil bent of fallen human nature, greed, selfishness, revenge, and other evils sway the rich to use their wealth in ways that serve their own interests at the expense of the less fortunate. Because it is usually the rich who have the power and status in a society, it is the rich who typically are the lawmakers. And so often laws are established that make it legal for the rich to oppress the poor in various ways with impunity.

In the Roman Empire, 90 percent of the population lived in poverty by today's standards. But rather than referring strictly to their economic resources, James uses the appellations "rich" and "poor" to label ethical constructs in the context of an apocalyptic dualism. He defines the "rich" as friends of the world, as those who love the things of the world, who make their plans to increase their wealth without consideration of God and their dependence on him for life itself (4:13–17). They fail to realize their own temporality in their evil, pretentious boasting. The "rich" that James has in mind oppress others even to the point of violence to get what they want (5:1–6). They blaspheme and drag the poor into court because they can (2:6–7). In James's understanding, the rich exercise earthly wisdom, which in the context of eschatological dualism is in reality demonic wisdom that does not come from God (James 3:13–18). In James the "poor" are those who love God and who seek wisdom from him to face their trials. Even if they have been blessed with a measure of wealth, they boast in their lowliness before the cross rather than their own means. In other words, in James the "poor" and "lowly" are on God's side of the dualism, but the "rich" are not.

There has been much debate about whether the "rich" in James are Christians or unbelievers. That distinction is actually irrelevant to James's point, for if believers of means rely on their resources rather than God, if they expect to be treated with privileged status, if they oppress others to sustain self-interest, then they are "the rich" who are condemned. And unbelievers are already on the side of the fallen world, for whom such attitudes and actions come naturally as if that is the way things should be. James's point is that Christians with resources must live differently than "the rich" by caring for the poor; otherwise they have not truly understood and believed the gospel.

> "What causes fights and quarrels among you? Don't they come from your desires that battle within you?"
>
> James 4:1

The essence of God's kingdom as Jesus taught it is the redemption of humanity from the power of evil, necessarily involving social, political, and economic reversals. James's moral exhortation stems from his apocalyptic worldview that rejects current social realities with their injustices that will be judged by God, and it redefines a social reality and its moral obligations in terms that honor God in Christ. Specifically, James is addressing the problem that Christians were too enamored by the wealth of those who had more than they themselves did. James condemns those who are so impressed by the clothing and jewelry that a rich person wears that they give him preferential treatment while neglecting and insulting the person who wears shabby clothes. He exhorts Christians who are impressed by wealth and therefore show favoritism to those who possess it, to repent of breaking the royal law, for they have not loved their economically disadvantaged neighbors (2:1–12). To the contrary, they have dishonored them. He rebukes Christians who are covetous of the things of the world and spend what they get on their own pleasures (4:1–10). To behave in these ways is to operate the way the fallen world does, with a worldly wisdom that advises currying favor with those who have wealth. It assumes the fallen social order in which the rich are honored and the poor are exploited.

James teaches that how we treat the rich and the poor displays our allegiance either to the world's ways or to God's. The criterion of wealth for assigning honor is false, and God will reverse it when the rich perish and the lowly are honored with their place in God's kingdom (1:9–10). To assign a person's value and honor based on wealth or lack of it is to violate the supreme law that sums up all of God's law: Love your neighbor as yourself. Treat your neighbors the way you would want to be treated regardless of whether they have more or less than you do. Anything else is injustice in God's eyes. And God will judge those who claim to have faith in Christ but who do not love their neighbors as themselves. If God has chosen and blessed the poor by granting them a place in his kingdom, why, James asks, do you bless the rich who oppose and oppress (2:6–7)?

Ring with nicolo intaglio engraved with Theseus, Roman, (2nd century AD)/ Private Collection/Photo © Heini Schneebeli/The Bridgeman Art Library

A second-century Roman ring. "Suppose a man comes into your meeting wearing a gold ring . . ." (James 2:2).

Three times throughout the letter James points to the dynamics between the rich and the poor in the Christian community as an issue that his readers must correct. In 2:15 – 17 he points out that to see a brother or sister in need of daily food and clothing but to do nothing about it is to be a hearer of the word but not a doer and to possess a faith that cannot save because it lacks the deeds characteristic of saving faith. In 4:13 – 17 he points out that the desire to make money may lead one to a presumption of control over life and a forgetfulness of God's will. And the most extreme situation is found in 5:1 – 6 where James thunders judgment against those who defraud the poor of even what little wages they are due. The very wealth they have accumulated unjustly is actually a corrosive agent that will bring their lives to destruction (vv. 2 – 3).

Jay King

A corroded Roman coin. "Your gold and silver are corroded. . . . you have hoarded wealth in the last days" (James 5:3).

Rather than continuing to live by the values and standards of the world, James exhorts his Christian readers to repent and to live in a manner consistent with God's reign and rule. The gospel presents a leveling of rich and poor, for wealth or lack of it means nothing to God, who does not show favoritism (Rom. 2:11). The withering of the rich (James 1:10) suggests a leveling that shows the rich and poor to have the same status: both will die and face judgment; both are sinners saved by God's grace. Their bank balance doesn't impress or dismay God, and any consideration of it is irrelevant to their place in his kingdom. The final leveling of all will be on judgment day when what little or much we have is left behind and we stand or fall based only on our relationship to God in Christ. Because of that ultimate reality, the Christian community is to express that great truth in its dealings here and now.

But James is no Marxist, and Jesus himself said there will always be poor people among us (Mark 14:7). For no matter the dollar amounts involved, there will always be some who have more than others, creating a relative disparity.

> "Blessed are you who are poor, for yours is the kingdom of God."
>
> Jesus, Luke 6:20

The issue of the rich and poor in James is not about how much money one has. No matter how rich, there may be those who have more. And no matter how poor, there may be those who have less. God calls those who have more to love those who have less and to provide food, shelter, and the basic human necessities to those who lack them. James is not concerned with how much or how little his readers have; rather, he rebukes the "rich" person in each of us.

CHAPTER SUMMARY

James presents his readers with ethical exhortation intended to motivate them to live rightly under the reign and rule of God, as taught by Jesus. The royal law of love for God and love for neighbor as oneself was Jesus' summary of all the Law and Prophets of ancient Judaism, and everything that James teaches is related to that moral concept. By choosing to love one's neighbor as oneself, the Christian is choosing the way of wisdom, living toward life's highest good of a relationship with God and others that will survive into the afterlife. Any claim to Christian faith that dismisses the call to care for those in need, to speak well and wisely, and to have a godly attitude toward one's wealth and resources is not a faith that can stand in the judgment of God. For true saving faith motivates and enables the believer to live in a way that God had always intended for humanity. James's most challenging and countercultural exhortation, then and today, is the call to repent of the false values that a love for increasing wealth and possessions instills.

KEY TERMS

- apocalyptic
- eschatology
- faith and works
- Golden Rule
- Hellenistic age
- kingdom of God
- royal law
- sapiential theology

QUESTIONS FOR REVIEW OR DISCUSSION

1. If you were asked what is life's greatest good, what would you say? What do you think are society's answers to that question?
2. Is James the most unchristian book of the New Testament? Defend your answer.
3. Explain why many readers have seen a contradiction between James and Paul. How do you understand the relationship between the two?
4. What is the relationship between eschatology and ethics?
5. Some people read the ethical teaching of James as equivalent to the teachings of other world religions, such as Judaism, Islam, and Buddhism. Do you agree? What are the similarities? What, if anything, makes the ethical teaching of James distinct from that of other religions?
6. Discuss the pros and cons of government-funded welfare for the poor versus church-sponsored assistance to those in need.

GOING FURTHER

Bauckham, Richard. *James: Wisdom of James, Disciple of Jesus the Sage.* New Testament Readings. London: Routledge, 1999.

———. "The Wisdom of James and the Wisdom of Jesus." Pages 75–92 in *The Catholic Epistles and the Tradition.* Edited by J. Schlosser. BETL 176. Leuven: Leuven University Press, 2004.

Cheung, Luke. *The Genre, Composition and Hermeneutics of the Epistle of James.* Paternoster Biblical and Theological Monographs. Waynesboro, Ga.: Paternoster, 2003.

Donelson, Lewis R. *From Hebrews to Revelation: A Theological Introduction.* Louisville: Westminster John Knox, 2001.

Jobes, Karen H. "The Greek Minor Prophets in James." In *Devotion, Vision, and Worship in Early Jewish and Christian Interpretation of Scripture.* Edited by Craig Evans. London: T&T Clark, forthcoming.

Sider, Ronald J. *Rich Christians in an Age of Hunger: Moving from Affluence to Generosity.* 20th Anniversary Revision. Dallas: Word, 1997.

Tiller, Patrick A. "The Rich and Poor in James: An Apocalyptic Ethic." Pages 169–79 in *Conflicted Boundaries in Wisdom and Apocalypticism.* Edited by Benjamin G. Wright III and Lawrence M. Wills. SBLSymS 35. Atlanta: Society of Biblical Literature, 2005.

Verseput, Donald. "Wisdom, 4Q185, and the Epistle of James" *JBL* 117 (1998): 691–707.

Wachob, Wesley Hiram. *The Voice of Jesus in the Social Rhetoric of James.* SNTSMS 106. Cambridge: Cambridge University Press, 2000.

Wall, Robert W. *Community of the Wise: The Letter of James.* New Testament in Context. Valley Forge, Pa.: Trinity Press International, 1997.

CHAPTER 8

Jude

JESUS' BROTHER WARNS THE CHURCH

Your Goals for This Chapter

- To learn who is the most likely author of the letter.
- To be able to identify the most likely original recipients of the letter.
- To understand the challenges presented by the letter.
- To reflect on Jude's use of **pseudepigraphal** material in relation to your doctrine of Scripture.
- To articulate the original significance of the letter and its relevance to the church today.

WHY THE BOOK OF JUDE IS IMPORTANT TO YOU

We live in spiritually confusing times. Some people who think of themselves as Christians proclaim a message of God's grace as a reason to accept beliefs and practices that Scripture clearly condemns. We live in an age when shadows are being cast on Christianity by media stories of clergy who commit sexual crimes against children and by scholars who claim that we have it all wrong and that orthodox Christian doctrine is actually a later perversion of a more primitive, purer form of faith in Jesus. Anyone who wants to live and be known as a Christian in these times has to decide how to live and what church to join as he or she faces the discouragement and confusion within and about the Christian faith today. One might even wonder if Christianity as it has been known in America will survive into the next century. The letter from Jude tells us that such immorality and confusion *within* the church have plagued it from its infancy. The fact that the gospel of Jesus Christ has survived these two thousand years and is still transforming lives today is perhaps one of the greatest evidences that it is a work of God's Holy Spirit and not dependent on any race, culture, nation, or historical period for its power.

Jude was distressed by the immorality and licentious living that he observed in the church by people who called themselves Christians and whom others received in good faith as Christians. It is true that no one is sinless, and every Christian's life is tainted by sin to some degree. Yet it is one thing to yield to sin in a momentary temptation or from

Key Verses

v. 1: Jude, a servant of Jesus Christ and a brother of James....

v. 3: Dear friends, although I was very eager to write to you about the salvation we share, I felt compelled to write and urge you to contend for the faith that was once for all entrusted to God's holy people.

v. 9: But even the archangel Michael, when he was disputing with the devil about the body of Moses, did not himself dare to condemn him for slander....

vv. 14–15: Enoch, the seventh from Adam, prophesied about them: "See, the Lord is coming with thousands upon thousands of his holy ones to judge everyone, and to convict all of them of all the ungodly acts they have committed in their ungodliness, and of all the defiant words ungodly sinners have spoken against him."

vv. 24–25: To him who is able to keep you from stumbling and to present you before his glorious presence without fault and with great joy—to the only God our Savior be glory, majesty, power and authority, through Jesus Christ our Lord, before all ages, now and forevermore! Amen.

ignorance; it is another to believe that immoral behaviors, such as lust and selfish greed, are in fact acceptable practices for a Christian and, what's worse, to teach this to others by word and deed. Jude wrote to Christian communities that had people within them who had personal power and influence, whether they were official leaders of the church or not. When those influential people began living and teaching in ways that contradicted "the faith that the Lord has once for all entrusted" to his people (Jude 3), the congregation was in great spiritual danger. Jude wrote his brief letter into just such a situation, one not so very different from the times in which we live. For one's own life and to make disciples in the church, Jude's voice must be heard today.

Challenges Presented by the Book of Jude

- Its use of material from the pseudepigrapha.
- Its indirect use of the Old Testament through Jewish interpretive tradition.
- The judgment on Sodom and Gomorrah as condemnation of homosexual behavior.

CHAPTER OUTLINE

I. Who Wrote This Letter and When?
  A. Author
  B. Date
II. To Whom Did Jude Write?
III. Why Did Jude Write? The Warning against False Christians
IV. Jude's Theology
  A. God—Father, Savior, Judge
  B. Jesus Christ
  C. The Holy Spirit
  D. The Christian Life
V. How Did Jude Use the Old Testament?
VI. Jude's Use of the Pseudepigrapha
VII. Jude's Relationship to 2 Peter
VIII. Text and Canonicity of Jude
IX. Outline of Jude's Letter

Please read the book of Jude in one sitting before reading this chapter.

WHO WROTE THIS LETTER AND WHEN?

Author

The name Jude may be best known in our times from the lyrics of the 1968 Beatles hit, "Hey, Jude, don't make it bad; take a sad song and make it better. . . ." The name Jude is the English form of the ancient name Judas (Gk. *Ioudas*), which in New Testament times was very common. In the New Testament there are four men named Judas. Of those, perhaps the most famous is Judas Iscariot, one of Jesus' twelve disciples, whose betrayal led directly to Jesus' execution. Then there is Jude, the son of a man named James, who was also, like Iscariot, one of the twelve disciples (Luke 6:16). (Yes, Jesus apparently had two disciples named Judas.) There is also Judas Barsabbas who accompanied Paul, Barnabas, and Silas to Antioch after the Council at Jerusalem (Acts 15:22). And finally there is Judas, one of the four half brothers of Jesus who is named in the Gospels (Matt. 13:55; Mark 6:3).

The author of the New Testament **epistle** we call Jude says that he is "a brother of James" (Jude 1). Because Jude mentions this without further description or explanation of who James is, he apparently expected his readers to know. The most likely man who was well known enough was probably James, a half brother of Jesus who became the leader of the church in Jerusalem after the apostle Peter had to flee because of persecution (Acts 12, esp. v. 17; Acts 15, esp. v. 13; Acts 21, esp. v. 18; Gal. 1:19).

Both the gospels of Mark (6:3) and Matthew (13:55) list the names of Jesus' four "brothers": James, Joseph, Judas, and Simon, all of which were very common names at the time.[1] Their biological relationship to Jesus is of course defined by Christian theology of the incarnation and, in some quarters, Christian tradition concerning the perpetual virginity of Mary. Because Jesus had no human father, if these four men were the sons of his mother, Mary, and Joseph, they are properly his half brothers and would have been younger than Jesus. Or they may have been Jesus' stepbrothers, the sons of Joseph by a wife previous to Mary. Some have argued that the Greek word "brother" (Gk. *adelphos*) could also be used of a more distant male relative, such as a cousin. For the sake of brevity and without wishing to decide this issue, here we will refer to these men simply as Jesus' brothers. In any case, these four men and the two female siblings of Jesus also mentioned would have formed his immediate family group.

1. The Gospels also mention that Jesus had two sisters, and later Christian tradition claims their names were Mary and Salome. So there would have been seven children in Jesus' immediate family, including him.

Judas (Jude) Was a Common Name

- Judas Iscariot: one of the Twelve; he betrayed Jesus (Matt. 27:3; Mark 14:10; Luke 6:16; John 6:71)
- Judas: son of James, one of the Twelve (Luke 6:16)
- Judas Barsabbas: he accompanied Paul, Barnabas, and Silas to Antioch after the Council at Jerusalem (Acts 15:22)
- Judas: one of four brothers of Jesus (Matt. 13:55; Mark 6:3)

Jesus Had (Half/Step) Brothers

"Isn't this the carpenter's son? Isn't his mother's name Mary, and aren't his brothers James, Joseph, Simon and Judas?"

Matthew 13:55

"Isn't this the carpenter? Isn't this Mary's son and the brother of James, Joseph, Judas and Simon? Aren't his sisters here with us?" And they took offense at him.

Mark 6:3

Throughout the history of the church there has been debate about the exact relationship of these four men to Jesus because of belief in the virgin birth of Jesus and later, in the Roman Catholic Church, the perpetual virginity of Mary. The virgin birth of Jesus obviously means that any other children Mary may have subsequently had with Joseph were technically half siblings. For those who believe in the perpetual virginity of Mary, these brothers may have been stepbrothers, sons of Joseph by a previous marriage. Others have claimed that "brother" should be read more loosely as a relative, such as a cousin. The Greek word for "brother" (Gk. *adelphos*) in this context would most naturally be read to refer to either a half brother or stepbrother.

Although Jesus' brothers did not follow him as a spiritual authority during his itinerant public ministry, they apparently did come to faith and later traveled as preachers of the gospel after Jesus' resurrection (1 Cor. 9:5).[2] Paul tells us that Jesus had appeared to James (1 Cor. 15:7), so possibly he appeared to others in his family as well.

The author of Jude, who is the brother of James, is therefore also most likely the brother of Jesus and was himself apparently well known in the early church.

Eusebius of Caesarea, a Christian writer who lived at the turn of the third to fourth century cites an earlier writer, Hegesippus, saying that Jude's grandsons were also leaders in the church and were interrogated by the Roman emperor Domitian (**AD** 81–96) (*Hist. eccl.* 3.19.1–20.6).

The name Judas (Gk. *Ioudas*) appears as the third leader of the Jerusalem church on the list preserved (or created) by Epiphanius, a fourth-century bishop of Cyprus, following the names James (Gk. *Iakōbos*) and Simon (Gk. *Symeōn*).[3] These three names—James, Simon, and Judas—happen also to be the names of three of the four brothers of Jesus (Matt. 13:55; Mark 6:3). In the *Apostolic Constitutions* the third bishop of Jerusalem is further specified as "Judas of James," but the fourth century date of this writing may reflect only the later tradition of the church that the third bishop was the brother of James and not necessarily reliable historical information.[4] Furthermore, it is difficult to know with any certainty if the third name on the Jerusalem bishop list refers to the same man who wrote the epistle of Jude. First, the name was very common; second, there are differing

2. See Richard Bauckham, *Jude and the Relatives of Jesus in the Early Church* (Edinburgh: T&T Clark, 1990).
3. Epiphanius, *The Panarion of St. Epiphanius, Bishop of Salamis*, trans. Philip R. Amidon (Oxford: Oxford University Press, 1990), 229.
4. Burnett H. Streeter, *The Primitive Church Studied with Special Reference to the Origins of the Christian Ministry* (New York: Macmillan, 1929), 186.

A Story about Jude's Grandchildren

"Now there still survived of the family of the Lord grandsons of Judas [Jude], who was said to have been his brother according to the flesh, and they were delated [reported] as being of the family of David. These the officer brought to Domitian Caesar, for, like Herod, he was afraid of the coming of the Christ. He asked them if they were of the house of David and they admitted it.... They were asked concerning the Christ and his kingdom, its nature, origin, and time of appearance, and explained that it was neither of the world nor earthly, but heavenly and angelic, and it would be at the end of the world, when he would come in glory to judge the living and the dead to reward every man according to his deeds. At this Domitian did not condemn them at all, but despised them as simple folk, released them, and decreed an end to the persecution against the church. But when they were released they were the leaders of the churches, both for their testimony and for their relation to the Lord, and remained alive in the peace which ensued until Trajan."

Eusebius, *Hist. eccl.* 3.20

bishop lists on which the name Judas does not appear; and third, Judas Barsabbas was also a prominent leader in the Jerusalem church (Acts 15:22, 27, 32).[5] It would not be surprising that the brothers of Jesus successively became leaders in the Jerusalem church, given the esteem the Lord's family was accorded in Palestine, but it cannot be proven. The list of Jewish leaders of the Jerusalem church given by Eusebius includes fifteen men, starting with James, up until the Bar Kokhba revolt in AD 135, which makes for an average term of seven years each. James led the church until his death in AD 62, making the average terms of office for the subsequent fourteen leaders about five years each. It is therefore not out of the realm of possibility that Simon and Jude were still alive to succeed James following his death; though for this to be true, they probably would have been younger than James. In any case, the tone and content of Jude's letter are certainly consistent with what might be expected from the leader of the church in Jerusalem. On the other hand, had Jude written his letter as the leader of the church in Jerusalem, one assumes that he would have been known in his own right, making his self-description as a "brother of James" likely unnecessary. Therefore the question of Jude's identity and role must remain uncertain.

Beyond identifying the author of the epistle of Jude as the brother of James, the content of the epistle indicates that his background was in the religious tradition of Palestinian Judaism. He appears to use the Hebrew version of the Scriptures, not the Greek **Septuagint**, although he does employ some common religious expressions also found in the Septuagint. Jude 3 mentions the author's intent to write, undercutting the theory that the letter originated as a sermon.

Date

The close parallels between the content of Jude and 2 Peter imply that the date of one book informs the date of the other. The consensus of current New Testament scholarship is that Jude was written first and then used in 2 Peter, which means that the latest date

5. Bauckham, *Jude and the Relatives*, 71.

for the appearance of Jude would be somewhat before 2 Peter was written, a date that is also unknown. (See the discussion of their literary relationship in chapter 12.) If Jude, the brother of Jesus, wrote this letter, then it would have to have been written within the life of that generation, suggesting a date not later than AD 80. If Jude was an older stepbrother of Jesus (by a previous marriage of Joseph), AD 65 is probably the latest date; if he was a younger half brother, the date could be extended toward AD 80.

Many scholars date the book well past the probable lifetime of Jesus' brother Jude, believing it is a **pseudonymous** epistle written by some later unknown Christian leader using Jude's name. If this should be true, the pseudonymous author apparently would have viewed the brothers of Jesus as having significant spiritual authority. In this case, one wonders why "Jude, brother of James," would be chosen as the pseudonym rather than simply James himself. (See discussion of pseudonymous letters in the introduction.) Some scholars read Jude's reminder in verse 17 as evidence that the apostolic age is over: "remember what the apostles of our Lord Jesus Christ foretold." This construal must overlook the beginning phrase of the next verse (emphasis added), "They said *to you*. . . ." This is most naturally read as referring to personal contact between the apostles and Jude's readers, though it could be taken as the apostles speaking to all subsequent generations.

Courtesy of the Pitts Theology Library, Candler School of Theology, Emory University

Jude in a woodcut by Johann Christoph Weigel, 1695.

Some have construed the false Christians against whom Jude rails as **Gnostics**, an assumption that tends to push the date into the early second century. Although a gnostic form of Christianity developed that did embrace a licentious lifestyle, it also held an errant **Christology**. There is no evidence of doctrinal heresy in Jude; the teachers are heretical because of their cavalier attitude toward immorality. Certainly Gnostics were not the first or only ones to live licentiously, and therefore the nature of this heresy does not help date the letter.

Others argue for a later dating by suggesting that the letter belongs to the "early Catholic" period because of the reference to "the" faith in verse 3. Such a reading sees the definite article as indicating an established body of doctrine more characteristic of the later church. The article could just as plausibly refer to the oral tradition of the apostolic witnesses of the teaching of Jesus, a corpus that existed from the time of Jesus' death onward. Furthermore, the most salient issues of those who identify an early Catholic period is the delay of the **parousia** and an emphasis on ecclesiastical structure and authority. Neither of these concerns the author of Jude. Contra that view, **apocalyptic** elements and exhortations for a Spirit-controlled life of faith argue more strongly for an earlier rather than later date.

Although there is little in the content of the book that can be reliably used to date it, there is also nothing that compels the conclusion that it is pseudonymous. The most solid position is a date within the lifetime of Jesus' brother Jude, AD 80 at the latest. If 2 Peter borrows material from Jude's letter and if the apostle Peter is the author of that letter, then Jude would have been written not later than the mid-60s, since Peter was martyred in AD 65/66 during Nero's reign.

TO WHOM DID JUDE WRITE?

Every author assumes certain shared knowledge with his or her readers, knowledge that begins with the decision in which language to write. Correspondence to a person or group implies the most specific shared knowledge because of the author's intent to communicate, not to anyone who happens to read it, but to the specific people he or she has in mind. Identifying the original audience of the biblical writings that lack a specific address usually involves making inferences based on what shared knowledge is assumed by the content of the book.

The fact that Jude is composed in Greek of a fairly advanced style and vocabulary implies that the original readers, who may have read it aloud to Christian assemblies, had good proficiency in Greek. It may imply that Jude himself was highly capable in Greek or only that he employed an **amanuensis**. If Jude himself wrote this letter as a Palestinian Jew whose native language was Aramaic, this letter would count as evidence for the proficient knowledge and use of Greek by Jews even within Roman Palestine, adding to increasing evidence that Greek was used throughout Palestine, even in Jerusalem, in the first century. Josephus mentions that both freemen and even slaves could acquire skill in Greek in Palestine if they so desired.[6]

Notable thinkers who left their legacy through their writings in Greek, such as Josephus, Theodorus the rhetorician, Meleager the poet, and Philodemus the philosopher, all came from Galilee, and so this was clearly not a region of complete illiteracy.[7] While there is still room for debate about the proficiency and scope of Greek language in first-century Palestine, there is mounting evidence that many of its people were bilingual at least and quite possibly trilingual.[8] Aramaic would have been the native language, Hebrew the reli-

---

6. Joseph A. Fitzmyer, "Did Jesus Speak Greek?" *BAR* 18 (September–October 1992): 59.
7. J. Daryl Charles, "Literary Artifice in the Epistle of Jude," ZNW 82 (1991): 118.
8. See Fitzmyer, "Did Jesus Speak Greek?" 58–63, 76–77; Martin Hengel, *The "Hellenization" of Judaea in the First Century after Christ*, trans. John Bowden (Philadelphia: Trinity, 1989); *Judaism and Hellenism*, 2 vols., trans. John Bowden (Philadelphia: Trinity, 1981); Ben Witherington III, *Letters and Homilies for Jewish Christians: A Socio-Rhetorical Commentary on Hebrews, James, and Jude* (Downers Grove, Ill.: InterVarsity, 2007), 563–67.

Even Slaves Could Learn Greek in First-Century Palestine

"But I labored hard to steep myself in Greek prose ... after having gained a knowledge of Greek grammar; but the constant use of my native tongue hindered my achieving precision in pronunciation. For our people do not welcome those who have mastered the speech of many nations ... for they consider that such skill is not only common to ordinary freedmen, but that even slaves acquire it, if they so choose."

Josephus, *Antiquities* 2.11.264

gious and sacred language, and Greek the language of commerce and civic affairs. It is no longer permissible to dismiss the family and twelve disciples of Jesus as necessarily incapable of writing the Greek found in the New Testament books.

Even if Jude was a native Semitic speaker, he chose to write in Greek, which may imply that the people he had in mind were living outside of Palestine in the Greek-speaking **Diaspora** or that the New Testament preserves a Greek translation of a letter originally written in Aramaic (though the Greek does not seem to have strongly the character of "translation" Greek). Because Greek was the lingua franca throughout the Roman Empire, the fact that Jude is written in Greek gives no clue that would specify where his original readers were located. What is somewhat surprising is that while writing in Greek, Jude nevertheless used the Hebrew version of the Scriptures rather than one of its Greek translations. Furthermore, the quotation from *1 Enoch* 9 in verses 14–15 shows the imprint of an Aramaic, not Greek, source. This, of course, is more telling about the author than about the recipients. The use of Hebrew and/or Aramaic was more narrowly limited to a geographical location at the far eastern end of the Roman Empire in Palestine, Syria, and perhaps the most eastern reaches of Asia Minor. Because of Jude's association with the family of Jesus, a Palestinian provenance is the most likely of the Aramaic-speaking regions.

Gustave Dore

Jude 11 accuses the heretics of the same error as Balaam (Num. 22).

What is clear from the letter itself is that Jude expected his readers to be familiar with people and events found in the Old Testament. In verse 5 he acknowledges that his readers "already know all this" before he reminds them of the lessons of the exodus, fallen angels, Sodom and Gomorrah, Michael the archangel, the way of Cain, and the error of Balaam. However, each of these people and events had a longstanding place in the traditions of Judaism that had developed beyond the text of Scripture alone. Balaam, for instance, had by the time the New Testament was written become known for his greed, and it is that association that Jude seems to assume and invoke in verse 11 (and 2 Peter 2:15).[9] Similarly, Jude refers to (v. 9) and quotes (vv. 14–15) pseudepigraphal literature known in Jewish circles of that day, not as Scripture, but as valued religious writings that had standing with the audience to whom Jude writes.

Jude's allusions to persons and events of the Old Testament indicate that he had the Hebrew Old Testament in mind, even though he writes in Greek to people who could

9. Geza Vermes, "The Story of Balaam," in *Scripture and Tradition in Judaism*, StPB 4 (Leiden: Brill, 1961), 127–77, esp. 131–33.

presumably read it. He nevertheless uses the Scripture in the form that would have been familiar to Palestinians. (See further discussion below, How Did Jude Use the Old Testament?)

Jude's original readers were clearly Jewish Christians who would receive and respect his authority as the brother of James, the (late?) head of the Jerusalem church. Without further information, it is probably best to surmise that Jude's original audience was located within the area of influence of the Jerusalem church, and therefore within Palestine, possibly its near environs such as Antioch in Syria. The fact that Jude had been planning to write to them anyway, even before the crisis of heresy (v. 3), may imply he had an ongoing relationship previously established with his original readers. Given that many fled persecution of the church in Jerusalem in its earliest days (Acts 8:1), Jude's letter may be directed at one or more of the communities throughout Judea and Samaria where the church had taken root. Had it been written to one specific church, one might expect some indication of that in the address of the letter; instead, Jude writes to "those who have been called, who are loved in God the Father and kept for Jesus Christ" (v. 1). Such a general address suggests that the letter was intended for more than one church congregation.

WHY DID JUDE WRITE? THE WARNING AGAINST FALSE CHRISTIANS

Jude makes his purpose explicit. Although he would have written about "the salvation we share" (v. 3a), Jude is compelled to write urging his readers "to contend for the faith that the Lord has once for all entrusted to God's holy people" (v. 3b). The letter is a plea to hold to apostolic orthodoxy in the presence of "ungodly people" who "have secretly slipped in" among Jude's readers, ungodly people "who pervert the grace of our God into a license for immorality and deny Jesus Christ our only Sovereign and Lord" (v. 4).

Most modern works and commentaries refer to these people as "false teachers," but there are no words in the Greek that would indicate that these people held any official role as teachers in the church(es). Jude himself most often refers to those he denounces as "these people" (Gk. *houtoi* in vv. 8, 10, 12, 16, 19). The fact that they had been able to "secretly slip in" suggests that in every observable way they would fit a Christian image. They probably did not hold any official leadership position, compared, for instance, to 3 John 9, which concerns a leader of a church who has stepped outside the bounds of apostolic orthodoxy. Rather, these people apparently exerted a type of personal power that was very influential, whether because of their socioeconomic status, their education, their political connections, or some other reason.

Jude does not denounce them for holding an errant Christology (cf. 1 John 2:18, 22–23), but he does condemn them for being guided by their own dreams and knowledge that is rooted in base human nature (vv. 8, 10). This has led them to

- reject apostolic authority and teaching (v. 18),
- prefer their own ideas about spirituality and morality to revelation (v. 8),
- practice sexual immorality driven by animal instincts and unnatural lust (vv. 6–8, 10), and
- not apprehend or respect the power and position of spiritual beings (vv. 8–9).

As Jude points out in verse 3, the Lord entrusted the revelation of his redemptive plan to "his people," ancient Israel, the ancestors of Second Temple Judaism. As the Jewish Messiah, Jesus consummated God's message of redemption. Christ's apostles stood within this Judaic tradition, announcing its truth to the Roman world. But the Christian gospel also underscored the coming of the Holy Spirit into the world in a new way, transforming those who came to faith in Christ. This more direct access to God than humanity had ever previously known led some Christians, both then and now, to believe that knowledge allegedly coming directly from the Holy Spirit should supplant the prophetic and apostolic revelation that came throughout the centuries and that culminated in the written Scriptures we have today. Jude is apparently writing to denounce such Christians who, "on the strength of their dreams," reject any spiritual authority other than their own instincts. It is important to note that the work of the Holy Spirit, as taught in the New Testament, is (1) to open the eyes of people to the truth of the gospel of Jesus Christ and (2) to transform the moral character of the Christian believer in conformity to God's will for his human creatures. The work of the Spirit does not impart new revelation upon which doctrine or practice can be justified that is not consistent with the apostolic teaching. This misunderstanding about the Spirit imparting new knowledge forms the basis of much of the heresy condemned by New Testament writers, as well as modern heretical movements today.

Those who look inward for spiritual truth apart from apostolic teaching find only knowledge that originates in their own base human instincts. Such "knowledge" usually results in a form of moral antinomianism varnished with a claim that freedom, in Christ, from the law means that previously understood moral constraints on behavior no longer apply. Such knowledge, Jude says, perverts "the grace of our God into a license for immorality" (v. 4). Although such people may claim to be Christian, in fact they "deny Jesus Christ our only Sovereign and Lord" (v. 4), who came to set humanity free from sin so that we live in obedience to God's moral standards, which are in opposition to the base instincts of our fallen human nature. The Holy Spirit always works in concert with the revealed word of Scripture, empowering a transformation aligned with the arc of biblical morality.

Where a new message apart from Scripture is claimed, it always tends toward the base instincts of human desire—lust and greed. False beliefs about the work of the Holy Spirit apparently also gave them the false idea that the indwelling Spirit gave them power equal to that of the angels, which motivated them "to heap abuse on celestial beings" (v. 8). Ancient ideas about angels and their sexual relationship to humans are quite foreign to modern thinking and beyond the scope of this work, but suffice it to say that God has consigned angels and humans to two different spheres of existence, and to cross those boundaries was to bring down God's overwhelming wrath. Although modern interpreters want to reinterpret the sin of Sodom and Gomorrah as a failure to extend hospitality, Jude explains the destruction of those towns as the consequence of an unnatural sexual immorality similar to that perpetrated by the "Watchers," who were fallen angels who had sexual relations with human women, producing giants with a superhuman bent toward evil (*1 Enoch* 12–16). Nothing less than Noah's flood was necessary to wash the earth of that evil (Gen. 6). Jude explains that the ungodly "in the very same way" (i.e., sexually) pollute their own bodies, reject authority, and heap abuse on celestial beings (v. 8), raising the possibility that Jude's letter was a polemic against the practice of homosexuality in the early church, which was living in a society where it was widely tolerated.

The teachings of Judaism condemned homosexual practice; Greco-Roman society tolerated it. It is not difficult to see how the early Christian church, emerging from Judaism yet quickly comprised primarily of Greco-Roman Gentiles, would have to deal with diverse opinions in the churches about homosexual practice. Jude's letter appears to be an early condemnation of those within the churches teaching that sexual immorality was consistent with freedom from the Jewish law that Christianity preached.

Jude explains that "these people" are guilty of a fundamental misunderstanding and abuse of God's grace. Their way of thinking and living was causing division in the churches they influenced (v. 19) as the congregation struggled to find the truth. Jude unequivocally pronounces that though "these people" self-identify as Christians, in fact they do not have the Holy Spirit (v. 19) and are therefore not true followers of Christ.

Perhaps "these people" were Jews attracted to the Christian gospel because of the misunderstanding that as Christians they could throw off what they perceived to be the shackles of the moral laws of Judaism. However, the behavior of Jewish converts documented elsewhere in the New Testament tends toward the imposition of Jewish legalism, not toward antinomianism. More likely, this letter gives us a glimpse into the consequences of **Gentile** Christians coming into congregations of primarily Jewish believers. While in the apostle Paul's writings we see the effect of Jewish believers trying to assert spiritual influence over Gentile converts, here we may be seeing Gentile converts using their liberty in Christ to assert spiritual influence over their more conservative Jewish brothers and sisters. In this scenario Jude would be concerned that the Jewish believers, who have been formed by the Hebrew Scriptures and have a good grasp on God's authority, the basis of morality, and the consequences of sin, would be pulled toward the heretical views of Gentile Christians who "slander whatever they do not understand" (v. 10). Jude pleads with his readers to contend for the faith that the Lord Jesus entrusted, not to the Gentiles, but "to us, his people" (v. 3).

K. H. Jobes

Jude describes the heretics as a twice-dead tree.

As Christianity spread into the Gentile world of the Roman Empire, various problems and heresies developed as those shaped by the world of pagan thought and behavior became Christians. The Corinthian church is perhaps the best example of this as indicated by the apostle Paul's correspondence with them and by a letter from Clement of Rome that suggested the problems continued even decades later. In Jude's letter we may be seeing the converse problem of the Gentile world coming into Palestine with greater influence. We know that itinerant preachers and prophets moved among the churches in the late first century, not all of whom were true and worthy of welcome (3 John; *Didache* 11 – 13). False Christians who designated themselves as teachers or prophets made demands for extended hospitality and sought financial gain as they exerted their influence in the churches.

The *Didache* on Christian Hospitality

> Let every apostle who comes to you be welcomed as if he were the Lord. But he is not to stay for more than one day, unless there is need, in which case he may stay another. But if he stays three days, he is a false prophet. And when the apostle leaves, he is to take nothing except bread until he finds the next night's lodging. But if he ask for money, he is a false prophet.
>
> *Didache* 11:4–6*

The *Didache* (or *The Teaching of the Twelve Apostles*) is a text discovered in 1873 that may contain material dating to the first century that summarizes instruction for those preparing for Christian baptism and church membership and instruction about food, baptism, fasting, prayer, the Eucharist, and offices of church leadership. Its place of origin is unknown, but Syro-Palestine seems likely. Because it was not continually preserved through church history and because there were apparently relatively few copies of it made, it was never accorded the same esteem as the apostolic writings, but it is a very interesting historical piece.

*The full text in both Greek and English translation can be found in *The Apostolic Fathers*, ed. Michael W. Holmes (Grand Rapids: Baker, 1999).

Jude's response to this spiritually dangerous situation is to reassure the churches that nothing completely new or surprising is happening. In fact, he says that the condemnation of such people "was written about long ago" (v. 4) and then mentions that even Enoch, the seventh generation from Adam, prophesied a message of judgment of the ungodly when "the Lord [comes] with thousands upon thousands of his holy ones ... to convict all of them of all the ungodly acts they have committed in their ungodliness, and of all the defiant words ungodly sinners have spoken against him" (vv. 14–15). This emphatic reminder of judgment may imply that an element of false teaching involved the denial of coming judgment. Jude reminds his readers that more recently the apostles of Jesus Christ also predicted that scoffers would come who would "follow their own ungodly desires" (v. 18). Jude cuts through the confusion to say that not only do "these people" not have the truth because they do not have the Holy Spirit, but that they will be condemned for spreading such an ungodly message through their words and deeds.

Although Jude is not surprised that "these people" have infiltrated the churches, he is certainly not complacent about them, and he warns his readers to stand against them. His exhortation in verses 17ff. is the main point of the letter that follows his lengthy introduction about why such an exhortation is necessary. His exhortation is that his readers are to be the rescuers of those who are about to fall under the influence of these false Christians and become like them. But first, Jude says, you must be sure to keep yourselves in God's love "by building yourselves up in your most holy faith and praying in the Holy Spirit" (vv. 20–21). Although it is a bit uncertain what exactly Jude meant by "building up" oneself in the faith, presumably it involved becoming better acquainted with the apostolic teachings of "the faith" so that the errors of "these people" could be recognized. Second,

Jude instructs them to pray in the Holy Spirit. While a misunderstanding about the work and power of the Holy Spirit may lie at the root of the heresy of false Christians, Jude does not shy away from the third member of the Trinity. Almost surprisingly, he wants his readers to pray in the Spirit, confident that it is only by the Spirit of God that heresy in the church can be overcome. His readers are to do this "as you wait for the mercy of our Lord Jesus Christ to bring you to eternal life" (v. 21). Jude reminds his readers that they have not reached the eschatological final state—perhaps another element in false teaching that denies any further judgment—and that they must live faithfully while they wait for it. Moreover, the final state is "eternal life" to which Jesus Christ in his mercy will bring believers. Therefore all three members of the Godhead are involved in Jude's exhortation.

After exhorting them to guard themselves in this spiritually dangerous situation, he continues his exhortation that they must be merciful to those who are confused by the teaching of these false Christians (v. 22). Moreover, they are not to stand idly by while fellow congregants fall under the influence of this heresy, but are to move quickly and decisively to "snatch" those about to be consumed by the false teaching out of the fire of this spiritual danger (v. 23).

Jude is confident that the Savior God is able to keep them safe from stumbling and bring them into God's presence "without fault and with great joy" (v. 24). This confident thought of God's power over his churches compels Jude to a beautiful doxology announcing "glory, majesty, power and authority" to God *through* Jesus Christ in eternity past, now, and forevermore (v. 25). The closing doxology and other statements throughout the letter reveal much about Jude's theology.

JUDE'S THEOLOGY

New Testament theology has to be read out of the content of letters that are themselves not theological treatises. But the fact that the epistles are not theological treatises does not mean they contain no theology or cannot be used for understanding early Christian theology, as Jude's statements about God, Jesus Christ, the Holy Spirit, **soteriology**, and **eschatology** show. Paul's letters reveal Christian theology as it was expressed to Greek-speaking Gentile converts; Jude's thoughts are especially valuable, for they, along with those of James, likely represent theological ideas of the Aramaic-speaking church of Palestine. What's more, if Jude, the author of this letter, was in fact Jesus' brother, then Jude's theology gives some glimpse into the religious thought in which Jesus was raised.

God—Father, Savior, Judge

Jude's thoughts are hemmed in by God on all sides. He opens his letter by addressing it "to those ... who are loved in God the Father" (v. 1) and closes it by ascribing glory, majesty, power, and authority to "the only God our Savior" (v. 25). Both concepts of God as Father and of God as Savior are present in the Old Testament, on which Jude's theology heavily depends. Psalm 89:26–27 provides a starting point, noting that God's servant, David, will call out to him, "'You are my Father, my God, the Rock my Savior.' And I [God] will appoint him to be my firstborn, the most exalted of the kings of the earth." In the New Testament, Jesus is revealed as both son of David and Son of God. And God is revealed most specifically in the New Testament as the Father of our Lord Jesus Christ (Rom. 15:6; 2 Cor. 1:3; Eph. 1:3; Col. 1:3; 1 Pet. 1:3). By virtue of faith in Jesus Christ, God's Son, all Christian believers are spiritually reborn as children of God. Jude notes that his readers are "loved *in* God," a phrase that accords with exhortations found in the **Johannine** writings about remaining in Christ's love (John 15:9–10). The apostle Paul often speaks of believers being "in Christ," but the phrase "in God" is found elsewhere only in the opening verse of 1 and 2 Thessalonians. Jude defines his targeted readers as those who have been spiritually born again of God and describes the nature of their relationship with God as a loving Father.

The concept of God as Savior frequently occurs in the Psalms and Prophets of the Old Testament as Israel cried out for deliverance. For instance, Psalm 79:9 would be especially relevant to Jude's readers: "Help us, God our Savior, for the glory of your name; deliver us and forgive our sins for your name's sake." The idea that God is "our only God and Savior" might echo Isaiah 45:21, "And there is no God apart from me, a righteous God and a Savior; there is none but me." It is this one true God whom Jude teaches is able to keep Christians from stumbling and to present them before his presence without fault and with great joy (vv. 24–25).

God is both Father and Savior, but Jude also knows him to be the ultimate and final Judge. Even at the time of the exodus, it was insufficient to be numbered among God's people but not to live faithfully. Jude points out that even in ancient times the one who delivered his people also destroyed those among them who did not believe (v. 5). And so by implication Jude explains that it is not enough to call oneself a Christian and fellowship in the church among Christians without truly living out the faith in obedience to God's Word. Judgment deferred is not judgment forgotten, for according to Jude, God has the power to bind even the primordial rebellious angels and keep them chained for a day of great judgment (v. 6). To scoff at the return of Christ is to forget that the day of God's judgment is coming.

But God is able to keep Christ's followers from stumbling and to present them before his presence without fault and with great joy (v. 25). Although God is Judge, for those who live out their faith in Christ in obedience to God's Word there will be joy, for God is also Savior (vv. 24–25).

Jesus Christ

If the Jude of this letter was in fact the earthly brother of Jesus, then his Christology is all the more striking. After all, what would it take for you to come to a place where you could worship your older brother—the one who sat at the family dining table, whom you played with and squabbled with—as "our only Sovereign and Lord" (v. 4)? Jude makes himself subservient to Jesus Christ (v. 1a), referring to Jesus not as his brother but as his Lord. Although the early church may have held the earthly family of Jesus in high regard, and understandably so, it is clear from both Jude's letter and that of James that these men recognized their half brother Jesus as more than an earthly religious leader or founder of a movement. Jude subordinates himself to Jesus Christ and joins all other believers in the inclusive pronoun *our* when describing Jesus as Sovereign and Lord. Jude recognizes Jesus Christ to be the eternally permanent ruler of God's kingdom (v. 25).

Jude describes his readers to be those who are being kept for Jesus Christ, presumably by God's power (v. 24, cf. 1 Thess. 5:23; John 17:11), though the Greek could be construed as "kept by" or even "kept in" Jesus Christ. This description casts Jude's readers and their situation into an eschatological framework oriented toward the future. It is a particularly reassuring thought at the opening of a letter intended to warn them of the grave spiritual danger of the influence of false Christians.

The title that Jude uses for Jesus, "Sovereign" (Gk. *despotēs*), is striking because it is used in Luke 2:29; Acts 4:24; and often in the Septuagint to address God. Jude thus implies an equality of Christ's sovereignty with God's. Furthermore, by denying to live within the moral constraints of "the faith" that was once for all entrusted to his people, the false Christians have in fact denied not only Christ but God. "The faith" refers to that understanding of humanity's relationship to God as imparted by the ministry, death, and resurrection of Jesus Christ, which was "once for all entrusted" to the apostles. In other words, the orthodox gospel of Christ is for all people and all places and all times. Jude underscores the idea that no new revelation will supplant that which has been handed down from Jesus through his apostles to the church (cf. similar teaching in Hebrews). In fact, the apostles of Jesus predicted the very situation that had arisen — that some people would scoff at the truth because they want to follow their own ungodly desires (vv. 17 – 18). The warning is pointed: those who follow the false Christians deny Christ and therefore deny God.

Jude's Glorious Doxology

"To him who is able to keep you from stumbling and to present you before his glorious presence without fault and with great joy — to the only God our Savior be glory, majesty, power and authority, through Jesus Christ our Lord, before all ages, now and forevermore! Amen."

Jude 24 – 25

The title most used by Jude for Jesus is Christ (Gk. *christos*), the Greek equivalent of the Hebrew *Messiah*, revealing Jude's fundamental understanding of his brother as the Messiah. Jesus is God's anointed whose every teaching and deed is by God's authority. Jude portrays Christ's lordship as the lordship of God; the faith Christ has entrusted is the truth of God, which must be obeyed. It is the mercy of Jesus Christ that keeps Christians safe while they live out their earthly lives waiting for him to bring them to eternal life (v. 21).

The concluding doxology found in Jude 25 is one of the most beautiful in the New Testament. Jude declares that human beings see Jesus, God's Messiah, and ascribe praise to God's eternal attributes of glory, majesty, power, and authority. Jude calls God the Savior, but it is a salvation that comes through Jesus, the Sovereign and Lord who will bring us to eternal life. As with other writers in the New Testament, to see Jesus Christ in his life, death, and resurrection is to know the true nature of God. Jesus reveals the character and attributes of the invisible God.

The Holy Spirit

Jude mentions the Holy Spirit only twice (vv. 19 – 20). In verse 19 the false Christians who are dividing the church are following merely natural instincts that they mistake as divine guidance, for they "do not have the Spirit." Jude implies by this that a person must have the Holy Spirit in order to know spiritual truth that does not deny the faith. He further implies that it is not the Holy Spirit who leads people to beliefs and life choices that deny Jesus Christ; it is their own ungodly desires and mere natural instincts.

Jude instructs his readers to fortify themselves in the faith by praying "in the Spirit" (v. 20). He assumes that those who truly have the Spirit of God will not fall to the influence of false Christians, for the Spirit will give them discernment and power. Although Jude emphasizes that God will keep believers till the end, he nevertheless also underscores the believer's responsibility to be fortified in the faith and to pray, not formal, cold, lifeless prayers, but prayers that are fired by the Holy Spirit. Despite a heresy that may have claimed new revelation from the Holy Spirit, Jude shows the Spirit to be the transforming power that overcomes mere natural instincts and empowers a life lived in God's love (vv. 20–21).

The Christian Life

Not only does Jude exhort his readers to pray in the Holy Spirit, but also to keep themselves in God's love (v. 21) as they wait for Jesus' mercy to bring them to eternal life, a pleasantly euphemistic way to describe death. In other words, for as long as a Christian lives, he or she is to live in such a way that pleases God, and so remain in his love, as opposed to an unbelieving life that brings judgment (cf. John 15:10). While modern slogans imply that God loves the sinner and hates the sin, Jude's exhortation implies that it is possible to step outside the love of God by stepping outside of the bounds of orthodoxy. The Christian is to think of life as a time of waiting for that great moment of being brought into God's presence, faultless and with great joy. Because of the eternal consequences at stake, Jude exhorts his faithful readers to be merciful toward, not condemn, those who doubt. They are to "snatch" others from the danger the false Christians present. While it isn't clear exactly what Jude intended his readers specifically to do, which may have depended on individual situations, he communicates a sense of urgency and great danger. Even though the apostles predicted that false Christians would come, Jude exhorts his readers not to be complacent about it. Deal with the danger, he says, in a way that protects both yourself and others among God's people.

HOW DID JUDE USE THE OLD TESTAMENT?

Once while listening to a sermon, I heard a preacher mention Noah. He didn't explain who Noah was; he didn't quote any verse from Genesis; he didn't even mention the flood. Because of the audience he was preaching to, he assumed, probably rightly, that everyone in the congregation knew the story of the great flood and had likely read the Genesis account more than once. Because of their knowledge about Noah, the simple mention of his name was sufficient to bring to mind the whole story of the flood. Jude's use of the Old Testament is very similar. He does not quote Old Testament verses, but he refers often to people and events from the Old Testament stories—and from other literature that would have been well known to his audience as well.

What's more, if someone today mentions the name Noah, what comes to mind may be more than what is said about him in Genesis. For instance, additional information about Noah comes from what the New Testament says about him, that he was a "preacher of righteousness" (2 Peter 2:5) even though the Genesis story says nothing about him being a preacher. The modern search for the remains of Noah's ark centers on Mount Ararat in the region of eastern Turkey. No one really knows where Noah's ark landed when the flood waters receded, but this location might also be brought to someone's mind today when Noah is mentioned, and an author could allude to that location by virtue of its association with Noah.

Similarly, Jude's allusions to the Old Testament characters and events often assume not only what the Old Testament says about them, but also what Jewish tradition said about those people and events at the time Jude was writing. "Jewish tradition" generally refers to a body of beliefs built on and developed from Scripture that has been preserved in other religious writings that were valued within Judaism, which Christians today typically refer to as the **Apocrypha** and the **pseudepigrapha**. The writings of Philo, Josephus, and other Jewish writers also preserve a window into how the Bible was interpreted in the first century. There is analogously a large corpus of Christian tradition today contained in books written by Christian authors that are not at all considered Scripture or canonical but that are nevertheless valued and considered to be a source of spiritual truth.

Jude 11, which pronounces woe on false Christian teachers who "go the way of Cain" is a good example of how Jude relies on the *interpretive tradition* of the story of Cain rather than on the biblical story alone. What we know of Cain from Genesis 4 is that his offering was inferior to that of his brother Abel's, whom he murdered in jealous anger. It is not clear from Genesis 4 alone in what way the false teachers condemned by Jude are like Cain—they weren't actual murderers, were they? Considering the tradition associated with Cain at the time Jude wrote solves the puzzle. At the time Jude was writing, Cain had become the archetypal sinner in Jewish tradition, who taught others to sin because there is no divine judgment coming. Josephus characterizes him by greed, violence, and lust (*Ant.* 1.52–66). Several other Jewish writings, such as Philo's writings, *Targum Neofiti*, *Wisdom of Solomon* 10.3, and the *Testament of Benjamin* 7.5, also elaborate similarly on the wickedness of Cain. Jude is comparing the evil influence of the false Christians in the churches to how Cain was understood at the time, as someone who should be a brother but who is driven by ungodly motives that lead others away from God.

Jude often refers to the false Christians as "these people" whose sin is like that of the fallen angels and the cities of Sodom and Gomorrah, both of which serve typologically as examples of certain and irreversible judgment in Jewish tradition (vv. 6–7). While biblical scholars today debate exactly what was the sin of Sodom and Gomorrah, Jude makes it quite clear that he viewed it as sexual sin of a severe nature. Minimally the sin was of a homosexual nature, but because Lot's visitors were in fact angels, Jude's reference also seems to imply the even more egregious sin of species crossing, for the same sin of Genesis 6:1–8 is alluded to in Jude 7, which reads more literally in the Greek, "they likewise went after flesh of another kind." The bizarre statement in Genesis 6:4 that "the sons of God came in to the daughters of men and they bore children to them" (NKJV) provoked much debate throughout the centuries. *First Enoch* documents one interpretation that the "sons of God" were fallen angels who through cross-species sexual relations introduced unprecedented evil into the human gene pool that motivated God to cause the great flood. The incident at Lot's house came dangerously close to a similar sexual encounter; Jude considers the immorality of the false Christians to deserve the same catastrophic judgment.

Several other references to the Old Testament are named, including the exodus (v. 5), Moses (v. 9), Cain (v. 11), Balaam (v. 11), Korah (v. 11), Enoch (v. 14), and the archangel Michael (v. 9), most of which can be only partially understood on the basis of the biblical text by itself. Furthermore, vivid images of judgment from the Old Testament color Jude's message: wind-driven clouds without rain (Prov. 25:14) and wave-tossed mud (Isa. 57:20), though he doesn't actually quote the Bible verses.

Jude exhorts his readers in verse 23 to "save others by snatching them from the fire; to others show mercy, mixed with fear—hating even the clothing stained by corrupted flesh." Here we have phrases of more than one word that likely allude to Zechariah 3:2, where Joshua, the high priest and representative of God's people, stands before Satan and the angel of the Lord. In Zechariah 3:2 the Lord asks, "Is not this man [Joshua] a burning stick snatched from the fire?"[10] In the context of Zechariah, the fire was an image for exile, a precarious situation for God's chosen people. Jude is probably using the image, which may have become a common one in Jewish tradition, to represent the immediate spiritual danger of being under the influence of false teachers.

Zechariah 3:3 also refers to the filthy clothing that Joshua the high priest was wearing as he stood before the angel of the Lord. The Hebrew word refers specifically to filth from excrement or vomit, a disgusting image that connotes how repulsive was the sin that clung to God's people even after the restoration. Together the images of the firebrand and the removal of filthy clothing indicate that the charges of the accuser, also present in this scene, cannot stand before the Lord's sovereign mercy. In the context of Jude, those on the verge of following the false teachers into sin are to be plucked from the danger; mercy is to be extended, but without tolerance for the teaching of the false teachers, which is to be regarded as disgusting as clothing soiled by bodily excrement.

By referring to so many people and events from the Old Testament Scriptures, Jude is drawing a line of continuity between his day and the history of God's relationship to humanity that is based on God's unchanging character and standards, the persistent and unchanging nature of sin, and the certainty of judgment for even those who count themselves among God's people but who don't live lives of faith. What's different for Jude is that the Messiah has come, acting as God's agent of salvation and mercy who will bring believers who keep themselves in God's love to eternal life (v. 21). And this comes from Jude, the Messiah's own brother!

An important clue about a New Testament writer and his audience is given by whether he uses the Hebrew version of Old Testament Scripture or one of the standard Greek translations. Even though Jude doesn't fully quote an Old Testament verse, a couple clues point to his use of the Hebrew Scriptures. One of these clues is found in the likely allusion to Zechariah 3:3 in Jude 23. The Hebrew word for "filth" in Zechariah 3:3 (Heb. *ṣōʾîm*) more specifically defines the source and kind of filth than does the corresponding word in the **Old Greek** translation (Gk. *rhupara*). So it seems that Jude must have had the Hebrew

10. The uncommon English word "brand" used in the ESV, NASB, NKJV, and NRSV refers to a smoldering stick of wood that is about to ignite into flames.

Left: Jude describes heretics as clouds without rain — promising life giving water but not providing it. *Right:* Jude describes the heretics as dangerous as a billowing sea.

text in mind, for in verse 23 he adds the prepositional phrase "from the flesh" to make the allusion to the repulsive image of the Hebrew expression clearer (Gk. *rhupara apo tēs sarkos*, "filth from the flesh").

Perhaps more decisive is the allusion to Proverbs 25:14 in Jude 12, which is more fitting to Jude's context in its Hebrew version ("Like clouds and wind without rain is one who boasts of a gift never given") than in its Greek translation ("As winds and clouds and rains are exceedingly apparent, so are they who boast over a false gift").

Similarly, the reference to shepherds who feed only themselves in Jude 12 stands closer to the Hebrew of Ezekiel 34:2 ("Ah, you shepherds of Israel who have been feeding yourselves!") than the Greek ("Oh, you shepherds of Israel, do shepherds feed themselves?").[11] Finally, the allusion to Isaiah 57:20 in Jude 13 can be compared in its Hebrew and Greek versions:

Hebrew: "But the wicked are like the tossing sea that cannot keep still; its waters toss up mire and mud."

Greek: "But thus shall the unrighteous be tossed like waves and shall not be able to rest."

Based on this evidence, it seems more likely that Jude was thinking of the Hebrew Scriptures even though he, or his amanuensis, was writing in Greek. In spite of this, Jude also uses expressions that are found in the Greek version of the Old Testament, probably because these expressions had become common idioms among Jewish people who used Greek, even if not as their first language.

JUDE'S USE OF THE PSEUDEPIGRAPHA

It is beyond doubt that Jude uses literary sources from the pseudepigrapha. The term *pseudepigrapha* is how scholars have denoted a corpus of ancient Jewish writings that date

11. Bauckham, *Jude and the Relatives*, 137.

from the century before and after the birth of Christ and that are characterized by the literary feature of claiming to have been written by various heroes of the ancient past, such as Adam, Enoch, and the twelve sons of Jacob. Clearly none of these people actually could have written the books ascribed to them because they all lived many centuries before the books were written. This genre of fictional authorship seems to have arisen and thrived in the late Hellenistic and early Roman periods of foreign occupation of the Promised Land, first by the Greeks and later the Romans. The pseudepigraphal books seem to have been written to tell the Jewish people what Adam or Enoch or the patriarchs would have said about the condition of the people and the situation they found themselves in had they been alive at that time. It is unclear whether the ancient readers of the pseudepigraphal books understood the fictive authorship as a literary device or whether they somehow believed that these texts had survived through time immemorial.

It would be as if a modern scholar today took the opportunity of, for instance, Martin Luther King Day, to pen an open letter to America from the great civil rights leader commenting on the state of minority life some fifty years after his death in the light of the way things were during his life. Although no one would believe the letter to have been actually written by Dr. King, reading what that inspirational preacher might say if alive today could be a very poignant and effective literary device.

Pseudepigrapha: Jewish writings ascribed to various patriarchs and prophets but composed within two hundred years of the birth of Christ.

Oxford American College Dictionary

One scholar put it this way, though in reference to another corpus of Jewish tradition, the Targums:

> In this retelling of biblical history, the lives and deeds of earlier personages were not recounted for the mere sake of history. Biblical characters tended to become vehicles of later tradition. They could easily become types of certain sections of humanity, prototypes of good and evil or perpetual reminders of the eternal truths of God's relationship with humanity.[12]

Much of the message of the pseudepigraphal books is along those lines, with the additional element of **pesher interpretation** of prophecy related from an apocalyptic perspective. Not familiar with "pesher" or "apocalyptic"? That's exactly why the pseudepigraphal books make so little sense to modern readers. A "pesher" interpretation relates a previously written prophecy to current events, suggesting that what is happening is the direct fulfillment of ancient prophecy. Usually the author then capitalizes on that prophetic perspective either to encourage his readers that everything they are experiencing is under God's control or to condemn them by showing that they will come to a fated destiny.

Jude refers to the condemnation of "certain individuals " as having been written "long ago" (v. 4). He also points out that what the Lord's apostles had previously predicted (vv. 17 – 18) was coming to pass at that very moment in the churches (v. 19). The apocalyptic worldview involves seeing current events from a cosmic perspective such that events on earth are representations of a universal spiritual battle between good/God and evil/Satan, a

12. Martin McNamara, *The New Testament and the Palestinian Targum to the Pentateuch* (Rome: Pontifical Biblical Institute, 1966), 155.

Pesher

Pesher refers to a distinct type of ancient interpretation of biblical prophecy or to a text that represents that type of interpretation. The term is a Hebrew word whose verbal root, *pšh*, means to "loosen" or "interpret." This mode of interpretation is exemplified in the sectarian documents found at Qumran (e.g., the Habakkuk commentary [1QpHab]), in which the meaning of obscure ancient texts was interpreted to refer to the Qumran community itself by employing an array of specific techniques. This understanding of the ancient prophecies gave the community an unprecedented dignity and significance in their own eyes, as they perceived themselves as the *telos* of prophecy given centuries before.

battle God is sure to win. Jude expresses an apocalyptic worldview by associating the angels being held for judgment with the destiny of the false Christians. Modern readers of the New Testament may be perplexed because the writers assume their readers will be familiar with books such as *1 Enoch* and the *Assumption of Moses*, or will recognize apocalyptic imagery and themes, such as being bound by everlasting chains in darkness or the ongoing battles between the archangel Michael and Satan.

The Archangel Michael Vanquishing the Devil, Viani, Antonio Maria/Palazzo Ducale, Mantua, Italy/The Bridgeman Art Library

The archangel Michael in battle with Satan. Antonio Maria Viani (1555/60–1629).

Jude is the only New Testament writer who explicitly quotes *1 Enoch* and refers specifically to material from the *Assumption of Moses*. (It is interesting that if 2 Peter uses Jude as a source, that author does not include the material from pseudepigraphal books in his letter. See chapter 12.) The author of 1 Peter, especially 3:17–22, likely has material from *1 Enoch* in mind that he expects will be familiar to his readers, but he doesn't explicitly quote or allude to the text of *1 Enoch* like Jude does. Jude refers to Enoch and Michael's dispute with the devil over Moses as they were understood in Jewish tradition of that day to develop the themes of ungodliness and the certainty of judgment. Whatever else those books may contain, they affirm the truth of the themes with which Jude is concerned.

Jude's use of pseudepigraphal material is perhaps the greatest challenge of the book of Jude, for depending on how one understands divine inspiration, it can raise big questions that seem to threaten the boundaries of canon or the nature of inspiration. It is very likely this is exactly the issue that caused even ancient Christian leaders to question whether Jude's letter should be accepted as canonical Christian Scripture.

However, rather than feeling threatened or insecure about what we find in Jude, we have an opportunity to think more deeply about whether our assumptions about divine inspiration and the inferences we draw from it match the way God demonstrably did things based on the actual texts of the New Testament.

Jude 9 refers to a dispute between the archangel Michael and the devil over the body of Moses, an incident that is neither preserved in Scripture nor in any **extant** ancient text. But a second-century Christian writer, Clement of Alexandria, mentions in his *Fragments on the Epistle of Jude* that this story is from a text he knew as the *Assumption of Moses*. (Note that an archaic meaning of the word *assumption* is "reception into heaven.") Unfortunately, the surviving copies of that work are incomplete and do not include this incident.

Although Jude obviously is familiar with the material in the *Assumption of Moses*, he does not assert the incident between Michael and the devil as though it is Scripture. Such an incident would have had to be revealed to the author of the *Assumption*, since that author could not have historically observed it, and that would involve accepting the *Assumption of Moses* as divinely inspired. But Jude is not elevating the *Assumption* to the level of Scripture; he simply uses a well-known story in Jewish tradition that indicts the false Christians' cavalier attitude toward spiritual authority. The point is that they should have more respect for the power and authority of what they are apparently speaking abusively about.

The nature of Jude's use of *1 Enoch* is somewhat different and more difficult. Jude introduces his quotation from *1 Enoch* with, "Enoch, the seventh from Adam, prophesied about them" (v. 14). While there is nothing unusual about a New Testament writer quoting a prophet, the quote that follows is not from the Bible but from *1 Enoch* 1:9, suggesting that Jude accepted it as an authentic prophecy that was being fulfilled by the false teachers of his day. Moreover, although Genesis 5:22 and 24 state twice that Enoch "walked with God," he is not called a prophet, and none of his words are recorded in the Bible.

The recognition of this problem motivated two opposite tacks in the early church. Since Jude is inspired and he seems to quote *1 Enoch* as a true prophecy, *1 Enoch* should also be in the canon (e.g., Tertullian took this view).[13] Others argued the opposite; if *1 Enoch* is not inspired and Jude quotes it as authoritative, then Jude shouldn't be in the canon. In fact, it was this issue that caused such debate over the book for so long. Is there a way we can cut between these two extremes with integrity?

---

13. See Tertullian, *Cult. fem.* (*The Apparel of Women*) 3.3. The Christian debate over the canonicity of *1 Enoch* concluded negatively (see Jerome, *Vir. ill.* 4; *Apostolic Constitution* 6.16.3) (Halton, FC). Despite Tertullian's opinion, the book of *1 Enoch* has never stood in any canon of Scripture, Jewish or Christian.

Apocalyptic Worldview

Apocalyptic worldview is a belief about the end of the world in catastrophic destruction based on divine revelation. This outlook is not unique to Christianity, but a Christian apocalyptic worldview has distinctive, unique elements. In the Judeo-Christian Scriptures, God reveals through dreams, visions, and angelic announcements a coming day of catastrophic judgment of evil that will end the world as we know it. The apocalyptic worldview includes a sharp dualism between good and evil that is based on faith in Jesus Christ, the intervention of the returning Christ in judging and putting an end to evil once and for all, and the existence of a new place purged of all evil following the judgment.

Last Judgement, from the Luther Bible, c.1530, German School/ Bible Society, London, UK/The Bridgeman Art Library

Last Judgement, from the Luther Bible, c.1530 (coloured woodcut).

Jude does not indicate that he thought *1 Enoch* to be Scripture, for he never refers to it as *graphe*, the Greek word adopted to refer to inspired Christian writings. Moreover, the book of *1 Enoch* has never been canonical in *any* Jewish or Christian canon. It isn't even within the Apocrypha that appears as **deuterocanonical** books in Roman Catholic versions of the Bible. But this raises the question of whether citing pseudepigraphal material is worthy of inspired authors. It should be quickly said that the doctrine of inspiration must allow God to inspire the biblical authors to use whatever material suits his purposes. The apostle Paul, for instance, quotes *Phaenomena*, a work by the pagan poet Aratus in Acts 17:28, because it was a work of cultural value to the Greek philosophers with whom Paul was arguing. Paul didn't consider that pagan poet to have been inspired, nor would he want his readers to infer that *Phaenomena* was an authoritative text. Jude is no doubt doing something similar to this. The orthodox doctrine of inspiration does not imply that inspiration must be assumed of extrabiblical works simply because they are quoted.

Clement Knew of the Assumption of Moses

"'When Michael, the archangel, disputing with the devil, debated about the body of Moses.' Here [Jude] confirms the *Assumption of Moses*."

Clement of Alexandria, *Fragments on the Epistle of Jude*

But, you might observe, Paul does not claim that Aratus was a prophet; nor does he use the allusion to the poet to announce with certainty the future event of divine judgment. Note, however, that Jude says only, "Enoch prophesied," which must not be taken to mean that Enoch wrote an inspired book (contra Augustine's view). In the book of *1 Enoch*, Enoch speaks as a prophet, and the anonymous author of this work is building on a biblical theme that is true: the theme of God's certain judgment of the ungodly. In other words, Jude does not have to think that *1 Enoch* is an inspired book or even a true book in general; he cites one small part of it that *is* in accord with biblical truth.

> "If Jude overlaps in content with one element found in, say, *1 Enoch*, it does not necessarily follow that Jude buys into all that *1 Enoch* says on the subject."
>
> D. A. Carson, "Jude," in *Commentary on the New Testament Use of the Old Testament*

Recalling the two passages of the New Testament most relevant to the doctrine of inspiration might be enlightening at this point as well. Second Timothy 3:16 attributes inspiration ("God-breathed") to the *written texts* of Scripture. The divine origin of Scripture may also be considered in light of 2 Peter 1:21: "prophets, though human, spoke from God as they were carried along by the Holy Spirit." Neither passage implies that every word ever spoken, much less every thought of the biblical writers, was inspired apart from the production of their writings that became Scripture. It is impossible to know from the letter Jude left whether he believed that Enoch actually spoke the prophecies that were preserved for millennia in the text of *1 Enoch* or what authority he gave to that book. Jude uses these writings only to make a point, much the same way a preacher today might refer to Harry Potter or Lord of the Rings to make a point.

What is undeniably inspired is the way Jude *uses* this material as a summary of his denunciation of the false Christians who will be convicted at the divine judgment for "all

Augustine's Thoughts on *1 Enoch**

"Certainly, we cannot deny that Enoch (the seventh in descent from Adam) wrote a number of things by divine inspiration, since the apostle Jude says as much in a canonical epistle. But there was good reason for the exclusion of these writings from the canon of the Scriptures, which was preserved in the temple of the Hebrew people by the careful custody of the priestly succession. The reason was that these books were judged of doubtful reliability because of their antiquity; and it was impossible to discover whether they were what Enoch had written, since those who put them forward are not found to have preserved them with the due formality, that is, through an appointed succession. That is why responsible judges have decided that we should reject the attribution to Enoch of the documents put forward under his name, containing stories about giants who are said not to have had human fathers. Many other writings are similarly put forward under the names of other prophets, and more recent productions under the names of apostles. All these have been excluded from canonical authority as a result of careful examination."

*Augustine, *City of God* 15.23, in *Concerning the City of God against the Pagans*, trans. Henry Bettenson (New York: Penguin, 1972).

Photo Clara Amit, courtesy Israel Antiquities Authority

7qEnoch. A fragment of 1 Enoch in Greek from Qumran.

the ungodly acts they have committed in their ungodliness, and of all the defiant words ungodly sinners have spoken against him" (v. 15). Just as Paul cites material that would have been familiar and apparently valued by his audience, Jude is most likely quoting *1 Enoch* not because he considered it Scripture but because of its familiarity and value to his readers, perhaps especially to the false Christians. There is some evidence in the Greek of Jude 14 (*de kai*) that it should be construed as "even [your own] Enoch."[14] This explanation makes good sense of both the indisputable fact that Jude quotes *1 Enoch* and also of the fact that there is no other evidence that *1 Enoch* was ever regarded as canonical Scripture by either Jews or Christians. Although fragments of *1 Enoch* in Greek were found at Qumran, they were not in the same storage pots as the biblical books.[15]

JUDE'S RELATIONSHIP TO 2 PETER

That Jude stands in close relationship to the text of 2 Peter, primarily in chapter 2, cannot be denied. Explaining the nature and direction of that relationship is one of the challenges of these books. Traditionally it was believed that Jude must have copied the thoughts of 2 Peter because Peter's stature as one of the greatest of Christ's apostles made it unseemly for him to copy from a lesser-known figure such as Jude. However, more recent work has shown that the family of Jesus was both well known and held great authority in some parts of the church, especially in Palestine. The consensus of scholars today is that the author of 2 Peter, even if the apostle Peter himself, did in fact copy the flow of Jude's argument, because both were dealing with essentially the same problems in different geographical areas of the church. See the chapter on 2 Peter for a detailed discussion of the reasons for this consensus.

TEXT AND CANONICITY OF JUDE

Most readers of this book will not likely become textual critics or scholars of the history of the biblical canon. Even so, it is worth knowing in at least a general sense on what historical evidence the text of a New Testament book came to be received as Scripture.

The earliest extant manuscripts of Jude are from the fourth century: the great **codex** Vaticanus and **papyrus** 72 ($\mathfrak{P}^{72}$).

---

14. J. Daryl Charles, "Jude's Use of Pseudepigraphical Source-Material as Part of a Literary Strategy," *NTS* 37 (1991): 144.

15. Peter H. Davids, *The Letters of 2 Peter and Jude*, Pillar New Testament Commentary (Grand Rapids: Eerdmans, 2006), 76.

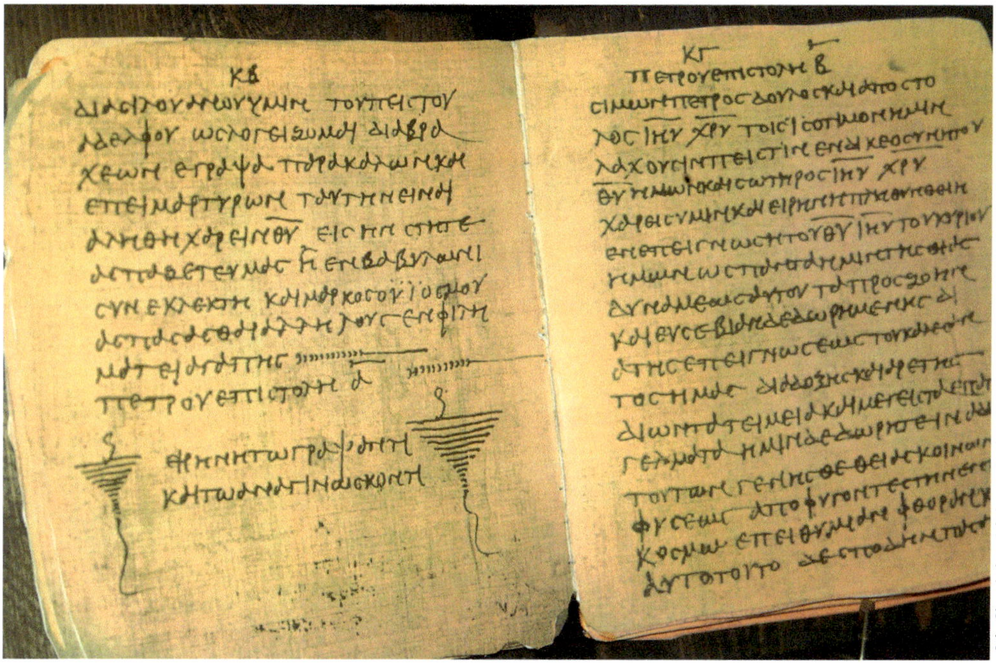

Baker Photo Archive. Sola Scriptura—the Van Kampen Collection on display at the Holy Land Experience, Orlando, Florida.

A facsimile of P72, a manuscript from the 3rd or 4th century AD that contains the earliest extant text of Jude.

If Jude was used by 2 Peter, as modern New Testament scholars believe, then 2 Peter would of course be the earliest attestation of Jude's existence, requiring Jude to have been written sometime earlier. Other than 2 Peter, the earliest clear references to Jude or his letter among Christian writers comes from the late second or early third century from Clement of Alexandria (d. c. AD 215), Tertullian (c. AD 200), and Origen (d. AD 253/54). The book is well known to Eusebius (c. AD 300) and Jerome (d. AD 420).[16] The New Testament Institute at Münster has identified eleven readings in the new *Editio Critica Maior* that differ from the NA27.[17]

The concept of canon in the sense of authoritative texts existed before the second-century development of the codex. The lists of which books were authoritative, and therefore in the canon, and which were not seems to have been motivated when (1) decisions had to be made about which books to bind together between two covers, and (2) the publication of many spurious books forced the church to list which writings may be read in the church services as Scripture, and (3) influential leaders, such as Marcion, began to teach falsely concerning the boundaries of Scripture. One item of evidence concerning the standing of a given book comes in the form of canon lists, and the earliest surviving canon list from the late second century is known as the **Muratorian Canon**. Though damaged at

16. See Charles Bigg, *A Critical and Exegetical Commentary on the Epistles of St. Peter and St. Jude*, ICC (New York: Scribner, 1909), 305–10, for further discussion of the nature of these references.

17. These readings can be found in Peter M. Head, 'Editio Critica Maior: An Introduction and Assessment', *Tyndale Bulletin* 61.1 (2010),152, available online at https://www.academia.edu/3633883/_Editio_Critica_Maior_An_Introduction_and_Assessment_Tyndale_Bulletin_61.1_2010_131-152 (accessed May 2, 2016).

both the beginning and end, it does include Jude, though in a way that suggests some have questioned its place in the canon. This debate is known also from the surviving writings of Origen, Eusebius, Didymus, and Jerome, which describe doubts raised by Jude's use of the *Assumption of Moses* and *1 Enoch*. Origen did not seem to doubt it himself but knew that others did. In Alexandria, Didymus defended Jude despite its use of pseudepigrapha. Eusebius seems to question its authenticity (*Hist. eccl.* 3.25.3). Questions about its place in the canon persisted as late as the sixth century when the Syrian church finally acknowledged it as Holy Scripture.

OUTLINE OF JUDE'S LETTER

I. Address of the Letter and Greeting (vv. 1–2)

II. Crisis in the Church (vv. 3–23)

- A. Jude's Reason for Writing (vv. 3–4a)
- B. Three Examples of Condemnation of the Ungodly (vv. 4b–7)
    1. Destruction of the exodus generation (v. 5)
    2. Imprisonment of rebellious angels until judgment day (v. 6)
    3. Sodom and Gomorrah as example of eternal punishment (v. 7)
- C. Characteristics of the Ungodly in the Church (vv. 8–16)
    1. The ungodly take their dreams as their guide (v. 8a)
        - a. They pollute their bodies (v. 8b)
        - b. They reject authority (v. 8c)
        - c. They heap abuse on celestial beings, which even Michael didn't do (vv. 8d–9)
    2. Their knowledge comes from their base nature (v. 10)
        - a. They are like Cain (v. 11a)
        - b. They are like Balaam (v. 11b)
    3. They are blemishes on Christian fellowship (v. 12a)
    4. They are clouds without rain (v. 12b)
    5. They are twice dead trees (v. 12c)
    6. They are waves of the sea (v. 13a)
    7. They are wandering stars (v. 13b)
    8. They are doomed by prophecy (vv. 14–15)
    9. They are grumblers and faultfinders (v. 16a)
    10. They follow their own evil desires (v. 16b)
    11. They boast and flatter others (v. 16c)
- D. Jude's Call to Persevere (vv. 17–23)
    1. Remember what the apostles said (vv. 17–19)
    2. Keep yourselves in God's love (vv. 20–22)
        - a. Build yourselves up in the faith (v. 20)

b. Pray in the Holy Spirit (v. 20)
c. Wait for eternal life (v. 21)
d. Be merciful to doubters (vv. 22–23)

III. Doxology (vv. 24–25)

CHAPTER SUMMARY

The letter of Jude is a stern warning to the church and a scathing condemnation of ungodly, false Christians who pollute their bodies and reject authority because they seek spiritual guidance through means that reflect their own base nature. Jude warns that such people in the church will be condemned and cautions others in the congregation not to follow them. Jude points faithful Christians back to the apostolic teaching and exhorts them to persevere in faith, prayer, and mercy.

KEY TERMS

apocalyptic
Assumption of Moses
doxology
1 Enoch
Muratorian Canon
papyrus 𝔓[72]
pesher
pseudepigrapha
relationship to 2 Peter
Sodom and Gomorrah
Watchers

QUESTIONS FOR REVIEW OR DISCUSSION

1. List the men who possibly could have written this letter and discuss the pros and cons of each possibility. State in your own words the argument that Jude the brother of Jesus wrote the letter.
2. What are the pseudepigrapha? Where does Jude use material from the pseudepigrapha? Why is this an important issue?
3. Summarize what Jude says or necessarily implies about God, Jesus Christ, the Holy Spirit, and the Christian life. What important points of Christian doctrine cannot be read from this book?

4. What are the major points about the false Christians that Jude denounces?
5. Identify a situation in today's church for which Jude's letter would be relevant.
6. How does this study of Jude's letter affect your understanding of divine inspiration? Of canonicity?

GOING FURTHER

Bauckham, Richard. *Jude and the Relatives of Jesus in the Early Church.* Edinburgh: T&T Clark, 1990.

Carson, D. A. "Jude." Pages 1069–79 in *Commentary on the New Testament Use of the Old Testament.* Edited by Gregory K. Beale and D. A. Carson. Grand Rapids: Baker Academic, 2007.

Charles, J. Daryl. "Jude's Use of Pseudepigraphical Source-Material as Part of a Literary Strategy." *New Testament Studies* 37 (1991): 144.

Charlesworth, James, ed. *Old Testament Pseudepigrapha.* 2 vols. New York: Doubleday, 1983–85.

Chester, Andrew, and Ralph P. Martin. *The Theology of the Letters of James, Peter, and Jude.* New Testament Theology. Cambridge: Cambridge University Press, 1994.

Donelson, Lewis R. *From Hebrews to Revelation: A Theological Introduction.* Louisville: Westminster John Knox, 2001.

Gilmour, Michael J. *The Significance of Parallels between 2 Peter and Other Early Christian Literature.* Academia Biblica 10. Atlanta: Society of Biblical Literature, 2002.

Guthrie, Donald. *New Testament Introduction.* 3rd ed. Downers Grove, Ill.: InterVarsity, 1970.

Harner, Philip B. *What Are They Saying about the Catholic Epistles?* What Are They Saying Series. New York: Paulist, 2004.

Perkins, Pheme. "Christ in Jude and 2 Peter." Pages 155–65 in *Who Do You Say That I Am? Essays on Christology.* Louisville: Westminster John Knox, 1999.

Commentaries

Bauckham, Richard. *Jude, 2 Peter.* Word Biblical Commentary 50. Waco, Tex.: Word, 1983.

Charles, Daryl J. "Jude." Pages 541–69 in *Hebrews–Revelation. Expositor's Bible Commentary.* Vol. 13. Edited by Tremper Longman III and David E. Garland. Rev. ed. Grand Rapids: Zondervan, 2006.

Davids, Peter H. *The Letters of 2 Peter and Jude.* Pillar New Testament Commentary. Grand Rapids: Eerdmans, 2006.

Green, Gene. *Jude and 2 Peter.* BECNT. Grand Rapids: Baker Academic, 2008.

Moo, Douglas J. "Jude." Pages 228–43 in *ZIBBC.* Vol. 4. Edited by Clinton E. Arnold. Grand Rapids: Zondervan, 2002.

———. *2 Peter, Jude.* NIVAC. Grand Rapids: Zondervan, 1996.

Neyrey, Jerome H. *2 Peter, Jude.* AB 37C. New York: Doubleday, 1993.

Reese, Ruth Anne. *2 Peter and Jude.* Two Horizons New Testament Commentary. Grand Rapids: Eerdmans, 2007.

Richard, Earl J. *Reading 1 Peter, Jude, and 2 Peter.* Macon, Ga.: Smyth & Helwys, 2000.

Schreiner, Thomas R. *1, 2 Peter, Jude*. New American Commentary. Nashville: Broadman and Holman, 2003.

Senior, Donald P., and Daniel J. Harrington. *1 Peter, Jude and 2 Peter.* Sacra Pagina 15. Collegeville, Minn.: Liturgical, 2003.

Witherington, Ben, III. *Letters and Homilies for Jewish Christians: A Socio-Rhetorical Commentary on Hebrews, James and Jude.* Downers Grove, Ill.: IVP Academic, 2007.

PART 3

Letters from Peter

CHAPTER 9

"The True Grace of God"

INTRODUCING 1 PETER

Your Goals for This Chapter

- To understand who Peter was.
- To be able to list the evidence against Petrine authorship and its counterevidence.
- To describe the original audience of this letter.
- To be able to state Peter's **Christology**.
- To understand the role of suffering in the Christian's life.
- To read the "household codes" within their first-century historical setting.

WHY THE BOOK OF 1 PETER IS IMPORTANT TO YOU

It seems that we are now living in a post-Christian society that appears to be growing more similar to first-century Roman society year by year, even though the technology has changed vastly since the time Peter wrote this letter. The values by which most Americans live have shifted significantly even during my lifetime. When I was a child, the majority of people were at least nominally Christian. Sundays were quiet days, boring for a restless child desiring entertainment, because stores, movie theaters, and most businesses were closed. To become pregnant before marriage was such a stigma that girls of my generation were whisked away from school to deliver their babies in maternity homes and then place them for adoption. Fifty years ago morality was still based on Judeo-Christian values. Much less so today, even if the majority of Americans still claim some Christian affiliation.[1]

As it was in first-century Roman society, today it is fine to believe in Jesus, but it is offensive to many if he is preached as the only way to God. These days the very idea of any absolute standard of moral truth is viewed with hostility. Truth is considered to be relative to one's own needs and judgments, so to argue that one's beliefs represent truth for all people is often viewed as a socially unacceptable attempt to assert one's personal power over others. Religious pluralism has made the exclusive claims of Jesus Christ distasteful to many in our society, just as it did in the polytheistic Roman Empire. However, the idea that any and all of the world's major religions are paths to the one God is monotheism gone bad. Theological truth seems irrelevant to most people in our society. The heated controversies about same-sex marriage and parenting have relativized the biblical standard of a man and a woman joined in God-ordained holy matrimony as the right and best home into which a baby should be brought. Sexual immorality of all forms is as public as it was in licentious Roman society. The popularity of violence in entertainment rivals the blood-thirsty audiences that crowded the Colosseum to watch gladiators slaughter and be slaughtered.

And yet Christ's church is called as it has been in every time and place to be a winsome witness to the gospel. As one contemporary Christian leader puts it, "We are called to faithful witness and compassionate ministry. In the context of post-Christian America, our task is to preach the gospel and to proclaim the truths of God's Word."[2]

Because modern Western society and its values are growing more and more similar to that of the pagan first-century Roman Empire, the apostolic writings from that time giving instruction on how to live as a Christian in such a time and place grows more and more directly relevant. The apostle Peter presents the hermeneutical and theological foundation on which he offers practical instruction for living wisely as a Christian in a pagan society. His exhortation to live for Christ faithfully—even when it hurts—is a challenging but necessary message for Christians today who want to be bearers of the gospel in this generation.

---

1. See Brian J. Grim and David Masci, "The Demographics of Faith," http://www.pewresearch.org/fact-tank/2015/08/27/10-facts-about-religion-in-america/ (accessed May 2, 2016).

2. Al Mohler, "Transforming Culture: Christian Truth Confronts Post-Christian America," www.albertmohler.com/2004/07/15/transforming-culture-christian-truth-confronts-post-christian-america/?action=print&id=2401 (accessed December 28, 2009).

Key Verses

1:1–2: Peter, an apostle of Jesus Christ, To God's elect, exiles scattered throughout the provinces of Pontus, Galatia, Cappadocia, Asia and Bithynia, who have been chosen according to the foreknowledge of God the Father, through the sanctifying work of the Spirit, to be obedient to Jesus Christ and sprinkled with his blood: Grace and peace be yours in abundance.

1:3b–4a: In his [God's] great mercy he has given us new birth into a living hope through the resurrection of Jesus Christ from the dead, and into an inheritance that can never perish, spoil or fade.

2:9: But you are a chosen people, a royal priesthood, a holy nation, God's special possession, that you may declare the praises of him who called you out of darkness into his wonderful light.

2:13–14: Submit yourselves for the Lord's sake to every human authority: whether to the emperor, as the supreme authority, or to governors, who are sent by him to punish those who do wrong and to commend those who do right.

2:21: To this you were called, because Christ suffered for you, leaving you an example, that you should follow in his steps.

Challenges Presented by the Book of 1 Peter

- The question of its authorship and date.
- Its perspective on sin and suffering.
- Its teaching that Christ preached to the spirits after his death (see chapter 10).
- Its teaching on order in the household.

CHAPTER OUTLINE

I. Who Was Peter?

II. Authorship and Date of 1 Peter

III. Purpose and Major Themes

  A. An Overview of Peter's Christology

    1. Crucifixion and resurrection
    2. The Living Stone (1 Peter 2:4–8)
    3. The Suffering Servant (1 Peter 2:21–25)
    4. The Victorious Savior (1 Peter 3:18–22)

B. Transformation of the Christian's Identity
1. Living as foreigners
2. The "household codes"

IV. The Text and Canonicity of 1 Peter
A. The Greek Text of 1 Peter
B. The Canonicity of 1 Peter

V. Structure and Outline of 1 Peter

Please read the book of 1 Peter in one sitting before reading this chapter.

The brief New Testament book of 1 Peter began its life more than two thousand years ago as a letter from the apostle Peter to Christians scattered across what is now known as northern Turkey. In the closing of the letter, Peter refers to its contents as "the true grace of God," and he exhorts readers to "stand fast in it" (5:12). First Peter has been called "the most condensed New Testament resume of the Christian faith and of the conduct that it inspires."[3] The great Reformer Martin Luther called it "one of the noblest books in the New Testament," on par with even Romans and the gospel of John, and containing all that is necessary for a Christian to know. Peter's letter contains not only the essentials of what Christians believe, but also how those beliefs energize Christian life. What is so striking about Peter's letter is that in it he teaches that the life of the Christian believer is inseparable from the life of Jesus, who is not only the object of Christian faith but the pattern of the Christian's destiny as well.

WHO WAS PETER?

The letter of 1 Peter presents itself as written by the apostle of Jesus whom we know as Simon Peter. Although some scholars today dispute that claim (see below), even if it is a **pseudonymous** letter, it apparently was intended to be read as if from the apostle Peter, with all that was known about Peter in mind.

The apostle Peter is a pillar in church history, known almost universally even by the youngest of churched children, who first learn the story of this endearing fisherman on flannelgraphs in church school. But he is also revered as a great apostle of Jesus Christ and believed by millions of Roman Catholics to have been the first pope of the church. From what we know of him, Peter was an unlikely person to achieve such renown in history to still be remembered and to have his brief writings not only still read, but also preached as God's Word, two thousand years after his death. But had he not met Jesus, he would have been one of the countless myriads of human beings who have passed their time on this earth without leaving any historical memory of themselves.

Born into a lower-class working family in first-century Palestine during its time of Roman occupation, Simon was given a very common name shared by many men of his time. He grew up in Galilee, apparently in the town of Bethsaida (Matt. 4:18; 10:2; Mark

---

3. Edmund Clowney, *The Message of 1 Peter: The Way of the Cross*, ed. J. R. W. Stott, The Bible Speaks Today (Downers Grove, Ill.: InterVarsity, 1988), 15.

Simon Peter lived in Capernaum and made his living fishing on the Sea of Galilee. Most of Jesus' public ministry took place in Galilee.

1:16; John 1:44). About **AD** 27 Simon was living in the town of Capernaum on the northern shore of the Sea of Galilee, where he made his living in the fishing business with his brother Andrew (Matt. 4:18; Mark 1:16; John 1:40; 6:8) and his partners, James and John, all of whom also later became disciples of Jesus (Luke 5:10).

Apparently Simon had heard the preaching of John the Baptist, who announced himself to be the harbinger of the long-awaited Messiah (John 1:40). When his brother Andrew met Jesus, the first thing he did was run and tell Simon, "We have found the Messiah!" (John 1:41–42). Andrew introduced Simon to Jesus, and from that simple moment in Simon's life, the history of the embryonic church began to unfold.

One day as Jesus was preaching the word of God by the Sea of Galilee (also called the Lake of Gennesaret in the New Testament), he saw nearby two fishing boats at the water's edge. Getting into one of them, he asked to be pushed out so he could teach the people from the boat (Luke 5:1–3). The boat happened to belong to Simon. After Jesus finished speaking to the crowd, he suggested that Simon take him out fishing. Even though Simon had been out all night and had nothing to show for it, out of respect for this preacher of God's word, Simon agreed. Amazingly their net filled with such a large number of fish that

Baker Photo Archive

Todd Bolen/www.BiblePlaces.com

Left: Simon's boat was probably similar to this one discovered in the mud by the Sea of Galilee in 1986. *Right:* This model shows what Peter's boat may have looked like. It could carry 15–20 people.

Simon had to call for his partners to come help them. This abundant blessing of fish made Simon realize that Jesus was a truly holy man, which made Simon all too aware of his own sinfulness (Luke 5:4–8). When Jesus reassured Simon and suggested that he start fishing for people, he and his partners pulled their boats up on shore, left everything, and followed Jesus (Luke 5:10–11). Apparently this boat often would be used to transport Jesus to the towns that ringed the Sea of Galilee as he trained these men to fish for the souls of people.

St. Peter, Ribera, Jusepe de (lo Spagnoletto)/Galleria Doria Pamphilj, Rome, Italy/Alinari/The Bridgeman Art Library

No ancient representations of Peter exist, but he has often been the subject of painters. Saint Peter Penitent by Jusepe de Ribera (1591–1652).

The New Testament writers tell us that Simon was married to an unnamed woman, who at some point also became a follower of Jesus Christ and who later traveled with Simon far from home (1 Cor. 9:5). While they still lived in Capernaum, Peter's ill mother-in-law was in his home during one of Jesus' visits (Matt. 8:14; Mark 1:29; Luke 4:38; 1 Cor. 9:5). Jesus healed her of a fever quickly enough and completely enough that she was able to get up and wait on them.

Simon was among those whom Jesus chose to accompany him during his public ministry, to witness his teaching and miracles and whom were designated as apostles to preach and exercise spiritual authority in Jesus' name (Matt. 10:1–2; Mark 3:14–16; 6:7; Luke 6:13; 9:1). Not only was Simon Peter one of the Twelve, but he was part of Jesus' inner circle, privy to exclusive events. For instance, Simon Peter, along with the brothers James and John, witnessed the transfiguration of Jesus as he spoke with Moses and Elijah (Matt. 17:1–13; Mark 9:2–13; Luke 9:28–36).

Simon seems to have become a spokesman for the Twelve (Matt. 15:15; 26:40; Mark 1:36; 10:28; 14:37; Luke 8:45; 12:41;

18:28; John 6:68; 13:24, 36; Acts 2:37–38). When Jesus asked, "Who do people say the Son of Man is?" it was Simon Peter who first verbalized Jesus' identity as "the Messiah, the Son of the living God" (Matt. 16:13, 16; Mark 8:27, 29; Luke 9:18, 20). When Simon was the first to publicly identify Jesus as the Messiah, Jesus gave Simon the nickname Peter, which means "rock" (Gk. *Petros*; Ara. *Cephas*), and gave him the "keys of the kingdom" (Matt. 16:19). Jesus used the Aramaic form of the nickname *Cephas*, but the New Testament writers who were writing in Greek translated the name as *Petros*, which then came into English as "Peter." Interestingly, the apostle Paul almost always refers to the apostle Peter by his Aramaic nickname, *Cephas* (1 Cor. 1:12; 3:22; 9:5; 15:5; Gal. 1:18; 2:9, 11, 14). Perhaps this is because, when Paul was a new believer, he spent two weeks with Peter in Jerusalem, where Aramaic was the local language, and would have first known Simon by the Aramaic form of his nickname (Gal. 1:18).

Family of Dewitt Jayne

The Transfiguration. Painting by Dewitt Jayne (1992).

Peter's extended companionship with Jesus and the other disciples gave him a unique perspective from which to interpret Jesus' life. Eusebius claims that Peter's memories and teaching stand behind the gospel of Mark.

Even though Peter was apparently the first of the Twelve who dared to name Jesus as the Messiah, Peter's understanding of the role of the Messiah was seriously deficient. Once Jesus' disciples began to believe that he was indeed the Messiah, Jesus immediately began to teach them that it would mean he must suffer many things and be rejected by the elders, the chief priests, and the teachers of the law, and be killed, but after three days rise again (Mark 8:31–33). Peter took Jesus aside to set him straight. One can almost imagine him saying, "Jesus, you've got this all wrong! The Messiah goes into Jerusalem as a conquering hero, raises up a successful revolt against the Romans, and restores the Davidic kingdom to Israel. What do you mean 'suffer, be rejected, and die'?" Jesus wanted all of his disciples to have their understanding of the role of the Messiah corrected, and in front of them he gives Peter a sharp rebuke, saying, "Get behind me, Satan! You do not have in mind the concerns of God, but merely human concerns" (Mark 8:33). This stunning reprimand no doubt stayed with Peter for the rest of his life and became key in his

Did Mark's Gospel Originate with Peter?

"Mark became Peter's interpreter and wrote accurately all that he remembered, not, indeed, in order, of the things said or done by the Lord. For he had not heard the Lord, nor had he followed him, but later on, as I said, followed Peter, who used to give teaching as necessity demanded but not making, as it were, an arrangement of the Lord's oracles, so that Mark did nothing wrong in thus writing down single points as he remembered them."

Eusebius, *Hist. eccl.* 3.39.15

thinking, for it was Peter who led the way in understanding why the long-awaited Messiah should be rejected by the very people who were being prepared for centuries to expect him. For it is in Peter's first letter that we find the clearest exposition of Jesus as God's Suffering Servant, predicted centuries before Jesus was born by the prophet Isaiah (1 Peter 2:18–25; cf. Isa. 52:13–53:12). How beautifully ironic that the Lord's discipline opened the way for such a powerful transformation of Peter's thinking, a transformation that would make him a Christian leader still renowned two thousand years later.

As a frequent companion of Jesus, Peter witnessed many of the miracles recorded in the Gospels. Jesus was apparently staying in Peter's home after returning to Capernaum, for the tax collectors found Jesus there. Children of kings didn't have to pay taxes, and because Jesus is the Son of the King of the universe, he could have thought of himself as exempt. But Jesus didn't want to unnecessarily offend, so he sent Peter out to do what Peter was so good at—fish. Peter was probably expecting to sell a large catch of fish, such as Jesus had previously provided, to raise the money for the temple tax. But instead, Jesus told him to open the mouth of the first fish he caught and in it he would find a four-drachma coin! Jesus miraculously paid not only for his own two-drachma tax but for Peter's as well (Matt. 17:24–27).

Perhaps the most famous miraculous event of Peter's life was when he and the Twelve were out on the Sea of Galilee in a storm and Jesus, who had stayed behind to dismiss the crowds and pray, came out to meet the boat by walking on the water! (Matt. 14:22–32). From this story, we know that Peter was quite adventurous in his faith—some might even say he was impetuous. He tests the identity of the mysterious water-walker by calling out, "Lord, if it's you, tell me to come to you on the water" (Matt. 14:28). Jesus agrees to this test, and Peter bravely climbs out of the boat and begins to walk toward Jesus! But the wind-stirred waves suddenly make Peter realize the precarious position he has put himself in, and in his fear he begins to sink, calling out to Jesus to save him. Immediately, Matthew tells us, Jesus reaches out, grabs Peter, and walks him back to the boat! (Matt. 14:29–31). Jesus chides Peter about how short a time his faith had lasted, that Peter had so quickly let the danger he saw around him overcome his belief in Jesus' power to make him stand. But Jesus had been in command of the danger all the time, which he revealed when, on another occasion, he stilled a storm (Mark 4:35–41; Luke 7:22–25).

Wikimedia Commons

Peter had faith enough to get out of the boat. Christ Walking on Water by Julius Schnorr von Carolsfeld (1794–1872).

Peter played a large role in the final days and moments of Jesus' earthly life. He was responsible for preparing Jesus' final Passover (Luke 22:8). During that final evening, he again questioned Jesus, this time on the matter of foot washing (John 13:6, 8). After declaring his intent to even die with Jesus, he is again gently rebuked by the prediction that his faith is weak and that he will, in fact, deny even knowing Jesus before the night is over (Luke 22:31–34).

Along with the Twelve, Peter accompanied Jesus to a private place in the garden of Gethsemane (Matt. 26:37; Mark 14:33, 37) and attempted to defend Jesus at his arrest by wounding the high priest's servant with a sword (John 18:10–11). Despite this, he boldly followed Jesus after his arrest into the courtyard of the high priest (Matt. 26:58; Mark 14:29; Luke 22:54–55; John 13:37; 18:15–18, 25–27). When his identity as Jesus' disciple was suspected, Peter denied it three times and was devastated by his loss of courage (Matt. 26:69–75; Mark 14:66–72; Luke 22:54–62). Nevertheless, Peter remained with the Twelve as they mourned and was, along with the beloved disciple, the first to witness the empty tomb (Luke 24:12; John 20:2–7). The resurrected Jesus singled him out (Luke 24:34; 1 Cor. 15:5) to receive special forgiveness and reinstatement (Mark 16:7; John 21:2–3, 7, 15–19).

Peter denies Jesus three times. William Brassey Hole (1846-1917).

Peter is apparently able to forgive himself enough to remain with Jesus' other disciples. When the 120 followers are gathered in the upper room, Peter is not only among those filled with the Holy Spirit but becomes a spiritual leader and a powerful preacher of the gospel (Acts 1:13, 15; 2:14, 37–38; 4:1, 8; 8:25). He works miracles in the name of Jesus (Acts 3:1–12; 5:15; 9:32–35, 36–41). His denial of Jesus is never repeated, even when he is dragged in to appear twice before the Sanhedrin (Acts 4:7–13, 18–20; 5:29). To the contrary, the Sanhedrin is amazed at his power and boldness, even noting that he possesses qualities surprising of one not rabbinically trained (Acts 4:13).

Peter finds himself in a position of leadership in the expanding church and along with Paul is one of the two great apostles whose deeds are documented in the book of Acts. The Lord does great things through Peter, as he judges Ananias and Sapphira (Acts 5:3, 8–9), as the Holy Spirit is bestowed on believers in Samaria through him (Acts 8:14, 17), and as he judges Simon the sorcerer (Acts 8:20). While staying in Joppa with a tanner also named Simon, Simon Peter has a startling vision that signals the transformation of God's dealings with the **Gentiles** (Acts 10:9–16). That vision gives Peter the understanding that allows him to bring the gospel to Gentiles living in Caesarea (Acts 10:23–48). He is then called upon to explain in Jerusalem why he felt free to cross that cultural barrier (Acts 11). From that time on, the kingdom has been open to Gentiles.

The belief of Gentiles in Jesus the Jewish Messiah inevitably caused problems that the Lord's apostles had to hammer out in the earliest years of the Christian religion. Peter, along with Paul and James, played a key role at the council of Jerusalem where epoch-changing decisions were made about how Christian Gentiles would relate to God's previous revelation in the Torah (Acts 15). Recognized by the apostle Paul as the apostle to the Jews (Gal. 2:7–8), at some point Peter had a run-in with the apostle Paul in Antioch over fellowship between Jewish and Gentile believers (Gal. 2:11, 14).

Despite his earlier denial of knowing Jesus to avoid possible arrest, Peter finds the courage of his convictions, leading to his arrest in Jerusalem by Herod and to a miraculous escape (Acts 12:3, 5–7, 14, 16). Little is known with certainty about Peter after he leaves Jerusalem "for another place" (Acts 12:17). A strong and uncontested tradition associates Peter with the city of Rome. When forgiven and reinstated by Jesus those many years before on the shores of the Sea of Galilee, Jesus hinted at Peter's death by execution (John 21:18–19). After many years of apostolic leadership in the emerging Christian church, Peter finally met that predicted death when he was executed by crucifixion during Emperor Nero's reign in the mid-60s.

The two letters included in the New Testament that bear his name, 1 Peter and 2 Peter, are a large part of Peter's legacy. All this happened because one day he met Jesus.

Peter's Vision (Acts 10:9–20). Margaret Gere (1878–1965).

AUTHORSHIP AND DATE OF 1 PETER

When 1 Peter is read against the background of what the Gospels say about Peter, the disciple who misunderstood Jesus' mission and denied him in his final hours, an interesting irony emerges from observing how the apostle's thought later developed. In the book of Acts, when the One killed by the Romans afterward appears alive, it prompts his followers to ask, "Lord, are you at this time going to restore the kingdom to Israel?" (Acts 1:6). If Peter thought the Messiah was to overthrow Roman occupation and restore the Davidic kingdom, who better to do that than a Messiah who can withstand death? Judging from this letter, Peter had come to see the resurrection of Jesus not as the secret weapon against the Romans but the means by which God in his great mercy has given new birth into a living hope to those who believe in Christ (1 Peter 1:3–5). At some point, Peter had come to understand Jesus in light of the redemptive concerns of God rather than merely human concerns (Mark 8:33). He had come to realize that through rejection, suffering, and execution, Jesus was fulfilling the messianic role of God's Suffering Servant that centuries before had been prophesied by Isaiah (Isa. 52:13–53:12). The irony of it all is that God inspired Peter, the one who dared to rebuke Jesus for his prediction of suffering and death, to present the New Testament's clearest understanding of Jesus as the Suffering Servant of God (1 Peter 2:18–25; see chapter 10).

Tradition Says that Peter Was Crucified Upside Down

"At Nero's hands he received the crown of martyrdom, being nailed to the cross with his head towards the ground and his feet raised on high, asserting that he was unworthy to be crucified in the same manner as his Lord.... Buried at Rome in the Vatican near the Triumphal Way, he is venerated by the whole world."

Jerome, *De viris illustribus* 1.2, 6

It is ironic that the one who first boldly marched into the home of the high priest only to cower before a servant girl and deny Jesus is the one Jesus singled out for such a prominent leadership role in the early church. When the Holy Spirit filled Peter at Pentecost (Acts 2), he received at last the courage of his convictions that allowed him to stand before any and all threats. He had learned well the lesson of Jesus' statement, "Whoever wants to be my disciple must deny themselves and take up their cross and follow me" (Mark 8:34). And it is this inseparability of the life of Christ and the life of the believer that undergirds Peter's instructions for Christian living, starting with the foundational thought that "Christ suffered for you, leaving you an example, that you should follow in his steps" (1 Peter 2:21).

Planet Art

Peter's martyrdom by Michelangelo Merisi da Caravaggio (1600–01). Peter's crucifixion was the subject of many later artists.

In spite of such congruencies between 1 Peter and what is known of the life of Peter, most New Testament scholars today argue that this letter is pseudonymous, that it was written by an unknown author, perhaps a disciple of Peter who adopted Peter's name for his writing. There are several reasons given for denying Petrine authorship, including:

1. The Greek of 1 Peter is just too good for a former fisherman to have written; its style and rhetorical features indicate some formal education of the kind not available to Galilean fishermen.
2. The letter reflects a situation both in church structure and in social hostility to Christians that best fits a time decades after Peter had died.
3. First Peter exhibits a dependence on the later books of Paul, also considered by many scholars to be pseudonymous, therefore pushing the date of composition well after the death of the two apostles.
4. Christianity could not have reached the remote areas of Asia Minor to which the letter is addressed and therefore could not have become a target for persecution until decades after Peter died.

Such reasons, and their counterarguments, are largely subjective and will strike different people with different force. But all of these arguments can be countered to the extent that they no longer compel one to deny Petrine authorship.

The quality of the Greek, an argument we have encountered before, is perhaps the strongest evidence that Peter did not write the book. Even some scholars who defend Peter's authorship concede that the Greek is better than could be expected of Peter himself when they offer the explanation that the apostle used an **amanuensis**, that is, a secretary who took dictation in some form and wrote down the apostle's message. It was common practice in the first century to use an amanuensis, and perhaps it is the proficiency of the amanuensis displayed in the Greek of the letter. On the other hand, the opinion that the Greek is too good for a Galilean fisherman to have written is based on many assumptions about the use of Greek in Galilee and about what level of proficiency a person could achieve after years of living in the Greek-speaking world outside of Palestine, as Peter apparently did. Furthermore, the syntax of the Greek of 1 Peter exhibits bilingual interference from a Semitic language, such as might be expected if Greek were the second language of an author whose native language was Aramaic.[4] Specifically, the Greek of 1 Peter shows a less than native proficiency in (1) the use of prepositions, (2) the use of the genitive personal pronoun, (3) the position of the attributive adjective, and (4) the use of the dative case with the Greek preposition *en*. Of course, such a syntactic analysis cannot compel the conclusion that Peter wrote the letter himself, but it can seriously weaken the argument that an anonymous native Greek-speaker in Asia Minor wrote it.

The second category of objection to Petrine authorship has to do with the stage of development in church structure reflected in the letter and the type of social hostility directed at the church. Those who oppose Petrine authorship argue that on both counts the letter better matches the historical situation of later decades long after Peter's death. However, a close examination of the letter does not suggest a well-developed hierarchy in church leadership or any other structure that did not exist in even the earliest days of the church. Moreover, the church may have developed at a different pace in different locations, making it specious to so precisely correlate church structure with a particular historical period. The period of ecclesiastical development reflected in 1 Peter is a complicated issue. The evidence the letter presents is too general to be used for purposes of dating. Peter is not writing to churches, as the apostle Paul did, but to scattered Christians across a vast geographical area. The only direct reference to church structure is 1 Peter 5:1–4, which mentions only elders (Gk. *presbyteroi*) who ought to shepherd (Gk. *poimainō*) the flock. The Greek participle *episkopountes* in 5:2, often translated *overseer* or *having oversight of*, has been argued to be a reference to the office of the monarchical bishop of the second century. If this letter could be dated to the second century on other grounds, then it would be appropriate to construe the meaning of *episkopountes* consistent with its second-century usage. But the word had a long history of more general usage before it came to be adopted as the official term for a bishop. Furthermore, the vast geographical area to which the letter is written would have been the territory of more than one bishop, as later history attests.

4. See Karen H. Jobes, "The Syntax of 1 Peter: Just How Good Is the Greek?" *BBR* 13 (2003): 159–73; idem, *1 Peter*, BECNT (Grand Rapids: Baker Academic, 2005), 7–8, 325–38.

Moreover, the word *episkopountes* is a textual variant, introducing considerable doubt about its presence in the original text of the letter. The scant evidence presented by the letter is insufficient and cannot be used to date its origin. The wording is consistent with known church structure in even the earliest days of the church.

A similar inconclusive situation pertains to the type of persecution reflected in 1 Peter. The **extant** letters of Pliny the Younger, a Roman official who wrote letters to the emperor Trajan about AD 110, describe persecution of Christians in Bithynia and have tilted some interpreters of 1 Peter to see it as also addressing persecution at the time of Trajan. However, the persecution in view in 1 Peter does not seem to be the severe physical persecution and martyrdom that Christians of Asia Minor later experienced under Trajan's rule (AD 98–117) but rather to be limited to slander, malicious talk, and false accusations (1 Peter 1:6; 2:12, 15; 3:9, 16; 4:12, 16). Even Nero's severe persecution of Christians in the mid-60s, in which the apostle Peter himself died, was limited to Rome itself and had no apparent effect in the areas of Asia Minor mentioned. The current consensus of New Testament scholars that the persecution faced by the Christians to whom Peter wrote was sporadic, individual, and unorganized social ostracism renders this evidence useless for dating the letter, for this type of persecution of Christians was present during the first two hundred years of the church, beginning with Jesus himself. However, the irenic attitude toward the Roman emperor expressed in 1 Peter 2:13–14, 17 may suggest that the letter was written either before Nero's horrendous torture of Christians in Rome or, if 1 Peter were to be found to be pseudonymous on other grounds, during the period of relative peace and stability in Asia Minor before the persecution of Christians that the Roman writer Pliny documented under the reign of Trajan. In any case, the nature of the persecution mentioned in the letter does not provide sufficient evidence for dating its origin.

A third objection to Petrine authorship is 1 Peter's reliance on Paul's letters. The assured consensus of an earlier generation of source critics in the first half of the twentieth century argued that 1 Peter could not have been written before Paul's Ephesians and Romans because it exhibits a distinct dependency on Pauline thought, if not on the text of Paul's letters. This theory, which is still held by some today, suggests that an anonymous author of the Pauline school wrote 1 Peter to bring Pauline ideas to an audience that revered Peter. If Ephesians is also believed to be pseudonymous, then the date of 1 Peter would likely be late

The Roman Emperor Trajan Writes to Pliny about the Christians

"You have followed the right course of procedure, my dear Pliny, in your examination of the cases of persons charged with being Christians, for it is impossible to lay down a general rule to a fixed formula. These people must not be hunted out; if they are brought before you and the charge against them is proved, they must be punished, but in the case of anyone who denies that he is a Christian and makes it clear that he is not by offering prayers to our gods, he is to be pardoned as a result of his repentance however suspect his past conduct may be. But pamphlets circulated anonymously must play no part in any accusation. They create the worst sort of precedent and are quite out of keeping with spirit of our age."

Pliny, *Epistulae* 10.97

Free from "Pauline Captivity"

"It can no longer be claimed that the Petrine author was dependent on Paul for his thoughts and formulations, that he was representative of exclusively Pauline theology, that he was a member of a Pauline or post-Pauline circle, or that he was in dialogue or dispute with Pauline theology or its distortions.... It is high time for 1 Peter to be liberated from its 'Pauline captivity' and read as a distinctive voice of the early Church."*

*John H. Elliott, *1 Peter*, AB 37B (New York: Doubleday, 2000), 40.

in the first century or early second. However, when the passages in Romans that are alleged sources for 1 Peter (Rom. 9; 12; 13) are examined, much of it is material that ultimately came from the Old Testament, material related to Christian responsibility to civic authority, while the remaining alleged parallels consist of single words.[5] At best, one can conclude that both Romans and 1 Peter draw from a common Old Testament interpretive tradition and a common view of "church and state" relations, so to speak. Much the same can be said about the evidence of 1 Peter's dependence on Ephesians, which apart from Old Testament material includes the use of some of the same words—words such as "hope," "inheritance," and "power"—that are too common to indicate a literary relationship. The household codes (Eph. 5:21–6:9; cf. 1 Peter 2:18–3:7) cannot be used as evidence for a literary relationship, because they differ substantially in content, and their form is a common form found in Hellenistic moral philosophy. The similar theological ideas found in both writers (e.g., the concept of "in Christ") are more plausibly explained by reliance on common Christian tradition that had developed, perhaps through liturgy or catechism, and plausibly by the apostles themselves. And so the nature of the alleged similarities when closely examined does not support a literary relationship between 1 Peter and Paul's writings.

Of special note perhaps is the similarity between 2 Thessalonians and 1 Peter.[6] Past scholars have observed parallels in the wording of the Greek between 2 Thessalonians 2:13–17 and various verses in 1 Peter, primarily from chapter 1. This consideration, combined with noting that Silas may have been involved in the composition of the Thessalonian letters has suggested to some that Silas may have served as the amanuensis of 1 Peter, since he is mentioned in 1 Peter 5:12 by his Latin name Silvanus.

A further objection to Petrine authorship has to do with a historical reconstruction of the advance of Christianity into the areas to which 1 Peter is addressed. In the absence of any conclusive evidence, it has been assumed that the gospel spread gradually to these remote areas of Asia Minor through indigenous evangelization by unknown persons, probably sent out by the Pauline churches in southern Asia Minor or in Antioch. Such a process would have taken probably more than a decade or two after the deaths of Peter and Paul in the mid-60s for a Christian population to attract the kind of social persecution that the letter addresses. Representing this view, John Elliott writes:

5. See Paul J. Achtemeier, *1 Peter*, Hermeneia (Minneapolis: Fortress, 1996), 15–19.

6. For extensive discussion, see Edward G. Selwyn, *The First Epistle of St. Peter: The Greek Text with Introduction, Notes and Essays* (London: Macmillan, 1958), 383.

> The large amount of territory ... indicates expansion of the messianic mission in Asia Minor that could have occurred only subsequent to the activities of Paul. In addition, sufficient time must be allowed for the social conflict between Jesus-followers and their neighbors mentioned in 1 Peter to have developed generally throughout these Roman provinces.... Thus the address of this letter as well as the situation that it reflects point to a date no earlier than 70 or 75 CE.[7]

Following this theory, one of those unknown evangelists wrote 1 Peter in order to bring apostolic teaching to northern Asia Minor. If this is the case, it is a wonder why Peter's name would be the chosen pseudonym, especially if Paul had founded the sending churches. But this objection would become moot if Christianity in fact arrived rather suddenly on the scene in northern Asia Minor, even during the lifetime of Peter. Rather than taking root through a slow evangelization process, Christianity could have come quickly through the establishment of Roman colonies in which displaced Christians were among the colonists.[8]

The early Roman period saw extensive expansion of the empire to lands that then needed to be integrated culturally and administratively under Roman governance. To accomplish this, the emperors established Roman colonies in the lands annexed, either by designating an existing city as worthy of such status or by building a new city. Caesarea in Palestine was an example of a Roman city built as the center of Roman administration of that province to be a comfortable place for the Roman officials to live. The Roman emperor Claudius, who reigned AD 41–54, established Roman cities in all five of the regions named in 1 Peter 1:1. In Pontus Claudius conferred the status of a Roman colony on the old settlement of Andrapa, which then took the name Neoclaudiopolis.[9] In Galatia the ancient city of Iconium received a new political advantage from Claudius and took the name Claudiconium.[10] Claudius also established another colony in the Galatian area of Trocmi called Claudiopolis.[11] The ancient settlement of Archelais in the newly annexed Cappadocia was given the status of a Roman colony.[12] In the province of Asia, the Seleucid community of Laodicea became romanized with the name Claudiolaodicea.[13] And finally, in Bithynia the town of Boli was conferred with a new status that required its name to become Bithynium-Claudiopolis.[14] Elsewhere in Asia Minor Claudius also established five colonies in Pisidia and Lycaonia.[15]

---

7. John H. Elliott, *Conflict, Community, and Honor: 1 Peter in Social-Scientific Perspective*, Cascade Companions (Eugene, Ore.: Cascade, 2007), 5.

8. For a fuller discussion of Roman colonization and the origin of 1 Peter, see Jobes, *1 Peter*, 28–41.

9. A. H. M. Jones, *The Cities of the Eastern Roman Provinces*, 2nd ed. (Oxford: Clarendon, 1971), 159; David Magie, *Roman Rule in Asia Minor to the End of the Third Century after Christ*, 2 vols. (Princeton: Princeton University Press, 1950; repr., New York: Arno, 1975), 1:546–47; CAH, 10:679.

10. Magie, *Roman Rule*, 1:547.

11. CAH, 10:679.

12. Jones, *Cities*, 179; CAH, 10:679; Magie, *Roman Rule*, 1:547; Barbara Levick, *Claudius* (New Haven: Yale University Press, 1990), 158, 178.

13. Magie, *Roman Rule*, 1:547.

14. Jones, *Cities*, 164; CAH, 10:679; Magie, *Roman Rule*, 1:546.

15. CAH, 10:680; see also Levick, *Claudius*, 158, 178; Magie, *Roman Rule*, 1:547; Arnaldo Momigliano, *Claudius: The Emperor and His Achievement*, trans. W. D. Hogarth (Oxford: Clarendon, 1934; repr., Cambridge: Heffer, 1961), 64–65.

Roman colonies typically were populated by at least three hundred colonists who had cultural and political loyalties to Rome. If the colony was a strategic military outpost, retired Roman soldiers usually populated it. But it was not uncommon for the emperor or senate to deport a group from Rome it viewed as troublemakers because of their religion, ethnicity, or occupation. Unlike modern concepts of citizenship, one was not a citizen by virtue of birth at a location. And Roman citizenship could be held by people living far away who had never set foot in Rome. (The apostle Paul was such a person, who held Roman citizenship long before visiting Rome for the first time.) Because those people who held Roman citizenship had legally protected rights and privileges, those deported as colonists were usually "foreigners" (Lat. *peregrini*; Gk. *parepidēmos*) because they did not have citizenship even if they had been born in Rome and lived there all their lives. Sometimes Roman citizenship was offered as an incentive to colonists willing to move to the far-flung outposts of the empire. Perhaps the most famous deportation of a group from Rome (usually referred to as an expulsion) was during the reign of Claudius, who expelled the Jews from Rome in AD 49 because of trouble caused by "Chrestus," which may be a reference to the Greek word *Christos*, or Messiah. If the uproar was between Jews who believed in Jesus as the Messiah and those who opposed this movement, Claudius's expulsion probably would have included Christians.

Claudius's Expulsion

Iudaeos impulsore Chresto assidue tumultuantis Roma expulit.
"Since the Jews constantly made disturbances at the instigation of Chrestus, he [Claudius] expelled them from Rome."
Suetonius, *Divus Claudius* 25.4

Added to this historical fact is Peter's association with Rome long before his execution there during the reign of Nero, the emperor who followed Claudius. Peter left Jerusalem about AD 42 "for another place" (Acts 12:17), but there is no historically reliable information about where he went. If he did go to Rome, it would explain the ancient tradition of Peter's twenty-five-year "episcopate" in the Roman church. Moreover, if the Christians of northern Asia Minor had once been part of the church at Rome and subsequently emigrated among colonists to northern Asia Minor, they would have had knowledge of and some connection to the apostle Peter.

K. H. Jobes

The Roman Emperor Claudius.

A Greek equivalent of the Latin word *peregrinus*, or "foreigners" eligible for deportation, is *parepidēmos*, the very term used in 1 Peter 1:1 to address the original recipients of this letter scattered throughout the five provinces. Because Peter's original readers were not citizens of the dominant power, they may have been displaced and consequently found themselves to be foreigners both in Rome and in their new location. Even if the reference was originally literal, the spiritual sense of sojourning is nonetheless implied, for being foreigners in their world is exactly the point that allows the metaphorical interpretation of Christians as pilgrims sojourning in this world to later emerge.

If this theory, or something like it, is correct, Christianity could have come rather suddenly to northern Asia Minor during the lifetime of Peter, and the letter could have been written by the apostle himself, perhaps with the aid of an amanuensis.

PURPOSE AND MAJOR THEMES

The purpose of Peter's letter can be inferred from 5:12: "This is the true grace of God. Stand fast in it." The two parts of this statement reflect, first, Peter's intent to present truth about God's grace extended in Jesus Christ and, second, his exhortation that his readers might embrace that grace and stand firm by continuing to live faithfully for the Lord, despite their challenging circumstances. The major themes of the book can, therefore, be divided into those addressing Christology and those addressing the spiritual development of the Christian's identity. Each of these two topics will be discussed in greater depth in the next two chapters, but that discussion will be facilitated by an overview here. Peter's Christology forms the basis of his teaching about Christian life. The two topics can be distinguished but not separated, so as we survey his Christology, there will also be references related to Christian living.

An Overview of Peter's Christology

Peter reminds his readers of the efficacy of the death and resurrection of Jesus Christ in establishing the new covenant (1:2) and enabling the new birth (1:3) of those who are redeemed from the empty way of life that leads to God's judgment (1:17–19). The death and resurrection of Jesus are foundational for Peter's theology, and both events in Christ's life are seen to have correspondences in the Christian's life.

Crucifixion and resurrection.

Peter's theology is very Christ-centered, but his Christology is grounded in a Trinitarian understanding of God's relationship to the Christian believer. In the opening of the letter, Peter first refers to his readers as "God's elect" (1:1) who have been

1. chosen according to the foreknowledge of God the Father,
2. chosen through the sanctifying work of the Spirit, and
3. chosen for obedience and sprinkling of the blood of Jesus Christ.

Peter begins his letter by pointing out that a Christian's relationship with God involves all three members of the Godhead. It has its origin in the initiative of God the Father, as accomplished through the work of the Holy Spirit, and for the purpose of entering the covenant ratified by the blood of Jesus. This third point comes from recognizing that "obedience and sprinkling" is a phrase that alludes to the covenant confirmation in Exodus 24, when Moses presented the revealed words and laws of God and the people responded with

What Martin Luther Said about 1 Peter

Martin Luther considered 1 Peter, along with Romans and the gospel of John, to be "the true kernel and marrow" of all the sacred books. "For here you find depicted in masterly fashion how faith in Christ overcomes sin, death, and hell, and gives life, righteousness and salvation."

Martin Luther, "Preface to the New Testament"

a statement of obedience. Then Moses sprinkled them with "the blood of the covenant that the LORD has made with you" (v. 8). The blood of animal sacrifice ratified that covenant, but Peter recognizes a covenant that has been ratified by the blood of Jesus Christ, a clear reference to the crucifixion. And so the work of the Holy Spirit is not to bring people to some generic spirituality as the goal of God's electing purposes; rather, it is specifically to bring people into a covenant relationship with God through Jesus Christ and him alone. The blood of Jesus ratified the new covenant, but according to Peter it was through the resurrection of Jesus that God "has given us new birth into a living hope" (1:3), and consequently a new identity in Christ. (See more on this below under Transformation of the Christian's Identity.) By this we see that Peter's Christology starts with the crucifixion and resurrection of Jesus Christ, the essential center of all New Testament Christology.

The blood that ratified the new covenant is the blood that redeems human beings from the Father's judgment (1:17–19). Although God is presented in 1 Peter as the Judge, it is God's mercy, not wanting people to fall under judgment, that has motivated his plan of redemption (1:3). Judgment is certain in Peter's theology, and it will include God's household as well (4:17–18). For this reason, those who claim God's grace must persevere in obedience and faithful living (1:6–8; 4:19).

The call to persevere from various New Testament writers went out to original audiences in somewhat differing situations, reflecting a range of life circumstances that are still faced by Christians today. In the case of 1 Peter, the challenges of social ostracism and rejection by even family and friends called for a new way of thinking about self-identity that would allow and support perseverance in the Christian faith. Believers in Christ are both chosen by God and marginal in society, both elect and alien. Human psychology "resists the combination of these apparent opposites.... In order to move forward with faith and in faithfulness, we need new ways of making sense of things, new values and commitments, and this is what Peter seeks to provide."[16] That original purpose is no less pressing today, as people search for meaningful self-identity amid a cacophony of voices. The Christian's self-identity must be based soundly on the true grace of God, which Peter lays out in his letter with the call to stand fast in it.

The Living Stone (1 Peter 2:4–8).

Although the origin of an individual's Christian faith is in God's election (1:1), Peter also recognizes that people must come to Christ in a willful conversion. The Christ to whom believers come is the Living Stone (2:4); he is living because of the resurrection, and he is a Stone because he is the first and foundational human being in God's great plan of redemption.

The image of the Lord laying a foundation stone for his redemptive work is found in three Old Testament passages—Psalm 118:22–23 and Isaiah 8:14–15 and 28:16—and all three of them are quoted here in 1 Peter. In pre-Christian biblical interpretation, the stone image of these three passages came to be understood as a reference to the Messiah, as attested in the Greek translation of Isaiah 28:16–17a as well as *Targum Jonathan* of Isaiah

16. Joel B. Green, "Living as Exiles: The Church in the Diaspora in 1 Peter," in *Holiness and Ecclesiology in the New Testament*, ed. Kent E. Brower and Andy Johnson (Grand Rapids: Eerdmans, 2007), 318.

28:16 and Qumran material 1QS8.8. When Jesus came, he identified himself with that Stone, indicating his identity as the Messiah and predicting his rejection (Matt. 21:42; Mark 12:10; Luke 20:17).

The christological image of the Living Stone is closely related to the image of Christian life. When believers come to the Living Stone, they too, said Peter, are like living stones, built into a spiritual temple, taking their places to serve God through Jesus (2:5). The placement of the Living Stone with living stones in the temple implies the close relationship of Christ with believers and their common nature as human beings. Believers are *living* stones because their nature derives from the nature of the life of the resurrected Christ. In Peter's imagery Christ himself is part of the spiritual temple alongside believers, but he is the foundational, first, and preeminent stone, a stone that holds a unique place; apart from him the temple would not exist. This image of the living stones being built into a spiritual house whose cornerstone is Christ also speaks of the unity, significance, and purpose of all believers, which are concepts essential for Christian self-understanding. This important metaphor also has much to say about the Christian's relationship to other believers. We will reflect more deeply on that in chapter 11.

The experience and destiny of those who come to Christ are bound up with the experience and destiny of Christ himself. Because the Living Stone was rejected and suffered, the living stones will also suffer, not in spite of being chosen by God but *because* they are chosen by God. Suffering is arguably the most prominent theme in the letter, and it forms both the heart of Peter's Christology and his fundamental principle of the Christian life.

The Suffering Servant (1 Peter 2:21–25).

Unlike the stone passages of the Old Testament, the Suffering Servant passage of Isaiah 52:13–53:12, hereafter referred to simply as Isaiah 53 for brevity, was not so clearly understood as messianic in pre-Christian times. But the New Testament writers clearly see Jesus' suffering as the fulfillment of that prophetic passage, for it is quoted by Matthew, Luke, John, Paul, and Peter at six places in their writings.[17]

The identification of Jesus as Isaiah's Suffering Servant began with Jesus himself on the last evening of his life. On that fateful evening, Peter, in a moment of sincere bravado, told Jesus, "Lord, I am ready to go with you to prison and to death" (Luke 22:33). Jesus immediately predicted that instead, before that very night was over, Peter would three times deny that he even knew Jesus. Jesus then quoted Isaiah 53:12, saying, "It is written: 'And he was numbered with the transgressors'"

Isaiah's Prophecy of the Suffering Servant Is Quoted Often in the New Testament

Luke 22:37 quoting Isaiah 53:12
Matthew 8:17 quoting Isaiah 53:4
John 12:38 quoting Isaiah 53:1
Romans 10:16 quoting Isaiah 53:1
Acts 8:32–33 quoting Isaiah 53:7–8
1 Peter 2:22–24 quoting Isaiah 53:4–6, 9

17. For a survey discussion of the use of Isaiah 53 in the New Testament, see Karen H. Jobes, "'He Bore Our Sins': Apostolic Reflections on Isaiah 53," in *Ears to Hear and Eyes to See: Biblical and Theological Essays in Memory of J. Alan Groves*, ed. Peter Enns, Douglas J. Green, and Michael Kelly (Phillipsburg, N.J.: P&R, 2010), 92–105.

(Luke 22:37), and concluded, "and I tell you that this must be fulfilled in me. Yes, what is written about me is reaching its fulfillment."

Poignantly, the clause in Isaiah 53:12 immediately before the one explicitly quoted by Jesus is "he poured out his life unto death." By quoting just a phrase, Jesus invoked the entirety of Isaiah 53 when he said, "and I tell you that this must be fulfilled in me. Yes, what is written about me is reaching its fulfillment" (Luke 22:37).

Although several New Testament books quote different parts of the Isaiah 53 passage in various contexts, 1 Peter gives us the most fully developed reflection on how Jesus' suffering fulfilled Isaiah 53. He does so, however, not as an exposition of Isaiah 53, but as a reflection on the last hours of Jesus' life. Peter creatively weaves a description of Jesus' suffering with phrases and allusions from Isaiah 53 in the LXX that interpret various aspects of his trial and suffering, choosing those that bear similarities to the experience of Peter's original readers. (See discussion in chapter 10.)

In citing Isaiah 53, Peter puts the **atonement** at the center of this teaching, writing that Jesus "himself" bore our sins (1 Peter 2:24; cf. Isa. 53:4a, 12), but then adding "in his body upon the cross." The unjust and undeserved suffering of the crucifixion and all that preceded it is clearly the heart of atonement in Peter's reflection on the significance of Jesus Christ as understood through Isaiah's prophecy. Contra liberal Protestantism, which places Jesus' moral and ethical teachings at the heart of the Christian gospel, Peter describes the Suffering Servant as atoning, not by providing ethical and religious instruction, but by bearing our sin—and just to make certain what "bearing our sin" involved, Peter explicitly referred to Jesus' crucifixion as his body hung on the cross.

Peter's foundational principle for Christian life emerges from his christological reflections on Isaiah 53. The purification envisioned by Isaiah means that those for whom the Servant suffered are to separate themselves from sins and live righteously (1 Peter 2:24). However, choosing not to sin in a society that doesn't know the meaning of the word will inevitably lead to suffering at times and to some extent for those whose lives reflect countercultural values based on God's Word. Just as it was God's will that his Servant should suffer (Isa. 53:10), Peter writes that it is God's will for Christians to follow in Jesus' footsteps and to choose to suffer rather than to sin (1 Peter 3:17). Consequently, Peter presents the christological pattern of the life of faith, directly linking the suffering of Christ to the suffering of a Christian. (See further discussion in chapters 10 and 11.)

The Victorious Savior (1 Peter 3:18–22).

Jesus' footsteps lead not just to death but also onward to glory. Although the Suffering Servant is at the heart of Peter's Christology, the apostle also points his readers to the victorious Jesus Christ ascended to heaven and sitting at God's right hand, who has been victorious over unjust suffering and death, with angels, authorities, and powers in submission to him (1 Peter 3:22). Although believers share in suffering by following the example of Christ, they also share in the sure victory of the one who has gone ahead of them and should therefore be encouraged to persevere in faithfulness. By virtue of his vicarious and atoning suffering, Jesus opened the way for those who follow him to approach God. As Peter puts it, "Christ also suffered once for sins, the righteous for the unrighteous, to bring you to God."

The emphasis in this letter on the suffering, death, and ultimate victory of Jesus is remarkable considering that it was written by the disciple who had previously so adamantly rejected any thought of a suffering Messiah, when Jesus announced what lay ahead (Matt. 16:22; Mark 8:32). The Greek phrase *peri hamartiōn*, translated "for sins," is used repeatedly throughout the LXX of the Pentateuch to refer to the sin offerings of the sacrificial system. By the time he wrote this letter, Peter had come to understand that Christ's suffering and death were necessary as the ultimate atonement for sin that opens the way to God.

Jesus has led the way.

Though Jesus was put to death in this life, the resurrection inaugurated a new realm where death does not intrude and where evil has been conquered. Christ's death opens the way for Christians to follow him through death and into eternal life in the presence of the Father. When Christians are given new birth, it is into life in that new realm. But until our bodies die, we still live on the earth in societies for whom Christ is not Lord and where evil still too often prevails. This is why Peter wants his readers to understand who they are as followers of Christ and how their new lives must be lived out here. The worst that the authorities and powers could do to Jesus is the worst they can do to any human being. But if death is not an end but the doorway to the afterlife, then Christians can take heart as they face the future, especially those being persecuted. Peter directly connects his Christology to his exhortation for faithful Christian living by pointing out in 1 Peter 2:21, "Christ suffered for you, leaving you an example, that you should follow in his steps." But to follow in the footsteps of Jesus requires a radical transformation in the way Peter's readers are to think of themselves and their relationship to their society.

Transformation of the Christian's Identity

The second book of the New Testament that bears Peter's name refers explicitly to this transformation of one's thinking that must occur for a Christian to mature spiritually: "Dear friends, this is now my second letter to you. I have written both of them as reminders *to stimulate you to wholesome thinking*" (2 Peter 3:1, emphasis added). The teaching Peter presents about Jesus Christ is intended to ground and motivate a transformation in the way Christians understand themselves in every season of life and in every situation.

This transformation begins by recognizing that, because the believer has been given new birth, God has become his or her Father. Although in popular thought God is the Father of all people because he created them, in the New Testament the concept of new birth through faith in Jesus Christ is the *only* way one becomes a child of God the Father. There is a no more sweeping image of new identity than that of new birth, which implies a new life. For Peter, conversion to faith in Jesus Christ is not limited to one aspect of life; it is an all-encompassing transformation of oneself into a child of God, with all the rights, responsibilities, and privileges that entails. More on this in chapter 11, but an overview here will prepare for that discussion.

Living as foreigners.

The first reference Peter makes to the identity of his readers is that they are *parepidēmoi*, variously translated as "exiles" (NIV, NRSV, ESV), "strangers in the world" (NIV), and "those who reside as aliens" (NASB) in some of the major English versions. The sense of the Greek word is "foreigners," and traditional interpretation has understood this to mean that, because Christians' eternal home is in heaven, as long as they are in this world, they are foreigners away from home (hence the NIV's interpretive translation "strangers in the world"). But given the way Peter develops this image throughout the letter, rather than understanding *parepidēmoi* as describing believers' transitory life on this earth as a journey toward their heavenly home, it should be understood primarily as defining the relationship between Christians and unbelieving society. The Christian is a foreigner in a society whose values are based on other philosophies. If the theory is correct that Peter's original readers were actually displaced persons from elsewhere in the empire, then the term would have poignant meaning for those who had suffered literal "foreignness" firsthand. But regardless of the original historical situation, Peter uses the term "foreigner" to distance his readers from the hold their society has over them. Because of their new birth in Christ, they are children of God, citizens of the kingdom of God, and therefore they have become "foreigners" to the society in which they are living. Peter wants his readers to recognize themselves as having purpose, values, and standards that come from another place, not from Roman society. And that is a truth for all Christians at all times, regardless of where or when they may live.

> "The tension between the addressees' homelessness in society and 'at-home-ness' in the household of God is a theme that runs through 1 Peter like a golden thread."
>
> JOHN H. ELLIOTT, *CONFLICT, COMMUNITY, AND HONOR*

The second time that Peter refers to his readers as *parepidēmoi* is in 2:11, where the context is behavior among the Gentiles. "Dear friends, I urge you as foreigners and exiles to abstain from sinful desires, which wage war against your soul. Live such good lives among the pagans that when they accuse you of doing wrong, they may see your good deeds and glorify God on the day he visits us" (1 Peter 2:11–12). Peter uses this concept of the foreignness of the Christian to discuss engagement with society, a topic we will take up in chapter 11.

Suffering enters the picture when a Christian lives by a standard foreign to his or her society and is reviled for it. If you have tried to live for Christ in high school or college, you may have experienced such ostracism, teasing, and hostility from peers who accused you of a "holier-than-thou" attitude or of being a party-pooper because you didn't join in activities that violated your Christian values. That is the kind of suffering Peter is talking about, suffering *because* one lives as a Christian. Peter describes the persecution and resulting suffering as worldwide (1 Peter 5:9), suggesting not the execution of official Roman policy in any one place, but a type of persecution that potentially threatens all Christians everywhere simply because they are striving to live a faithful Christian life. One scholar describes the nature of the persecution described in 1 Peter as "due more to unofficial harassment than to official policy, more local than regional, and more at the initiation of the general populace as the result of a reaction against the lifestyle of the Christian than at the initiation of Roman officials because of some general policy of seeking out and punishing Christians."[18]

Peter's instructions in this case of facing harassment and ostracism because of being a Christian is to commit oneself to the faithful Creator and continue to do good (1 Peter 4:19) despite the suffering it may generate. That's perseverance! And it is following in the footsteps of Jesus, who experienced harsh rejection, persecution, and execution simply because in his incarnation he was the ultimate foreigner.

The "household codes."[19]

There are three passages in the New Testament—one in 1 Peter (3:1–7) and two in Paul's writings (Eph. 5:21–6:9; Col 3:18–4:1)—that Martin Luther referred to as the "household codes" (Ger. *Haustafeln*) in the headings of his translation of the Bible into German. That label stuck and has affected the way these passages came to be interpreted. Today they are often viewed as if they are a biblical marriage manual proscribing the nature of relationships between husbands and wives in modern marriages. While it is true that these passages do have something to say about Christian marriage, each of the three New Testament household codes had a function in the respective letter that needs to be considered before applying these instructions to marriage today. Furthermore, the form taken by the household code, presenting pairs that comprised the ancient household (husband-wife, father-child, master-slave), and the type of exhortation directed at each were common in ancient writings of the Greek moral philosophers. Instructions not unlike the New Testament household codes can be found in Plato's *Republic* (384–70 **BC**), Xenophon's *Oeconomicus* (c. 430–355 BC), Aristotle's *Oeconomica* (384–322 BC), Plutarch's *Advice to Bride and Groom* (c. AD 46–120), Seneca's *Epistulae Morales* (c. 4 BC–AD 65), and Dio Chrysostom's *On Household Management* (AD 40–c. 112).[20] Although these writers had different views on how slaves and women should be treated, all shared a common belief that order in the household, which they believed to be divinely ordained, was the constituent basis for a strong, orderly, and prosperous society. And the head of the Greek household was the husband/father/master, who was expected to maintain proper order as part of his *civic* duty, regardless of his religious beliefs. It is important to appreciate the role of the household codes in Greco-Roman culture of the first century in order to understand the point of their use in the New Testament. The copious writings concerning household management and their prominent place in the Greco-Roman culture suggest that no religion or philosophy entering that moral world could ignore addressing this topic.

Peter and Paul, whose theology and ethics are deeply rooted in the tradition of the Old Testament, nevertheless include household codes in their letters to Greco-Roman audiences

18. Achtemeier, *1 Peter*, 35–36.

19. This section draws heavily on Jobes, *1 Peter*, 174–212.

20. For an extensive comparison of these Greek writers to 1 Peter, see David L. Balch, *Let Wives Be Submissive: The Domestic Code in 1 Peter*, SBLMS 26 (Chico, Calif.: Scholars, 1981).

whose worldview probably would have been influenced by the Greek moral writings. But even though both apostles address the topic of order in the household, neither simply affirms Greco-Roman expectations. The similarity in form indicates that the New Testament writers are deliberately engaging this aspect of Greco-Roman culture, but the differences between the New Testament and the Greek philosophers on this topic demonstrate that the apostles' views have been formed by the religious convictions of the Old Testament and not by the Greek thought they are engaging. Peter's Christology of the Suffering Servant (1 Peter 2:21–25) is placed within the household code where he addresses the proper behavior of the slave, for it provided the foundational principle for right Christian living within the most basic unit of Greco-Roman society, the household (which is not exactly the same as the family).

Peter's household code is in a unit of discourse that begins at 1 Peter 2:13, where the concern is apologetic:

> Submit yourselves for the Lord's sake to every human authority: whether to the emperor, as the supreme authority, or to governors, who are sent by him to punish those who do wrong and to commend those who do right. For it is God's will that by doing good you should silence the ignorant talk of foolish people. (2:13–15)

The very name "household codes" obscures the actual function of the teaching, which was intended by Peter to instruct on how Christians ought to fulfill their sociopolitical duty within greater society as a slave, a wife, or a husband. Because slavery is not an acceptable part of modern society today and readers of the letter in our age do not have household slaves, interpretation of 1 Peter 2:18–3:7 (as well as Eph. 5:21–6:9 and Col. 3:18–4:1) has primarily focused on the instruction addressed to wives and husbands as a type of marriage manual, obscuring its original sociopolitical message and function. Because of the importance of household relationships for social stability, religions introduced into the empire by foreigners were judged in large part by whether they complied with the expectations for household relationships, thus upholding the social and economic stability so important to Roman governance. One of the apologetic tasks for a religious group was to show compliance with the important elements of social order, as Josephus does for Judaism (*Against Apion* 2.158, 193, 220, 225, 235, 293). In contrast to Judaism, the Egyptian Isis cult was viewed as a threat to the Roman way of life because it permitted a woman authority over her husband.[21] Therefore, the household codes of the New Testament had important apologetic value as the newly formed religion of Christianity took root in Greco-Roman society. Peter writes a household code for Christians so that they might live within their households in ways that, first, honor Christ and, second, do so in a way that will silence the criticisms of Greco-Roman society against the gospel.

The emphatic description in the opening of 1 Peter of Christians as those who have been born again into a new life with new allegiances and the further description of Christians as a people set apart as God's own possession and as a kingdom of priests make it necessary for Peter to explain how the new life in Christ is to operate within the most basic social unit, the household. The apostle Peter informs Christians of their duties in a way that affirms part of the Greco-Roman social order while subtly rejecting those premises

21. Ibid., 29.

that were not compatible with the gospel. Peter is concerned that Christians do not use their moral freedom in such a way as to bring condemnation on the infant church for subverting social order. At the same time, the moral freedom that Christians have been given in Christ transforms their understanding of themselves in ways unparalleled in the Greek moral philosophy of their time.

The first distinctive difference between the Greek household codes and Peter's instructions is that Peter directly addresses the slave and the wife, which was not typically done by the Greek moral philosophers. Although instructions were often directed to masters about master-slave relationships in the Greek writings, slaves were not directly addressed as free moral agents as we find in the New Testament. In the Greek writings, wives, like slaves, received instruction through their husbands, because both slaves and wives were thought to be deficient, although not in the same way.[22] Aristotle understood the slave to be incapable of deliberative thinking, while the wife had the capability but not the commensurate authority.[23] Thus, it was proper to direct all instruction through the man, who had both the capability and the authority to reason fully. Moreover, the instruction of the wife should be the object of the husband's unstinting care (Aristotle, *Oeconomica* 3.2). While some modern interpreters consider the New Testament household codes to be hopelessly chauvinistic, they fail to read the codes against their contemporary literature, which shows that the New Testament writers actually subverted cultural expectations by elevating the slave and the wife with unparalleled dignity.

Goddess Vesta blesses a Roman wedding ceremony, Roman, (2nd century AD)/ Location Unknown/Ancient Art and Architecture Collection Ltd./The Bridgeman Art Library

Peter's "household codes" both uphold and subvert the social expectations of Greco-Roman society. This image shows a wedding ceremony from a second-century sarcophagus.

The second distinctive difference between Greek writings and Peter's instructions to Christian slaves and wives is that he rejects the cultural expectation that a slave must worship his or her master's god and a wife must worship her husband's. It is estimated that almost one-quarter of the empire's population were slaves, so their role was significant to socioeconomic stability. The slave's loyalty to the master's gods assured economic stability. In particular, any religion that advocated equality of any kind between slaves and masters would be met with swift and certain opposition. Wives were similarly expected to follow the husband's religion (e.g., Plutarch, *Mor.* 140.19). Peter does not follow society's expectations here but instead instructs the Christian wife married to an unbeliever to evangelize her husband through her lifestyle with the hope of winning him over to faith in Christ.

If Plutarch's view represents that of first-century Greco-Roman society, a pagan woman who became a Christian could appear rebellious for not worshiping her husband's gods, as

22. See, e.g., Xenophon, *Oeconomicus*, 7–10, where, when Socrates is concerned about a woman's views, he questions her husband about how he has instructed his wife.

23. Balch, *Let Wives*, 34–35.

> "A wife ought not to make friends of her own, but to enjoy her husband's friends in common with him. The gods are the first and most important friends. Wherefore it is becoming for a wife to worship and to know only the gods that her husband believes in, and to shut the front door tight upon all queer rituals and outlandish superstitions."
>
> Plutarch, *Moralia* (*Advice to Bride and Groom*) 2.311

well as for making friends in the Christian community who were not her husband's friends. Apparently first-century social expectations of the wife were quite different from those of our own society, where both husband and wife may have friendships apart from the other, as well as be of different religions without provoking accusations of perverting the social order. This large difference in social expectations suggests that we must be thoughtful about how these biblical instructions are to be observed by Christians today.

Furthermore, the expectation that a wife would worship her husband's gods raised a problem for the first-century husband who had converted to Christianity as well. He may have faced the problem of a wife who, though formally expected to follow his new Christian faith, in reality resented being socially demeaned by her husband's association with this strange new religion. Her rebellion against Christianity might in turn diminish her husband's status in society's eyes, because the man was responsible for order in his own household regardless of his religion. What was a man in such a position to do so that he could fulfill his duty as the head of the household while respecting the reality in which he lived? Peter saves his briefest instructions for married men (1 Peter 3:7), who are to live considerately with their wives and other females of the household. (The Greek word in the exhortation of 3:7 is the substantive adjective *gynaikeios*, "female," not *gynē*, "wife.")

In his household codes, Peter affirms the sociopolitical order on the one hand, while simultaneously reworking it on Christian principles, so that Christian households become a direct expression of an eschatological self-understanding lived out in that society. (More discussion on this in chapter 11.) The basis for Peter's reworking of social expectations is the example of Jesus Christ as the suffering servant of God, in whose footsteps all Christians, including slaves, wives, and husbands are to follow.[24]

THE TEXT AND CANONICITY OF 1 PETER

The Greek Text of 1 Peter

The Greek text of 1 Peter is well represented by over 550 manuscripts, the oldest being $\mathfrak{P}^{72}$, preserving the full text of 1 Peter (along with 2 Peter and Jude, and also some other extrabiblical material). It is a late third-/early fourth-century document now housed in the Vatican Library. The text is closely aligned to that of **codices** Alexandrinus and Vaticanus.

24. For a discussion of the important topic of domestic violence in relation to Peter's household code, see Steven R. Tracy, "Domestic Violence in the Church and Redemptive Suffering in 1 Peter," *CTJ* 41 (2006): 279–96.

When all manuscript evidence is considered, there are about forty notable textual variants in 1 Peter, but none significantly change the sense of the text. This suggests that the text was well accepted as it was received, presenting little motivation for scribal corrections.[25]

> **The Purpose of 1 Peter**
>
> "To mobilize the resources of faith and action which will enable the beleaguered addressees to stand firm and persevere as the community of God in a society from which they are estranged."
>
> John H. Elliott, *Conflict, Community, and Honor*

The Canonicity of 1 Peter

The first reference to 1 Peter may be in 2 Peter 3:1: "Dear friends, this is now my second letter to you"; but that statement is not relevant to the issue of canonicity. Although Clement's letter to the Corinthians (AD 96) shares more than three hundred words with 1 Peter, and some of them relatively uncommon, scholars are divided about whether this reflects Clement's use of the text of 1 Peter or simply a common tradition behind both letters. Polycarp uses enough distinctive phrases from 1 Peter in his letter to the Philippians to show that he clearly knew the text of 1 Peter. Polycarp, being the bishop of Smyrna, lived in Asia Minor and penned his letter soon after the martyrdom of Ignatius, bishop of Antioch, which was not later than AD 117. Irenaeus, born in Asia Minor about AD 140 and later the bishop of Lyon, is the first writer to cite Peter as the author of 1 Peter (4.9.2). Eusebius lists it among the authentic letters (*Hist. eccl.* 3.3.4). Even those ancient writers who doubt Petrine authorship of 2 Peter acknowledge 1 Peter as genuine (e.g., Origen, as quoted by Eusebius in *Hist. eccl.* 6.25.8). The clear and widespread knowledge of 1 Peter by the apostolic fathers led at least one scholar to conclude, "It was considered canonical as early as this word had a meaning."[26]

> "And Peter, on whom the Church of Christ is built, against which the gates of Hades shall not prevail, has left one acknowledged epistle, and it may be, a second also; for it is doubted."
>
> Origen, quoted in *Hist. eccl.* 6.25.8

First Peter does not appear in the late second century **Muratorian Canon** list (so named for the discoverer and first editor of the list in modern times, L. A. Muratori), but the extant manuscript of that list is incomplete. None of the Catholic Epistles appear in the first Syriac New Testament made in the late second century, probably because they had not yet been translated from Greek into Syriac. First Peter (as well as Acts, James, and 1 John) does appear in the Peshitta version introduced by the bishop of Edessa in the late fourth century.[27] The reception of 1 Peter into the universal canon does not seem to have been disputed, for there are no comments in the ancient writers opposing the authenticity of the letter as there are, for instance, concerning 2 Peter.

---

25. The thirty-two readings of 1 Peter in *Editio Critica Maior* that differ from NA27 can be found in Peter M. Head, 'Editio Critica Maior: An Introduction and Assessment', *Tyndale Bulletin* 61.1 (2010), 149–150, available online at https://www.academia.edu/3633883/_Editio_Critica_Maior_An_Introduction_and_Assessment_Tyndale_Bulletin_61.1_2010_131-152 (accessed May 2, 2016).

26. Donald Guthrie, *New Testament Introduction* (Downers Grove, Ill.: InterVarsity, 1970), 771, citing Charles Bigg, *The Epistles of St. Peter and St. Jude*, ICC (New York: Scribner, 1901), 15.

27. Encyclopedia Britannica Online, s.v. "Peshitta," http://www.britannica.com/topic/Peshitta (accessed May 2, 2016).

STRUCTURE AND OUTLINE OF 1 PETER

Although earlier scholarship argued that 1 Peter was a redacted work composed of at least two segments that had been joined, the weight of current New Testament scholarship understands it to be a unified work written by one author for one purpose at one time. There is no manuscript evidence that would suggest it is a composite work, and evidence of its unity outweighs alternate ideas about its composition. The themes in the epistolary framework (1 Peter 1:1–2; 5:12–15) introduce and are consistent with those found in the body of the letter.

The rejection of a composite origin for the book does not preclude the author's use of sources. Peter obviously uses a Greek version of the Old Testament, which is his primary literary and theological source. Scholars debate whether the letter contains preexisting hymns or liturgical material, the most likely candidates being the christological passages in 2:21–25 and 3:18–22. But those who have studied this issue most closely have reached no consensus, except that the author was dependent on some preexisting tradition. One leading Petrine scholar concludes, "The most that can be stated with certainty is that 1 Peter incorporates isolated phrases and formulas of christological and kerygmatic tradition but not that this material was embodied in demonstrable hymnic or creedal sources."[28]

Any sources used have been thoroughly integrated into the discourse of the letter, which should be understood as representing the thought flow of its author.

Outline of 1 Peter

- I. Greeting the **Diaspora** of Asia Minor (1:1–2)
  - A. The Author and Recipients (1:1)
    - 1. From the apostle Peter (1:1a)
    - 2. To foreigners of the Diaspora (1:1b)
      - a. Chosen by God's foreknowledge (1:2a)
      - b. Chosen by the consecration of the Spirit (1:2b)
      - c. Chosen for obedience and sprinkling (1:2c)
  - B. Grace and Peace Be Multiplied (1:2d)
- II. Reassurance for the People of God (1:3–2:10)
  - A. Doxology as the Basis for Christian Life (1:3–12)
    - 1. Opening doxology (1:3–5)
    - 2. Joy and suffering (1:6–9)
    - 3. The Christian's advantage (1:10–12)
  - B. Being What You Are (1:13–2:3)
    - 1. Children of the Father (1:13–21)
    - 2. Love is moral transformation (1:22–2:3)
  - C. Who God's People Are (2:4–10)
    - 1. Spiritual house and holy priesthood (2:4–8)
    - 2. Now, the people of God (2:9–10)

28. Elliott, *1 Peter*, 32.

III. Live Godly Lives (2:11 – 4:11)
   A. Social Behavior as God's People (2:11 – 3:7)
      1. Be a winsome witness (2:11 – 12)
      2. Submit to authority (2:13 – 17)
      3. Christ's example (2:18 – 3:7)
         a. For the slave (2:18 – 25)
         b. For wives and husbands (3:1 – 7)
   B. Inner Qualities of the Righteous (3:8 – 12)
   C. Suffering Unjustly (3:13 – 4:11)
IV. Consolation for the Suffering (4:12 – 5:11)
   A. Final Thoughts about Suffering (4:12 – 19)
   B. Exhortations to the Community (5:1 – 11)
V. Final Words and Greetings (5:12 – 14)

CHAPTER SUMMARY

The book of 1 Peter makes a distinctive contribution to developing Christian theology and practice and is a rich resource for the church today. When all factors are considered, there is no compelling reason to deny that the apostle Peter wrote this letter, perhaps with the aid of an amanuensis. Regardless of its author, the letter was intended to be read as if from the pen of one of Jesus' inner circle of disciples. Scripture tells us more about Peter than perhaps any of the other disciples, allowing us to see the development of Peter's thought between the time he was with Jesus and the time he wrote this letter.

The major themes of Peter's letter are as significant to readers today as they were when originally written more than two thousand years ago. Christians today grow up assimilating society's values and standards. The Holy Spirit works to develop spiritual maturity in the believer through a self-critique of those values and the transformation of one's Christian self-understanding of a new identity based on the new birth. The heart of orthodox Christianity is a correct understanding of Jesus' vicarious and atoning suffering, death, and resurrection. However, Peter corrects a popular view that because Jesus suffered, I don't have to, by explaining that suffering in the life of a Christian is part of one's calling to follow Christ.

KEY TERMS AND DATES

AD 49
AD 64 – 67
amanuensis
Claudius
household codes
papyrus $\mathfrak{P}^{72}$
pseudonymous
Roman colonization

QUESTIONS FOR REVIEW OR DISCUSSION

1. What are the reasons for dating 1 Peter beyond the lifetime of the apostle Peter? What are the counterarguments to pseudonymity?
2. Where did the original recipients of this letter live? What are the theories concerning them?
3. Write a statement describing Peter's Christology.
4. How might Peter's instructions for the household be applied in our modern setting today consistently with his intended purpose?

GOING FURTHER

Balch, D. L. *Let Wives Be Submissive*: *The Domestic Code in 1 Peter*. SBLMS 26. Chico, Calif.: Scholars, 1981.

Chester, Andrew, and Ralph P. Martin. *The Theology of the Letters of James, Peter, and Jude*. New Testament Theology. Cambridge: Cambridge University Press, 1994.

Donelson, Lewis R. *From Hebrews to Revelation*: *A Theological Introduction*. Louisville: Westminster John Knox, 2001.

Elliott, John Hall. *Conflict, Community, and Honor*: *1 Peter in Social-Scientific Perspective*. Cascade Companions. Eugene, Ore.: Cascade, 2007.

Green, Joel B. "Narrating the Gospel in 1 and 2 Peter," *Interpretation* 60 (2006): 262–77.

Harner, Philip B. *What Are They Saying about the Catholic Epistles?* What Are They Saying Series. New York: Paulist, 2004.

Howe, Bonnie. *Because You Bear This Name: Conceptual Metaphor and the Moral Meaning of 1 Peter*. Biblical Interpretation Series 81. Leiden: Brill, 2006.

Metzger, Bruce Manning. *Apostolic Letters of Faith, Hope, and Love: Galatians, 1 Peter, and 1 John*. Eugene, Ore.: Cascade, 2006.

Quast, Kevin. *Peter and the Beloved Disciple*: *Figures for a Community in Crisis*. JSNTSup 32. Sheffield: JSOT, 1989.

Tracy, Steven R. "Domestic Violence in the Church and Redemptive Suffering in 1 Peter," *CTJ* 41 (2006): 279–96.

Commentaries

Achtemeier, Paul J. *1 Peter*: *A Commentary on First Peter*. Hermeneia. Minneapolis: Fortress, 1996.

Charles, Daryl J. "1 Peter." Pages 277–356 in *Hebrews–Revelation*. *Expositor's Bible Commentary*. Vol. 13. Edited by Tremper Longman III and David E. Garland. Rev. ed. Grand Rapids: Zondervan, 2006.

Davids, Peter. "1 Peter." Pages 120–51 in *ZIBBC*. Vol. 4. Edited by Clinton E. Arnold. Grand Rapids: Zondervan, 2002.

———. *The First Epistle of Peter*. NICNT. Grand Rapids: Eerdmans, 1990.

Elliott, John H. *1 Peter: A New Translation with Introduction and Commentary*. AB 37B. New York: Doubleday, 2000.
Green, Joel B. *1 Peter*. Two Horizons New Testament Commentary. Grand Rapids: Eerdmans, 2007.
Harnick, Douglas. *1 and 2 Peter*. Brazos Theological Commentary on the Bible. Grand Rapids: Brazos, 2009.
Jobes, Karen H. *1 Peter*. BECNT. Grand Rapids: Baker Academic, 2005.
Michaels, J. Ramsey. *1 Peter*. Word Biblical Commentary 49. Waco, Tex.: Word, 1988.
Schreiner, Thomas R. *1, 2 Peter, Jude*. New American Commentary. Nashville: Broadman and Holman, 2003.
Senior, Donald P., and Daniel J. Harrington. *1 Peter, Jude and 2 Peter*. Sacra Pagina 15. Collegeville, Minn.: Liturgical, 2003.
Skaggs, Rebecca. *Pentecostal Commentary on 1 Peter, 2 Peter, Jude*. New York: Cleveland, Ohio: Pilgrim, 2004.
Witherington, Ben, III. *Letters and Homilies for Hellenized Christians: A Socio-Rhetorical Commentary on 1–2 Peter*. Downers Grove: IVP Academic, 2007.

CHAPTER 10

"Christ Has Left You an Example"

THE CHRISTOLOGY OF 1 PETER

Your Goals for This Chapter

- To describe what is distinctive about Peter's **Christology**.
- To name and explain the images Peter uses to teach about Jesus Christ.
- To reflect on how in Peter's thought the destiny of the Christian believer is inseparable from Jesus' destiny.

WHY THIS CHAPTER IS IMPORTANT TO YOU

First Peter shares with all New Testament writings the general contours of Christology—that Jesus Christ lived a sinless life, suffered an undeserved crucifixion that **atoned** for sin, was resurrected from the dead as vindication of his identity and proof of his power, and ascended into heaven where he reigns as God with God the Father. But Peter contributes a distinctive element to New Testament theology by discussing the suffering and victory of Jesus as the heart of his encouragement for suffering Christians. The life of Jesus is the pattern for the believer's life, for Jesus is not only the object of Christian faith; he is also the pattern of Christian destiny. Although for Peter the Christian life is very much the way of the cross, the faithful Christian is also assured of the same victory over evil that Jesus Christ has demonstrated in his resurrection and ascension. In other words, it is important to understand Peter's Christology in order to successfully live the Christian life and to disciple others to do so as well.

Key Verses

1:3: Praise be to the God and Father of our Lord Jesus Christ! In his great mercy he has given us new birth into a living hope through the resurrection of Jesus Christ from the dead, . . .

1:18–19: For you know that it was not with perishable things . . . that you were redeemed from the empty way of life handed down to you from your ancestors, but with the precious blood of Christ, a lamb without blemish or defect.

2:6: "See, I lay a stone in Zion,
a chosen and precious cornerstone,
and the one who trusts in him
will never be put to shame."

2:21, 25: To this you were called, because Christ suffered for you. . . . the Shepherd and Overseer of your souls.

3:18: For Christ also suffered once for sins, the righteous for the unrighteous, to bring you to God. He was put to death in the body but made alive in the Spirit.

3:21b–22: It [baptism] saves you by the resurrection of Jesus Christ, who has gone into heaven and is at God's right hand—with angels, authorities and powers in submission to him.

5:4: And when the Chief Shepherd appears, you will receive the crown of glory that will never fade away.

CHAPTER OUTLINE

I. Approaching Peter's Christology
II. The Hermeneutical Foundations of Peter's Christology (1 Peter 1:10–12)
III. Putting Peter's Christology in Context
IV. The Suffering Servant at the Heart of Peter's Christology (1 Peter 2:21–25)
V. The Victorious, Vindicated Savior (1 Peter 3:18–22)
VI. Other Images of Christ in 1 Peter
    A. Sacrificial Lamb
    B. The Living Stone

APPROACHING PETER'S CHRISTOLOGY

The **epistles** in the New Testament each were originally written to a Christian audience facing a different situation and needing different issues to be addressed. All of the writers of the Epistles relate these situations and issues to Jesus, but not in exactly the same way. As one New Testament scholar has put it, "Christ serves as an example to those virtues the author judges are most needed to address a particular need in the church. The 'biography' of Christ is retold in such a way as to reveal a particular character trait that the author seeks to instill in his audience."[1]

This is why there are four gospels that are not identical in their content and structure. And the epistles of the New Testament, while not retelling a narrative story of Jesus, emphasize aspects of an assumed narrative of Jesus that underlie the teachings and exhortations in their letters. Therefore, it is important to hear the distinctive voice of each New Testament author. While there is no need to pit what one writer says against the words of another, it is also unwarranted to try to make them all say exactly the same thing about Jesus.

Christology is the study of the person, nature, and role of Jesus Christ and his relationship to other branches of Christian theology, such as **soteriology**, **eschatology**, **pneumatology**, and the doctrine of God proper. Christian belief about Jesus did not appear fully formed the day after the resurrection or Pentecost. It was forged over time as the apostles hammered out the great truths of the faith on the anvil of real life situations. This development of apostolic thought is captured in the letters they wrote throughout the first century. And so by studying what one New Testament writer has to say about Jesus at one point in time, we get a perspective on some aspect of Christology as comprehension of the significance of Jesus Christ developed.

Peter's Christology does not highlight the preexistence of the Son as in John's gospel (though it does assume that idea in 1 Peter 1:20 and possibly 1:11) or the ethical teachings of Jesus as in the **Synoptics** (though the letter includes teachings that originated with Jesus). Peter focuses specifically on the suffering and execution of Jesus and his subsequent resurrection and ascension and presents these events as

1. J. De Waal Dryden, *Theology and Ethics in 1 Peter: Paraenetic Strategies for Christian Formation*, WUNT, 2nd ser., 209 (Tübingen: Mohr Siebeck, 2006), 172.

1. the blood of the new covenant (1:1 – 3),
2. the price of redemption (1:1 – 3),
3. a vicarious death for the sins of others (2:21 – 25),
4. and the means of reconciliation with God (3:17 – 22).

Peter's focus on the suffering of Jesus and the need to explain it in terms of the Jewish Scriptures suggest that this letter was written at a time when the crucifixion still remained a vivid memory in the church and especially in the mind of the man who wrote this letter. Moreover, this focus on Jesus' **passion**[2] represents an earlier stage of Christology in the emerging. Compared to Paul's in-depth teaching on the atonement, the Law, and the Spirit, Peter's Christology appears less involved and even primitive. This is not to say that Peter's theological understanding is inferior but only that it likely reflects a state of development closer to the crucifixion rather than more removed in time from it. The Christology that Peter presents is not as developed as that found in Romans or Revelation, but it is consistent with what is found there. Despite representing an early stage in the development of Christian theology, 1 Peter presents a rich theological understanding of Jesus.

Even the address of Peter's letter (1:1 – 2), while quite conventional in form, is replete with theology in general and Christology in particular. As mentioned in chapter 9, Peter writes to people who are "foreigners" in relation to their society but "chosen" in relation to God. Their chosen status is described further by three phrases: (1) according to the foreknowledge of God the Father, (2) through the sanctifying work of the Spirit, and (3) for the "obedience and sprinkling of the blood of Jesus Christ." This last phrase is often smoothed out in English Bibles as if it refers to two distinct parts, to be obedient to Christ and to be sprinkled with his blood. Instead, the phrase "obedience and sprinkling" is covenant language that alludes to Exodus 24:3 – 8, when God established the covenant with his people through Moses.[3] After meeting with God on Mount Sinai, Moses went and told the people what the LORD had said. When he read the book of the covenant to the people, they responded, "We will do everything the LORD has said; we will *obey*" (Ex. 24:7, emphasis added). That is the obedience part. And then Moses took the blood of young bulls that had been offered to the LORD, *sprinkled* it on the people, and said, "This is the blood of the covenant that the LORD has made with you in accordance with all these words." That's the sprinkling part.

Jesus taught that his blood shed on the cross instituted a new covenant between God and humankind (Mark 14:24).

During Jesus' last meal before he was crucified, he raised a cup of wine and defined it as a sacrament and symbol, saying, "This is my *blood of the covenant*, which is poured out for many" (Matt. 26:28; Mark 14:24; Luke 22:20, emphasis added). When Peter used the words "obedience and sprinkling" in 1 Peter 1:2, he alluded to the new covenant that is

2. The word *passion* has traditionally been used to refer to the suffering and death of Jesus, deriving from a sense of the word no longer in current usage.

3. This use of two words to refer to one concept is called hendiadys, a rhetorical term that comes from the Greek meaning "one through two." Some examples of hendiadys in English usage are "black and blue" to refer to bruising and "the birds and the bees" to refer to the basic teaching about sexual function and reproduction.

based, not on the blood of animals, but on the blood of Jesus. In other words, Peter says that being chosen by God is for the purpose of entering into the new covenant in Christ's blood. The sanctifying work of the Holy Spirit is not to draw people into some generic spirituality that is so popular in today's culture, but into covenant relationship with God in Christ. And so these three phrases show God the Father, the Holy Spirit, and Jesus Christ all working in concert with respect to the life of the Christian believer.

THE HERMENEUTICAL FOUNDATIONS OF PETER'S CHRISTOLOGY (1 PETER 1:10 – 12)

Peter's Christology is rooted in his interpretation of the Old Testament. The distinctive element of Peter's Christology is his identification of Jesus with Isaiah's Suffering Servant (1 Peter 2:21 – 24). Furthermore, he appropriates the language used in the Old Testament to describe ancient Israel and applies it directly to his Christian readers, which included **Gentiles**, perhaps even as a majority of the original readers (1 Peter 2:9 – 10). Peter is very explicit about the **hermeneutic** that legitimizes his interpretation. In 1 Peter 1:10 – 12a he writes:

> Concerning this salvation, the prophets, who spoke of the grace that was to come to you, searched intently and with the greatest care, trying to find out the time and circumstances to which the Spirit of Christ in them was pointing when he predicted the sufferings of Christ and the glories that would follow. It was revealed to them that they were not serving themselves but you, when they spoke of the things that have now been told you by those who have preached the gospel to you by the Holy Spirit sent from heaven.

Most obviously, Peter reads the Old Testament prophets as foretelling the coming of the Messiah, and Peter, like all New Testament writers, has identified Jesus as the Messiah. But Peter mentions very distinctive elements of his view of Israel's prophets — that it was the *Spirit of Christ* who inspired their prophecies, that the messages of the prophets were not for the prophets' own time but for Christians living after the Messiah had come, and that the things preached by Christian evangelists in Peter's time were the fuller revelation of the Old Testament prophets' messages. While other New Testament writers speak of Jesus fulfilling Old Testament prophecy, Peter brings a much closer identity to the work of the prophets inspired by the Spirit of Christ and the preaching of the evangelists by the Holy Spirit.

hermeneutic: a method or principle of interpretation

Merriam-Webster Online

In a move that distinguishes Christian interpretation of the Old Testament prophets from subsequent Jewish interpretation, Peter identifies what was foreknown by the prophets to be the very things that have now been preached to his readers about Jesus Christ. By showing how the Christian gospel forms continuity with the Old Testament prophetic message, Peter provides an **apology** for the cross and a foundation for his exhortations to his readers. It was not Peter's knowledge of the prophets that led him to recognize Christ; it was actually hearing and seeing Jesus. But *after* he recognized Jesus as the Messiah on the basis of Jesus' teachings and miracles, he realized that his generation and all subsequent generations were those people for whom Israel's ancient prophets ministered. The prophetic

In Israel's Ancient Past	In Peter's Christian Era
Prophets spoke these things.	Evangelists have now preached to you.
The Spirit revealed future things to the prophets.	The Spirit has now told you through evangelists.
Prophets inquired into the circumstances or time of the Messiah's sufferings and glories.	Angels eagerly desire to look into the Messiah's sufferings and glories.

fore-witness to the sufferings of the Messiah provided a basis in Scripture that enabled Peter to accept the suffering and death of the Messiah as the necessary center of God's plan of redemption, and not as an untimely accident or tragic mistake. By witnessing to the sufferings of the Messiah before they happened, the prophets provided a confirming fore-witness that a crucified man would indeed be the long-awaited Messiah. After Jesus came, suffered, and died, the prophecies became a confirmation for the benefit of those who would look back on that event to rightly understand the cross of Jesus.

apology: a reasoned argument or writing in justification for something, typically a theory or religious doctrine.

Oxford American College Dictionary

Furthermore, Peter's hermeneutic sees the Christian gospel as the full flowering of Israel's religion. Therefore, he is free to appropriate the language and moral vision of the Old Testament for his Christian readers, whether they are converts from Judaism or Gentiles. This is likely the reason scholars can't decide if Peter was writing to Jewish or Gentile converts; for Peter's purposes, there is no distinction. There could be no greater unity drawn between the Old Testament's religion and Christianity than the integral involvement of Christ in both. It was the preexistent Spirit of Christ, of this crucified Messiah, who inspired Israel's ancient prophets. And it is the Holy Spirit of God who preaches the Christian gospel through evangelists. Christian belief is not a new religion prompted by a new spirit, but of one piece with God's redemptive work begun through the chosen people, Israel. With that hermeneutical understanding, Peter draws heavily on Isaiah and the Psalms for his Christology.

PUTTING PETER'S CHRISTOLOGY IN CONTEXT

It is striking that Peter positions the center element of his Christology within what have traditionally been referred to as the "household codes." In 1 Peter 2:18–3:7, we find the apostle's instructions to slaves, wives, and husbands in a structure similar to what we find in Ephesians 5:21–33 and Colossians 3:18–4:1. Because in Greco-Roman thought the well-being of society was based on order in its smallest unit, the household, Peter provides instructions about how a Christian is to "live a good life" in relationship to others in the household as a witness to Christ.

In context Peter's Christology in 2:18–25 is informing his apologetic, in which he instructs Christians to "live such good lives among the pagans that, though they accuse you of doing wrong, they may see your good deeds and glorify God" (1 Peter 2:12). Peter is concerned about the relationship of the infant Christian church to society and wants to instruct Christians how to live as a winsome witness to the gospel. The "good lives" he has in mind means for his readers that they are to "submit [themselves] for the Lord's sake to every human authority: whether to the emperor, as the supreme authority, or to governors, who are sent by him" (1 Peter 2:13–14). While acknowledging that as Christians they are free people, Peter presses home the point that they are free to serve God, to live as "God's slaves" (1 Peter 2:16). Therefore, he uses the status of the slave in Roman society as the paradigm for every believer.

About one-quarter of the population of the first-century Roman Empire was comprised of slaves. Even though many slaves did jobs that would be considered professional today (such as teacher and physician), they were nevertheless owned by the family they served. The slave was the least empowered person in Roman society and had little control over his or her life. The reasons Peter sees the slave as a good model for Christian living will be discussed further in chapter 11, but two points are relevant to his Christology. First, Peter wants Christians to live their lives conscious of serving God and of having been bought by him (1 Peter 1:18; 2:16). Such obedience to God may invoke hostility from friends and neighbors, and even family. Peter's point is that it is better to choose to suffer such consequences than to sin. (More on this in chapter 11.)

Second, but of foundational importance for Peter's Christology, the Son of God came into this world as God's suffering servant (or slave; the Greek can be translated either way). Jesus, the Suffering Servant is the example for Christian life, and the two are inseparable in Peter's thought. For this reason, he places his teaching about Jesus in the center of his instructions about Christian life in the household. And because Jesus lived and died as God's suffering servant/slave, the slave is an apt paradigm for Christian life in Peter's instructions. Therefore, he puts his teaching about Jesus in the context of his instructions to slaves.

THE SUFFERING SERVANT AT THE HEART OF PETER'S CHRISTOLOGY (1 PETER 2:21–25)

It is an awesome point of theology that when the Son of God came into the world, he was not born into the palace of Caesar. He did not come into a wealthy, powerful Roman family. The King of the universe did not hold Roman citizenship. Nor was he born into the aristocratic priestly tribe of Israel's religious establishment. The Son of Man came not to be served but to serve. And his role as a servant was underscored when he was executed by the method the Romans usually reserved for slaves and criminals—crucifixion. Peter bases his instructions for *all* Christian members of society on the example of the lowly position in human society that Jesus himself willingly adopted.

Ironically, the suffering of Christ became central to the Christology of the apostle who most strongly objected to Jesus' prediction of his death (Matt. 16:21–23; Mark 8:31–33). Peter was among the first who recognized Jesus as the Messiah and who even rebuked Jesus when the Lord began to explain that the Messiah would in fact have to die to fulfill his role (Mark 8:27–33). Peter must have had to make big adjustments in his thinking as he pondered the shocking fact that when the long-awaited Messiah finally came, he had so little sociopolitical power that God's Anointed would end up dying a slave's death by crucifixion. And Peter knows that others need a similar transformation in their thinking too. The Jewish Scriptures played a large role in shaping the New Testament writers' understanding of the death and resurrection of Jesus. In fact, it is doubtful they could have made sense of it had they not had the Old Testament (see 1 Peter 1:10–12).

Erich Lessing/Art Resource, NY

A basin for footwashing. Peter objected at first when Jesus tried to wash his feet (John 13).

Isaiah's prophecies, especially those about God's "suffering servant" became central to the apostles' thinking as they pondered the significance of Jesus Christ. The passage often referred to as Isaiah 53 (which actually extends from Isa. 52:13 to 53:12) is quoted or otherwise referred to by five New Testament writers—Matthew (Matt. 8:17), Luke (Luke 22:37; Acts 8:32), John (John 12:38), Paul (Rom. 10:16; 15:21), and Peter (1 Peter 2:18–25).[4] For Peter, the Suffering Servant of Isaiah 53 becomes the centerpiece of his Christology.[5]

The identity of Jesus Christ as the Suffering Servant poignantly yet enigmatically portrayed in Isaiah 53 is well known in Christian tradition. Although other New Testament writers quote Isaiah 53 to make various points, we are indebted to the apostle Peter alone for his distinctive christological use of the Suffering Servant passage to interpret the significance of the suffering and death of Jesus. In a notably creative use of Old Testament material, elements of Christ's passion are interwoven with phrases and allusions from the **Old Greek** (OG) translation of Isaiah 53 that interpret aspects of his trial and suffering. As one New Testament scholar notes, Peter does not simply use Isaiah 53 as a proof text but moves beyond a "simple appeal to 'what is written' to the explanation of its *significance*" (emphasis original).[6] Quotations are indicated in boldface, allusions in italics:

2:20b: But if you suffer for doing good and you endure it, this is commendable before God.

4. For a survey discussion of the use of Isa. 53 in the New Testament, see Karen H. Jobes, "'He Bore Our Sins: Apostolic Reflections on Isaiah 53," in *Ears to Hear and Eyes to See: Biblical and Theological Essays in Memory of J. Alan Groves*, ed. Peter Enns, Douglas J. Green, and Michael Kelly (Phillipsburg, N.J.: P&R, 2010), 92–105.

5. For further discussion, see J. Ramsey Michaels, "St. Peter's Passion: The Passion Narrative in 1 Peter," *WW* 24 (2004): 387–94.

6. Morna D. Hooker, "Did the Use of Isaiah 53 to Interpret His Mission Begin with Jesus?" in *Jesus and the Suffering Servant: Isaiah 53 and Christian Origins*, ed. W. H. Bellinger and W. R. Farmer (Harrisburg, Pa.: Trinity), 93.

2:21: To this you were called, because Christ suffered for you, leaving you an example, that you should follow in his steps.

2:22: He committed no sin, and no deceit was found in his mouth (Isa. 53:9).

2:23: When they hurled their insults at him, he *did not retaliate;* when he suffered, *he made no threats* (Isa. 53:7c, d). Instead he *entrusted himself* (Isa. 53:6c, 12) *to him who judges justly* (Isa. 53:8a).

2:24: "He **himself bore our sins**" (Isa. 53:4a, 12) in his body on the cross, so that we might die to sins and live for righteousness.

"By his wounds you have been healed" (Isa. 53:6a).

2:25: For **"you were like sheep going astray"** (Isa. 53:6a), but now you have returned to the Shepherd and Overseer of your souls.

As commentators have noticed, Peter uses many of the phrases of Isaiah 53 but not in the same sequence as that passage. Instead, he seems to follow the sequence of events in the passion of Jesus, with 2:22–23 alluding to the trial and verse 24 to the crucifixion. Mark's gospel has traditionally been associated with Peter as its apostolic source, and three fundamental aspects of the passion narrative as it is found in Mark's gospel appear also in 1 Peter 2:22–25:[7]

1. Verbal abuse refers to slander by the Sanhedrin (Mark 14:65), ridicule by the Roman guards (Mark 15:16–20), and derision by the crucified thief (Mark 15:29–32).
2. Jesus accepts injustice without retaliating; in fact, he accepts it in silence (Mark 14:61; 15:5).
3. Jesus entrusts judgment to God, thereby leaving the preservation of justice to God the Father alone (Mark 14:62).

Jesus and St. Peter, detail from Jesus washing the feet of the apostle, Byzantine School, (12th century)/ Duomo, Monreale, Sicily, Italy/Giraudon/The Bridgeman Art Library

Peter's Christology of the Suffering Servant may have begun when Jesus washed Peter's feet. This 12th-century mosaic is from Sicily.

As Peter has already explained in 1:10–12, it was the Spirit of Christ who revealed to Isaiah and other prophets the sufferings of Christ and the glories that would follow, and this was done as a ministry for the generations who would look back on the Messiah's death and in their bewilderment need an explanation of its meaning. The resurrection of Jesus Christ is therefore not only a historical event but also a *hermeneutical* event that allowed a new understanding of the Old Testament. The significance of Jesus' death and resurrection is explained and interpreted by the prophecy provided by Isaiah so long before. Motivated by the need to explain how to live in the heat of society's hostility, Peter uses Isaiah 53 to focus on the way Jesus Christ responded during his own suffering. Peter picks up four phrases from Isaiah 53 and identifies them with Christ:

7. Paul J. Achtemeier, "Suffering Servant and Suffering Christ in 1 Peter," in *The Future of Christology: Essays in Honor of Leander E. Keck*, ed. A. J. Malherbe and Wayne A. Meeks (Minneapolis: Fortress, 1993), 180; Leonhard V. Goppelt, *A Commentary on 1 Peter*, trans. J. E. Alsup (Grand Rapids: Eerdmans, 1993), 211.

1. Christ, who did not commit sin and did not speak deceit (v. 22).
2. Christ, who did not retaliate when assailed with insults (v. 23).
3. Christ, who bore our sins in his body on the cross (v. 24a).
4. Christ, whose wounds heal those who accept his vicarious suffering and death (v. 24b).

These phrases from Isaiah 53 constitute the heart of 1 Peter's presentation of the significance of Jesus. First, Jesus Christ "did not commit sin, neither was deceit found in his mouth." Since this is a direct quote from the Old Testament, the Hebrew parallelism preserved in the Greek version Peter uses may suggest that the second phrase is a more specific restatement of the first, indicating that Jesus did not sin by lies and deception, even when being unjustly accused. Second, when Christ's adversaries hurled their insults at Jesus, "he did not retaliate"; when Jesus suffered, "he made no threats in return." Of all the various statements made in Isaiah 53 about the Suffering Servant, Peter chooses to emphasize the Servant's response to verbal insults and abuse as lived out by Jesus. Peter holds up this aspect of Jesus' behavior as the model whom his readers were to follow when they, too, were on the receiving end of abusive speech, ignorant talk, and the like (1 Peter 2:15; 3:9, 16; 4:14).

Peter's use of Isaiah 53 also explains why the prophecy both in the Hebrew and its Greek translation seems to shift in pronouns and syntax between the singular and plural. The Suffering Servant passage in Isaiah can be read to refer to an individual or collectively to the nation of God's people. The apostle Peter's reflections on Isaiah 53 in 1 Peter 2:24 explain that the purification envisioned by Isaiah means being separated from sins and living in righteousness. However, choosing not to sin in a society that doesn't know the meaning of the word will inevitably lead to suffering at times and to some extent. Just as it was God's will that his Servant should suffer (Isa. 53:10), Peter writes that it is God's will for Christians to follow in Jesus' footsteps and choose to suffer rather than to sin (1 Peter 3:17). In shifting between the singular and plural forms, Isaiah's prophecy envisioned both the singular suffering of the Servant and the consequential suffering for those who would follow him.

© hannahgleg/www.istockphoto.com

What would Jesus do?

A number of years ago, the acronym WWJD was very popular on Christian campuses. Young Christians even wore wrist bands intended to prompt them to ask "What would Jesus do?" as a guide to their behavior. Peter seems to be asking his readers to consider what Jesus would do if he was in their situation, because in fact Jesus had been the target of the same kind of rejection, even to the most extreme degree. What did Jesus do when he suffered insult, false accusation, and mockery? Jesus simply continued to trust God. He exercised a silence in the matter that exuded patient confidence in God's ability to vindicate him. Jesus' vindication came not by being rescued from crucifixion—the worst the world could do to him—but by something even greater, resurrection from crucifixion's death. Peter later instructs his readers about what it means to follow Jesus in 1 Peter 4:19, "So then, those who suffer according to God's will should commit themselves to their faithful Creator and continue to do good." Trust God who judges justly.

In 2:24 Peter continues to explain the significance of Jesus' undeserved capital punishment by conflating a phrase from Isaiah 53:12, "he himself bore," with a phrase from Isaiah 53:4, "our sins." Peter personalizes the quotation for the Christian community, speaking to his readers as those for whom Isaiah's suffering servant bore sin. One debate in modern New Testament theology has been between those who wish to center the significance of Jesus in his teachings as a great religious leader and those who center his significance in his crucifixion. Just so there will be no misunderstanding about specifically how Jesus Christ bore our sins, Peter adds two prepositional phrases not found in Isaiah 53, "in his body" and "on the tree," an explicit reference to the physical death of Jesus by crucifixion. Jesus' death achieved vicarious atonement for sin, and that is the heart of the gospel. But the purpose of Christ's vicarious atonement has direct implications for the lives of Peter's readers: "so that we might die to sins and live for righteousness" (2:24). Peter's understanding of Christian ethics is thoroughly grounded in the Christology of suffering and atonement.

So closely is Peter's Christology of Jesus as the Suffering Servant related to his instructions for Christian living that he presents the unjust suffering of slaves as the calling of all Christians. Jesus unjustly suffered, thereby "leaving you an example, that you should follow in his steps" (2:21). This is powerful imagery. If Christians are to live as servants of God (1 Peter 2:16), the essence of that identity is a willingness to suffer unjustly as Jesus did, exemplifying in suffering the same attitude and behavior he did. Jesus Christ left us this pattern over which we are to trace out our lives, in order that we might follow in his footsteps (2:21). (More on this in chapter 11.)

THE VICTORIOUS, VINDICATED SAVIOR (1 PETER 3:18–22)

Although Peter's Christology focuses on the suffering and death of Jesus, an equally important element is the vindication and victory of Jesus through his resurrection and ascension.

And because the pattern of Jesus' experience is the paradigm for the believer, the resurrection and ascension not only vindicate Jesus but also those who follow him. This glorious hope is the main point of 1 Peter 3:18–22, regardless of how one interprets this notoriously difficult passage.

The usually dogmatic Martin Luther admitted he struggled to understand this passage, but modern interpreters have an advantage that Martin Luther did not—the discovery of a manuscript that contains what is most likely the background of this passage, *1 Enoch*. This ancient text uses much of the same language as 1 Peter 3:18–20 and allows scholars today to make better sense of what Peter is saying about Jesus than has traditionally been understood.[8]

> "This is a strange text and certainly a more obscure passage than any other passage in the New Testament. I still do not know for sure what the apostle meant."
>
> Martin Luther, *Sermons on the First Epistle of St. Peter*

For most of the church's two-thousand-year history, the traditional understanding of this passage supported a

8. For a more extensive exegetical discussion, see Karen H. Jobes, *1 Peter*, BECNT (Grand Rapids; Baker Academic, 2005), 235–60.

An empty tomb was the first sign of Jesus' resurrection.

view that, between his crucifixion on Friday and resurrection on Sunday, Jesus in some disembodied state spent Saturday in hell, a day referred to as Holy Saturday in the Orthodox tradition. Though probably not originally intended to communicate this idea, the Apostles' Creed developed to the form we have it today, with its statement that Jesus "was crucified, died, and was buried. He descended into hell. The third day He arose again from the dead." The **extant** ancient manuscripts of the Apostles' Creed include the phrase "he was buried" *or* the phrase "he descended" (probably following the Old Testament language of "going down into **Sheol**," e.g., Gen. 37:35; Num. 16:30; 1 Sam. 2:6; Job 7:9; 21:13; Ps. 55:15). Later the two phrases—which both probably meant Christ was buried—were both included by copyists, giving the impression that the descent was something other than, and subsequent to, the burial.

The view that Christ descended into hell between his death and resurrection, sometimes referred to as the ***Decensus*** (Lat. for "descent"), was made famous by Dante in his literary masterpiece *The Inferno* and has been captured in many paintings.

Despite its long and venerable tradition in the church, the passage in 1 Peter thought to most strongly support this view does not actually mention that Jesus "descended," merely that he "went" and proclaimed. Furthermore, it does not mention hell or hades, just "imprisoned spirits." The Greek version of the Apostles' Creed states that Christ descended into *hades*, which is not a place of punishment but only the place departed spirits went, whether they were good or bad. When the Apostles' Creed was translated into English in the sixteenth century, the English word *hell* could refer to either the place of the departed spirits or the place of eternal punishment.[9] But in today's English, *hell* virtually always means a place of fiery punishment. So part of the problem, as with any ancient text that

9. Bruce M. Metzger, *Apostolic Letters of Faith, Hope, and Love: Galatians, 1 Peter, and 1 John* (Eugene, Ore.: Cascade, 2006), 54.

The Apostles' Creed

I believe in God, the Father Almighty,
the Creator of heaven and earth;

and in Jesus Christ, His only Son, our Lord:
Who was conceived of the Holy Spirit,
born of the Virgin Mary,
suffered under Pontius Pilate,
was crucified, died, and was buried.

He descended into hell.
The third day He arose again from the dead.
He ascended into heaven
and sits at the right hand of God the Father Almighty,
whence He shall come to judge the living and the dead.

I believe in the Holy Spirit,
the holy catholic church,
the communion of saints,
the forgiveness of sins,
the resurrection of the body,
and life everlasting.
Amen.

- The Apostles' Creed has a long tradition of use in the church, but it is not an official creed sanctioned by the early church councils.
- The Nicene Creed, which is an official creed of the early church, does not include the phrase "He descended into hell."
- The phrase first appeared around AD 400 in Rufinus's exposition of a Roman creed that included the phrase "He descended into hell" instead of the phrase "and was buried." It appears that at one time the phrase "to descend" was a graphic way of referring to burial or the "descent" into the grave (cf. "go down into Sheol" in the Old Testament).
- Many modern editions of the Apostles' Creed now omit the phrase "He descended into hell," since the consensus of scholarship has largely abandoned this interpretation.

has become part of liturgy, in that the meaning of the English word has changed since the creed was first formulated.

First Peter 3:19 also does not mention Christ's destination; that must be inferred from the description of it as the place in which the "spirits" of the dead are imprisoned. And then comes the problem of what Jesus proclaimed to them. Salvation? Doom? Given all the

Christ in Limbo, Previtali, Andrea/Gallerie dell'Accademia, Venice, Italy/Cameraphoto Arte Venezia/ The Bridgeman Art Library

The harrowing of hell has been the subject of many painters. Note that Adam and Eve are typically portrayed as the first to be released.

inferences that could be made in their various combinations, it is no wonder that a variety of views developed.

The church in Egypt, represented by Clement of Alexandria (c. AD 150–222), taught that Jesus descended into hell to preach the gospel and give the deceased the opportunity of postmortem conversion. He construed the "spirits" to be the souls of Noah's generation that perished in the flood as well as all Old Testament–era people, and understood the "prison" as the place that later developed into the Roman Catholic concept of purgatory. Those who objected to the idea of postmortem conversion inferred that the imprisoned spirits were the souls of the Old Testament saints awaiting the coming of Christ to the world so they could then fully participate in the salvation that he came to win. This was the interpretation most frequently portrayed in art and is usually referred to as the "**harrowing of hell**."

But this understanding seems to conflict with verse 19, which mentions that the spirits were of those who disobeyed at the time of Noah, which probably helped the development of the idea of purgatory as a place of punishment but also a place from which people

Harrowing of Hell

harrow: Old and Middle English term used in medieval literature to refer to Christ's disruption of hell, traditionally understood to be between the time of his crucifixion and resurrection. The noun *harrow* is still used to refer to a heavy farming implement with teeth or tines that is drawn over plowed ground to break up clods of earth in preparation for planting. In modern English the adjective *harrowing* refers to an experience that was very upsetting or disturbing.

could gain salvation. Origen and Cyril of Alexandria followed Clement, and this interpretation continued to enjoy popularity in the Eastern church. Even some today who argue a postmortem opportunity for conversion interpret 1 Peter 3:18–22 as suggesting that possibility, often reading 1 Peter 4:6 in the same light.

Andre Thevet

St. Augustine, Francesca, Piero della/National Museum of Ancient Art, Lisbon, Portugal/The Bridgeman Art Library

Left: Clement of Alexandria (ca. AD 150–222). *Right:* Augustine, a Latin father of the early church lived in North Africa in the late 4th to early 5th centuries.

Augustine, a Latin church father living at the turn of the fourth to fifth century in North Africa, was troubled by the idea of postmortem conversion, for Scripture clearly seems to teach that one's eternal destiny is determined in this life. He most likely was not aware of *1 Enoch*, which had disappeared from popular circulation by that time. Augustine, who could not read Greek very well and was more concerned with theological interpretation than with the syntax of the text, offered the alternate interpretation that the preincarnate Christ "went" to Noah's generation and preached repentance through Noah to those about to perish in the great flood, but who were dead at the time Peter wrote and so were "spirits in prison." This view would take its cue from Peter's statement in 1:10–12, that it was the Spirit of Christ who revealed to the Old Testament prophets the sufferings of the Messiah and the glories that would follow.

Nine Greek Words at the Heart of the Exegetical Debate

ἐν ᾧ καὶ τοῖς ἐν φυλακῇ πνεύμασιν πορευθεὶς ἐκήρυξεν (1 Peter 3:19)

1. Christ Preaches through Noah
   In his spiritual realm of existence, Christ went and preached through Noah to those who are now spirits in the prison of hell. He did this preaching through Noah's mouth when they formerly disobeyed, when the patience of God was waiting in the days of Noah while the ark was being built.
2. Christ Proclaims Victory by His Resurrection and Ascension
   In [this realm of the Spirit], Christ ascended ["went"] and, in so doing, proclaimed final defeat to the spirits in prison who were the fallen angels and who in times past disobeyed when the patience of God waited in the days of Noah while the ark was being built.
3. Christ Descends into Hell (Apostles' Creed)
   Christ's spirit descended [into hell] on Easter Saturday and preached grace to [and released] the imprisoned souls who in times past disobeyed when the patience of God waited in the days of Noah while the ark was being built.

The rediscovery of manuscripts of *1 Enoch* has recovered an important literary background that allows scholars to make better sense of this passage. While *1 Enoch* was probably never read as Scripture, it is mentioned in other ancient texts as a story that was well known in both Jewish and Christian tradition of the first and second centuries and that explained why God sent the great flood.[10] Moreover, the story explains where Enoch went when God "took him away" (Gen. 5:24) and that he was involved in proclaiming eternal doom to both the Watchers and the "spirits" whom God had locked up in the great abyss. An interpretation that many New Testament interpreters hold today is that in his resurrection and ascension (the "went" of 3:19), Christ proclaimed victory over the most powerful sources of evil—the offspring of the fallen angels ("spirits") that God imprisoned in the abyss according to *1 Enoch*. (The Greek word *kērussō* can be translated either "preach" or "proclaim"; the slightly different nuance of the English translation has tilted toward verbal proclamation in the English-speaking world, but that inference may be incorrect.)

Noah, the grandson of Enoch, provides the link connecting Peter's letter to Asia Minor with *1 Enoch*. Noah was the most famous of Old Testament people known among the pagan peoples of Asia Minor, the original destination of Peter's letter. This is primarily because the indigenous people of Asia Minor had a story about a great flood independent

10. *First Enoch* can be read in English translation in James H. Charlesworth, ed., *Old Testament Pseudepigrapha*, vol. 1, Apocalyptic Literature and Testaments (New York: Doubleday, 1983).

The "Discovery" of *1 Enoch* Manuscripts

First Enoch was well known in Jewish communities and in the Christian church at the time the New Testament was written. Jewish texts quote or refer to *1 Enoch* (*Jubilees* and the *Testament of the Twelve Patriarchs*), Jude 14–15, and early church fathers (Justin Martyr, Clement of Alexandria, Origen, Irenaeus, Tertullian, Eusebius, Jerome, Hilary, Epiphanius, and Augustine). Yet, despite its early prominence, there was a time when *1 Enoch* disappeared from the knowledge of the Western church. In the Eastern church, it was last quoted circa AD 800 by George Syncellus, a Byzantine chronicler.

In 1773 James Bruce, an English traveler in Egypt, discovered three manuscripts of *1 Enoch* written in Ethiopic, and he brought them to Europe, where they were translated into English in 1821 and into German in 1833.* Since that time, more Ethiopic manuscripts have been found that contain *1 Enoch*, most of which also include books of the Bible.†

While the only complete copies of *1 Enoch* were preserved in Ethiopic, portions of *1 Enoch* written in Aramaic were also discovered at Qumran in the mid-twentieth century. In addition, over a quarter of the text of *1 Enoch* "has been preserved in fragmentary texts of a Greek translation of the Aramaic original,"‡ and small portions of the book have been preserved in Latin.

Benjamin Ribbens

*See Emil Schürer, *The Literature of the Jewish People in the Time of Jesus*, ed. Nahum N. Glatzer (New York: Schocken, 1972), 54–55; George H. Schodde, *The Book of Enoch: Translated from the Ethiopic with Introduction and Notes* (Andover, Mass.: Draper, 1882), 1–11.

†George W. E. Nickelsburg, *1 Enoch*, Hermeneia (Minneapolis: Fortress, 2001), 16.

‡Ibid., 12.

The letter of 1 Peter, and probably also 2 Peter, was written to Christians living in the five Roman provinces in Asia Minor: Pontus, Galatia, Cappadocia, Asia, and Bithynia.

of the one told in Genesis. When Jewish colonists came to Asia Minor during the Seleucid period, they noticed the name of a town that had the Greek word for "ark" in it (Apameia *Kibotos*, modern Dinar) and assumed it to be the place where Noah's ark came to rest. At some point, Noah's name became identified with the great but anonymous Apamean flood hero, and consequently Noah became a part of the indigenous culture of Asia Minor. His fame in that region is attested by coins minted during the Roman period showing him and his wife in an ark.

Noah's fame in Asia Minor allowed Peter to allude to the tradition preserved in *1 Enoch*. Noah's story in the Bible follows after the disappearance of Enoch, who "walked faithfully with God; then he was no more, because God took him away" (Gen. 5:24). Noah's story begins with Genesis 6 and the mysterious statement that

Ancient coins recovered from Asia Minor attest to the popularity of Noah

> the sons of God saw that the daughters of humans were beautiful, and they married any of them they chose....
>
> The Nephilim were on the earth in those days—and also afterward—when the sons of God went to the daughters of humans and had children by them....
>
> The Lord saw how great the wickedness of the human race had become on the earth, and that every inclination of the thoughts of the human heart was only evil all the time." (Gen. 6:2, 4–5)

Although nothing further is said in Scripture about Enoch or the Nephilim, a large corpus of tradition developed within Judaism about them. The book of *1 Enoch* was a very popular version of Jewish tradition that brought Enoch and the Nephilim together. In

1 Enoch the "Watchers" were the fallen angels who slept with human women (*1 Enoch* 15:3) and produced children who were giants (the Nephilim), from whose bodies came "evil spirits" (*1 Enoch* 15:9) that incited the people of Noah's generation to the greatest and most depraved evil that consequently led to the great flood. And so when Peter wants to explain that Jesus Christ is victor over even the greatest evil, whether human or demonic, he alludes to the story of the great evil that preceded Noah's flood, because it would have been a cultural point of contact with readers in Asia Minor that would communicate his point well.

Over time the book of *1 Enoch* was lost to the knowledge of the church until its rediscovery in the eighteenth century. Without this literary background, interpreters in the early church began to read 1 Peter against the idea of Christ's descent, which had begun to develop independently to answer questions such as where Jesus' spirit was between his death and resurrection and how the saints who died before Christ's coming gained salvation. And that remained the dominant interpretation of the passage until the twentieth century.[11]

Because the language of the Enoch story is quite similar to this passage in 1 Peter and because the background of the Enoch story makes good sense in supporting Peter's point that Jesus has conquered even primordial evil, many New Testament interpreters today have abandoned the theories of the *Decensus* to hell and the idea that Christ preached through Noah.

But what about the traditional confession "He descended into hell" that many of us recite in church when we say the Apostles' Creed? Does it matter if Christ "descended into hell" or not? If the phrase "He descended into hell" originally conveyed the idea that Jesus "descended" into the grave, then it is redundant with the statement "He was buried" and could be edited from the creed. However, the phrase could, and perhaps should, be retained out of respect for the tradition but understood along the lines of Calvin's interpretation of 1 Peter 3:19–21. In Calvin's view, the descent to hell is a graphic image that speaks of the tortures of condemned and ruined humankind, which Christ vicariously bore in his own soul (*Institutes* 2.16.8–9). And so when the sin of the world was on Christ on the cross, he "descended" into the suffering due to sin, vicariously suffering "hell" for those he came to save.

Peter's point is clear, regardless of which of the three ways the passage has been interpreted. Christ's victory over all spiritual authorities and powers is a claim that Christianity is not a local, parochial religion but that Jesus Christ is Lord everywhere, having all authority. For Peter's original readers who were being maligned and losing status in their society, the vindication of Christ by his resurrection and ascension meant that good had, and would, triumph over even the greatest and most depraved evil.

OTHER IMAGES OF CHRIST IN 1 PETER

Other images for Christ in 1 Peter corroborate and contribute to Peter's Christology. The Suffering Servant theme is corroborated by Peter's reference to Christ as "a lamb without

11. The scholar primarily responsible was William J. Dalton, *Christ's Proclamation to the Spirits: A Study of 1 Peter 3:18–4:6* (Rome: Pontifical Biblical Institute, 1965).

blemish or defect" (1 Peter 1:19). The ongoing benefit of the resurrection is portrayed by the Living Stone imagery in 2:4–8.

Sacrificial Lamb

In 1 Peter 1:17–21, Peter writes that, just as Christians are chosen by God to enter into a covenant relationship with him (v. 1), Jesus Christ was also chosen before the creation of the world to shed the sacrificial blood that would end all sacrifice. In today's justice system, people convicted of wrongdoing are often fined or required to pay restitution to those injured or bereaved by their actions. But no amount of money can compensate for the wrongful death of a loved one due to the negligence or willful act of another. Money cannot redeem the situation or those involved. Peter similarly says that not even the most valuable things the world has to offer, its silver and gold, can redeem the evil people have done. It takes something far rarer and more valuable than silver and gold; it takes the precious blood of Christ, whom Peter describes as a lamb without blemish or defect (1:18–19).

The metaphor of Jesus as sacrificial Lamb has its roots in the Old Testament sacrificial system, which in turn had its origin in the Passover lamb slain to provide protection for God's people in Egypt when death struck down every firstborn male, both human and animal (Ex. 12:12). The recalcitrant evil of Egypt that refused to yield to a long series of plagues could be answered only with death. Yet God in his mercy wished to spare those who would by faith substitute for themselves the blood of a lamb without defect on their door (Ex. 12:5–7, 13). When Jesus appeared, he was heralded as the "Lamb of God, who takes away the sin of the world" (John 1:29, 36). The apostle Paul refers to Christ as "our Passover lamb" (1 Cor. 5:7), and the writer of Hebrews, while not referring explicitly to a lamb, does refer to the blood of Christ as the sacrifice that established the new covenant (Heb. 9:12–14; see chapter 3 on the Christology of Hebrews). John's letters understand Jesus to be "the atoning sacrifice" (1 John 2:2; 4:10) and mention three times his blood for purification from sin (1 John 1:7; 5:6, 8). The **apocalyptic** vision of the book of Revelation repeatedly portrays Jesus as the victorious Lamb who was slain. The several New Testament writers who use this metaphor attest that it was a foundational concept for understanding what Jesus' crucifixion achieved. If Jesus was not God in the flesh, his death would not have the power to atone for sin. The heart of Christian theology rests on the identity of Jesus as the perfect Son of God who had come in the flesh for just that purpose, to die as a redeeming sacrifice.

Todd Bolen/www.BiblePlaces.com

Modern Samaritans prepare a slaughtered sheep as part of the Passover ceremony on the holy mountain of Gerizim.

Peter, too, understands the suffering and death of Jesus as a redemptive act of God that redeems from evil those he came to save. In the context of Peter's letter, he uses the theological reality of the high cost of redemption from a former way of life to motivate and exhort his readers to "live out your time as foreigners here in reverent fear" (1 Peter 1:17). It was not with perishable things—though silver and gold are among the most valuable items known to humankind—that Peter's readers were redeemed, and therefore that redemption is permanent and imperishable as well. It was the "precious blood of Christ, a lamb without blemish or defect" that released them from the empty way of life of humanity left to itself. Peter explains that this redemptive plan was in God's mind even before the creation of the world! For that was when he chose Jesus Christ to be the sacrificial Lamb who would take away the sin of the world.

The Living Stone

First Peter 2:4 refers to Christ as the "living Stone," rejected by people but chosen by and precious to God. Peter's image of the Stone comes from three passages in the Old Testament—Isaiah 8:14; 28:16; and Psalm 118:22—which were interpreted within some streams of Judaism to be messianic even before Jesus came and the New Testament writers applied the image and these passages to him. In the **Synoptic Gospels** Jesus himself implies that he is that rejected Stone (Matt. 21:42; Mark 12:10–12; Luke 20:16–18), thereby identifying himself as the Messiah.

The apostle Peter also identifies Jesus as the Stone the builders rejected when he stands up to preach in Acts 4:1–12, where we find a reference to the resurrection juxtaposed with the verse from Psalm 118:22. If the Stone had been a reference to the Messiah in the

Bukvoed/Wikimedia Commons

In 1 Peter the risen Jesus is the living cornerstone of the church.

tradition of Judaism, the Living Stone reflects Peter's creative expression of a resurrected Messiah.

In the Synoptic Gospels, Simon Peter was the first to say that Jesus was the Messiah (Matt. 16:16; Mark 8:29), and it was at that moment Jesus gave him the nickname by which he is universally known today, Peter (Gk. *petros*, "rock"). Had Peter understood Jesus to mean that Peter would be the rock on which the church would be built (Matt. 16:18), his teaching about the cornerstone of the church in 1 Peter 2:4–10 would surely have at least hinted at that. As it is, Peter does not even give himself an honored place in the spiritual building of which Christ is the living cornerstone.

The image of Christ as the cornerstone in 1 Peter should be understood in reference to first-century Roman architecture and not in modern terms. Today many public buildings have a cornerstone on which is engraved the year the building was erected or some honorific inscription. Often this type of cornerstone is the last stone to be put in place when the building is dedicated for use. That is not the image first-century readers of Peter's letters would envision. In Roman architecture, the cornerstone was the very first stone to be put in place. It had to be perfectly level and perfectly square to the plan of the building, because the rest of the building would be plumbed to it. The integrity of the structure depended on laying the cornerstone well.

Centuries before Jesus came, God announced a grand building project. In Isaiah 28:16–17

> the Sovereign LORD says:
>
> "See, I lay a stone in Zion, a tested stone,
> a precious cornerstone for a sure foundation;
> the one who relies on it
> will never be stricken with panic.
> I will make justice the measuring line
> and righteousness the plumb line."

The birth, death, resurrection, and ascension of Jesus is the laying of that Stone that has been plumbed with justice and righteousness and to which, Peter says, all who come to Christ are joined (and plumbed) as they are placed into God's grand building project, a spiritual house "to be a holy priesthood offering spiritual sacrifices acceptable to God" (1 Peter 2:5).

Peter mentions other "builders" who reject this Stone for their project, disobeying the gospel message (1 Peter 2:4, 7). Therefore they trip and fall over the Living Stone. Their encounter with Christ is not a neutral thing, and their rejection of his message is not inconsequential. As one commentator has said:

> Christ is laid across the path of humanity on its course into the future. In the encounter with him each person is changed: one for salvation, another for destruction.... One cannot simply step over Jesus to go on about the daily routine and pass him by to build a future. Whoever encounters him is inescapably changed through the encounter: Either one sees and becomes a "living stone," or one stumbles as a blind person over Christ and comes to ruin, falling short, i.e., of one's Creator and Redeemer and thereby of one's destiny.[12]

12. Goppelt, *1 Peter*, 144, 146.

The sub-structure of the temple to Emperor Trajan (AD 98–117) in Pergamum in ancient Asia Minor illustrates the image of living stones in 1 Peter 2:4–5.

Those who come to Christ are built as "living stones" into God's great spiritual building, a new temple. This temple, whose foundation stone was laid in Zion, extends around the world and throughout time as people in every generation and on every continent come to Christ. God reclaims all the earth by building his temple globally. And his project is under way throughout history until Christ returns.

Peter's image presents the Living Stone and the living stones to be of the same material, communicating the truth that the Son of God took on human flesh in his incarnation, sharing in the nature of those he came to redeem. This beautiful image of Christ as the Living Stone to which believers are joined is suggestive of ideas that help Christians to understand their new identity in Christ, a goal that was apparently important to the apostle as he writes to believers in need of encouragement. This image speaks of the unity, significance, and purpose of all believers as their lives are taken up in God's redemptive plan. (More about this in chapter 11.) When the scaffolding of human history comes down, what will remain is the spiritual temple built of living stones, built on Jesus Christ, the Living Stone and foundation of God's redemptive project.

CHAPTER SUMMARY

The apostle Peter offers an understanding of Jesus that is distinct from, though complementary to, the teaching about Jesus found in other New Testament writers. The distinctive basis of Peter's Christology is in identifying Jesus as the Suffering Servant prophesied by Isaiah centuries earlier. According to Peter, the suffering of Jesus before and including his crucifixion was a sacrifice of atonement for the sin of others. The distinctive Christology of the Suffering Servant is presented within the context of exhortation to Christian living, indicating that the pattern of Jesus' life is also the pattern for the Christian's. Therefore, Christians are called to follow the footsteps of Jesus by choosing to suffer rather than to sin. Like other New Testament writers, Peter presents Jesus as the spotless sacrificial Lamb of God, chosen before the creation of the world, whose blood is the only thing valuable enough to atone for sin.

Peter extends his Christology to present the resurrected and ascended Christ as victor over all evil, even the most depraved primordial evil that led to catastrophic judgment at the time of Noah. As the Living Stone, the resurrected Jesus is the cornerstone of God's grand building project, into which believers are placed as living stones as they come to Christ.

KEY TERMS

apology/apologetics
Apostles' Creed
atonement
Christology
Decensus
1 Enoch
harrowing of hell
Isaiah 53
Living Stone
Messiah
Nephilim
Noah
passion, the
purgatory
sacrificial lamb
Suffering Servant
Watchers

QUESTIONS FOR REVIEW OR DISCUSSION

1. What is Christology? If the entire New Testament is about Jesus, how is it that different New Testament writers can teach distinctively about him?
2. What is Peter's view of the relationship between the Old Testament prophets and the gospel of Jesus Christ?
3. Explain how animal sacrifice as practiced during the time of the Old Testament is an important background for understanding Peter's teaching about Jesus.
4. Read Isaiah 52:13–53:12 in the New English Translation of the Septuagint (NETS). What language from this passage does Peter use to describe Jesus in 2:21–25?
5. Read Isaiah 8:14; 28:16; and Psalm 118:22. What points does Peter make when he uses these passages in 2:4–10?
6. State and contrast the three approaches to the difficult passage in 1 Peter 3:18–22.
7. Make a list of what the "living stone" image suggests to you about Christian identity in relation to Jesus and to other believers.

GOING FURTHER

In addition to the commentaries listed at the end of chapter 9, see the following:

Achtemeier, Paul J. "The Christology of 1 Peter: Some Reflections." Pages 140–54 in *Who Do You Say That I Am?* Edited by Mark Allan Powell and David R. Bauer. Louisville: Westminster John Knox, 1999.

Charlesworth, James, ed. *Old Testament Pseudepigrapha.* Apocalyptic Literature and Testaments. Vol. 1. New York: Doubleday, 1983.

Michaels, J. Ramsey. "St. Peter's Passion: The Passion Narrative in 1 Peter." *WW* 24 (2004): 387–94.

Oss, Douglas A. "The Interpretation of the 'Stone' Passages by Peter and Paul: A Comparative Study." *JETS* 32 (1989): 181–200.

Williams, Jocelyn. "A Case Study in Intertextuality: The Place of Isaiah in the 'Stone' Sayings of 1 Peter 2." *Reformed Theological Review* 66 (2007): 37–55.

CHAPTER 11

Foreigners and Resident Aliens

THE *IMITATIO CHRISTI* IN PETER'S ETHICS

Your Goals for This Chapter

- To reflect on what factors shape one's identity as a Christian according to 1 Peter.
- To describe how Peter's Christian readers were to reenvision themselves in relation to the expectations of the dominant society.
- To understand in what specific way Christians are to follow in the footsteps of Jesus.
- To gain insight into Peter's image of the living stones.
- To consider how moral transformation away from social norms and into God's character is the basis for faithful Christian living.

WHY THIS CHAPTER IS IMPORTANT TO YOU

Are you a Christian?[1] Do you live in this world? If so, the apostle Peter's teaching about Christian identity and lifestyle are essential for your continued growth toward spiritual maturity. Peter bases the origin of Christian identity in the new birth and the essence of Christian living in the imitation of Jesus Christ. But both of these concepts require careful understanding of what Peter meant at the time he wrote and thoughtful application to life today.

The relationships of the Christian with the society in which he or she lives and with other believers in the community of faith form the fabric of Christian living. It is by engagement with others that one's faith is tested or stretched or affirmed or weakened, depending on who is involved and in what kind of situation. I can sometimes feel very spiritual when I am alone with just me, myself, and I, but when I have to engage with colleagues having different agendas, difficult students, or neighbors hostile to my faith, that is where my mettle is tested. As society grows more post-Christian, believers face many challenging decisions about how to live faithfully. And the individualism of autonomous authority that is so highly valued in modern life creates isolation and alienation even in the church. Peter's first-century message grows increasingly relevant even at the same time it becomes more out of step with modern values, for it challenges those who follow Christ to know who they are and how to live in times like these.

CHAPTER OUTLINE

I. The Transformation of Values and Priorities in 1 Peter

II. The Christian's New Identity

III. Relationship to Pagan Society

- A. Foreigners and Resident Aliens
- B. The Foreigner's Relationship to the State
- C. Living as a Witness
- D. The Call to Suffering
- E. The Example of Christ

IV. Relationship to Other Believers

---

1. I welcome readers who do not claim the Christian faith as their own personal belief but envision that the majority of readers will probably be Christians. Presumably an unbeliever is reading this book to learn more about what Christians believe the New Testament says, and therefore this chapter is important for that purpose also.

Key Verses

1:1b: To God's elect, exiles scattered throughout the provinces of Pontus, Galatia, Cappadocia, Asia and Bithynia, . . .

1:3b: In [God's] great mercy he has given us new birth into a living hope through the resurrection of Jesus Christ from the dead, . . .

2:4–5: As you come to him, the living Stone . . . you also, like living stones, are being built into a spiritual house to be a holy priesthood, offering spiritual sacrifices acceptable to God through Jesus Christ.

2:11–12: Dear friends, I urge you, as foreigners and exiles, to abstain from sinful desires, which wage war against your soul. Live such good lives among the pagans that, though they accuse you of doing wrong, they may see your good deeds and glorify God on the day he visits us.

2:13a: Submit yourselves for the Lord's sake to every human authority: . . .

2:16–17: Live as free people, but do not use your freedom as a cover-up for evil; live as God's slaves. Show proper respect to everyone, love the family of believers, fear God, honor the emperor.

3:8–9: Finally, all of you, be like-minded, be sympathetic, love one another, be compassionate and humble. Do not repay evil with evil or insult with insult. On the contrary, repay evil with blessing, because to this you were called so that you may inherit a blessing.

4:3: For you have spent enough time in the past doing what pagans choose to do—living in debauchery, lust, drunkenness, orgies, carousing and detestable idolatry.

4:12: Dear friends, do not be surprised at the fiery ordeal that has come on you to test you, as though something strange were happening to you.

4:19: So then, those who suffer according to God's will should commit themselves to their faithful Creator and continue to do good.

5:8–9: Be alert and of sober mind. Your enemy the devil prowls around like a roaring lion looking for someone to devour. Resist him, standing firm in the faith, because you know that the family of believers throughout the world are undergoing the same kind of sufferings.

5:12: I have written to you briefly, encouraging you and testifying that this is the true grace of God. Stand fast in it.

THE TRANSFORMATION OF VALUES AND PRIORITIES IN 1 PETER

Human beings are always born into a social environment that from birth shapes and defines their identity. In turn, individuals have to learn who they are within that social context and what parameters they will accept as defining characteristics of who they are. First-century identity was rooted very much in membership in a community, where compliance with the priorities and values of that community was given great weight and brought status and honor. Modern Western society, in contrast, fosters the illusion of individualism, where growing up means deciding for oneself what priorities and values one will select from a smorgasbord of ethics and moral principles, rather than simply adopting those of a well-defined community. Societies that are still structured by community membership, such as the tribal culture of Afghanistan, are difficult for Westerners to comprehend and vice versa.

Religion is but one parameter that defines community in society, and to be an authentic Christian who follows Christ implies that there will be some difference in priorities and values compared to those of the greater society in which church and state are not only separate but growing steadily apart in worldview and moral values. Similarly, a Muslim living in a society governed by Sharia law would not be faced with the same kind of choices and decisions as a Muslim living in pluralistic America. As one recent study points out, "As members of a group interact with their non-group neighbors, they experience the painful reality of difference and estrangement" in proportion to the extent to which the group's worldview and practices clash with the dominant society.[2] The members of the group have to deal with the unpleasant feelings of alienation and difference. They may choose to reduce the difference and assimilate their society's view on especially those issues causing the pain, but this consequently diminishes their distinctive identity. Or they may choose to reduce contact with nongroup members to reduce their experience of alienation, choosing isolation instead, and consequently forfeit their influence on society. This give-and-take between maintaining a distinctive identity versus assimilating, and participating in society versus isolation, is a dynamic always in play for groups who do not share the dominant religion or worldview of their society.

> "Religion continues *to be a social force.* Religion is essentially a way of thinking and of living within a larger social context. Religious distance from the world is therefore always social distance."
>
> MIROSLAV VOLF

Christian community is defined by those who have experienced the new birth, who have chosen (and been chosen) to follow Jesus Christ as the north star of their philosophical and moral compass. The kingdom of God is the society in which Christians will ultimately find perfect congruity, but its realization awaits the end of this age. Until then, Christians in every location and at every period of time are called to live by priorities and values that will inevitably clash to some extent with the laws, governance, and social norms of any society in which they live. "Communities of those who are born anew and follow Christ live an alternative way of life within the political, ethnic, religious, and cultural institutions of the

2. J. de Waal Dryden, *Theology and Ethics in 1 Peter: Paraenetic Strategies for Christian Character Formation*, WUNT, 2nd ser., 209 (Tübingen: Mohr Siebeck, 2006), 133.

larger society,"[3] which inevitably presents the potential for painful alienation, even though the difference between the Christian community and society may vary from culture to culture. First Peter addresses issues necessary for navigating a life faithful to Christ in an unbelieving society.

Ernst Troeltsch wrote in *The Social Teaching of the Christian Churches* that the "idea" of Christianity produced at least three distinct social forms—church, sect, and mystic—in which Christians have lived out their faith.[4] And, indeed, when studying the church throughout history or observing its various forms in the world today, there are distinct and substantial differences in how various Christian communities have related and do relate to the society in which they live. Some Christians largely assimilate their culture and social norms, often with little critical thinking about whether they could defend their values and practices in the light of Scripture. At the opposite pole, many Christians have been drawn to a reclusive, separatist life, such as the great monastic movements of the medieval times. And yet again there is the vast middle, those who try to discern what it means to be "in the world" but not "of the world." All religions seem to express at least these three general approaches to life in this world.

Nouv Lat 3093 f.104 Monks taking prayers, from the 'Tres Belles Heures de Notre Dame de Duc de Berry', French School, (14th century)/ Bibliotheque Nationale, Paris, France/The Bridgeman Art Library

Some Christians have been drawn to a reclusive, separatist life, such as the great monastic movements of the medieval times.

Richard Niebuhr's classic work *Christ and Culture* identifies five stances Christian communities have taken throughout history and how these are mirrored in the various New Testament writings: Christ against culture, Christ of culture, Christ above culture, Christ and culture in paradox, and Christ the transformer of culture.[5] Such a schema is helpful for thinking through issues, but Christian communities often derail if they choose only one of these categories as the "right" way and try to define themselves accordingly. Human life is complex, and culture is complex; there are aspects of any given culture that might be affirmed by Scripture, others that will be condemned, others that can be transformed, and so on.

This means that it may be a lot of work for a Christian to think through how to live faithfully in a given social context. Much of the appeal of legalism is having a list of dos and don'ts that prescribe just how one is to live. Many people like that kind of approach because it frees them from having to constantly be evaluating and praying through decisions

3. Miroslav Volf, "Soft Difference: Theological Reflections on the Relation between Church and Culture in 1 Peter," *ExAud* 10 (1994): 20.

4. Ernst Troeltsch, *The Social Teaching of the Christian Churches*, trans. Olive Wyon, 2 vols. (London: Allen & Unwin, 1931), 2:994.

5. H. Richard Niebuhr, *Christ and Culture* (New York: Harper, 1975).

> "'Gospel' is never simply 'the good news,' not even the good news supported by a web of beliefs and practices. 'Gospel' always involves a way of living in a given social environment as a Christian community.... To ask about how the gospel relates to culture is to ask how to live as a Christian community in a particular cultural context."
>
> Miroslav Volf

and issues. And there are always those Christians whose temperament makes it appealing for them to prescribe the rules to others. But if God was calling the Christian to legalism, the New Testament probably would have been given in a very different form—a list of laws expanding on the Ten Commandments perhaps. Instead, it is a collection of letters written to specific Christian communities living in the Greco-Roman world of the first century, and each letter wrestles with different issues and problems within that social context.

Wikimedia Commons

Seneca, a Roman orator, was famous during the same period the New Testament books were being written.

Oddly, neither Troeltsch nor Niebuhr engage 1 Peter, the only book of the New Testament that directly addresses the issue of a Christian's engagement with the dominant society. This omission may or may not be intentional, but as another scholar points out, Peter's teaching refuses to conform to either Niebuhr's five neat categories or to Troeltsch's distinctions between church and sect.[6]

Considering ideas about moral living that were contemporary with the letter may enlighten the strategy that 1 Peter presents. Seneca (c. 4 BC–AD 65) was a Roman Stoic philosopher and statesman who lived at the same time as Peter and the other New Testament writers. In an interesting historical coincidence, both Seneca and the apostles Peter and Paul were executed by Nero in Rome. Seneca was no Christian, and Peter was no Stoic, but Peter's approach to faithful Christian living is better understood in light of Seneca's teaching on **paraenesis** in his *Epistulae morales*.[7] Seneca taught that one couldn't nurture the moral life by a list of instructions without grounding them in the beliefs of which they are representative (*Ep.* 95.12). In other words, legalism doesn't work, because the list of laws would be necessarily endless to address every life situation. What is needed is the ability to deduce the right decision and action for each situation and the power to do it, which necessarily depends on the beliefs from which one reasons. But false beliefs that are not molded by virtue obstruct moral development and render moral instruction ineffective. False beliefs must be checked by sound doctrine and molded by virtue (*Ep.* 95.34, 38).

6. Volf, "Soft Difference," 15–16.
7. This discussion of Seneca draws heavily from Dryden, *Theology and Ethics*, 58–61.

To live morally, as Seneca saw it, one must value things properly, and that can be skewed because people are controlled by what they admire or fear the most. In other words, a young person might emulate the behavior or looks of a celebrity they admire; or they might conform to the demands of a father they fear. So to value the things in life properly, and consequently to live morally, one needs a system of values that touches on all possible objects of admiration or fear, such as people, ideas, or possessions. For moral instruction to be effective, it must be grounded in "a universal map of fact and value—a worldview."[8] This suggests, "What is needed is an all-encompassing picture of reality that is able to relate the teleological place and ontological value of all things."[9] This is what Peter provides in his letter.

None of the New Testament writers give their Christian readers simple lists of dos and don'ts, but instead describe a moral universe and vision based in God's creation and redemption of his creation. Specifically, the incarnation of the Son of God as a human being generates a story that provides the "teleological place and ontological value of all things." The Christian's self-identity must be transformed by an understanding of their place in the narrative of God's redemptive plan: creation ("God created me"), fall ("I am a sinner accountable to God"), redemption ("Jesus saves me"), and consummation ("I will live forever after death in God's kingdom"). To become a Christian, being born anew, is to enter into something much larger than one's own individual life, giving one's life a significance that transforms values and priorities. "This new identity is rooted in a story—the metanarrative of God's saving actions," which takes those who once were not a people and transforms them now into God's people (1 Peter 2:10).[10] The imagery of the living stones being built into a spiritual house (1 Peter 2:4–5) is a powerful metaphor to encourage beleaguered believers to hope and courage, showing that they are not alone as individuals in their faith or in their suffering.

Within that metanarrative of Scripture, Peter tells the story of Jesus' suffering as an example of how to make daily choices of conduct that are honorable and commensurate with the grand story. The honorable conduct that Peter prescribes as normative for Christian living consists of four distinctives:[11]

8. Ibid., 60.
9. Ibid.
10. Ibid., 126.
11. John H. Elliott, *Conflict, Community, and Honor: 1 Peter in Social-Scientific Perspective*, Cascade Companions (Eugene, Ore.: Cascade, 2007), 73.

The Metanarrative of 1 Peter*

Peter assumes a narrative of redemption that spans human history.

Primordial Time	Time of Ignorance/ Emptiness	First Revelation of Jesus	Liberation from Sin	Time of Alien Life	Second Revelation of Jesus Christ

*Adapted from Joel B. Green, "Narrating the Gospel in 1 and 2 Peter," *Interpretation* 60 (2000): 269.

1. Honorable conduct is not based on public opinion but on the will of God.
2. Jesus is the example and enabler of such conduct.
3. Honorable conduct has a winsome effect as an evangelistic witness.
4. Honorable conduct may include suffering, which need not be a cause for shame.

As one scholar has said, "The metanarrative provides a context for moral instruction and transformation. The *telos* [i.e, the end goal] of the narrative worldview defines the *telos* for the individual."[12] Therefore, the story of redemption as revealed by Jesus Christ gives a context for Peter's ethical teaching and also imparts "a system of values and priorities that encourages the process of moral transformation."[13] The worldview that Peter represents "serves as a map of value for all reality" that he wishes his readers to adopt as a comprehensive system of values that will guide their conduct and reform their moral decisions. He wants his readers to be what they are so that they might live in right relationship to God (1 Peter 1:17) and might live honorably in their society (2:12).

THE CHRISTIAN'S NEW IDENTITY

There is arguably a no more sweeping concept for transforming self-identity than that of new birth. To have a new birth is to be a new person with a new life stretching out ahead. What characteristics that define your identity did you get from your parents? For starters, you almost certainly got your name and the native language you speak. Then there's the passport you carry identifying your citizenship. Your ethnicity and race, your physical characteristics, aspects of your personality, and your initial socioeconomic standing all came from your parents. Your religious affiliation (or the lack of one) was initially your parents' decision for you. We owe much of who we are to our parents, whether for weal or woe.

The New Testament writers use the concept of the new birth to describe what happens when a person comes to faith in Jesus Christ, being given new birth by the God and Father of the Lord Jesus Christ (1 Peter 1:3). The new birth defines a new reality for the believer that touches every aspect of one's life every day of one's life. Christianity is not simply a religion that can be added to one's activities, like a hobby or an academic degree. The New Testament teaches that being a Christian doesn't just mean adding church attendance on Sunday to our busy schedules. According to Peter, *every* part of who we are is transformed by the new birth, because as Christians we have a new identity and a new life. Because this new life is made possible through the resurrection of Jesus Christ from the dead, it is a life free from the constraints of those we inherited from our parents, like mortality, for instance. Faith in God's Son is a spiritual rebirth of an identity that will last for eternity, an identity that transforms the believer to look a lot like Jesus. The new birth brings us a "living hope" that underlies all that we are and do (1 Peter 1:3). If this is the case, "Which beliefs and practices of the culture that is ours must we reject now that our self has been reconstituted by new birth? Which can we retain? What must we reshape to reflect better the values of God's new creation?"[14]

12. Dryden, *Theology and Ethics*, 83.
13. Ibid., 84.
14. Volf, "Soft Difference," 19.

But the new birth isn't an individualistic experience, just God and me, as many spiritual Westerners would like it. The new birth is certainly personal and is, therefore, individual in that sense, just as one's physical birth was personal and individual. But just as physical birth brought you into a family who lived in a nation, Christian rebirth is also into a people, a family, a new nation. Christians are born again into a new people (the people of God), into a new family (the family of God), and they carry a new passport, so to speak, identifying them as citizens in the kingdom of God. And so the Christian does not have to invent new values and priorities, for the Christian culture that believers enter through the new birth has its values and priorities defined by Scripture and practiced through centuries of Christian living in various societies around the globe.

Anke van Wyk/www.BigStockPhoto.com

The Christian "family" circles the globe.

But since believers aren't immediately swept up to heaven upon their conversion, their new identity with its values and priorities has to coexist with the values and priorities of their birth family and the society in which they live out the rest of life. We don't stop being our mother's child when we are born again or stop being an American when we come to Christ. This dual identity presents ample opportunity for conflicting values and priorities about how to live. This is where Peter offers instruction.

Peter was writing to people who were suffering "grief in all kinds of trials" because they had been born again into God's people through their faith in Jesus Christ (1 Peter 1:6). They were being misunderstood, insulted, and verbally abused because of their Christian faith. And apparently the believers to whom Peter wrote thought this was a strange and abnormal situation (1 Peter 4:12). Peter spends most of his letter explaining how they need to reorient their self-understanding to their new lives in Christ. Because of who they are in Christ, their relationships with family, friends, coworkers, and society at large are different. Their new identity has changed everything.

"Christians are the insiders who have diverted from their culture by being born again."

Miroslav Volf

You have no doubt heard that old proverb "Like father, like son." In the natural order of things, a child is expected to bear a certain resemblance to his or her parent. Because God is the Christian's Father, he too expects to see a family resemblance. Peter writes, "But just as he who called you is holy, so be holy in all you do; for it is written: 'Be holy, because I am holy' " (1 Peter 1:15). That might be exasperating if you think it means that a Christian is to be as morally pure and perfect as God himself. But God expects not *divine* holiness of his children, but *human* holiness, and he sent his Son into the human race to exemplify what that holiness looks like. And so based on the new reality of their new birth with God as their Father, Peter holds up Jesus Christ, God's Son, as the one who has left us an example to follow (1 Peter 2:21).

It is just here, in this call to holiness, that the values and practices of the Christian who follows Jesus Christ will sharply differ from those of a society that by and large rejects Christ and believes in the autonomy of the individual as the highest spiritual authority. As New Testament scholar Joel Green observes:

> Today the language and practices of holiness suffer a debilitating anemia. This is especially true when it comes to any sense of community-based holiness—to the holiness of a people in contrast to personal piety, and to the holiness of God's people in the public realm.
>
> ... Basic to our notions and experience of authentic personhood are self-autonomy and self-legislation. If we have found it increasingly difficult to welcome or even contemplate an authority external to ourselves (our own conscience, our own experience, our own desires), if "growing up" is tied to achieving independence and autonomy, then we may not be surprised to discover that we hear so little of the holiness of God's people. The church may not be "of the world," but on these matters its contemporary views and practices have very much been shaped on the potter's wheel of the modern world.[15]

In this respect, the modern world in which we live is quite similar to the world in which Peter wrote. The people who read Peter's letter today are living in vastly different cultures and aren't facing exactly the same problems and trials as Peter's original readers. Nevertheless, all Christians everywhere at all times need to understand their new identity in Christ and how that will inevitably affect how others view them. In some places Christians live with hostility from their society that equals that of first-century Roman society and worse. In other places where Christianity is more the cultural norm, Christian identity faces different kinds of challenges. But all Christians at all times need to understand the basic principles that Peter teaches in this brief letter, for,

> Peter presents us with a paradox. He sets side-by-side two competing versions of the same reality, with our experience of the world portrayed as both the worst of times (ostracism, life on the margins, rejection) and the best of times (new birth, living hope, our lives as a journey of joy and faithfulness). Competing interpretations of the same situation rest on different perspectives from which to observe and make sense, and Peter wants his readers, us, to read our contemporary lives from within the perspective of the scriptural story of God and the life of Jesus. If we do, then we see that this lived reality, however perplexing and painful it may be, is deeply rooted in God's saving purpose.[16]

One of Peter's important points is that his Christian readers understand that the alienation and estrangement they feel, the suffering they experience for being a Christian, is part of the new reality into which they have been reborn and "deeply rooted in God's saving purpose." Rather than assimilate their Christian values and priorities to those of Greco-Roman society, Peter wants his readers to understand their identity in Christ, to embrace the values and priorities that define human holiness, and to stand fast in them even if and when suffering results.

The new birth consequently creates social distance. Volf describes this distance as:[17]

---

15. Joel B. Green, "Living as Exiles: The Church in the Diaspora in 1 Peter," in *Holiness and Ecclesiology in the New Testament*, ed. Kent E. Brower and Andy Johnson (Grand Rapids: Eerdmans, 2007), 311, 312.

16. Ibid., 313.

17. Volf, "Soft Difference," 18.

1. Distance from one's old way of life, inherited from one's ancestors (1 Peter 1:18) and transmitted by the culture at large—a way of life characterized by the lack of knowledge of God and by misguided desires (1 Peter 1:14). Peter does not rail at society or stir his readers to become social and political activists. He exhorts Christians to create distance from how they used to live (1 Peter 4:3) and identifies the struggle of Christians to be with their own inner desires (1 Peter 2:11).
2. Distance from the transitory nature of the present world, in which all human efforts ultimately end in death. The new birth is into a living hope that survives death. Because death was not the end for Jesus, so it shall not be for those who follow him. This creates a theological and philosophical difference between the Christian and the cynic or the existential nihilist, reorienting the Christian's priorities and values. As the old proverb says, "Only one life, will soon be past; only what's done for Christ will last."
3. Eschatological distance, for Christians are given a new home that comes from God's future in the midst of the world in which they live. The journey to this new home that commences with the new birth is realized by living toward that future, by appropriating that eschatological reality as one makes decisions in daily life reflecting God's values and priorities. What we believe about the future determines how we live today.

Unlike, for instance, the Essenes, whose religious convictions led them to isolate themselves in a community geographically distant from population centers, Peter does not encourage his readers to separatism but to engagement with their society. Their separation from the social norms is to be an internal barrier enabling good behavior in the midst of the **Gentiles**. This means (1) that they must maintain their moral distinctiveness while still living in close proximity to the pagan world, and (2) that their lives are on display before a watching world.[18] These emphases are found in Peter's teaching of the moral vision of the gospel and in his concern that his readers live a winsome witness for the gospel in their society. Furthermore, "Christian life in a social context demands holy conduct, reverent fear, duty to society, to others, and especially to fellow believers (1:15–16; 2:11–17), demands that invariably involve insiders and outsiders."[19]

"Only one life, will soon be past; only what's done for Christ will last."

UNKNOWN

RELATIONSHIP TO PAGAN SOCIETY

Peter's primary concern with respect to the pagan society in which his readers live, was that Christians conduct themselves honorably, even though the propensity of that society was hostility to the Christian message (1 Peter 2:12). Not only was Peter's concern for honorable conduct a largely apologetic and evangelistic concern, but it was also intended to fend off mistreatment of the Christian community (1 Peter 3:13). Peter was writing to people who

18. Dryden, *Theology and Ethics*, 131.
19. Earl Richard, "Honorable Conduct among the Gentiles—A Study of the Social Thought of 1 Peter," *WW* 24 (2004): 416–17.

were scattered over a wide geographical area and were no doubt facing different situations and problems. Because of the variety of personalities and temperaments of human nature, there may have been very different opinions among Christians about how to respond to those situations and problems. Peter provides a conceptual framework within which Christians could understand themselves as they navigated the troubled waters of living within a pagan society. His foundational image for Christians in society is as the foreigner and resident alien (1 Peter 1:1; 2:11), and from that identity he teaches about relationship with the governing authorities and living as a witness to unbelievers.

Foreigners and Resident Aliens

What is it like to be a foreigner? Think of a time when perhaps you were vacationing or living abroad. What made you feel different from the people around you? Language? The way you dressed? Certain customs and mannerisms, perhaps how people greeted one another? The food? I can remember crossing from Sweden into Norway on July 4 one year, feeling rather homesick for the parades and fireworks that were a part of my traditional celebrations. Of course, it was not a holiday in Scandinavia. The immigration officer at the border stamped my passport and with a broad smile said, "It's a big day in America today, isn't it?" I so much appreciated that offhanded remark. Although I was obviously a foreigner, his gesture was empathetic and welcoming.

Peter uses the Greek words *parepidēmoi* and *paroikoi* to describe his readers in 1:1 and 2:11. The first, *parepidēmoi*, means "foreigner," someone who is not a citizen of his or her current location and who consequently lacks the rights, responsibilities, and privileges of those who are. The second term, *paroikoi*, is a little more specific, referring to those who have taken up residence in a land not their own, and is often translated "resident alien." To be a foreigner or resident alien is to be in a somewhat precarious state politically and legally, as those not holding Roman citizenship experienced in the first century.

> "The word *paroikos* ('resident alien') in the Greek and Roman world was a technical term with specific legal and social implications. It designated those whose legal, economic, and social rights were limited because they were foreigners."
>
> John H. Elliott, *Conflict, Community, and Honor*

Both terms are found elsewhere in Scripture. Hebrews 11:13 speaks of God's people as those who were faithful to the end of their lives but nevertheless only saw the promises of God at a distance because they were foreigners (*parepidēmoi*) on earth. The ancient Greek version of Genesis 23:4 describes Abraham as a resident alien (*paroikoi*) and foreigner (*parepidēmoi*) while living among the Hittites. In the Greek Psalm 38:13 (39:12 in the Heb. and Eng.), the psalmist refers to himself as a foreigner (*parepidēmoi*) and resident alien (*paroikoi*) in relation to God.

It is a powerful concept that can be seen even where those particular words are not used. When Adam and Eve were expelled from Eden, they became foreigners in this world by their own doing (Gen. 3:24). Abraham, the father of God's people, was called to leave his home and to live out his life as a foreigner (Gen. 12:1). His descendants who lived in

Egypt had the same experience (Lev. 19:34). Even when God established his people in the land that he had promised, they were supposed to be different from the surrounding pagan nations in their religion, values, and practices. Abraham's further descendants sojourned in Babylon because of the failure to maintain that difference, and at the time Peter wrote, the Jewish people were familiar with the tension of needing to maintain a distinct identity while living within the demands of Greco-Roman life in **diaspora** and Roman occupation of the homeland.

Peter joins his readers' identity to this long heritage of God's people in the world. Once they were not a people, but now they are the people of God (1 Peter 2:10). "Indeed for Peter, 'the language and hence the reality of Israel pass without remainder into the language and hence the reality of the new people of God.'"[20] However, "the Israel into whose history Peter writes his audience is *Israel as interpreted* by the suffering, death, resurrection, ascension, and pending revelation of Jesus Christ."[21] Consequently, Peter uses the terms *parepidēmoi* and *paroikoi* in reference to the society in which his readers are living, to distance them from the hold that their society may have over them as they re-form their self-identity as people of God.

> "We live in strange times.
> Or the times we live in make
> strangers out of folks like me.
> I'm not sure which."
>
> Stan Gaede,
> *When Tolerance Is No Virtue*

Regardless of whether Peter's original readers were actual exiles living in a far-flung Roman colony in Asia Minor, Peter's point is that, because they have been chosen by God

---

20. Green, "Living as Exiles," 318, quoting Paul J. Achtemeier, *1 Peter: A Commentary on First Peter*, Hermeneia (Minneapolis: Fortress, 1996), 69.
21. Ibid., 316 (emphasis original).

Kim Walton

Races and gladiator fights were a popular form of entertainment and sport in the Roman period.

to be his people, his holy nation, spiritual rebirth with its consequential new identity has made them foreigners wherever they were living. The Christian as foreigner and resident alien implies "a 'clear distance in relation to society, a distance from its values and ideals, from its institutions and politics.'"[22]

Peter exhorts his readers to understand themselves as foreigners and alien residents and to interpret their experiences with family, friends, and neighbors through that grid. To be a foreigner often means to be misunderstood, scrutinized, and suspected, thereby exacerbating the sense of alienation. Foreigners can be unwelcome, and hostility might be covert or explicit. Christians were a suspect minority in the Roman world. The Roman writer Suetonius refers to Christians as a separate class (Lat. *genus*) of people given to a new and mischievous superstition (*Nero* 16). Because Christians lived by values counter to those of Roman society, they were accused of being antisocial "haters of mankind." They were perceived to repudiate pleasures (e.g., theater, races, gladiatorial fights), to break up homes and family ties (when one member of a family became Christian and others did not), to ruin businesses (perhaps by refusing to participate in dishonest gain), to abandon pagan religious ritual, and to avoid civic duties, all of which jeopardized the empire's standing with the gods. Perceptions like these led to attitudes and practices by Roman society that alienated Christians from the people of the empire. The Christian faith of Peter's readers evidently did nothing to enhance their social status and power when family, neighbors, and coworkers became aware of it. In fact, their faith in Christ was making them suspect in the eyes of their neighbors, and they were being accused of doing wrong (1 Peter 2:12). Apparently Peter's readers in northern Asia Minor were being insulted and mistreated. In 1 Peter 3:16 Peter mentions those who have spoken "maliciously against" his readers' good behavior in Christ. First Peter 4:4 tells us that those outside the faith were "heaping abuse on" them.

"The accusation 'You do not belong' holds little surprise for persons who know already that their true homeland is elsewhere. And the loss of honor among men and women loses its sting when this loss is parried by the reception of honor from God."[23] This is why Peter can say, "Dear friends, do not be surprised at the fiery ordeal that has come on you to test you, as though something strange were happening to you" (1 Peter 4:12). After all, in his incarnation, Jesus became the true resident alien. He came to that which was his own, but his own did not receive him (John 1:11). "He was a stranger to the world because the world into which he came was estranged from God. And so it is with his followers."[24] There is an innate and reciprocal foreignness and estrangement between Christians and the world that is the normal state of affairs for those redeemed from a fallen world.

By reassuring them that their unpleasant experiences are actually to be expected, and by reminding them that their honor and dignity are based on God's acceptance of them even while their society rejects them, Peter establishes the foundational principles that will transform their self-identity and allow them to make faithful decisions about how to live.

---

22. Volf, "Soft Difference," 17, quoting Richard Feldmeier, *Die Christen als Fremde: Die Metaphor der Fremde in der antiken Welt, im Urchristentum und im 1. Petrusbrief*, WUNT 64 (Tübingen: Mohr, 1992), 22.
23. Green, "Living as Exiles," 319.
24. Volf, "Soft Difference," 17.

By admonishing them to embrace their identity as "aliens and strangers," Peter constructs a "social barrier between the covenant community and the outside world."[25] The purpose of that barrier is not to isolate Christians from their society or to incite mutual animosity against society; it is to allow Christians to re-form their priorities, values, practices, and customs based on the principles of God's kingdom and not Caesar's, on the demands of the gospel of Jesus Christ and not those of a pagan lifestyle.

"Christians ... must exercise discernment as they sit loosely in relation to the institutions and ways of life that are respected and regarded as 'at home' in this world. And they must work out the terms of faithfulness according to the values and commitments determined by the age to come."[26]

When sociologists speak of the way minority groups maintain identity within a dominant society, they often speak in terms of the three A's: **assimilation** (the degree of social integration, including social interaction and practices), **acculturation** (the degree of linguistic, educational, and ideological achievement), and **accommodation** (whether to embrace or resist the surrounding culture).[27] Peter's letter subverts this approach to a large extent by showing that even those things that Christians do that look like assimilation and accommodation are done from a completely different motive and value system. Peter does not suggest that his readers pick and choose from their society certain activities or practices or beliefs that are consistent with Christianity; he puts the Christian's life choices on a completely different plane: to follow the footsteps of Jesus in obedience to God, even when it hurts. And so when Peter says, "honor the emperor" (1 Peter 2:17), it isn't to be a good Roman, but "for the Lord's sake" (1 Peter 2:13). When Peter's teaching for members of a household look surprisingly like that of the Greek moral philosophers, he isn't drawing from the Greek identity or capitulating to cultural norms; he is explaining how to live in God's grace within that social system (1 Peter 2:18–20; 3:1, 7). The Christian lives from values and priorities that are completely different from those of a society that rejects God, even when the Christian participates in society's structures and roles.

It is for this reason that Peter's message is so challenging to the believer, for it demands that every action and decision be motivated and justified by the values and priorities exemplified by Christ. "Dear friends, I urge you, as foreigners and exiles, to abstain from sinful desires, which war against your soul" (1 Peter 2:11). Christians are not at war with society but with the sinful desires within themselves. When those desires are acted upon with the approval and complicity of unbelieving society, it is an assimilation of culture that is at its root sin and a threat to Christian identity.[28]

The Foreigner's Relationship to the State

Christians may be foreigners and resident aliens, but "in the meantime [until Christ returns], however, they are citizens or wards of the Roman Empire (*paroikoi*) and owe corresponding

25. Dryden, *Theology and Ethics*, 131.

26. Green, "Living as Exiles," 320.

27. Ibid., 315, citing John M. G. Barclay, *Jews in the Mediterranean Diaspora: from Alexander to Trajan (323 BCE to 117 CE)* (Berkeley: University of California Press, 1996), 92–102.

28. For one analysis of this issue, which, however, does not refer to 1 Peter, see Stanley Hauerwas and William H. Willimon, *Resident Aliens: Life in the Christian Colony* (Nashville: Abingdon, 1989).

honor to officials and have their share of political and social duties."[29] While Peter recognizes that his readers then, as now, have responsibilities as residents of geopolitical states to the government and civic structures of their society, he grounds the Christian's relationship to the state in relationship to the Lord: "Submit yourselves *for the Lord's sake* to every human authority: whether to the emperor, *as the supreme authority*, or to governors" who represent his authority (1 Peter 2:13, emphasis added). Peter could recognize "the supreme authority" of the government under which his readers lived without diminishing the Lord's ultimate authority. Christianity, in Peter's view, is countercultural; but it is not incendiary. The Christians of Peter's day participated in civic duties, not to be good residents of the empire, but to be obedient to the Lord as winsome witnesses for Christ. This was the defining principle of the relationship of the Christian to the state. From that, Peter teaches that his readers should "honor the emperor" (1 Peter 2:17), bringing to mind Jesus' teaching that one should give to Caesar what is Caesar's and to God what is God's (Matt. 22:21; Mark 12:17; Luke 20:25).

Wikimedia Commons

Roman Emperor Nero, during whose reign Peter may have written his letters.

Even though Peter is writing into a situation that is unpleasant for his readers, he can apparently assume that, if they live as good residents, the ruling authorities will look with favor upon them, or at least not unduly trouble them. It is difficult to imagine such an irenic attitude during the time of Nero's horrific persecution of the church in Rome or anytime after Christians began being martyred by state-sponsored persecution, such as reflected in the book of Revelation where the emperor is portrayed as a demonic beast. This letter seems to have been written at a time when Peter could hope to maintain good relations with the state, evidence of an earlier rather than later date for his writing.

But it is probably no coincidence that immediately after exhorting his readers to honor the emperor, Peter begins his discussion of the role of suffering in the Christian's life. This shows that Peter was not compromising or accommodating Roman culture and realized that there comes a time when Christians out of obedience to God would not be able to honor the demands of the emperor and would suffer for it. Still, citizenship in the kingdom of God did not give one the freedom to thumb one's nose at the Roman authorities; to the contrary, Peter wanted Christians to silence any accusations against them by being sure those accusations were unfounded. Peter instructed his readers to "live such good lives among the pagans that, though they accuse you of doing wrong, they may see your good deeds and glorify God on the day he visits us" (1 Peter 2:12).

Living as a Witness

Peter describes the world of the unbeliever in 1 Peter 4:3 as the world in which his readers once lived, "For you have spent enough time in the past doing what pagans choose to do—living in debauchery, lust, drunkenness, orgies, carousing and detestable idolatry." And because his readers are no longer living in that way, they have caught the attention

29. Richard, "Honorable Conduct among the Gentiles," 420.

of friends and neighbors who criticize and malign them. "They are surprised that you do not join them in their reckless, wild living, and they heap abuse on you" (4:4). Debauchery refers to excessive indulgence in pleasures, such as gluttony and sex, and increasingly characterizes modern Western society just as it did the Greco-Roman social scene. And yet as Volf observes:

> We get no sense from 1 Peter, however, that the church should strive to regulate all domains of social life and reshape society in the image of the heavenly Jerusalem.... The Petrine community ... did not wish to impose itself or the kingdom of God on the world, but to live in faithfulness to God and to the values of God's kingdom, inviting others to do the same.... The community did not seek to exert social or political pressure, but to give public witness to a new way of life.[30]

The Christians to whom Peter originally wrote were living in a dictatorship, not a democracy. Social change was discouraged by the elite few at the top of the social order who held the power, for reasons of self-interest. Christians today, who live in democratic societies where change can be effected through the vote or through appropriate legal channels, should use those means to express their support of justice and social policy that honors God's principles and values. Of course, even among Christians with equally high views of the authority of Scripture there can be much debate on most issues about what is a God-honoring position, making it difficult to achieve Christian values in public policy.

Peter expects a negative reaction from unbelievers when Christians express different priorities and values by conducting themselves differently than the social norm, but it's interesting that he also sees an overlap between Greco-Roman and Christian values. We see this when he teaches that outwardly visible good deeds will cause non-Christians to see the truth and convert to Christianity (2:12, 15; 3:1, 16). There is probably within every human culture some values and ideals that are consistent with biblical principles. This is, first, because of God's common grace and, for modern Western societies, because of the long influence of the Judeo-Christian ethic. Attending church on Sunday is not something the majority of Americans do, but it does not generally cause hostility, because it is an understandable value given America's religious history. Attending that same worship service in a Muslim or Buddhist culture, however, would deviate more from the socially acceptable norm.

> "To make a difference, one must be different."
>
> Miroslav Volf

Even though debauchery and lust were acceptable in Greco-Roman society, such behavior was not the ideal of the Greek philosophers. Most societies have ideals that are honored more as abstractions than as practices, so that there is often considerable distance between society's ideals and its norms of practice. In the first-century Greco-Roman world, Seneca admonished philosophers to live up to the ideals of society by living above its norms, living by a higher standard of life, not a contrary standard.[31] Greek moral philosophy rejected the sensual indulgences of its society and exhorted people to live virtuously. Peter explained that his readers could win respect by living up to those recognizably high

---

30. Volf, "Soft Difference," 20.
31. Dryden, *Theology and Ethics*, 139.

standards of virtue in Greco-Roman society that were consistent with the spiritual virtues of the gospel. This does not mean that Seneca and Peter believed the same things or held the same philosophy. It doesn't mean that the apostle Peter had capitulated to a pagan system of belief. Peter's teaching was deeply rooted in obedience to God that transformed human conduct, not in a loyalty to Greek moral philosophy. Where the resulting conduct was favorable in comparison to society's highest ideals, so much the better for Christian witness. But as Peter showed in the household codes, the gospel is yeast that subverts social norms and ideals as well. For, as Volf observes:

> The call to follow the crucified Messiah was, in the long run, much more effective in changing the unjust political, economic, and familial structures than direct exhortations to revolutionize them would ever have been. For an allegiance to the crucified Messiah—indeed, worship of a crucified God—is an eminently political act that subverts a politics of dominion at its very core.[32]

The household codes. Peter both accommodates and subverts the existing social structures of the Roman world. Neither he nor the other New Testament writers mount a frontal attack on the social structures of the time, such as slavery. But as Christians lived out their calling in obedience to God, even within unjust social structures, they were subverting the status quo and opening the way for a new way of thinking.[33]

One part of the household code in 1 Peter 3:1–6 is notorious for admonishing wives to "submit" to their husbands and has become the target of critique when the passage is misinterpreted to hold women in situations of domestic abuse.[34] Part of the misinterpretation rests on the English word "submit" as a translation for *hypotassō*, which, in the context of "submitting for the Lord's sake to every human authority" (1 Peter 2:13), might be best understood as recognizing one's position and duty with respect to that authority. In the Greco-Roman household, that human authority was the male head of the household, who was the master of the slaves and had control over his wife and children. So important was order in the household in Greco-Roman society that instructions not unlike the New Testament household codes can be found in Plato's *Republic* (384–70 BC), Xenophon's *Oeconomicus* (c. 430–355 BC), Aristotle's *Oeconomica* (384–322 BC), Plutarch's *Advice to Bride and Groom* (c. AD 46–120), Seneca's *Epistulae Morales* (c. 4 BC–AD 65), and Dio Chrysostom's *On Household Management* (AD 40–c. 112). Although these writers had various views on how slaves and women should be treated, all shared a common belief

---

32. Volf, "Soft Difference," 23.

33. Two Petrine scholars, John H. Elliot and David L. Balch, represent two polarities in the debate whether the household codes reflected an attempt to protect Christian identity, emphasizing difference with the culture (J. H. Elliott) or acculturation by upholding social expectations (D. L. Balch). While drawing such sharp distinctions can be helpful for highlighting the contours of a debate, Peter's code does both. For an insightful critique of the Elliott-Balch false alternatives, see Volf, "Soft Difference," 22. See further David G. Horrell, "Between Conformity and Resistance: Beyond the Balch-Elliott Debate towards a Postcolonial Reading of First Peter," in *Reading First Peter with New Eyes: Methodological Reassessments of the Letter of First Peter*, ed. Robert L. Webb and Betsy Bauman-Martin, Library of New Testament Studies 364 (London: T&T Clark, 2007), 111–43.

34. E.g., see Steven Tracy, "Domestic Violence in the Church and Redemptive Suffering in 1 Peter," *CTJ* 41 (2006): 279–96. For a different voice, see Betsy Bauman-Martin, "Women on the Edge: New Perspectives on Women in the Petrine *Haustafel*," *JBL* 123 (2004): 253–79.

> **Aristotle on Order in the Household**
>
> "And now that it is clear what are the component parts of the state, we have first of all to discuss household management; for every state is composed of households. Household management falls into ... the parts of which [it] is composed; ... and the smallest parts of the household are *master and slave, husband and wife, father and children*."
>
> Aristotle, *Politics*, 1253a.37 (emphasis added)

that order in the household, which they believed to be divinely ordained, was the constituent basis for a strong, orderly, and prosperous society. Because prosperity and well-being were seen as dependent on religious forces, disorder in the home was a threat not only to the family but to society. While there were various opinions as to what should characterize the relationship between these pairs of relationships, every ethical system and religion was expected to take a position on order in the household. For centuries the Greek writers discussed order in the household under the categories of master/slave, husband/wife, and father/children.

As the apostles Paul and Peter led the infant Christian church, it is not surprising that both included instructions for Christians living in the household using the same categories when writing to audiences steeped in Greco-Roman culture. The motivation to respond to and correct pagan Greek ideas is clear, since there are no household codes in the Old Testament or in Jewish writings until Judaism engaged the Greek worldview, as exemplified in the works of Josephus and Philo. Even though neither Peter nor Paul simply taught what the Greek writers taught, it was important for the Christian church to have a position on household order. When writing to destinations holding a Greco-Roman worldview, both apostles gave instructions on how Christians who have realigned their sociopolitical loyalties with the kingdom of God are nevertheless to live responsibly in society.

Christians were frequently blamed as the cause of public calamity because they had introduced a new god, upsetting the religious status quo of the empire. For this reason, the apostles sought to strike a balance between upholding social expectations, so as not to bring unnecessary criticism to the church, and on the other hand, giving godly teaching about household relationships that had been transformed by the gospel of Jesus Christ.

While using the same form and even upholding the status quo to some extent, Peter nevertheless subverts the social order as he addresses slaves, wives, and husbands. As discussed in chapter 9, Peter directly addresses both the slave and the wife as moral agents, something not found in the pagan writers. A second difference is found where Peter applies the adjective "unjust" in reference to the treatment of slaves, implying an unprecedented status for the slave, to whom, according to Aristotle, no true injustice could be done. Furthermore, Peter does not talk about the husband "controlling" or "governing" the wife, as for instance, Plutarch does:

> And control ought to be exercised by the man over the woman, not as the owner has control of a piece of property, but, as the soul controls the body, by entering into her

feelings and being knit to her.... It is possible to govern a wife, and at the same time to delight and gratify her. (*Advice to Bride and Groom* 142. 33)

Instead, Peter instructs the husband, "in the same way" as the slave and wife, to live considerately with his female, treating her with respect, albeit as the "weaker partner" but also as a fellow heir of life (1 Peter 3:7). (The Greek word in the exhortation of 3:7 is the substantive adjective *gynaikeios*, "female," not *gynē*, "wife.")

Perhaps most significantly, Peter violates the social norm of his day by affirming the woman's choice to worship Christ instead of the god(s) of her unbelieving husband and not expecting the wife to abandon faith in Christ even if the husband was not a believer. This difference is seen again by a comparison with Plutarch, who wrote about the same time as Peter:

"The 'household codes' in 1 Peter are ... an example of differentiated acceptance and rejection of the surrounding culture."

MIROSLAV VOLF

> A wife ought not to make friends of her own, but to enjoy her husband's friends in common with him. The gods are the first and most important friends. Wherefore it is becoming for a wife to worship and to know only the gods that her husband believes in, and to shut the front door tight upon all queer rituals and outlandish superstitions. For with no god do stealthy and secret rites performed by a woman find any favor. (*Advice to the Bride and Groom* 140.19)

Within the "household code," Peter both upheld social expectations and at the same time subverted them with the good news of Jesus Christ, an example of Volf's point that "there are numerous ways of accepting, rejecting, subverting or transforming various aspects of a culture which itself is a complex pattern of symbols, beliefs, values, practices and organizations."[35]

The Call to Suffering

The most striking ethical principle of Peter's letter is that it is better to suffer for doing the right thing than to sin. In fact, there is a kind of suffering that Peter's readers were *called* to experience. It is not the kind of suffering that comes to all people because of illness or chronic pain or the declines of aging. And he isn't talking about the kind of suffering we bring on ourselves through bad choices and sin (1 Peter 4:15). He is talking about the kinds of suffering that persecution brings as a result of a person living a godly life as a Christian. Christians in North America do not experience the kind of persecution that Peter's readers did or that believers in other parts of the world today have to face continually.

To suffer persecution, even the threat of death, and to remain faithful to Christ is a profound act of self-denial and cross-bearing. Peter failed on this very point the night that Jesus was arrested, when he followed behind Jesus to the home of the high priest. He had declared earlier that evening that he was ready to die for Christ (John 13:37). How quickly his courage crumbled when asked if he was a follower of Jesus: three times he denied Christ rather than deny himself safety. Jesus said that those who wish to be his disciples must deny themselves and take up their cross and follow him (Matt. 16:24; Mark 8:34; Luke 9:23). Because the reference to the cross would have been understood at the time as a means of

35. Volf, "Soft Difference," 27.

execution, Jesus is making the radical statement that a Christian should be willing to die rather than renounce Christ.

Now if Christians should be willing to die for Christ, should we not also be willing to live for him? That is why Peter says Jesus died so that we "might die to sins and live for righteousness" (1 Peter 2:24). And so when presented with the temptation to sin and thereby avoid suffering, Peter says, "It is better, if it is God's will, to suffer for doing good than for doing evil" (3:17). Moreover, "those who suffer according to God's will should commit themselves to their faithful Creator and continue to do good" (4:19). How can suffering be a part of God's will? Even apart from persecution, the gospel calls us to self-denial, and self-denial hurts. Sometimes people choose to sin rather than face the suffering that would come from choosing to do what is right. For instance, being dishonest on an income tax return is an attempt to avoid suffering loss of money that we may feel we need more than the government does. For instance, cheating on a test is the unwillingness to suffer possible failure and loss of face. For instance, adultery and other sexual sins are the unwillingness to suffer unsatisfied physical and emotional needs. Sin is the path of least resistance. It is not the path of Jesus' footsteps.

"It is better to suffer than to sin."

Karen Jobes

Almost forty years ago, I was evangelized by someone explaining the "Four Spiritual Laws" to me. As a young Christian, I knew that "God loves me and has a wonderful plan for my life," and I understood vicarious **atonement**—that Jesus had died for my sins in my place so that I could be free from the penalty of death. But for a long time, I confused vicarious atonement with vicarious suffering. I thought that because Jesus suffered for me, I shouldn't have to suffer. I have long since known better, but I have also heard a lot of other Christians claiming that God wants us to be happy, that the "abundant life" in Christ is about our happiness.

A Christian who thinks like that is going to have a big shock when reading 1 Peter, for Peter says that Christians are "called" to suffer—and to suffer unjustly for doing good, at that (2:20–21)! This statement is within the instructions Peter gives to slaves, but in Peter's letter, all Christians are to "live as God's slaves" (2:16). And when the Son of God came as a man into this world, he wasn't born into the lap of luxury. The Son so humbled himself to the extent that he died the death of a slave, crucifixion, which was not a lawful execution for those who held Roman citizenship. And so we infer that Jesus and his family did not have the citizenship that would have given them certain rights. Jesus was a foreigner with respect to Roman law, even though he lived his whole life in the land where he was born. He lived and died without the privileges that citizenship would have provided. But beyond that, Jesus was the ultimate outsider, having come into a world that did not recognize him and rejected him all the way to execution. He was chosen by God but rejected by the world, just as Peter describes the Christians to whom he writes.

Peter writes that Christ "suffered for you, *leaving you an example*, that you should follow in his steps" (1 Peter 2:21, emphasis added). As Jesus walked across the stage of human history doing the will of the Father, he was in the crosshairs of Satan's evil intent. Jesus was misunderstood, slandered, rejected, and pursued by his enemies to a death on the cross. So the Christian who follows in his steps should not be surprised to find himself or herself in those same crosshairs, experiencing the same kinds of reactions by others. But hallelujah! The footsteps of Jesus don't stop in the grave; they lead through the grave and onward to the glory of eternal life and resurrection. In the meanwhile, Christians in every place and time in history should not be surprised if they experience hostility and rejection from a society that has rejected God. "Right(eous) living or good conduct, including the suffering that frequently results from living out a resurrection hope in a crucifixion world, is the chief outward mark of being a follower of Christ."[36]

The exclusivity of the Christian gospel is a primary offense to unbelieving society that has abandoned belief in truth that is not relative and self-defined. Jesus himself said, "I am the way and the truth and the life. No one comes to the Father except through me" (John 14:6). Because polytheism was culturally acceptable in Greco-Roman society, no one cared if Christians worshiped Jesus—after all, what's one more god? But the Christian claim that there is no God but Christ alone provoked the accusation that Christians were haters of humankind, for they rejected what was held dear by the majority of human beings. This is still the root cause of hostility to the Christian gospel today, as many postmodern thinkers see any claim to the exclusive truth of Christianity as a power play of imperialist domination, revealing a lack of respect for the beliefs of others. The suffering that perspective causes plays out for Christians in a myriad of ways.

The Example of Christ

When it comes to the ethical teachings of the Christian gospel, it's all about Jesus. Peter distinctively relates the redemptive role of Jesus Christ to his exemplary role for Christian living. As one scholar puts it, "The Christological narrative is . . . the story of both a gift and a call, at once indicative and imperative."[37] But in what way is the Christian to follow Jesus, and particularly in his suffering and death?

The ***imitatio Christi*** ("imitation of Christ") has been a spiritual quest since ancient times that has taken on various expressions. In recent times, during the 1960s, people in the Jesus movement often grew their hair long and wore sandals—though this was also the fashion of the wider culture in that decade—as part of the way they sought to follow Jesus. Later on young people wore wristbands with the letters WWJD? reminding themselves to ask, "What would Jesus do?" in every situation of daily life. But it might seem an unrealistic standard to ask what the perfectly holy, miracle-working Son of God would do.

Returning to the ancient world in which 1 Peter was written provides much help in understanding Peter's call for following Jesus. In Greco-Roman paraenesis, an exemplary hero would be described to foster admiration and love for the exemplar that would result in a commitment, not specifically to imitate the deeds he did, but to the virtues he embodied.[38] (This is probably how the example of Sarah functions in 1 Peter 3:6.) When a virtuous person is publicly praised, younger people would admire them and determine to follow their example. This is probably the motivation for the four gospels, which tell the story

36. Marc Kolden, "Are You Serious? First Peter on Christian Life in a Complicated World," *WW* 24 (2004): 425.

37. Dryden, *Theology and Ethics*, 185, quoting John B. Webster, "Christology, Imitability and Ethics," *SJT* 39 (1986): 311.

38. Ibid., 167.

"When blessing replaces rage and revenge, the one who suffers violence refuses to retaliate in kind and chooses instead to encounter violence with an embrace. But how can people give up violence in the midst of a life-threatening conflict if their identity is wrapped up in rejecting the beliefs and practices of their enemies? Only those who refuse to be defined by their enemies can bless them."

Miroslav Volf

of Jesus from four somewhat different perspectives, all intended to nurture love for Jesus and a commitment to the godly virtues by which he lived. And so to follow Jesus is not an expectation to reenact the things he did but to reenact his virtue. In this way, "Jesus is a normative pattern that can be creatively applied in different circumstances."[39]

And so in Peter's letter, Jesus is the Christian's example, because in the face of unjust suffering more intense than that suffered by Peter's readers, he did not retaliate with vengeance but continued to live in obedience to God's will. Peter places the example of Christ in his exhortation to slaves, who were the least empowered people of the Roman Empire and the most likely to suffer mistreatment and injustice. Christ did not meet evil with evil, but continued to do good even in the face of gross injustice. Jesus' disposition of forgiveness toward those who caused his suffering and his continued trust in the goodness of God is the exemplary pattern those walking in his footsteps must follow.

This is the disposition that Peter exhorted his readers to have in every situation of life. Of course, because of the Holy Spirit, Jesus is not *merely* an example. A spiritual bond exists between Jesus and his followers that did not exist, for instance, between the example of Pericles and the readers of Plutarch's *Lives*. Just as the law had no power to enable its obedience, an example had no power beyond that mustered by the human psyche. But because of Jesus' redemptive suffering and death, the Holy Spirit came to indwell the redeemed, transforming their character and enabling them to live in virtuous ways that could not be attained by a mere example.

However, the Spirit's transforming power works in concert with the human will, and the function of the will depends on knowledge. Peter exhorts his readers to know that it is better to suffer than to sin and to give that knowledge power in their decisions. To follow in Jesus' footsteps means to decide on the path of obedience to God's will, even when it hurts. This is achieved only by repeated choices through life at every decision point, whether large or small. Jesus followed "a long obedience in the same direction."[40] It is this principle that allows Peter to say, "Since Christ suffered in his body, arm yourselves also with the same attitude, because whoever suffers in his body is done with sin" (1 Peter 4:1).

Peter strongly associates the life of the Christian with the life of Christ. For one cannot step into the footsteps of Jesus and head off in any other direction than the direction he took, and his footsteps lead to the cross, through the grave, and onward to glory. Peter ends

39. Ibid., 172.

40. Eugene H. Peterson, *A Long Obedience in the Same Direction: Discipleship in an Instant Society*, 2nd ed. (Downers Grove, Ill.: InterVarsity, 2000).

Watch Your Step!

"Your future lies before you
Like a shining field of snow.
Be careful how you tread,
For every step will show."

Lillian Morrison,
Yours Till Niagara Falls

his teaching about Jesus in this passage with the image of believers who have returned to the Shepherd and Overseer of their souls, of the sheep following after the Shepherd, following in his footsteps so to speak. Peter's entire christological exposition is framed with the image that believers are to walk in Jesus' footsteps, embodying his virtues even through unjust suffering. For despite suffering along the way, it is nevertheless the Shepherd's path of safety, protection, and deliverance. First Peter joins **Christology** to paraenesis in a highly pastoral way. As one New Testament scholar describes it:

> The Christology of 1 Peter is a Christology of suffering.... By focusing on the sufferings of Christ, 1 Peter shows the intimate relationship between Christology and the Christian life: the *past* sufferings of Christ is the *present* condition of believers, while the *present* glory of Christ is the *future* glory of those who follow in the steps of the suffering Christ. While the Christology of 1 Peter may not be the most developed of the New Testament, it is among the most pastorally sensitive.[41]

The consequence of being willing to follow Jesus' exemplary disposition while suffering is that "holy life in the world is marked not by withdrawal or separation, but by an engagement of such profundity that it is capable of leading to ostracism, rejection, banishment, even wrongful death."[42] The Christians' willingness to suffer expresses "a far-reaching commitment to a worldview different from that of the societies around them. They are focused not on present pleasures but on the end of the present period of time, when their sojourning will be complete ... and God will bring justice to their oppressors."[43] The willingness to suffer injustice without retaliation has, therefore, even an evangelistic edge to it, for it exemplifies a presumption of God's justice.

Following in Jesus' footsteps.

Peter's ethics explains how Christians must be "in the world" but not "of the world," living honorably in a society that is hostile to some degree. Volf calls this mode of cultural engagement "soft difference":

> Soft difference is the missionary side of following in the footsteps of the crucified Messiah. It is not an optional extra, but part and parcel of Christian identity itself. To be a Christian means to live one's own identity in the face of others in such a way that one joins inseparably the belief in the truth of one's own convictions with a respect for the convictions of others.... To give up the softness of our difference would be to sacrifice our identity as followers of Jesus Christ.[44]

---

41. Frank J. Matera, *New Testament Christology* (Louisville: Westminster John Knox, 1999), 184 (emphasis original).
42. Green, "Living as Exiles," 320.
43. Frank Thielman, *Theology of the New Testament: A Canonical and Synthetic Approach* (Grand Rapids: Zondervan, 2005), 578.
44. Volf, "Soft Difference," 25.

The "soft difference" of the Christian must not be mistaken for a weak difference,[45] for it takes great spiritual strength to fearlessly find one's identity with God against the grain of one's society. Behind the "soft difference" lies a conviction as hard as flint but dressed in the velvet willingness to live a life of witness and invitation, not one of force, pressure, and manipulation. It is a soft difference to be willing to be thought wrong and foolish by an unbelieving world, all the while in word and deed testifying to the power of the gospel of Jesus Christ.

Sheep following the Shepherd.

This relationship of engagement with society is not based on how different a Christian is from the unbeliever in any given situation, "but rather on what *basis* Christian identity is established" (italics added).[46] As Green describes it:

> We are not against the world; the holiness of God's people is thus not found in reciprocal animosity with their opponents. We do not withdraw from the world. We do not work out our identity and sense of mission simply by negating the beliefs and behaviors of others. If we are different from the world, it is not because we set out to be so, but rather because our lives rest ultimately in a God who is different and we follow in the footsteps of Jesus Christ.[47]

Christians aren't called to simply reject elements of the dominant society as a way of creating difference; Christians must recognize that their new birth has made them a different person with different values, priorities, and goals. There *is* difference, regardless of whether a Christian happens to do the same thing as an unbeliever in an acceptance of the surrounding culture or abstains as a rejection of it. The basis of Christian identity calls for and allows a "differentiated acceptance and rejection of the surrounding culture" wherever the Christian lives.[48] As Volf explains:

> There is no single proper way for Christians to relate to a given culture as a whole. Instead, there are numerous ways of accepting, rejecting, subverting or transforming various aspects of a culture which itself is a complex pattern of symbols, beliefs, values, practices and organizations that are partly congruent with one another and partly contradictory.[49]

First Peter's model of how a Christian is to relate to the wider society does not permit the black-and-white thinking that is sometimes offered as a defense of Truth. Nor does it prescribe a list of rules and regulations that might have been relevant at that time but can no longer be observed today. Peter's sensitivity to the complexities of his readers' social situations allows his teaching to be relevant in any time or place. Society's response to the

45. Ibid., 24.
46. Dryden, *Theology and Ethics*, 135, quoting Volf, "Soft Difference," 20.
47. Green, "Living as Exiles," 324.
48. Volf, "Soft Difference," 22.
49. Ibid., 27.

Christian presence varies from place to place, from time to time, and even from individual to individual.

> We encounter evil people who persecute Christians and who will continue to do the same, blaspheming what is most holy to Christians (4:4, 12). We come across ignorant and foolish people who will be silenced by Christian good behavior (2:15). We meet people who know what is wrong and what is right and are ready to relate to Christians accordingly (2:14). Finally, we encounter people who see, appreciate, and are finally won over to the Christian faith (2:12; 3:1).[50]

RELATIONSHIP TO OTHER BELIEVERS

A self-identity based on new birth into the people of God also has implications for new relationships with other believers. Peter reminds his readers of their baptism "that now saves you ... by the resurrection of Jesus Christ" (1 Peter 3:21). Believers do not baptize themselves; there is no self-initiation ritual in the Christian faith. (And Holy Communion is also a communal sacrament.) The corporate nature of the Christian identity—that a believer is born again into a people, a nation—may be countercultural in places like modern North America, which prizes individualism in general but especially in religious matters.

The corporate identity is also a resource of strength and purpose, for the Christian believer is not alone as a foreigner and resident alien. Peter presents the image of the spiritual *oikos* ("building" or "home") into which the believer is being built. "As you come to him, the Living Stone—rejected by human beings but chosen by God and precious to him—you also, like living stones, are being built into a spiritual house to be a holy priesthood, offering spiritual sacrifices acceptable to God through Jesus Christ" (1 Peter 2:4–5).

Peter wants his readers to think of themselves in "the Old Testament categories of priesthood (called of God), sacrifice (offered to God), and temple (built by God); they have become the dwelling place of God's presence among humanity."[51] Furthermore, the call for Christian believers to live holy lives continues God's call to Israel, for "in order for Israel to fulfill its mission of being Yahweh's priesthood in the midst of the nations, they were to be

---

50. Ibid., 26.
51. Green, "Living as Exiles," 319.

The Unique Community

"The body of Christ becomes an overarching new identity that breaks down barriers of race and nationality and gender and makes possible a community that exists nowhere else in the world.... My identity as a Christian is more important than my identity as an American or as a Coloradan or as a white male or as a Protestant. Church is the place where I celebrate that new identity and work it out in the midst of people who have many differences but share this one thing in common. We are charged to live out a kind of alternative society before the eyes of the watching world."*

*Philip Yancey, *Grace Notes: Daily Readings with a Fellow Pilgrim* (Grand Rapids: Zondervan, 2009), 45.

'holy'—that is, 'different' or 'distinctive.' This was not at root a call for retreat from the world, but a vocation to identify with God's own character."[52]

Those who come to Christ are built as "living stones" into God's great spiritual building, a new temple.[53] This temple, whose foundation stone was laid in Zion, extends around the world and throughout time as people in every generation and of every nation come to Christ. God reclaims all the earth by building his temple globally.[54] And his project is under way throughout all of history, until the Lord returns. This beautiful image of Christ as the Living Stone to which believers are joined is suggestive of ideas that help Christians understand their new identity in Christ, a goal that was apparently important to the apostle as he wrote to believers in need of encouragement to continue on in faith in Christ.

Baker Photo Archive

Peter portrays the Christian community as a spiritual house in which each believer takes their place.

The spiritual house that Peter presents is a striking image of corporate or communal identity. He does not picture the living stones strewn across the landscape as if they are individual living stones unrelated to each other. Nor does he portray them as a heap of stones piled up without rhyme or reason. The image of a spiritual house in which each stone takes its place suggests purpose, unity, and strength, all under the supervision of the Great Architect. The image suggests many ideas about a believer's identity and relationship to others in the church.

- The Living Stone and the living stones are of the same material. The Son of God took on human flesh in his incarnation that he might share the nature of those he came to redeem.
- The Living Stone is the cornerstone of the spiritual house, to which the rest of the building is plumbed. Each of the living stones must be squared to the cornerstone, bringing their lives into conformity with the call of Jesus Christ.
- Being built of living stones joined to the Living Stone, the house represents the eschatological reality of the new life of believers that has intruded into this fallen world.
- As diverse as believers in Christ may be, each one has a place in God's project. Just as stones in a building are of different shapes, sizes, and purposes, yet each must be in place for the integrity of the structure, so the diversity of many peoples from various nations, cultures, and times with different skills, gifts, and abilities are nevertheless joined into one grand unity.
- Even though Peter is writing to believers who are "scattered" across a vast area of northern Turkey, he does not present the image of living stones scattered across a

52. Ibid., 322.

53. John H. Elliott reads the Greek phrase *oikos pneumatikos* as referring to God's household, a place where those who are foreigners and aliens in their society find a true home. See John H. Elliott, *A Home for the Homeless: A Social-Scientific Criticism of 1 Peter, Its Situation and Strategy* (Minneapolis: Fortress, 1990).

54. See Gregory K. Beale, *The Temple and the Church's Mission: A Biblical Theology of the Dwelling Place of God*, New Studies in Biblical Theology 17 (Downer's Grove, Ill.: InterVarsity, 2004).

The Great Walls of Sparta

A Spartan king was boasting to a visiting monarch about the famed walls of Sparta. As the visiting king looked around, he could see no walled city and asked, "Where are the renowned walls of Sparta?" The Spartan king pointed to his army and replied, "These are the walls of Sparta, every man a brick."*

*S.v. "Brick of a Man," *The Facts on File Encyclopedia of Word and Phrase Origins: Definitions and Origins of More Than 12,500 Words and Expressions*, ed. Robert Hendrickson, 3rd ed. (New York: Facts on File, 2004), 104.

vacant lot or even of stones heaped up together in a pile. No matter how isolated or alone a Christian may feel, he or she is not alone, but is joined to all other believers past, present, and future for God's great redemptive purposes.

- The needs of the building require that stones be cut and chiseled and fit into the master plan. As a living stone takes its place, he or she grows spiritually in ways that fit into the needed shape.
- The image of the living stones joined to the Living Stone also imparts significance to the believer that is greater than one's own life. As each living stone takes its place in the living temple, he or she occupies a position that only he or she can fill. And the significance of one life takes on new meaning when viewed as part of that grand structure that will be complete and ready to be revealed only at the end of history.

Peter prefaces the image of the living stones in 2:4–5 with moral exhortation in 2:1–3: "Therefore, rid yourselves of all malice and all deceit, hypocrisy, envy, and slander of every kind. Like newborn babies, crave pure spiritual milk, so that by it you may grow up in your salvation, now that you have tasted that the Lord is good."[55] And prior to that in 1:22, a love command establishes the basis for relationships between believers: "Now that you have purified yourselves by obeying the truth so that you have sincere love for each other, love one another deeply, from the heart." After explaining that their new life is to be characterized by love, Peter defines the quality of that love as being a moral transformation as believers relate to others. The goal of God's redemptive purposes in this life is to restore right relationships, first, between a person and God, but between people as well.

The vices listed in 2:1 that must be put off are those that destroy community. The social alienation that Christians experience from society is to be remedied by the genuine fellowship characterized by love, respect, and like-mindedness found within the community of believers. Peter strongly implies that the maverick Christian, one who believes that it's all just "Jesus and me" with no need for the church, will never attain true spiritual maturity apart from the fellowship of the church. For that is a denial of the new birth into a people, a community of believers that provides a spiritual home for the foreigner.

55. See Karen H. Jobes, "Got Milk? Septuagint Psalm 33 and the Interpretation of 1 Peter 2:1–3," *WTJ* 63 (2002): 1–14.

CHAPTER SUMMARY

Theology and morality are inextricably linked in Peter's letter. The new birth through the resurrection of Jesus Christ motivates a great doxology of praise to a merciful God who gathers his children as living stones into a living temple. The great privilege of having been chosen by God effectively counters all the social alienation that conversion to Christ might provoke. Jesus was the ultimate foreigner and resident alien, who came as God's Son into a world that rejects God and therefore rejected Christ. Those who follow Christ are likewise exposed to the possibility of suffering rejection to some degree. The basic principle of Peter's ethics is that such suffering is to be embraced, for it is better to suffer for being a Christian than to sin by capitulating to the social pressure that would lead to a renunciation of God. Like Jesus, Christians are to continue to entrust themselves to God and live faithfully even when it hurts, for they will be vindicated by God's judgment. As a Christian's self-identity is transformed by the knowledge of all that is implied by the new birth into the people of God, increasing devotion to him motivates moral transformation, which allows the Christian to live a winsome witness among unbelievers and to build community with others following in the footsteps of Jesus.

KEY TERMS

accommodation
acculturation
assimilation
holy nation
imitatio Christi
living stones
paraenesis
people of God

QUESTIONS FOR REVIEW OR DISCUSSION

1. Think about how your parents have shaped your identity. What does Peter say about how God reshapes a Christian's identity?
2. In what ways can a minority group relate to the dominant society (hint: the three A's)? What ways have you observed by which minorities protect their distinctive identity?
3. Does Peter's exhortation to "honor the emperor" surprise you? Why or why not? What would this principle look like as applied to our modern lives?
4. What principles does Peter's "household code" exemplify?
5. What is the role of suffering in Christian life today and how is it related to the suffering of Jesus?
6. List and reflect on the implications suggested by Peter's image of Christians as living stones being built into a spiritual house.

GOING FURTHER

Bauman-Martin, Betsy. "Speaking Jewish: Postcolonial Aliens and Strangers in First Peter." Pages 144–77 in *Reading First Peter with New Eyes: Methodological Reassessments of the Letter of First Peter.* Edited by Robert L. Webb and Betsy Bauman-Martin. London: T&T Clark, 2007.

Dryden, J. de Waal. *Theology and Ethics in 1 Peter: Paraenetic Strategies for Christian Character Formation.* WUNT 2/209. Tübingen: Mohr Siebeck, 2006.

Elliott, John H. "The Church as Counter-Culture: A Home for the Homeless and a Sanctuary for Refugees." *Currents in Theology and Mission* 25 (1998): 176–85.

———. *Conflict, Community, and Honor: 1 Peter in Social-Scientific Perspective.* Cascade Companions. Eugene, Ore.: Cascade, 2007.

———. *A Home for the Homeless: A Social-Scientific Criticism of 1 Peter, Its Situation and Strategy.* Philadelphia: Fortress Press, 1990.

Gilmour, Michael J. "Crass Casualty or Purposeful Pain? Psalm 34's Influence on Peter's First Letter." *WW* 24 (2004): 404–11.

Green, Joel B. "Faithful Witness in the Diaspora: The Holy Spirit and the Exiled People of God according to 1 Peter." Pages 282–95 in *The Holy Spirit and Christian Origins: Essays in Honor of James D. G. Dunn.* Edited by Graham N. Stanton, Bruce W. Longenecker, and Stephen C. Barton. Grand Rapids: Eerdmans, 2004.

———. "Identity and Engagement in a Diverse World: Pluralism and Holiness in 1 Peter," *Asbury Theological Journal* 55 (2000): 85–92.

———. "Living as Exiles: The Church in the Diaspora in 1 Peter." Pages 311–25 in *Holiness and Ecclesiology in the New Testament.* Edited by Kent E. Brower and Andy Johnson. Grand Rapids: Eerdmans, 2007.

———. "Narrating the Gospel in 1 and 2 Peter." *Interpretation* 60 (2006): 262–77.

Hauerwas, Stanley, and William H. Willimon. *Resident Aliens: Life in the Christian Colony.* Nashville: Abingdon, 1989.

Horrell, David G. "Between Conformity and Resistance: Beyond the Balch-Elliott Debate Towards a Postcolonial Reading of First Peter." Pages 111–43 in *Reading First Peter with New Eyes: Methodological Reassessments of the Letter of First Peter.* Edited by Robert L. Webb and Betsy Bauman-Martin. Library of New Testament Studies. London: T&T Clark, 2007.

Howe, Bonnie. *Because You Bear This Name: Conceptual Metaphor and the Moral Meaning of 1 Peter.* Biblical Interpretation Series 81. Leiden: Brill, 2006.

Kolden, Marc. "Are You Serious? First Peter on Christian Life in a Complicated World." *WW* 24 (2004): 421–29.

McKnight, Scot. "Aliens and Exiles: Social Location and Christian Vocation." *WW* 24 (2004): 378–86.

Rensburg, Fika J. Janse van. "Metaphors in the Soteriology in 1 Peter: Identifying and Interpreting the Salvific Imageries." Pages 409–35 in *Salvation in the New Testament: Perspectives on Soteriology.* Edited by Jan G. van der Watt. Supplements to Novum Testamentum. Leiden: Brill, 2005.

Richard, Earl. "Honorable Conduct among the Gentiles—A Study of the Social Thought of 1 Peter." *WW* 24 (2004): 412–20.

Tracy, Steven. "Domestic Violence in the Church and Redemptive Suffering in 1 Peter." *CTJ* 41 (2006): 279–96.

Volf, Miroslav. "Soft Difference: Theological Reflections on the Relation between Church and Culture in 1 Peter." *ExAud* 10 (1994): 15–30.

CHAPTER 12

2 Peter

AN APOSTLE'S LAST WORDS TO THE CHURCH

Your Goals for This Chapter

- To be able to identify the issues of author, date, audience, and purpose.
- To evaluate the arguments about the genre of 2 Peter, specifically whether it is a **pseudonymous** apostolic last testament.
- To discuss the major themes and issues of 2 Peter and apply them to current life situations.
- To understand arguments concerning the literary relationship between 2 Peter and Jude.

WHY THE BOOK OF 2 PETER IS IMPORTANT TO YOU

Whether Christian or not, each of us has to decide how to live. We do this every day with each decision we make. Should I go to that place with those people to do those things? How should I spend my time? Should I be diligent in my studies or skip class? Is it important that I respect authority, or is it more grown-up to do my own thing? I once read about a near-death experience of a woman thrown from a capsized boat who thought she would drown. She related how after her initial panic a serene calm came over her. One of her thoughts was, *Well, no more decisions at least!* Deciding how to live today depends more than we may realize on what we believe about the future. For instance, if a young person believes there is no way she will ever be able to go to college, she is less likely to give her all to her studies in high school.

Peter wrote this letter because he believed that his readers cared about how they lived; that they wanted to increase in their knowledge of God and grow closer to him through faith in Jesus Christ. He wanted to remind them that the world is not always going to continue as it has and that judgment is coming. In light of that future, Peter wanted his readers to live well today by growing in virtue (1:5–8), by not being taken in by false teachers (2:1–2), and by not losing patience or growing weary with the Christian life (3:9). The wisdom Peter offers in his parting words to the church is needed ever more today as collectively and individually Christians must decide what kind of people we ought to be.

Key Verses

1:5(–8): For this very reason, make every effort to add to your faith goodness; and to goodness, knowledge;...

1:21: For prophecy never had its origin in the human will, but prophets, though human, spoke from God as they were carried along by the Holy Spirit.

2:1a: But there were also false prophets among the people, just as there will be false teachers among you.

3:1: Dear friends, this is now my second letter to you. I have written both of them as reminders to stimulate you to wholesome thinking.

3:11a: Since everything will be destroyed in this way, what kind of people ought you to be?

3:15–16: Bear in mind that our Lord's patience means salvation, just as our dear brother Paul also wrote you with the wisdom that God gave him.... His letters contain some things that are hard to understand.

3:17b: [B]e on your guard so that you may not be carried away by the error of the lawless and fall from your secure position.

Challenges Presented by 2 Peter

- The question of its author and genre.
- Its **eschatology**.
- Its relationship to Jude.
- The reference to Paul's letters as Scripture in 3:15–16.

CHAPTER OUTLINE

I. Author, Genre, Date
    A. Arguments for Pseudonymity
        1. Style, vocabulary, and syntax
        2. Influence of Greco-Roman concepts
        3. A ***Sitz im Leben*** after Peter's lifetime
            a. Paul's letters as Scripture
            b. Scoffing at the delay of the **parousia**
            c. The nature of the heresy
            d. The motive for **pseudepigraphal** authorship
    B. The Big Question of Genre
    C. Summary of Author, Genre, Date
II. To Whom Was 2 Peter Originally Written?
III. Why Was 2 Peter Written?
IV. The Theology of 2 Peter
    A. God
    B. Jesus Christ
    C. Holy Spirit
    D. Eschatology
V. The Christian Life of Ethical Virtue
VI. Peter's Knowledge of Paul's Letters
VII. 2 Peter's Relationship with 1 Peter
VIII. 2 Peter's Relationship with Jude
IX. Text and Canonicity
    A. The Greek Text of 2 Peter
    B. Canonicity
X. Outline of 2 Peter

Please read the book of 2 Peter in one sitting before reading this chapter.

AUTHOR, GENRE, DATE

The question of when a New Testament book was written is obviously bound up with the dates of the author who wrote it. If a book is **pseudonymous**, then the dates of the author named do not limit the date the book was actually written; in fact, pseudonymous authorship obliterates any indication of date other than possibilities based on inferences from internal evidence that usually are quite inconclusive at best. Although the occurrence of legitimate pseudonymous **epistles** is highly suspect (see discussion in the introduction), pseudonymity was a feature of ancient **testamental literature**, in which the wisdom of a long-deceased hero was presented as his last testament and brought to bear on a current situation. Because of arguments put forth that 2 Peter is indeed a **testament**, the issue of the genre of this book also enters the discussion about authorship and, consequently, when it was written. Moreover, 2 Peter and Jude have a unique relationship that also enters into the discussion of their respective dates. If 2 Peter borrows language and thought from Jude, as most scholars now think, then clearly it must be dated after Jude, bringing all the exigencies of Jude's authorship into play. The intertwined issues of author, date, and genre are probably more complicated for 2 Peter than for any other book of the New Testament. Unless new evidence comes to light, it is doubtful we will ever resolve these questions with certainty.

The Apostle Peter statue in the Basilica of St. John Lateran in Rome.

Whatever literary features 2 Peter may have, it clearly comes to us as a letter from "Simon Peter, a servant and apostle of Jesus Christ, To those who through the righteousness of our God and Savior Jesus Christ have received a faith as precious as ours" (1:1). Consequently, it is meant to be read as penned by the great apostle whose given name was Simon (or Simeon), whom Jesus nicknamed Peter and, though one of the Lord Jesus' closest disciples, nevertheless denied knowing Jesus on the night of his arrest. This was the Peter who witnessed the transfiguration (2 Peter 1:16–18; cf. Matt. 17:1–9; Mark 9:2–9), the Peter who, emboldened by the power of the Holy Spirit, became the first leader of the church in Jerusalem and the apostle through whom God first brought the gospel to the **Gentiles** (Acts 10). Peter, as the author of this book, would also have been the author of what we know as 1 Peter and, in fact, that book may be the reference in 2 Peter 3:1: "This is now my second letter to you. I have written both of them as reminders to stimulate you to wholesome thinking."

> "Second Peter is a mystery wrapped in an enigma cloaked in a conundrum."
>
> Ben Witherington III, *Letters and Homilies for Hellenized Christians*

In spite of the letter's claim to be from the apostle, from its earliest days there have been serious doubts that Peter himself wrote it.[1] One recent scholar concludes, "No document

1. See Charles Bigg, *A Critical and Exegetical Commentary on the Epistles of St. Peter and St. Jude*, ICC (New York: Scribner, 1909), 199–210, for a detailed presentation of the ancient evidence.

included in the New Testament gives such thorough evidence of its pseudonymity as does 2 Peter. The arguments against authenticity are overwhelming."[2] Even the most conservative doctrine of Scripture does not allow us to prejudge whom the Holy Spirit may or may not have inspired to write, so the evidence for pseudonymous authorship needs to be seriously considered.

The Transfiguration by Giovanni Battista Paggi (1554–1627).

Arguments for Pseudonymity

Style, vocabulary, and syntax.

The two epistles of Peter exhibit very different styles, vocabulary, and syntax and, as some argue, could not have come from the same man. Such an argument, however, is generally not a reliable indicator of different authors, for even the same author will use greatly different style, vocabulary, and syntax depending on the recipient(s) and purpose for writing. Think about the difference between the style you use when writing email messages to your friends and your style when writing term papers. Furthermore, one's writing style changes over one's lifetime, as anyone who has looked back at a high school paper later in life can admit. Nonetheless, the style of the Greek causes most to doubt that it could have come from a Palestinian fisherman even with years of experience in the language. But since we know virtually nothing of Peter's life and experience after he fled Jerusalem (Acts 12:17), any conclusion from this argument must be held lightly.

In fact, however, the distinctive features of 2 Peter do raise legitimate questions about its authorship. Of its 565 Greek forms, 57 of them are not found elsewhere in the New Testament, although 25 of them occur in the Greek Old Testament.[3] Of its 32 biblical *hapaxes*,[4] 15 occur in other Hellenistic Jewish writers. Although 2 Peter and Jude share much material, there are only four words found in Jude and 2 Peter that do not occur elsewhere in the New Testament. Many of the distinctive words in 2 Peter seem to have been used in preference over more common words, perhaps with a view toward euphony and rhythm, which tends toward iambic rhythm as found in secular Greek writing, though there were many Jewish writers in Alexandria who also used this style. The overall effect is the impression that the author of 2 Peter is aiming for a literary style recognized as "Asiatic" rhetoric by the Greek rhetoricians Quintilian (*Inst.* 12.10.16) and Cicero (*Opt. gen.* 3.8).[5] These Roman orators looked down on this style, associated with Asia Minor in the Roman

2. David G. Meade, *Pseudonymity and Canon: An Investigation into the Relationship of Authorship and Authority in Jewish and Earliest Christian Tradition* (Grand Rapids: Eerdmans, 1986), 179.

3. See Richard Bauckham, *Jude, 2 Peter*, WBC 50 (Waco, Tex.: Word 1983), 135; cf. Bigg, *Peter and Jude*, 224.

4. A ***hapax legomenon*** is a term that refers to a word that occurs only once in the given corpus of writings. The term is Greek and literally means "said once."

5. All references to ancient writers are from the Loeb Classical Library unless otherwise noted.

world, and preferred the more elegant revival of Attic style. Because of the distinctive style of the rest of the letter, at least one scholar sees a difference between 2 Peter 1:12–21 and the rest of the book, which he describes as "Asiatic Greek on steroids."[6] If 2 Peter is correctly identified as fitting the Asiatic Greek style of writing, it strengthens the association of the letter with Asia Minor, to which 1 Peter was written (2 Peter 3:1). It does not necessarily imply that the author lived in Asia Minor, as he may have chosen a style appreciated by his audience rather than dictated by his own location. But it does indicate a familiarity with the culture of that area.

Influence of Greco-Roman concepts.

Not only does the author of 2 Peter use vocabulary, syntax, and style that are commonly found in Greek secular writings, but he is apparently influenced by concepts found in Greek philosophy. Second Peter is the only book of the New Testament to mention **Tartarus**, the most desolate place of the mythological underworld where the fallen Greek gods known as the Titans were cast (2 Peter 2:4; note that some modern English translations obscure that reference by translating it as "hell"). The author of 2 Peter uses the name of the place of divine judgment that would have been familiar to pagan readers when relating the Jewish tradition of the fallen angels in Genesis 6. The omission of references to the Jewish writing *1 Enoch* that are found in Jude and the inclusion of Tartarus indicate that 2 Peter and Jude were addressed to different target audiences, despite the similarities of the content of the two letters.

A second Greek idea, that of the believer's participation in the divine nature (2 Peter 1:4), is not elsewhere found in the New Testament, but it had a long history in pagan Greek thought, which divided all existence between the material, mortal world and the divine world of permanence and purity. Jewish Hellenistic writers prior to 2 Peter suggest that the destiny of the human soul after death was to attain the purity and permanence associated with the divine sphere (e.g., 4 Macc. 18:3; Wisd. Sol. 2:23). Even the phrase "to share in the divine nature" can be found in both pagan and Jewish writings, but only in 2 Peter in the New Testament. While at first glance it could be taken by modern readers to mean a deification of the human that blurs the creator-creature distinction, it more likely would have been taken by the original readers to mean that through God's promises in Jesus Christ human beings may come to the purity and immortality associated with God.

The author of 2 Peter adopts other words from the tradition of the Greek moral philosophers such as *aretē* ("moral goodness"), *egkrateia* ("self-control"), and *eusebeia*, ("godliness") to talk about distinctively Christian virtue found only in Jesus Christ. He uses language that would have been familiar to readers acquainted with Greek literature to exhort them to participate in Christ's life through moral goodness. This influence of the secular Greek tradition and a relative paucity of references to the Old Testament could be construed to suggest that someone other than the apostle Peter penned this letter.

---

6. Ben Witherington III, *Letters and Homilies for Hellenized Christians: A Socio-Rhetorical Commentary on 1–2 Peter* (Downers Grove: IVP Academic, 2007), 264, esp. n. 18.

A *Sitz im Leben* after Peter's lifetime.

Some references in 2 Peter seem to pertain to a time later than Peter's death, which occurred by order of Emperor Nero sometime between **AD** 64 when Rome burned and AD 68 when Nero killed himself. Obviously, if the book was written after Peter's death, it is pseudonymous.

a. Paul's letters as Scripture.

The author of 2 Peter knows that the apostle Paul has also written to these people, teaching things that are hard to understand, things that the false teachers are twisting as they do also the "other Scriptures" (2 Peter 3:15–16). This statement is used to argue for pseudonymous authorship by (1) taking the mention of Paul's letters as a reference to the collection of Pauline letters that likely began to circulate after the apostle's death late in the first century and (2) assuming that the word "Scripture" implies reference to an established canon. The statement could be more naturally read to mean that the author of 2 Peter knew that his audience had also received, possibly indirectly, at least one letter from the apostle Paul.

Sitz im Leben is a technical term coined by German scholars to refer to the "setting in life" from which the various biblical books were written.

When apostolic letters were read in the Christian worship assembly along with writings from the Old Testament, the concept of "Scripture" would easily have been extended to the apostolic letters. The thought of 2 Peter 3:16 indicates the author's awareness of the contents of one or more of Paul's letters that contain difficult things, but it does not necessarily mean that a corpus of Pauline letters was in circulation. Therefore, this statement need not indicate a time later than Peter's life (or even Paul's, for that matter); nevertheless, it is a remarkable statement, suggesting that the apostles did not work in a vacuum but were aware of each other's teachings.

b. Scoffing at the delay of the parousia[7]

> Above all, you must understand that in the last days scoffers will come, scoffing and following their own evil desires. They will say, "Where is this 'coming' he promised? Ever since our ancestors died, everything goes on as it has since the beginning of creation." (2 Peter 3:3–4)

7. The Greek term *parousia* is still used today to refer to the second coming of Jesus Christ when he will judge the world.

> "Bear in mind that our Lord's patience means salvation, just as our dear brother Paul also wrote you with the wisdom that God gave him. He writes the same way in all his letters, speaking in them of these matters. His letters contain some things that are hard to understand, which ignorant and unstable people distort, as they do the other Scriptures, to their own destruction."
>
> 2 Peter 3:15–16

Did the apostles and earliest Christians expect Jesus to return in their own lifetimes? Statements such as Mark 9:1 have been understood to mean just that. As time went on the apostles and first generation of Christians died and Jesus had not returned. This led some scoffers (both ancient and modern) to lose faith in Jesus' teaching and in the subsequent teaching of the apostles. It is an interesting question of how Jesus' predictions and promises were understood and whether there was a crisis in the church after that first generation had passed without the parousia happening. Perhaps the church allowed that fact simply to correct any false understanding of what Jesus had meant. But this statement in 2 Peter is used to argue for pseudonymity by understanding the "fathers" (some translations, "ancestors") to be the apostles, rather than the Old Testament patriarchs. If so, Peter himself would have been among those who had died, and still the Lord had not returned, clearly making 2 Peter a pseudonymous work.

But the point of this statement in 2 Peter is that the scoffers mistake the patience of God, who is giving opportunity for repentance, as evidence that there will be no judgment. Such an attitude is certainly not unique to the postapostolic period, for similar thoughts are found even in the Old Testament book of Malachi (3:13–18), where arrogant people come to the false conclusion that there is no point in serving God. Moreover, 2 Peter 3:3 is a prediction and a warning that scoffers *will* come to Peter's readers in the future, not that such doubt about the parousia is necessarily a present reality. In fact, the apostle may have foreseen that at the death of the apostles such an understanding of Jesus' teaching would

Marie-Lan Nguyen/Wikimedia Commons

Liturgical art has represented the parousia by a monogram of Christ surrounded by a sunburst, as in St. Peter's at the Vatican.

lead to the disillusionment of some. Therefore, one must *assume* that 2 Peter was written after Peter's lifetime in order to read this future tense in the Greek as reflecting the *present* circumstance of the pseudonymous author projected back into Peter's lifetime as a prediction. This is not evidence for pseudonymous authorship; it is circular reasoning.

c. The nature of the heresy.

The letter of 2 Peter is clearly written as a warning about heresy that leads to immorality, as Peter fears for the churches after he is gone. Arguments for dating the letter, and hence determining if its authorship is authentic or pseudonymous, have often tried to determine the nature of the heresy and how that lines up with heresies at various times in early church history known from other sources. Perhaps the best-known heresy in the early church was a Christian form of **Gnosticism** that flourished in the second century. There was a time when every heresy of the New Testament was read as an incursion of second-century Gnosticism, usually to date the Epistles long past the lifetimes of any of the original apostles.[8] Of course, Gnosticism did not suddenly appear fully formed in the second century without its precursors in the first. The New Testament epistles do seem to argue against heretical strains of thought that have points of contact with Gnosticism, but consequently a first-century date is not necessarily precluded.

Rather than Gnosticism, the heresy in 2 Peter may reflect the incursion of **Epicureanism** into Christian thought of the first century. The apostle Paul mentions this school of thought by name as he debates with the philosophers in the **Areopagus** (Acts 17:18). The nature of the heresy reflected in 2 Peter is discussed further below, but suffice it to say that second-century Gnosticism is neither the only, nor even the best, background against which to read 2 Peter. And if the heresy is a form of Epicureanism, the letter could certainly be dated to the lifetime of the apostles.

d. The motive for pseudepigraphal authorship.

Those who read the New Testament epistles as pseudonymous often argue that—far from being an attempt to deceive or usurp undue honor—writing in the name of an apostle who was known to be deceased provided continuity between contemporary church leadership and apostolic orthodoxy. Rather than subsequent church leaders writing in their own names, they adopted the name of an apostle with whom they shared kindred belief. Therefore, pseudonymity is motivated by the assumption of Spirit-inspired interpretation (2 Peter 1:21) given to an authorized group of teachers to indicate continuity between an apostolic source and its later interpreters.[9] On this argument the ascription of a New Testament letter to Peter indicates only that authoritative Petrine tradition is presented but not the true identity of the actual author of the letter. This would be a valid conclusion if it could be established on independent grounds that the ascribed author did not write the letter. On the other hand, such a claim and defense of authoritative orthodoxy as 2 Peter

8. David G. Meade is a striking example of this approach when he cites characteristics, none of which was unique to Gnosticism, and then declares, "There is little reason to doubt that this [the heresy in 2 Peter] was some form of Gnostic sectarianism" (*Pseudonymity and Canon*, 181).

9. Ibid., 182.

Erich Lessing/Art Resource, NY

Noah's flood was a sign of God's power to judge the human race. The Flood Rises by Kaspar Memberger (died before 1662).

contains would equally well pertain to the apostolic author himself in the face of false teachers claiming to bring new revelation.

As mentioned, of the evidence presented for pseudonymous authorship of 2 Peter, it is probably the vocabulary, syntax, and style that have given interpreters the greatest pause throughout church history. No less an interpreter than Calvin sought a nuanced way to harmonize the name of Simon Peter given in 1:1 with the character of the letter he read. Calvin wrote:

> Since it has his [Peter's] name inscribed ... it would have been a fiction unworthy of a minister of Christ, to have [im-]personated another individual. So then ... *it must have proceeded from Peter*; *not that he himself wrote it*, but that some one of his disciples set forth in writing, by his command, those things which the necessity of the times required.... He allowed this testimony of his mind to be recorded shortly before his death.... In every part of the Epistle the majesty of the Spirit of Christ appears ... though I do not here recognize the language of Peter.[10]

Calvin raised an interesting question: When does an **amanuensis** shade into a pseudonymous author?[11] It has long been known and accepted that the apostles probably used an amanuensis for at least some of their letters. This theory has been used by even the most conservative modern interpreters to explain differences in the Greek syntax, style,

10. John Calvin, *Commentaries on the Catholic Epistles*, trans. John Owen (Grand Rapids: Eerdmans, 1948), 363–64.

11. An *amanuensis* (Greek term) was a secretary or scribe who was employed to represent the thoughts of an author.

vocabulary, and rhetoric between books of the New Testament that are attributed to the same author. Calvin suggests that the apostle Peter "allowed this testament of his mind to be recorded shortly before his death," but how long after Peter's death could such a record be legitimately attributed to Peter? At what point would an amanuensis who knew the "testimony of Peter's mind" be considered a pseudonymous author, especially if he was a close disciple of the apostle? At what point would such a document be considered a forgery? The question of pseudonymity of the New Testament books in relationship to the death of the apostle may not be as clear-cut as we might wish.

A scribe, or amanuensis, was commonly employed in the ancient world. St. Gregory writing with scribes below, Franco-German School, c.850–875 (ivory).

St. Gregory writing with scribes below, Franco-German School, Carolingian School (9th century)/ Kunsthistorisches Museum, Vienna, Austria/The Bridgeman Art Library

The Big Question of Genre

While the question of at what point the writing of an amanuensis becomes pseudonymous is gray, those who argue for pseudonymous authorship of New Testament books are generally not thinking of an amanuensis. There is some evidence that in the narrowly limited relationship between a master and his student-disciples in the Greco-Roman schools, some writings were produced in the master's name, because to do otherwise would have been to claim the master's ideas as one's own. The example of Iamblicus's description of the writings of the Pythagorean school that were ascribed to Pythagoras provide one commonly cited example.[12] While this may have been an accepted practice, it presumed a close relationship between a disciple and the master during the master's lifetime. The tradition that Mark's gospel preserves Peter's teaching about Jesus would be somewhat parallel—though neither Peter's nor Mark's name appears in the text—as would an apostle's use of an amanuensis from among his close associates.

However, the practice also led to abuses that were condemned as forgeries when writers who had no reputation used the pseudonym of a well-known author to gain a reading for their own ideas that did not represent those of the one whose name they assumed and with whom they had no personal relationship. Such pseudonymity was considered forgery in the ancient world, and based on considerable **extant** evidence, it was condemned. One famous example is found in Tertullian, who documents the defrocking of a presbyter who wrote *The Acts of Paul and Thecla* using Paul's name.

Though this pseudepigrapher made every effort to portray Paul with verisimilitude and acted only from love for Paul, he was nevertheless disciplined by the church for *forgery* (*Bapt.* 17).[13] A second condemnation of pseudonymous writing is found in Eusebius speaking about Serapion, bishop of Antioch, about AD 180, who forbade the reading of

12. See Terry L. Wilder, "Pseudonymity and the New Testament," in *Interpreting the New Testament: Essays on Methods and Issues*, ed. David A. Black and David S. Dockery (Nashville: Broadman and Holman, 2001), 296–335, for a discussion of this example within the wider context.

13. Tertullian, *On Baptism* 17 (*ANF* 3:677).

The Church Did Not Tolerate Pseudonymous Letters

"In Asia, the presbyter who composed that writing [the Acts of Paul and Thecla], as if he were augmenting Paul's fame from his own store, after being convicted, and confessing that he had done it from love of Paul, was removed from his office."

Tertullian, *De Baptismo* 17

the *Gospel of Peter* in the churches, saying, "We receive both Peter and the other apostles as Christ, but the writings which falsely bear their names (*pseudepigrapha*) we reject, as men of experience, knowing that such were not handed down to us" (Eusebius, *Hist. eccl.* 6.12).[14] The *Gospel of Peter* was an early anti-Semitic retelling of the passion narrative that used the canonical Gospels as sources. If pseudepigraphal *narrative* material was rejected by the early church as forgeries, how much more so would be the use of another's name in *personal correspondence*, such as in 2 Peter.

On the other hand, if what to modern eyes looks like a letter is in essence some other less familiar ancient genre, and if one of the features of that genre was pseudonymity, then as some argue, the question boils down simply to genre identification without any moral or ethical wrong being committed. Even the most conservative doctrine of Scripture does not presume to prescribe what genres the Holy Spirit may or may not have chosen when inspiring Scripture, and so the pseudonymity of 2 Peter cannot be ruled out without due consideration.

Perhaps the best articulation of this approach is found in Richard Bauckham's defense of the theory that 2 Peter is actually an ancient testament, which was a Jewish genre popular in the intertestamental period just before the time of the New Testament writings.[15] While not denying that 2 Peter began as a letter sent to an actual destination, its content seems to some scholars to fit the form of a testament. Ancient testaments reported the last words of a hero of the faith and generally include both ethical exhortations that his people were to live by, usually given in light of **apocalyptic** revelation, and predictions that those close to death were believed to experience. A number of testaments are extant, such as the *Testament of the Twelve Patriarchs* and the *Testament of Moses*, and sometimes a testament is found within a larger work, for instance, *1 Enoch* 91–104.[16] The hero delivers an oral address in anticipation of his death, which an anonymous writer records in the name of the dying hero; hence pseudonymity is one of the assumed literary features of these writings. In the case of extant testaments, it seems obvious that they were written many centuries or even millennia after the named hero lived, and the alleged farewell speech was created by the anonymous writer. It is quite a different thing if the testament was written so shortly

14. For a fuller discussion of this important issue, see Bruce M. Metzger, "Literary Forgeries and Canonical Pseudepigrapha," *JBL* 91, no. 1 (1972): 3–24; Donald Guthrie, *New Testament Introduction: The Pauline Epistles* (Chicago: InterVarsity Press, 1964), 282–94; Stanley E. Porter, "Pauline Authorship and the Pastoral Epistles: Implications for Canon," *BBR* 5 (1995): 105–23.

15. Bauckham, *Jude, 2 Peter*, 130–35.

16. Testaments in English translation can be found in James H. Charlesworth, ed., *Apocalyptic Literature and Testaments*, vol. 1 of *The Old Testament Pseudepigrapha* (New York: Doubleday, 1983).

after the alleged author's death that its readers may or may not have known that the alleged author was deceased.

The rhetorical features of 2 Peter show that it almost certainly began as an oral sermon. It includes many of the features of Greco-Roman oral rhetoric, such as metaphors, hyperbole, metonymy, synecdoche, and the use of new and rare words (Cicero, *De or.* 3:153–55). Second Peter 1:12–15 explicitly mentions Peter's knowledge of impending death, and 1:3–11 is a farewell speech that summarizes Peter's ethical and religious teachings that are to be followed after his death. These two features are almost universal in surviving testaments. We gain apocalyptic insight from 2 Peter 3:7–11, where Peter reveals that the earth will be destroyed by fire in God's good time, and we find predictions in 2 Peter 3:3–6 about scoffers who will come into the community and live by a false understanding of God's grace. Peter's life ended at Rome, so turning his oral testament into a letter was the obvious way for the church at Rome to communicate Peter's final words to churches elsewhere late in the first century when and where such correction was needed. Therefore, it is argued that pseudonymous authorship, at least as practiced when producing a testament, was recognized as a legitimate literary device, and that the pseudepigraphal testamentary letter would have been the ideal genre to communicate apostolic teaching after the death of an apostle. By this theory the original readers of 2 Peter would have known that the apostle Peter was deceased and his final words were coming to them in a letter penned by some anonymous person—in other words, that 2 Peter was a legitimate pseudepigraphal letter without moral suspicion.

The theory that 2 Peter is an epistolary testament is the most cogent way of understanding it as also being a pseudonymous letter. But there are a number of objections to the theory.[17] Verses 3:1 and 15 seem to argue against the theory that Peter's farewell speech at Rome was written as a testament and circulated later for the benefit of the wider church, as they limit the original destination of the letter to those to whom both the author and the apostle Paul have previously written. Perhaps the largest objection is that if the testament genre was such an effective way to assert apostolic authority, could not Peter himself have written a farewell letter, possibly using an amanuensis, when he knew his days were numbered? How would we be able to distinguish an authentic farewell letter from a later pseudonymous testament written in Peter's name? If the evidence for Peter's authentic authorship is in fact weak, then the testament theory helps us to make sense of how the letter came into existence. This would mean that the earliest readers of the letter would have known that it had not come from the apostle personally, assuming they recognized the testament genre and read accordingly. But if 2 Peter was so clearly recognized and accepted by the churches in the late first century as a legitimate testament of the apostle Peter, why did the early church fathers of the late second century so question its authenticity? (See discussion of canonicity below.)

Moreover, content that includes both ethical admonition and apocalyptic or eschatological revelation is neither unique to the testament genre nor distinctive of someone near

17. See Peter H. Davids, *The Letters of 2 Peter and Jude*, Pillar New Testament Commentary (Grand Rapids: Eerdmans, 2006), 143ff.; Michael Green, *2 Peter and Jude*, TNTC (1987; repr., Grand Rapids: Eerdmans, 1993).

death. The apostle Paul's second letter to the Thessalonians contains both, with its prediction about the man of lawlessness. The *distinctive* mark of 2 Peter that suggests it may be a testament is Peter's knowledge that he is about to die (2 Peter 1:13–14). Without that statement, there would be little to commend the letter as a testament. But could that knowledge have been the motive that prompted Peter himself to put pen to paper, perhaps through an amanuensis, and to express his concern for the future of the church as the apostolic age passed?

Summary of Author, Genre, Date

Even if we believe that the apostle Peter wrote 2 Peter, we must feel the weight of the evidence for pseudonymity, for if any book of the New Testament is pseudonymous, it would almost certainly be 2 Peter. The great exegete and Reformer John Calvin believed that Peter "allowed this testimony of his mind to be recorded shortly before his death" by one of his disciples.[18] But what if that writing of Peter's teaching was done shortly *after* his death?

If the author was:	*then the likely date was:*	*and the location was:*
the apostle Peter	before AD 68	probably Rome
one of Peter's personal disciples	between AD 65 and 100	probably Rome
otherwise pseudonymous	between AD 65 and 150	possibly Asia Minor

If the apostle Peter wrote this letter, even through an amanuensis, then obviously it dates from his lifetime, and given his sense of impending death, a date after the burning of Rome in AD 65 and before Nero's death in AD 68 seems most fitting.

If a close personal associate of Peter wrote it sometime after his death, then it would have to be within the lifetime of that associate, probably making AD 100 the latest point. Second Peter does have distinctive affinities with the noncanonical but historically important books of *1* and *2 Clement* that originated in Rome in the last decade of the first century.[19] If Calvin is right that a disciple of Peter wrote 2 Peter, Linus, an associate of both Peter and Paul mentioned in 2 Timothy 4:21, is the man often suggested for this role. There is strong tradition preserved in Irenaeus, Jerome, Eusebius, Chrysostom, and elsewhere that Linus was an early leader of the church in Rome ordained by the apostle Paul. However, the tradition is conflicting, with Eusebius reporting that Linus died in AD 80 (*Hist. eccl.* 3.2, 13; 5.6) and another anonymous writer reporting that Linus died before Peter, who then ordained Clement as successor (*Apos. Con.* 7.46). Wherever the author was located, he apparently had access to Jude's letter and at least some of the letters of Paul, making Rome a plausible location. Ben Witherington has put forward the theory that 2 Peter was compiled by a leader of the Roman church, plausibly Linus, by taking Peter's farewell sermon and combining it with Jude's letter, "making it the very first encyclical addressed to the whole church in the postapostolic era."[20] Since by one dating, Linus was bishop of Rome from

18. Calvin, *Catholic Epistles*, 363–64.
19. Bigg, *Peter and Jude*, 210.
20. Witherington, *1–2 Peter*, 285.

Sebastian Bergmann

Tradition suggests that Linus, an early bishop of Rome, may have written 2 Peter shortly after Peter's death in his city.

AD 56 to 67, he may still have been alive when Peter died, heard Peter's farewell speech, and committed it to writing not long before his own death.

Finally, there are those who argue that 2 Peter originated in Asia Minor or elsewhere and was written by a completely unknown author who had a very high degree of literacy and rhetorical skill, and whose motives and circumstances are lost to us.[21] The acceptance of this type of pseudonymous authorship assumes that writers who were both chronologically and geographically removed from the apostles may nevertheless take a place alongside them as guardians of the orthodox, apostolic tradition. If this person was not a personal associate of the apostle Peter and had no authority to write in his name, it is most difficult to square this type of pseudonymity with either the extant traditions of the early church or the doctrine of Scripture.

Because the quality of its Greek text is unique in the New Testament and because of its relationship to Jude, 2 Peter presents unique issues of authorship, date, location, and genre. Unless further historical evidence comes to light, it is unlikely that we will ever settle these issues with great certainty. This lengthy discussion of the possible relationship of the letter to the apostle Peter is necessary because the issue of authorship and genre is one of the most challenging issues 2 Peter presents. Nevertheless, the lack of certainty on how the book came into existence does not impede understanding its message and taking it to heart.

TO WHOM WAS 2 PETER ORIGINALLY WRITTEN?

Even though the letter of 2 Peter has rhetorical qualities that suggest it originated as an oral sermon, it has come to us in the form of a letter addressed "To those who through the righteousness of our God and Savior Jesus Christ have received a faith as precious as ours" (2 Peter 1:1). This very broad address seems to support the theory that in its written form 2 Peter was intended for all Christians of that day and beyond, except that 3:1 and 15 seem

21. This approach is represented, for instance, by Jerome H. Neyrey, *2 Peter, Jude*, AB 37C (New York: Doubleday, 1993).

Second Peter may have been written to the same destinations in Asia Minor as 1 Peter.

to limit its original destination to those to whom both the author and the apostle Paul have previously written.

In 2 Peter 3:1 the author refers to this letter as "my second letter to you." Perhaps Peter wrote many letters to many churches, but only one other has survived in the canon, 1 Peter, which is addressed to "God's elect, exiles scattered throughout the provinces of Pontus, Galatia, Cappadocia, Asia and Bithynia," that is, to Christians in northern Asia Minor. Even this address is provocatively general. Unlike Paul who writes to the church of a specific city, Peter writes to Christians scattered over a fairly large area of what is now northern Turkey. If the first letter referred to in 2 Peter 3:1 is 1 Peter, then those same scattered Christians, about whom we know very little, would be the original recipients of 2 Peter.

A little further, in 2 Peter 3:15, there is a reference to "our dear brother Paul" who "also wrote you." The letters Paul wrote to the cities of the province of Asia would include Ephesians, Colossians, 1 and 2 Timothy, and Philemon. The exact destination of his letter to the Galatians is debated, but the province of Galatia is also in the list of addressees of 1 Peter. There is no evidence that Paul wrote to Pontus, Cappadocia, or Bithynia or that he ever traveled there. In fact, when he tried to enter Bithynia, "the Spirit of Jesus would not allow" him (Acts 16:7). Despite no evidence of contact between Paul and the Christians of northern Asia Minor, it is often assumed that Paul or missionaries from his churches in southern Asia Minor originally evangelized Peter's readers. So either Paul wrote to Pontus, Cappadocia, and Bithynia or 2 Peter was intended for only those Christian communities in Asia and Galatia that had received both 1 Peter and correspondence from Paul. However, because we know that not every apostolic letter was later canonized (e.g., Paul's letter to the Laodiceans), Peter's first letter to these recipients may not have survived, so inferences based on the addresses of 1 Peter should be held lightly.

Because of the strong Greco-Roman character of 2 Peter (e.g., its "Asiatic" style and references to Greek mythology and philosophy), the recipients were probably not located in Aramaic-speaking Syria or Palestine. This seems to be confirmed when 2 Peter 2 is compared to Jude, which was almost certainly written to Palestinian, Aramaic-speaking Christians and relies heavily on the extrabiblical literature of Judaism (see chapter 8). When 2 Peter appropriates that material, all such references are removed, suggesting that the recipients would be either unfamiliar with that material or find it irrelevant. Furthermore, the inclusion of Greek philosophical terms and a reference to Tartarus suggest Peter wrote to an audience steeped in Greco-Roman thought. Nothing more can be said of the original recipients that is not sheer speculation.

WHY WAS 2 PETER WRITTEN?

"False teachers among you ... will secretly introduce destructive heresies" (2 Peter 2:1). While it is evident that 2 Peter originates as a farewell speech motivated by the author's sense of impending death (1:12–15), his major concern as he writes is to warn his readers about destructive heresies that will enter the church after his demise. He wants them to remain "firmly established in the truth you now have" (v. 12), especially the truth of "the coming of our Lord Jesus Christ in power" (v. 16), which power he affirms was witnessed by himself, James, and John in the transfiguration (Matt. 17:1–9; Mark 9:2–9; Luke 9:28–36). Furthermore, Peter refers to the prophetic message of the Old Testament (2 Peter 1:19), alluding to its predictions of the day when the Lord will come in judgment ("day of the Lord"). Apparently the destructive heresies had to do with teaching that denied the return of Christ in judgment and consequently encouraged a licentious lifestyle that followed "the corrupt desire of the flesh" (2:10).

Project Gutenberg

Lot flees the destruction of Sodom and Gomorrah by Gustave Doré.

Furthermore, these false teachers despised authority and were exploiting the churches with "fabricated stories" (2 Peter 2:3, 10) that opposed the eyewitness testimony of apostolic orthodoxy (1:16–18). With the passing of the apostles, the danger of heresy intensified, so Peter wrote that he would "make every effort to see that after my departure you will always be able to remember these things" (v. 15). After pronouncing scathing condemnation on the false teachers in 2 Peter 2:3–22, Peter includes a reaffirmation of teaching concerning the end of the world (3:1–10) and an exhortation that his readers live holy and godly lives in light of the coming judgment (v. 11).

These false teachers identified themselves as Christian believers. By living according to the corrupt desires of the sinful nature, they apparently failed to recognize sin as sin.

The Nature of the Destructive Heresy in 2 Peter

1. Rejects apostolic authority.
2. Fails to recognize a sinful lifestyle for what it is.
3. Blasphemously discounts coming judgment.
4. Denies the Lord's return.

Whenever sin is rationalized or ignored, a denial of Jesus Christ is involved, because Jesus died to **atone** for sin, and his costly **atonement** is demeaned by those who wish to call themselves Christian but at the same time live without recognizing the need for a profound transformation of their character, values, and lifestyle. Such "Christians" bring "the way of truth into disrepute" (2 Peter 2:2) and in the end will be judged as false believers no better than pagans.

Peter's authority as a church leader is of a different quality than that of the false teachers who did not see Jesus and who were not appointed by Jesus to be apostolic witnesses of the gospel. Through Jesus' teaching and by personally witnessing miraculous events, Peter had received knowledge about Jesus' identity (Matt. 16:17), about the coming of false teachers into the churches (Matt. 24:11, 24), and about the parousia (Matt. 24:29–31). Moreover, he had been transformed by the work of the Spirit from a cowardly follower of Jesus to a bold apostle accredited by the miracles the Lord had performed through him (Acts 3:12; 9:34, 40; 12:11). Against his apostolic authority, false teachers who had no such credentials and probably didn't even have the written Gospels were asserting their own fabricated teachings.

Their heresy erred in two ways. One involved a denial of the end of the world in judgment, as they apparently argued, "Where is this 'coming' he promised? Ever since our ancestors died, everything goes on as it has since the beginning of creation" (2 Peter 3:4). The stability of human life on earth over eons of time has certainly led many throughout history to believe in the eternity of the universe, a view that was popularly held during the apostolic period (though today has been replaced by the Big Bang theory of a beginning point of the universe in modern cosmology). The Christian gospel came into a world already full of religions and philosophies. As people came to faith in Christ from these

Gnosticism

Derived from the Greek word for knowledge (*gnosis*), the term denotes a philosophical system that flourished in the second century of this era. Its distinctive beliefs influenced many different religions, including streams of Christianity and Judaism of that time, and included the belief that the human soul was trapped in its material body and that a successful afterlife involved acquiring esoteric and mystical knowledge before death. The Christian version of this belief made Jesus' teaching a source of ***gnosis*** but disdained any atoning efficacy of his crucifixion and bodily resurrection. The attendant belief that the material world was inferior at best and evil at worst, created by an evil demigod was rooted in **Neoplatonic dualism**.

various backgrounds, they carried with them ideas and practices that distorted their understanding of the Christian faith. The particular false teachers addressed in 2 Peter (as well as in Jude) seem unwilling to let the gospel critique their former beliefs and have instead allowed those beliefs to critique the gospel. Then, as now, revelation is often wrongly judged by the philosophical currents of the day.

Gnosticism was a philosophical system that came to its fullest development in the second century and provided a convenient identification of the heresy for those inclined to date the origin of 2 Peter and other New Testament books to that late period. Gnosticism made inroads into all religions, including Judaism and Christianity. Based on a cosmological **dualism** rooted in **Neoplatonism**, in its heretical Christian form, it led to the rejection of the full humanity of Christ and the denial of the resurrection of the body. Salvation was defined as the attainment of the soul released at death from the prison of the material body to the highest heaven, based on a mystical and esoteric *gnosis* ("knowledge") acquired in life that was independent of ethical and moral standards. Embrace of such Gnostic ideas could lead to a very licentious lifestyle and a denial of divine judgment. Furthermore, Peter is concerned with knowledge of God, which he grounds in Scripture and the revelation of Jesus rather than in mystical experience (2 Peter 1:3; 3:18). Even in the first century, ideas later labeled as Gnostic were at work. Certainly the knowledge the false teachers claimed was based on some kind of individualistic experience, probably attributed to the Holy Spirit, and led to an unholy way of living. But 2 Peter does not seem to be concerned with a dualistic philosophy or christological heresy, such as found, for instance, in John's letters.

The false teachers of 2 Peter may have distorted the gospel to be compatible with Epicurean philosophy of that time.

Most recently scholars have turned to a philosophical system known to be active in the first century and before, namely, Epicureanism. We know from Acts 17:18 that Paul preached the gospel to Epicurean and **Stoic** philosophers in Athens. Epicurus (c. 341–c. 270 **BC**), the founder of this school of thought, lived three centuries before Christ, but the philosophy he proposed developed over time and was current in the first-century Roman world.

The philosophical school of Epicureanism believed that life's highest good was pleasure, defined by Epicurus as the tranquility of a life undisturbed by conflict, pain, or trouble. Later forms of Epicureanism had devolved into hedonism and the seeking of sensual pleasures, a thought apparently consistent with the false teaching described in 2 Peter (2:13). One of the principles of Epicureanism was a materialistic worldview that denied an afterlife, and consequently the denial of any judgment of this life became one of their defining characteristics. After all, fear of death and judgment would certainly trouble the tranquility of the soul.

Plutarch's *De Sera Numinis Vindicta* (548C, 549B) presents a first-century debate between the Epicureans and other Greco-Roman thinkers of the day on the issue of **theodicy**. In this work the "slowness" (Gk. *bradutēs*) of the deity to punish the wicked was a primary argument against divine judgment. This is a remarkable parallel to 2 Peter 3:9, where Peter refers to the Lord's "slowness" with the same Greek word, occurring only here in the Greek Old and New Testaments. And the false teachers seem to misconstrue the Lord's "slowness" along the same lines as Plutarch writes. In contrast in Peter's theodicy, God's slowness to judge is not an indication of his indifference or inability, but rather of his patience as he waits for people like the false teachers themselves to come to repentance and a true knowledge of his grace. For if he acted swiftly enough to please his critics, those who accuse him of slowness would themselves be destroyed in his judgment.

Epicureanism

A philosophical system founded by Epicurus (c. 341 – c. 270 BC), who taught a materialistic view of the universe that precluded an afterlife and promoted as life's highest good a peaceful and tranquil life based on knowledge, friends, and moderate and virtuous living.

In his *Obsolescence of Oracles* (420B), Plutarch writes that the Epicureans referred to stories of divine judgment as "myths" (Gk. *muthos*). In reaction to accusations influenced perhaps by such Epicurean thought, Peter responds in 1:16 that the gospel he preaches is not "cleverly devised stories" (same Greek word, *mythos*). Furthermore, the Epicureans rejected the authenticity of prophecy (Plutarch, *Obsolescence of Oracles* 434D; *Pythiae* 414E, 418E; *A Pleasant Life is Impossible* 1110D – E), which may account for the emphasis on Spirit-inspired prophecy in 2 Peter 1:19 – 21. Peter is turning the tables on the false teachers by exhorting his readers not to trust in cleverly devised "stories," such as those of the Epicureans, but in the true authority of the revelation of the Spirit through the prophets, who certainly spoke of "the day of the Lord" as a time of judgment by fire (cf. 2 Peter 3:10 – 12).

A third point of contact between Epicurean belief and the false teachers in 2 Peter is the drive for "pleasure" defined as carousing, reveling, and sexual immorality (2:13 – 14). While Epicurus himself would have disavowed such behavior, by the first century his pursuit of pleasure as life's highest good had devolved into hedonism.

theodicy: a defense of divine goodness and justice in light of the persistence and prosperity of evil.

While it may not be possible to label the false teachers, and perhaps they themselves had a mixture of wrong beliefs, many of the attitudes apparent among them are still expressed in the church today by Christians who defend a blatantly sinful lifestyle, a materialistic worldview that denies an afterlife, and living as if God will not judge. Peter ends his message with a restatement of the danger such ideas present: "since you have been forewarned, be on your guard so that you may not be carried away by the error of the lawless and fall from your secure position" (2 Peter 3:17). Instead, he exhorts them to "grow in the grace and knowledge of our Lord and Savior Jesus Christ" (v. 18), echoing his opening in 1:3 that Christians have everything needed "for a godly life through our knowledge of him who called us by his own glory and goodness."

THE THEOLOGY OF 2 PETER

The second letter of Peter is placed in canonical position following 1 Peter to provide the fullest possible voice of the Petrine witness to the Christian gospel. While 1 Peter is outward looking in its orientation, giving instructions for Christian living within unbelieving society, 2 Peter turns its attention to the internal issues of orthodoxy within the Christian community. Second Peter, like all the New Testament epistles, is not a discourse in theology. Nevertheless, as Peter responds to the danger of false teachers, he refers or alludes to many of his theological beliefs.

God

Statements about God in 2 Peter are made primarily within the context of judgment and salvation from judgment. God is he who by his word created the earth through water and also destroyed the world of Noah through water (3:5–6). Judgment preceding punishment is the fate of the ungodly, whether they are angels (2:3), people of the Old Testament era (2:5–6), or the spiritually immature and self-deluded who think of their Christian faith in God's grace as a license for immorality (e.g., "If I'm saved, then it doesn't matter what I do").

Beyond his sovereignty as Creator and Judge, the most prominent characteristic of God presented in 2 Peter is his patience. By his longsuffering of those who reject or distort his grace, blaspheme that which they don't understand, and revel in immorality, even enticing others to the same, God's inscrutable sense of time may give the appearance that he lets the ungodly get away with it, but in fact he is expressing his patience with the slowness of people to come to repentance (3:8–9). This patient lapse of time where daily life seems to go on forever, generation after generation, should not be construed to mean that it doesn't matter whether one lives a godly or ungodly life. The "day of God" (3:12) will come, and it will be a day of punishment for the unrighteous (2:9). But God is also a Savior, who knows how to deliver the righteous (2:9) who look forward, not to judgment, but to a new heaven and new earth (3:13).

A second observation about God in 2 Peter that is consistent with the synoptic tradition, but independent from it, is that he bestows honor and glory on Jesus at the transfiguration when the voice of the Majestic Glory declares Jesus to be the beloved Son (1:17). Peter clearly refers to God, the divinity of Jesus Christ as Son of God, and the Holy Spirit as the medium of God's revelation, thereby showing his Trinitarian belief about the Godhead.

Jesus Christ

The explicit reference to a previous letter (2 Peter 3:1) invites us to read the **Christology** of 2 Peter in light of 1 Peter. Peter's first letter centered its Christology in the atonement of the crucifixion. In this second letter, the coming judgment and return of Christ takes greater prominence. The final judgment of God is emphasized in 2 Peter, and Christ provides salvation for the believer from that judgment. When taken together, these two books give a fully orbed Christology.

In 2 Peter 1:1 Peter identifies himself as a servant and apostle of Jesus Christ, indicating his call as a prophet and witness of the message of Christ, who is further identified as "our God and Savior." It is through the righteousness of Christ, who is also God, that faith comes to Peter's readers. He is the sovereign Lord who "buys" sinners (2:1), enabling their freedom from the corruption of this world (2:20) and offering an eternal kingdom (1:11) in the new heaven and earth where righteousness dwells (3:13).

Although all three **Synoptic Gospels** present the transfiguration of Jesus in the presence of Peter, James, and John, this epistle alone understands it to have been a vision of the glory and power of Jesus at his future second coming (2 Peter 1:16), an event denied by the false teachers (3:3–4). It is Peter's eyewitness revelation of Christ's power that makes his teachings superior to those of the false teachers, who rely merely on their own instincts (2:12) as they appeal to the lustful desires of human nature (2:18) and entice young believers to follow them away from the truth (2:19). Their arrogant presumption in spiritual matters leads them to blaspheme by professing a Christianity devoid of Christ himself. This errant **soteriology** and eschatology inevitably result in immoral ethics and a licentious lifestyle.

Holy Spirit

In 2 Peter only one statement is made about the Holy Spirit, and that is his role as an agent of divine inspiration of prophecy. He "carried" the prophets who spoke from God (1:21). In contrast to the false teachers' own interpretation of things spiritual, the prophecy of Scripture was not by the prophet's own interpretation, but the Holy Spirit was the agent who moved the prophets to speak the words of God. Peter's witness of Jesus' transfiguration has further confirmed the prophecies of Scripture, and he points to both to refute the claims of the false teachers.

It is probably Peter's recognition of the Holy Spirit in the production of Scripture that allows Peter to refer to Paul's writings as he does (2 Peter 3:15–16). Paul does not interpret spiritual matters from his own wisdom but writes with the wisdom God gave to him (v. 15) as he too, according to Peter, speaks of the Lord's patience providing the space for repentance. Recognizing the unstated role of the Holy Spirit in Paul's apostolic teaching allows Peter to refer to Paul's letters as on par with the words of past prophets in Scripture, which ignorant and unstable people distort to their own destruction.

"The heavens will disappear with a roar; the elements will be destroyed by fire" (2 Peter 3:10).

Eschatology

Peter speaks of a world beyond this one in which Jesus Christ will reign eternally (2 Peter 1:11) and where righteousness will dwell in the new heaven and new earth (3:13). Just as God created the heavens and the earth that we know, there will be another divine re-creation after God's day of judgment and destruction of this world.

That day will come "like a thief" (2 Peter 3:10), a phrase found also in Paul's eschatology (1 Thess. 5:2) and that echoes Jesus' teaching on eschatology in Matthew (24:43) and Luke (12:39). The ongoing existence of human life as it has been from the beginning should not be misunderstood as evidence of God's inaction, inability, or indifference to unrighteousness and evil. Scoffers who make this mistake that all will go on regardless of how they live are themselves part of what characterizes the last days (3:3). Their rejection of the theology of Christ's second coming in judgment and power allows them to live according to their own evil desires, accountable to no higher authority than their own instincts. As suddenly and unexpectedly as a thief will come the day of judgment, a day when the heavens and "the elements" (see commentaries) will be destroyed by fire and the earth and everything done in it will be disclosed (2 Peter 3:10, 12). Without announcement, the world as we know it will end. This thought leads Peter to ask, "Since everything will be destroyed in this way, what kind of people ought you to be?" (v. 11). His question brings us to the major theme of Christian living and ethics in 2 Peter.

> "Bad eschatology leads to bad ethics."
>
> Ben Witherington III, *Letters and Homilies for Hellenized Christians*

THE CHRISTIAN LIFE OF ETHICAL VIRTUE

The major reason Peter wrote as he did was to point out the great danger of false teachers who claimed to be Christian but who were denying the return of Christ and the certainty of divine judgment. Their way of thinking led to a licentious lifestyle in which those who claimed to be spiritually enlightened could live as their instincts demanded without thought of the standards by which God would judge them. On the threshold of death, the great apostle sees this pressing danger and reinforces what he knows of Jesus and God's judgment based not on his own imagination but on what he experienced as an eyewitness (Gk. *epoptēs*) of Christ's death and glory. His emphasis on the reality of God's sovereignty in both the creation of the world and its final end in judgment is given not primarily to correct the false teachers, who were probably not receptive to his teaching anyway, but to prevent his readers who had regard for his apostolic authority from abandoning their knowledge of the truth to follow the easier path to doom (2 Peter 3:17). In other words, in light of the eventual destruction of this world and God's judgment on its inhabitants, how should people live who have received faith "through the righteousness of our God and Savior Jesus Christ" (1:1)?

In the very midst of false teaching by those who claim to be Christian and in a world filled with pagan idolatry and corrupt morality, Peter claims that Christ has given his people "everything we need for a godly life through our knowledge of him" (2 Peter 1:3), the very knowledge of Christ that brings us grace and peace (1:2). The godly ("divine") life that Christians are called to live is removed from the corruption of the world caused by evil desires (1:4). The false teachers were promising freedom to those who would follow, without recognizing that they themselves were slaves to depravity (2:19). A right understanding of salvation does not grant the Christian freedom to sin; it delivers Christians *from* a sinful lifestyle to the freedom to live in a way that pleases God.

The Christian life begins with faith (1:5) that Jesus is the Son of God who will deliver those who are his from the coming destruction and judgment to a place where righteousness dwells, the new heaven and new earth (3:13). But Peter teaches that to escape the world's corruption one must have a change of character. To faith in Christ one must add goodness, and to goodness, knowledge; to knowledge one must add self-control and then perseverance; to perseverance one must add godliness followed by mutual affection and, finally, love (1:5–8). In other words, Peter sees the Christian life that pleases God as one of growing virtue, or as theologians might put it, of sanctification. The apostle Paul says something very similar in his passage on the fruit of the Holy Spirit in Galatians 5:22–24. Peter acknowledges that his readers already know these things but considers it right that he continually remind them of it, for the world's corruption continually presses in, even making inroads into the church through false teachers.

Steps to Spiritual Maturity: 2 Peter 1:5–7

"Make every effort to add to your faith goodness; and to goodness, knowledge; and to knowledge, self-control; and to self-control, perseverance; and to perseverance, godliness; and to godliness, mutual affection; and to mutual affection, love."

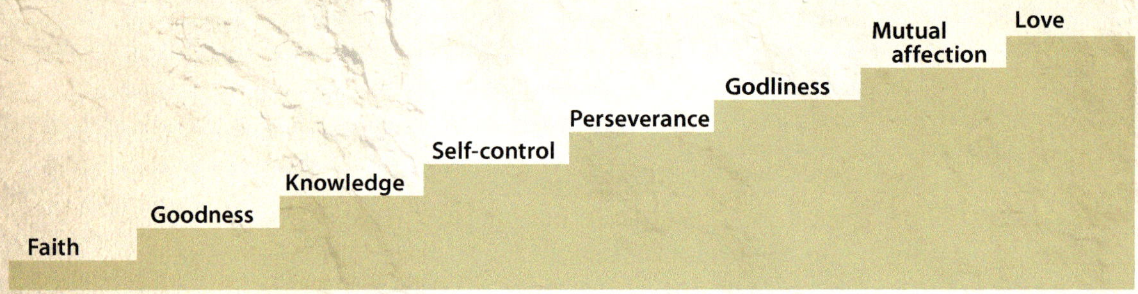

Peter presents the Christian virtues in a rhetorical form that suggests progression and growth—to this, add that. It should not be read as stages of sanctification through life; for instance, that only after one has accomplished knowledge can one then move on to self-control. The point is that the Christian life is one of moral growth and transformation, a concept that would also have been familiar from the moral philosophy of the Greco-Roman period, a tradition that also commended the development of virtue throughout one's life. In fact, even our own modern culture has some implicit expectation that growth from childhood to adult life will be accompanied by an increasing measure of moral maturity. The problem is that there is little consensus about what constitutes morality in a pluralistic, democratic society that rejects accountability to God yet wishes to cling to some association with historic Christianity. In this rhetorical chain of Christian virtues, Peter presses home the point that the life that pleases God is the life of moral responsibility, contra the false teachers who argue that since there will be no judgment, moral standards are an unnecessary guide in living one's life. The radical individualism and rejection of all authority that characterized the 1960s in North America parallels the apparent beliefs of the false teachers. "If it feels good, do it!" was one '60s slogan that sounds very much like Peter's description of "creatures of instinct" (2:12) whose "idea of pleasure is to carouse in broad daylight" (2:13). Peter's second letter is quite applicable to those today who wish to think of themselves in some sense as Christians yet resent the biblical claim that they are accountable to God and will be judged by the standard of his revealed word in Scripture.

A Christian who becomes entangled in the corruption of the world is like a sow returning to the mud (2 Peter 2:22).

And so while Peter is concerned with correct doctrine concerning eschatology, his pressing issue is the danger of moral and ethical collapse within the church(es). What one believes about the future determines how one lives today. Bad eschatology breeds bad ethics. But as Peter reminds his readers, God's divine power has already provided everything needed to live the life pleasing to him and to keep the Christian life from being ineffective and unproductive (1:8). However, to neglect one's moral responsibility as a Christian is to forget one's cleansing from past sins. It is to be nearsighted, thinking only of the moment, and blind to the bigger picture of eternity (1:9). Peter exhorts his readers to grow in the virtues, which confirms their calling and election in Christ and assures a rich welcome into the eternal kingdom of the Lord and Savior Jesus Christ (1:10–11).

PETER'S KNOWLEDGE OF PAUL'S LETTERS

From reading Acts and the New Testament epistles, one might wonder how much the apostles knew of one another's work and writings. Certainly a select group were together at least briefly at the Jerusalem Council (Acts 15). Did these men have ongoing contact throughout the years of their ministries? Did Peter know of Paul's whereabouts and the churches he planted? Did Jude and Peter know each other later in their lives? The New Testament gives virtually no information about such questions. But 2 Peter includes the intriguing reference to Paul's letters (3:15–16) that calls attention to exactly these issues.

The apostles Paul and Peter by Carlo Crivelli (1435/40–1493).

It seems that the false teachers had read at least some of Paul's letters and were using ideas from them to defend their own view of spiritual liberty. Paul wrote several letters to churches in Asia Minor (Ephesians, Colossians, Galatians, 1 and 2 Timothy, and the lost letter to Laodicea), and these letters were copied, exchanged, and read even during the apostle's lifetime (Col. 4:16). Yet we need not think that Peter is writing to the same churches in Asia Minor that Paul founded and to whom he wrote, for apostolic letters probably reached most if not all churches in Asia Minor without many decades of delay. (The **Rylands fragment** of John's gospel found in Egypt dating to just one or two decades after being written attests to the speed at which some writings traveled through the Roman world.) It also is not necessary to assume that this reference to Paul's letter signals a time long after Paul's death when the writings that would become the New Testament were beginning to be collected and bound.

What is more intriguing is that Peter himself seems to be familiar with Paul's letters, even though we have no historically verifiable evidence that Peter resided in the several cities where Paul's churches were located. (Although 1 Cor. 1:12 could be construed to mean that Peter had visited at least the Corinthian churches.) Even so, it would be remarkable timing if Peter arrived after each had received a letter from Paul. It seems more likely that Peter had access to Paul's letters in a different location, possibly Rome. This would suggest that copies of apostolic correspondence may have been frequently, if not routinely, exchanged. This also could help explain the relationship between 2 Peter and Jude (see below).

Those who date 2 Peter well after the apostle's lifetime argue that the reference to Paul's letters as "Scripture" would require a date well into the process of canon formation. Extending the Jewish concept of the Old Testament as Scripture, Paul referred to Jesus' teachings as Scripture (1 Tim. 5:18 apparently referring to teaching recorded in Matt. 10:10; Luke 10:7). Inasmuch as Jesus was the Messiah promised by the Old Testament and the gospel of his life, death, and resurrection is the consummation of the old covenant, the gospel of Jesus Christ as preached by the apostles was easily included within the extended concept of Scripture, especially if the apostolic teaching was thought to be inspired by the same Holy Spirit who inspired the prophets of old (cf. 1 Peter 1:10–12). It is therefore no stretch to understand Peter referring to Paul's letters as Scripture, because they proclaim the Spirit-inspired truth of Jesus Christ.

Peter implies a unity between his message and that of Paul by pointing out that any interpretation of Paul's letters that puts the two at odds is a twisting of Paul's teaching, some of which is admittedly difficult to understand (3:16).[22] False teaching that claims to be based in Scripture but that in fact twists and distorts it is a particularly insidious danger in the church. One does not have to think too hard to recall contemporary issues in which twisted interpretations have distorted biblical truth.

2 PETER'S RELATIONSHIP WITH 1 PETER

The books within the New Testament that are most similar to 2 Peter are 1 Peter and Jude. Both epistles of 1 Peter and 2 Peter present themselves as written by the apostle Peter, although 2 Peter uses both Peter's given name (Simon) and his nickname Peter (Gk. *petros*, "rock"). Furthermore, 2 Peter 3:1 refers to a previous letter that is either 1 Peter or that has not survived. The main difficulties of authentic Petrine authorship of both arise when the original Greek text of the two letters are compared and found to be very different in their Greek vocabulary, syntax, and style. Of the 735 forms in 1 Peter, about half are not used in 2 Peter, and about 230 forms in 2 Peter are not used in the first epistle.[23] Moreover, 2 Peter includes fifty-four words not used elsewhere in the New Testament (***hapax legomena***)—a very high number considering how brief the epistle is. As discussed above, the style of 2 Peter is observed to tend toward iambic rhythm, a feature suggesting very strong Greek literary influence that is lacking in 1 Peter. First Peter abundantly uses connecting particles; 2 Peter more sparsely. First Peter is full of quotations, allusions, and images from the Old Testament; 2 Peter much less so. None of these differences need compel the conclusion of a different author, although they do seem compelling enough that many interpreters suggest a native Greek amanuensis penned 2 Peter on behalf of the apostle. To others the differences do compel the conclusion of pseudonymous authorship (see discussion above).

"No document in the New Testament is so like 1 Peter as 2 Peter."

CHARLES BIGG

On the other hand, after detailing the differences between 1 and 2 Peter, Charles Bigg concludes, "No document in the New Testament is so like 1 Peter as 2 Peter."[24]

22. For a list of similar concepts found in Peter's and Paul's letters, see Neyrey, *2 Peter, Jude*, 133.
23. Bigg, *Peter and Jude*, 224–32.
24. Ibid., 232.

- The greetings in 1 Peter 1:2 and 2 Peter 1:2, "Grace to you and peace be multiplied" (Gk. *charis hymōn kai eirēnē plēthuntheiē*) are identical to each other but different from every other New Testament epistle and include the relatively rare optative form of the verb. Of course, such a thing would be easy for a pseudepigrapher to mimic.
- Despite differences in vocabulary overall, 2 Peter 1:12–2:3 shares eighteen common words with 1 Peter, including some relatively rare words, such as *apothesis* ("removal"), that do not occur in other books of the New Testament. Such overlap in such short letters is probably not accidental.[25]
- God's role in 2 Peter is primarily as Creator and Judge (2:4; 3:5), which is the same portrayal as in 1 Peter (3:20; 4:19).
- Both books mention the inspiration of the prophets (1 Peter 1:10–12; cf. 2 Peter 1:16–21).
- Both letters not only mention Noah as evidence of God's ability to save, but Noah and seven others (1 Peter 3:20; cf. 2 Peter 2:5).
- Only these two letters in the New Testament use the words "spotless" (Gk. *aspilos*) and "blameless" (Gk. *amōmos*) together (1 Peter 1:19; 2 Peter 3:14).
- Both 1 and 2 Peter assume familiarity with the Jewish book known as *1 Enoch*, though neither letter quotes it (1 Peter 3:19–20; 2 Peter 2:4–5).

In addition to these commonalities, there is a similarity of ideas when the opening verses of each letter are compared, albeit with differences in expression and emphasis:[26]

Comparison of Sequence of Thought
So I will always remind you of these things. (2 Peter 1:12)

1 Peter 1:3–9	2 Peter 1:3–11
Through the resurrection of Christ, we have hope of an incorruptible and undefiled inheritance, reserved for us in heaven. This inheritance is for those guarded by faith until salvation "in the last time" and is a cause of rejoicing in the grief of present trials or temptations. Faith, tested and proved by suffering, will issue in glory, honor, and salvation "when Jesus Christ is revealed" (i.e., at the parousia).	Christ's divine power and glory are sources of all things pertaining to life and godliness, as well as of precious promises that allow us to avoid corruption. To faith other spiritual virtues must be added. This will promote the necessary knowledge of Jesus Christ and be in keeping with cleansing from former sins. Make your calling and election sure, as well as your entry into Christ's eternal kingdom.

Those who believe 2 Peter to be the work of an anonymous pseudepigrapher would explain all these similarities of shared distinctive words, references, and sequence of ideas as careful attention to and mimicking of 1 Peter. However, they could also be the fingerprint of a common author.

25. Ben Witherington, *1–2 Peter*, 264.

26. G. H. Boobyer, "The Indebtedness of 2 Peter to 1 Peter," in *New Testament Essays: Studies in Memory of Thomas Walter Manson*, ed. A. J. B. Higgins (Manchester: Manchester University Press, 1959), 40.

2 PETER'S RELATIONSHIP WITH JUDE

One has only to read Jude and 2 Peter one after the other to notice that almost all of Jude's polemic, with some interesting omissions, is included in the second chapter of 2 Peter. Of Jude's twenty-five verses, nineteen of them appear in 2 Peter. Although 2 Peter and Jude are addressed to different audiences—Jude probably to a Palestinian audience and 2 Peter to Christians living in Asia Minor—the problematic circumstances in each place were apparently similar enough to warrant condemnation in the same terms. This relationship between the text of the two letters raises the question that any professor facing two student papers with such overlap would ask: Who copied from whom? Of course, in the case of 2 Peter and Jude, it is also possible that both copied from a third source no longer extant—for instance, the apostolic **kerygma**, or preaching, that may have been repeated orally in a much more crystallized form than sermons of today.

A Comparison of Jude and 2 Peter

Jude 1:4–25	2 Peter 2:1–3:3
Jude 4 For certain individuals whose condemnation was written about long ago have secretly slipped in among you. They are ungodly people, who pervert the grace of our God into a license for immorality and deny Jesus Christ our only Sovereign and Lord.	*2 Peter 2:1* But there were also false prophets among the people, just as there will be false teachers among you. They will secretly introduce destructive heresies, even denying the sovereign Lord who bought them—bringing swift destruction on themselves.
Jude 6 And the angels who did not keep their positions of authority but abandoned their proper dwelling—these he has kept in darkness, bound with everlasting chains for judgment on the great Day. *Jude 7* In a similar way, Sodom and Gomorrah and the surrounding towns gave themselves up to sexual immorality and perversion. They serve as an example of those who suffer the punishment of eternal fire.	*2 Peter 2:4* For if God did not spare angels when they sinned, but sent them to hell, putting them in chains of darkness to be held for judgment; *2 Peter 2:5* if he did not spare the ancient world when he brought the flood on its ungodly people, but protected Noah, a preacher of righteousness, and seven others; *2 Peter 2:6* if he condemned the cities of Sodom and Gomorrah by burning them to ashes, and made them an example of what is going to happen to the ungodly; . . .
Jude 8 In the very same way, on the strength of their dreams these ungodly people pollute their own bodies, reject authority and heap abuse on celestial beings. *Jude 9* But even the archangel Michael, when he was disputing with the devil about the body of Moses, did not himself dare to condemn him for slander but said, "The Lord rebuke you!" *Jude 10* Yet these people slander whatever they do not understand, and the very things they do understand by instinct—as irrational animals do—will destroy them.	*2 Peter 2:10* This is especially true of those who follow the corrupt desire of the flesh and despise authority. Bold and arrogant, they are not afraid to heap abuse on celestial beings; *2 Peter 2:11* yet even angels, although they are stronger and more powerful, do not heap abuse on such beings when bringing judgment on them from the Lord. *2 Peter 2:12* But these people blaspheme in matters they do not understand. They are like unreasoning animals, creatures of instinct, born only to be caught and destroyed, and like animals they too will perish.

Jude 1:4–25	2 Peter 2:1–3:3
Jude 11 Woe to them! They have taken the way of Cain; they have rushed for profit into Balaam's error; they have been destroyed in Korah's rebellion. *Jude 12* These people are blemishes at your love feasts, eating with you without the slightest qualm—shepherds who feed only themselves. They are clouds without rain, blown along by the wind; autumn trees, without fruit and uprooted—twice dead. *Jude 13* They are wild waves of the sea, foaming up their shame; wandering stars, for whom blackest darkness has been reserved forever. *Jude 14* Enoch, the seventh from Adam, prophesied about them: "See, the Lord is coming with thousands upon thousands of his holy ones *Jude 15* to judge everyone, and to convict all of them of all the ungodly acts they have committed in their ungodliness, and of all the defiant words ungodly sinners have spoken against him." *Jude 16* These people are grumblers and faultfinders; they follow their own evil desires; they boast about themselves and flatter others for their own advantage. *Jude 17* But, dear friends, remember what the apostles of our Lord Jesus Christ foretold. *Jude 18* They said to you, "In the last times there will be scoffers who will follow their own ungodly desires." *Jude 19* These are the people who divide you, who follow mere natural instincts and do not have the Spirit.	*2 Peter 2:13* They will be paid back with harm for the harm they have done. Their idea of pleasure is to carouse in broad daylight. They are blots and blemishes, reveling in their pleasures while they feast with you. *2 Peter 2:14* With eyes full of adultery, they never stop sinning; they seduce the unstable; they are experts in greed—an accursed brood! *2 Peter 2:15* They have left the straight way and wandered off to follow the way of Balaam son of Bezer, who loved the wages of wickedness. *2 Peter 2:16* But he was rebuked for his wrongdoing by a donkey—an animal without speech—who spoke with a human voice and restrained the prophet's madness. *2 Peter 2:17* These people are springs without water and mists driven by a storm. Blackest darkness is reserved for them. *2 Peter 2:18* For they mouth empty, boastful words and, by appealing to the lustful desires of the flesh, they entice people who are just escaping from those who live in error. *2 Peter 2:19* They promise them freedom, while they themselves are slaves of depravity—for "people are slaves to whatever has mastered them." *2 Peter 2:20* If they have escaped the corruption of the world by knowing our Lord and Savior Jesus Christ and are again entangled in it and are overcome, they are worse off at the end than they were at the beginning. *2 Peter 2:21* It would have been better for them not to have known the way of righteousness, than to have known it and then to turn their backs on the sacred command that was passed on to them. *2 Peter 2:22* Of them the proverbs are true: "A dog returns to its vomit," and, "A sow that is washed returns to her wallowing in the mud." *2 Peter 3:1* Dear friends, this is now my second letter to you. I have written both of them as reminders to stimulate you to wholesome thinking. *2 Peter 3:2* I want you to recall the words spoken in the past by the holy prophets and the command given by our Lord and Savior through your apostles. *2 Peter 3:3* Above all, you must understand that in the last days scoffers will come, scoffing and following their own evil desires.

Although the two texts are similar enough to suggest a relationship, note that they do not display the same kind of literary relationship as the Synoptic Gospels. Consider for instance:[27]

Example of the Literary Relationship of the Synoptic Gospels		
Matthew 9:14–15	*Mark 2:18–20*	*Luke 5:33–35*
Then the disciples of John came to him, saying, "Why do we and the Pharisees fast, but your disciples do not fast?" And Jesus said to them, "Can the wedding guests mourn as long as the bride- groom is with them? The days will come, when the bridegroom is taken away from them, and then they will fast."	And people came and said to him, "Why do John's disciples and the disciples of the Pharisees fast, but your disciples do not fast?" And Jesus said to them, "Can the wedding guests fast while the bridegroom is with them? As long as they have the bridegroom with them, they cannot fast. The days will come, when the bridegroom is taken away from them, and then they will fast in that day."	And they said to him, "The disciples of John fast often and offer prayers, and so do the disciples of the Pharisees, but yours eat and drink. And Jesus said to them, "Can you make wedding guests fast while the bridegroom is with them? The days will come when the bridegroom is taken away from them, and then they will fast in those days."

This example from the Synoptic Gospels shows a close lexical similarity that characterizes the Synoptics, but the same episode is found in a different sequence in the narrative flow. In Jude and 2 Peter we find generally the same sequence of thoughts, some of the same language and images of condemnation, but it is not as if one "cut and pasted" from the other, as could be argued for the synoptic relationships.

A Closer Look at the Similarity

Jude 10 (NIV)

Yet these people slander whatever they do not understand, and the very things they do understand by instinct—as irrational animals do—will destroy them.

2 Peter 2:12–13a

But these people blaspheme in matters they do not understand. They are like unreasoning animals, creatures of instinct, born only to be caught and destroyed, and like animals they too will perish.

Despite the obvious similarities, some interesting differences should also be observed:

27. Reproduced from Kurt Aland, ed., *Synopsis of the Four Gospels* (New York: United Bible Societies, 1982), 43.

- Second Peter refers to the heretics as "false teachers" (Gk. *pseudodidaskaloi*), whereas Jude does not, preferring instead the more general "certain individuals" and "these people." This may suggest that the churches in Asia Minor were facing problems with heretical leadership, while the heretics in Palestine were personally influential but did not hold a leadership role in the church(es).
- Jude freely quotes from a noncanonical Jewish text known to us as *1 Enoch* and relates a story about the archangel Michael and the body of Moses probably found in a second noncanonical text, the *Assumption of Moses*.[28] The author of 2 Peter omits this material, though he seems to assume a familiarity with *1 Enoch*.[29]
- The false teaching in 2 Peter concerns a denial of the return of Christ and the end of the world in judgment; this doctrinal issue does not seem to be a factor in Jude.

Therefore, while some sort of relationship between 2 Peter and Jude seems undeniable, it is not simply a matter that one copied from the other without making deliberate modifications presumably best suited for the new purpose. Because firm dates are unknown for either letter, the question of which was written first and who borrowed from whom must rest primarily on external assumptions and on matters of style, which will always strike different people subjectively. Martin Luther affirmed that Jude copied from 2 Peter, a position that was widely held until modern critical times. This was based largely on the thought that the lesser borrows from the greater. Peter is a great apostle about whom much is known from the Gospels, but Jude, though a brother of Jesus, never attained the same degree of celebrity. However, the work of Richard Bauckham has convincingly demonstrated that the immediate family of Jesus took up the work of the gospel after his resurrection, preached throughout Palestine, and enjoyed considerable authority and fame, at least in that region.[30] It appears that one or more of them may have led the Jerusalem church after James, the brother of Jesus, was martyred. These findings have blunted the argument that an apostle would not borrow material from a brother of Jesus, but those scholars who still argue for the priority of 2 Peter observe that Jude 17–18 sounds very much like a quotation of 2 Peter 3:3, where the heretics only predicted in 2 Peter had subsequently arrived when Jude was written:

2 Peter 3:3

Above all, you must understand that in the last days scoffers will come, scoffing and following their own evil desires.

Jude 17–18

But, dear friends, remember what the apostles of our Lord Jesus Christ foretold. They said to you, "In the last times there will be scoffers who will follow their own ungodly desires."

Comparisons of the two texts yield observations such as the order followed by each writer when listing God's judgment:[31]

---

28. At the time this text was named, the English word *assumption* referred to one's ascent and reception into heaven.

29. For the significance of *1 Enoch* to Peter's writings, see Karen H. Jobes, *1 Peter*, BECNT (Grand Rapids: Baker Academic, 2005), 235–56.

30. Richard Bauckham, *Jude and the Relatives of Jesus in the Early Church* (Edinburgh: T&T Clark, 1990).

31. Bigg, *Epistles*, 221.

Order of Events Mentioned from the Old Testament	
2 Peter	*Jude*
1.———	Israel in the wilderness
2. Fallen angels	Fallen angels
3. The flood (Noah)	———
4. Sodom and Gomorrah	Sodom and Gomorrah
5.———	Cain
6. Balaam	Balaam
7.———	Korah's rebellion

Note that the references in 2 Peter are arranged in chronological order, but those in Jude are not. Should strict chronological order count as evidence for the priority of 2 Peter? There is no logical necessity to this conclusion, but some find it appealing. Based on various observations about the comparison of the texts in light of redaction theory, the consensus of New Testament scholarship today is that the author of 2 Peter borrowed his material from Jude's letter, to which he had access. If both letters are considered authentic, then this relationship between 2 Peter and Jude is further evidence that the apostles had access to copies of each other's letters, even when not residing in the same geographical locale.

Modern sensibilities may be offended that the author of 2 Peter—even if and especially if the great apostle Peter—would so freely copy another's words. Does the literary relationship between these two letters in itself constitute a moral infringement? Actually, when understood in its own cultural moment, it does not. The modern concept of plagiarism as theft of published material is based in the monetary value of intellectual property that the copyright laws define. Plagiarism between students is morally wrong because it presents another's work as if it were one's own, even though another student's work is not copyrighted, and is a matter of integrity. We cannot not assume that the values of modern society that plagiarism violates were values in ancient society.

Correspondences between 2 Peter and Jude*

2 Peter passage:	*Jude passage:*
2:1	4
2:2	4
2:3	4
2:4	6
2:6	7
2:9	6
2:10	7b – 8
2:11	9
2:12	10
2:15	11
2:13	12a
2:17	12b – 13
2:18	16
3:1 – 2	17
3:3	18
3:14	24
3:18	25

*Gene Green, *Jude and 2 Peter*, BECNT (Grand Rapids: Baker Academic, 2008), 159.

Bildarchiv Preussischer Kulturbesitz/Art Resource, NY

The false teachers have followed the way of Balaam (Num. 22–24). Painting by Luca Giordano (1634 – 1705).

In fact, in the Greco-Roman literary culture, there was the acceptable practice of ***imitatio*** (Gk. *mimēsis*), in which an author would incorporate material from a well-known work into his own with the expectation that its source would be recognized.[32] The borrowed material would not simply be pasted into the new text, but it would be reworked to some extent in order to display the creativity and suit the new purposes of the borrower. The borrowed material, while recognizable, was transformed and remade into a new work, much as we see in the relationship between Jude and 2 Peter. *Imitatio* preserved and propagated classic texts while at the same recontextualizing them for a new audience through the reworking of the borrowed material. Cicero, Quintilian, Dionysus of Halicarnassus, and Longinus refer to the practice as applied to a range of genres from history to poetry. Seneca explains that Ovid appropriated material from Virgil "with no thought of plagiarism, but meaning that his piece of open borrowing should be recognized" (Seneca the Elder, *Suasoriae* 3.7). As the saying goes, "Imitation is the sincerest form of flattery," and the practice of *imitatio* was perceived as ascribing honor to its author. So if Peter's use of Jude is *imitatio*, then Peter is indeed ascribing honor to the brother of Jesus (or vice versa, as the case may be). As Gene Green explains:

> Peter's intertextual methodology transforms Jude's thought, making it his own to advance his own argument . . . and offering us an example of *imitatio*. While he uses Jude extensively, he

32. Gene Green, *Jude and 2 Peter*, BECNT (Grand Rapids: Baker Academic, 2008), 161 – 62.

adapts the language and thought to his own ends, making the work at hand his very own. In this process, the new situation before him calls on him to expand the original.[33]

While it may never be known with certainty in which direction the borrowing went, the relationship between 2 Peter and Jude demonstrates the legitimate sharing of common material within the common mission shared by the leaders of the first-century church around the Mediterranean world. Given the relative ease of travel and communication, it is not a stretch to assume that either Peter or Jude knew of the other's writing. It also shows that the problem of people in the churches who wished to believe themselves Christian yet live an immoral life based on a presumed spiritual superiority derived from unbiblical concepts was not an isolated problem but one fought on many fronts by the early church.

TEXT AND CANONICITY

The Greek Text of 2 Peter

The earliest extant (i.e., surviving) copy of 2 Peter is a **papyrus** fragment dating from the late third or early fourth century known as 𝔓[72], which contains 2 Peter 1:1–3, 18. It is among the Bodmer papyri housed at the Bibliotheca Bodmeriana in Cologny, Switzerland. The Bodmer papyri were discovered in Egypt in 1952 and are named for Martin Bodmer who purchased them. The earliest complete copy of 2 Peter is in the fourth-century Codex Sinaiticus at the British Library in London, a **codex** that contains all of the books of the New Testament canon.

The twenty-four readings of 2 Peter in *Editio Critica Maior* that differ from NA27 can be found in Peter M. Head, 'Editio Critica Maior: An Introduction and Assessment', *Tyndale Bulletin* 61.1 (2010), 150–151, available online at https://www.academia.edu/3633883/_Editio_Critica_Maior_An_Introduction_and_Assessment_Tyndale_Bulletin_61.1_2010_131-152 (accessed May 2, 2016).

Canonicity

Just as many, and perhaps most, New Testament scholars today doubt that 2 Peter was written by the apostle Peter, ancient writers expressed similar doubts for similar reasons. In the third and early fourth century, Eusebius wrote, "And Peter, on whom the Church of Christ is built, against which the gates of Hades shall not prevail, has left one acknowledged epistle, and, it may be, a second also; for it is doubted" *(Hist. eccl.* 6.25.8). Writing about that same time, Jerome noted the "discrepant" style and character between the two epistles bearing Peter's name and spoke about the use of different "interpreters" to explain those differences, but he did not question the letter's authority or place in the canon:

> He [Paul], therefore, had Titus as an interpreter just as the blessed Peter also had Mark, whose Gospel was composed with Peter narrating and him writing. Further, two epistles also, which are extant as of Peter, are discrepant among themselves in style and character and structure of the words, from which we understand that he used different interpreters as necessary (*Letters* 120.11).[34]

Modern observers note that 2 Peter does not appear on several early extant canon lists. The early doubts about the letter's authorship and its absence from canon lists, such as the

33. Ibid., 162.
34. Quoted in Green, *Jude and 2 Peter*, 143.

The Authenticity of 2 Peter Was Questioned Even in Ancient Times

"Of Peter, one epistle, that which is called his first, is admitted and the ancient presbyters used this in their own writings as unquestioned, but the so-called second Epistle we have not received as canonical, but nevertheless it has appeared useful to many, and has been studied with other Scriptures."

Eusebius, *Hist. eccl.* 3.3.1

Muratorian Canon (AD 175), have led some to conclude that the book is not only pseudonymous but was written in the late second century, making it perhaps the last book written that was eventually included in the New Testament canon. However, its absence from any given canon list means only that the churches or individual associated with that list either did not consider 2 Peter to be canonical or did not know of the book—or in some cases that the extant canon list itself is in poor condition and that the original inclusion of a given book has been lost. Given the parochial nature of the earliest canon lists, the absence of any given book is not airtight evidence against its existence or authority, for it took time for books known and accepted by the churches in one geographical area to be known and accepted by all. The earliest extant list of canonical books as we know it today dates from the fourth century with Athanasius's Easter letter (*Ep. fest.* 39.4–5; AD 367), but the full extent of the canon may have already been recognized for decades if not centuries. The books of the New Testament did not appear simultaneously to the church everywhere as soon as they were written; therefore discrepancies between which churches knew which books at which point in time are not surprising. The exchange and travel of authoritative writings among the churches is well attested, beginning with Paul's letters (Col. 4:16). Polycarp, bishop of the churches in Smyrna, also attests to the practice of forwarding letters by copying them, "We are sending to you the letters of Ignatius that were sent to us by him together with any others that we have in our possession.... They are appended to this letter" (*Phil.* 13). This probably means that a letter by a given authority would be better attested within the locale of its origin and the network of churches associated by personal contact. It could therefore take quite some time for an apostolic letter to be copied and reach all the churches. When the bishops gathered for councils, authentic apostolic letters that had originally been received by their respective churches could be validated as authentic. By the time of the Council of Laodicea (AD 360), the church universally received 2 Peter as canonical, though its authorship was still debated.

Evidence for the existence of a given letter or book and attitudes toward its authority are provided by authors who subsequently quote, refer to, or discuss the writing. It is true that extant Christian writings of the early second century do not directly quote 2 Peter, unless it should be that Jude used 2 Peter as his source. There may be allusions to it in *Shepherd of Hermas*, *1* and *2 Clement*, and other second-century writings, but they are ambiguous enough to question if their source was specifically 2 Peter or early Christian tradition more generally.[35] The first possible quotation of 2 Peter (3:8) is found in the *Epistle of*

35. See Bauckham, *Jude, 2 Peter*, 162, for more details.

Barnabas (15:4), in reference to a day with the Lord being like a thousand years. The *Epistle of Barnabas* dates from the late first or early second century, but the reference in 15:4 may not be a quotation of 2 Peter at all, since the source of the statement may be Psalm 90:4. Origen, in the early third century, expresses doubt about the authorship of 2 Peter but nevertheless quotes it six times and alludes to it twice more, referring to it as Scripture.[36] Such evidence suggests that the early fathers, while perhaps doubting that the apostle Peter wrote the letter himself, nevertheless believed that whoever put pen to paper reliably represented the apostle's thoughts.

It is true that the early church fathers record the doubts of others or their own about the authenticity of 2 Peter, doubts that may have delayed its wider circulation and consequently its acceptance. It is true that no other book of the New Testament is so poorly attested in the early church as 2 Peter; but on the other hand, in comparison to the books rejected by the early church, it has "incomparably better support for its inclusion" in the canon.[37] As with all discussions of the formation of the canon, the evidence will be judged differently by those predisposed on other grounds to reject apostolic authenticity than by those predisposed to accept it. In any case, 2 Peter stands firm in the accepted canon of our New Testament. Its position following 1 Peter invites us to read these two together, giving us the fullest scope of Petrine theology.

OUTLINE OF 2 PETER

I. Salutation and Greeting (1:1 – 2)

II. Exhortation to Confirm One's Calling and Election (1:3 – 11)

- A. God Has Enabled Us to Live a Godly Life (1:3 – 4)
- B. Grow in Spiritual Virtues (1:5 – 9)
- C. Assuring a Rich Welcome (1:10 – 11)

III. The Divine Origin of Peter's Message (1:12 – 21)

- A. Words to Remember Peter By (1:12 – 15)
- B. The Transfiguration Not Made Up (1:16 – 18)
- C. Prophets Spoke from God (1:19 – 21)

IV. The Destruction of False Teachers (2:1 – 22)

- A. Peter Predicts False Teachers Will Come (2:1 – 3)
- B. The Lord Will Rescue the Righteous and Punish the Unrighteous (2:4 – 9)
- C. Description of the False Teachers (2:10 – 22)

V. The Day of the Lord (3:1 – 18)

- A. Scoffers Will Come (3:1 – 4)
- B. Answer to Scoffers (3:5 – 10)
- C. How Then to Live? (3:11 – 18)

---

36. Bigg, *Peter and Jude*, 201. Bigg notes that these quotes are extant only in Latin versions that come through Rufinus, raising the question of whether they can be ascribed to Origen himself.

37. Michael Green, *2 Peter Reconsidered* (London: Tyndale, 1961), 5.

CHAPTER SUMMARY

We live in an age that assumes life as we know it and the planet we live on will go on for astronomical times into the future that might as well be forever relative to the human life span. The challenges of nuclear holocaust, global warming, and population growth have sometimes cast a dark shadow over that assumption, but most people live in denial that the world will end in a day of reckoning before God's judgment.

We also live in an age when people in the Christian church, and even its leaders, are rewriting the biblical commands of virtue in favor of a lifestyle that seems right in their own eyes and that appears to be guided by the spirit of this age rather than the truths of Scripture. Paul's letters, probably the same letters known to Peter, do contain things that are just as hard for our age to hear now as they were in the first century, and sincerely deluded false teachers distort biblical truth now as they did in Peter's time. It is no wonder that 2 Peter is seldom taught or preached, for it is a scathing indictment of false teachers and leaders in the church, those who tell people what they want to hear so they can follow their own desires and still maintain the delusion of being Christian. Certainly our time no less than Peter's needs to hear the apostolic warning to be on guard so that we may not be carried away by the error of the lawless and fall from a secure position of salvation found only in Jesus Christ. Read together with 1 Peter, the voice of the apostle for our times is clearly heard.

KEY TERMS AND DATES

AD 64–68
Assumption of Moses
1 Enoch
Epicureanism
imitatio
Muratorian Canon
papyrus $\mathfrak{P}^{72}$
parousia
pseudepigraphal authorship
Sitz im Leben
Tartarus
testament (genre)
theodicy

QUESTIONS FOR REVIEW OR DISCUSSION

1. Discuss what is at stake for you if 2 Peter is pseudonymous in one of the ways discussed in this chapter, especially with reference to your doctrine of Scripture. Defend your opinion.
2. What message did the author apparently most wish to impart on the threshold of his death?
3. What are the possibilities for the identity of the original recipients of 2 Peter?
4. Describe the nature of the relationship between 2 Peter and Jude. How is it best explained?

5. What does this letter say about God? Jesus Christ? The Holy Spirit?
6. How does the eschatology of 2 Peter compare to that of other major religions? (You will need to rely on sources outside this textbook.)
7. How does the reception history of 2 Peter affect your view of the book as Scripture?

GOING FURTHER

Charles, J. Daryl. *Virtue amidst Vice: The Catalog of Virtues in 2 Peter 1.* JSNTSup 150. Sheffield: Sheffield Academic Press, 1997.

Charlesworth, James H. *The Old Testament Pseudepigrapha.* 2 vols. New York: Doubleday, 1983–85.

Chester, Andrew, and Ralph P. Martin. *The Theology of the Letters of James, Peter, and Jude.* New Testament Theology. Cambridge: Cambridge University Press, 1994.

Donelson, Lewis R. *From Hebrews to Revelation: A Theological Introduction.* Louisville: Westminster John Knox, 2001.

Gilmour, Michael J. "Reflections on the Authorship of 2 Peter." *EQ* 73 (2001): 291–309.

———. *The Significance of Parallels between 2 Peter and Other Early Christian Literature.* Academia Biblica 10. Atlanta: Society of Biblical Literature, 2002.

Green, Joel B. "Narrating the Gospel in 1 and 2 Peter," *Interpretation* 60 (2006): 262–77.

Harner, Philip B. *What Are They Saying about the Catholic Epistles?* What Are They Saying Series. New York: Paulist, 2004.

Perkins, Pheme. "Christ in Jude and 2 Peter." Pages 155–65 in *Who Do You Say That I Am? Essays on Christology.* Louisville: Westminster John Knox, 1999.

Wall, Robert. "The Canonical Function of 2 Peter." Biblical Interpretation 9 (2001): 64–81.

Commentaries

Bauckham, Richard. *Jude, 2 Peter.* Word Biblical Commentary 50. Waco, Tex.: Word, 1983.

Charles, Daryl J. "2 Peter." Pages 359–411 in *Hebrews–Revelation. Expositor's Bible Commentary.* Vol. 13. Edited by Tremper Longman III and David E. Garland. Rev. ed. Grand Rapids: Zondervan, 2006.

Davids, Peter H. *The Letters of 2 Peter and Jude.* Pillar New Testament Commentary. Grand Rapids: Eerdmans, 2006.

Green, Gene. *Jude and 2 Peter.* BECNT. Grand Rapids: Baker Academic, 2008.

Harnick, Douglas. *1 and 2 Peter.* Brazos Theological Commentary on the Bible. Grand Rapids: Brazos, 2009.

Moo, Douglas. "2 Peter." Pages 153–75 in *ZIBBC.* Vol. 4. Edited by Clinton E. Arnold. Grand Rapids: Zondervan, 2002.

———. *2 Peter, Jude.* NIVAC. Grand Rapids: Zondervan, 1996.

Neyrey, Jerome H. *2 Peter, Jude.* AB 37C. New York: Doubleday, 1993.

Perkins, Pheme. "Christ in Jude and 2 Peter." Pages 156–65 in *Who Do You Say That I Am? Essays on Christology.* Edited by Mark Allan Powell and David R. Bauer. Louisville: Westminster John Knox, 1999.

Reese, Ruth Anne. *2 Peter and Jude.* Two Horizons New Testament Commentary. Grand Rapids: Eerdmans, 2007.

Richard, Earl J. *Reading 1 Peter, Jude, and 2 Peter.* Macon, Ga.: Smyth & Helwys, 2000.

Schreiner, Thomas R. *1, 2 Peter, Jude.* New American Commentary. Nashville: Broadman and Holman, 2003.

Senior, Donald P., and Daniel J. Harrington. *1 Peter, Jude and 2 Peter.* Sacra Pagina 15. Collegeville, Minn.: Liturgical, 2003.

Witherington, Ben, III. *A Socio-Rhetorical Commentary on 1–2 Peter.* Letters and Homilies for Hellenized Christians. Vol. 2. Downers Grove: IVP Academic, 2007.

PART 4

Letters from John

CHAPTER 13

1 John

REASSURANCE FOR CHRISTIANS IN CONFUSING TIMES

Your Goals for This Chapter

- To list various options for the referent of "we" in 1 John.
- To know the ancient evidence for authorship of 1 John.
- To learn how 1 John is similar to and different from John's gospel.
- To understand the major themes of 1 John.

WHY THE BOOK OF 1 JOHN IS IMPORTANT TO YOU

Have you ever felt that we live in a spiritually confusing age? What does it really mean to be a Christian? What does one have to believe and do in order to be a true Christian? Can one have a true knowledge of God apart from Jesus Christ? These questions are very relevant for our lives today, and there are no clearer answers to them than are given in 1 John.

There are many different religions and conflicting approaches to God. Even if we are sure of what we believe about Jesus Christ, we cannot avoid hearing the many other voices that claim spiritual truth—from those who teach Eastern ideas about reincarnation to spiritualists who communicate with the dead, to the beliefs espoused in sacred synagogues, mosques, and temples that dot the land. Many today do not believe that there is any one truth about God, but that any religion is worthy if one only believes it sincerely. Sometimes such ideas make inroads even into the Christian church and cause confusion about the essence of the gospel of Jesus Christ, resulting in growing rifts about Christian belief and practice. Is Jesus the only way to God? Doesn't the command to love one another mean that we have to accept, or at least tolerate, all manner of behavior, especially of those who profess to be Christian? The gospel of Jesus Christ first came into a world that was also filled with voices claiming various truths through a multitude of religions and philosophies. Into that world Jesus proclaimed, "Now this is eternal life: that they know you, the only true God, and Jesus Christ, whom you have sent" (John 17:3). What does it mean to know God and Christ in such a spiritually pluralistic world?

Judging from John's letter, things apparently weren't much different in the church of the first century. The author of 1 John writes his **epistle** to assure Christian believers who were being confused by conflicting views about who Jesus was and what is important to believe about him for eternal life. First John 5:13 says, "I write these things to you who believe in the name of the Son of God so that you may know that you have eternal life." John wanted the people he pastored to live with the confidence of knowing that they had the truth about eternal life when apparently there were those in the congregations who identified themselves as Christians but were speaking a very different message about what it meant to know God and to have eternal life.

If eternal life is to know God and Jesus Christ whom he has sent, how does one acquire that knowledge, and what is essential to know about Jesus? There are many different opinions, even among professing Christians, about the significance of Jesus. Is it enough to believe that Jesus was a man who lived, taught good moral lessons to live by, and was unfortunately misunderstood by the Jews and Romans and killed? Are Jesus' teachings the very heart and essence of why God sent him into this world? Is it sufficient to believe that God's Spirit animated the man Jesus as a godly example for Christians, so that what is really important for a believer is the guidance of the Holy Spirit? Is the brutal violence of the crucifixion really essential to the significance of Jesus? In other words, the confusion that the brief epistle of 1 John seeks to clarify concerns the very heart of Christianity. John's epistle defines what one must believe in order to know that he or she has eternal life. What could be more important to you?

Key Verses

1:1: That which was from the beginning, which we have heard, which we have seen with our eyes, which we have looked at and our hands have touched — this we proclaim concerning the Word of life.

1:5: This is the message we have heard from him and declare to you: God is light; in him there is no darkness at all.

1:8 – 9: If we claim to be without sin, we deceive ourselves and the truth is not in us. If we confess our sins, he is faithful and just and will forgive us our sins and purify us from all unrighteousness.

2:1 – 2: My dear children, I write this to you so that you will not sin. But if anybody does sin, we have an advocate with the Father — Jesus Christ, the Righteous One. He is the atoning sacrifice for our sins, and not only for ours but also for the sins of the whole world.

2:18: Dear children, this is the last hour; and as you have heard that the antichrist is coming, even now many antichrists have come. This is how we know it is the last hour.

2:23: No one who denies the Son has the Father; whoever acknowledges the Son has the Father also.

3:1: See what great love the Father has lavished on us, that we should be called children of God! And that is what we are! The reason the world does not know us is that it did not know him.

3:16 – 17: This is how we know what love is: Jesus Christ laid down his life for us. And we ought to lay down our lives for our brothers and sisters. If anyone has material possessions and sees a brother or sister in need but has no pity on them, how can the love of God be in that person?

4:2 – 3: This is how you can recognize the Spirit of God: Every spirit that acknowledges that Jesus Christ has come in the flesh is from God, but every spirit that does not acknowledge Jesus is not from God. This is the spirit of the antichrist, which you have heard is coming and even now is already in the world.

4:8: Whoever does not love does not know God, because God is love.

5:3a: In fact, this is love for God: to keep his commands.

5:5: Who is it that overcomes the world? Only the one who believes that Jesus is the Son of God.

5:13: I write these things to you who believe in the name of the Son of God so that you may know that you have eternal life.

5:16c: There is a sin that leads to death. I am not saying that you should pray about that.

Challenges Presented by the Book of 1 John

- Identifying the referent of the first person plural "we."
- Understanding the statement in 3:9 that Christians do not sin.
- Contemplating what the sin is that leads to death.
- Comprehending the abrupt ending of the letter with its command to "keep yourselves from idols."

CHAPTER OUTLINE

I. Authorship and Date of 1 John
  A. Who Is the "We" of 1 John?
  B. The **Johannine** Community
  C. Traditional Authorship
II. Relationship to the Gospel and Other Letters of John
  A. 1 John and John's Gospel
  B. 1 John's Relationship to 2 and 3 John
III. Genre and Purpose of 1 John
IV. Major Themes of 1 John
  A. Truth
  B. God Is Light: John's Conceptual **Dualism**
  C. The **Christology** of 1 John
    1. Denying that Jesus is the Son of God
    2. Denying that Jesus was fully human
    3. Cerinthus and **adoptionism**
    4. **Docetism**
    5. Perhaps a misunderstanding of John's gospel?
  D. The **Hamartiology** of 1 John
    1. Three errors about sin
    2. The sin that leads to death (1 John 5:16)
  E. Love is the Opposite of Sin
V. The Text and Canonicity of 1 John
  A. The Greek Text of 1 John
  B. Canonicity
VI. Structure and Outline of 1 John

Please read the book of 1 John in one sitting before reading this chapter.

AUTHORSHIP AND DATE OF 1 JOHN

The book of 1 John is anonymous. It does not say who wrote it, as would be expected if it were a personal letter. But the first four verses make it clear that the author, though anonymous to us, asserts his authority over the topics presented in the discourse and was probably well known to the original readers. He claims to speak truth based in the historical reality of eyewitness testimony:

> That which was from the beginning, which we have heard, which we have seen with our eyes, which we have looked at and our hands have touched — this we proclaim concerning the Word of life. The life appeared; we have seen it and testify to it, and we proclaim to you the eternal life, which was with the Father and has appeared to us. We proclaim to you what we have seen and heard, so that you also may have fellowship with us. And our fellowship is with the Father and with his Son, Jesus Christ. We write this to make our joy complete. (1 John 1:1 – 4)

The verbs of sensory experience pile up — hearing, seeing, touching — emphasizing a physical reality that grounds what the author is about to write. He presents himself as a part of a group he refers to as "we" who have had physical contact with the revealed "Word of life," an allusion to not just the man Jesus, but to a privileged understanding of the significance of his life. There is also a clear echo of the prologue of John's gospel ("In the beginning was the Word ..."), which is an indirect echo of Genesis 1 ("In the beginning God created the heavens and the earth"). These first four verses of 1 John introduce what will be discussed in the body of the discourse, the Word of Life as the authoritative interpretation of the significance of Jesus' life with its implications for Christian living. These verses also include a statement of purpose for the writing and a veiled consequence for the reader who does not respond to the author's message. The author writes to include his readers in the fellowship that the authoritative tradition bearers have with each other, with God, and with Jesus Christ. To ignore or reject the message will result in the reader not partaking of, or continuing in, that fellowship.

In the world of ancient rhetoric, this opening would function to set up the readers for an argument that would persuade them to remain faithful to beliefs and values they already hold by refuting competing claims. The echoes to the prologue of John's gospel in these opening verses bring that gospel to mind, perhaps so the readers would compare and contrast the letter's message with their understanding of that gospel.[1] (This, of course, presumes that 1 John was written after John's gospel was in circulation; see Relationship to the Gospel and Other Letters of John below.) In such cases of ancient rhetoric intended to reinforce truth, the strongest influence for the case being made was that the rhetor (or author in this case) was believed to be a good man and an absolutely reliable witness.[2] Both John's gospel and 1 John present themselves as testimony, or witness, not only to the life of the man Jesus but also to the true interpretation of the significance of his life, death, and resurrection. John's gospel does not just tell the story of Jesus but interprets that story,

1. See, e.g., Duane F. Watson, "'Keep Yourselves from Idols': A Socio-Rhetorical Analysis of the *Exordium* and *Peroratio* of 1 John," in *Fabrics of Discourse: Essays in Honor of Vernon K. Robbins*, ed. David B. Gowler, L. Gregory Bloomquist, and Duane F. Watson (Harrisburg, Pa.: Trinity Press International, 2003), 281 – 302.

2. Ibid., 284.

presenting its significance. This is the likely reason why 1 John 1:1 includes two verbs of sight. The first, *horaō*, is sight with the eyes. The second, *theaomai*, is perception that goes beyond what is seen with eyes — in this case the true significance of Jesus.

Who Is the "We" of 1 John?

In the opening verses, 1 – 4, the author of 1 John refers to himself with the first person plural pronoun "we." Is it a genuine plural, suggesting that the author is part of a group? If so, is it inclusive, that is, including the readers, such as I used at the opening of this chapter? Or is it exclusive, that is, referring to a group that does not include the readers? Or perhaps it is not a true plural at all, but a singular use of "we," sometimes called the editorial use or the authoritative use, by which the speaker or writer wishes to distinguish his or her privileged vantage point from the readers, often for the purpose of asserting authority.

First John uses the first person plural pronoun (Gk. *hēmeis*) fifty-six times and the first person plural verb form ninety-six times; in contrast, it contains only fifteen first person singular verb forms, and they are all forms of the verb *graphō*, "I write." In these places the author most explicitly refers to himself as the writer of the letter, in contrast to 1:4 where the first person plural form of *graphō* is found, "we write." This suggests that the first person plural "we" of the opening verses is in fact a genuine plural, where the author of 1 John is counting himself among a group of witnesses to the Word of Life, in some distinction from his readers, whom he invites to fellowship with that group, with God, and with Jesus Christ (1:3). But in the body of the discourse that follows, there is a rhetorical assumption (and hopefully a realized assumption) that the readers are in fact enjoying the fellowship to which the opening verses refer. In these sections "we" (whether explicit or implied by the verbal form) is primarily inclusive, as the author joins his readers as followers of Jesus Christ (e.g., 1 John 3:14, "*We know* that *we have passed* from death to life, because *we love* each other"; emphasis added).

How Does 1 John Employ the First Person Plural Pronoun?

"we" = "I"
"we" = "you and me"
"we" = "my colleagues/community and I"

Most Johannine scholars today construe the "we" of verses 1 – 4 to refer to a group, but there is great disagreement over the identity of that group. The most natural reading of the text suggests that this group was comprised of those who had heard, seen, and touched Jesus; in other words, they were the eyewitnesses of his life. But they were not just witnesses of the man Jesus; they were also authoritative interpreters of the significance of Jesus' life, death, and resurrection, an interpretation 1 John refers to as "the Word of life" (1:1). The apostle John was among the twelve apostles who had been chosen by Jesus himself and who subsequently testified about him as they preached the gospel. Because these apostolic eyewitnesses comprised the earliest possible group matching the description in 1 John 1:1 – 4, the apostle John, son of Zebedee, has traditionally been viewed as the author of the gospel and the letters. Modern Johannine scholarship, however, has suggested as many as five different authors whose work produced the gospel and three epistles.

While all scholars agree that the similarities between the gospel of John and 1 John show that they were both produced within the same theological milieu, there is disagreement as to what extent this evidence implies that the same author wrote both. Those who argue for different authors stress differences between how even the same language is used. Those who argue for one author stress that these differences are due to different purposes for different historical moments. Refer to the commentaries listed at the end of this chapter (especially Marshall, 1978, 31–42) for discussion of this complex topic.

The Johannine Community

Most Johannine scholars today do not believe that 1 John was written by an eyewitness to the life of Jesus, but by someone who was a member of a community that embraced the eyewitness tradition. The eyewitness of Jesus' earthly ministry who provided the material found in John's gospel—identified only as the "beloved disciple"—preached to, discipled, and led a group of Christian converts who resided near each other and worshiped in house churches. Modern scholarship identifies the "we" as the Johannine community, a group of Christians who were closely associated with the "beloved disciple" of John's gospel and who continued to write in that tradition after his death, preserving the testimony of his eyewitness. Some would identify the beloved disciple as the apostle John; others have suggested it was Lazarus or a disciple unknown to history. Upon the death of the beloved disciple, someone close to him put the fourth gospel into the form in which it has survived today. Either that person or another with authority in the churches of the beloved disciple also wrote the epistles, either before or after the gospel, and possibly as trouble arose in the power vacuum that followed after the beloved disciple's death.

Bildarchiv Preussischer Kulturbesitz/Art Resource, NY

The apostle John by Giovanni Francesco Guercino (1591–1666).

John's letters are, therefore, attributed to one or more members of that community. The late Raymond Brown developed the idea of the Johannine community arguably further than any other scholar, concluding that there were at least four people involved in the production of the Johannine corpus over several decades:[3] (1) the beloved disciple, who provided the oral authoritative eyewitness to Jesus on which John's gospel is based, (2) the evangelist who produced the gospel's material in an earlier form (3) the redactor who put the fourth gospel into its final form, and (4) the elder(s) who wrote John's letters. Other scholars propose variations, such as one author for the final form of the gospel and 1 John, and a second author for 2 and 3 John. Still others argue that one person wrote the gospel and the letters but that the author was not the apostle John.

Although the existence of the Johannine community has been assumed in modern biblical scholarship for such a long time and to such an extent that it may seem an unassailable theory, it is built on very slim evidence that is found primarily in the epilogue of John's gospel, where the first person plural pronoun is also used in 21:24: "This is the disciple who testifies to these things and who wrote them down. *We* know that his testimony is

3. Raymond E. Brown, *The Epistles of John*, AB 30 (New York: Doubleday, 1982), 14–35.

Early Information about John

"John the disciple of the Lord, who leaned back on his breast ... published the Gospel while he was resident at Ephesus in Asia."

Irenaeus, *Against Heresies* 3.1.2

"Now the church at Ephesus was founded by Paul, but John stayed there until the time of Trajan."

Eusebius, citing Irenaeus, *Hist. eccl.* 3.23.4

"That very disciple whom Jesus loved, John, at once apostle and evangelist, still remained alive in Asia and administered the churches there, for after the death of Domitian, he had returned from his banishment on the island."

Eusebius, citing Irenaeus and Clement of Alexandria, *Hist. eccl.* 3.23.1 – 2

"[John] used to go [from Ephesus] to the neighboring districts ... in some places to appoint bishops, in others *to reconcile whole churches*, and in others to ordain some one of those pointed out by the Spirit."

Eusebius, citing Clement of Alexandria (c. AD 155 – 220), *Hist. eccl.* 3.23.6

"John, who leaned on the Lord's breast, who was a priest wearing the mitre, and martyr and teacher ... sleeps at Ephesus."

Eusebius, citing Polycrates, bishop of Ephesus, *Hist. eccl.* 3.31.3)

true" (emphasis added). Because much critical biblical scholarship of the last two centuries has rejected the possibility of the supernatural and the miracles with which the Gospels abound, it has rejected *any* of the Gospels as (near-)eyewitness accounts,[4] usually dating them into the second century and therefore well beyond the lifetimes of any of the eyewitnesses. Consequently it was logical to read the first person plural "we" as a reference to a group who had written and/or redacted the fourth gospel at some time following the death of the beloved disciple.

It is beyond the scope of this chapter to fully discuss the exegesis of the fourth gospel's epilogue, which is certainly complex. But an alternative reading of the "we" in the epilogue as a singular can be offered. It has long been recognized that John's gospel has strong concerns with its witness or testimony to the truth about Jesus Christ. Some scholars have attempted to show that in language and form it follows conventions of Greco-Roman legal testimony known from the surviving documentary papyri.[5] If it could be shown from ancient Greek documents that the first person plural pronoun in the gospel epilogue is the *author's* self-reference in following the convention of recording testimony in the ancient world, the theory of an anonymous member(s) of the Johannine community as the author(s) of the gospel and letters would be largely undercut.[6] There is no reason to

4. By "(near-)eyewitness" I mean an eyewitness of Jesus himself (including the apostle Paul) or a close associate of an eyewitness, such as Mark and Luke.

5. E.g., see Andrew T. Lincoln, *Truth on Trial: The Lawsuit Motif in the Fourth Gospel* (Peabody, Mass.: Hendrickson, 2000).

6. For one such proposal, see Howard M. Jackson, "Ancient Self-Referential Conventions and Their Implications for the Authorship and Integrity of the Gospel of John," *JTS* 50 (1999): 1 – 34.

doubt that a community of Christian believers developed in the locale where the apostle John resided, traditionally Ephesus, during his long life. And so in that sense the Johannine community is most likely a historical fact. The question is whether and to what extent that community was involved in producing the gospel and letters attributed to John.

Traditional Authorship

From the earliest days of the church, the apostle John, son of Zebedee, who was one of the Twelve and was within Jesus' inner circle of three, was believed to have written the gospel and the three letters that bear the name of John. Tradition claims that at some point, John left Palestine and relocated to Ephesus in Asia Minor, taking Mary, the mother of Jesus with him (cf. John 19:27).

The earliest witnesses to John's authorship come from Polycarp, bishop of Smyrna (d. **AD** 156), and Papias, a contemporary of Polycarp, whose testimony is preserved through the **extant** writings of Irenaeus and Eusebius. Both Polycarp and Papias lived in western Asia Minor in the greater vicinity of Ephesus, thus in proximity to where John is said to have lived. In what appears to be a chain of direct personal contact, Irenaeus, who was bishop of Lyon (c. AD 175–195) but born in Asia Minor, writes from personal memory that Polycarp reported he had conversed with John and with others who had seen the Lord, the eyewitnesses of the Word of Life (*Hist. eccl.* 5.20.6). (Polycarp is said to have been appointed bishop of

Wikimedia Commons

The Roman Emperor Trajan. The apostle John may have lived into the reign of Trajan (AD 98–117).

Baker Photo Archive

A church in Ephesus built to commemorate Mary, the mother of Jesus.

Smyrna in western Asia Minor [modern Turkey] by eyewitnesses of the Lord, and met a martyr's death in AD 156 at the age of eighty-six.)

The apostle John is believed to have lived in western Asia Minor into the reign of the Roman emperor Trajan (AD 98–117), when Polycarp would have been in his late twenties and John would have been an elderly man. (If John had enjoyed the same longevity as Polycarp, he would have been a teenager when he met and began to follow Jesus.) Irenaeus, who personally remembered Polycarp well, also states that John the disciple of the Lord, who was with Jesus in the upper room, wrote the gospel while living in Ephesus (*Haer.* 3.1.2). This is a remarkable chain of historical witness not known to any other book of the New Testament. Even though our sources are subject to the same scrutiny of all historical documents, this evidence cannot be ignored.

Tradition claims that the apostle John lived in Ephesus for many years and that he had great influence over the churches in nearby places such as Smyrna, Sardis, Philadelphia, and Laodicea. Note the island of Patmos, which was a Roman penal colony and the place where the book of Revelation was written.

The witness of Papias, preserved in Eusebius, is a second ancient witness from the turn of the first to second centuries, who made use of 1 John in his own writings (*Hist. eccl.* 3.39.17). But Eusebius read Papias as referring to John in such a way as to suggest that there may have been two men by the same name (*Hist. eccl.* 3.39.3–5), and that John the apostle wrote the gospel but that John the Elder wrote the book of Revelation. This possibility of two men named John in Ephesus allows some to argue that John the Elder wrote the letters, especially 2 and 3 John, which present themselves as explicitly from "the elder." Eusebius bases his reading of Papias on the fact that John is mentioned as both a "disciple of the Lord" and as an "elder." But Eusebius overlooks the fact that, even when Papias refers to Peter and James, he does not at first call them "apostles," but "elders," suggesting that perhaps the two titles were not mutually exclusive in Papias.

Jerome also believed there were two different men involved in the production of John's gospel and John's letters, that the apostle John wrote the gospel and 1 John, and a second John the Elder wrote 2 and 3 John. In his day, Jerome could not conceive of an apostle referring to himself as simply an "elder."[7] But such a view is anachronistic, for in the very earliest days of the church, "elder" was the highest office of the church organization, and apostles were referred to as elders of the church(es) in their local vicinity. First Peter 5:1 is

7. Jerome, *Vir. ill.* 9.5 (Halton, FC).

K. H. Jobes

Tomb marker of St. John in Ephesus.

another example where the alleged apostolic author refers to himself as a "fellow elder" for the purpose of creating solidarity with other leaders in the church.

There is an indisputable affinity between John's gospel and 1 John, to the extent that if both were not written by the same author, 1 John was written by someone thoroughly familiar with the concepts, vocabulary, and theology of John's gospel. The ambiguity Eusebius introduces has allowed many scholars to conclude that the final redaction of the fourth gospel, with the epilogue's first person plural "we," and the letters of John should be attributed not to John the son of Zebedee, but to an elder John associated with him in Ephesus.

The date of John's letters is, of course, bound up with the date of the fourth gospel and their relationship to it. Most scholars believe the letters to have been written after the gospel had circulated for a while, and that 1 John attempts to correct a misreading of the fourth gospel that was leading to an aberrant Christology. But this order is reversed in a recent argument that the gospel was written after 1 John to provide an authoritative narrative of Jesus' life that could set the record straight against heretical claims. (See Relationship to the Gospel and Other Letters of John below.)

Regardless of the order in which the gospel and 1 John were written, the **Rylands fragment** of John's gospel, dated to around AD 125 and found in Egypt, refuted any claim that the gospel was written well into the second century. Most scholars now date it toward the end of the first century, as early as AD 80–85 or as late as the 90s, with the letters being written within a decade. Given the limited evidence, it is not possible to date these books more precisely than sometime during the final decades of the first century.

One or Two Men Named John?

Papias (early second century) wrote:

> If ever anyone came who had followed the elders, I inquired into the words of the elders, what Andrew or Peter or Philip or Thomas or James or John or Matthew, or any other of the Lord's disciples *had said* [Gk., *eipon*] and what Aristion and the elder John, the Lord's disciple, *were saying* [Gk., *legousin*].
>
> *Interpretation of the Oracles of the Lord*, excerpts preserved by Eusebius, *Hist. eccl.* 3.39.4 (emphasis added)

Eusebius comments on Papias's statement:

> It is here worth noting that he [Papias] twice counts the name of John, and reckons the first John with Peter and James and Matthew and the other apostles, clearly meaning the evangelist, but by changing his statement places the second [John] with others outside the number of the apostles, putting Aristion before him and clearly calling him a presbyter [i.e., elder]. This confirms the truth of the story of those who have said that there were two of the same name in Asia, and that there are two tombs in Ephesus both still called John's.
>
> Eusebius, *Hist. eccl.* 3.39.5–6

But critiquing Eusebius:

> Both times the name John appears, it appears with both the designations "elder" and "Lord's disciple." By contrast, Aristion — even though designated a "Lord's disciple" — lacks the title "elder" when mentioned alongside John. This contrast points toward a single individual named John. Papias wanted to make plain the single identity of John by repeating the designation "elder," just used for the apostles but omitted with Aristion; and Papias mentioned John a second time because John was the only one of the Lord's disciples still living and speaking who was also an apostle. [Note the distinction between the aorist and present tenses in Papias's statement.] Admittedly, Eusebius interpreted Papias as referring to two different men named John and even claimed a tradition of two men named John having different memorials in Ephesus. But one and the same person may have more than one memorial and sometimes does. Because Eusebius disliked the book of Revelation, he wanted to find a way around its apostolic authorship. So he conjured up an Elder John allegedly distinct from the Apostle John to enable an ascription of Revelation to someone lacking apostolic authority.*
>
> Robert H. Gundry

*Robert H. Gundry, *A Survey of the New Testament*, 4th ed. (Grand Rapids: Zondervan, 2003), 257.

Although it may not be possible to remove all reasonable doubt about the identity of its author and the date of its composition, what is clear is that the author of 1 John is an official bearer of the apostolic tradition that was based in the eyewitness testimony about Jesus' public ministry, death, and resurrection. This testimony trumps any reinterpretation of the "Word of life" by those far removed from personal knowledge of Jesus. The emphasis on the author's span of knowledge "from the beginning" not only echoes John's prologue, but underscores the authority of his message. First John 1:1–4 makes three essential points before launching into the major themes of the letter: (1) it stresses the historical basis and eyewitness character of the apostolic tradition as the only basis for true knowledge about Jesus; (2) it corrects any Christology that denies importance of Jesus' earthly life; and (3) it presents the possibility of forsaking fellowship with the author by not receiving his message, and consequently, forsaking fellowship with God and Christ.

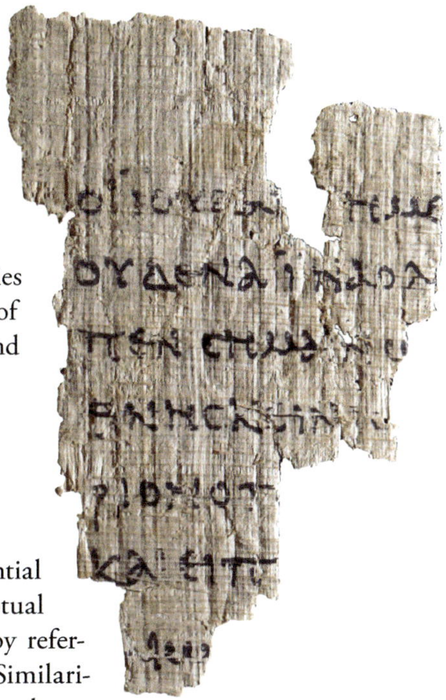

Mal Hamilton

The Rylands fragment (P52) is the earliest witness to the Gospel of John, dating to ca. AD 125.

RELATIONSHIP TO THE GOSPEL AND OTHER LETTERS OF JOHN

1 John and John's Gospel

Even a casual reading of John's gospel and 1 John reveals substantial similarities of vocabulary (e.g., truth, love, light), syntax, conceptual structures, and interpretation of Jesus. The dualism constructed by references to light/darkness and to truth/falsehood is found in both. Similarities of language and thought are found between 1 John and the prologue of the gospel (John 1:1–18) and between the letter and the Upper Room Discourse (John 13–17). Both books state the reason each was written (cf. John 20:30–31 with 1 John 5:13):

> Jesus performed many other signs in the presence of his disciples, which are not recorded in this book. But these are written *that you may believe that Jesus is the Messiah, the Son of God, and that by believing you may have life in his name.* (John 20:30–31, emphasis added)

> I write these things to you who believe in the name of the Son of God *so that you may know that you have eternal life.* (1 John 5:13, emphasis added)

The gospel presents the reasons why someone should believe in Jesus as the Messiah and Son of God and, as a result, have eternal life, and 1 John seems to be reassuring those who have so believed.

Furthermore, the distinctive Greek word ***paraclete***, often translated "advocate," is found only in John's gospel and the first epistle (John 14:16 cf. 1 John 2:1). Common themes and motifs—such as witness and testimony, light and darkness, truth, abiding in truth, a new commandment, loving one another, believers having passed from death into life, the threefold theme of water, blood, and Spirit—show the close relationship between the gospel and the letters that bear John's name. The apostle Paul wrote thirteen books of

The Similarity between the Gospel and Letters Was Noted in the Ancient World

"In a word, it is obvious that those who observe their character throughout will see at a glance that the Gospel and Epistle have one and the same complexion."

Eusebius, *Hist. eccl.* 7.25.21

the New Testament, but even his Galatians and Romans do not stand in such close thematic and verbal relationship. In fact, there are no other two books of the New Testament that mirror each other as closely as John's gospel and letters.

On the other hand, some scholars emphasize the differences between the gospel and the epistles, pointing out that the difficult relationship between the disciples of Jesus and the Jewish synagogue found in the gospel is absent from the epistles. Others argue that even though much of the same vocabulary is used, the words are used in somewhat different senses, indicating different authors.

Because of the similarities between the two, the consensus of scholarship has been to argue that the letters were composed some ten years or so after the gospel, as a corrective to a misreading and distortion of the gospel by some within the church. As an example of a possible misunderstanding, consider perhaps the most famous verse of the fourth gospel, John 3:16, "For God so loved the world that he gave his one and only Son, that whoever believes in him shall not perish but have eternal life." If God loves the world, shouldn't his children love the world too? And if so, what would love of the world look like? Is it, therefore, a coincidence that 1 John 2:15 says, "Do not love the world or anything in the world. If anyone loves the world, love for the Father is not in them"? Are these two different and opposing ideas that suggest two different minds at work? Or is 1 John an explanation of what the gospel means by the "world" and by "love" and why it is that God can love the world but Christians shouldn't?

Heresy in the church was perhaps being caused by "an influx of **Gentile** believers who 'no longer had a direct link with the Jesus tradition' and instead tended 'to think of the revelation of new truth through the Spirit of Truth.'"[8] Jesus himself had promised that the Holy Spirit would guide believers into truth (John 14:17; 15:26; 16:13). Now that the Spirit has come, some may have claimed that the Spirit had given them new spiritual insight. If they had no personal or direct connection to Jesus, their philosophical and ideological premises in contradiction to apostolic teaching may have shaped their new insight. If the gospel was already written, with Jesus' promise of the Spirit of Truth, they were distorting its interpretation, for all spiritual truth that can be legitimately called Christian must conform to the apostolic witness.

But if John's gospel was not yet available to those making the claims, their heresy may have prompted it to be written as the authoritative, apostolic narrative of the significance of

8. Tom Thatcher, *Why John Wrote a Gospel: Jesus–Memory–History* (Louisville: Westminster John Knox, 2006), 67–68, citing John Painter, "The Farewell Discourses and the History of Johannine Christianity," *NTS* 27 (1981): 525–43.

Jesus himself. One recent argument is that the gospel was written after 1 John to provide an authoritative narrative of Jesus' life to "end debate over 'what happened' and limit discussion to the interpretation of what happened.... AntiChrists can no longer dispute whether or not Jesus did or said certain things; [they] can only discuss the correct interpretation of the data in the text."[9]

Clearly the teaching of the fourth gospel stands behind 1 John, even if the gospel was not in final written form before 1 John was written.

We may never know which came first, the gospel or the epistle. But the many verbal and thematic parallels between them suggest that one was intended to be read in light of the other.

9. Thatcher, *Why John Wrote*, 154.

Some Similarities between John's Gospel and the Epistles of John			
John 1:1 In the beginning was the Word, and the Word was with God, and the Word was God. *John 1:14* The Word became flesh and made his dwelling among us. *John 15:26* "When the Advocate comes, whom I will send to you from the Father—the Spirit of truth who goes out from the Father—he will testify about me." *John 15:27* "And you also must testify, for you have been with me from the beginning."	*1 John 1:1* That which was from the beginning, which we have heard, which we have seen with our eyes, which we have looked at and our hands have touched—this we proclaim concerning the Word of life.		
John 3:21 But whoever lives by the truth comes into the light	*1 John 1:6* If we claim to have fellowship with him and yet walk in the darkness, we lie and do not live out the truth.	*2 John 4* It has given me great joy to find some of your children walking in the truth.	*3 John 3* It gave me great joy when some believers came and testified about your faithfulness to the truth, telling how you continue to walk in it.
John 1:5 The light shines in the darkness, and the darkness has not overcome it.	*1 John 2:8* ... because the darkness is passing and the true light is already shining.		

continued on next page...

Some Similarities between John's Gospel and the Epistles of John			
John 8:12 When Jesus spoke again to the people, he said, "I am the light of the world. Whoever follows me will never walk in darkness, but will have the light of life."	*1 John 1:5* This is the message we have heard from him and declare to you: God is light; in him there is no darkness at all. *1 John 2:9* Anyone who claims to be in the light but hates a brother or sister is still in the darkness.		
John 1:12 Yet to all who did receive him, to those who believed in his name, he gave the right to become children of God— *John 1:13* . . . children born not of natural descent, nor of human decision or a husband's will, but born of God.	*1 John 5:1* Everyone who believes that Jesus is the Christ is born of God,		
John 15:12 "My command is this: Love each other as I have loved you."	*1 John 3:23* And this is his command: to believe in the name of his Son, Jesus Christ, and to love one another as he commanded us.	*2 John 5* And now, dear lady, I am not writing you a new command but one we have had from the beginning. I ask that we love one another.	
John 15:7 "If you remain in me and my words remain in you, ask whatever you wish, and it will be done for you."	*1 John 2:24* As for you, see that what you have heard from the beginning remains in you. If it does, you also will remain in the Son and in the Father.	*2 John 9* Anyone who runs ahead and does not continue in the teaching of Christ does not have God; whoever continues in the teaching has both the Father and the Son.	
John 13:34 "A new command I give you"	*1 John 2:8* Yet I am writing you a new command.		
John 14:16 "And I will ask the Father, and he will give you another advocate to help you and be with you forever."	*1 John 2:1* But if anybody does sin, we have an advocate with the Father—Jesus Christ, the Righteous One.		

Some Similarities between John's Gospel and the Epistles of John			
John 17:3 "Now this is eternal life: that they know you, the only true God, and Jesus Christ, whom you have sent."	*1 John 2:25* And this is what he promised us—eternal life. *1 John 5:11* And this is the testimony: God has given us eternal life, and this life is in his Son.		
John 14:6 Jesus answered, "I am the way and the truth and the life. No one comes to the Father except through me."	*1 John 2:23* No one who denies the Son has the Father; whoever acknowledges the Son has the Father also.		
	1 John 2:18 Dear children, this is the last hour; and as you have heard that the antichrist is coming, even now many antichrists have come. This is how we know it is the last hour.	*2 John 7* Many deceivers, who do not acknowledge Jesus Christ as coming in the flesh, have gone out into the world. Any such person is the deceiver and the antichrist.	
John 13:30 As soon as Judas had taken the bread, he went out. And it was night.	*1 John 2:19* They went out from us, but they did not really belong to us.		
John 20:31 But these are written that you may believe that Jesus is the Messiah, the Son of God, and that by believing you may have life in his name.	*1 John 5:13* I write these things to you who believe in the name of the Son of God so that you may know that you have eternal life.		

1 John's Relationship to 2 and 3 John

As the chart shows, the similarities between 1 John and the fourth gospel extend also into 2 and 3 John. One distinct difference between 1 John and the other two is that 2 and 3 John are clearly in the form of Hellenistic correspondence, letters written from the elder to the elect lady and her children (2 John), and to Gaius (3 John). The sequence in which the letters are presented in the New Testament canon—1, 2, and 3 John—is not necessarily the order in which they were written, and scholars have proposed just about every permutation of order possible. The theory of the Johannine community has conveniently

1 John and the Dead Sea Scrolls*

There are several parallels in the dualistic concepts and language of John's gospel and epistle with Qumran, especially with the *Manual of Discipline* (1QS):

- light and darkness / truth and deceit (1QS 3:19)
- two groups of people: sons of light (1QS 3:13) and sons of darkness (1QS 1:10)
- spirit of truth / spirit of deceit (1QS 3:18, 19)
- angels or princes of light and darkness (1QS 3:20–25)
- brotherly love (1QS 2:24–25; 5:4, 24–25)
- community (1QS 1:1; 3:12; 5:1; 8:1, 5, 19)
- knowledge (1QS 4:22; 9:17–18)
- confession of sin (1QS 1:23–26)
- idols (1QS 2:11, 17; 4:5)

These are concepts common to ancient religion and do not necessarily imply that there was any literary influence between the scrolls and John's writings.

*Adapted from Colin G. Kruse, *The Letters of John*, PNTC (Grand Rapids: Eerdmans, 2000), 32.

provided a pool of potential authors for the books of the Johannine corpus, opening up a place for arguments that would probably not be possible if one author wrote them all. (See Raymond Brown's extensive discussion of the complicated sets of relationships between the Johannine epistles.)[10]

Both 1 and 2 John are concerned with the threat of false teachers. In 1 John these **secessionists** have already stirred trouble for the author's congregation; in 2 John the author is afraid that those who left are heading for the Christian communities to whom he wrote in warning. This suggests that both letters were written at about the same time and likely by the same author. Some have suggested that 2 John was a cover letter for 1 John, which had originally been delivered as a sermon in the author's church and then sent to one or more nearby churches.[11] Third John, which may have been sent at the same time, is a letter to an individual, Gaius, and seems to assume the same troubled waters as 1 and 2 John. It is concerned with how the schism will affect hospitality toward itinerant missionaries sent out by the elder.

It is possible that all three letters were originally sent together to a congregation at some distance from the author, but over which the author had standing and spiritual authority.[12] This would help explain why only one letter of John is mentioned in the early canon lists (see The Text and Canonicity of 1 John below), if the two short notes were considered part of the same package with 1 John and subsequently preserved and copied only together with

10. Brown, *Epistles of John*, 14–106.

11. L. T. Johnson, *The Writings of the New Testament: An Interpretation*, rev. ed. (Minneapolis: Fortress, 1999), 560–61.

12. Robert W. Yarbrough, *1–3 John*, BECNT (Grand Rapids: Baker Academic, 2008), 329, citing Luke Timothy Johnson, *The Writings of the New Testament: An Interpretation*, rev. ed. (Minneapolis: Fortress, 1999), 560–61.

it. Irenaeus might provide ancient evidence for this, for he refers to John's first letter but then quotes from 2 John (*Haer.* 3.16.5).[13] There is simply no evidence from which to conclude with any certainty the order in which John's letters were written.

GENRE AND PURPOSE OF 1 JOHN

Although 1 John is typically referred to as a letter, it does not take the form and conventions of Hellenistic personal correspondence, lacking the typical "to" and "from" in the opening verse. Nevertheless, the author uses the phrase "I write to you" a dozen times in this brief text. First John reads more like an essay or sermon that was written with the intention of being sent to one or more destinations, perhaps accompanied by a cover letter that has not survived or that might have been what we know as 2 John.

The letter refers to people, often called "secessionists" in modern scholarship, who "went out from us, but ... did not really belong to us" (1 John 2:19). The content of the letter suggests that the author was attempting to reassure his readers of the truth in the wake of this departure of dissenting members of the church. He deals with the secessionists obliquely, making it difficult to know specifically how they disagreed with the apostolic tradition or under what circumstances they left. For instance, consider 1:8, "If we claim to be without sin, we deceive ourselves and the truth is not in us." It sounds as if someone had made just that claim and had led some of the believers in the Johannine church(es) to go out from fellowship, creating a schism. They left behind them much confusion and doubt.

First John, as well as the other two Johannine epistles evidently were written in a climate where false teaching about the true nature of Christianity had made inroads into the church, and where the authority of the author is being severely tested. The central foci of John's Christianity are truth and love, but both were evidently being understood and practiced in ways that distorted and corrupted the apostolic gospel of Jesus Christ. The epistles were written to reassert the elder's authority and to correct the heretical teaching of those who had seceded from the churches, apparently saying that it was not necessary to believe in Jesus as the Son of God in order to have true knowledge of God and salvation.

Although 1 John had its origins during a period of false teaching, the author's main purpose is not to confront heresy, but to reassure those who remain that they do indeed know the truth about Jesus, and consequently do have eternal life (5:13 cf. John 17:3). Analysis of the rhetorical elements of 1 John shows it to be "**epideictic rhetoric** that is aimed to increase the audience's adherence to values it already holds,"[14] which seems to be the consensus of scholarship. As one scholar explains it:

> Since this is epideictic rhetoric, we should not expect formal arguments carefully laid out. The author is not attempting to persuade the audience about something that they do not already affirm or believe, nor is he seeking to alter their behavior in the near future, nor is he attacking or defending actions taken in the past. This homily is all about praise and blame in the present for things already believed and done.[15]

---

13. Robert M. Grant, *The Formation of the New Testament* (New York: Harper & Row, 1965), 155.

14. Watson, "Keep Yourselves from Idols," 282.

15. Ben Witherington III, *A Socio-Rhetorical Commentary on Titus, 1–2 Timothy and 1–3 John*, vol. 1 of *Letters and Homilies for Hellenized Christians* (Downers Grove, Ill.: IVP Academic, 2006), 436.

The Author of 1 John States His Purpose for Writing

I write …

to you who believe in the name of the Son of God so that you may know that you have eternal life (5:13).

to make our joy complete (1:4).

so that you will not sin (2:1).

because your sins have been forgiven (2:12).

because you know the Father (2:14).

because you know him who is from the beginning (2:14).

because you are strong, and the word of God lives in you, and you have overcome the evil one (2:14).

because you do know [the truth] (2:21).

Much scholarship on 1 John for the past thirty years has attempted to reconstruct the precise nature of the schism, usually labeled as docetism, **Cerinthianism**, or incipient **Gnosticism**, and this has led to scholarly reconstructions of the Johannine community and its relationship to the seccessionists that have far exceeded the evidence available. More recently, some are arguing for what they call a nonpolemical reading of the letter that does not depend so heavily on identifying what the secessionists believed and why they left.[16] This corrective to scholarship on 1 John seems to sit better with the author's own statements about why he wrote. The true concern of the author is pastoral, not dealing with the secessionists in any direct way, but assuring those under his spiritual care that they remain within the fellowship of apostolic orthodoxy.

MAJOR THEMES OF 1 JOHN

Truth

Can you recall a time when you were unsure, and maybe even fearful, about a situation in your life and needed reassurance? The last thing you needed was someone's empty words, perhaps well-meant fibs but incapable of offering any true reassurance. True assurance must be based on nothing less than, or other than, the truth. The topic of truth and the importance of truth run throughout the Johannine writings, though the concept of the Johannine "truth" is not simply the opposite of "false." Most generally, Johannine truth refers to the gospel of Jesus Christ, the one who claimed to be the Truth (John 8:32; 14:6), and its necessary implications for life (1 John 3:19–20; 2 John 1–3; 3 John 1, 8). Following from this definition, the Johannine writings refer to truth as the ethical standards that God has established. This is most clearly seen in the distinctive idiom "to do the truth" (Gk., *poiein tēn alētheian*; John 3:21; 1 John 1:6). To modern thinking, truth is something

16. E.g., see Judith M. Lieu, "'Authority to Become Children of God': A Study of 1 John," *NovT* 23 (1981): 210–28; T. Griffith, "A Non-Polemical Reading of 1 John: Sin, Christology and the Limits of Johannine Christianity," *TynBul* 49 (1998): 253–76; Hansjörg Schmid, "How to Read the First Epistle of John Non-Polemically," *Bib* 85 (2004): 24–41.

that one knows cognitively; in the Johannine world, truth was something that one did. Furthermore, "truth" is a reference to God's sanctifying presence, imparted by the Holy Spirit, allowing the believer to display character traits consistent with a profession of faith in Jesus Christ (1 John 1:8; 2:4, 20–21; 4:6; 5:6). "Truth" in the Johannine writings is a shortened way of referring to everything on God's side of the dualism between light and darkness (see below).

In the fourth gospel, truth is important because the beloved disciple is a witness to Jesus' life, his teachings, his miracles, and his death. Just as reassurance based on a lie is worthless, a false witness is worthless. First John was written to provide assurance, and truth is no less important a theme in that letter. Clearly, there was contention for the truth about Jesus at the time John's letters were written. First John provides a witness to the truth, pointing to the Spirit's testimony as mediated, not through those who claimed new revelation through the Spirit, but through the authoritative bearers of the apostolic tradition (1 John 5:6; cf. 1 John 1:1–4).

God Is Light: John's Conceptual Dualism

The letter of 1 John makes two theological statements about God that form the basis of an **apocalyptic** dualism found in both the letter and the gospel. Within the Jewish literary tradition, it was common to divide all humanity into two groups: God's people and everyone else (the "Gentiles" or "nations"). Apocalyptic writers built on that distinction using antonyms to create a black-and-white distinction that was characterized by opposing values and destinies. The basic conceptual premise in 1 John is theological, namely, "God is light; in him there is no darkness at all" (1 John 1:5). From that truth, the author frames a dualism in which the antonyms of light and darkness form a polarity between God and "the world," which in Johannine thought refers to the value system of fallen humankind in opposition to God. (There is also another use of the word *world* in Johannine thought, as expressed in John 3:16: "For God so loved the world ...," referring to fallen humankind in need of redemption.)

> "I have never read a book written in simpler words than this one, and yet the words are inexpressible."
>
> MARTIN LUTHER

John's gospel is an invitation to leave the dark side and, through faith in Jesus Christ, come into the light where eternal life is found. John's first letter assumes the fellowship of those who have done so, who join those who hold the apostolic faith in fellowship with God and Christ, and encourages them to continue to live in the light. This implies that either through the embrace of false teaching or through wrong ethical behavior, or both, John's readers were in a place of vulnerability and needed reassurance and persuasion to continue in what they had embraced as the source of eternal life. On the side of God and light is truth, which in 1 John refers to the content of the apostolic gospel about Jesus Christ. In John's gospel, Jesus famously proclaims, "I am the way and the truth and the life" (John 14:6). The fourth gospel explains the truth of Jesus through interpretive narrative as well as through various signs, symbols, and metaphors. The opening of 1 John (1:1) refers not to a "who" (Gk. masc. rel. pron., *hon*), but to "what" (Gk. neut. rel. pron., *ho*), which was the apostolic message of the "Word of life" that interpreted the Life that had come into the world. Whatever teaching or belief that is not consistent with that proclamation is deemed "lies" and "deception," standing in opposition to the truth. Those who spread such deception stand in opposition to Christ and therefore are labeled **antichrists** in 1 John, the only place in the New Testament to use that term. (Though "antichrist" is most often associated with the book of Revelation, the word does not occur in that book.)

Continuing the dualistic structure, those who embrace the truth of Jesus Christ do so because they are "of the Father," while those who reject the truth are "of the world." Those who are "of God" are the children of God who live in the righteousness defined by his holy character and are destined for eternal life; those who are "of the world" live in the darkness of sin as children of the devil. Some professing Christians in the Johannine churches apparently had ideas about Jesus Christ and Christian living that differed from that taught by the apostles. These Christians had not remained in the truth but went beyond its boundaries, perhaps justifying it by an appeal to what they presumed was the Spirit's work. The author of 1 John is concerned that his readers, who have professed faith in Christ, remain in the apostolic truth of Jesus Christ, deal rightly with sin, and love one another. These three pillars uphold true Christian faith as John teaches it, and they comprise the major themes of the letter.

Conceptual Dualism in 1 John	
God	World
light	darkness
truth	lies/deception
of God the Father	of the world
Christ	antichrist
righteousness	sin
children of God	children of the devil
eternal life	death
love one another	hating the brother
remaining	going ahead/beyond

The Christology of 1 John

First John's Christology is woven together with the themes of sin and love, showing that proper Christian living flows from a proper understanding of who Jesus Christ is. Heresy concerning who Jesus is produces aberrant Christian behavior, and it is likely that christological error was at the heart of the schism mentioned in 1 John 2:19: "They went out from us, but they did not really belong to us. For if they had belonged to us, they would have remained with us; but their going showed that none of them belonged to us." If you have ever experienced a similar situation in your church life, you know that such a departure, especially if some of those leaving were respected leaders, can be very disorienting and creates the need for a reassurance about the truth, especially for those young in their Christian life. This christological error had given rise to wrong thinking about sin in the life of Christians and about what it means to love one another, and so was threatening to disrupt Christian life and practice in John's church(es).

Every chapter of the letter speaks to the topic of the nature of Jesus Christ and the efficacy of his life and work:

The Three Major Topics of 1 John: Christ, Sin, and Love

1:5–2:2	Christ and our sin
2:3–9	Christ and love for others
2:18–27	Christ and antichrist
3:1–3	love
3:4–10	sin
3:11–24	love
4:1–6	Christ came in the flesh
4:7–21	love
5:1–12	Christ came by water and blood
5:16–21	sin

CHAPTER 1

vv. 1–4: Emphasizes the physical reality of Jesus' life and work. The Word of Life was revealed as a real person who taught, did miracles, and lived in close association with men he had chosen to be his witnesses when he was gone.

vv. 5–7: The blood of Jesus (note the physical emphasis), God's Son, purifies us from all sin.

CHAPTER 2

v. 1: Jesus is our *paraclete* with the Father who intercedes on our behalf. A *paraclete* in Greco-Roman society was someone who acted as an advocate, often in the courtroom.

v. 2: Jesus is the atoning sacrifice (Gk. *hilasmos*) for our sins and for the sins of the whole world. In John's view, Christ's death is the ground on which we may be cleansed when we confess our sins. This verse has been used to support the idea of universalism, that because of Jesus, all people will be saved whether they know Christ or not. At the time John wrote, religion and sacrifice were parochial, each local deity requiring its offering. But Jesus Christ is the **atonement** that is universally applicable; there is no other efficacious atoning sacrifice for sins wherever one goes in the world. When John says, "and not for ours only," he is making a huge claim for the universal scope and efficacy of the gospel but not for salvation.

Moreover, John is making a further huge claim that Jesus' blood is sufficient to forgive and cleanse every sin ever committed from Adam until present day by every human being who ever lived. But neither of these thoughts implies that every person will be saved.

vv. 21–22: No one who rejects Christ can know God, for in rejecting Jesus Christ, one is rejecting God himself.

CHAPTER 3

v. 2: Jesus Christ will reappear, and those who are children of the Father will be like him when he does.

CHAPTER 4

vv. 1–6: The truth is that Jesus Christ has come *in the flesh*. He was not some elusive spirit-presence but a real flesh and blood person. John here underscores the incarnation, also emphasized in the prologue of John's gospel. To teach otherwise is to be antichrist. In verses 5–6 the author again reasserts the apostolic authority of the "we" first mentioned in 1:1–4.

vv. 14–15: God sent his Son to be Savior of the world, a statement that presumes readers know from what the world needs to be saved. The confessed belief that "Jesus is the Son of God" brings God into one's life, joining the believer to God.

CHAPTER 5

vv. 1, 10–12: The new birth depends on believing, not just that Jesus was truly a man, but that he is the Christ. To reject Christ is to make God a liar, a statement that implicitly claims that the apostolic tradition as developed by the eyewitnesses is God's own testimony about his Son (an implicit claim to the divine inspiration of their writings). There is no eternal life apart from Jesus Christ, the Son of God.

In 1 John what one believes about Jesus Christ is of utmost importance and is the indicator of on which side of the apocalyptic dualism one stands. It is not enough to believe sincerely in one's religious doctrines; faith, regardless of its sincerity, must have the right objective content centered in a proper understanding of Jesus Christ. There is no true Christianity without doctrine, but that doctrine must be according to what the apostles who heard, saw, and touched Jesus taught about the significance of his person and work.

We, too, live in spiritually confusing times, just as John's readers did. There are many opinions about Jesus today, as there were in the first century. Church history has shown that the origin of denominations is most often due to schism in the church. To have the assurance of eternal life, 1 John says one must believe correctly about Jesus Christ. John wants to vigorously defend against any belief that

- denies that the man Jesus is the Christ (1 John 2:22; 5:1).
- denies that Jesus is the Son of God (1 John 2:23; 3:23; 5:11–12).
- denies that Christ has come in the flesh (1 John 4:2–3; 2 John 7).
- denies that Jesus Christ came *both* by water and blood—a metaphor of debated meaning, but probably a reference to both the baptism and death of Jesus (1 John 5:6; see commentaries). By ignoring the death of Jesus and paying attention only to his baptism when the Spirit descended upon him, some could claim that his Spirit anointing produced the divine revelation of his teaching. Similarly, they claimed to be Spirit anointed and having direct access to the same source of revelation as Jesus, thus elevating the Spirit and diminishing the role of Jesus.

Denying that Jesus is the Son of God.

Most people today have no problem believing that Jesus was a fully human man who lived in the first century. But according to 1 John, it is not enough to believe that Jesus was just a human being, even if one considers him to be a great prophet (as Muslims do) or a great teacher of religious values (as many liberal Protestants and those of various non-Christian religions do). According to 1 John 3:21–23, God has commanded that to please him one must believe in the name of *his Son*, Jesus Christ. First John further says that those who claim to believe in God the Father but not in Jesus are deceived and aren't believing in the true God, for "no one who denies the Son has the Father; whoever acknowledges the Son has the Father also" (1 John 2:23). John would correct those people both in the first century and today who want to give Jesus some special role as a human being but who deny that he was the incarnate Son of God. He would also correct those who believe in some spiritual presence of Christ that is not grounded in the historical reality of his life and death.

Denying that Jesus was fully human.

To modern thinking, Jesus' humanity is the most believable part of the gospel. But not so in the ancient world. Because some disputed that Jesus was fully human, we will need to explore why it was that John had to explain that to have reassurance of eternal life it was necessary to acknowledge that Jesus Christ had "come in the flesh." In what ways could someone deny that the Christ and Son of God was fully human?

Those readers who have studied Greek philosophy might remember that the greatest of the Greek philosophers whose thinking has had the longest reach across history was Plato (c. 427–347 **BC**). Plato taught many ideas, but his thought that has come to be known as **Platonic dualism** is most relevant, in its Neoplatonic form, to first-century thought about Jesus. Plato taught that this material world and everything in it had a corresponding spiritual counterpart in the perfect, eternal world of ideal forms. Individual things in this world are merely the fleeting, temporary manifestations of their higher, perfect, eternal "forms" or "ideals" that constitute true and absolute Being. Corresponding to this metaphysical system is a theory of knowledge that the human soul existed in this world of ideal forms before it was birthed into this world in a human body in which it temporarily resides. The ultimate goal for a person was to acquire the mystical *gnosis* (knowledge) needed for his or her soul to escape the prison of the body at death and return to the eternal world.

By the time Jesus came into the world, various Greek philosophers had expounded Plato's ideas into a variety of theories that were applied to religious thought. In one such school of thought, the material world was not just inferior to the spiritual world of ideal forms, because everything in it is temporary and perishing, but the material world was ethically and morally evil. When those with this philosophical bent applied this thought to the Christian gospel, the Christ-spirit who dwelt "above" in the spiritual world of perfect

Jesus Is Mentioned by the Roman Historian Tacitus

Writing about the persecution of Christians by Nero, Tacitus (AD 56–117) explained the origin of their name as derived from that of their founder Chrestus, who "suffered the extreme penalty during the reign of Tiberius at the hands of one of our procurators, Pontius Pilate."

Tacitus, *Annales* 15.44

forms could not *really* have become a material human being, for such perfection could not comingle with the corruption of human flesh. This basic philosophical assumption when applied to the Christian gospel led to two well-known christological heresies in the second century, Cerinthianism and docetism (cf. the apostle Paul's warning in Col. 2:8). Both of these schools of thought attempted to understand Jesus in ways that were compatible with philosophical currents of the time, and both denied the humanity of Jesus, though each in a different way. John's letter does not dwell on the christological errors that were current at his time, and therefore it is unwise to lean heavily on either of these as the specific background of the book. They are simply two examples from the ancient world of the kind of thinking that John would oppose; the actual situation of his day may have had nothing to do with either of these schools of thought.

Cerinthus and adoptionism.

Around the end of the first century there lived a man who taught that Jesus was the naturally born son of Mary who had had relations with Joseph or some other man. For whatever reason, God chose this man Jesus to be the human bearer of the Christ-spirit, which came upon Jesus at his baptism (Matt. 3:16; Mark 1:10; Luke 3:22), enabling Jesus to do miracles and to reveal truth about God, but then left Jesus before his crucifixion. Irenaeus is said to have told a story that the apostle John and Cerinthus actually both lived in Ephesus at the same time, and that one day when John happened to learn that Cerinthus was in the same bathhouse, he ran from the building.

If one were to hold such an opinion of Jesus as Cerinthus did, then clearly the significance of Jesus for Christianity would be Jesus' life and miracles but not his passion and death (much less any idea of the resurrection of the body, which would have defeated the goal of the soul's escape). In this way of thinking, Jesus becomes a revealer of divine truth but is himself not divine. The man Jesus was simply used (in the worst sense of that word) as a vehicle for divine revelation.

Docetism.

A second way Neoplatonic thought warped early Christian understanding of the nature of Jesus was through a belief later called *docetism* by Christian theologians. Docetism (from

Cerinthus and the Apostle John at the Bathhouse

Irenaeus ... in the third book has committed to writing a narrative, which deserves not to be forgotten, stating how, according to the tradition of Polycarp, the apostle John once went into a bath-house to wash, but when he knew that Cerinthus was within leapt out of the place and fled from the door, for he did not endure to be even under the same roof with him, and enjoined on those who were with him to do the same, saying, "Let us flee, lest the bath-house fall in, for Cerinthus, the enemy of the truth, is within."

Eusebius, *Hist. eccl.* 3.28.6

Todd Bolen/www.BiblePlaces.com

Ruins of the bath house in Ephesus, reported to be the scene of Polycarp's story about John and Cerinthus.

the Greek verb *dokein*, to seem) denies the humanity of Jesus by claiming that the Christ was a pure spirit being who only seemed to be in human form but was not truly human.

First John would vehemently disagree with both Cerinthianism and docetism, arguing that Jesus is the eternally preexistent Word (1 John 4:2) and the fully human incarnate Son of God, whose blood purifies from sin (1 John 1:7). As significant as Jesus' teachings, miracles, and life example are for Christians, his crucifixion is the essence of the gospel message according to 1 John, for it is the atoning sacrifice that enables reconciliation and fellowship with God (1 John 1:7).

Perhaps a misunderstanding of John's gospel?

Johannine scholars are discussing a theory about what it meant to deny that Christ had come in the flesh based on the close relationship the epistle has to John's gospel. In the

Ignatius of Antioch against Docetism

Around AD 110, in his letter to Smyrna, Ignatius wrote against a docetist who was defending Ignatius in the face of martyrdom.

"For what good does it do me if someone praises me but blasphemes my Lord by not confessing that he was clothed in flesh? Anyone who does not acknowledge this thereby denies him completely."

Ignatius, *Smyrn.* 5.2

gospel we read the promise of Jesus to send "another paraclete," the Holy Spirit (John 14:16), and that Jesus had much more truth to impart than he could at that time, probably because it required his disciples to witness his death and resurrection before they could understand it. Once the Holy Spirit came (Acts 2), some Christians felt that whatever knowledge they needed about God and guidance for life came directly from the Spirit, making Jesus and his significance a past event that was largely irrelevant to Christian life. Of course, the fact that the disciples could not receive the truth Jesus had for them until after his crucifixion and resurrection argues for how crucial history is for revelation and against the idea that the Spirit imparts revelation in some direct, mystical way apart from that historical basis.

Christian orthodoxy today insists that the Holy Spirit illumines Scripture and his work is necessarily integral for anyone to understand the story of Jesus and his significance. But imagine that the New Testament was not yet in existence as a book that Christians had easy access to. In that situation, the work of the Holy Spirit could have been more easily perceived as separate and distinct from the story of Jesus (as perhaps was part of the problem with the "super spiritual" believers of Corinth). Even today Christians experience the presence of God through the Holy Spirit, for we do not now see Jesus in the way the eyewitnesses saw him. Any claim of Spirit-led spiritual insight must be tested against the New Testament, the repository of the apostolic, divinely inspired truth about the gospel.

In addition, Jesus taught that eternal life meant *knowing* God (John 17:3). In the first century, the developing idea of Gnosticism as divine knowledge (Gk. *gnosis*) needed for the afterlife reinforced such ideas that the Holy Spirit, not the man Jesus, was the revealer most central to Christianity. In such an environment, one can easily imagine the promise of Jesus to send "another paraclete" being misconstrued to mean that the additional truth

Z. Radovan/www.BibleLandPictures.com

Ephesus was a center of Christianity for centuries.

Jesus promised was in fact being imparted through the Holy Spirit apart from the witnesses he had chosen to authenticate the events of his life. Moreover, such a view would allow someone to go beyond the orthodox teaching of the apostles, venturing into spiritually imaginative concepts and claiming that it was a new work of the Holy Spirit. John called those who believe that Jesus Christ has not come in the flesh antichrists, so strongly did he oppose their heretical teachings.

If one rejects the idea of Jesus Christ's atoning death as central to the Christian gospel, then the concept of a necessary atonement for sin is also diminished or eliminated. Consequently, Christian behavior is affected. It is therefore no coincidence that a proper view of sin is the second major topic in John's letter.

The Hamartiology of 1 John

Jesus taught that knowing God and the One he sent, Jesus Christ, is the defining requirement of eternal life (John 17:3). John's writings agree with other New Testament writers that the great problem that prohibits knowing God is human sin, which has separated human beings from fellowship with God ever since the fall in the garden of Eden (Gen. 2). Throughout human history people have attempted many solutions to this felt problem. One failed attempt is to deal with the problem of sin through education. If people just had more knowledge or knew the right things, they would act better and the sin problem would go away. Gnosticism best represents the ancient form of this approach, but it is centered on the acquisition in this life of a spiritual, mystical knowledge that could be used in the afterlife to successfully ascend to the desired destination. The apostolic witness of 1 John disagrees. Because of the nature of sin and evil, it is not knowledge but atonement that is at the heart of John's teaching about Jesus.

Hamartiology is the term theologians use to refer to the nature of sin and its consequences (from the Greek word for sin, *hamartia*). *Sin* is not a word often heard in modern culture, except perhaps to deny its existence. That would certainly be one way for someone to claim, "I have no sin" (see 1 John 1:8, 10). If sin doesn't exist, no one can be guilty of it. But the human conscience is hard to avoid, so another tactic when we hear that inner voice accusing us would be to rationalize sin. "Sure, I may have done something that bothers my conscience (at least a little), but . . . ," and then we recite to ourselves a litany of reasons to justify what we did and define our act or thought as something other than sin. Apparently John is writing to people who have claimed in some way "to be without sin," and he is quick to label such claims as self-deception and a lie (1 John 1:8).

First John teaches that to have reassurance of eternal life, one must deal rightly with sin by confessing it and not denying or rationalizing it. In fact, John's Christology (what he teaches about Jesus Christ) meets his hamartiology at just this point because Jesus' death (which John refers to as Jesus' "blood") cleanses from confessed sin, provides forgiveness, and sustains fellowship with God the Father—that is, allows us to know God (1 John 1:7–8; 2:2). For assurance of eternal life, it is the death of Jesus that is of crucial significance. And if sin made it necessary for the Word who became a human being to suffer a brutally violent death, then Christians who know that should not take sin lightly.

Three errors about sin.

While we cannot be certain if John was writing specifically against an incipient Gnosticism in any of its various forms, we can discern from the letter itself some elements of the teaching John was writing to refute:

THREE ERRORS IN THINKING ABOUT SIN

The error:	*John's response:*
1. *1:6* If we claim to have fellowship with him and yet walk in the darkness, we lie and do not live out the truth.	1. *1:7* But if we walk in the light, as he is in the light, we have fellowship with one another, and the blood of Jesus, his Son, purifies us from all sin.
2. *1:8* If we claim to be without sin, we deceive ourselves and the truth is not in us.	2. *1:9* If we confess our sins, he is faithful and just and will forgive us our sins and purify us from all unrighteousness.
3. *1:10* If we claim we have not sinned, we make him out to be a liar and his word is not in us.	3. *2:1b* But if anybody does sin, we have an advocate with the Father—Jesus Christ, the Righteous One.

These three errors all amount to the same claim: "Sin does not affect me." First John, however, states that sin is central to the Christian message because it was for this very reason that Jesus Christ died and is today our advocate (*paraclete*) with the Father (2:1).

The first error, that one can have fellowship with God while walking in darkness, is the belief that sin is unimportant to one's relationship with God. There are many people today who would claim a relationship with God yet don't seem to take sin in their lives seriously. In John's day there were those who also claimed to have fellowship with God yet walked "in the darkness"—a way of saying that their behavior was according to the values of this fallen world and not consistent with the behavior God prescribed. Since "God is light," in whom "there is no darkness at all" (1 John 1:5), any behavior that God does not condone is not a part of him and is therefore darkness. People who live in such a way, John writes, lie and are not living the truth (v. 6). What are those people lying about? What they claim—to have fellowship with the God in whom is no darkness. Impossible, John says. Any claim of fellowship with God is a lie for those whose lives are lived in the moral darkness of this world. In fact, a person who is unconcerned that his or her life is characterized by habitual sin has not been reborn into the light and remains on the wrong side of the Johannine dualism.

The second error about sin is for a Christian to claim, "I am without sin." There is more than one way to make such a claim. Some might reason that if they are Christians, and if there is no darkness in God, then it follows that they are in the light and nothing they do can actually be deemed sinful. John's own statement in 1 John 3:9, "No one who is born of God … they cannot go on sinning," might be construed to reinforce such an idea (but see discussion on this verse below). And so while a certain behavior might be sinful for a nonbeliever, a Christian might attempt to define what amounts to the same behavior as somehow not sinful by rationalizing it.

The third erroneous claim is for a person to say that he or she has not sinned. This perhaps is most similar to modern thought of our day that dispenses with the need for atonement by claiming that we haven't sinned. We haven't sinned in the garden of Eden (i.e., there is no such thing as "original sin"), and we haven't sinned individually and personally (sure, everybody makes mistakes, but ...). Such a claim, John says, is to make God a liar (strong language!), because God not only says we *have* sinned, but he has taken the most drastic measure to deal with sin: sending his Son Jesus Christ to die for the sin of the world so that those who believe might not perish but have eternal life (John 3:16). So when any human being individually or the world collectively says they have not sinned, they contradict God and call him a liar.

The issue of sin works counter to John's purpose of reassuring his readers they have eternal life. On the one hand, sin is on the dark side of the conceptual dualism and has no place in the life of a Christian (1 John 2:1a); yet on the other, Christians do commit sins from which they are to seek cleansing by Christ's blood (1 John 2:1b–2). John wishes to reassure those who believe in Christ that they do in fact have eternal life even though they sin. And so he must explain sin in terms that clarify why those who "walk in darkness" do not know God and therefore do not have eternal life, but why even those who have believed in Christ yet still sometimes sin nevertheless have eternal life. And he must do this all the while reinforcing the point that sin is definitely not okay. First John is not self-contradictory or inconsistent, but is explaining how a Christian can have assurance of eternal life while living in an "already–not yet" world.

The dualism that John constructs facilitates, on the one hand, his reassurance of eternal life for those believers who, he must admit, *do* sin and, on the other, upholds his condemnation of sin as belonging to the dark side. It also sheds light on those most difficult verses, 1 John 3:9, which states that those who are born of God cannot sin, and 1 John 5:16, which distinguishes between sin that leads to death and sin that does not. John is thinking in an apocalyptic and dualistic framework in which God, light, sinlessness, and life broke into this world of darkness, sin, and death when the Word became flesh. Those who have been born again of the Father have been brought into the light, have eternal life, and can choose not to sin. However, because the darkness has not yet been eliminated, Christians sometimes do sin, but they do not thereby lose their eternal life. Nevertheless, it is imperative that they choose not to sin, for "no one who is born of God will continue to sin" (1 John 3:9). To do so is evidence that one has not been born of God, and therefore is good reason to doubt one's eternal life. There can be no assurance of eternal life when a professing Christian is aware of sin in his or her life but does not deal with it through confession and seeking the cleansing that God has provided by Jesus' blood (1 John 1:9).

First John focuses the issue of sin not on individual sins, but on whether a person is on God's side of the dualism through new birth in Christ and therefore must deal rightly with sin. The difference between the Christian and the unbeliever who commit the same sin is that the Christian can seek cleansing and continual restoration because of Christ's blood;

the unbeliever has no such recourse. (Of course, an unbeliever's sin may be the catalyst that drives that person to become a Christian as he or she seeks relief from guilt.)

The sin that leads to death (1 John 5:16).

All sin is unrighteousness (darkness) that is of the devil, but 1 John teaches there is sin that does not result in the forfeiture of eternal life, for it can be confessed and cleansed by the blood of Christ. Christians are to pray for those brothers and sisters who sin, that they might repent and seek cleansing (1 John 5:16). It is a common assumption today that Christians pray for one another, but in ancient religion intercession was restricted to the priests. In that context, John's claim that any believer can effectively intercede for a brother or sister in sin is quite remarkable.

However, there is a sin unto death (5:16; Gk. *estin harmartia pros thanaton*) about which there is no point in praying. In Roman Catholic tradition, this verse forms the basis for the doctrine of "mortal" sin and "venial" sin. Mortal sins forfeit grace (sins that lead to death) and require formal confession and penance. Venial sins do not. Protestant interpreters move in a different direction. This is the sin of those who are yet in darkness, even if they profess to be Christian. It is the sin of those unwilling to accept the heart of the apostolic gospel—that Jesus died to atone for sin—but who still want to believe in him in some sense, perhaps as a teacher of good morals, for instance. Their sin cannot be forgiven, because they reject the very means of grace, the blood of Jesus. In the words of one commentator, "the 'sin unto death' is simply violation of the fundamental terms of relationship with God that Jesus Christ mediates."[17] John most likely has in mind a kind of person rather than a type of sin. (See commentaries for further discussion.)

17. Yarbrough, *1–3 John*, 310.

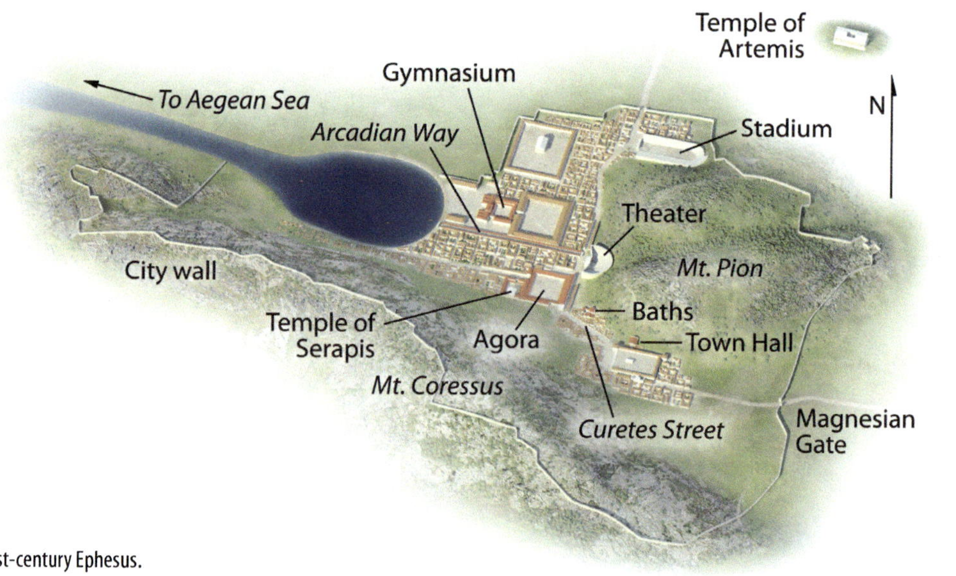

First-century Ephesus.

K. H. Jobes

Saint John's Basilica in Ephesus, shown in this model, was built by the Emperor Justinian in the 6th century.

Love Is the Opposite of Sin

The third strand of the author's concern in 1 John is that Christians love one another. This is the message heard from the beginning: "We should love one another" (1 John 3:11). First John relates this command to his purpose of reassurance: "We know that we have passed from death to life, because we love each other" (3:14a). Love for others is evidence that one has crossed from darkness into light, from death into life, for "anyone who does not love remains in death" (3:14b). The preeminent characteristic of Christian living is love for others, especially fellow believers.

> "All you need is love. All you need is love. All you need is love, love. Love is all you need."
>
> "All You Need Is Love," first performed by the Beatles, June 25, 1967

There is probably no topic in human history that has been written about, sung about, satirized, lauded, and lamented more than that of love. But what is love? If you took a poll on a street corner, you would no doubt get a wide spectrum of definitions, ranging from warm, fuzzy emotion, to political unity, to inner harmony, to sex. When the world's many definitions of love are lined up against what the New Testament writers say love is, it is easy to see that, as one writer has observed, "love is a terribly debased term today, almost beyond rescue as a description of the good news of the kingdom come in Jesus Christ.... We must work to recover an understanding and practice of love.... Salvation is living in the way of love."[18]

Invoking the love command may sound biblical, but the concept of loving others can be easily used in ways that are counter to the truth and therefore produce only counterfeit love. Love has been cited as a great ecumenical creed by those who wish to unite people with religious beliefs that are otherwise quite incompatible, as well as by those who wish

18. Jonathan R. Wilson, *God So Loved the World: A Christology for Disciples* (Grand Rapids: Baker, 2001), 131.

to practice no religion at all. One New Ager and producer of a TV program on spirituality was asked about his personal religious experience.[19] He described "an experience in which I felt what is defined as love, or oneness, or God." When asked what people should learn from faith and deeds, he replied, "Ultimately, our faith and deeds give us an experience of love and connectedness. The more good we do, the more experience we have with God, or love." He defined his personal goal in life: "To experience more love, more compassion, more faith and more surrender." And finally, when asked what his message to the community was, he announced, "We are all made of love, *God is love*, and we are God."

First John does indeed twice affirm that "God is love" (1 John 4:8, 16), but it is wrong to see that as an identity whose predicates can be interchanged.[20] Love is arguably God's first and foremost attribute, though never at the expense of his other innate attributes, such as holiness. "God is love" does not simply mean that God does loving things, but that *everything* God does originates in his love for his creation. When God redeems, it is because he loves; when he judges, it is out of love; whatever God does flows from his love. Consequently, God is love, but love is not God. This text gives no warrant to consider the quality of love in the abstract more supreme than the God whose being defines it.

"Love doesn't trump holiness."

KAREN JOBES

The concept that God is love is found among many religions and is used as a foundational principle for ethics. Since God is love, we as God's children should love one another and live in love. If we do this, we are living as God expects us to live, harmony with nature and others will result, and all will be well as God intended. In fact, if we were to understand spiritual truth as that which is common to all religions, there would not be a better principle to unite us than "God is love." Following that line of thinking, Jesus, some would argue, is simply another expression of God's love, a love that is found among all peoples and religions embodied in some other form. Following that logic, Christians should be loving people who are accepting of other religions also based on the principle of divine love. After all, John himself says, "Dear friends, let us love one another, for love comes from God. Everyone who loves has been born of God and knows God" (1 John 4:7). Does this not mean that love is the great common grace that God has given to unite everyone? So when we claim to have exclusive knowledge of the truth, when we assert that Jesus is the only way to the Father, are we not in fact violating the transcendent principle of our own religion? Isn't it really true that all the world really needs is love, sweet love? This line of thinking may very well have played into the error of the secessionists, for 1 John defines genuine love in relation to truth.

"What the world needs now is love, sweet love."

"WHAT THE WORLD NEEDS NOW," FIRST PERFORMED BY JACKIE DESHANNON, 1965

Of course, spiritual truth cannot be determined by the least common denominator of otherwise incompatible religious thought; it is determined by God's self-revelation in Jesus Christ as recorded by the inspired witnesses who wrote the biblical books.

---

19. Bob Barber, "Profiles in Faith," *Santa Barbara News Press*, January 3, 1998.

20. For a helpful further discussion, see R. W. L. Moberly, " 'Test the Spirits': God, Love, and Critical Discernment in 1 John 4," in *The Holy Spirit and Christian Origins: Essays in Honor of James D. G. Dunn*, ed. Graham N. Stanton, Bruce W. Longenecker, and Stephen C. Barton (Grand Rapids: Eerdmans, 2004), 296–307.

The author of 1 John has much to say about love. In fact, he mentions it more than fifty times in thirty verses out of the about one hundred verses in the book. The command to love is, as 1 John says, both ancient and new (2:7). First and foremost of the commandments of ancient Israel is love for God:

> "Love the LORD your God with all your heart and with all your soul and with all your strength." (Deut. 6:5)

> "Love the LORD your God and keep his requirements, his decrees, his laws and his commands always." (Deut. 11:1)

But love for God is no mere emotional experience or spiritual high. To love God means to keep his commandments, and when those commandments are considered, they involve how to treat other people.

Jesus brought God's love for humankind to earth, and he reaffirmed that the greatest commandment is to love God with all oneself, and the second is to love one's neighbor as oneself (Matt. 22:37, 39; Mark 12:30–31; Luke 10:27). In other words, the Bible teaches that love for others is rooted in a love for God. All genuine ethics and morality flow from that. Anything else is counterfeit, even though it may be sincere.

"Love doesn't trump truth."
KAREN JOBES

John also reaffirms this principle for Christians: "This is love for God: to keep his commands" (1 John 5:3), and "This is love: that we walk in obedience to his commands" (2 John 6). Love for God is not a feeling, but an obedient response to his moral commandments; and love for others is a way of behaving toward them that is rooted in how God defines the moral life. Love does not steal from its neighbor, bear false witness, kill, commit adultery, or even covet. It gives special honor to parents and respects the Sabbath need for rest by not driving others into exploitive circumstances. What passes for love in the world is only a poor counterfeit of the riches of love in Christ.

Love as Scripture defines it is the sign that a believer has passed from death to life and therefore should produce reassurance. But counterfeit love that is not rooted in the truth about God can never produce reassurance of eternal life. Just as genuine reassurance, as opposed to false hope, can rest only on the truth, reassurance can rest only on genuine love.

Love must be joined to truth to be genuine. First John teaches that we love because God first loved us (4:19) and sent his Son as an atoning sacrifice for our sins (4:10). Christology and Christian ethics are closely joined throughout the New Testament. As 1 John explains it, the moral basis of humankind is God's love for his creation. To return God's love in right relationship with him, one must keep his commands, and "this is his command: to believe in the name of his Son, Jesus Christ" (3:23a). God's love for the world is expressed specifically through the sacrifice of Jesus Christ for sin. Only by embracing that truth can one love others "as he commanded us" (3:23b). Those who reject Jesus Christ reject God's love and can never love others as God intended. That is not to say that people who aren't Christian can't have sincere *emotions* for loved ones, or even a self-sacrificing commitment to them, but to love others as 1 John defines it requires knowing God.

The expression of love for others is also defined in 1 John: "This is how we know what love is: Jesus Christ laid down his life for us. And we ought to lay down our lives for our brothers and sisters" (3:16). God's love for us becomes the model of how we are to love others. God saw the need of humankind and met that need in Christ. John relates this to how Christians are to love others: "If anyone of you has material possessions and sees a brother or sister in need but has no pity on them, how can the love of God be in you?" (3:17). Jesus defined love the same way in the parable of the good Samaritan (Luke 10:25–37). Love as God defines it is not having warm feelings toward others, but a considerate response to others, especially to those in need.

THE TEXT AND CANONICITY OF 1 JOHN

The Greek Text of 1 John[21]

The Greek text of 1 John is preserved in about six hundred manuscripts, the earliest of which is $\mathfrak{P}^{9}$ (third century; P.Oxy 402) and $\mathfrak{P}^{74}$ (seventh century; P.Bodmer XVII). $\mathfrak{P}^{9}$ is among the famous Oxyrhynchus **papyri** discovered by Grenfell and Hunt in 1896–97 in Egypt.

There are about forty variants in the Greek text of 1 John,[22] but they have resulted in only three revisions in *Novum Testamentum Graecum Editio Critica Maior* compared to the NA27/UBS[4] Greek text, at 1:7; 5:10; and 5:18.[23] A list of those variant readings can be found in Peter M. Head, 'Editio Critica Maior: An Introduction and Assessment', *Tyndale Bulletin* 61.1 (2010), 151–152, available online at https://www.academia.edu/3633883/_Editio_Critica_Maior_An_Introduction_and_Assessment_Tyndale_Bulletin_61.1_2010_131-152 (accessed May 2, 2016).

The ***Johannine comma***. A famous textual critical problem is found at 1 John 5:7–8 and is referred to as "the Johannine comma." We think of a comma as a punctuation mark, but here it is the Latin term for a clause. In manuscripts from the fourteenth century onward, an additional clause not original to 1 John creates the reading (with the clause in italics),

> Because there are three who testify *in heaven*:
> *Father, Word, and Holy Spirit;*
> *and these three are one;*
> *and there are three who testify on earth:*
> the Spirit and the water and the blood;
> and these three are one.

Only Bibles in the King James tradition, which venerate the Greek text as it existed in the sixteenth century, continue to include this additional material, in spite of the virtually universal consensus that these words are a very late addition to the text and in full knowledge of the historical situation that gave rise to them.

Although the Johannine comma is certainly not part of what John originally wrote, its origin was a colorful moment in the history of the Greek New Testament.[24] The first

21. For a good overview of the Greek of 1 John, see Martin M. Culy, *I, II, III John: A Handbook on the Greek Text* (Waco, Tex.: Baylor University Press, 2004).

22. See Bruce M. Metzger, *A Textual Commentary on the Greek New Testament*, 2nd ed. (Stuttgart: German Bible Society, 1994); Barbara Aland et al. eds., *Novum Testamentum Graecum Editio Critica Maior*, vol. 4: *Catholic Letters*, pt. 1: Text, installment 3: *The First Letter of John* (Stuttgart: Deutsche Bibelgesellschaft, 2003).

23. Yarbrough, *1–3 John*, 4–5.

24. See Bruce M. Metzger, *The Text of the New Testament: Its Transmission, Corruption, and Restoration* (New York and Oxford: Oxford University Press, 1980), 62, 101–2.

Greek New Testament to be printed rather than hand copied was produced by Erasmus in 1515, followed by editions in 1516 and 1519. One of the criticisms of Erasmus's Greek text was the absence of the testimony of the three heavenly witnesses found in the Latin version at 1 John 5:7–8. Erasmus answered the criticism by explaining that he did not include it because it was not in any of the Greek manuscripts he used, although he recognized that the clause did appear in the Latin Vulgate. In the heat of the moment, Erasmus promised he would include it in a future printing if even one Greek manuscript could be found that included it. Before his next edition appeared, he was shown a manuscript that did indeed have the missing material, and Erasmus reluctantly included what we know as the Johannine comma at 1 John 5:7–8, though with a note expressing his suspicion that the manuscript had been made to order for the occasion! As it turns out, that manuscript (Greg. 61) was most likely written in Oxford in 1520 by a Franciscan friar who translated the disputed words from the Latin Vulgate to provide a Greek manuscript for Erasmus.

When modern textual critics examine the thousands of manuscripts of the Greek New Testament, the Johannine comma appears in only two as a margin note where it was clearly added and a third whose date is disputed to either the fourteenth or sixteenth century. Although the additional phrase was included in the Latin Vulgate at the time of Erasmus, it does not appear in any Latin manuscripts earlier than AD 800.[25] There it appears as a scribal gloss in the margin that had found its way into the body of subsequent Latin manuscripts, creating the cause of Erasmus's troubles.

The most recent reconstruction of the Greek text of 1 John is found, not in Nestle-Aland *Novum Testamentum Graece* (NA27, 1993), but in Barbara Aland et al, *Novum Testamentum Graecum Editio Critica Maior*, vol. 4: *Catholic Letters*, pt. 1: *Text*, installment 3: *The First Letter of John* (Stuttgart: Deutsche Bibelgesellschaft, 2003). The sixteen readings that differ from NA27 can be found in Peter M. Head, 'Editio Critica Maior: An Introduction and Assessment', *Tyndale Bulletin* 61.1 (2010), 151–152, available online at https://www.academia.edu/3633883/_Editio_Critica_Maior_An_Introduction_and_Assessment_Tyndale_Bulletin_61.1_2010_131-152 (accessed May 2, 2016).

Canonicity

There is no evidence that the canonicity of 1 John was ever disputed (though there is skepticism in ancient writings about 2 and 3 John). The first time all three epistles are mentioned is by Origen (c. AD 250), who wrote that John "left also an epistle of a very few lines and, it may be, a second and a third, for not all say that these [the second and third] are genuine" (quoted in Eusebius, *Hist. eccl.* 6.25.10). Irenaeus quotes both 1 and 2 John as if they were the same text, which may be evidence that both circulated together (*Haer.* 3.16.8). Eusebius himself lists 1 John among the "recognized" (Gk. *homologoumena*) books, along with 1 Peter (*Hist. eccl.* 3.25.2–3). In the same place he lists 2 and 3 John among the disputed books (Gk. *antilogoumena*). The **Muratorian Canon**, a seventh-century Latin manuscript that likely preserves a much earlier canon list, refers to only two letters of John. There is, however, some thought that the very brief 2 John originally may have functioned

25. Ibid., 102.

as a cover letter for 1 John, in which case they may have circulated together and counted as one. Only after 2 John was separated from 1 John did it become suspect. All three epistles are included in Athanasius's canon list (AD 367).

The designation of 1 John as a "**catholic**" epistle is early. Recall that in the ancient world, the Greek word *katholikos* meant "general" or "universal," and had nothing to do with the much later development of the Roman Catholic Church (which title lays claim to being the universal church). Dionysius, bishop of Alexandria (c. AD 250), is quoted as referring to 1 John as John's "catholic" epistle (*Hist. eccl.* 7.25.7, 10). At about that same time, Origen also calls it "catholic" (*Comm. Matt.* 17.19). Debates about the authorship of 1 John persisted through the centuries to our own times, but not about its canonicity.

STRUCTURE AND OUTLINE OF 1 JOHN

The structure of 1 John is notoriously difficult to discern and articulate. Often the letter's structure is described as a braid or a spiral, with its major themes recurring throughout. If it was written to be delivered orally, its structure may reinforce memory of its public reading.[26] The letter's lack of structure at the topical level led one scholar to comment, probably an exaggeration, "The author's logic is so obscure that one could move around units almost at will and still 1 John would read just as well as it does now."[27] Interpreters forced to divide 1 John into **pericopes** to structure their commentaries have suggested from two to twelve divisions. The following outline is intended only to give an overview of the topics as the letter unfolds.

I. Witness to the Word of Life (1:1 – 4)

II. God Is Light (1:5 – 4:6)

- A. Walking in the Light (1:5 – 2:11)
    1. Confessing sin (1:5 – 2:2)
    2. Keeping the commands of God (2:3 – 11)
- B. Reasons for Writing (2:12 – 14)
- C. Warnings (2:15 – 29)
    1. Do not love the world (2:15 – 17)
    2. Do not deny the Son (2:18 – 29)
- D. Being Children of God (3:1 – 4:6)
    1. Children who do not sin (3:1 – 10)
    2. Children who love one another (3:11 – 18)
    3. Children who know the truth (3:19 – 24)
    4. Children who test the spirits (4:1 – 6)

III. God Is Love (4:7 – 5:12)

- A. Love One Another (4:7 – 21)
- B. Believe in the Son of God (5:1 – 12)

IV. Concluding Assurances and Warnings (5:13 – 21)

26. E.g., see Russ Dudrey, "1 John and the Public Reading of Scripture," *SCJ* 6 (2003): 235 – 55.
27. Brown, *Epistles of John*, 117.

A. The Assurance of Eternal Life (5:13–15)
B. The Sin That Leads to Death (5:16–17)
C. Final Assurances (5:18–20)
D. Keep Yourselves from Idols (5:21)

CHAPTER SUMMARY

First John is a message from an elderly leader of the first-century church, most likely the apostle John, son of Zebedee, reflecting a lifetime of preaching, ministry, and church leadership. Based on the eyewitness testimony about Jesus Christ, it provides reassurance for believers living in troubling times of confusion and doubt. The assurance of eternal life is attained by (1) believing rightly about Jesus, the Son of God, who became fully human to atone for sin; (2) dealing rightly with sin by calling it what it is, confessing it, and seeking the cleansing of the Lord, not by denying or rationalizing it; and (3) loving others as God defines love, which is not a matter of how one feels, but is living by the moral commands of God with a considerate responsiveness to the needs of others, especially those in dire need. This is a message as relevant in our times as when it was first penned.

KEY TERMS

antichrists
Cerinthianism
docetism
epideictic rhetoric
Erasmus
Eusebius
Irenaeus
Johannine comma
Johannine community
NA27
Papias
papyrus $\mathfrak{P}^{9}$
pericope
Polycarp
prologue
secessionists

QUESTIONS FOR REVIEW OR DISCUSSION

1. How might the referent of the pronoun "we" of 1 John be resolved? How does this bear on theories of authorship?
2. Much of what we know of John and the apostles comes from Eusebius. How trustworthy do you consider this information and why?

3. What situation apparently precipitated 1 John to be written?
4. Describe the kinds of thinking that were apparently leading some in the Johannine church(es) into error.
5. Why is truth a necessary foundation for reassurance? How does the truth of Jesus relate to sin and, its opposite, love?
6. Do you think people who are not born again can genuinely love others? Why or why not?

GOING FURTHER

Abbott, Edwin A. *Johannine Vocabulary: A Comparison of the Words of the Fourth Gospel with Those of the Three.* London: A. & C. Black, 1905. Repr., Eugene, Ore.: Wipf & Stock, 2005.

Brown, Raymond. *The Community of the Beloved Disciple: The Life, Loves, and Hates of an Individual Church in New Testament Times.* New York: Paulist, 1979.

Burge, Gary. *The Anointed Community: The Holy Spirit in the Johannine Tradition.* Grand Rapids: Eerdmans, 1987.

Culpepper, R. Alan. "The Christology of the Johannine Writings." Pages 66–87 in *Who Do You Say That I Am? Essays on Christology.* Edited by Mark Allan Powell and David R. Bauer. Louisville: Westminster John Knox, 1999.

———. *John, the Son of Zebedee: The Life of a Legend.* Studies on Personalities of the New Testament. Columbia: University of South Carolina Press, 1994.

Culy, Martin M. *I, II, III John: A Handbook on the Greek Text.* Waco, Tex.: Baylor University Press, 2004.

Dudrey, Russ. "1 John and the Public Reading of Scripture." *Stone Campbell Journal* 6 (2003): 235–55.

Harner, Philip B. *What Are They Saying about the Catholic Epistles?* What Are They Saying Series. New York: Paulist, 2004.

Hill, Charles E. *The Johannine Corpus in the Early Church.* New York: Oxford University Press, 2004.

Kruse, Colin G. "Sin and Perfection in 1 John." *Australian Biblical Review* 51 (2003): 60–70.

Lieu, Judith. *The Theology of the Johannine Epistles.* New Testament Theology. Cambridge: Cambridge University Press, 1991.

Longacre, Robert E. "Towards an Exegesis of 1 John Based on the Discourse Analysis of the Greek Text." Pages 271–86 in *Linguistics and New Testament Interpretation: Essays on Discourse Analysis.* Edited by David Alan Black, Katharine G. L. Barnwell, and Steven H. Levinson. Nashville: Broadman, 1992.

Metzger, Bruce M. *Apostolic Letters of Faith, Hope, and Love: Galatians, 1 Peter, and 1 John.* Eugene, Ore.: Cascade, 2006.

Moberly, R. W. L. "'Test the Spirits': God, Love, and Critical Discernment in 1 John 4." Pages 296–307 in *The Holy Spirit and Christian Origins: Essays in Honor of James D. G. Dunn.* Edited by Graham N. Stanton, Bruce W. Longenecker, and Stephen C. Barton. Grand Rapids: Eerdmans, 2004.

Painter, John. *The Quest for the Messiah: The History, Literature, and Theology of the Johannine Community.* 2nd ed. Nashville: Abingdon, 1993.

Richards, W. Larry. *The Classification of the Greek Manuscripts of the Johannine Epistles.* SBLDS 35. Missoula, Montana: Scholars, 1977.
Tan, Randall K. J. "A Linguistic Overview of 1 John" *Southern Baptist Journal* (2006): 68–80.
———. "Should We Pray for Straying Brethren? John's Confidence in 1 John 5:16–17." *JETS* 45 (2002): 599–609.
Thatcher, Tom, ed. *What We Have Heard from the Beginning: The Past, Present, and Future of Johannine Studies.* Waco, Tex.: Baylor University Press, 2007.
———. *Why John Wrote a Gospel: Jesus–Memory–History.* Louisville: Westminster John Knox, 2006.
Watt, Jan van der. *An Introduction to the Johannine Gospel and Letters.* T&T Clark Approaches to Biblical Studies. London: T&T Clark, 2007.

Commentaries

Brown, Raymond. *The Epistles of John*. AB 30. Garden City, N.Y.: Doubleday, 1982.
Bultmann, Rudolf K. *The Johannine Epistles: A Commentary on the Johannine Epistles.* Edited by R. W. Funk. Translated by R. P. O'Hara, L. C. McGaughy, and R. W. Funk. Hermeneia. Philadelphia, Fortress, 1973.
Burge, Gary. *Letters of John*. NIVAC. Grand Rapids: Zondervan, 1996.
Culpepper, R. Alan. *The Gospel and Letters of John.* Interpreting Biblical Texts. Nashville: Abingdon, 1998.
Jobes, Karen H. *1, 2, 3 John*. Zondervan Exegetical Commentary on the New Testament 19. Grand Rapids: Zondervan, forthcoming.
Kruse, Colin G. *The Letters of John.* Pillar New Testament Commentary. Grand Rapids: Eerdmans, 2000.
Lieu, Judith. *I, II and III John*. New Testament Library. Louisville: Westminster John Knox, 2008.
Lindars, Barnabas, Ruth B. Edwards, and John M. Court. *The Johannine Literature.* Sheffield New Testament Guides. Sheffield: Sheffield Academic Press, 2000.
Marshall, I. Howard. *The Epistles of John*. NICNT. Grand Rapids: Eerdmans, 1978.
Schnackenburg, Rudolf. *The Johannine Epistles*. Translated by Reginald Fuller and Ilse Fuller. New York: Crossroad, 1992.
Smalley, Stephen S. *1, 2, 3 John.* Word Biblical Commentary 51. Waco, Tex.: Word, 1984.
Strecker, Georg. *The Johannine Letters*. Hermeneia. Minneapolis: Fortress, 1996.
Talbert, Charles H. *Reading John: A Literary and Theological Commentary on the Fourth Gospel and the Johannine Epistles.* Reading the New Testament Series. New York: Crossroad, 1994.
Thatcher, Tom. "1 John." Pages 414–505 in *Hebrews–Revelation. Expositor's Bible Commentary.* Vol. 13. Edited by Tremper Longman III and David E. Garland. Rev. ed. Grand Rapids: Zondervan, 2006.
Thompson, Marianne Meye. *1–3 John*. IVPNTC. Downers Grove, Ill.: InterVarsity, 1992.
Witherington, Ben, III. *A Socio-Rhetorical Commentary on Titus, 1–2 Timothy, and 1–3 John.* Vol. 1 of Letters and Homilies for Hellenized Christians. Downers Grove, Ill.: IVP Academic, 2006.
Yarbrough, Robert W. "1 John" Pages 176–211 in *ZIBBC.* Vol. 4. Edited by Clinton E. Arnold. Grand Rapids: Zondervan, 2002.
———. *1–3 John*. BECNT. Grand Rapids: Baker Academic, 2008.

CHAPTER 14

2 and 3 John

NOTES OF GRACE AND TRUTH

Your Goals for This Chapter

- To learn the major theme(s) of 2 and 3 John.
- To consider how truth and love are related.
- To gain insight into the realities of a congregation in the early church.

WHY 2 AND 3 JOHN ARE IMPORTANT TO YOU

Have you ever cleaned out a grandparent's attic or basement? Often that task comes at a sad moment when someone has passed away, but it can be exciting to find mementos, letters, or documents from a time before we were born. Such finds often give insight into a side of our loved one we never saw, or what kind of life they lived before we were a part of it. Similarly, archaeologists get very excited when an ancient text is discovered, untouched by human hands for centuries or millennia. Such discoveries—for instance, the Dead Sea Scrolls or the Code of Hammurabi—provide valuable information about the times and cultures of antiquity.

Baker Photo Archive, courtesy of the British Museum

The Code of Hammurabi is the earliest known law code from the ancient Near East.

The books of the Bible must be appreciated as artifacts of antiquity if they are to be fully understood as God's Word. In 2 and 3 John (and Philemon) we find actual personal notes written more than two thousand years ago yet continuously read since the time of their writing. That's pretty exciting! Third John presents a real situation in the ancient church that involved four men, and we know the actual names of three of them. Reading 2 and 3 John is like opening a time capsule and realizing from its contents how connected we are to the past because of our human nature and shared beliefs with the early church. God has allowed us to look over the shoulder of the elder into a situation that was troubling to the Christians who first read these notes. In them we see the elder's heart as he speaks grace and truth into a distressing situation. And because the elder was an apostolic writer, these letters allow him to speak into similarly distressing situations today.

Key Verses

2 John 1: The elder, To the lady chosen by God and to her children, whom I love in the truth . . .

2 John 6: And this is love: that we walk in obedience to his commands. As you have heard from the beginning, his command is that you walk in love.

2 John 9: Anyone who runs ahead and does not continue in the teaching of Christ does not have God; whoever continues in the teaching has both the Father and the Son.

3 John 4: I have no greater joy than to hear that my children are walking in the truth.

3 John 8: We ought therefore to show hospitality to such people so that we may work together for the truth.

3 John 11: Dear friend, do not imitate what is evil but what is good. Anyone who does what is good is from God. Anyone who does what is evil has not seen God.

Challenges Presented by the Books of 2 and 3 John

- The identity of the elder of 2 and 3 John.
- The identity of the lady, her children, and her chosen sister mentioned in 2 John.
- Discerning the situation that gave rise to these letters.

CHAPTER OUTLINE

Please read the books of 2 and 3 John in one sitting before reading this chapter.

THE ELDER

The letters of 2 and 3 John are among the briefest books of the New Testament with 2 John comprised of 212 words and 3 John of 190.[1] Each would easily have fit on one **papyrus** sheet, used for such personal correspondence. In most Bibles, each book takes up only one page, and the books are easy to miss as one thumbs through the New Testament. Seldom does one hear a sermon taken from either of these letters.

Both books take the form of a Hellenistic personal letter, with an opening salutation and closing remarks. Both name "the elder" (Gk. *presbyteros*), with no further identity given, as the person sending these notes. One of the mysteries of these books is the identity of "the elder" and his relationship to the John whose name titles these books.

The titles, of course, were not a part of the original letters and were added later, necessarily when the letters came to be bound together with other writings. The titles in the

1. As enumerated by Accordance 8.4 counting words in the NA27GNT text.

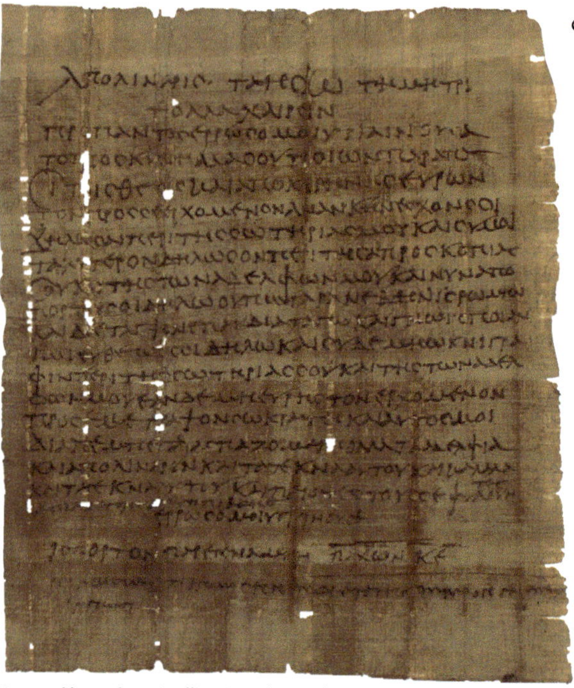

Personal letter from Apollinarius to his mother Taesion, stating that he has safely reached Ostia and, later on the same day, Rome, where he received his appointment to Misenum (2nd century AD).

earliest manuscripts of the first **epistle** vary, but all include the same name, John.[2] The question remains whether 1 John was also written by "the elder" and whether the elder was the apostle John or another Christian leader of the same name. (See the discussion in chapter 13, which concludes that apostles could be referred to as elders, in the sense of church office.) The same Greek word, *presbyteros*, was also used to refer to an elderly man quite apart from church office. Even if the apostle John was too old to be active in church oversight beyond writing notes and occasional visits (2 John 12; 3 John 14), the word "elder" would be apt. In either sense of the word *presbyteros*, the author felt no need to further identify himself as he was writing to people who evidently knew him and with whom he had a warm and personal relationship, especially in the case of 3 John.

There is little textual reason to reject one author having written all three of these letters. Second John seems particularly close to 1 John, sharing the same concern about the "**antichrists**" (1 John 2:18, 22; 4:3; cf. 2 John 7), reminding of the joy that results from living in the truth (1 John 1:4; cf. 2 John 4; 3 John 3), and defining love as obedience to God's commands (1 John 5:3; cf. 2 John 6). Third John bears affinities with 2 John, indicating a unity of content and syntax among all three.

The sequence of John's three letters in the New Testament may or may not have been the order in which they were written. In any case, 2 and 3 John would make much less sense if it were not for 1 John. It may be that all three were written at about the same time and sent as a package.[3] By that theory, the courier, Demetrius, carried a letter of introduction to Gaius (3 John), along with a letter to be read in Gaius's church (2 John) as an introduction to the sermon to be delivered (1 John). Regardless of the specifics, these three letters clearly have a closely related history.

2 JOHN

The Chosen Lady and Her Children

The note we know as 2 John is addressed to the "lady chosen by God and to her children." Its final greeting is from the "children of your sister" who are also chosen. Was the chosen lady a real individual or a metaphorical reference to a sister congregation? Although a few interpreters throughout the church's history have suggested the former, most take the note

2. For a list of titles found in the early manuscripts, see Robert W. Yarbrough, *1–3 John*, BECNT (Grand Rapids: Baker Academic, 2008), 12–13.
3. Luke Timothy Johnson, *The Writings of the New Testament: An Interpretation*, rev. ed. (Minneapolis: Fortress, 1999), 560–61.

to be addressed to a sister church. First, neither of the words translated "chosen" and "lady" (Gk. *eklektē* and *kyria*) were known to be personal names in the first century. Second, there are no personal references within the note that would suggest the author had a specific individual in mind. There are no names or other specific personal information mentioned. Furthermore, assemblies or congregations were sometimes personified as a female, perhaps because personification often adopts grammatical gender. The Greek word used to refer to a church congregation (*ekklēsia*) was grammatically feminine, and so personification of a church as a female would be conventional. Third, 1 John addresses its readers as "children" several times, in what is almost certainly a spiritual sense. The repetition of that in 2 John 1 suggests that the same or a similar group is in the author's mind. The final verse 13 refers to "the children of your sister," suggesting that this is a greeting from the elder's congregation to a sister church at some distance, but in the same vicinity and having the same spiritual values.

The note conveys warm encouragement that the elder has found this congregation to be living in the truth of the gospel of Jesus Christ (v. 4). The elder reminds this congregation of the command to love one another (v. 5) and ties this exhortation to living in obedience to God's commands (as discussed in chapter 13). He then immediately refers to the antichrists who have gone out to spread their false gospel, denying that Jesus Christ has come in the flesh. The elder apparently felt the need to clarify that the command to love one another did not imply that such "Christians" were to be received or welcomed with hospitality. In fact, they should not be given even the slightest consideration — not even an opportunity for a greeting (v. 10). Here we see that the elder's exhortation to love one another does not trump the truth of the gospel. The elder feared that by welcoming the antichrists with hospitality and giving them an opportunity to speak their errant beliefs, the congregation would be sharing in their wicked work (v. 11). In fact, the elder's concern for this congregation was such that he himself planned to travel to visit them in the near future (v. 12).

Courtesy of the Pitts Theology Library, Candler School of Theology, Emory University

The book of 2 John is concerned with truth (*veritas*).

Even though we do not know the exact social and historical situation that prompted its author to write, the concerns expressed are as timely and relevant today as when they were first written. How wrong it would be in the name of Christian love to aid and assist those who have a distorted and erroneous understanding of the person and work of Jesus Christ in spreading heresy. In fact, the elder implies that if the chosen lady and her children are to continue to walk in truth and love, they must side squarely with the elder. Taking sides is never pleasant in arguments between Christians, but the elder's concern is that by exposing themselves to errant teaching and aiding the evil work of heretics, these "children" will prove the elder's work in vain and lose the reward of their faith (v. 8).

Christian Hospitality

At the time the letter was written, the practical matter in view was hospitality. For various reasons, Christians opened their homes so traveling missionaries and preachers could work in their area. Moreover, when they departed, it was the practice to send them on their way with enough food and resources to reach their next destination. Such hospitality was necessary, and it greatly aided the spread of the gospel in the Roman world, but it also helped heresy to spread, and that is the elder's concern in 2 John.

An ancient text entitled the *Didache* is among the earliest of Christian writings, a compilation of material that likely dates from the first century.[4] It claims to contain the teaching (Gk. *didache*) of the twelve apostles, from which it takes its name. The practice of Christian hospitality in the early church flowed from a more general practice of generosity:

> Do not be someone who stretches out his hands to receive, but withdraws them when it comes to giving. If you earned something by working with your hands ... you shall not turn away from someone in need, but shall share everything with your brother, and not claim that anything is your own. For if you are sharers in what is imperishable, how much more so in perishable things! (*Didache* 4:5–8)

Of course, such generosity could be abused, especially by the unscrupulous who saw an opportunity to exploit Christian hospitality. The *Didache* also addresses that situation:

> Everyone "who comes in the name of the Lord" is to be welcomed. But then examine him, and you will find out—for you will have insight—what is true and what is false. If the one who comes is merely passing through, assist him as much as you can. But he must not stay with you for more than two or, if necessary, three days. However, if he wishes to settle among you and is a craftsman, let him work for his living. But if he is not a craftsman, decide according to your own judgment how he shall live among you as a Christian, yet without being idle. But if he does not wish to cooperate in this way, then he is trading on Christ. Beware of such people. (*Didache* 12:1–5)

Although the *Didache* is not Scripture (and it may not accurately reflect the practices of the apostles), it does indicate some of the practices and concerns of the early church. In 2 John the elder is addressing a situation in which the practice of Christian hospitality should be withheld—the arrival of people known to be false teachers. Some interpreters find the elder to be inconsistent on this point: on the one hand, he admonishes his readers to love one another, and then, on the other, he instructs them to withhold food and shelter, an act some interpreters consider to be very unloving.

Bringing Love and Truth Together

Although this little book of 2 John is so often overlooked in the church, its message is vital for the health of the church in every age. How do we, as individuals and as congregations, bring truth and love together? Does Christian love mean tolerance of whatever ideas come down the pike? First, the elder is not shy to stake a claim to truth and demand that it must be obeyed. Sociologists might argue today that such exclusive claims to truth are power plays that exhibit cultural or personal arrogance. Furthermore, they may argue that what is truth

4. For both the Greek and English texts, see Michael W. Holmes, *The Apostolic Fathers Greek Texts and English Translations*, rev. ed. (Grand Rapids: Baker Academic, 1999).

for you isn't necessarily truth for me. But the metaphysical claims of divine self-revelation must transcend the social construction of truth. The claim for an exclusive truth was as unpopular in the first century as it is today. The truth about Jesus Christ was given as he revealed himself to those he chose to be with him through his public ministry and to be witnesses of his death and resurrection. The responsibility of the truth about Jesus Christ rested on those original apostles who preached and taught others but who eventually also brought the New Testament into existence. At the time the letters of John were written, living apostolic authority was still in play, either through the apostle John himself, or through one who had close access to the apostolic eyewitnesses. Just as Luke wrote as an associate of the apostle Paul, and Mark wrote as an associate of Peter, it is possible that the Holy Spirit chose a man close to the apostle John to inscripturate the apostle John's authoritative message about Christ. This is the claim of 1 John 1:1–4, that the authority of those who know the eyewitness truth trumps those who may have been claiming some direct revelation from the Spirit, or who made their claims based on human reasoning or observation, such as the Greek philosophers did. The authoritative truth about Jesus Christ today rests in the New Testament writings, such as the letters of 2 and 3 John. The church can and should boldly proclaim the authority of Scripture against all distorted and erroneous beliefs about Jesus that circulate today.

St. Benedict finds flour and feeds the monks, from the Life of St. Benedict, Signorelli, L. & Sodoma, G./Monte Oliveto Maggiore, Tuscany, Italy/The Bridgeman Art Library

Early Christians tried to practice generosity and hospitality.

Love enters the picture, not by being tolerant of any and all claims to truth, but by asserting the authority of Scripture and not allowing people to continue in spiritual error and sin. It is not loving to see someone, especially someone who claims to be a Christian, living with false beliefs or habitual sin, and simply look the other way. Love demands that in gentleness and humility, but with the full authority of God's Word, the gospel be shared. But with those who identify themselves as Christian yet persist to believe other than what Scripture says, and to teach others the same, no true fellowship can be maintained. The elder tells his readers to do nothing that would assist pseudo-Christians to spread lies about Jesus Christ.

An Outline of 2 John

I. Salutation (vv. 1–2)

II. The Greeting (v. 3)

III. Affirmation and Exhortation (vv. 4–6)

- A. Affirmation of Faithfulness (v. 4)
- B. Exhortation to Continue to Love (vv. 5–6)

David Bivin/www.LifeintheHolyLand.com

Hospitality was important in the ancient world. Birket-Ram, Israel, is a volcanic crater lake on the Golan Heights. According to legend, the lake covers a village punished for its lack of hospitality.

IV. Warning against the Antichrists (vv. 7–9)

V. Exhortation to Withhold Hospitality (vv. 10–11)

VI. Letter Closing (vv. 12–13)

A. Promise of a Visit (v. 12)

B. Closing Greeting (v. 13)

3 JOHN

The letter of 3 John is the shortest book of the New Testament, comprised of only 190 words,[5] and is easy to overlook in the Bible. Like the letter to Philemon written by the apostle Paul, 3 John is addressed to one specific individual, whose name is Gaius. And yet in this small slice of life from the earliest days of the church, we have four Christians identified, two delegations of itinerant preachers, and two or more congregations involved.

The Purpose of the Note

If there are any today who would nostalgically long for those early days of the Christian church because they believe everyone got along in perfect harmony, this brief note will disabuse them of such romantic ideas. The tensions, personality conflicts, and issues between the elder and the church of Diotrephes are intense and serious. The note holds both instruction for those who were confused by the situation and a warning for those leaders who would let their personal ambition go unchecked.

5. As enumerated by Accordance 8.4, counting the NA27 GNT text.

The elder and Gaius are personal friends. The elder has received a good report about Gaius from some traveling Christians who had enjoyed the hospitality of Gaius. The elder affirms such acts of generosity and encourages him to continue to show hospitality to those itinerant preachers who go out to spread the gospel of Jesus. But all is not well in the area where Gaius lives. The elder apparently fears that Gaius will be influenced by Diotrephes, a man who "loves to be first" and who will have nothing to do with the elder for reasons that aren't given. Diotrephes has been "spreading malicious nonsense" about the elder and those associated with him. The hostility is such that Diotrephes refuses to extend hospitality to those brothers the elder sends, and furthermore, he stops others in the church from extending hospitality as well. The elder fears that because of the tense conflict of this unfortunate situation, Gaius might also begin to refuse such hospitality to those sent by the elder.

The specifics of why Diotrephes is hostile to the elder are not known. If his hostility is viewed in light of the antichrists in 1 John, it may be that Diotrephes is on their side and therefore views the elder's beliefs as aberrant. Ironically, Diotrephes may be practicing the elder's message of 2 John, turning the elder's exhortation against him by refusing to welcome those he believes teach an errant gospel. Or the breech in relationship between Diotrephes and the elder may have had nothing to do with doctrine, but may have been more personal, such as a rejection of the elder's authority because of his age or clashes of personality. We have no way of knowing.

One debate is whether Diotrephes held an official position of leadership in the church or was a layman with a dominant personality who used personal influence to sway others. Since the elder had written "to the church" (v. 9), it is likely he wrote to the pastor. Since Diotrephes is mentioned in the next clause, it seems likely that he was the pastor or held some official leadership position, though the theory that he was among the first bishops of a monarchical episcopacy goes beyond the text.

Both in 2 and 3 John, "the truth" was central to the elder's thinking, as it is in 1 John (see chapter 13), which indicates that protection of the correct interpretation of the gospel was an issue at this time. This issue would have been most acute between the time of the apostles' passing and the time their writings were being gathered and circulated for a wider audience. Given the competing philosophies and religions that were making inroads into Christian thinking in the late first century, the transition of authority in the church was a precarious time for the gospel.

3 John's Cast of Characters

The elder — author of the note who asserts spiritual authority
Gaius — a dear friend of the elder's who lives at some distance
Diotrephes — a man who has considerable influence over a congregation and who is spreading malicious gossip about the elder
Demetrius — a well-respected man from the elder's congregation who brings the note to Gaius
Itinerant brothers — missionaries sent from the elder

A Letter of Introduction from Oxyrhynchus, Egypt, AD 25*

"Theon, to the most honored Tyrannus, very many greetings. Heraclides, the bearer of this letter, is my brother, therefore I entreat you with all my power to take him under your protection. I have also asked your brother Hermias by letter to inform you about him. You will do me the greatest favor if you let him win your approval. Before all else I pray that you may have health and the best of success, unharmed by the evil eye. Goodbye."

*Slightly adapted from *Selected Papryi* #106 (Hunt and Edgar, LCL).

The elder had to send this brief note that we know as 3 John in the hands of a messenger, Demetrius, and hoped that Gaius would provide him with food and shelter when he arrived. Such letters of introduction were a necessary part of that culture of hospitality, and many such notes have been discovered by archaeologists in Egypt. The purpose of 3 John therefore seems to have been to raise with Gaius the problem Diotrephes had presented and to test the waters with Gaius, to see if he would continue to provide a home away from home for those sent out from the elder's congregation(s).

No one knows if Gaius did receive Demetrius, or how the issue between the elder and Diotrephes subsequently played out in those congregations. We don't know what happened to the antichrists, though some scholars suggest that they evolved into the late second-century Montanists who flourished in that area of Asia Minor and whose leader, Montanus, claimed to receive direct revelation from the Holy Spirit. The claim of new revelation from the Spirit that involved a rejection of apostolic orthodoxy comports well with the concerns of the **Johannine** letters. After a few generations, the Nicene Council declared **Montanists** heretical. We can't know for sure if they had any relationship to the situation of 3 John. But the fact that 3 John was preserved in the New Testament and placed with 1 and 2 John suggests that the elder's authority did prevail.

An Outline of 3 John

- I. Salutation (v. 1)
- II. Letter Opening (vv. 2–4)
  - A. Greeting (v. 2)
  - B. The Joy of a Faithful Report (vv. 3–4)
- III. Exhortation to Continue Hospitality (vv. 5–8)
- IV. The Problem of Diotrephes (vv. 9–10)
- V. Exhortation to Receive Demetrius (vv. 11–12)
  - A. Exhortation to Imitate the Good (v. 11)
  - B. Introduction of Demetrius (v. 12)
- VI. Letter Closing (vv. 13–14)
  - A. Promise of a Visit (vv. 13–14a)
  - B. Closing Greeting (v. 14b)

THE TEXT AND CANONICITY OF 2 AND 3 JOHN

Canonicity

If 2 and 3 John were known only in isolation from the rest of the New Testament, it is not likely these brief, anonymous notes would have been preserved. The fact that they were preserved and fit so well with the context provided by 1 John suggests that the three letters had a history closely related to one another, a history that was likely also tied to the gospel of John and perhaps the book of Revelation. The fact that none of the three letters states the name of the author suggests that he was a well-known figure among the original readers, either the apostle John or someone known to be closely associated with the apostle.

Irenaeus (c. **AD** 140 – c. 202) quotes both 1 and 2 John as if they were the same text, which may be evidence that both circulated together (*Haer.* 3.16.8). Judith Lieu observes from the earliest witnesses to 2 and 3 John by the church fathers that the attitudes toward them fall into three different patterns.[6] First, there were those ancient writers who, like Irenaeus, knew of 1 and 2 John but did not explicitly mention 3 John. Second, there were those, like Tertullian and Cyprian, who were familiar with 1 John but did not explicitly mention 2 or 3 John. This is the normative pattern observed among the Syriac churches. Such confusion in their numbering would be natural if all three originated as a package. A third pattern is observed among those who knew of 2 and 3 John but question whether they should be received as canonical. Origen, whose writing is the earliest surviving to mention all three letters, represents this viewpoint:

> Why need I speak of him who leaned back on Jesus' breast, John, who has left behind one gospel, confessing that he could write so many that even the world itself could not contain them; and he wrote also the Apocalypse.... He has left also an epistle of a very few lines, and, it may be, a second and a third; for not all say that these are genuine. Only, the two of them together are not a hundred lines long. (quoted by Eusebius, *Hist. eccl.* 6.25.9 – 10)

It is understandable that given the brevity and content of 2 and 3 John, there may have been those who doubted their canonical value. In fact, it is difficult to see a reason for their acceptance other than the celebrity of their author and their value in illustrating the tensions caused by the antichrists mentioned in 1 John. For whatever reasons, these two brief letters were given the benefit of the doubt, as all three letters listed individually do appear in the canon list of Athanasius (AD 367) and were affirmed by later church councils in AD 393 and 397. Although the debate about their authorship has continued throughout church history to this very day, their canonicity has been accepted by some part of the church since the second century.

The Greek Text of 2 and 3 John

The number of variant readings introduced by scribal activity in the manuscripts of a New Testament book is generally proportional to the number of times the text was copied. This means that books that had a more limited circulation generally have a more stable textual

---

6. Judith M. Lieu, *I, II, and III John: A Commentary*, NTL (Louisville: Westminster John Knox, 2008), 26 – 27.

basis than the more popular books. In the case of 2 and 3 John, the paucity of textual variants may have as much to do with the brevity of the texts as with the frequency they were copied. The small number of textual variants in 2 and 3 John compared to 1 John[7] is consistent with the reception patterns described above, which imply that because 2 and 3 John were perhaps less universally known than 1 John, their text had been copied less frequently.

The most recent, painstaking work by The Institute for New Testament Textual Research in Münster, Germany, based on an expanded selection of manuscripts has found only two readings in 2 John and three in 3 John that differ from the NA27.[8] These can be found in Peter M. Head, 'Editio Critica Maior: An Introduction and Assessment', *Tyndale Bulletin* 61.1 (2010), 152, available online at https://www.academia.edu/3633883/_Editio_Critica_Maior_An_Introduction_and_Assessment_Tyndale_Bulletin_61.1_2010_131-152 (accessed May 2, 2016).

CHAPTER SUMMARY

The brief letters of 2 and 3 John focus on the immediate issue of Christian hospitality but reflect concerns about the bigger question of the source of authority in regard to the gospel of Jesus Christ. Does the authoritative teaching come from the apostolic eyewitnesses or from Christian leaders who had no personal experience of Jesus but claimed direct revelation from the Holy Spirit?

The letters of 2 and 3 John are two sides of the same issue: when to extend hospitality to itinerant preachers and when to deny it. The elder exhorts the congregation, represented by the "chosen lady and her children," to deny hospitality to those professing Christians who arrive with a message about Jesus Christ that does not square with the apostolic teaching based on personal eyewitness experience with Jesus (reading 2 John in light of 1 John). But when those sent by the elder are denied hospitality by Diotrephes and the congregation(s) associated with him, the elder writes to Gaius to be reassured that he can count on Gaius to continue to provide the hospitality needed by those sent from the elder.

The larger issue is that of spiritual authority. The elder's authority is being questioned by Diotrephes, and that is putting other believers in the awkward situation of having to choose which man they will follow. The elder, who is most likely the author of 1 John, represents the apostolic teaching and an authority that went back to Jesus Christ himself. These remarkable notes from the elder give us a window into church dynamics at a moment when the early church was transitioning from apostolic to postapostolic leadership. Would it remain faithful to the apostolic truth about Jesus Christ? That is still a most pressing question for Christian churches today.

7. Barbara Aland et al, eds., *Novum Testamentum Graecum Editio Critica Maior*, vol. 4: *Catholic Letters*, pt. 1: *Text*, installment 4: *The Second and Third Letter of John* and *The Letter of Jude* (Stuttgart: Deutsche Bibelgesellschaft, 2003), 35.

8. Ibid., 37.

KEY TERMS

the chosen lady
Demetrius
Diotrephes
the elder
Gaius
Montanists, Montanus
NA27
papyrus 𝔓[9]

QUESTIONS FOR REVIEW OR DISCUSSION

1. List reasons that the addressee of 2 John may have been an individual and her family and reasons it may have been a congregation of Christians.
2. If the author of 2 and 3 John was the apostle John, in addition to being an "elder" in the sense of spiritual authority, he would also have been a very elderly man. In what ways might that have added to the tension between him and those who had gone out from the church?
3. How does studying 2 and 3 John affect your image of the early Christian church?
4. What place do you give to ancient writings about the Christian church, such as the *Didache*, that are not part of the biblical canon? Why?

GOING FURTHER

Abbott, Edwin A. *Johannine Vocabulary: A Comparison of the Words of the Fourth Gospel with Those of the Three.* London: A. & C. Black, 1905. Repr., Eugene, Ore.: Wipf & Stock, 2005.

Brown, Raymond. *The Community of the Beloved Disciple: The Life, Loves, and Hates of an Individual Church in New Testament Times.* New York: Paulist, 1979.

Burge, Gary. *The Anointed Community: The Holy Spirit in the Johannine Tradition.* Grand Rapids: Eerdmans, 1987.

Culpepper, R. Alan. "The Christology of the Johannine Writings." Pages 66–87 in *Who Do You Say That I Am? Essays on Christology.* Edited by Mark Allan Powell and David R. Bauer. Louisville: Westminster John Knox, 1999.

Culy, Martin M. *I, II, III John: A Handbook on the Greek Text.* Waco, Tex.: Baylor University Press, 2004.

Harner, Philip B., *What Are They Saying About the Catholic Epistles?* What Are They Saying Series. New York: Paulist, 2004.

Hill, Charles E. *The Johannine Corpus in the Early Church.* New York: Oxford University Press, 2004.

Lieu, Judith. *The Theology of the Johannine Epistles.* New Testament Theology. Cambridge: Cambridge University Press, 1991.

Painter, John. *The Quest for the Messiah: The History, Literature, and Theology of the Johannine Community.* 2nd ed. Nashville: Abingdon, 1993.
Thatcher, Tom, ed. *What We Have Heard from the Beginning: The Past, Present, and Future of Johannine Studies.* Waco, Tex.: Baylor University Press, 2007.
Watt, Jan van der. *An Introduction to the Johannine Gospel and Letters.* T&T Clark Approaches to Biblical Studies. London: T&T Clark, 2007.

Commentaries

Brown, Raymond. *The Epistles of John*. AB 30. Garden City, N.Y.: Doubleday, 1982.
Bultmann, Rudolf K. *The Johannine Epistles: A Commentary on the Johannine Epistles.* Edited by R. W. Funk. Translated by R. P. O'Hara, L. C. McGaughy, and R. W. Funk. Hermeneia. Philadelphia, Fortress, 1973.
Burge, Gary. *Letters of John*. NIVAC. Grand Rapids: Zondervan, 1996.
Culpepper, R. Alan. *The Gospel and Letters of John*. Interpreting Biblical Texts. Nashville: Abingdon, 1998.
Jobes, Karen H. *1, 2, 3 John.* Zondervan Exegetical Commentary on the New Testament 19. Grand Rapids: Zondervan, forthcoming.
Kruse, Colin G. *The Letters of John.* Pillar New Testament Commentary. Grand Rapids: Eerdmans, 2000.
Lieu, Judith. *I, II and III John*. New Testament Library. Louisville: Westminster John Knox, 2008.
Lindars, Barnabas, Ruth B. Edwards, and John M. Court. *The Johannine Literature.* Sheffield New Testament Guides. Sheffield: Sheffield Academic Press, 2000.
Marshall, I. Howard. *The Epistles of John*. NICNT. Grand Rapids: Eerdmans, 1978.
Schnackenburg, Rudolf. *The Johannine Epistles.* Translated by Reginald Fuller and Ilse Fuller. New York: Crossroad, 1992.
Smalley, Stephen S. *1, 2, 3 John.* Word Biblical Commentary 51. Waco, Tex.: Word, 1984.
Strecker, Georg. *The Johannine Letters*. Hermeneia. Minneapolis: Fortress, 1996.
Talbert, Charles H. *Reading John: A Literary and Theological Commentary on the Fourth Gospel and the Johannine Epistles.* Reading the New Testament Series. New York: Crossroad, 1994.
Thatcher, Tom. "2 John." Pages 509–23 in *Hebrews–Revelation. Expositor's Bible Commentary.* Vol. 13. Edited by Tremper Longman III and David E. Garland. Rev. ed. Grand Rapids: Zondervan, 2006.
———. "3 John." Pages 527–38 in *Hebrews–Revelation. Expositor's Bible Commentary.* Vol. 13. Edited by Tremper Longman III and David E. Garland. Rev. ed. Grand Rapids: Zondervan, 2006.
Thompson, Marianne Meye. *1–3 John*. IVPNTC. Downers Grove, Ill.: InterVarsity, 1992.
Witherington, Ben, III. *A Socio-Rhetorical Commentary on Titus, 1–2 Timothy, and 1–3 John.* Letters and Homilies for Hellenized Christians. Vol. 1. Downers Grove, Ill.: IVP Academic, 2006.
Yarbrough, Robert W. *1–3 John*. BECNT. Grand Rapids: Baker Academic, 2008.
———. "2 John" pp. 212–19 in *ZIBBC*. Vol. 4. Edited by Clinton E. Arnold. Grand Rapids: Zondervan, 2002.
———. "3 John" pp. 220–27 in *ZIBBC*. Vol. 4. Edited by Clinton E. Arnold. Grand Rapids: Zondervan, 2002.

Glossary

Aaronic priesthood. The priesthood established by God to perform acts of worship and atonement for ancient Israel (see Ex. 29).

AD. An abbreviation of the Latin phrase *Anno Domini* (*Nostri Iesu Christi*), "in the year of our Lord Jesus Christ."

adoptionism. *See* Cerinthianism.

allegory. A method of thinking, writing, or reading that takes material things and persons to represent ideals with no concern for the historical reality of the things or persons.

amanuensis. A scribe or secretary who put pen to paper on behalf of the person who commissioned him.

antichrist. The term used in the Johannine writings to designate those professing Christians who held heretical beliefs about Jesus Christ.

antitype. *See* typology.

apocalyptic. A belief about history ending in divine judgment that will destroy the wicked and vindicate the oppressed righteous. Christianity is not the only religion with apocalyptic beliefs.

Apocrypha, the. Religious writings from the intertestamental period that were highly esteemed but not considered authoritative in Judaism or in the early church.

apology. A reasoned argument to justify a policy or belief.

apostasy. The recanting of one's Christian faith and deliberate rejection of Christ.

archtype. *See* typology.

Areopagus. A building on Mars Hill in first-century Athens that housed philosophical debates.

atone (-ment). To make amends or reparation. In Christian theology, to reconcile humankind to God through Jesus.

BC. Before Christ.

canonical reading. Reading a New Testament book or passage in association with other passages of the Bible that contain similar language, themes, symbols, or motifs.

catholic. From the Greek phrase that meant "referring to the whole" and was used to refer to the whole, or universal, church before the Protestant Reformation.

Cerinthianism. An ancient heresy that claimed the Christ-spirit descended on the merely human man Jesus at his baptism and left him before the crucifixion. Also known as adoptionism.

Christology. The theological study of the person, nature, and work of Jesus Christ.

circumcision. The surgical removal of the foreskin of the penis as a sign of a man's covenant relationship with God practiced by ancient Israel and other religions of the ancient Near East.

codex (-ices). The format of ancient manuscripts whose sheets of papyrus or parchment were stitched together on one edge to form a book.

decensus. Latin for "descent." Used to refer to the descent of Christ into hell on Holy Saturday.

deuterocanonical. *See* Apocrypha.

dialectical Hegelian philosophy. A philosophy of the history of ideas that defines issues in terms of thesis, philosophy, antithesis, and synthesis. It was applied to the origin of the New Testament writings by viewing them as a synthesis of conflicting viewpoints among the apostolic churches.

Diaspora, the. From the Greek, meaning "scattered." It refers to the emigration or deportation of the Israelites and later Jewish people out of Palestine to various locations in the ancient world, or more generally to any mass movement of people away from their homeland.

Diatessaron. *See* Tatian's Diatessaron.

docetism. An ancient heresy that claimed Jesus only appeared to be human.

dualism. A conceptual viewpoint that polarizes and contrasts two aspects of reality.

Epicureanism. An ancient Greek philosophical school that believed the highest ideal for humanity was pleasure, defined not as sensual pleasure but as a well-being that could be attained only through avoiding anything that might disturb the tranquility of the soul.

epideictic rhetoric. One form of Greco-Roman oration that was intended to affirm an audience's values and increase their adherence to it.

epistle. A written communication that includes personal correspondence, sermons, or essays. The traditional designation for a major section of the New Testament canon.

eschatology. The study of or doctrine of the last things, usually related to the end of the world.

exhortation. A style of address intended to persuade the hearer or reader to observe some practice, rule, ethic, or moral standard.

extant. Surviving until our time.

Gentile(s). In the worldview of the Old Testament, humankind was divided into two groups: God's covenant people and the "Gentiles" or "nations," undifferentiated with respect to race, ethnicity, and so forth. This division is employed by some New Testament writers to distinguish believing Christians from the rest of humankind.

gnosis. The Greek word for "knowledge," from which the label Gnosticism was taken.

Gnostic. *See* Gnosticism.

Gnosticism. A worldview built on Plato's idealistic dualism that influenced religious thought in the ancient world. It characteristically viewed the material world as inferior to the spiritual world of ideals, or as innately evil. It had far-reaching consequences for Christology and Christian living.

Halakhah. The complete body of Jewish laws that included the biblical commandments, rabbinic rules, and traditional customs.

hamartiology. The theological study or doctrine of sin.

hapax legomena. Greek for "once said." A term used to refer to a word that occurs only once in a given corpus.

harrowing of hell. An archaic phrase used to refer to Christ's disruption of hell on Holy Saturday.

hendiadys. Greek for "one through two." A rhetorical term referring to a figure of speech in which two words joined by a conjunction are used to refer to one notion.

hermeneutic(s). An interpretative approach.

historical-grammatical. Reading a text in light of its historical setting and authorial intention, in contrast to a canonical reading, in which a text is read in light of other biblical books.

illocutionary force. The effect a speaker or writer intends by his or her statement or message.

imitatio. A Greco-Roman literary practice in which an author would incorporate material from a very well-known work into his own.

imitatio Christi. A Latin phrase meaning "the imitation of Christ," which throughout church history has been a spiritual goal for Christians, though defined in many ways.

Johannine. The adjective used to refer to writings associated with John.

Johannine comma. An additional clause (Lat. *comma*) found in a few late manuscripts of 1 John 5:7–8.

Judaizers. An early sect of Christianity that taught that a Gentile must become a Jew when converting to faith in Jesus, the Jewish Messiah.

***koine* Greek.** *Koine* ("common") Greek was the lingua franca of the first-century Roman Empire.

***kerygma*.** A Greek word meaning "proclamation." It has come to be used as a technical term in New Testament studies to refer to the oral tradition about Jesus before the Gospels were written.

literary genre. A category of writing defined by a certain style, form, or conventions, e.g., fairy tale, parable, historiography.

locution. A term from speech act theory referring to a statement made with an intent.

metonymy. A rhetorical term in which one word is substituted for another with which it is closely associated, e.g., "kingdom of heaven" rather than "kingdom of God," where "heaven" is a metonymy for "God."

midrash. An ancient interpretive writing that expands, amplifies, and glosses biblical stories of the Old Testament.

Mishnah. The first written version of the oral tradition of Judaism.

Montanists. A second-century Christian sect of Phrygia in Asia Minor whose founder, Montanus, claimed direct revelation from the Holy Spirit. The Montanists were declared heretical by the Nicene Council.

Muratorian Canon. A second-century list of canonical books preserved in a seventh-century Latin manuscript, so named for the discoverer and first editor of the list in modern times, L. A. Muratori.

Neoplatonic dualism. *See* Neoplatonism.

Neoplatonism. A revival of the philosophy of Plato's idealistic dualism in the centuries surrounding the birth of Jesus.

occasional writings. A term used to distinguish literary writings from those originating as a response on a specific occasion.

Old Greek (OG). The designation for the oldest Greek translation of the Old Testament books. For the Pentateuch, it is referred to as the Septuagint (LXX).

ossuary. A stone box used in first-century Palestine to hold the skeletal remains of a body that had been entombed.

papyrus. The earliest known form of paper made from the papyrus plant. This material gives its name to the earliest manuscripts of the New Testament books.

***paraclete*.** A Greek word that meant "advocate" and is found in the Johannine writings to refer both to Jesus and to the Holy Spirit he promised to send.

paraenesis. A Greco-Roman literary genre marked by certain rhetorical conventions that was intended to argue a point based on the personal convictions of the reader.

parousia. A Greek word meaning "arrival," used in the New Testament to refer to the second coming of Jesus Christ.

passion, Jesus'. An archaic use of the English word *passion*, which persists only in reference to the suffering of Jesus Christ.

pericope. A unit of written text.

pesher interpretation. A form of interpreting current events as the direct fulfillment of ancient prophecy. It was characteristic of how the Scriptures were read at Qumran but is also practiced by some interpreters today.

Platonic dualism. An ancient philosophical concept that divides all reality into the material world and the world of ideals.

pneumatology. The theological study of or doctrine of the Spirit.

Pseudepigrapha. A collection of writings from the Hellenistic period of Judaism whose authors wrote in the name of an ancient hero of the faith.

pseudonymity (-ous). The practice of writing under a false name.

Q. *See* Q-document.

Q (*Quelle*) -document. A hypothetical document constructed by scholars that is claimed to represent an actual ancient document containing the earliest form of the sayings of Jesus.

Rylands fragment. A papyrus fragment found in Egypt that dates to the early second century and contains portions of the gospel of John.

secessionists. The term typically used to refer to those who went out from the Johannine churches.

Septuagint. The ancient Greek translation of the Old Testament made first of the Pentateuch in the third century BC. All other books were translated into Greek sometime before the birth of Christ.

Sheol. A Hebrew word denoting the place of the dead.

Sitz im Leben. A term coined by German scholars, meaning "setting in life," to refer to the situation that gave rise to various biblical books or the parts from which they were composed.

soteriology. The theological study of or doctrine of salvation.

speech act theory. A technical term in linguistics that refers to the action performed by a statement or discourse.

Stoicism. *See* Stoics.

Stoics. An ancient Greek philosophical school that believed the universe is controlled by impersonal Reason and that life's highest good is to live in harmony with it.

Synoptic Gospels. The first three Gospels, Matthew, Mark, and Luke, because they present a similar view of Jesus' life. Synoptic means "viewed together."

tabernacle. The portable tent used for worship by ancient Israel during the wilderness wanderings and early years in the land (see Ex. 25–27).

Tartarus. The location of the underworld in ancient Greek mythology where the fallen Greek gods known as the Titans were cast.

Tatian's Diatesseron. A second-century work produced by Tatian that interwove material from all four Gospels into a single narrative of the life of Jesus. The name derives from the Greek *dia tesserōn*, "through, or out of, four."

testament/testamental literature. An ancient literary genre presenting the parting words of a hero, usually pseudonymous.

theodicy. An apologetic argument that explains how, if God is all good and all knowing, there can be evil in the world.

type. *See* typology.

typology. A method of understanding previous historical events, persons, and institutions, referred to as types, that anticipate later events, persons, or institutions referred to as the corresponding antitypes or archtypes.

Scripture Index

2 Peter

1 John

2 John

3 John

Index of Extrabiblical Ancient Texts

New Testament Apocrypha and Pseudepigraphical Texts

Index of Authors

Subject Index

G

H

I

T